FIFTY-NINTH EXCAVATION MEMOIR

EDITED BY ALAN B. LLOYD

QAṢR IBRÎM THE LATE MEDIAEVAL PERIOD

BY

WILLIAM Y. ADAMS

EGYPT EXPLORATION SOCIETY
3 DOUGHTY MEWS, LONDON WC1N 2PG
1996

LONDON

SOLD AT

THE OFFICES OF THE EGYPT EXPLORATION SOCIETY

3 Doughty Mews, London WC1N 2PG

British Library Cataloguing-in-Publication Data

A catalogue record for this book is available from the British Library

ISBN 0-85698-134-6

PRINTED IN GREAT BRITAIN

Typeset by Unicus Graphics Limited, Horsham, West Sussex

Printed by Whitstable Litho Ltd., Whitstable, Kent

CONTENTS

LIST OF TABLES

LIST OF FIGURES

LIST OF PLATES

Plate

ABBREVIATIONS

Journals

BASP	*Bulletin of the American Society of Papyrologists*
JARCE	*Journal of the American Research Center in Egypt*
JEA	*Journal of Egyptian Archaeology*
LAAA	*University of Liverpool Annals of Archaeology and Anthropology*
SNR	*Sudan Notes and Records*

Condensed Titles

Ceramic Industries	William Y. Adams, *Ceramic Industries of Medieval Nubia* (Memoirs of the UNESCO Archaeological Survey of Sudanese Nubia 1) (Lexington, 1986)
Études	*Études Nubiennes; Colloque de Chantilly, 2–6 Juillet 1975* (Institut français d'archéologie orientale, Bibliothèque d'étude 77) (Cairo, 1978)
Michalowski, *Faras*	Kazimierz Michalowski, *Faras, Fouilles Polonaises 1961* (Warsaw, 1962)
Michalowski and Gerster, *Faras*	Kazimierz Michalowski and Georg Gerster, *Faras, die Kathedrale aus dem Wüstensand* (Zurich and Cologne, 1967)
Kunst	Erich Dinkler, ed., *Kunst und Geschichte Nubiens in Christlicher Zeit* (Recklinghausen, 1970)
La Nubia	Ugo Monneret de Villard, *La Nubia Medioevale* (2 vols.) (Cairo, 1935)
Adams, *Nubia*	William Y. Adams, *Nubia, Corridor to Africa* (London, 1977)
Michalowski, *Nubia*	Kazimierz Michalowski, ed., *Nubia, récentes recherches* (Warsaw, 1975)
Objects	W. M. Flinders Petrie, *Objects of Daily Use* (London, 1927)
The Scrolls	J. Martin Plumley, *The Scrolls of Bishop Timotheos* (Egypt Exploration Society, Texts from Excavations, 1) (London, 1975)
Storia	Ugo Monneret de Villard, *Storia della Nubia cristiana* (Pontificium Institutum Orientalium Studiorum, Christiana Analecta 118) (Rome, 1938)
Tools	W. M. Flinders Petrie, *Tools and Weapons* (London, 1917)
Travels	J. L. Burckhardt, *Travels in Nubia* (London, 1819)

PREFACE

This is the first of what I hope will be a long and distinguished series of monographs dealing with one of the world's most extraordinary archaeological sites. At Qaṣr Ibrîm, the combination of long, continuous occupation and the almost total preservation of every kind of archaeological material provide a nearly unique opportunity to reconstruct the life and lifeways of a vanished community, and that is what I have attempted in these pages.

Excavations in the citadel at Qaṣr Ibrîm began in 1963, and have continued on a more or less regular biennial basis down to the present. (For more detail on the history of the excavations see Part 1, Chapter 1.) Remains of the late mediaeval period (c. 1172–1500) were, of course, among the uppermost on the site, and therefore some of the first to be investigated. Some excavation was carried out in late mediaeval structures and deposits in each season between 1963 and 1984, at which time it was believed that investigation of these remains was substantially complete. Consequently, it seems appropriate now to offer a monograph summing up what the Qaṣr Ibrîm excavations have revealed about this very important interval in Nubian history, in which Qaṣr Ibrîm played a pivotal role (see Part 1, Chapter 1).

My own association with the Qaṣr Ibrîm excavations began in 1972, and continued until 1984. I was present during all or part of each excavation season during that interval, and served as co-director of the excavations in 1978 and 1980. Much of the late mediaeval material that is reported in these pages was dug under my immediate supervision, but a great deal more of it was not. For structures and artifacts excavated in the seasons between 1963 and 1969, and also for part of the 1974 season, I am obliged to rely on such documentation as has been provided by others. I have spent two protracted periods and several shorter ones in Cambridge, working with artifactual finds and documentary records from the earlier Qaṣr Ibrîm seasons, and this has given me at least a second-hand familiarity with the work of the 1963, 1964, 1966, and 1969 seasons. I have to stress that my interpretation of the remains excavated in those seasons may in some cases be at variance with that of the original excavators, as reported after each season in the *Journal of Egyptian Archaeology*.[1]

The monograph that follows reflects to some extent the personal proclivities of its author. My primary interest has always been in the life, culture, and history of the Nubian people rather than in their material productions and remains per se, and my report is aimed at others who share the same interests. In terms of its organization it reads more like an ethnography than like a typical archaeological site report. It will not necessarily serve as a model for subsequent reports on Qaṣr Ibrîm, which may be written by other archaeologists with different interests.

Acknowledgements

I have first of all to acknowledge the generous financial support that has made possible the excavations at Qaṣr Ibrîm over so many seasons. During the years of my own field work the Egypt Exploration Society and the Smithsonian Foreign Currency Program contributed in just about equal measure to the budget of the expedition, and my thanks go to both of them. I have also to acknowledge the generosity of the University of Kentucky, which allowed me released time to work at Qaṣr Ibrîm while continuing to pay my regular academic salary over a number of seasons. Finally I must not forget the Egyptian Antiquities Organization, which year after year provided us with houseboats, tugs, and boat personnel at what can only be described as a nominal rental, and whose personnel in the Aswân and Abu Simbel offices served us as an invaluable support network.

Among personal obligations I must mention first Professor J. Martin Plumley, who launched the Qaṣr Ibrîm citadel excavations in 1963 and continued to direct them for many seasons thereafter. The difficulties under which he laboured in the earliest seasons are briefly reviewed in Part 1, Chapter 1. It was he who first invited me to join the dig in 1972, thereby inaugurating (perhaps unexpectedly for both of us) what was to be an equally long involvement on my own part. His personal generosity and professional collaboration during my long periods of research in Cambridge must also be acknowledged.

In the seasons since 1963, more than 100 specialists and experts of one kind and another have taken part in the Qaṣr Ibrîm excavations, and at least in an indirect way this report owes something to all of them: the architects, the photographers, the epigraphers, the registrars, the specialists in food remains, textiles, basketry, and leather, and certainly also the Egyptian inspectors. I have not space here to cite them all by name, but they are listed in the

[1] For a complete list of published preliminary reports see Part 1, Chapter 1, footnotes 65 through 69.

preliminary reports that have appeared after each season in the *Journal of Egyptian Archaeology.* I hope they will accept the collective citation here as an expression of my very genuine appreciation for all of their contributions.

I must however single out for individual recognition those individuals who have contributed in a direct way to the making of this report, by reading and commenting on the text and sometimes by contributing to it. For the artifactual chapters (Part 3) I have had the assistance of Peter Rowley-Conwy (on food remains), Peter French (on shoes and coins), Boyce N. Driskell (on basketry and cordage), and Elisabeth Crowfoot (on textiles). I owe a special debt to Nettie K. Adams, who wrote the whole of Chapter 14 as well as contributing sections of text for several of the other chapters. Indeed, the work stands indebted to her for much else besides.

For the textual chapters (Part 4) I have had to rely heavily upon the help of specialists in the various mediaeval languages that were employed at Qaṣr Ibrîm. In particular I must thank Professors J. Martin Plumley of Cambridge and K. H. Kuhn of Durham (on Coptic), Professor J. David Thomas of Durham (on Greek), Professor Louis Swift of the University of Kentucky (on Latin), Professor Gerald M. Browne of the University of Illinois (on Old Nubian), and the late Professor Martin Hinds of Cambridge and Mrs. Elizabeth Sartain of Cairo (on Arabic). I owe a very special debt to Professor Browne for his promptness and courtesy in responding to a steady stream of demands and inquiries, usually within a week of receiving my letters. Without his collaboration, this report would certainly have been delayed much longer than it has been already.

Mark Horton has provided invaluable help in the preparation of the published illustrations, as well as some suggestions about the text. Any remaining deficiencies are however my sole responsibility. This applies to the line drawings as well as to the written text, since I was obliged to execute most of them myself. At age 62, my hand is not as steady as it once was.

PART I
BACKGROUND

CHAPTER 1
THE SITE AND ITS EXCAVATION

LOWER Nubia is the name given to a portion of the Nile Valley, about 350 km in length, extending from the First to the Second Cataract of the Nile. This region, which in the recent past has been entirely submerged by the waters of the Aswân High Dam, lies in the most southerly part of Egypt and the adjoining northern part of the Republic of the Sudan. In past centuries, as today, Lower Nubia was often under Egyptian political control, but its people and their history were alike different from those of Egypt proper. In appearance and in their native speech the inhabitants of Nubia were and are more akin to neighbouring peoples of inner Africa than to the inhabitants of the Mediterranean rim. For many centuries their culture has been largely derivative from Egypt, but here also certain African and non-Egyptian traits have persisted. While at times under Egyptian control, the Nubians at other times developed important kingdoms and even empires of their own, and on occasion they exerted a major influence on the history of Egypt itself.

For much of the last three thousand years, the single most important community in Lower Nubia was Qaṣr Ibrîm, located about 240 km to the south of the first Nile cataract (Fig. 1). Unlike most other settlements in Egypt and Nubia, Qaṣr Ibrîm was not situated on or near the Nile floodplain. It was perched on the top of a rocky eminence some 70 m above the river which lapped directly against the base of the bluff below the site. The setting of Qaṣr Ibrîm was at the northern tip of a long, narrow finger of elevated land separating two deep *wadis*, so that the only level approach to the site was across the denuded desert plateau from the south (Pl. 1, a). On the east, west, and north sides, bluffs of varying steepness dropped away directly below the ramparts. Strategic and defensive considerations played an important part in the history of the community, although during most periods it had important administrative, commercial, and religious functions as well.

The most important installations at Qaṣr Ibrîm were apparently always on the mountain-top, but at some periods of history there was also settlement at the foot of the bluffs, close to the river's edge. This was certainly true in the later Middle Ages,[1] and perhaps earlier as well. Certain industrial activities like pottery making, brick making, and iron smelting, which require large amounts of fuel or water, must always have been carried out close to the riverbank.[2] Unfortunately these low-lying remains were never subject to archaeological investigation before their final destruction by the Aswân Dam waters, and nothing can be said for certain about their age or extent.

In addition to settlement areas there were extensive cemeteries, dating from many different periods, below the bluffs to the east and west of the Qaṣr Ibrîm citadel (Pl. 1, a). Altogether these contained several thousand graves, of which the most important were excavated in the archaeological campaigns of 1932[3] and 1961.[4] Additional cemeteries—so far not excavated—are located on the desert plateau immediately to the south of Qaṣr Ibrîm. Surface examination suggests that there are graves of the Meroitic, Ballana, and Christian periods and perhaps earlier graves as well.

Historical resumé

The earliest history of Qaṣr Ibrîm is, for the time being, very imperfectly known. This is in part because the site is not mentioned in early documentary sources and in part because archaeological excavations have not yet penetrated very extensively into the earliest levels of occupation (Table 1).

[1] 'Lower Ibrîm' is specifically mentioned in one of the late mediaeval legal documents (74.1.30/6, no. 5) found at Qaṣr Ibrîm. For the translation see Gerald M. Browne, *Old Nubian Texts from Qaṣr Ibrîm* III. (Egypt Exploration Society, Texts from Excavations) (in press).

[2] For evidence of pottery making beside the riverbank see Somers Clarke, *Christian Antiquities in the Nile Valley* (Oxford, 1912), 78–81.

[3] W. B. Emery and L. P. Kirwan, *The Excavations and Survey between Wadi es-Sebua and Adindan 1929–1931* (Cairo, 1935), 268–77.

[4] See Anthony J. Mills, *The Cemeteries of Qaṣr Ibrîm* (Egypt Exploration Society, Excavation Memoir 51) (London, 1982).

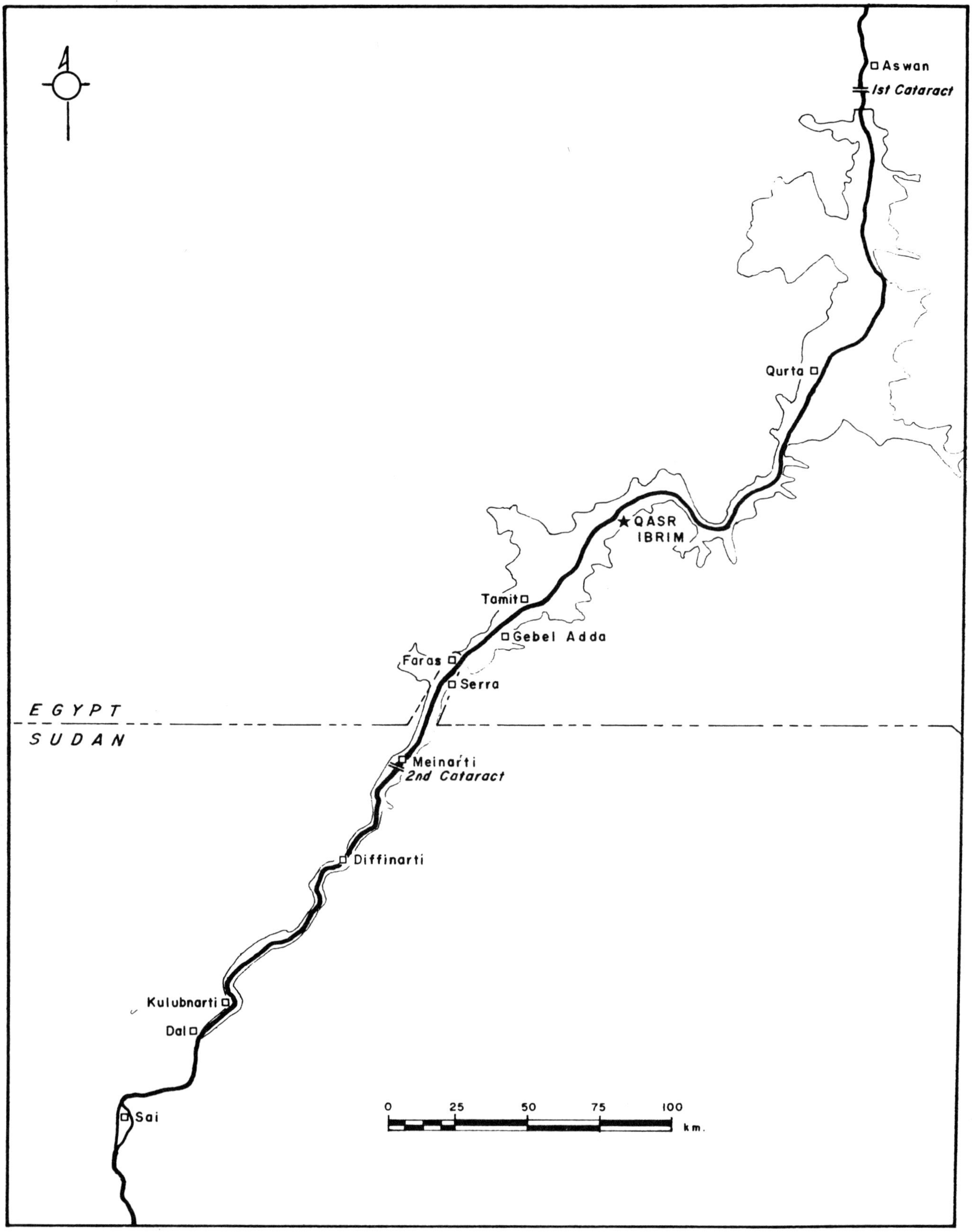

Figure 1. Map of Lower Nubia and the *Baṭn el-Hajjar* showing the location of Qaṣr Ibrîm and other major settlements of the late mediaeval period. The fine line indicates the maximum pool contour of Lake Nasser/Lake Nubia.

TABLE 1
CHRONOLOGY OF ACTIVITIES AND REMAINS AT QAṢR IBRÎM
(Dates AD unless otherwise stated)

			Archaeological remains		
Dates	Period	Activities	Houses	Religious structures	Fortifications
1550–1811	'Bosnian'	Ottoman garrison point'; local commercial centre	Large and small stone house all over citadel	Part of Cathedral 293 converted to mosque	Girdle wall repaired and heightened
1400–1500	Terminal Christian	Main religious centre of Kingdom of Dotawo	Few large brick castle-houses	Cathedral 293 and Cupola Church 839	Girdle wall kept in repair?
1172–1400	Late Christian 1 and 2	Administrative, commercial, and religious centre	Fairly numerous stone and brick houses	Cathedral 293; Churches 287 and 294	Girdle wall entirely rebuilt
700–1172	Early Christian 2; Classic Christian	Primarily religious centre	Few houses west of Cathedral	Cathedral 293 and Church 287	Girdle wall largely in ruins
500–700	Late X-Group and Early Christian 1	Thriving commercial and religious centre	Tight cluster of stone houses over most of site	Temple 287 converted to church; adjoining monastery	Girdle wall in disrepair
350–700	Earlier X-Group	Major commercial and administrative centre	Tight cluster of stone houses all over site	Meroitic Temples 287 and 290 continued in use	Girdle wall neglected?
		(Limit of systematic excavation)			
100–350	Late Meroitic	Important religious centre; other functions uncertain	Numerous brick and stone houses	Taharqa Temple 287 restored, Temples 289 and 290 built	Girdle wall maintained? Main gate moved from south to east
100 BC–100 AD	Ptolemaic and Roman	Military garrison point	Only one house found so far	None known; Temple 287 in disrepair	Girdle wall built and later enlarged
?–100 BC	Late Dynastic	Uncertain	None found yet	Podium built?	Napatan revetment walls
690–? BC	Napatan	Religious centre; other functions uncertain	None found yet	Taharqa Temple 287 built	Revetment walls built?
?	New Kingdom	Religious and military outpost?	None found yet	Foundations of stone Temple 290 laid?	No evidence
?	C-Group or Kerma?	Uncertain	None found yet	Round stone tower 283 built; later cased in brick?	Rubble-filled girdle wall 284 built?

It seems that Qaṣr Ibrîm must have been a place of some importance in the later New Kingdom; for half a dozen Egyptian votive shrines were cut into the rock face below the citadel top.[5] The site at this time probably formed a kind of outlier to the more important administrative centre of Aniba (Miʿam), situated just across the river on the west bank.[6] A few centuries later, the 'Ethiopian' Pharaoh Taharqa chose the Qaṣr Ibrîm mountain-top as the site for at least one of the many temples that he commissioned in Nubia and the Sudan.[7] The Ibrîm temple was a relatively small and unprepossessing affair of mud brick, but it was nevertheless to remain in use for over 2000 years, first as a pagan shrine and later as one of Nubia's first Christian churches.[8] Apparently dating also from the time of Taharqa are two other monumental constructions which look decidedly un-Egyptian. One is a very oddly constructed, rubble-filled enclosure wall, and the other a rubble-filled round tower which was later encased within a pentagonal skin-wall of mud brick. For the time being these structures have only been partly cleared of overburden, and nothing definite can be said about their origins or functions.[9]

After the time of Taharqa there is little evidence of further activity at Ibrîm for several centuries. Archaeology suggests that Lower Nubia at this time was largely, if not entirely, devoid of inhabitants, and was of little economic or strategic consequence either to the Egyptians or to the Nubians, who in the meantime were consolidating their Empire of Kush further to the south.[10] A small religious and/or military establishment might have been maintained at Qaṣr Ibrîm, but there is no certain evidence even of this.

Sometime in the second or first century BC, the Ptolemaic rulers of Egypt took possession of Qaṣr Ibrîm, apparently for strategic purposes. They built the first unmistakable fortification wall around the mountain-top; a feature which, with numerous rebuildings, was to remain prominent during the subsequent two millennia of the site's existence (Pl. 1, c). The total area enclosed within the girdle wall was about two hectares (five acres). This in all later centuries was the full extent of the mountain-top settlement, although, as previously noted, there was also a town-site at the base of the bluffs in the Middle Ages.

Under the Ptolemies Qaṣr Ibrîm was apparently a garrison site, with no important administrative, commercial, or religious functions. The Taharqa mud-brick temples appear at this time to have been very much dilapidated and were probably not in use. The same situation evidently continued for a time under the Romans, who succeeded the Ptolemies as rulers of Egypt and Lower Nubia in 30 BC.

Qaṣr Ibrîm makes its first appearance on the pages of written history in 23 BC, in the works of Pliny[11] and Strabo[12] In that year an invading force of Nubians drove out the Roman garrison and took temporary possession of the citadel before proceeding north to attack Philae. A Roman retaliatory expedition under the Prefect Petronius soon dislodged the Nubians and reclaimed the fortress. Two years later, according to written sources, a treaty was negotiated which fixed the frontier between Roman and Nubian dominions at Maharraqa, a place about 80 km to the north of Qaṣr Ibrîm.[13] This would seem to imply that Qaṣr Ibrîm was once again handed back to Nubian control, but archaeological evidence suggests a continuing Roman presence on the site until at least the end of the first century AD.[14] During all this time the place seems to have had almost exclusively a military character. The original Ptolemaic fortress walls were strengthened and heightened several times, and tens of thousands of stream pebbles were brought in from the desert *wadis* and piled up along the ramparts to serve as sling ammunition. Several hundred larger stone balls, carefully shaped from sandstone, were evidently made as ballista projectiles.[15]

In the accounts of Pliny and Strabo, and in a number of later classical texts, Qaṣr Ibrîm is given the name Primis. This is evidently a Latinization of the indigenous toponym Pedeme, which begins to appear on Meroitic funerary stelae at about the same time.[16] The name subsequently underwent further mutations, appearing in mediaeval Coptic texts as Phrim and finally, at the end of the Middle Ages, as Ibrîm.[17] The Arabic forename Qaṣr ('castle') is an accretion of recent times, possibly following the abandonment of the site; for in Ottoman documents the place is always named as Qal'at ('fortress') Ibrîm rather than as Qaṣr Ibrîm.[18]

[5] See Ricardo A. Caminos, *The Shrines and Rock-Inscriptions of Ibrîm* (Egypt Exploration Society, Archaeological Survey of Egypt, Memoir 32) (London, 1968).

[6] Op. cit., 6–8.

[7] See William Y. Adams, *Nubia, Corridor to Africa* (London, 1977), 264–6.

[8] See Plumley and Adams, *JEA* 60 (1974), 228–36.

[9] See R. D. Anderson, W. Y. Adams *et al.*, *JEA* 65 (1979), 33–5.

[10] See Adams, *JEA* 50 (1964), 108–20; id., *Meroitic North and South* (Meroitica 2) (Berlin, 1976), 12–16. See also id., *Nubia*, 241–5.

[11] Pliny vi: 35, 181–2.

[12] Strabo xvii, 1, 54.

[13] Ibid.

[14] For discussion see Adams, *JARCE* 20 (1983), 95–104; id. in Francis Geus and Florence Thill (eds.), *Mélanges offerts à Jean Vercoutter* (Lille, 1985), 9–17.

[15] See Adams, Alexander, and Allen, *JEA* 69 (1983), 58.

[16] See F. Ll. Griffith, *Karanòg, the Meroitic Inscriptions of Shablul and Karanòg* (Eckley B. Coxe Junior Expedition to Nubia, Vol. 6) (Philadelphia, 1911), 82. See also Griffith, *JEA* 15 (1929), 71.

[17] For further discussion of the name see Caminos, op. cit., 4–5.

[18] See Martin Hinds and Hamdi Sakkout, *Arabic Documents from the Ottoman Period from Qaṣr Ibrîm* (Egypt Exploration Society, Texts from Excavations, Memoir 8) (London, 1986), 2–3.

Although the length of Roman occupation is not certainly known, it is clear the Qaṣr Ibrîm had been reoccupied by the Nubians by the middle of the second century. This event marks a major turning point in the history of the site; for the new occupants evidently neglected the fortifications while restoring and enlarging the religious installations. The old and apparently badly decayed Taharqa brick temple was put back into repair, and a new and much larger stone temple was built adjoining its western end.[19] Qaṣr Ibrîm was evidently the seat of important civil as well as religious officials; for many of the notables buried in the great cemetery of Karanòg, a few kilometers to the north and across the river, specifically mention a connection with Pedeme in their funerary memorials.[20]

Gradually, too, a major commercial settlement grew up around the precincts of the temples. These developments coincided with, and were spurred on by, a wholesale repopulation of Lower Nubia, probably resulting from the introduction of the ox-driven waterwheel (*saqia*).[21] The newcomers seem to have come from the more northerly and westerly provinces of the Empire of Kush, and it may have been they who brought to Lower Nubia an early version of the present-day Nubian speech.[22]

The collapse of the Kushite Empire, sometime before AD 350, brought economic ruin and political chaos to the central Sudan, but the effects on the frontier province of Lower Nubia were much less severe. The region became a battleground for contending local kinglets, and Qaṣr Ibrîm itself apparently changed hands at least twice, but the settlement actually reached an apogee of size and importance during the so-called Ballana period which followed the collapse of Kushite authority. A large part of the mountain-top, within the fortification walls, was overbuilt with stoutly constructed stone houses, arranged along a regular system of intersecting streets and passages. In many respects these represent a continuation and an expansion of the townsite of Meroitic times, but most of the houses were rebuilt and enlarged in the Ballana period. Many of the buildings were two storeys high, the lower floors apparently serving as commercial shops and the upper floors as habitations.[23] There were extensive local manufacturing industries in wood, leather, pottery,[24] and cotton textiles, as well as large scale importation of wine and other luxury goods from Egypt. Recurrent military disturbances, in which the rulers of the Blemmye (Beja) and Nobatae (Nubian) succeeded one another as masters of Ibrîm,[25] apparently did not disrupt the commercial prosperity of the settlement. Worship continued in the old Meroitic temples, as is attested by scores of late Roman and early Byzantine coins laid down as offerings on the temple pavements.[26] An old brick temple, possibly from Taharqa's time, was now converted to the celebration of the Isis mystery cult, popular throughout the Roman Empire in the late pagan period.[27] The main seats of royal power in the Ballana period have not been definitely identified, but there is evidence that at different times both Blemmye and Nobatae kings resided at Qaṣr Ibrîm.[28]

The official conversion of Nubia to Christianity occurred between 543 and 570, according to ecclesiastical historians.[29] However, archaeological evidence points to the establishment of Christianity at Qaṣr Ibrîm somewhat earlier, perhaps near the beginning of the sixth century.[30] At that time one of the Taharqa brick temples was converted into a church by the insertion of a half-round apse within its original sanctuary chamber and the addition of a western narthex. The building soon came to be adjoined on its north, west, and south sides by contiguous rooms which may have been part of a monastic complex. Meanwhile the other Taharqa temple, which had lately served as an Isis shrine, was systematically dismantled and its contents smashed and scattered.[31] Elsewhere newly built secular buildings, mostly for the storage of goods, intruded upon the former areas of the temple precincts, which had apparently lost their sacred status. In other respects the introduction of a new faith had little immediate impact on the life or the fortunes of Qaṣr Ibrîm, which remained an important commercial and manufacturing centre in the Early Christian Nubian period.

[19] It is not yet clear whether a second small mud-brick temple, located further north on the site, was also restored to use at the same time.

[20] See n. 16.

[21] See Adams, *Nubia,* 345–8.

[22] See Adams, *Nubia,* 419–21; id. in Christopher Ehret and Merrick Posnansky (eds.), *The Archaeological and Linguistic Reconstruction of African History* (Berkeley, 1983), 11–38.

[23] See especially Plumley and Adams, *JEA* 60 (1974), 214–27; Plumley, *JEA* 61 (1975), 6–13; Plumley, Adams and Crowfoot, *JEA* 62 (1977), 31–7.

[24] See Plumley and Adams, *JEA* 60 (1974), 236–8; Plumley, Adams and Crowfoot, *JEA* 62 (1977), 42–7. See also Clarke, op. cit., 78–80.

[25] See C. L. Woolley and D. Randall-MacIver, *Karanòg, the Romano-Nubian Cemetery* (Eckley B. Coxe Junior Expedition to Nubia, Vol. 3) (Philadelphia, 1910), 103. Also Kirwan, *LAAA* 24 (1937), 77–8; W. B. Emery, *Egypt in Nubia* (London, 1965), 236.

[26] See Plumley, *JEA* 61 (1975), 16–17.

[27] See Driskell, Adams and French, *Archéologie du Nil Moyen* 3 (1988), 11–54.

[28] See n. 25.

[29] John of Ephesus, *Ecclesiastical History,* trans. Payne-Smith (London, 1860), Part III; John of Biclarum, *Chronicle,* ed. Mommsen (Berlin, 1894), 207–20.

[30] The date is established by potsherds built into the newly constructed church walls. See below, p. 259.

[31] See Driskell, Adams. and French, op. cit., 12.

A major transformation took place in the late seventh or early eighth century, by which time Qaṣr Ibrîm and Lower Nubia had come under the control of the more southerly Christian Kingdom of Makouria. Political power and activity now shifted largely to the southern region, and a decision was taken to convert Qaṣr Ibrîm from a primarily commercial and administrative centre to a primarily religious one. A new cathedral, the largest in Nubia, was built in the most elevated position on the mountain-top, and at the same time most of the secular houses in its vicinity were evacuated. Their upper storeys were deliberately razed, the brick and stone rubble being used to fill up the lower rooms and the adjacent streets so as to form a level, elevated terrace extending from the temple-church to the newly built cathedral. This apparently served as a gathering and a camping place for pilgrims, whose visits are attested by a great many inscriptions on nearby rock surfaces and mountain-tops.[32] A few houses within the citadel continued to be occupied during the early Middle Ages, but the bulk of secular occupation was probably banished to the lower townsite beside the Nile.

A kind of reverse transformation, equally abrupt and drastic, took place in the second half of the twelfth century. The old Ptolemaic and Roman fortification walls had been neglected for many centuries and were in an advanced state of disrepair, but they were now entirely rebuilt and heightened. Simultaneously the open plaza areas surrounding the churches began to suffer encroachment by secular houses, until at least a part of the mountain-top became once again a congested townsite. Letters found in some of the later mediaeval houses make it evident that Qaṣr Ibrîm had now become the principal residence of the Eparchs of Nobadia; the Viceroys of Lower Nubia.[33] Religious functions meanwhile were carried on as before, and a new church was built alongside the cathedral, presumably to accommodate the new settlers on the mountain-top. In later centuries still a fourth church, of the late Nubian cupola type, was built on the easternmost extremity of the citadel.[34]

In the abrupt refortification and resettlement of Qaṣr Ibrîm it is tempting to see the aftermath of the destructive invasion of Lower Nubia by the Ayyubid Shams ed-Dawla, in 1172–3.[35] This event brought to a close a period of more than five-hundred years of uninterrupted peace between Christian Nubia and Muslim Egypt, made possible by a treaty that was negotiated soon after the Arab conquest of Egypt.[36] Coupled with the rising tide of military adventurism in the Near East and elsewhere, it evidently reawakened in the Nubians a concern for their defences. In the later Middle Ages military architecture became more and more prominently a feature of the Nubian landscape, while ecclesiastical architecture declined in proportion.[37] It could be said of Qaṣr Ibrîm itself that it was converted from an acropolis to a castle. This architectural transformation was so thorough and so abrupt that it marks a convenient starting point in time for what we call the Late Christian period at Qaṣr Ibrîm—the period covered in the present monograph.

The refortification of Qaṣr Ibrîm nevertheless did not immediately signal a period of heightened military activity. Relations between the Nubians and the later Ayyubid sultans were generally peaceable, and even the periodic Mamluk incursions after 1250 did not immediately affect the fortunes or the prosperity of Qaṣr Ibrîm. Archaeology suggests that the settlement continued to thrive and to carry on a lively commerce at least until the middle of the fourteenth century, with trade in textiles, leather, wood products, pottery, and slaves. Glazed pottery, glass, fancy metal goods, luxury fabrics, and even some wine continued to arrive regularly from Egypt. Christian worship continued in the cathedral and churches, even though the ruler of the Kingdom of Makouria after 1323 was a Muslim.[38]

The fourteenth century was, however, a time of political anarchy in the more southerly reaches of the kingdom, and by the end of the century Makouria had ceased to exist. Its place was taken by a dozen or more warring principalities in which power was often in the hands of newly arrived Arab nomads. Lower Nubia, with its scanty pastoral resources, was relatively unaffected by the Arab migrations, and here a somewhat mysterious splinter-state called Dotawo managed to preserve some of the traditions and the institutions of Christian Nubia until near the end of the fifteenth century.[39] The principal seat of royal power in Dotawo seems to have been at Gebel Adda, a place about 40 km. to the south of Qaṣr Ibrîm, but textual finds suggest that Ibrm continued to be the principal religious centre in Lower Nubia.[40]

The Dotawo period was in general a time of economic and political decline, mirroring the chaotic conditions which prevailed in Egypt under its Mamluk

[32] See Plumley and Adams, *JEA* 60 (1974), pl. LI.

[33] See Plumley in Kazimierz Michalowski (ed.), *Nubia, récentes recherches* (Warsaw, 1975), 104–6.

[34] Reported in Ugo Monneret de Villard, *La Nubia medioevale,* I (Cairo, 1935), 109–11, and II, pl. LV.

[35] Reported by Abu Salih. See B. T. A. Evetts and A. J. Butler (eds.), *The Churches and Monasteries of Egypt and Some Neighbouring Countries* (Oxford, 1895), 266–7.

[36] For a translation and commentary see Forand, *Der Islam* 48 (1971), 111–21.

[37] See Adams, *Nubia*, 511–20.

[38] Op. cit., 529.

[39] See Adams in Michalowski, op. cit., 11–17.

[40] See especially Plumley in *Études nubiennes* (Institut français d'archéologie orientale, Bibliothèque d'étude, 77) (Cairo, 1978), 231–41.

rulers. A group of Arabized Beja warlords called the Beni Kanz for a time terrorized both Upper Egypt and Lower Nubia, defying the authority alike of Mamluk sultans and Nubian kinglets. These conditions seriously interfered with trade and probably contributed to the gradual abandonment of the Qaṣr Ibrîm settlement. By the year 1400 most of the later mediaeval houses were evidently disused and filled with rubbish. On top of their filled-up remains there arose a small cluster of castle-like two-storey brick structures of a type that began to appear all up and down the Nile at the end of the Middle Ages.[41] These may well have been the only inhabited dwellings left on the mountaintop in the latter part of the fifteenth century. The last traces of Christian Nubian polity had apparently disappeared before the end of the century; for no documents relating to the Kingdom of Dotawo have been found bearing a date later than 1484.[42]

Egypt was conquered by the Ottomans in 1517, and Lower Nubia was annexed a generation or two afterward. The date of this latter event has been in some dispute,[43] but textual finds from Qaṣr Ibrîm suggest that it was shortly after the middle of the sixteenth century.[44] An Ottoman garrison, which according to tradition was made up initially of Bosnian mercenaries,[45] took complete possession of the hilltop fortress, and its descendants remained there until they were finally evicted in the year 1811. Qaṣr Ibrîm for most of that time was the main centre of Ottoman military control in Lower Nubia. Whether or not there were any of the previous inhabitants left on the site when the troops arrived is uncertain, but certainly the place was in an advanced state of decay. Except for the castle-like brick houses to which we have previously alluded, the 'Bosnians' made no use of any of the existing installations on the site, but instead pulled them down and built their own houses from the resulting rubble. The Taharqa temple-church, now more than 2000 years old, was finally abandoned and filled with rubbish, as was the small church beside the cathedral. In time both were overbuilt with secular houses. The nave and south aisles of the cathedral were converted to serve as a kind of makeshift mosque,[46] while other parts of the building were given over to secular occupation.

Although the original Ottoman troops at Qaṣr Ibrîm are reported to have been of European origin, their numbers were maintained in succeeding generations entirely by intermarriage with Nubian women. As a result the racial, cultural, and linguistic distinctness of the garrison largely disappeared. Certainly the archaeological remains of the Ottoman period at Qaṣr Ibrîm are little different from those of the same period in other parts of Nubia.[47] The inhabitants, however, continued to designate themselves as 'Bosnians,' and to take pride in this special identity right down to the time of their final expulsion in 1811.[48]

Very little survives archaeologically from the earliest years of Ottoman occupation, but it seems probable that initially Qaṣr Ibrîm was almost purely a garrison site, with a largely male population. However, as the soldiers married and settled down, the place resumed more and more the character and appearance of a normal townsite. Letters and documents found in the houses relate to military matters—especially pay matters—but also bear witness to a lively trade in textiles, slaves, dates, and grain.[49] The houses of the late Islamic period, which in time spread over the entire citadel area, do not have the appearance of barracks but of large family dwellings.[50]

In the course of their occupation the Ottoman inhabitants carried out one final 'urban renewal' at Qaṣr Ibrîm. Large areas appear to have been stripped of the surviving stumps of earlier buildings, both from the Late Christian and from the early Ottoman periods. The resulting rubble was piled up behind the girdle wall which was once again repaired and heightened.[51] The effect of this activity was to create, on the mountain-top, a much more nearly level 'plateau' than had been present in earlier times. Additional family houses were then built on top of the newly created terraces. It is not clear from the archaeological evidence whether this transformation was carried out in a single burst of activity or whether it went on piecemeal over a considerable period of time, but it probably coincided with an interval of renewed prosperity at Qaṣr Ibrîm in the seventeenth century. The town-site at this time appears to have been more populous and more congested than in any previous period since the Ballana.

Economic and political decline set in again after the seventeenth century: it is reflected in the abandonment and the dilapidation of the Islamic houses, in a declining volume of imported goods, and in a paucity of texts

[41] Reported by Frend, *JEA* 60 (1974), 33–6. For discussion see Adams, *Nubia*, 515–18, 18 and id., *Archéologie du Nil Moyen*, 6 (1994), 11–46.

[42] Found at Gebel Adda but so far unpublished. The date is furnished in a personal communication from Nicholas B. Millet.

[43] See Plumley, *Nubia Christiana*, 1 (1982), 20; Hinds and Sakkout, op. cit., 2–3.

[44] See Adams, Alexander and Allen, *JEA* 69 (1983), 49.

[45] J. L. Burckhardt, *Travels in Nubia* (London, 1819), 133–5.

[46] See Plumley, *JEA* 50 (1964), 3.

[47] E.g. at Faras and Kulubnarti. See Kazimierz Michalowski, *Faras, fouilles polonaises 1961* (Warsaw, 1962), 173–81; and Adams in Erich Dinkler (ed.) *Kunst und Geschichte Nubiens in Christlicher Zeit* (Recklinghausen, 1970), 143–6.

[48] See Burckhardt, *Travels*, 134–5.

[49] See Hinds and Sakkout, op. cit.

[50] Adams, Alexander and Allen, *JEA* 69 (1983), 43–9.

[51] See Plumley, Adams and Crowfoot, *JEA* 62 (1977), 37–9.

relating to commercial activities. Conditions were evidently both impoverished and chaotic in the later eighteenth and early nineteenth centuries, on the evidence of Norden and other early European visitors.[52] By the nineteenth century the garrison force must have been fairly weak; for the last of the 'Bosnians' were evicted with little difficulty by Mamluk refugees fleeing from Egypt in 1811. A few months later the Mamluks in their turn were driven out by artillery fire, and the 3000-year history of Qaṣr Ibrîm came to an end.[53] (Pl. 1, b is a drawing made a few months after the final abandonment.) It ceased, in effect, to be a community and became an archaeological site, although 150 years were to elapse before any systematic excavation was undertaken.

The nature of the archaeological deposits

Because of its elevated situation, Qaṣr Ibrîm has been very little affected by natural forces either of deposition or destruction. With insignificant exceptions there is neither wind-blown nor waterborne nor tumbled deposit on the mountain-top; whatever is there is the result of intentional or unintentional human activity. There has also been no flooding, fire, earthquake, volcanic eruption, or any appreciable amount of rainfall. Even the normal processes of organic decay that affect most archaeological deposits have been absent; for the totally dry midden deposits at Qaṣr Ibrîm do not provide a viable habitat for insects or micro-organisms. The conditions of preservation are, in consequence, those that are usually encountered only in deep rock tombs or in dry caves. It can be stated with only slight exaggeration that whatever remains on the Qaṣr Ibrîm mountain-top has been placed there by the hand of man, and whatever does not remain has been removed by the hand of man.

The deposits within the citadel have essentially three components: the standing remains of buildings, the fallen or displaced remains of buildings, and the midden (refuse) deposit that accumulated within and around the buildings. The amount of surviving wall material obviously varies from area to area and from period to period. In densely settled and well-preserved sections of the town-site, such as those of the Ballana period, standing walls may be calculated as comprising about one-fourth of the total volume of archaeological deposit (Pl. 1, d). Fallen or displaced rubble from older buildings also varies considerably in density and distribution. Earlier construction on the citadel was mostly in either mud brick or cut stone. Displaced or fallen brick was seldom reused and is found rather thickly scattered through some of the refuse deposits. Cut stone, on the other hand, was consistently taken for use in later buildings and is rarely encountered as rubble. From Roman times onwards, the great majority of construction was always in roughly shaped stone blocks, laid up in heavy mud mortar and chinked with potsherds and stone chips. The larger stones from these walls were fairly consistently recycled in later buildings, while decomposed mortar and chinking became a significant component of the refuse deposits on the site.

Midden is the name usually given to archaeological refuse deposits resulting from human habitation. That part of the deposit at Qaṣr Ibrîm that is not made up of standing or fallen walls—at least 85% of the total volume—consists almost exclusively of dry, densely bedded midden. This material has many components: decomposed building material, human and animal dung, straw and chaff, small sticks and wood chips, ash and charcoal, animal bone and plant food refuse, and a vast amount of cultural debris. A midden deposit which had accumulated along the southern ramparts during the Roman occupation at Qaṣr Ibrîm was found to contain, for every 10 cu. m of deposit, an average of 2660 potsherds, 124.5 pieces of cloth, 3.5 registered objects of stone, 5.5 registered objects of metal, 3.9 registered objects of pottery, 1.95 objects of mud, 2.5 objects of glass, 8.8 objects of wood, 20.9 objects of leather, 11.7 fragments of basketry and cordage, 1.2 registered textile objects, 14.2 whole and fragmentary specimens of inscribed material on papyrus, stone, and potsherds, 1.35 coins, and 3.6 other registered objects.[54] For a Late Christian refuse deposit found within one of the houses reported in this volume the figures were 1530 potsherds, 98.5 pieces of cloth, .7 registered objects of stone, .7 registered objects of metal, 7.1 registered objects of pottery, 1 object of mud, 7.5 objects of glass, 21.8 objects of wood, 9.6 objects of leather, 5.4 fragments of basketry and cordage, 0.7 registered textile objects, and 57.8 whole and fragmentary inscriptions per 10 cu. m.[55]

The content and density of the midden deposit also varies from area to area and from level to level, reflecting in part the different uses to which space was put. The deposit in streets and plazas is usually relatively soft and contains a great deal of fine straw and chaff, indicative of the large amount of winnowing activity that was carried on at Qaṣr Ibrîm. There are also sub-

[52] Frederick Norden, *Travels in Egypt and Nubia,* trans. Tempelmann (London, 1757); W. G. Browne, *Travels in Africa, Egypt, and Syria from the Year 1792 to 1798* (London, 1799), 134–9.

[53] Reported in Thomas Legh, *Narrative of a Journey in Egypt and the Country Beyond the Cataracts* (London, 1817), 165–6.

[54] South Rampart Street, Section B, Level 3.

[55] House 763, Room 3.

a

b

c

d

e

Plate 1. General views of the site. a, Aerial view showing Qaṣr Ibrîm (centre) and the adjacent wadis, before flooding. b, Thomas Legh's sketch of Qaṣr Ibrîm in 1813, as viewed from downstream. c, View along the western fortifications, before flooding. d, General view over excavated houses of the 'X-Group' period, seen from the Cathedral tower. e, Storage pits excavated into the deposits west of the Cathedral.

stantial quantities of human and animal faeces; the dung of sheep, goats, cattle, horses, donkeys, and camels has been specifically recognized. Outdoor deposits contain also enormous quantities of small potsherds but very few large sherds, stone and brick fragments, or other material that would have been an impediment to traffic. Indoor deposits, on the other hand, may contain fallen wall material, large potsherds, wooden sticks, and all kinds of large and small cultural debris. Much of this material was clearly deposited after the abandonment of the buildings, when they were very often used as rubbish dumps. Even while the buildings were in use, however, a good deal of rubbish was brought in accidentally or deliberately at the time when floor levels were renewed and raised. Moreover, the mediaeval inhabitants at Qaṣr Ibrîm were in the habit of burying valuables of one kind or another beneath their floors, and for this reason the deposits within houses are sometimes found to contain intact objects, especially pottery vessels. Floor surfaces themselves are usually free from refuse, except in the few instances where there is evidence of precipitate abandonment. However, deposits of sheep and goat dung are more or less ubiquitous on the house floors at Qaṣr Ibrîm.

Although there is, in most areas, a total preservation of organic debris, deposits are occasionally encountered in which all organic material is absent and the midden deposit itself has turned to a fine dust. Some of this material may be wind-blown, but by far the larger part is thought to be the result of prolonged water spillage. There was no running water and virtually no rainfall on the site, but water was of course required for the daily consumption of the inhabitants, and there must have been a steady parade of human and animal water-carriers up and down the mountainside. Some areas within the citadel would appear to have served as water depots or distribution points for extended periods, resulting in the soaking and partial dissolution of the underlying deposits.

Mound or *tell* sites in the Near East often grow in a regular and consistent fashion, with the steady accumulation of later deposits on top of the earlier ones.[56] This was found to be true at Meinarti [57] and other village sites of mediaeval Nubia, where houses had a predictable life cycle from initial building through successive uses as dwellings, storehouses, animal pens, and finally rubbish dumps or latrines, before being overbuilt with new houses. At Qaṣr Ibrîm, however, the processes of urban growth and decay were seldom orderly or consistent. Three factors seem to have contributed to this anomalous situation. First, the site was not subject to the usual processes of wind-borne and waterborne deposition which tended gradually to raise the street and floor levels in other town-sites. Second, many of the buildings were of a monumental character and did not undergo the cycle of building, rebuilding, and decay that is normal in domestic structures. They tended to be kept in repair, and free from accumulated fill for centuries at a time and then to be dismantled wholesale for the reuse of their building stones. Activities of monumental building and dismantling sometimes had an impact on neighbouring habitation areas as well. Finally, from Roman times onward the majority of building at Qaṣr Ibrîm was in stone rather than mud brick, and the stones from earlier structures were consistently reused in later ones rather than being left to accumulate as rubble, as usually happened in the case of mud brick. These factors, together with others that will be discussed presently, combined to produce a singularly irregular pattern of stratification in the Qaṣr Ibrîm deposits.

The one natural force that has had any significant destructive impact at Qaṣr Ibrîm is wind. The mountain-top is naturally exposed and wind-swept, and the steady erosion of bricks and stones, and even more of the mud mortar between them, has visibly weakened some of the higher standing walls. The effects of wind damage are particularly apparent on the northern, or windward, side of the cathedral, but centuries of wind action probably contributed also to the periodic collapse of sections of the girdle wall. The weight of continually accumulating refuse deposits and buildings within and upon the girdle wall would presumably have been another contributing factor. Collapse of the wall resulted, at times, in the slumpage of the immediately adjacent deposits within. Apart from these episodes, however, the destructive agencies at Qaṣr Ibrîm have nearly all been the intentional or unintentional handiwork of man.

Human destructive activity at Qaṣr Ibrîm has been of four kinds: warlike depredations, wholesale urban renewals, the dismantling of old buildings to obtain stone for new ones, and pit digging. The first of these is of course the most dramatic, but at Qaṣr Ibrîm it was the least destructive in any permanent sense. A number of raids and several actual captures are historically attested, but here (as in most other urban sites) [58] the resulting damage seems to have been fairly promptly and completely repaired. In the archaeological record there is only one clear-cut indication of violent destruction: a mass of burned brick and other debris resulting

[56] For discussion see Seton Lloyd, *Mounds of the Near East* (Edinburgh, 1963), 13–21.

[57] See Adams, *Kush* 12 (1964), 222–34; *Kush* 13 (1965), 149–61; and in K.-C. Chang (ed.), *Settlement Archaeology* (Palo Alto, 1968), 174–207.

[58] For discussion see Adams, *Antiquity* 42 (1968), 207–8; and in Art Gallaher, Jr., and Harland Padfield (eds.), *The Dying Community* (Albuquerque, 1980), 30–1.

apparently from the destruction of churches and houses by Shams ed-Dawla in his well-known raid of 1172–3.[59] The very odd and apparently somewhat hasty wall repairs that were carried out in some of the Ballana period houses may also indicate rebuilding following one or another of the raids and counter-raids of that period.

For the rest, far more destruction has been wrought upon the installations at Qaṣr Ibrîm by the inhabitants of the place than by its enemies. Confined within its fortification walls, the settlement had no way to grow except upward. Houses could be built directly on the filled-up remains of older houses, without a great deal of preliminary dismantling, but the preparation of the ground for temples and churches usually involved a wholesale dismantling of earlier structures. There were at least two major 'urban renewals' in the mediaeval and early modern periods: one in the Early Christian period, when large areas of domestic habitation were cleared to provide an open plaza adjoining the Qaṣr Ibrîm churches, and one in the early Islamic period, when many Late Christian houses were apparently dismantled to provide material for rebuilding and heightening the girdle wall. Apart from these large-scale demolitions, abandoned buildings were more or less routinely robbed of their building stones, until in many cases only the foundations were left in situ. This process of continual recycling probably accounts for the successively smaller average size of building stones in the house walls of the Ballana, Early Christian, Late Christian, and Islamic periods.

Recycling of materials has affected not only the preservation of houses, but that of artifactual remains as well. Materials like pottery, glass, and most kinds of stone had no intrinsic value, and little remaining utility once the original vessels or implements were broken. Hence it is common to find these artifacts in large fragments, and sometimes even intact. Some kinds of pottery were so little esteemed that they were commonly discarded or abandoned while still unbroken, especially in the Ballana period.[60] On the other hand wood was obviously scarce and valuable, so that large items of wood were routinely refashioned into smaller ones and perhaps ultimately were burned as fuel, after they had served their original purposes. Thus, for example, the site has yielded literally hundreds of wooden keys and lock tumblers but only a few known examples of lock housings and bolts. Only one door has been found *in situ*, although there are stone sockets to indicate that they were originally present in a great many doorways. Similarly wooden spindles, spindle whorls, and shuttles are found in profusion, but larger loom parts such as beams, shed rods, and battens have not been identified.

Large pieces of iron were probably often melted down for reuse. Small items like knives, needles, and awls are quite common in the refuse deposits, but large ones such as axes and *turiya* blades are very rare. The case of bronze is even more ambiguous; for it is not certain that there was an indigenous bronze-founding industry in mediaeval Nubia. Items of bronze found in the archaeological deposits are probably small and relatively scarce, not because they were melted down for reuse but because they were expensive, imported luxuries.

Large pieces of plaited basketry and matting could be, and nearly always were, used to line storage pits after they were too broken or worn to serve their original purposes. Over 95% of all the plaited basketry found at Qaṣr Ibrîm has in fact come from storage-pit linings. On the other hand the smaller coiled baskets and lids had little remaining utility once they were worn out, and consequently these are often found discarded in the refuse deposits. A good many lids and some other baskets seem to have been discarded not because they were worn or broken but simply because they were soiled.

Textiles, whatever their original function, nearly always ended their days as rags. These are found by the tens of thousands in each season's excavations, but in fewer than 1% of cases is it possible to recognize the original form of the garment, drapery, or bag from which they came. The only garments that have been found intact in any numbers are doll's dresses, but these themselves probably represent a secondary use of older material.

Perhaps the most consistently destructive of all human activities at Qaṣr Ibrîm was the digging of storage pits. Throughout its later history the citadel was prized as a place for the safe storage of goods and foodstuffs, not only from human enemies but also and more importantly from the action of moisture and parasites. Grain stores, cached in mud bins or simply in excavated pits, would remain viable and edible for years at a time. Storage facilities in the form of bins or crypts or whole rooms are a conspicuous feature of most mediaeval houses at Qaṣr Ibrîm, yet it is apparent that only a fraction of the storage was done indoors. Virtually every square metre of the street and plaza areas of the site is dug through with deep storage pits which in total probably number several thousand (cf. Pl. 1, e). The typical pit is about a metre in diameter and a metre deep, with straight sides and a rounded bottom. Some, however, are far larger: one pit dug in late Islamic times was nearly 5 m in diameter and 3 m deep.[61] Pits, large and small, are found in profusion at every level of occupation from the Meroitic period

[59] See n. 35.

[60] See Plumley and Adams, *JEA* 60 (1974), 225–6.

[61] Pit no. 82/131 (Index no. 842).

onward. They intrude indiscriminately through whatever deposits underlie, destroying parts of walls and floors no less than the surrounding midden. It is a rare building at Qaṣr Ibrîm, either monumental or domestic, that has not been extensively damaged by the digging of pits after the time when it was abandoned and filled in.

The collective effect of urban renewals, the dismantling of buildings, and pit digging at Qaṣr Ibrîm has been to produce a very irregular and almost chaotic stratigraphy. It can never be taken for granted that the remains of any particular period will be directly underlain by those of the next preceding period; for the accumulated debris of several centuries may have been cleared away before the new buildings were overbuilt. Thus, over a considerable part of the site the Islamic town-remains are directly underlain by those of the Ballana period, 1000 years earlier. It is also usual to find that potsherds and other cultural debris from later periods have been intruded into much older deposits in the course of the digging and filling of storage pits. Further complicating the archaeologist's job is the fact that thousands of potsherds were employed as chinking in stone walls. When the walls were subsequently destroyed or dismantled, the sherds were redeposited in contexts long postdating the time of their manufacture. These circumstances have necessitated the development of very careful and somewhat specialized excavation procedures and controls, which will be detailed in later paragraphs.

The excavations at Qaṣr Ibrîm

In 1910, after a century of abandonment, the ruins at Qaṣr Ibrîm were visited by Gaston Maspéro, then the Director General of Antiquities in Egypt. On his recommendation some repair and restoration work was carried out in the cathedral and in one of the Meroitic temples.[62] This was not, however, accompanied by any formal archaeological investigation, which had to await the threatened destruction of Qaṣr Ibrîm by the Aswân High Dam waters.

A licence to excavate at Qaṣr Ibrîm was granted to the Egypt Exploration Society in 1961, as a contribution to the International Campaign to Save the Monuments of Nubia.[63] An initial season in 1961 was devoted to work in the riverside cemeteries,[64] and in 1963 work began on the citadel itself. There were further seasons of excavation in 1964,[65] both at the beginning and at the end of 1966,[66] in 1969,[67] in 1972,[68] and in every even-numbered year thereafter down to the present time.[69] In 1972 the University of Kentucky and the American Research Center in Egypt became associated with the Egypt Exploration Society as sponsors of the Qaṣr Ibrîm excavations, a connection that continued through subsequent seasons until 1986. Funding for the American contribution was provided largely by the Smithsonian Institution.

The early seasons at Qaṣr Ibrîm were in a sense a race against the rising waters of Lake Nasser, and it was this that dictated the excavation of the low-lying cemeteries before the citadel itself was undertaken. The cemeteries were finally submerged in 1964, and by 1969 the flood had reached and destroyed the lowest portion of the citadel fortifications, along the east side of the site. Among the first features to disappear was the ornamental gateway which, at least since Meroitic times, had provided the main ingress to the citadel. The waters continued to rise until in 1975 they finally reached the maximum pool contour, leaving the once lofty citadel as a small island separated by 70 m. of open water from the eastern shore of Lake Nasser. Since 1975 the lake surface has fluctuated considerably from season to season, reaching maximum pool contour more than once. However, since 1984 it has been at a level well below that which was reached in 1969 so that all of the previously inundated parts of the fortress have reemerged.

Inundation, even though temporary, has damaged or destroyed about one-fifth of the original surface area of the Qaṣr Ibrîm citadel along its eastern and south-eastern sides[70] (Fig. 2). The remains chiefly affected were 'Bosnian' houses that had been built directly on the *gebel* rock; for there was not much prior habitation at the eastern end of the Qaṣr Ibrîm mountain-top. There were, however, a small Meroitic temple (Temple 289) and an even smaller Christian church (Church 839); both have now been very largely destroyed by the lake waters. Elsewhere, no part of the citadel has been directly inundated, but the action of high waves during the periodic windstorms on Lake Nasser has undermined and brought down large parts of the fortification walls. The only part of the girdle wall which today survives in anything like its original condition is a short section at the west side of the site.

The earliest excavations on the Qaṣr Ibrîm citadel were concentrated on the clearance of overburden from the Cathedral and the Podium, two of the most prominently visible architectural features on the site. This was followed in later seasons by the digging of

[62] See Caminos, op. cit., 19.

[63] For a comprehensive history of the campaign see Torgny Säve-Söderbergh, *Temples and Tombs of Ancient Nubia* (London, 1987).

[64] Mills, op. cit.

[65] Plumley, *JEA* 50 (1964).

[66] Plumley, *JEA* 52 (1966), 9–12; id., *JEA* 53 (1967), 3–5.

[67] Plumley, *JEA* 56 (1970), 12–18.

[68] Plumley and Adams, *JEA* 60 (1974), 212–38.

[69] Plumley, *JEA* 61 (1975) 5–27. Plumley, Adams and Crowfoot, *JEA* 62 (1977) 29–47. Anderson and Adams, *JEA* 65 (1979) 30–41. Adams, Alexander, and Allen, *JEA* 69 (1983) 13–60.

[70] See Adams, Alexander and Allen, *JEA* 69 (1983), 45.

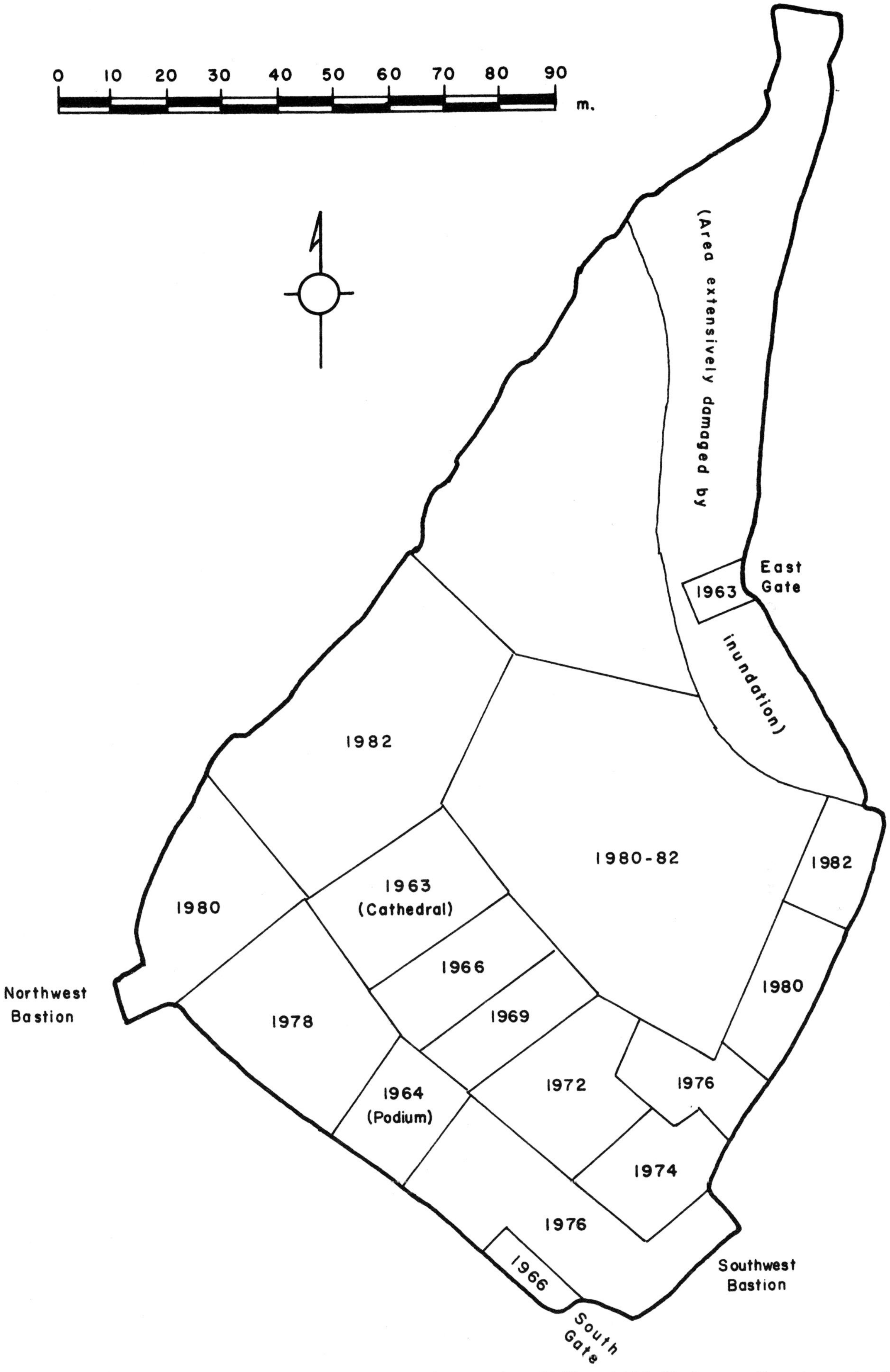

Figure 2. Plan of Qaṣr Ibrîm showing principal areas of excavation, 1963 to 1982. No late mediaeval remains have been excavated since 1982.

deep trenches and sondages in a number of areas, revealing the presence of extensive town-site remains of many different periods. Beginning in 1972 there was a shift toward a more long-range and coordinated excavation programme, involving the clearance of large contiguous areas down to a common level. The seasons from 1972 to 1976 were mostly devoted to the clearance of town-site remains of the Ballana period, as these had been extensively penetrated and disturbed by the sondage excavations of earlier seasons. Work in 1978 concentrated mainly on the mediaeval town-site remains west of the cathedral and on clearance of the large Meroitic temple adjoining the older Taharqa brick temple (cf. Fig. 2).

Beginning in 1980 there was another basic change of strategy. It was decided then to cease all work in the earlier horizons, except where necessitated by the threat of damage from wind or wave action, and to begin stripping all of the surviving remains phase by phase. The investigation of each major occupation episode would, in theory, be completed before work was begun on the next underlying stratum, and this would make possible the completion and publication of final excavation reports as each layer was completed. The 1980 and 1982 seasons were accordingly devoted mainly to investigation of the remaining 'Bosnian' (Ottoman-period) structures, which still covered the site surface wherever they had not been removed by the excavations of earlier years (see Fig. 2). This work was completed in the 1982 season, making possible the publication of a final report on the Islamic remains which will constitute a later volume in the present series.

Removal of the Islamic stratum revealed that there were, in the underlying deposits, very few surviving structures of the late mediaeval period, apart from those that had already been cleared in earlier seasons. Accordingly, the season of 1984 was sufficient to complete the investigation of the Late Christian remains at Qaṣr Ibrîm, making possible the preparation of the present monograph. Subsequent campaigns will concentrate similarly on the Early and Classic Christian periods (which can be treated as a single occupation episode), on the Ballana period, on the Meroitic period, and then on the earlier levels about which very little is currently known. Each major phase of occupation will form the basis for an excavation monograph to be prepared when the excavation of that particular level has been completed.

Excavation controls and documentation

The excavation and recording methods employed at Qaṣr Ibrîm developed over many seasons, and are still evolving. The account that follows here is descriptive of the procedures that were followed in the seasons between 1963 and 1986; that is, during the period when late mediaeval remains were being excavated. They are not necessarily the same procedures in use today, when it is no longer necessary to approach the Ibrîm dig as a salvage operation. It seems nevertheless desirable to give a description of the earlier procedures, since these will help to explain some of the kinds of documentation that are and are not found in the present monograph.

Earth removal is done basically by means of the *turiya* and basket, as has long been traditional in Egyptian archaeology (Pl. 2, a). In recent seasons a force of about sixty labourers has been employed, of whom about 20 are engaged in loosening and sifting deposit with the *turiya* (a heavy, short-handled hoe). The remaining forty men carry away the excavated earth in baskets after the removal of all potsherds, textile fragments, and other cultural material. Spoil is dumped over the citadel walls rather than within the townsite, since further excavations are planned in nearly every part of the site. House floors, burials, and other sensitive features are, of course, cleared by exceptionally skilled labourers, usually working with trowel and brush. Sieving of the deposit is carried out only in special circumstances or for special purposes, such as the recovery of plant remains or in deposits containing a large number of manuscript fragments. Because of the volume of organic material the work of sieving is enormously tedious and time-consuming, and experience has shown that is it normally not justified by the results.

Digging is mostly supervised by the Excavation Directors, with the assistance of one or two additional field archaeologists (Pl. 2, b). It is their task to establish and maintain controls, to bag and/or label all collections as they come from the ground, and to produce detailed field notes, sketch plans, and profiles. At the end of each season these records are made up in triplicate: one set to remain on the site, one to be deposited at Cambridge University, and one at the University of Kentucky. The total volume of field notes compiled since 1972 now includes more than 1000 pages of single-spaced typescript and more than 300 pages of sketch plans and profiles. In earlier years the archaeologists were also responsible for site photography, but since 1982 this task has been turned over to a full-time photographer. Survey and mapping, including the preparation of accurate profiles and elevations, has always required the services of one or more cartographic specialists, since continuous and accurate mapping is an essential feature of the excavation programme at Qaṣr Ibrîm. All buildings and features are routinely planned at a scale of 1:50. Over 100 individual building plans, profiles, and elevations have

Plate 2. Excavation and registration procedures. a, Excavations in the West Plaza area. b, Excavation supervision. c, Object registration on board the *Gerf Hussein*. d, Sorting potsherds on the *Gerf Hussein* upper deck. e, Examining and tallying textile fragments. f, The *Gerf Hussein* moored alongside the site.

been completed since the beginning of excavations in 1963.

The tangle of architectural remains at Qaṣr Ibrîm dictates the use of 'natural' rather than arbitrary excavation units. Every building, burial, pit, street, or plaza is given a separate identification number, and this becomes the basic unit of horizontal control. Within buildings each room is separately numbered, beginning with 1, while in streets and plazas the surface is divided up arbitrarily into sectors designated as A, B, C, and so on. Vertical controls are based on observable stratigraphy. Within any room or street the uppermost deposit is normally designated as Level 1, and each successive layer beneath this, as well as each floor surface, is numbered sequentially. A fairly typical control designation for sherds or textile material would therefore by 'House 763, Room 7, Level 3.' The location of more important artifacts is, of course, more accurately recorded with reference to walls, floors, or other datum points.

A word must be said about the system of numbers used to identify houses and other archaeological units throughout this report. They are not the same numbers which appear in preliminary excavation reports published in the *JEA*, or in field notes before 1982.

In the earliest seasons there was no consistent system of house numeration at Qaṣr Ibrîm. Buildings were simply identified descriptively as 'The Cathedral,' 'the vaulted brick complex,' and so on. As more and more buildings were uncovered, however, these designations proved insufficient, and in 1972 a uniform system of house numbers was introduced. Every building was assigned to a particular stratigraphic level, and all buildings belonging to any one level were numbered in sequence. This system resulted in designations such as X-17 (the seventeenth house found in the X-Group level), EC1-5 (the fifth house found in the Early Christian I level), and so on. Identification numbers of this kind appear in *JEA* reports between 1972 and 1982. However, the stratigraphic numbering system also proved to have its drawbacks. Many houses had continued to be occupied through several periods and thus had to be given a separate number for each period. The Meroitic and X-Group Tavern, for example, bore successively the numbers M-4, X-4, EC1-1, CC1-1, LC1-8, and LC2-11. Another difficulty arose from the fact that the proper stratigraphic context could not always be determined when houses were first discovered, yet numbers had to be assigned immediately for purposes of note-taking and the labelling of sherd and artifact finds. At times we guessed incorrectly, with the result that notes, plans, and artifact records had later to be altered. Still another shortcoming was the fact that the system of numeration applied only to buildings and did not provide designations for streets, plazas, or pits.

In 1982 a comprehensive system of index numbers was adopted, and every archaeological feature on the site was renumbered in accordance with this system. Every discrete feature, whether house, street, stairway, storage pit, burial, or whatever, was given a unique three-digit or four-digit identifying number, and it continued to carry the same number through all the different phases of its occupation or use. Stratigraphy was indicated by a prefix before the number, while a single letter following the index number indicated whether the feature was a house, street, pit, or some other kind of feature. Under this system the Meroitic and X-Group Tavern was given the unique index number 178, and its designation at different levels was M2-178-H, X1-178-H, X2-178-H, and so on through all the stratigraphic levels to LC2-178-H. The suffix H identifies the feature as a house. Other suffix designations are A, streets; C, churches, D, sub-floor deposits; M, monumental constructions; O, open plazas; P, storage pits; R, single rooms; T, temples; U, storage crypts; W, fortifications walls; X, unidentifiable features; Y, refuse dumps; and Z, stairways.

Three-digit identifying numbers of the kind introduced in 1982 are employed throughout the present report, but stratigraphic prefixes and indicative suffixes have generally been omitted, as they are not necessary for purposes of general discussion. They are employed in on-site documentation primarily in order to facilitate the computerization of the expedition's records, which is now underway. Correspondence between the building numbers employed in this report and those appearing in earlier published reports is indicated in Tables 4.1, 5.1, and 6.1.

Something must be said also about directional orientations given in this and other archaeological monographs on Qaṣr Ibrîm. The layout of the 'Bosnian' town-site which finally covered the top of the citadel was more or less at a 45° angle to the cardinal points of the compass, and this was found to repeat and perpetuate the orientation of all earlier townsite remains, at least as far back as Meroitic times. Even the Qaṣr Ibrîm churches have a northeast-to-southwest orientation, in contrast to all other churches in Nubia which are very nearly on an east-west axis.[71] Thus buildings at Qaṣr Ibrîm cannot be described accurately as having north, east, south, and west walls, nor can streets be characterized as running from north to south or from east to west. However, the continual use of the designations northeast, northwest, southeast, and southwest is awkward, and does not permit immediate visualization on the part of most readers. Accordingly it was decided long ago to adopt, for descriptive convenience, a set of directional orientations based on the fiction that the cathedral and other churches have

[71] See Adams, *JARCE* 4 (1965), 120

TABLE 2
REFERENCES TO QAṢR IBRÎM IN HISTORICAL WORKS

Era, AD	Author	Work	Language	Information given
Early 1st century	Strabo	*Geography*	Greek	Roman campaign of Petronius in 23 BC; capture of Ibrîm and establishment of Roman garrison
Late 1st century	Pliny	*Natural History*	Latin	(Same information as Strabo)
End of 2nd century	Ptolemy	*Geography*	Greek	Lists 'Primis minor' with other places in Lower Nubia
5th century	Olympiodorus	*History*	Greek	Tells of visiting Ibrîm at invitation of Blemmye king
Late 5th or early 6th century	Silko	*Graffito at Kalabsha*	Greek	Account of campaign against Blemmyes; tells of driving them from Ibrîm
Early 13th century	Abu Salih	*Churches and Monasteries*	Arabic	Description of Cathedral; Ibrîm called residence of Eparch; account of the raid of Shams ed-Dawla in 1172/73
Early 13th century	Ibn el-Athir	*The Perfect One in History*	Arabic	Account of the raid of Shams ed-Dawla in 1172/73
13th century	Abu Shama	*Two Gardens*	Arabic	(Same information as Ibn el-Athir)
13th century	Yahya el-Intaki	*Chronicle*	Arabic	Recounts an Egyptian invasion and capture of Ibrîm in 956
Late 13th century	Ibn Wadil	*History of Ayyubids*	Arabic	(Same information as Ibn el-Athir)
Early 14th century	Mufaddal	*The Straight Way*	Arabic	Ibrîm and Gebel Adda placed under direct rule of Mameluke Sultan following Egyptian invasion in 1275/76
Early 15th century	Maqrizi	*Geography*	Arabic	Mentions fortress of Ibrîm in his excerpt from Ibn Selim's 9th century travel accound; also recounts Egyptian invasion of 956, using information from Yahya el-Intaki
Early 15th century	Maqrizi	*Book of Dynasties*	Arabic	Raid of Shams ed-Dawla in 1172/73, as in Ibn el-Athir. Recounts a Mameluke raid and capture of Ibrîm in 1365/66. Egyptian emir reportedly met with Nubian king at Ibrîm
Late 17th century	Evliya Çelebi	*Travels*	Turkish	Lists Ibrîm as one of the Ottoman *sanjaks* of Egypt. Later recounts a personal visit in 1672. Reports horses were kept on citadel
1817	Thomas Legh	*Narrative of a Journey*	English	Reports expulsion of last inhabitants from Ibrîm by artillery fire in 1811

an east-west axis. What is technically the northeast wall of the cathedral is therefore designated as the east wall, the northwest wall is called the north wall, and so on around the building, and the same conventions are applied to all other buildings and streets on the site which have a northeast-to-southwest or a northwest-to-southeast orientation.

The same conventions are applied also to the orientation of the Nile Valley itself. The river as it passes Qaṣr Ibrîm is flowing approximately from southwest to northeast, but neighbouring areas upstream from the citadel are referred to for convenience as lying west of the site, and those downstream as lying east of the site.

The processing of collections

As in any townsite excavation, the primary emphasis at Qaṣr Ibrîm has always been on the uncovering, recording, and interpretation of the architectural and stratigraphic record. Recovery of artifactual material is an important but secondary objective. Nevertheless, the effort to cope with unprecedented quantities of small finds not only engages the attention of about two-thirds of the supervisory team, but is responsible for some of the most novel and unconventional features of the Qaṣr Ibrîm excavations. While two or three archaeologists have always been sufficient to direct and to oversee the

TABLE 3
EXCAVATION SEASONS AT QAṢR IBRÎM

Year	Dates	Principal areas worked	Preliminary Report, *JEA*
1961	Oct. 16–	Cemeteries 192 and 193, below citadel	—
1963	Jan. 20– Feb. 28	Cathedral	Vol. 50: 3–5
1964	Dec. 21– Feb 27	Cathedral; Christian houses overlying Podium	Vol. 50: 3–5 Vol. 60: 30–59
1966	Feb. 1– March 19	Deep sondage west of Cathedral; Christian houses east of Podium; Church 294	Vol. 52: 9–12
1966	Dec. 9– Dec. 13	Stairways to Cathedral terrace; South Gate	Vol. 53: 3–5
1969	Jan. 25– March 9	South Gate; Christian houses south of Church 294; Tavern	Vol. 56: 12–18
1972	Oct. 9– Dec. 4	X-Group houses along Tavern Street; Church 287	Vol. 60: 212–38
1974	Jan. 23– March 25	X-Group houses along Tavern Street; Meroitic, X-Group, and Christian structures south of Church 287; test excavation in East Gate	Vol. 61: 5–27
1976	Jan. 21– March 11	X-Group houses along lower Tavern Street and Magazine Street; Christian houses and plaza west of Church 287	Vol. 63: 29–47
1978	Jan. 15– March 30	Christian houses west of Cathedral; Meroitic Temple 290; South Bastion structure 283	Vol. 65: 30–41
1980	Jan. 17– March 13	'Bosnian' houses north of Cathedral; Ptolemaic and Roman deposits along southern ramparts; south Bastion structure 283	Vol. 69: 43-60
1982	Jan. 14–	'Bosnian' houses east and south of Cathedral; Late Christian houses north of Cathedral	Vol. 69: 43-60

actual work of digging, in recent years it has been necessary to engage two full-time registrars, two philologists, two textile analysts, and a basketry analyst, just to keep up with the daily accumulation of artifactual material (Pl. 2, c). Other specialists in the analysis of animal bone and of plant food remains have also joined the excavations for shorter periods.

For many seasons it has been the policy at Qaṣr Ibrîm to collect and examine *all* cultural debris, insofar as this could be done without resorting to special procedures like sieving. In front of each *turiya* digger there are placed, at a minimum, three collection baskets, each with a tag identifying the excavation unit and level. One basket is exclusively for the collection of potsherds, one for textile fragments, and one for all other finds. Depending on the nature and content of the deposit, additional baskets may be placed for the collection of basketry remains and of animal bone. The baskets are, of course, replaced with others as rapidly as they are filled. A typical day's excavation will produce altogether perhaps 20 full baskets of sherds, 10 baskets of textile material, and 5 baskets of other material.[72]

Baskets of sherds, when filled, are taken for washing and then await study by the archaeologists at the conclusion of each day's digging (Pl. 2, d). Textile material is taken to a protected area in the Qaṣr Ibrîm Cathedral, which serves as an on-site work laboratory; here the two textile analysts are continually at work throughout the day. Each fragment is examined, and at least minimally recorded as to type and provenance, while a great many specimens receive more detailed examination (Pl. 2, e). The unprecedented masses of material found at Qaṣr Ibrîm have necessitated a radically new, quantitative approach to the study of textiles, somewhat akin to the archaeologist's traditional treatment of potsherds. The methodology

[72] For the total quantities of various materials recovered in 1982 see Adams, Alexander, and Allen, *JEA* 69 (1983), 49.

employed has been described in detail in another place.[73]

Baskets of material other than sherds and textiles are delivered to the object registrars, who then undertake a further sorting. Recognizable and describable artifacts are numbered and set aside for drawing, cataloguing, and photography. Materials such as leather, cordage, and basketry scraps, animal bone, and plant remains are passed along to the appropriate specialists, if they are present on the team, or are bagged for later study. All manuscript finds, after initial registration, are passed to the epigraphers for more detailed recording and analysis. In recent seasons there have usually been two epigraphers, one for Arabic and Turkish and one for the mediaeval languages (Greek, Coptic, and Old Nubian).

The Qaṣr Ibrîm Expedition has always been somewhat handicapped by the lack of a fixed operational base in Egypt. The team is housed entirely on boats obtained from the Egyptian Antiquities Organization, but these must be returned to Aswân at the conclusion of each season. They are comfortably furnished and provide adequate living and working space, but there is of course no facility for the storage of finds between seasons. Anything of value which is found must necessarily be registered, packed, and shipped to Cairo at the conclusion of each campaign.[74] The result is that the study and documentation of finds can never be deferred from one season to the next. A part of the professional and technical staff is, therefore, obliged to remain on the site for a period of several weeks after the conclusion of digging to make sure that this work is fully completed.

In the study of artifactual remains, all objects which give evidence of human workmanship are initially collected, whether they are whole or fragmentary. They are given identifying numbers according to the day of finding; e.g. 78.2.4/33, the 33rd object found on the 4th of February, 1978. All objects are recorded and drawn, either singly or in groups, on standard recording slips. A typical season's work will yield about 1500 completed slips. The actual total of objects will be far larger, since in many cases a group of similar objects from the same provenance will be recorded on a single slip. Most whole and many fragmentary objects are also photographed. There is, as a result of these procedures, a dual system of registration numbers for artifacts. Every object has a day-number, and all those that are officially registered have also a registration number. Registration numbers are sequential for each season; thus Reg. No. 72/56 is the 56th object registered during the 1972 season.

Throughout the present report, reference is made from time to time to individual artifacts. In these cases identifying numbers are usually given in parentheses or in a footnote. Official registration numbers are used by preference, since these are the numbers appearing in the records of the Egyptian Antiquities Organization and its museums. However, day-numbers are given for all objects that were not officially registered and also in cases where the registration number does not provide a complete identification (because several finds were registered under one number). Museum accession- or catalogue-numbers have also been given in a few instances, but, for the most part, we are not informed of the numbers that are assigned by the different Egyptian museums once the objects are taken in division.[75]

It has to be acknowledged frankly that the documentation for the later seasons of excavation at Qaṣr Ibrîm is much more complete than that from the earlier seasons. In the 1960's, especially, there was uncertainty about the rate of flooding of Lake Nasser and about the extent to which the Qaṣr Ibrîm citadel would be affected. There was also, in the absence of any previous excavation, no very definite knowledge about what might be expected in the underlying levels, and to what extent they would repay excavation. There was, in consequence, a certain amount of haste in the early campaigns, and buildings were sometimes dismantled without being very fully or accurately documented. There was, in addition, a severe shortage of personnel and of time, which precluded the collection and detailed description of many kinds of remains that are now routinely studied. The total of registered finds from the earlier seasons is, in consequence, only a fraction of that from the later seasons. After 1972 conditions were somewhat alleviated by the availability of Smithsonian funding, which made possible both a larger excavation staff and a longer season. These circumstances should be borne in mind by readers of this and other reports on the Qaṣr Ibrîm excavations, for they will find the documentation for some buildings and artifacts to be less complete than could be desired.

Even today, the excavation procedures at Qaṣr Ibrîm are not always up to textbook standards. The dig is not, and by its nature cannot be, an exercise in method; for it still remains a race against time. With limited resources, and within a finite span of years, we are endeavouring to recover the 3000-year history of a five-acre site, with the certain knowledge that waves, capillary action, and the depredations of fishermen will in time destroy whatever we do not excavate. (The site is wholly unguarded during the intervals between our excavations.) In these circumstances we are inclined to

[73] Nettie K. Adams, *Wissenschaftliche Zeitschrift der Humboldt-Universität zu Berlin, Geisteswissenschaftliche Reihe,* 35 Jg., Heft 1 (1986), 21–6.

[74] Finds from Qaṣr Ibrîm have variously been allotted to the Egyptian, Coptic, and Islamic Museums in Cairo. Many will probably ultimately go to the Nubian Museum now under construction in Aswân.

[75] See n. 74.

introduce methodological refinements when, and only when, they produce measurable results. By more painstaking procedures we would surely recover much that now escapes us, but we would end by recovering only a 1000-year history of the site, or perhaps the 3000-year history of a fraction of the site. Because of the unique position of Qaṣr Ibrîm in Nubian history, we have opted, as it were, to paint a large picture with a broad brush, rather than a smaller picture with a finer brush.

Chronology and chronological controls

At Qaṣr Ibrîm both structures and artifacts can be dated much more accurately than is usually possible in town-site excavations in the Nile Valley. In part this is due to the extraordinary number of whole and fragmentary written texts that are preserved in the site; they are recovered by the hundreds and sometimes by the thousands in each season's excavations. Only a fraction of the texts bear actual dates, but others can be roughly dated either by the events or personalities referred to, or on palaeographic grounds. In either case the dates can of course be applied to the deposits in which the texts are found and to any other objects discovered in the same deposits.

Even where texts are absent, the method of total ceramic analysis which we have employed at Qaṣr Ibrîm since 1972 will usually permit the dating of deposits within an interval of 100 years, and often of 50 years or even less. This methodology, previously developed in a series of excavations in Sudanese Nubia, has been extensively described elsewhere and need not be detailed here.[76] Suffice it to say that all potsherds from all excavation units are routinely saved, sorted, and tallied, according to a taxonomic scheme of 102 known and dated pottery wares.[77] The relative proportion of wares present or absent in each level of deposit serves to fix its date within fairly narrow time limits. The continual study of potsherds is thus an essential key to deciphering the tangled stratigraphy at Qaṣr Ibrîm. It is for this reason that the study of accumulated sherds is undertaken each day by the excavation supervisors themselves, rather than being delegated to specialists as in the study of other kinds of finds.

The present monograph deals specifically with those phases of Nubian history which elsewhere have been designated as Late Christian and Terminal Christian.[78] At Qaṣr Ibrîm these correspond to the interval between the rebuilding of the fortifications and reoccupation of the mountain-top, probably shortly after 1173, and the putative depopulation at the end of the fifteenth century (see Table 1). The period involved was not, of course, one of complete stability or stagnation; it was marked at the beginning by rapid growth and at the end by rapid decay. In the interval there were changes in the prevailing canons of architecture, pottery, textiles, and most other material goods. Accordingly the chapters that follow cannot give a wholly static picture but must attempt to characterize the life and culture of Qaṣr Ibrîm at a number of different points in time. For purposes of descriptive and analytical convenience the period covered by this monograph has been subdivided into phases which are designated as Late Christian I (LC1 for short),[79] Late Christian II (LC2), and Terminal Christian (TC).[80] The first of these is believed to have extended from 1173 to about 1300, the second to about 1400, and the last to about 1500. In the pages that follow both architecture and artifacts will often be designated chronologically or typologically according to the three aforementioned phases.

It should not be supposed that the chronological phases designated as LC1, LC2, and TC correspond to distinct building episodes in the history of Qaṣr Ibrîm, or that they are marked by abrupt changes in pottery and other items of material culture. Like most other archaeological periodizations they are purely heuristic; that is, they provide a convenient device for placing architectural remains and artifacts in a chronological context relative to one another. It would of course be still more desirable to place the Qaṣr Ibrîm finds in an absolute chronological context (i.e. as belonging to the thirteenth, fourteenth, or fifteenth century), but our chronological controls in most cases are simply not that precise.

[76] William Y. Adams, *Wissenschaftliche Zeitschrift der Humboldt-Universität zu Berlin, Geisteswissenschaftliche Reihe,* 35 Jg., Heft 1 (1986), 27–45; id., *Ceramic Industries of Medieval Nubia* (Memoirs of the UNESCO Archaeological Survey of Nubia, 1) (Lexington, 1986), 617–33.

[77] See Adams, *Ceramic Industries.*

[78] For details of the Christian Nubian chronology see Adams, *Kush* 12 (1964), 241–7; and T. Säve-Söderbergh in C. J. Gardberg, *Late Nubian Sites* (Scandinavian Joint Expedition to Sudanese Nubia Publications, Vol. 7) (Stockholm, 1970), 14–21.

[79] It is important to notice that the Late Christian I period at Qaṣr Ibrîm, as described in this monograph, does not correspond precisely to the Late Christian I period for Nubia as a whole, as described in Adams, *Kush* 12, and Säve-Söderbergh in Gardberg, *Late Nubian Sites.* The LC1 period for Nubia as a whole is estimated to begin around 1100 A.D., whereas at Qaṣr Ibrîm we begin this period with the raid of Shams ed-Dawla in 1172–13.

[80] See n. 78.

Logistics

The rather forlorn surroundings and the lack of immediate human neighbours create an impression of isolation and privation at Qaṣr Ibrîm that is not fully justified. There are no habitable buildings on the site, or indeed within 40 km of it, but the expedition has been comfortably housed for many years in houseboats provided by the Egyptian Antiquities Organization (Pl. 2, f). One of these, the *Zoser*, is equipped with running water, showers, and, intermittently, with electricity. This vessel provides the basic housing, eating, and working space for the expedition members. In a number of seasons an older boat, the *Gerf Hussein*, has also been available to provide additional working and storage space. The Egyptian labour force is housed on a third vessel, a large and partly covered barge. Motive power is provided by tugboats which tow the houseboats and barge from Aswân to Qaṣr Ibrîm at the beginning of each season and back to Aswân at the end. One tugboat remains with the expedition throughout the season, providing a means of communication, when necessary, with Abu Simbel, five hours away to the south. Here are several small shops, a clinic, a post office, and an airport with several daily flights to Aswân. The recent completion of a tarmac road has resulted also in the opening of bus service between Aswân and Abu Simbel. Another tug regularly plies back and forth between Aswân, Qaṣr Ibrîm, and Abu Simbel, making the round trip about every fortnight and bringing fresh supplies and mail. Basic supplies of food and other provisions are purchased in Aswân at the start of each season, but they are supplemented by fresh provisions brought by the tug on its fortnightly trips. Fresh fish is plentifully available from fishing crews on the lake. The working and living conditions at Qaṣr Ibrîm are thus somewhat unusual by Nile Valley standards, but they do not compare to the isolation and privation that are routine features of many excavations in Latin America, Africa, or many parts of Asia.

CHAPTER 2
CHRISTIAN NUBIA: THE HISTORICAL AND CULTURAL SETTING

WE have a much fuller picture of the history and the culture of mediaeval Nubia than we have for any earlier period. This is due in considerable part to the accounts left by Arab travellers and scholars, who showed a good deal more interest in Nubia and the Nubians than did any of the country's earlier neighbours. The eye-witness report of Ibn Selim el-Aswâni, written near the end of the tenth century,[1] is of especial value, but altogether there are more than a hundred references to Nubia in mediaeval Arabic works.[2] The available source material was brought together half a century ago by Monneret de Villard to produce his pioneering *Storia della Nubia cristiana,* [3] but since that time a mass of additional material has come to light. This has enabled Fr. Giovanni Vantini to undertake two recent works of synthesis[4] which substantially augment the earlier work of Monneret de Villard. Archaeology has meanwhile rounded out our picture of the social and cultural life of mediaeval Nubia. Medieval sites were largely ignored in the earlier archaeological campaigns in Nubia,[5] but this deficiency was more than rectified by the large number of churches and villages that were investigated between 1960 and 1970 as part of the Aswân High Dam salvage campaign.[6] The archaeological record of Christian Nubia has been most fully synthesized by W. Y. Adams in *Nubia, Corridor to Africa.* [7]

The *Baqt* treaty and its consequences

Throughout the historic period the shadow of Egypt, the 'northern colossus,' has seldom been absent from Nubia. Even in times of political independence the fortunes and misfortunes of the Nubians have been closely bound up in their relations with their northern neighbours. In times when Egypt was exceptionally strong politically she usually tried to subjugate or even to annex Nubia, with unhappy consequences for the native population. When Egypt was weak or impoverished, on the other hand, there was little market for the exported luxury goods (gold, ivory, ebony, slaves, etc.) on which the prosperity of the Nubian kingdoms depended to a considerable degree. The most flourishing periods in Nubian history were, therefore, those in which Egypt was relatively well off economically but was divided or disorganized politically. To a very large extent this was the case during the Middle Ages.

The Arab conquerors of Egypt attempted almost at once to extend their dominion into Nubia, but two separate invasions, in 642 and 652, were successfully repulsed. After the second of these incursions a treaty, called the *Baqt,* was concluded, which largely shaped the course of Egyptian-Nubian relations for the next 600 years. Under its terms the Nubians were protected from further attempts at subjugation or Islamization but in return were required to deliver an annual tribute of 400 slaves to the Emir of Aswân. They were also obliged to grant safe conduct and privileges to Egyptian and other Muslim merchants travelling in Lower Nubia, and to return any runaway slaves to the Egyptians.[8] According to some accounts the Nubians on their side were to receive annual payments of wine, grain, textiles, and other goods.[9] There has been much dispute over the terms and the meaning of the *Baqt* treaty,[10] but a document found at Qaṣr Ibrîm in 1972 confirms that the version of the treaty which is preserved in the fifteenth century geography of Maqrizi is substantially correct.[11]

The *Baqt* treaty provided the climate of peaceful relations and of active commercial intercourse in which Nubia's mediaeval civilization was nurtured. Freed

[1] The original is lost, but excerpts are preserved in Maqrizi's fifteenth century geography, *al-Khitat.* For translations see J. L. Burckhardt, *Travels in Nubia* (London, 1819), 493–521, and G. Troupeau, *Arabica* 1 (1954), 279–88.

[2] For an encyclopaedic compendium of these sources see Giovanni Vantini, *Oriental Sources Concerning Nubia* (Heidelberg and Warsaw, 1975).

[3] Pontificium Institutum Orientalium Studiorum, Orientalia Christiana Analecta 118 (Rome, 1938).

[4] Vantini, op. cit.; id., *Christianity in the Sudan* (Bologna, 1981); id., *Il cristianismo nella Nubia antica* (Verona, 1985).

[5] The only significant exception was the survey of Nubian churches made by Ugo Monneret de Villard and published in *La Nubia medioevale*, I–IV (Cairo, 1935 and 1957).

[6] See William Y. Adams, *Nubia, Corridor to Africa* (London, 1977), 83–6; Torgny Säve-Söderbergh, *Temples and Tombs of Ancient Nubia* (London, 1987).

[7] Adams, *Nubia*, Ch. 14–16.

[8] For translations of the treaties see Burckhardt, op. cit., 511–12, and Forand, *Der Islam* 48 (1971), 114–15.

[9] Burckhardt, *Travels,* 512.

[10] See Forand, op. cit., and Hinds and Sakkout in Wadad al-Qadi (ed.), *Studia Arabica et Islamica* (Beirut, 1981), 209–16.

[11] For the text and translation see Hinds and Sakkout in al-Qadi (ed.), *Studia,* 217–24.

from the continual threat of military invasion and from the political instability which is often engendered by a large military establishment, the Nubians devoted themselves to commerce and building and achieved for a time a kind of golden age second only to the Empire of Kush. In later centuries there were frequent complaints that the Nubians were not living up to the terms of the *Baqt*, [12] but the Egyptians kept their side of it at least to the extent that for more than 500 years they made no attempt to subjugate the Nubians or to propagate the Islamic faith. The raid of Shams ed-Dawla in 1172–3, which apparently caused considerable damage and led to the refortification of Qaṣr Ibrîm, was the first serious breach of the compact.[13] Yet even this was only a brief and temporary interruption in the general course of peaceful and profitable intercourse. It was not until after the advent of Mamluk rule in Egypt in 1250 that serious military disturbances began, disturbances that were to contribute to the weakening and ultimate dissolution of the Kingdom of Makouria. Significantly, the pretext originally cited by the Mamluks to justify their incursions was that the *Baqt* tribute of slaves was in arrears.[14]

The Kingdom of Makouria

In the sixth century AD there appear to have been three major kingdoms in Nubia: Nobadia in the north, Makouria in the Dongola region, and Alwa or Alodia in the region around the junction of the Blue and White Niles. A century or two later Nobadia was absorbed into the Kingdom of Makouria, although the name Nobadia persisted for many centuries as a toponym for the more northerly part of the kingdom, in which Qaṣr Ibrîm was situated.[15]

We have little detailed information about the political or administrative structure of the mediaeval Nubian kingdom of Makouria. The capital and principal royal residence was at Dongola, about halfway between the Third and Fourth Cataracts of the Nile.[16] According to an Arab chronicler the power of the king was in theory absolute; he was regarded as the owner of all the land, and all of his subjects were nominally his slaves.[17] These powers were, however, tempered by the concessions granted to Muslim merchants under the terms of the *Baqt*. Later Arab historians, including Ibn Khaldûn, reported that the royal succession was, or could be, transmitted in the female line,[18] but there are only one or two recorded instances when this rule is known to have been applied.[19] Surrounding the king were various court functionaries who bore Byzantine titles: *domestikos*, *protodomestikos*, *meizon*, *protomeizoteros*, *primikerius*, and others.[20] Apart from the titles themselves we know little or nothing about the functions of these officials, either in central or in provincial administration.

In addition to the court bureaucracy there was evidently some kind of feudal order. Abu Salih mentions that the 'Great King' at Dongola was overlord to thirteen lesser kings.[21] In Lower Nubia there are late mediaeval inscriptions of a certain 'King Tienossi of Ilenat,' and of another king called Koudlaniel.[22] However, the local monarchy which is most frequently mentioned in texts is Dotawo, which was evidently centered in the region around Qaṣr Ibrîm. In the fifteenth century, after the collapse of Makouria, Dotawo was to emerge as a fully independent state, but at Qaṣr Ibrîm there are documents referring to the monarchy going all the way back to the year 1155, when the sovereignty of Makouria was still paramount.[23] Probably the King of Dotawo and other local feudatories provided what provincial government there was in the Kingdom of Makouria.

The one civil official about whom we have some concrete information is the Eparch of Nobadia, who was in effect the Viceroy of Lower Nubia.[24] Under the

[12] Op. cit., 209–16; Forand, op. cit., 116–21; Adams, *Nubia*, 454–8.

[13] Reported by Abu Ṣalih. See B. T. A. Evetts and A. J. Butler, trans., *The Churches and Monasteries of Egypt and Some Neighbouring Countries* (Oxford, 1895), 266–7.

[14] See Adams, *Nubia*, 526–7.

[15] For discussion of the unification of Nobadia and Makouria see Ugo Monneret de Villard, *Storia della Nubia cristiana* (Pontificium Institutum Orientalium Studiorum, Orientalia Christiana Analecta 118) (Rome, 1938), 79–83. See also Kirwan, *The Geographical Journal* 140 (1974), 43–51, and Adams, *The Geographical Journal* 142 (1976), 381–4.

[16] Now known as Old Dongola to distinguish it from the more recently founded New Dongola (Dongola el-Urdi), some 110 km to the north.

[17] Ibn Selim el-Aswâni, cited in Monneret de Villard, *Storia*, 169.

[18] This was reported by Abu Salih and Ibn Khaldûn, among others. See Evetts and Butler, op. cit., 271–2, and J. Spencer Trimingham, *Islam in the Sudan* (London, 1949), 71–2.

[19] For an enumeration and discussion of the known kings of Makouria see Stuart Munro-Hay, 'Kings and Kingdoms of Ancient Nubia' (MS). See also Vantini, *Cristianismo*, 311–20.

[20] For discussion see Monneret de Villard, *Storia*, 189–91.

[21] Evetts and Butler, op. cit., 272.

[22] See F. Ll. Griffith, *The Nubian Texts of the Christian Period* (Abhandlungen der Königlichen Preussischen Akademie der Wissenschaften, 1913, Phil.-Hist. Classe, no. 8) (Berlin, 1913), 52. See also Monneret de Villard, *La Nubia* I, 174–5.

[23] See Plumley in *Études nubiennes* (Institut français d'archéologie orientale, Bibliothèque d'étude, 77) (Cairo, 1978), 231–41.

[24] His title in Arabic is usually read as *sahib al-gebel*, translated as 'Lord of the Mountain.' In some texts, however, it is read as *sahib al-khayl*, translated as 'Lord of the Horses.' Hinds suggests that the latter is the correct reading, and that renderings as 'Lord of the Mountain' are erroneous; see Plumley, *JEA* 56 (1970), 14. Still more recently, however, G. M. Browne has observed that both the titles 'Lord of the Mountain' and 'Lord of the Horses' are employed in Old Nubian texts; see *Old Nubian Texts from Qaṣr Ibrîm*, II (Egypt Exploration Society, Texts from Excavations) (London, in press).

terms of the *Baqt* Egyptian traders were allowed to circulate freely in Lower Nubia, whereas above the Second Cataract all foreign commerce was a royal monopoly.[25] The supervision of trade, and of Nubian-Egyptian relations in general, was evidently the special responsibility of the Eparch. Some commentators have suggested that the office was hereditary,[26] but letters found at Qaṣr Ibrîm have shown clearly that it was appointive.[27] The Eparch was, however, invested with some of the trappings of royalty: he wore a special horned headdress and is depicted in wall paintings as a founder of churches, and even as receiving the blessings of the Holy Family.[28] Fluency in the Arabic language must have been one of the qualifications of the office, for at Qaṣr Ibrîm much of the correspondence addressed to the Eparchs is in Arabic.[29] In the early Middle Ages the principal residence of the Eparch may have been at Faras, but after the time of the Shams ed-Dawla raid it was certainly at Qaṣr Ibrîm. At least three of the houses within the citadel have been identified by their contents as eparchal residences (see below, pp. 42–58).

The splinter-state of Dotawo

After the disintegration of Makouria, the formerly vassal state of Dotawo evidently became fully independent. Although increasingly impoverished, it does not seem to have been severely beset either by foreign or domestic enemies until near the end of the fifteenth century, and in the meantime it managed to keep alive some of the traditions and the institutions of Christian Nubia. Its situation must have been an isolated one; for the existence of Dotawo is not mentioned in any Arabic or European work. Our only information comes from internal records in the Old Nubian language, nearly all of which have been found either at Qaṣr Ibrîm or at Gebel Adda.[30] In the Mahas-Fadidja (Nobiin) dialect of Nubian the name Dotawo means 'under Do,' and probably derives from the mediaeval name of Gebel Adda (Daw in Arabic manuscripts).[31] Thus Gebel Adda is usually regarded as the principal seat of royal authority, but the number of documents found at Qaṣr Ibrîm make it evident that this was also a place of major importance.[32]

The surviving records of Dotawo are nearly all legal documents, and they are far from being fully understood at the present time. They do, however, furnish a fairly lengthy list of titles, both civil and ecclesiastical, and the juxtaposition of these suggests that there was no longer a clear line of distinction between church and state.[33] How far the territory of Dotawo extended can only be conjectured; for nearly all of the surviving texts have been found within a single small area surrounding Qaṣr Ibrîm and Gebel Adda. Of the ten or so Kings of Dotawo who are known to us by name,[34] the most active was apparently the last, a certain King Joel, whose name is attached to a number of dedicatory and legal inscriptions dated between 1464 and 1484.[35] After the latter date the historical record of Dotawo, and indeed of Christian Nubia, comes to an end.

Christianity and the church

In mediaeval Nubia, no less than in Europe, the church provided an administrative structure more universal in scope, and hardly less powerful or wealthy, than that of the monarchies. The evangelization of Nubia took place at a time when there was active and frequently hostile competition between the Melkite (Byzantine) and Monophysite (Coptic) factions in Egypt. Both attempted to convert the Nubians to their respective causes, and both had some initial success. However, the Arab conquest of Egypt in the seventh century assured the final ascendancy of the Monophysites, who had largely sided with the invaders, and this was ultimately reflected in Nubia as well. The Nubian church became, and throughout the Middle Ages remained, simply a territorial extension of the Coptic Orthodox Church of Egypt.[36]

The character of Coptic Christianity was, and is, relatively hierarchical and exclusive, probably reflecting the persistence of ancient Egyptian religious traditions. The sanctuary of each church is separated by a solid *higab*, or ikonostasis, from the nave and aisles, so that the congregation is excluded not only from participation in but even from witnessing most of the holy service. In the small late Nubian churches there is even a suggestion that the entire building was reserved for the clergy, the sermon being delivered to the congrega-

[25] See Burckhardt, *Travels,* 494–5.

[26] See Adams, *Nubia*, 466.

[27] Discussed below pp. 245–6.

[28] See Monneret de Villard, *Storia*, 182–6, and Adams, *Nubia*, 466.

[29] See Plumley in Kazimierz Michalowski (ed.), *Nubia, récentes recherches*, 106.

[30] These documents are enumerated in Adams, *Nubia*, 532–3, and in Plumley, *Études* , 234–5.

[31] For discussion of the name see Monneret de Villard, *Storia,* 141–2, and Adams, *Nubia,* 535.

[32] See Gerald M. Browne, *Old Nubian Texts from Qaṣr Ibrîm*, III (Egypt Exploration Society, Texts from Excavations) (London, in press). See also pp. 225–6 and 244–5, below.

[33] Adams, *Nubia*, 534.

[34] Op. cit., 532–3; Plumley, *Études*, 234–5.

[35] See Adams, *Nubia*, 532–4.

[36] For further discussion see Monneret de Villard, *Storia,* 158–68, and Adams, *Nubia,* 471–3.

tion from the church door.[37] The frequent presence of small churches alongside the great cathedrals (as at Qaṣr Ibrîm) suggests too that the cathedrals were not for everyday services, the laity being admitted perhaps only once or twice a year on the occasion of special festivals. In Nubia, the somewhat exclusive and esoteric character of the church must have been further reinforced by the fact that many of the higher clergy were Egyptians rather than Nubians.[38]

According to a late ecclesiastical history there were seven episcopal sees in the Kingdom of Makouria, of which those at Qurta, Qaṣr Ibrîm, Faras, Sai, and Dongola can be substantiated from archaeological and textual records.[39] There was no archbishop or overall governing official comparable to the Abuna of Abyssinia; the Nubian bishops were all appointed, independently of one another, by the Coptic Patriarch, and were responsible directly to him. Insofar as there was any *primus inter pares* among the Nubian bishops, it was probably the Bishop of Faras in the early Middle Ages and the Bishop of Ibrîm later.[40]

Clerical personnel included bishops, presbyters, archdeacons, deacons, 'epideacons,' and 'hypodeacons.'[41] Parochial or congregational organization must have been fairly strong, for many communities boasted a number of different church buildings. In places like Qaṣr Ibrîm and Serra, which grew significantly by accretion in the later Middle Ages, new churches may have been built by and for the newly arriving settlers.[42] There were also monks, living both in monastic communities and in isolated desert caves, but monasticism never flourished in Nubia as it did in Egypt. Abu Salih, who never actually visited Nubia, wrote glowingly of the many and wealthy Nubian monasteries,[43] but only a handful of these have ever been recognized archaeologically. All of them were relatively small, at least by Egyptian standards, and all seem to have gone out of existence by the late Middle Ages.[44]

The lower ranks of the Nubian clergy may have been filled from the native populace, but many of the bishops and monks were evidently Egyptians, as is attested by their tombstones and mural inscriptions in the Coptic language. Notwithstanding this fact, and the administrative unity of the Nubian and Egyptian churches, the liturgical language of mediaeval Nubia was always Greek rather than Coptic. In architecture and in art too there were significant differences between the Nubian and Egyptian churches. Nubian church buildings retained, at least until the thirteenth century, an elongated basilican form which had long gone out of vogue in Egypt. They had, in addition, certain peculiarly Nubian features: the building was entered from the north and south sides rather than from the west, and at the east end there was a narrow passage behind the sanctuary, connecting the sacristy and the baptistry. This latter feature is known from only a handful of occurrences outside Nubia.[45] In the thirteenth century a radically simplified and smaller form of church, nearly square in plan, made its appearance. These buildings have parallels among the late mediaeval churches of Anatolia and Greece, but again they are not closely similar to the church buildings of Egypt.[46]

The mural art of the Nubian churches, although in the beginning closely similar to that of contemporary Egypt, evolved through a series of phases which became more distinctly Nubian over time. The various developmental phases are best represented in the magnificently preserved Cathedral of Faras,[47] but they are also exemplified at Tamit,[48] Abdullah Nirqi,[49] Sonqi Tino,[50] Kulubnarti,[51] and other churches that were excavated during the High Dam salvage campaign. Whether or not there were also independent developments in the field of religious literature is questionable, but a good many familiar religious texts were translated into the Old Nubian language.[52]

In spite of its concessions to local artistic and linguistic traditions, the church in Nubia was never in any real sense a Nubian church. It was a foreign institution without deep local roots, and was dependent for its survival on periodic infusions of clergy from abroad. When, at the end of the Middle Ages, the link with Alexandria was broken, the demise of Nubian Christianity inevitably followed. The Nubians sent first to Egypt[53] and then to Abyssinia[54] requesting the send-

[37] See especially Adams, *JARCE* 4 (1965), 118.

[38] See Adams, *Nubia*, 485–6.

[39] Op. cit., 472.

[40] For further discussion see Adams, op. cit.

[41] Op. cit., 473; Monneret de Villard, *Storia*, 166–8.

[42] See Adams, *Nubia,* 478.

[43] See Evetts and Butler, op. cit., 261–4.

[44] For further discussion see Adams, *Nubia*, 478–80.

[45] See Monneret de Villard, *La Nubia*, III, 3–8.

[46] See Adams, *Nubia*, 118.

[47] See especially Kazimierz Michalowski and Georg Gerster, *Faras, die Kathedrale aus dem Wüstensand* (Zurich and Cologne, 1967), and Michalowski, *Faras* (Warsaw, 1974).

[48] Università degli Studi di Roma, Missione Archeologica in Egitto, *Tamit (1964)* (Rome, 1967).

[49] Paul van Moorsel *et al.*, *The Central Church of Abdullah Nirqi* (Leiden, 1975).

[50] Donadoni in Erich Dinkler (ed.), *Kunst und Geschichte Nubiens in Christlicher Zeit* (Recklinghausen, 1970), 200–16.

[51] Adams in Dinkler, op. cit., 146 and pl. 121; id., *Kulubnarti* I (Lexington. 1994), ch. III.

[52] See Griffith, *The Nubian Texts;* Adams, *Nubia*, 485–6; J. Martin Plumley and Gerald M. Browne, *Old Nubian Texts from Qaṣr Ibrîm, I* (Egypt Exploration Society, Texts from Excavations, 9) (London, 1988).

[53] Yusuf Fadl Hasan, *The Arabs and the Sudan* (Edinburgh, 1967), 126.

[54] Francisco Alvarez, *The Prester John of the Indies*, trans. Lord Stanley (Cambridge, 1961), 461.

TABLE 4
CHRONOLOGY OF MEDIAEVAL NUBIAN HISTORY

Year, A.D.	Cultural phase*	Main historical events
1550	Post-Christian	Ottoman annexation of Lower Nubia
1500	——	Probable end of organized Nubian Christianity
		Probable end of Dotawo Kingdom
1450	Terminal Christian	Independent Kingdom of Dotawo
1400	——	
		Disintegration of Kingdom of Makouria
1350	Late Christian II	Further Mamluk incursions
1300	——	
		Beginning of Mamluk incursions
1250		
1200	Late Christian I	
		Invasion of Shams ed-Dawla
1150		
		Eparch of Nobadia resides at Qaṣr Ibrîm
1100	——	Close relations with Fatimid Egypt
1050	Classic Christian II	
1000	——	
950	Classic Christian I	Era of general peace
900		
850	——	
800	Early Christian II	
750		
		Union of Nobadian and Makourian kingdoms
700	——	
850		
	Early Christian I	Arab invasions and Baqt Treaty
	——	
	Transition II	
600	——	
	Transition I	
500	——	Conversion of Nubians to Christianity

*See W. Y. Adams in *Kush*, 12 (1964), pp. 241–247.

ing of priests; for there was within the country no authority and no institution capable of anointing priests or of maintaining the traditional forms of worship. The requested help was never given, and Nubian Christianity degenerated into a fragmentary system of folk beliefs and practices, a few of which are still present in Nubia today.[55]

Economic life

The basis of subsistence in mediaeval Nubia, as in all earlier historical periods, was irrigation agriculture. Wheat and durra (sorghum) were the most important crops, along with barley and a considerable number of fruits and vegetables. Dates were probably the only agricultural product grown for export. The most productive lands were those irrigated by the *saqia* (ox-driven waterwheel), which was fundamental to the agricultural productivity of mediaeval Nubia. Fodder crops were also grown along the sloping banks and foreshores left each year by the receding of the high Nile, as they still are today.[56] Most agricultural land was probably held in small holdings, although there were evidently sizable royal estates in Upper Nubia.[57] A good deal of productive land must also have been in the hands of the church, to judge from a number of legal documents found at Qaṣr Ibrîm (see below, 231ff).

[55] See A. and W. Kronenberg, *Kush* 11 (1963), 304, 311; id., *Kush* 12 (1964), 285–6; Vantini, *Christianity,* 208–15.

[56] See Trigger in Dinkler, op. cit., 354–5, and Hassan Dafalla, *The Nubian Exodus* (London, 1975), 70–6.

[57] As reported by Ibn Selim. See Burckhardt, *Travels,* 496.

Most families evidently kept a few sheep and goats, which provided wool and milk as well as a small amount of meat. Cattle were probably more important for plowing and for turning the *saqia* than as a food source, but they would also have provided a certain amount of meat and dairy products.[58] Pigs were kept in considerable numbers, at least at Qaṣr Ibrîm.[59] Overland transport was carried on mainly by donkeys, though horses and camels were also kept in small numbers. So far as Lower Nubia was concerned, however, the great avenue of commerce was always the river, and most cargoes certainly arrived at Qaṣr Ibrîm by boat.

Irrigation agriculture was the basis of survival, but trade was the real key to prosperity in mediaeval Nubia. A variety of manufactures such as ironwork, pottery, textiles, leatherwork, and woodwork were locally produced and circulated within the country. The main centres of manufacturing were evidently at Qaṣr Ibrîm and other large towns, from which finished goods were distributed to the villages in exchange for raw foodstuffs and fibres. Long-distance trade was, however, a more important source of wealth, as it was in nearly all periods of Nubian history. Exports, in addition to slaves, almost certainly included dates, acacia and other woods, hides, and probably raw or woven cotton. Cotton weaving had been a mainstay of Nubia's export economy in the immediate pre-Christian period, and although production had dropped off in the early Middle Ages, it seems to have revived again later.[60] Shams ed-Dawla in 1172/3 is reported to have carried off a large quantity of raw cotton which he found at Qaṣr Ibrîm.[61]

To what extent tropical exotica such as ivory, ebony, ostrich feathers, and leopard skins were involved in the trade of mediaeval Nubia is uncertain. The sources of these commodities were not under the direct control of Makouria; they lay within and beyond the territories of the more southerly Kingdom of Alwa, which was often on bad terms with Makouria.[62] On the other hand such goods could hardly have reached Egypt from the Upper Nile without passing through Makouria, and a tax on riverain traffic may have contributed substantially to the prosperity of the northern Nubian kingdom.

Some of the goods received by the Nubians in exchange for their exports are specifically enumerated in the various recorded versions of the *Baqt* treaty. In the early centuries they certainly included wine; this is attested both textually[63] and by the finding of tens of thousands of amphora fragments in archaeological contexts.[64] Wheat, barley, various fine textiles, and horses are also mentioned in historical texts,[65] while archaeology provides abundant examples of glass, glazed pottery, bronze, and other luxury goods of undoubted Egyptian manufacture. Items which cannot be specifically verified, but which were important in the trade of earlier times, were honey, sesame and olive oil, and perfumes.[66]

We have it on the first-hand authority of Ibn Selim that trade was unrestricted in Lower Nubia, where Arab merchants travelled freely, and money was in circulation.[67] These assertions are borne out in part by the volume of commercial texts in the Arabic language found at Qaṣr Ibrîm,[68] and by the finding of mediaeval Arabic tombstones at various places in Lower Nubia.[69] On the other hand the number of Arabic or other coins that have been found is extremely small, and it is doubtful that coined money really played a significant role in mediaeval Nubian commerce. Textual records suggest that pieces of cloth often served as media of exchange in lieu of money.[70]

According to Ibn Selim, private traders were not allowed to proceed beyond the Second Cataract, on pain of death.[71] All cargoes were taken over at that point by royal commissioners, and the profits presumably went to the king in Dongola. How much this system of royal monopoly acted to restrict the importation of goods into Upper Nubia will not be determined until more excavation has been carried out in Upper Nubian sites. Certainly, however, the volume of imported goods found at Kulubnarti, in the *Batn el-Hajjar*, is only a fraction of what is found at comparable sites in Lower Nubia.[72]

Social life

Mediaeval Nubia, like modern Nubia, was a land of village dwellers. In the early Middle Ages settlements

[58] Cattle bones were found to be fairly common in the refuse deposits at Qaṣr Ibrîm; see Adams, Alexander and Allen, *JEA* 69 (1983), 50.

[59] According to Abu Salih, Shams ed-Dawla Turan Shah slaughtered 700 pigs in the course of his raid on Qaṣr Ibrîm in 1172–73: see Evetts and Butler, op. cit., 267.

[60] N. K. Adams, in *Wissenschaftliche Zeitschrift der Humboldt-Universität zu Berlin, Geisteswissenschaftliche Reihe*, 35 Jg., Heft 1 (1986), 21–6.

[61] Evetts and Butler, op. cit., 267.

[62] See Adams, *Nubia*, 526–8.

[63] See Forand, op. cit., 114–16.

[64] See especially Plumley and Adams, *JEA* 60 (1974), 218–19.

[65] See Burckhardt, *Travels*, 512.

[66] See Torgny Säve-Söderbergh, *Ägypten und Nubien* (Lund, 1941), 21.

[67] Burckhardt, *Travels*, 493.

[68] Plumley in Michalowski (ed.), *Nubia*, 106.

[69] See Monneret de Villard, *Storia*, 118; Adams, *Nubia*, 468.

[70] See Burckhardt, op. cit., 512.

[71] Op. cit., 495.

[72] See Adams in Dinkler, op. cit., 150.

were small and widely scattered, though they were most concentrated along the more fertile reaches of the Nile floodplain. Later, when defence became a consideration, there was a tendency for the Lower Nubian population to draw together into fewer and larger settlements. Places like Qaṣr Ibrîm, Gebel Adda, and Serra grew at the expense of the outlying villages, many of which were abandoned after 1200. At the same time however there was a wholesale dispersal of population into what may be termed refuge areas: the islands and rocky promontories of the Second Cataract and the *Batn el-Hajjar* region beyond it.[73]

The principal urban centres of Lower Nubia would appear to have been Qurta, Qaṣr Ibrîm, Gebel Adda, and Faras. Of these only Qaṣr Ibrîm has been subjected to systematic archaeological investigation.[74] The place in its heyday, between 1200 and 1300, probably never numbered as many as a thousand inhabitants, and except for the cathedral and the girdle wall its appearance would have differed little from that of ordinary villages. Though there was evidently a flourishing commerce, there were no specialized shops. Stocks of goods for sale must have been kept in ordinary dwellings at night but by day were carried out into the open streets and plazas where most business was undoubtedly transacted.[75] There are no specifically identified market areas at Qaṣr Ibrîm, but there was plenty of open space between and around the houses. Manufacturing activities were presumably also carried out largely out of doors, since the late mediaeval houses were mostly without windows or other sources of light. Pottery-making and other manufacturing activities requiring either fuel or water were undoubtedly carried on along the riverbank rather than within the citadel walls. Towns like Qaṣr Ibrîm would have been differentiated from villages by the volume of commerce and the amount of manufacturing carried on within them, not by the possession of elaborate civic facilities that could not be found in the villages.[76] The only major exceptions would have been the cathedrals at Qurta, Qaṣr Ibrîm, and Faras.

The basic unit of mediaeval Nubian society was evidently the monogamous nuclear family. This is not recorded in texts, but is readily inferable from archaeological evidence. Dwellings of the mediaeval period are quite standardized in plan, having at a minimum one general-purpose living room, one store room, and a passage ending in a latrine. Variations in size and plan are reflected chiefly in the presence or absence of additional store rooms and/or an entrance parlour, but in no case can we recognize facilities for the accommodation of two or more married couples under the same roof.[77] Houses did not, moreover, grow by accretion over a period of time, nor can we recognize the kind of multi-family dwelling clusters that are common in the post-Christian levels at Qaṣr Ibrîm.[78] Indeed, the evidence of funerary inscriptions and other texts suggests that familism was not a significant component of the social ideology of mediaeval Nubia, and that the wider ties of kinship were relatively unimportant.

Despite the strictly monogamous structure of the family, the status of women in Christian Nubia does not appear to have been significantly higher than in Muslim Egypt. They were evidently barred alike from civil and from ecclesiastical office. The *Ñonnen*, or queen mother, appears to have been an honoured personage at the royal court, but it is not at all certain what role she played in practical affairs. Texts found at Qaṣr Ibrîm show that women could and did own and sell property (see below, pp. 233–4), but there are no texts suggesting their involvement in commerce. Only in the rarest instances do we find women commemorated by funerary inscriptions or elaborate tombs.

Mediaeval Nubian society was unquestionably stratified, distinguishing at least between royalty, commoners, and slaves. Yet distinctions of rank and even of wealth are surprisingly difficult to recognize archaeologically. There are variations in the size and ostentation of houses from one period to another, and to some extent from one site to another, but at any given time and in any given place there is a surprising uniformity in the dwellings. Inequalities in the distribution of luxury goods are difficult to document because these are usually found where they were discarded rather than where they were used, and there are no funerary offerings to give a clue to the relative wealth or the social status of the mediaeval Nubian dead. The size and ostentation of tomb superstructures varies a good deal, but whether or not this is a reflection of real status differences is uncertain. On the whole it appears that Nubian society was relatively egalitarian as mediaeval societies went, and that such wealth as existed was fairly equitably distributed. Differences in rank were probably expressed more in terms of deference and privilege than of material ostentation. Slaves were present but were apparently not numerous, if only because the exactions of the *Baqt* tribute obliged the Nubians to hand over to the Egyptians most of the

[73] See Adams and Nordström, *Kush* 11 (1963), 42–4, and Adams, *Nubia*, 513.

[74] The excavations in the Gebel Adda townsite were very limited in extent; those at Faras were confined to the ecclesiastical buildings and did not extend to the town-site.

[75] Cf. Burckhardt's description of Shendi market in the early nineteenth century (*Travels*, 289–324).

[76] I have discussed this phenomenon further in 'Urban Dynamics in Microcosm: the Life and Death of a Nubian Frontier Settlement' (MS).

[77] For a detailed discussion of mediaeval Nubian house architecture see Adams, *Nubia*, 489–93, 514–8.

[78] See Adams, Alexander and Allen, *JEA* 69 (1983), 46.

slaves in their possession. Indeed it was a frequent complaint of the Nubians that they could not meet the annual quota of slaves imposed under the *Baqt.*[79]

The question of ethnic diversity in mediaeval Nubia is a tangled but potentially an important one. Unfortunately it is one on which neither archaeology nor written history sheds much light. Whatever differences existed would presumably have shown up at urban centres like Qaṣr Ibrîm, rather than in the villages with their traditionally homogeneous culture and society. The Kingdom of Makouria included territory which in more recent times has been inhabited by three different Nubian language groups: the Kanuz (*sing.* Kenzi) in the north, the Mahas in the middle, and the Danagla (*sing.* Dongolawi) in the south.[80] These groups have traditionally not felt a very strong sense of affinity,[81] and it must have been even less in the Middle Ages, before they were collectively enclaved within an Arabic-speaking majority. The native population in and around Qaṣr Ibrîm spoke the Mahasi dialect and used its written equivalent, Old Nubian, as a major vehicle for legal and other written records. The language spoken in and around the royal capital was, however, Dongolawi, as the name suggests, and it therefore seems quite possible that Dongolawi officials would have visited or even resided from time to time at Qaṣr Ibrîm.

The presence of Egyptian and other Arab traders in Lower Nubia is well attested textually, and is further confirmed by the large volume of Arabic correspondence found in mediaeval contexts (see below, p. 223). Yet other ethnic elements were probably represented in the slave population, since slaves would have been taken by choice from the non-Nubian and non-Christian tribes of the central and southern Sudan rather than from the indigenous population[82] Finally there is the possibility that metalwork, pottery-making, and other low-status occupations were in the hands of endogamous 'pariah castes' of putative slave origin, as has been true in both Egypt and the Sudan in the more recent past.[83] Despite, however, the probable ethnic and linguistic diversity there seems to have been no generally recognized *lingua franca,* at least for written communication. Greek, Coptic, Arabic, and at least two different varieties of Old Nubian were all used for different kinds of documents.[84]

[79] See Forand, op. cit., 116–8.

[80] For discussion of the Nubian languages and their historical significance see Millet in Robert A. Fernea (ed.), *Contemporary Egyptian Nubia,* I (New Haven, 1966), 59–71; Adams, *JEA* 52 (1966), 153–5; and id. in Christopher Ehret and Merrick Posnansky (eds.), *The Archaeological and Linguistic Reconstruction of African History* (Berkeley, 1982), 11–38.

[81] Cf. Burckhardt, *Travels*, 138.

[82] Adams, *Nubia,* 505.

[83] For Egypt see Winifred S. Blackman, *The Fellahin of Upper Egypt* (London, 1927), 135–53. For the Sudan see Bentley and Crowfoot, *Sudan Notes and Records* 7, no. 2 (1924), 21; and Robertson and Mohammed in P. L. Shinnie (ed.), *Canadian Archaeology Abroad* (Calgary, 1976), 93.

[84] The linguistic situation is described by Shinnie in Abdelgadir M. Abdalla (ed.), *Studies in Ancient Languages of the Sudan* (Sudan Research Unit, Sudan Studies Library, no. 3) (Khartoum, 1974), 41–8. See also Adams, *Nubia*, 484–6.

PART 2
THE ARCHITECTURAL RECORD

CHAPTER 1
THE TOWN PLAN

SURVIVING architectural remains at Qaṣr Ibrîm do not give a complete picture either of the extent of settlement or of the layout of the town in late mediaeval times. Unlike the remains of earlier and subsequent periods, late mediaeval structures were not found to be continuously distributed within the area of the fortification walls. They were almost entirely confined to the more westerly portion of the site, and even here their distribution was very irregular (cf. Figs. 3, 4, and 5). However, this may not be a true indication of the original state of affairs. Stratigraphic evidence makes it apparent that large areas were systematically levelled prior to their overbuilding in the Islamic period, and, since the Late Christian houses were uppermost, these buildings would have suffered the most destruction.

With one or two exceptions to be noted later, the 'Bosnian' inhabitants of the Islamic period made little or no use of the pre-existing buildings. Instead the older houses were systematically dismantled to provide stone for newly built houses, for the heightening of the girdle wall, and to fill in behind the heightened wall. In this process some Late Christian houses were probably destroyed altogether. Buildings or portions of buildings that were not dismantled were probably, for the most part, those that had already been filled with refuse prior to the time of the 'Bosnian' overbuilding. The extent of preservation in the Late Christian remains would, therefore, be a measure of the extent to which refuse had already accumulated in them in Late Christian times.

For purposes of discussion, five areas of Late Christian occupation can be distinguished; they are designated in Figures 3 and 4 as Zones A, B, C, D, and E:

Zone A comprises a large area in the southwestern part of the site, between the Cathedral (Church 293) on the north and the Taharqa Temple-church (Church 287) on the south. This area had been an open plaza in the Classic Christian period, but in the LC1 and LC2 periods it gradually filled up with a dense cluster of irregularly built stone houses (Figs. 3 and 4). However, all these buildings seem to have been abandoned in the Terminal Christian period (Fig. 5).

Zone B adjoins the west fortification wall, and specifically that part of it that is formed by the famous Qaṣr Ibrîm Podium[1] (see pl. 1c). Here in the Terminal Christian period there were three massive brick 'castle-houses' which may have been the only occupied structures on the site at the end of the Christian period. These houses were underlain by remains of earlier stone and brick buildings, apparently also of Late Christian date. Unfortunately the underlying houses were dismantled in one of the earliest excavation seasons at Qaṣr Ibrîm, and the available documentation for them is very scanty.[2]

Zone C, to the west of the Cathedral, was occupied by houses originally built in the Early and Classic Christian periods. They suffered severe damage during the Shams ed-Dawla raid of 1172–3. There was, nevertheless, a certain amount of continued occupation in the earliest years of the LC1 period, but before long the whole area was abandoned and became a dump. If there was any subsequent occupation here in the late Middle Ages, all traces of it were destroyed in the course of 'Bosnian' overbuilding after 1550. Preservation of the Late Christian remains in Zone C is very poor, with only the lowest courses of any of the walls surviving.

In *Zone D*, near the Northwest Bastion, there were four houses with rather different histories. The large House 763 was built in the Classic Christian period but continued to be occupied until the end of LC1, at which time it was abandoned and deeply filled with rubbish. Because of this filling, House 763 is one of the very few Late Christian structures that is reasonably well preserved (see pl. 4b). The adjoining House 781 was a much older building which, after an interval of disuse, was rehabilitated for a time in the LC1 period. Directly over the Northwest Bastion the two small Houses 206 and 207 were newly built in the LC1 period, and continued in use until the TC period.

In *Zone E*, along the northern scarp of the citadel, there were four Late Christian houses in a contiguous row, but each had a different history. House 210 was a much older building, dating back originally to X-Group times. It had been abandoned and filled with rubbish in

[1] See Frend, *JEA* 60 (1974), 30–59.

[2] The only available documentation is in op. cit., 34–6 and 41–2.

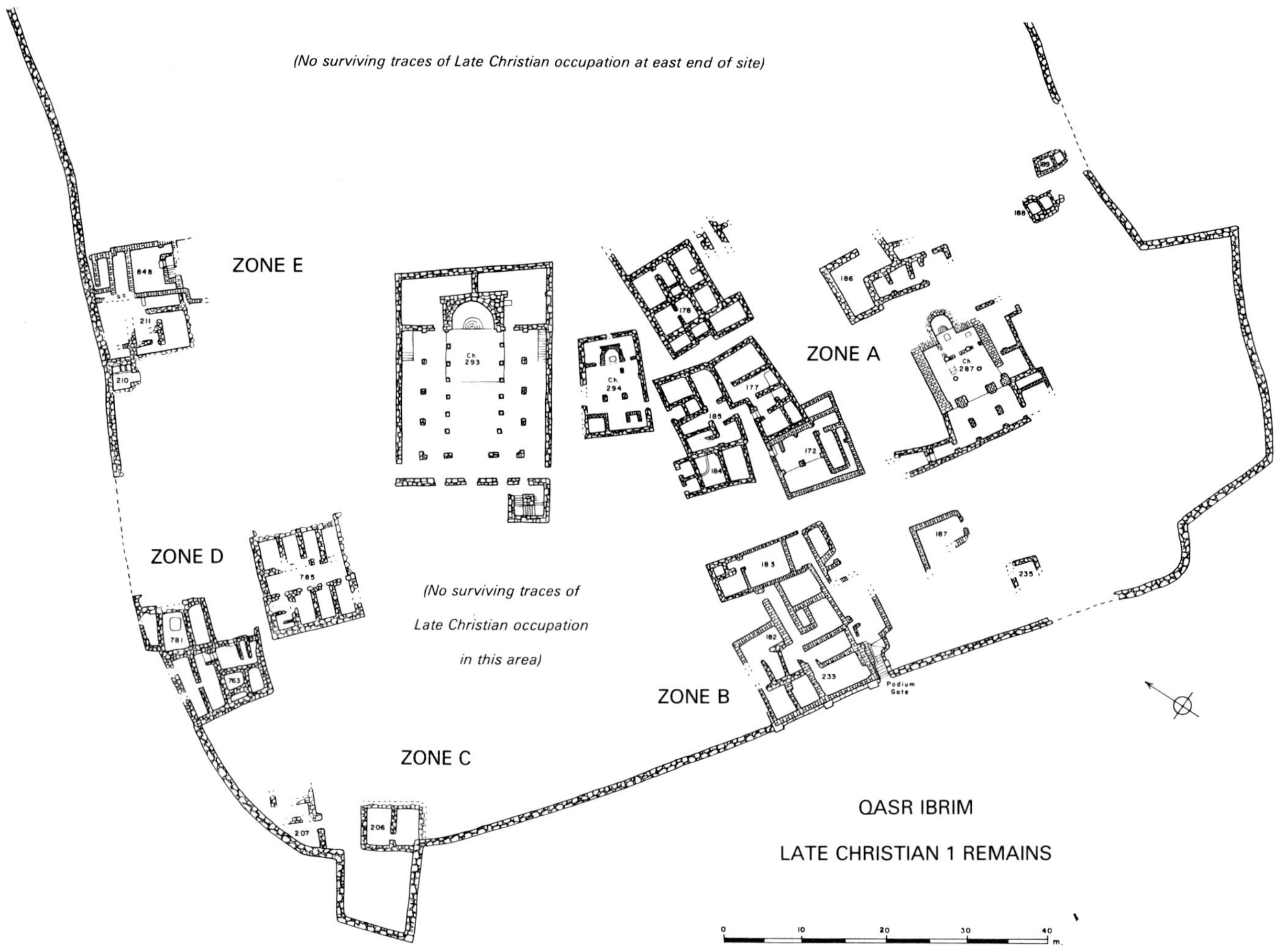

Figure 3. Surviving architectural remains from the Late Christian 1 period, on the western half of the Qaṣr Ibrîm citadel. There are no surviving Late Christian remains on the eastern half of the site. Numbers entered in each building are building numbers. Note different shading conventions for stone and brick construction.

the Classic Christian period, but one room was dug out to serve as a partially subterranean store room in the LC1 period. Next door to it, House 211 was built in the Early Christian period but continued in use until the end of the LC1 period, after which it was filled with refuse. House 848 was a Roman or Meroitic brick building which, after a very long hiatus, was restored to use in the CC2 and LC1 periods, then was once again abandoned. Finally, House 849 was built and occupied entirely in the LC2 period. It was destroyed by fire, which brought down the remnants of its brick upper storey as fill into the lower-storey rooms. Because of this deep filling, the houses in Zone E were among the best preserved Late Christian structures on the site.

It will be apparent from the foregoing discussion that the pattern of occupation was by no means stable during the late mediaeval period. Altogether 43 buildings can be assigned wholly or in part to the LC1, LC2, and TC periods, but it is probable that there were never more than twenty-six buildings in use at any one time. Table 5 shows the chronological relationships of the various Late and Terminal Christian buildings.

The occupation history of Qaṣr Ibrîm in the late Middle Ages has been revealed partly by pottery (cf. Ch. 1), partly by stratigraphy, and partly by architectural typology. Briefly, it may be summed up as follows:

LC1 period. At the beginning of the Late Christian period the main area of domestic occupation was to the west of the Qaṣr Ibrîm Cathedral (Zones B and C). However, these areas were already falling into disuse because of the dilapidated condition of the houses, and before long they were abandoned altogether.[3] A little further to the north, in Zone D, occupation continued in the stoutly built House 763, and the older House 781 adjoining it was restored to use. Two new houses,

[3] For more detail see Anderson, Adams *et al.*, *JEA* 65 (1979), 36–7.

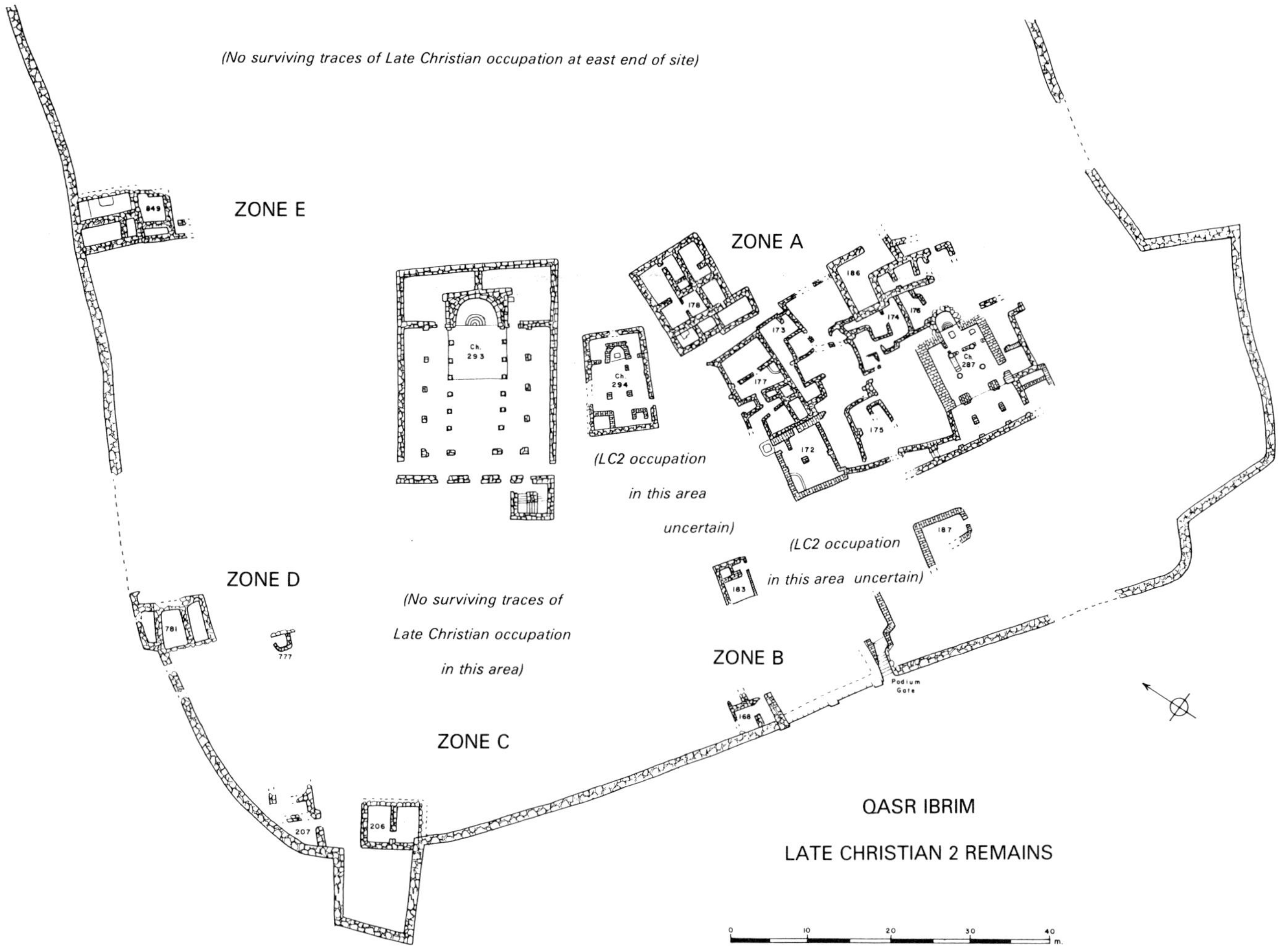

Figure 4. Surviving architectural remains from the Late Christian 2 period, on the western half of the Qaṣr Ibrîm citadel. There are no surviving Late Christian remains on the eastern half of the site. Numbers entered in each buiding are building numbers. Note different shading conventions for stone and brick construction.

206 and 207, were also built in this area. In Zone E, House 211 continued in use from the Classic Christian period, and the much older brick House 848 was restored to use after a long hiatus.

Meanwhile, new houses began to appear in the area between Church 293 and Church 287 (Zone A), which had been an open plaza all through the Classic Christian period. The small Church 294 was also built at this time, and the old Meroitic and X-Group Tavern (House 178) was restored to use as a dwelling or a storehouse. To the south of these dwellings, there was still a small open plaza adjoining the north side of Church 287. Buildings which can be assigned wholly or in part to the LC1 period are shown in Figure 3.

LC2 period. The LC1 houses in Zone A continued to be occupied, and new ones were added alongside them until the former plaza area between the churches was entirely overbuilt. This clearly became the main concentration of settlement in the LC2 period. In areas further to the north (Zones D and E), several of the older houses went out of use and were filled with refuse. The small houses 206 and 207 remained in use, and one new house, 849, was built alongside the north battlement. Buildings assignable to the LC2 period are shown in Figure 4.

TC period. In this final century of Christian occupation all of the houses in Zones A and E were abandoned, as were the earlier brick structures in Zone B. These latter, however, were overbuilt by the massive brick 'castle-houses' 169, 170, and 171. They and the two small houses 206 and 207 in the Northwest Bastion area (Zone D) are the only dwellings at Qaṣr Ibrîm that exhibit signs of occupation during the Terminal Christian period. Ceramic evidence makes it clear that Church 293 (the Cathedral) and Church 287 also remained in use until the end of the Christian era, but Church 294 may have gone out of use after the LC2 period. Nothing can be said about Church 839,

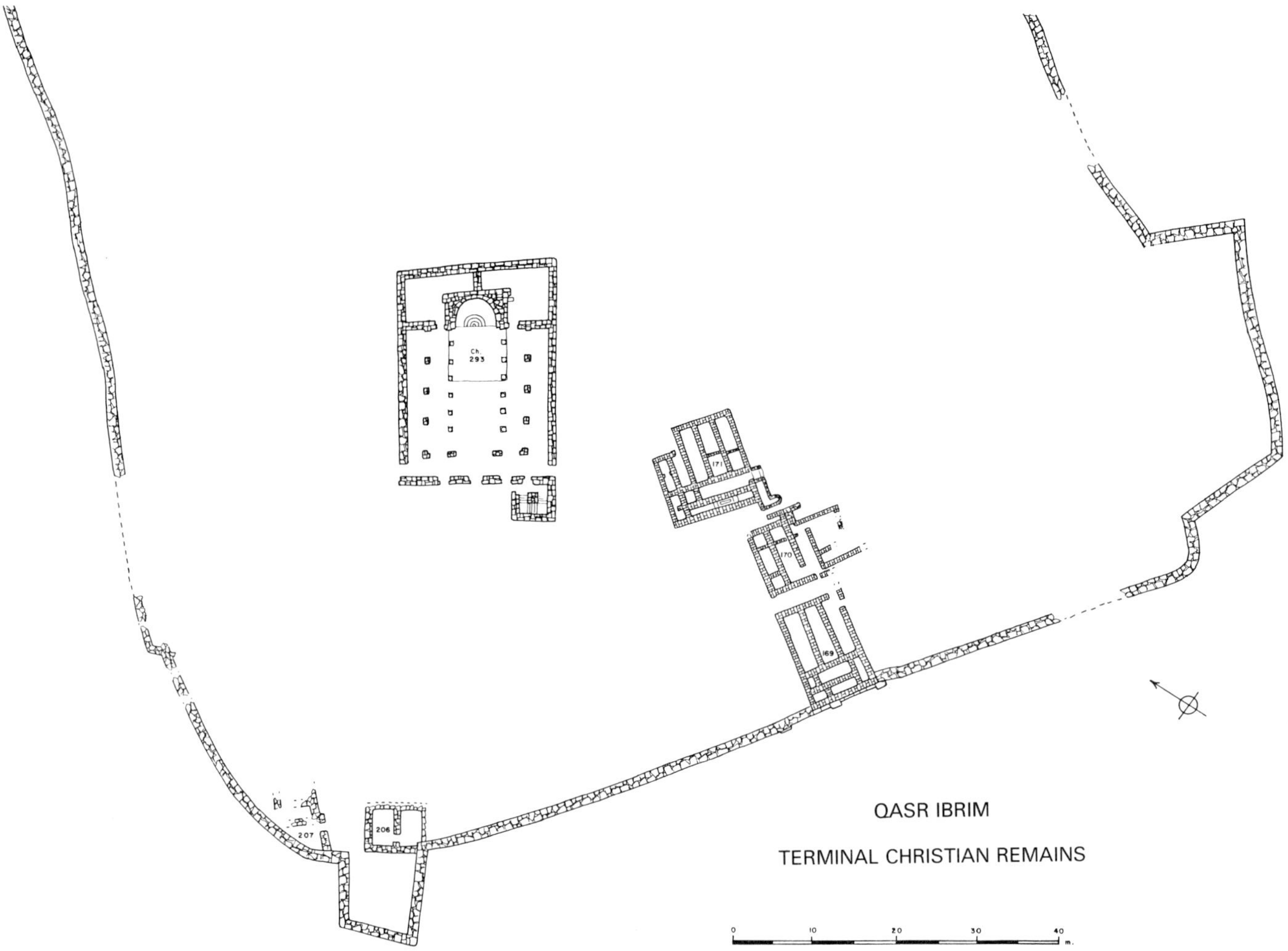

Figure 5. Surviving architectural remains from the Terminal Christian period, on the western half of the Qaṣr Ibrîm citadel. There are no surviving Late Christian remains on the eastern half of the site, except for Church 839 (not shown). Numbers entered in each buiding are building numbers. Note different shading conventions for stone and brick construction.

where no excavations were carried out, except that it is architecturally of a very late type.[4] Buildings assignable to the Terminal Christian period are shown in Figure 5.

The foregoing discussion applies, of course, only to the western half of the Qaṣr Ibrîm citadel. Nothing can be said about what was going on in the eastern area, where no Late Christian remains were preserved. Since, however, the entire girdle wall was restored in Late Christian times (see Ch. 7), it is reasonable to suppose that some use was made of the whole mountaintop. One possibility is that animals were penned in the more easterly portion of the site area, at least in militarily disturbed times.

[4] See Adams, *JARCE* 4 (1965), 116–19.

CHAPTER 2
HOUSES AND HOUSE ARCHITECTURE

Of the forty-three surviving buildings of the late mediaeval period, thirty can be identified tentatively as dwellings. In the LC1 and LC2 periods they were built mostly of stone, and the general method of their construction differed little from that of the Early Christian and pre-Christian houses at Qaṣr Ibrîm. There was also some use of mud-brick construction, but only one house (172) was built entirely of brick. In the Terminal Christian period there was no more building in stone; the only structures newly built at this time were the massive brick 'castle-houses' 169, 170, and 171. The brick houses of Late and Terminal Christian times represent the first regular use of mud-brick construction at Qaṣr Ibrîm since the Meroitic period. This is in marked contrast to the situation at other mediaeval Nubian sites, where construction was always primarily in brick.[1] The difference is undoubtedly a consequence of Qaṣr Ibrîm's elevated situation, close to stone quarries but far from the riverbank where brick had to be made.

The stone houses

All of the Late Christian stone houses were built of relatively small and irregularly shaped stone blocks, laid up in heavy mud mortar and with abundant use of stone chips and potsherds as chinking. In this respect they differed little from the houses of the X-Group, Early Christian, and Classic Christian periods. Indeed a good deal of building material was undoubtedly 'recycled' from the older buildings. In other respects, however, the Late Christian houses give an impression of technical retrogression. For the most part they were neither as stoutly nor as carefully built as were the houses of earlier times.

Plans

A conspicuous feature of the Late Christian stone houses at Qaṣr Ibrîm was their irregularity of size, shape, and interior plan. At least nine houses were preserved to their full horizontal extent, and their floor areas varied from a low of about 35 m^2 to a high of 80 m^2. The smallest house had four rooms, and the largest eleven. No two houses were closely similar in plan; the most that can be said is that they generally had two large rooms and two or more smaller ones. Most of the better preserved houses were roughly square or rectangular in plan, but none was precisely so. Indeed there was hardly such a thing as a 90° corner in any stone house. Houses typically had two outside walls that were roughly parallel, while the other two outside walls might diverge from each other by as much as 20°. In the most elaborate of the Late Christian houses, House 763, there were no two parallel walls anywhere in the building (see Fig. 6).

Two observations may be made in regard to the skewed construction of the Late Christian houses. First, this was a feature specifically of the stone-built houses; it was not found in the brick buildings either at Qaṣr Ibrîm or elsewhere in Nubia. Second, it seems to have been deliberate; for it occurred not only in nearly all of the dwellings but in the stone-built churches 294 and 839 (see Chapter 6). Moreover, similarly irregular stone houses were found in the late mediaeval sites of Kasanarti[2] and Kulubnarti,[3] alongside more regularly built brick houses. In these places, too, the stone houses were notably variable in plan, while the brick houses were much more uniform. The evidence suggests that brick houses, but not stone houses, were built by itinerant professional builders, as are the more elaborate houses in Nubia today.[4]

Only two of the Late Christian stone houses, 763 and 849, appear to have had a second storey. This is established by inference rather than by direct evidence. The two aforementioned houses had exceptionally thick walls, in comparison to the neighbouring buildings, and both included ground-floor rooms that could be entered only from above (see figs. 6 and 12). Elsewhere in Nubia such blind cellars were found to be a consistent feature of two-storey houses.[5] Neither House 763 nor House 849 had an interior stairway, but in House 763 there appears to have been a stairway ascending from the outside. House 849 might possibly have been entered at the second storey by means of a ladder, as was the case in a number of two-storey houses in the *Batn el-Hajjar region*.[6] In both Houses 763 and 849 the upper storey rooms appear to have

[1] See William Y. Adams, *Nubia, Corridor to Africa* (London, 1977), 491–3.

[2] See Adams, *Kush* 12 (1964), 221.

[3] See Adams in Erich Dinkler, (ed.), *Kunst und Geschichte Nubiens in Chrislicher Zeit* (Recklinghausen, 1970), 142–3. See also Adams, *Nubia*, 581, fig. 82.

[4] See Adams, *Nubia*, 357; Jaritz in Robert A. Fernea and Georg Gerster, *Nubians in Egypt* (Austin, 1973), 49.

[5] Adams, *Nubia*, 515–7.

[6] Op. cit., and Adams in *Archéoloie du Nil Moyen* 6 (1994), 11–46.

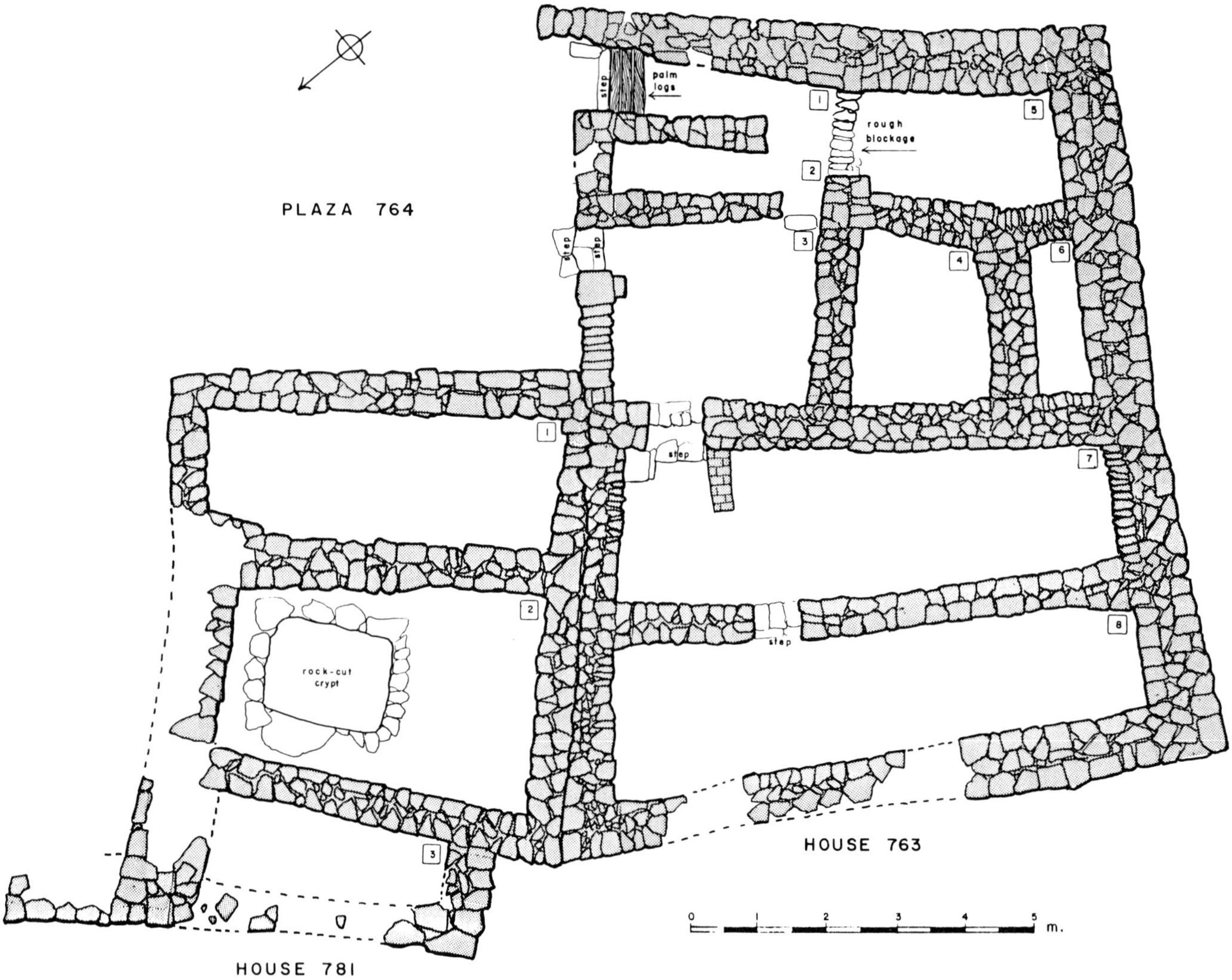

Figure 6. Plan of eparchal House 763, and adjoining House 781. Figures in squares are room numbers.

been constructed of mud brick rather than of stone, as was true also in many two-storey dwellings at Tanjur,[7] Kulubnarti,[8] and elsewhere.[9] Nothing survives to indicate the actual plan of the second-floor apartments in the two houses. In other Late Christian stone houses at Qaṣr Ibrîm, the walls do not appear thick enough to have supported an upper storey.

Wall construction

Walls were built of relatively small and highly irregular sandstone chunks, few of which show any evidence of deliberate dressing (pl. 3a). There was no true coursing, but occasionally rows of rather thin slabs might be inserted in upright or 'herringbone' position. Such rows seldom ran for the full length of any wall, and they can have served no purpose except perhaps to relieve the monotony of the builders. Once the wall surfaces were plastered over, the contours of the individual stones could not be seen. Building stones were laid up in a heavy mortar of mud and dung, with small stone chips, potsherds, and rags used to fill in the interstices. Both interior and exterior wall surfaces were generally bumpy and uneven. Interior walls were covered with a rather thin coating of mud plaster, but only rarely were whitewashed. No evidence of painted decoration or of mural inscriptions was found.

Longer stone walls were frequently somewhat curving (cf. Fig. 6). As in the case of skewed house plans, this appears to be a deliberate feature, designed to impart greater strength or stability. Walls often varied substantially in thickness. The typical thickness was about 70 cm, but variation from a low of 50 cm to a high of more than a metre can sometimes be found along the length

[7] See Erich Dinkler in Dinkler (ed.), *Kunst,* 262.

[8] Adams in Dinkler (ed.), *Kunst,* 142–3; id., *Kulubnarti* I (Lexington, 1994), Ch. II.

[9] Op. cit.

of the same wall. Inside partitions that did not support the roof were sometimes no more than 40 cm thick, and occasionally were of brick. Stone walls were almost entirely without features. In one room in House 849 there were two small niches in the wall, about one metre above the floor, but nothing similar was found in any other stone house.

Floors and floor features

The Qaṣr Ibrîm Cathedral (Church 293) had a fine paving of cut stone, and Church 287 had a rough but well-laid flagstone floor installed in the Late Christian period (see Ch. 6). However, no dwelling had anything other than a hard-packed mud floor. The original floor in each house was usually wet-laid, hard, and fairly smooth. Some houses, like 763 and 849, were built on sloping *gebel* surfaces, and in these buildings the floors themselves sometimes had a considerable slope.

Most Late Christian houses were refloored at least twice in the course of their occupation, though this varied from house to house and even from room to room in the same house. The maximum number of deliberately laid floors in any Late Christian house was five. There might be anywhere from 5 to 40 cm of densely compacted midden deposit or wet-laid mud between successive floor surfaces. In most cases this did not consist of material accidentally accumulated in the course of occupation, but material deliberately brought in when a new floor was laid. Later floors were often not as carefully laid as were the original floors; sometimes they had rather uneven contours and were not very hard packed. The installation of floors at successively higher levels would, of course, have reduced the amount of headroom in any room. There is no way of knowing whether roof levels were concurrently heightened, as they sometimes were in X-Group and Early Christian houses at Qaṣr Ibrîm.[10] Obviously this would have been possible only in one-storey houses.

An extraordinary characteristic of Late Christian house floors at Qaṣr Ibrîm was their consistent lack of floor features. The inhabitants made a regular practice of burying valuables beneath the floors, but they did not make use of built-in crypts as they did in X-Group and Early Christian times.[11] Instead they simply dug rather irregular holes through the floors, usually but not always in the room corners (pl. 3c). These would be filled with soft earth, but they were seldom afterward paved over, so that there were very conspicuous soft spots in most floors. An exception to this general rule was House 781, an Early Christian structure with sub-floor storage crypts, some of which were restored to use in the Late Christian period. Otherwise, deliberately constructed storage crypts were nearly always located outside the houses rather than within them (see Ch. 5). Even more striking is the absence of pottery jars buried in the house floors. Almost the only examples found at Qaṣr Ibrîm were in the atypical House 177, to be described in detail later. Elsewhere such vessels are ubiquitous in Nubian houses of nearly all ages, down to modern times. They are usually found in room corners, and are buried so that the rim of the vessel comes just flush with the floor. They served both as braziers for small charcoal fires and as repositories for valuables.[12] Large mud *somas* were often used for storage within houses, but they were usually not built-in features. They either rested on the floor surface (pl. 36) or were sunk into irregular holes dug in the floors (pl. 3c). There was also no place for a fire or any cooking apparatus in most of the Late Christian houses.

Mud-built *mastabas* were another generally absent feature, in contrast to Late Christian houses elsewhere in Nubia.[13] Only two mastabas were found, one in House 177 and one in House 849 (pl. 3d). The latter was an original feature of the house, while the mastaba in House 177 was a later addition. Both of these two houses will be more fully described in later paragraphs.

Doors and windows

Exterior doorways and also many interior doorways were fitted with wooden doorframes and, presumably, pivoting wooden doors. Several large fragments of plank have been found that were probably parts of doors. No doorframe or door was found *in situ,* but impressions were often visible where wooden jambs had been removed. Sockets where the original door had pivoted were occasionally found *in situ.* They were usually stones with a hemispherical depression, but were occasionally blocks of wood. Doors were closed by means of a sliding bolt and a wooden lock and key mechanism similar to those still in use in Egypt and the Sudan. Locks and keys will be described in Part 3, Chapter 5.

A peculiarity of most Late Christian houses was the absence of short buttresses just beside the doorways. These were regular features of X-Group and Early Christian houses at Ibrîm, and elsewhere in Nubia they are found in houses of all ages down to the present.

[10] This is particularly conspicuous in House 217 (formerly X-17). For the preliminary report see Plumley, Adams and Crowfoot, *JEA* 63 (1977), 34–5. For discussion of similar modifications at Meinarti see Adams in K.-C. Chang (ed.), *Settlement Archaeology* (Palo Alto, 1968), 190–1.

[11] See Plumley and Adams, *JEA* 60 (1974), 215; Plumley, Adams and Crowfoot, *JEA* 63 (1977), 34.

[12] See Adams, *Nubia*, 491.

[13] Op. cit.

a

b

c

d

Plate 3. Features of house construction. a, Stone wall construction. b, Storage *somas* in House 168. c, Storage pit in floor of House 763. d, Mud mastaba in House 849, Room 5.

Their purpose was to provide support for a stout timber that ran across the top of the doorframe and held in place the upper end of the doorpost (i.e. the timber on which the door pivoted).[14] It can only be assumed that at Qaṣr Ibrîm the upper end of the doorpost was secured by some other mechanism, perhaps by a loop of rope anchored into the wall masonry. In most doorways, both interior and exterior, there was a threshold of rather rough stone masonry which was integral with the adjoining walls. In only two or three instances was the threshold comprised of a single cut-stone slab, as was common in earlier houses. Thresholds typically projected 10 to 15 cm above the levels of the original floors which adjoined them. However, they were not usually raised when new floors were installed, so that in time they came to be flush with the adjoining floor surfaces or were even buried beneath them.

No trace of a window was found in any Late Christian house at Qaṣr Ibrîm. In most houses the walls were not preserved to a sufficient height so that windows could be expected. It may be noted, however, that windows are not a usual feature of mediaeval Nubian houses even where they are well preserved.

Roof construction

Definite evidence of roof construction was found in only two stone houses, 763 and 849. In the former case at least four of the rooms had been covered by mud-brick barrel vaulting, the springings of which were still *in situ.* House 849, however, had had a flat roof supported on well-shaped palm logs, over which were laid *gerid* (palm-leaf ribs) and packed mud. This roof had been destroyed by fire, and its remnants were found within the rooms below. Most other stone houses at Qaṣr Ibrîm probably also had flat rather than vaulted roofs, as is suggested by their irregular shapes and rather thin walls.

Toilets

Indoor toilet arrangements were a regular feature of late mediaeval houses in other parts of Nubia,[15] but at Qaṣr Ibrîm they were found in only two of the stone houses. In Room 7 of House 177 there was a a raised platform about a metre above the floor, which was mounted by means of a ramp at one side (see Fig. 8). The platform's upper surface was formed of palm logs which were still in situ, but there was no ceramic toilet fixture of the type found elsewhere in Nubia.[16] The cess pit beneath the platform could be cleaned out through a small hole in the outer house wall at ground level. In House 763, one ground-floor room was full of excrement and rubbish, but there was no evidence of a platform or steps leading to it. Presumably this was a cess pit beneath a toilet located on the upper floor. Again, there was a small cleanout hole at ground level.

Four of the most elaborate and best preserved of the Late Christian stone houses will be individually described in later pages (see below, p. 41ff). Other stone houses are listed and briefly described in Table 5.

Late Christian brick construction

Mud brick was the usual building material in other mediaeval Nubian communities, but it was used very sparingly at Qaṣr Ibrîm. Only eight buildings from the LC1 and LC2 periods show some evidence of brick construction, and only two of these were built exclusively of brick. Only House 848 could be identified specifically as a dwelling. This was in reality a restoration of a much older house, and it will be dealt with more fully in a later section (p. 41). Another brick building, House 172, was apparently designed as an audience chamber for the Eparch of Nobadia; it too will be more fully described later (pp. 50–2).

In Zone B, overlying the Qaṣr Ibrîm Podium, there was a complex arrangement of rooms built partly of brick and partly of stone. They were excavated and dismantled in an early season (1964),[17] and the surviving notes and plans do not furnish a very coherent picture. Professor Frend's published description speaks only of stone construction,[18] while Mr. Frazer's plan shows a very irregular combination of brick and stone walls.[19] The plan suggests that the rooms excavated in 1964 formed parts of three separate buildings, but none was excavated to its full extent at that time.[20] The published description states: 'These were the lowest row of dwellings which in Late-Nubian times formed a series of houses rising in tiers above each other until the foundations of those furthest from the podium were as much as 6 m above its floor. The terracing, however, was due entirely to the houses being constructed on accumulated deposits which had formed during the Late-Nubian period... The pottery from these deposits

[14] For an illustration see Friedrich Hinkel, *Auszug aus Nubien* (Berlin, 1978), 9th photo after 64.

[15] Adams, *Nubia*, 491.

[16] Op. cit. For an illustration of one of these fixtures, incorrectly identified as an amphora stand, see Ugo Monneret de Villard, *La Nubia medioevale*, I (Cairo, 1935), 221, fig. 212.

[17] For preliminary excavation reports see Plumley, *JEA*, 50 (1964), 4–5, and Frend, *JEA* 60 (1974), 36–9.

[18] Frend, *JEA* 60 (1974), 38.

[19] The excavation plans of Kenneth Frazer are the basis for the plans appearing in this report (Part 2, Chapter 1, figs. 3, 4, and 5).

[20] The remaining portions of these houses must have been destroyed in the course of the 1966 and 1969 excavations, for in most cases we were unable to find any surviving trace of them in the excavations after 1972.

TABLE 5
CONSPECTUS OF LATE AND TERMINAL CHRISTIAN HOUSES AT QAṢR IBRÎM

House no.	Former no.	Periods of occ.	Stories	No. of rooms*	Area (m^2)	Condition of preservation: Floor plan	Condition of preservation: Walls	Years excav.	Reports, JEA
						Houses continuing in use since CC times			
168	LC2–1	?	1?	4?	?	Not fully excavated	Not clearly indicated	1964	60: 45
182	LC1–2	CC–LC1?	1	6+	120?	Apparently incomplete	Not clearly indicated	1964	60: 41–42
183	LC1–3	CC–LC1?	1	4+	50+	Incomplete	Not clearly indicated	1964	60: 42
194	LC1–17	EC–LC1	1	4	48	Complete?	Very denuded	1978	None
195	LC1–18	?–LC1	1	1+	20+	Incomplete	Very denuded	1978	65: 37
197	LC1–20	EC–LC1	1	3+	25+	Incomplete	Very denuded	1978	65: 37
202	CC1–6 LC1–25	EC–LC1	1	3	35	Complete	Fairly well preserved	1978	65: 37
211	CC1–5	EC2–LC1	1	5?	45	Largely complete	Parts well preserved, Parts badly destroyed	1972 1982 1984	None
233	LC1–2	CC–LC1?	1	5+	85?	Complete?	Not clearly indicated	1964	60: 38–39
763	—	CC2–LC1	2	8	70	Complete	Lower floor well preserved	1982	69: 54
						Disused houses restored to use			
178	LC1–8 LC2–11	M–EC--- LC1–LC2	2?	11	80	Complete	LC levels rather poorly preserved	1969 1972	56: 13–15
186	LC1–9	X–EC--- LC1–LC2	1	5+	25+	Incomplete	LC levels very denuded	1974	63: 36
781	—	EC--- LC1–LC2	1	3	35	Complete	Somewhat denuded	1982	None
848	—	R–M--- LC1	1	5	55	Nearly complete	Mostly well preserved	1982	None
						Newly built stone houses			
173	LC2–6	LC2?	1	4+	45+	Incomplete?	Very denuded	1972	None
174	LC2–7	LC2–TC	1	4+	30+	Incomplete?	Very denuded	1972	None
175	LC2–8	LC2?	1	1+	30+	Incomplete	Very denuded	1972	None
176	LC2–9	LC2?	1	2+	12+	Incomplete	Very denuded	1972	None
177	LC1–6	LC1–LC2	1	8	70	Complete	Fairly well preserved	1969 1974	56: 13 61: 6–7
184	LC1–4	LC1?	1	4	35	Complete	Not indicated	1966	52: 11–12
185	LC1–5	LC1?	1	8	55	Complete	Not indicated	1966	52: 11–12
195	LC1–18	LC1?	1	1+	18+	Incomplete?	Very denuded	1978	None
206	LC1–29	LC1–TC	1	2+	25+	Incomplete	Very denuded	1980	None
207	LC1–30	LC1–TC	1	2+	?	Incomplete	Very denuded	1980	None
849	—	LC2	2			Complete	Lower floor well preserved	1982 1984	69: 55
						Newly built brick houses			
169	LC2–2	TC	2	8	75	Complete	Lower floor well preserved	1964	60: 33–36
170	LC2–3	TC	2?	4+	45+	Not fully excavated	Not clearly indicated	1964 1966	60: 36
171	LC2–4	TC	2	11	90	Complete	Lower floor well preserved	1966 1969	52: 9–10 56: 13
172	LC1–7 LC2–5	LC1–LC2	1	5	70	Complete	Fair to good	1969 1972	56: 13
187	LC1–10	LC1–LC2	1	1?	1+	Incomplete	Very denuded	1976	None

*Ground floor rooms.

indicated that none of the houses over the podium can be much earlier than the second half of the Classic Christian period, *c.* AD 1000.'[21] The few pottery vessels described and illustrated in the report are mostly of Classic Christian II types (c. 1000–1100),[22] but include some LC1 types as well. This suggests that the houses were abandoned fairly early in the LCl period, as were those in the adjoining Zone C to the north. They were certainly abandoned and filled with refuse before the Terminal Christian period, when the whole area of Zone B was overbuilt with massive brick castle-houses (see p. 58ff, below). For further information the reader is referred to Professor Frend's published description.[23] It should be noted, finally, that mud brick was used for the upper storeys of at least two Late Christian stone houses, 763 and 849, and also apparently for the upper walls of House 177. All of these buildings will be described in more detail later (see p. 42ff).

Reuse of older buildings

Only a few Classic Christian houses remained in use in the LC1 period. A peculiar feature of the Late Christian periods, however, was the rehabilitation of older buildings that had been disused during the Classic period, and sometimes in the Early Christian period as well. Both houses and storerooms were renovated, sometimes by digging out a substantial amount of refuse that had accumulated during the intervening centuries. Reused buildings are indicated by special shading on the LC1 town plan (fig. 3). Three of the more interesting cases of renovation or reuse will be described here.

House 848 was a large house in Zone E that was built entirely of brick (fig. 12; pl. 4a). The bricks throughout were of typical Meroitic size (33 × 16 × 9 cm),[24] and the lowermost deposits within the house were also of late Roman or early Meroitic age. The two best preserved rooms (Rooms 2 and 3) each had three successive floor levels, of which the earliest was accompanied by late Roman and early Meroitic sherds (index clusters R2 and M1),[25] the second by Late Classic Christian sherds (index cluster CC2), and the uppermost by LC1 sherds. There was no surviving trace of any occupation between the Meroitic and the Classic Christian—an interval of 800 years or more—yet the house had evidently remained in good condition throughout that time. Some of its walls were found standing to a height of more than 150 cm, and all of the surviving brickwork appeared to be original. The only sign of rebuilding that could be recognized anywhere in the house was at the north end, where a new brick stairway had been laid on top of an older and very worn flight of steps in Room 4. The excellent preservation of the house is probably best explained by the assumption that it was deeply filled with refuse during the 800-year interval between its abandonment and its reoccupation. This deposit would then have been dug out by the Classic Christian reoccupants, as was done also in other parts of the site.

House 848 was built immediately beside the cliff edge at the northern edge of the citadel. It consisted essentially of four rooms: two very narrow chambers (Rooms 1 and 2) at the north, a much larger chamber (Room 3) further to the south, and a narrow stair chamber (Room 4) beside the southern house wall (fig. 12). It seems probable that the stairs led not to an upper storey but to the outside doorway of the house; for the building was built on a fairly considerable slope, and the street level on the south side was substantially higher than were the floors within the house.

The most northerly room (Room 1) was provided with two narrow, vaulted cellars, 90 cm high, running the full length of the room beneath the floor. Cellars of this kind were also found in Meroitic brick structures at Faras[26] and Meinarti.[27] The neighbouring Rooms 2 and 3 had no interior features, either from the Meroitic or from the Christian occupations. In the Classic or Late Christian period a doorway had been hacked through the wall at the southwest corner of the house, opening onto a narrow alleyway between House 848 and House 211. It was provided with jambs of rough stone masonry and a masonry threshold. Just inside the doorway were two foetus burials, sealed in pottery jars (82.3.3/32 and 82.3.3/34) and buried under the Classic Christian floor.[28]

House 848 was again abandoned and was filled with densely compacted rubbish before the end of the LC1 period. It then became an outside working surface connected with the neighbouring House 849. The original north wall was entirely dismantled and was replaced with a stout stone wall as part of a general renewal of the northern fortifications at this time. House 848 was fully excavated in the 1982 season.

[21] Frend, *JEA* 60 (1974), 36–8.

[22] Op. cit., 51–9.

[23] Op. cit.

[24] See Adams, *Kush* 13 (1965), 155, n. 13.

[25] For an explanation of ceramic index clusters and their use in dating see William Y. Adams, *Ceramic Industries of Medieval Nubia* (Memoirs of the UNESCO Archaeological Survey of Sudanese Nubia, 1) (Lexington, 1986), 627–33.

[26] Griffith, *LAAA* 13 (1926), 21–3 and pl. XIII.

[27] Adams, *Kush* 13 (1965), 161–3 and 152, fig. 1, B.

[28] Foetal burials of this kind were very common in the Late Christian levels at Qaṣr Ibrîm.

House 781, excavated in the 1982 season, was a three-room stone house in Zone D, and was used primarily for storage (fig. 6). Like House 848 it was built directly along the cliff edge at the northern side of the citadel. It was built on top of very denuded brick remains of the X-Group period. House 781 appears to have been constructed in the Early Christian period, abandoned or at least disused in the Classic Christian period, and then restored to use for a time in the LC1 period. In the LC2 period it was again filled with refuse, and then was largely dismantled in the course of a 'Bosnian' over-buiding. Only the lowest 40 to 80 cm of the walls were left *in situ.*

House 781 was originally entered through a doorway at the southeast corner, leading into Room 1 (fig. 6). This had been solidly blocked with masonry in the LC1 period, and there is no evidence as to how the house was subsequently entered. Within Room 1 there were five floor levels, each comprising a smooth, wet-laid mud surface. The upper floor levels were separated from each other by from 10 to 15 cm of soft refuse. The two oldest floors (Floors 4 and 5), however, were separated from each other by 10 cm of dense, wet-laid mud. Surprisingly, this material had been laid directly over and around a collection of more than a dozen small cups and bowls (82/63; 82/141–143), which had been resting on Floor 5 and were sealed intact below Floor 4.[29] Both Floor 5 and Floor 4 were associated with Early Christian II pottery (c. 700–850 AD), while the three later floors were associated with LC1 pottery exclusively. The hiatus between the earlier and later occupations would, therefore, have been on the order of 250 years. Small pottery jars (82/162 and 82.2.15/62A) were buried up to their rims in both of the earlier floors, but there were no features of any kind in the three Late Christian floors.

Room 1 was adjoined on the north by Room 2, but there was no surviving trace of any interconnection between them. Room 2 had only two floor levels, both associated with refuse of LC1 date. A large part of the floor area was occupied by storage crypts cut into the *gebel* rock which immediately underlay the original floor. The large rectangular Crypt 1 measured about 175 × 150 m, and was 190 cm deep. It had presumably been roofed over at one time with poles and mud, but no trace of roofing was found *in situ,* and the whole crypt was filled with refuse of LC2 date. The original digging of the crypt dates in all probability from X-Group or Early Christian times, when most of the other rock-cut crypts at Qaṣr Ibrîm were made.[30]

A second storage crypt in Room 2 (Crypt 2) was made by roofing over a deep natural crack in the *gebel,* leaving only a small square aperture which was covered by a stone slab. Just below the opening, foot-holds cut in the rock made it possible to descend into the bottom of the crypt, which was 235 cm below the opening. The crypt extended northward beyond the area of Room 2 and formed also the lowermost of two crypts under Room 3. It was filled with soft, wind-blown deposit containing only a few sherds of LC2 date.

Room 3, the most northerly room in House 781, was considerably smaller than its neighbours. Very little survived above the level of the original floor. The floor in most of the room was formed of palm trunks overlaid with mud. Beneath them was a small white-washed crypt, partly dug out of *gebel* rock and partly constructed of masonry. The floor of the crypt, at a depth of 135 cm below the ceiling, was again formed of palm timbers and mud; below this was the natural crack which was a northward extension of Crypt 2 in Room 2. The upper crypt (Crypt 3) was filled with refuse of Early Classic Christian (CC1) date.

Structure 785 was excavated in the 1984 and 1986 seasons. This unusually large and unusually symmetrical building (fig. 8) dates back at least to X-Group and possibly to Meroitic times. In plan and layout it bears a considerable resemblance to the Meroitic magazines at Meinarti.[31] The building evidently continued in use during the Early and Classic Christian periods, after which it suffered the same fiery destruction that was visited upon many of the Classic Christian buildings at the time of the Shams ed-Dawla raid. Although it was never fully restored, there is some evidence of subsequent use in at least the more westerly rooms (Rooms 1–6), where substantial Late Christian refuse deposits were found. The partition walls separating Rooms 1, 2, and 3 appear to date from Late Christian times (fig. 8). Whether Structure 785 served as a dwelling or for some other purpose could not be determined.

Another very interesting reused structure was the old Meroitic and X-Group Tavern, House 178. Since it shows signs of use as an eparchal residence, it will be described in a later section (see p. 53). Other reused buildings of the Late Christian periods are listed and briefly described in table 5.

The eparchal residences

Five Late Christian structures at Qaṣr Ibrîm stood out from the others by virtue of their unusual construction, interesting contents, or both. They were among the

[29] A very large cache of Early Christian vessels was also found under the floor of a house excavated in 1964 (not yet reported in print).

[30] See Plumley and Adams, *JEA* 60 (1974), 215 and pls. XLIV–XLV.

[31] See Adams, *Kush* 13 (1965), 162–3 and 152, B.

best preserved Late Christian buildings on the site. Four of them can be specifically associated with Eparchs of Nobadia, and the fifth was clearly also more than an ordinary house. These buildings merit description in some detail, partly because of their special historical role and partly because they provide unusually good examples of many features of Late Christian architecture.

House 763, excavated in its entirety in the 1982 season,[32] was the oldest of the five buildings which could be identified as eparchal (fig. 6; pl. 4b). It was originally built in the later Classic Christian (CC2) period, perhaps around AD 1050, and was then occupied for about 250 years. The lower floor rooms were found in a fairly good state of preservation, with most walls standing to a height of 150 to 200 cm The highest surviving section of wall, near the southwest corner, survived to a height of nearly 3 m.

House 763 was built on a sloping area immediately beside the cliff which forms the northern limit of the Qaṣr Ibrîm settlement. The more northerly rooms rested directly on *gebel,* and there were no underlying structures or deposit. The more southerly rooms, however, were built on an accumulation of refuse from the Early Christian and Classic Christian periods. Just at floor level in Room 3 (fig. 6) were three large cut-stone foundation blocks from an older monumental building that had otherwise been entirely dismantled. Two of the blocks formed a kind of floor paving within the room, while a third, higher block provided a step up to the level of the room threshold.

House 763 was built alongside an older house, 781, which by Classic Christian times had already been abandoned. (It was later to be restored to use for a time in the LC1 period.) There were no adjoining structures to the south and west, and to the north the cliff face fell away directly below the house wall. Because it was built on sloping ground, and partly on an accumulation of refuse, the house had a considerable downward slope from south to north, i.e., the floors in the most northerly rooms were at lower levels than were those in the southerly rooms.

The plan of House 763 was very roughly trapezoidal (fig. 6), though in fact there were no exactly parallel walls anywhere in the building. The quality of stone construction was generally not very good, both interior and exterior surfaces being markedly uneven. Interior surfaces were somewhat thinly mud plastered, though this had only survived in places. The sharp ends of building stones protruded through the plaster at various points. Walls averaged about 75 cm in thickness but varied from a low of 45 cm to a high of just over one metre.

[32] For the preliminary report see Adams, Alexander and Allen, *JEA* 69 (1983), 54.

The ground floor rooms in House 763 were entered through a rather narrow doorway in the southern part of the east wall, which communicated with an open plaza area (Plaza 764). Here there was already a considerable accumulation of refuse before the house was built, which was not removed at the time of construction. Consequently there was always a descent of two or more steps from the outside ground surface to the interior of House 763. As the level of refuse continued to build up in the outdoor plaza, additional descending steps were added in the LC1 period. In the original plan the threshold itself formed one step, and there was a second descending step within the house (figs. 6 and 7). The house door had originally neither buttresses nor jambs, though a socket in the threshold stone shows that it was fitted with a pivoting door. During a later rebuilding a rather crude buttress was added just beside the northern side of the doorway (fig. 6).

The first room to be entered on coming into the house from outside was a rather small antechamber (Room 3). This had no interior features, but it was the best floored room in the house. It was constructed from the beginning with a very hard, smooth, wet-laid mud floor, except where the floor was formed by the building blocks of an older, buried building. The room was subsequently refloored three times (fig. 7), raising the original level by a total of 45 cm; in each case the new floor was as hard and as well laid as was the original. The floors had been dug away in the north-east corner of the room, where a large cache of dom nuts was buried in a sub-floor pit.

From the antechamber, two doorways led into other parts of the house. An opening in the southern wall gave access to two small closets (Rooms 1 and 2) underneath the stairway to the upper floor. Floors in these rooms were not particularly hard or well laid, reflecting the fact that they were not put to much use. The very soft nature of the fill within these rooms, and the total lack of organic content in them, was probably due to extensive water spillage and suggests that the rooms were used in part for the storage of water jars. However, a shallow stone grinding mortar was set into the floor of Room 2. The passage from Room 3 into Rooms 2 and 1 apparently always stood open; for there was no evidence of a pivoting door here.

A fairly wide doorway with a pivoting door led from Room 3 into the much larger Room 7, and to Room 8 beyond it. In the original plan there were two descending steps from the level of Room 3 to that of Room 7; one within the doorway itself and the other a rather low, wide platform within Room 7. As the floor levels were raised by later refloorings in both Room 3 and Room 7, it was necessary to build new steps and a new door threshold at a higher level (fig. 7). The descending steps were now enclosed between buttresses on either side of the door. In the course of a later reconstruction,

a

b

c

d

Plate 4. Houses of the Late Christian 1 period. a, House 848. b, House 763. c, House 172, Room 1. d, House 172, Rooms 2–5.

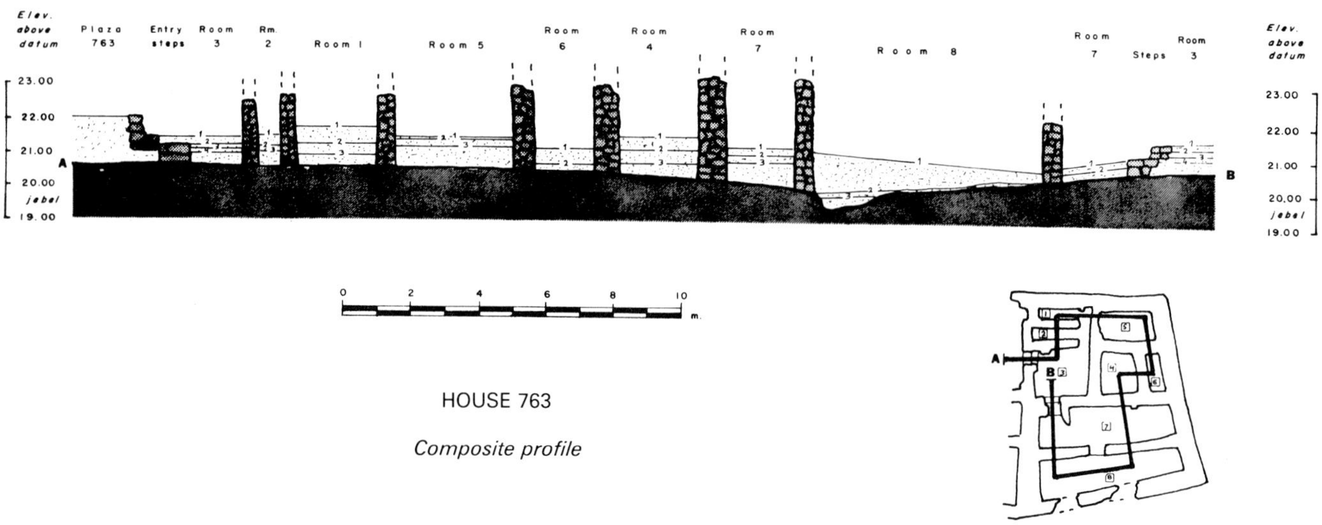

Figure 7. Composite profile of House 763, showing floor levels in each room.

the buttress to the west of the door was extended to form a kind of brick wing-wall, running halfway across the width of Room 7 (fig. 6).

The original floor in Room 7 had a pronounced downward slope from east to west, reflecting the slope of the underlying *gebel.* This was corrected in the course of later refloorings by inserting more fill material at the west end of the room than at the east, so that the third and uppermost floor surface (Floor 1) was nearly level (fig. 7). All the floors in this room were hard, smooth, wet-laid mud surfaces, but all of them had been dug through at various places by storage pits made while the house was still in use. The pits were concentrated mainly in the western half of the room, where there was abundant earth fill overlying the *gebel.* At the eastern end of the room the level of *gebel* was only about 10 cm below the original floor surface.

Room 8, a second large room at the northern end of the house, was originally entered through a rather narrow doorway from Room 7. This had neither buttresses nor jambs and apparently was not fitted with a closing door. In the course of a later modification the doorway was solidly blocked with well-laid stone masonry and mortar, leaving Room 8 without any lateral entry. Presumably at this time it became a cellar, entered from above, like the neighbouring Rooms 4 and 6.

The *gebel* surface beneath Room 8 had a very pronounced slope from east to west, like that in Room 7. In this room, however, the original floor was nothing more than a thin plastering of mud laid directly on the uneven *gebel* rock. Only at the western end of the room, where the slope was steepest, was a small amount of fill material inserted to level this part of the floor. In the course of renovations more material was brought in, and new floors were established in the western half of the room, while the level at the eastern end remained the same. Only in the fourth and final reflooring was a level surface achieved throughout the whole length of the room (fig. 7). As in Room 7, considerable areas of the floor at the west end of the room had been dug through with storage pits.

The storage pits in Rooms 7 and 8 contained no forgotten treasures, but an extraordinary concentration of artifactual refuse. Altogether the two rooms yielded over 150 discarded objects, exclusive of inscriptions, that were deemed worthy of cataloguing: 2 objects of stone, 2 of metal, 3 of mud, 20 of pottery, 21 of glass, 61 of wood, 27 of leather, 15 of basketry and cordage, and 2 of textile. Most extraordinary of all, however, was the content of written material, which numbered 1279 individual pieces of paper bearing text. Most of this was in highly fragmentary condition, having in many cases been chewed to bits by mice, but there were also about a dozen intact letters and several large fragments. None of this material showed any evidence of intentional or careful deposition; it was simply a part of the refuse deposited in the pits. Of the texts 604 were in Old Nubian (82/14), 396 were in Arabic (82/13), 134 had material in both languages (82/15), 4 were in Greek or Coptic (82/16), and in 141 cases the fragments were too small for linguistic identification.

The textual finds from Rooms 7 and 8 identify House 763 as the residence of a certain Eparch Isra'il. His name appears on a number of the documents, both in Arabic (82.1.25/49) and in Old Nubian (81.1.25/19). One is a letter from the son of Isra'il, congratulating his father on his appointment as Eparch. The textual finds from House 763 and other Late Christian dwellings will be much more fully discussed in Part 4.

Room 8 did contain one intentionally buried and, apparently, forgotten treasure. Just beside the door threshold within the room was buried a beautiful sculptured bronze standard of Hellenistic type (82/49), topped by a lion head and a Dionysus figure (pl. 55d–e). This was perhaps originally part of a tripod stand, but the remaining portions were missing by the time the standard was buried. It is unlikely that this already ancient and pagan object served any practical purpose in Late Christian times; probably it was a valued antique whose owner prized it enough to bury it beneath his house floor.

The three rooms at the southwest corner of House 763 had no lateral access. Rooms 4 and 6 were simply storage cellars, entered from the floor above. Both rooms originally had hard floors laid directly on *gebel.* The very small Room 6 was never refloored, but Room 4 had a later floor installed at a level 55 cm above the original. No features were found in either room.

Room 5 was a sewage pit beneath a toilet that must have been on the second floor, since there was no lateral access to the ground-floor room. It was designed to be cleaned out through a small opening at the base of the south wall, but this was apparently not used for long. In time the faecal material within the room built up to a level much higher than the top of the cleanout hole. It was probably this accumulation, with its high moisture content, that caused the east wall of Room 5 to collapse at some time during the occupation of the house. It was later rebuilt with very roughly piled stone masonry. Damage was also apparent along the north wall of Room 5, where much of the mortar between the building stones had dissolved away. This may have been one factor contributing to the final abandonment of the house.

Traces of mud brick vaulting were preserved at the western end of Rooms 7 and 8, and along both the east and west walls of Rooms 4 and 6. It is apparent that these rooms had brick vaulted roofs, and the same can be assumed for Room 3. The vaulting in all cases ran parallel to the long axis of the room; that is, east west in the case of Rooms 7 and 8, and north-south in the case

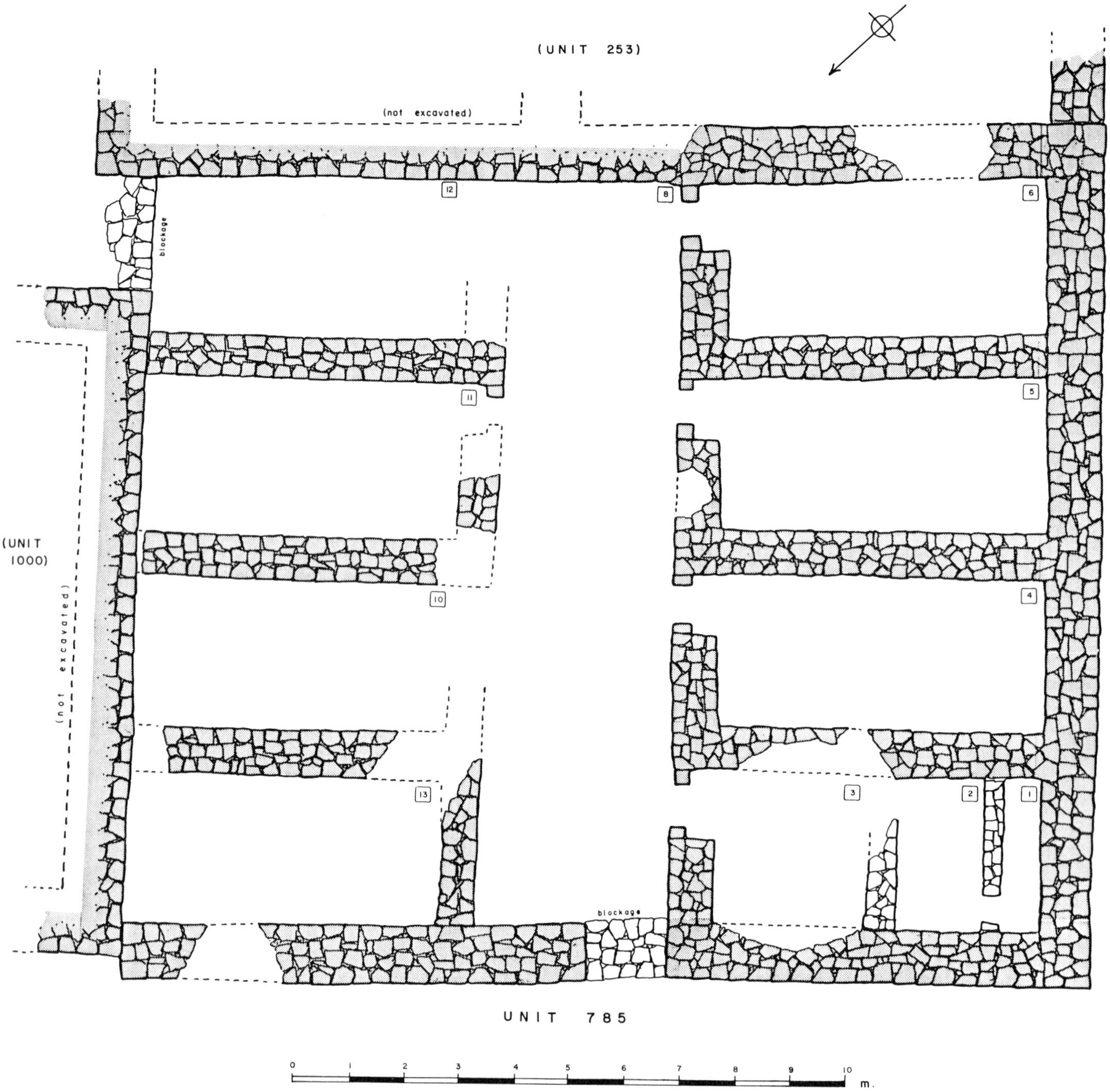

Figure 8. Plan of Meroitic and X-Group Unit 785, as reused in Late Christian times. Figures in squares are room numbers.

of Rooms 4 and 6, and presumably Room 3. The method of roofing in Room 5 is less certain; elsewhere in Nubia toilets usually rested on a flat, wooden platform. The roof in the small Rooms 1 and 2 was, of course, formed by the underside of the stair treads leading to the second floor.

Although no part of it was actually preserved, the presence of a second storey in House 763 can be deduced from three factors: first, the house had exceptionally thick outside walls; second, there was almost certainly a stairway at the southeast corner of the house, ascending over Rooms 1 and 2; finally, there were blind cellars (Rooms 4 and 6, and later also Room 8) that could be entered only from above.

Along the top of the highest surviving portion of wall, west of Rooms 7 and 8, there were a few surviving courses of mud brick. This suggests that the upper-storey construction throughout the house was of mud brick, as was true also in House 849 (see below). It may be noted that two-storey construction involving a lower storey of stone masonry and an upper storey of brick is common at many places in the *Batn el-Hajjar,* [33] whereas there is no known instance of a two-storey house built entirely of stone.

Access to the second-floor rooms in House 763 was through a narrow doorway at the southeast corner of the house (fig. 6). The threshold of this doorway was originally somewhat higher than the adjoining plaza surface, so there were three low steps ascending to it from the plaza outside. The two upper steps were built of mud brick, while the lowest was formed by two stone slabs. An eastward extension of the southern house wall perhaps served as a kind of balustrade beside the outside steps. No part of the doorway survived except the threshold slab itself; consequently there was no trace of jambs or doorframe. There would almost certainly have been a pivoting wooden door to close off access to the upstairs rooms, but a pivot stone was not actually found.

Immediately within the doorway, three roughly squared palm logs formed both the ceiling of Room 1 and the first tread of the stairway. All three logs had small rectangular perforations which had subsequently been stuffed with small stones and mud, suggesting that they had previously served in some other context. No other traces of the stairway were preserved, but it is a safe assumption that the higher treads were also formed by wooden beams set into the side walls; for a stairway either of brick or of stone would have required a solid filling in the underlying Rooms 1 and 2. It is evident that the stairway ascended in a westerly direction above Room 1, then returned to ascend eastward above Room 2. At the top, it must have given onto an antechamber directly over the ground-floor antechamber (Room 3). No actual features of the second floor plan were preserved, but it may be noted that barrel vaults of the kind found in House 763 are not strong enough to support the weight of heavy stone or brick walls. Second-floor partitions can only be built directly on top of ground-floor partitions, so that the arrangement of rooms on the upper and lower floors has to be essentially the same. This was found to be true in a number of late Nubian two-storey houses in the *Batn el-Hajjar,* where parts of the second floors are preserved.[34]

Late in the LC1 period, or perhaps at its conclusion, all of the ground-floor rooms in House 763 were abandoned and deeply filled with rubbish. The reason for this is not apparent, but a weakening or partial collapse of the brick vaulted ceilings is the most probable explanation, since the house by this time would have been somewhere around 250 years old. There was also some visible deterioration of the north wall, adjoining the sewage chamber.

Subsequent to the refuse filling, deep, brick-lined storage crypts (766) were sunk into the accumulated fill in Room 7, adjoining its south wall. These in their turn were later refilled with material of LC2 date. Still later, the 'Bosnians' sank other brick-lined crypts into the west ends of both Room 7 and Room 8, and they also dug out and reused Rooms 4 and 6 as storage crypts. Finally a new 'Bosnian' house, 126, was built directly over the filled-up House 763, using some of its wall tops as footings.

It cannot be certainly established that the second floor rooms in House 763 went out of use at the same time as did those on the ground floor. They might have remained in use after the lower storey had been filled in, as happened in some two-storey houses in the *Batn el-Hajjar.* [35] It may be noted, however, that brick-lined storage crypts of the kind that were sunk into Room 7 are a common feature of the LC1 and LC2 periods, but they are nearly always found outside of houses rather than within them. This suggests that the upper storey was no longer functioning as such at the time when Crypts 766 were intruded.

In sum, House 763 appears to have been the residence of a wealthy and influential family, one of whose members achieved the office of Eparch of Nobadia in the twelfth or thirteenth century. The deposition of the Isra'il letters belongs to a relatively late period in the occupation of House 763, and it should, therefore, not be assumed that the house was designed from the beginning as an eparchal residence. Since the office of Eparch was appointive rather than hereditary, it is probable that there was no official or public residence. The evidence from House 763, and from Houses 177 and 172 to be discussed below, suggests that the Eparch used his own home for official functions, making whatever modifications were necessary for that purpose. What we have preserved, in any case, are only the ground-floor cellars in House 763, and they tell us less than we should like to know about the family's living arrangements, which were probably mainly on the upper floor. Fortunately this deficiency is partly rectified in House 177, another eparchal residence which did not have a second storey.

House 177 was one of a tight cluster of houses in Zone A, the area between Church 287 and Church 294 (see fig. 3). All the structures were built on a dense accumulation of refuse from the Early and Classic Christian periods, when Zone A was an open plaza between the churches. The earliest houses to be built, 185 and 177, were also underlain by a small amount of LC1 deposit,

[33] See Adams in Dinkler (ed.), *Kunst,* 142–52; and id., *Archéologie du Nil Moyen* 6 (1994), 11–46.

[34] Op. cit. Additional well-preserved 'castle-houses' have been recorded at Dal, but are not yet reported in print.

[35] Adams in Dinkler (ed.), *Kunst,* 143.

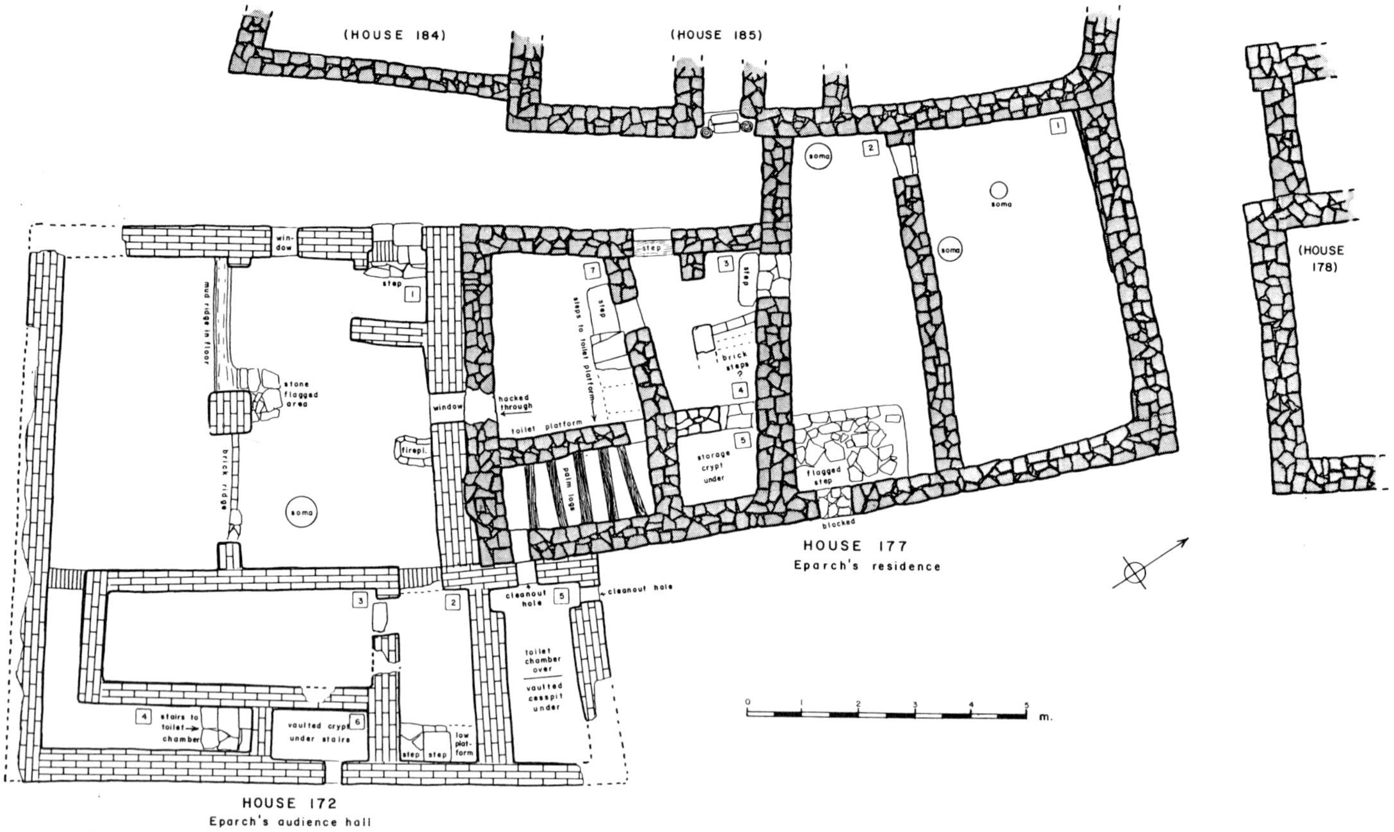

Figure 9. Plan of eparchal House 177, and adjoining audience chamber 172. Stone construction indicated by shading; brick construction indicated by simulated brick. Figures in squares are room numbers.

suggesting that they were built early in the LC1 period but not actually at its beginning. A date around 1175 AD, immediately following the Shams ed-Dawla raid and the rebuilding of the girdle wall, seems most likely.

The earliest house to be rebuilt in the plaza was evidently House 185, since Houses 184 and 177 were abutted against it. In the LC2 period more houses were added to the south of this group, until the formerly open plaza between the churches was entirely built over. In the same area several older buildings from the X-Group and Early Christian periods were also dug out and restored to use (see p. 42, above).

House 177, then, was originally built alongside the previously built House 185. In the beginning there were no adjoining structures on the east, south, or west. Before long however the brick structure 172 was built adjoining the west side of House 177 (fig. 9). It was not properly a house but a kind of annex to House 177 and will be described more fully in later paragraphs. In the LC2 period additional stone Houses 173 and 175 were built alongside the south wall of House 177, so that it was surrounded by contiguous structures on three sides. On the east, there was always a narrow open street separating House 177 from House 178.

[36] For the preliminary reports see Plumley, *JEA* 56 (1970), 13, and id., *JEA* 61 (1975), 6–7.

Excavation in House 177 was begun in 1969, continued in 1972, and completed in 1974, when all surviving parts of the house were dismantled. The post-abandonment fill and some of the upper floor surfaces were taken out in 1969 without careful documentation and without any collection of sherds, so that the later history of the house cannot be reconstructed with as much certainty as can the original occupation.[36]

House 177 was found in a fair state of preservation, with walls standing in places to a height of between 100 and 125 cm The higher parts of the walls had been systematically dismantled prior to the time of the 'Bosnian' overbuilding. The surviving walls were mostly of stone masonry similar to that in House 763. They were, however, notably thinner than the walls in House 763, with an average thickness of 45 cm and a maximum thickness of 65 cm. In Room 1 the lower walls had been thickened by leaning heavy upright slabs against them; these, as well as the regular masonry of the walls, were enclosed within a heavy coating of mud plaster. Both Room 1 and the neighbouring Room 2 had been whitewashed. (For the plan of the house see fig. 9.)

The highest surviving portions of wall were capped by one or two courses of brick masonry. This suggests that the upper parts of the house, above a height of

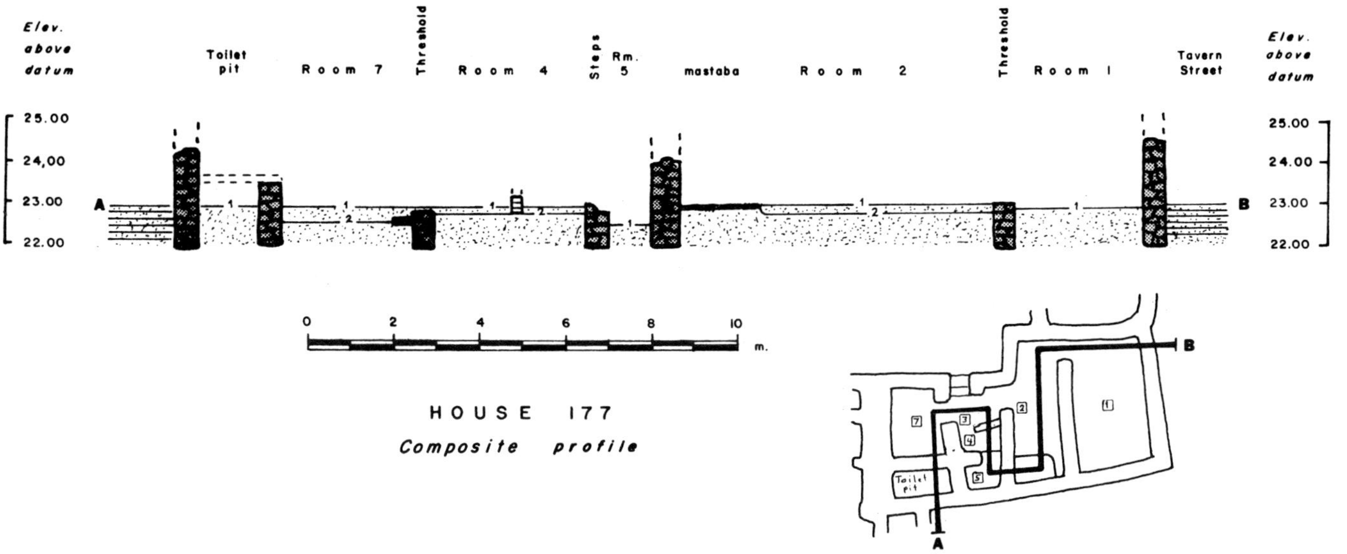

Figure 10. Composite profile of House 177, showing floor levels in each room.

120 cm, may have been built of brick. In view of the rather thin and curving walls, however, it is unlikely that the building had a vaulted brick roof. The surviving bricks averaged 44 × 22 × 8 cm in size, larger than the typical size of bricks found in Late Christian houses elsewhere in Nubia.[37]

House 177 from the time of its original construction was somewhat irregular in plan (fig. 9). It was essentially rectangular, but the northern wall had a set-back to allow for a narrow passage between House 177 and House 185. This provided the only access to House 185, and later also to Houses 177 and 172 (see fig. 4). House 177 was originally entered from the south through a narrow doorway near the middle of the south wall. Like the original doorway to House 763, this had neither jambs nor buttresses, and there is no surviving evidence to show how it was closed. The doorway had a raised masonry threshold 15 cm higher than the outside ground level, and higher also than the floors within the house. The original doorway to House 177 gave onto a large chamber (Room 2) which ran the full width of the house. From the actual threshold there was a step down of 10 cm to a low stone-flagged platform and then a further step down of 15 cm to the original floor of the room. During a subsequent renovation the floor level throughout the room was raised by 15 cm, so that it came flush with the top of the older platform (fig. 10). At the north-east corner of Room 2, a doorway led into the equally large Room 1. Here again there was a raised masonry threshold but no trace of jambs or buttresses. There was no evidence of a closing door here or anywhere in the house. As previously noted, the lower walls of Room 1 had been reinforced by the addition of heavy upright slabs.

Rooms 1 and 2 were obviously the most important in House 177, and they were almost the only Late Christian rooms at Qaṣr Ibrîm that had any number of floor features. Room 1 had two large mud *somas* buried under the floor, as shown in the plan (fig. 9), and also three pottery jars buried in the northeast corner of the room (74.1.31/7–9). All of these vessels were buried so that their rims were flush with the original floor surface. One pot had a stone slab cover still in place and was devoid of contents; the other pots and the *somas* were filled with the same loose rubbish found elsewhere in the room. Room 2 also had a single jar buried in its north-east corner (74.1.31/6) and a *soma* beneath the floor in the north-west corner. In the very centre of the floor in Room 1, a large burden basket full of durra grain (74/15) had been buried. The overlying floor was afterward firmly repaved with mud, so that the basket was in effect sealed beneath the floor.

House 177, like House 763, yielded a treasure trove of documents. In the loose fill beneath the floor of Room 1 were found several small folded papers which appeared to be letters to the Eparch (69.2.8/3, 7, 8; 69/26; 74/12). In the fill beneath the stone-flagged entrance step in Room 2 were more papers, bearing texts both in Arabic and in Old Nubian (74.1.29/11). These were in very fragmentary condition; they appear to have been cached within a large jar that was subsequently crushed.[38] The most important documents from House 177, however, were those buried in a sealed pottery jar at the base of the west wall of Room 2 (74/13–14). The contents included 10 leather scrolls, 1 paper scroll, 6 documents on parchment, and 17

[37] See Adams, *Kush* 13 (1965), 155, n. 13.

[38] Plumley, *JEA* 61 (1975), 7. This find is described in Part 4, Chapter 1 as Cache no. 4.

letters on paper, all intact. These were legal documents from the late mediaeval Kingdom of Dotawo; they will be more fully discussed in Part IV.[39]

Among the various documents found in House 177, a certain Adam, or Adama, is mentioned twelve times as being Eparch of Nobadia (and also, concurrently, as Domesticus of Faras).[40] It seems very probable, therefore, that Adam was at least one of the eparchal residents of this house. Four of the documents bearing his name have dates between the years between 1188 and 1200;[41] the others are undated.

At the west side of Room 2, a small doorway with a cut-stone threshold slab led into the smaller chambers in the western half of House 177 (Rooms 3, 5, and 7). From the threshold there was a second step leading down to the floor level in Room 3, which was 20 cm lower than that in Room 2, and there was a further step down of 25 cm from Room 3 into Room 5. Both Room 3 and Room 5 appear originally to have been store rooms, with no interior features. The partly subterranean Room 5, whose floor level was 50 cm below that outside the house, was perhaps designed for the cool storage of wine or water.

From Room 3 another doorway led into Room 7 at the western end of the house. The floors in Rooms 3 and 7 were at the same level, as was the stone masonry threshold between them. Room 7 was designed from the beginning and was used throughout its history as a toilet chamber. The southern side of the room was occupied by a platform 175 cm wide and 90 cm.high, formed of palm logs resting on a stone masonry partition at the front and socketed into the house wall at the back. Access to the top of the platform was apparently by means of a sloping ramp made of logs, whose lower ends were held in position by two heavy stones set into the floor (see fig. 9). The space beneath the platform was unmistakably a cess pit. It was originally designed to be cleaned out through a small hole within Room 7, directly beneath the ramp leading to the platform top. However this hole was later blocked, and a somewhat larger hole was hacked through the south wall of the house from the outside. This was perhaps concurrent with the building of an adjoining toilet chamber in House 172, to be described later.

At some time after its original building, but still within the LC1 period, House 177 underwent a series of modifications. Floor levels throughout the house were raised by 15 to 25 cm (fig. 10). The original entryway into Room 2 was firmly blocked with masonry, and a hard mud mastaba was built along the south wall of Room 2, where the doorway had formerly been. (It was the closing of this doorway which made possible the subsequent building of House 173 adjoining the south side of House 177.) Meanwhile a new and wider doorway was cut through the north wall of the house, leading into Room 3 which now became an entrance chamber. The newly made doorway was provided with a cut-stone threshold slab, and a stout brick buttress was built beside the door. A squared palm log set into the floor provided a step down from the level of the threshold to that of the floor in Room 3. At the same time a brick partition was run part way across Room 3; this may have been a retainer for a flight of steps leading up and over Room 5. The original doorway to the latter room was now firmly blocked with stone masonry, leaving it accessible only from above.

From the evidence it is possible to deduce that all of the aforementioned changes in House 177 were carried out at the same time, and that they were concurrent with the building of House 172 alongside. It may also be surmised that this signals the time when the occupant of House 177 became Eparch of Nobadia.

House 172, unlike any other LC1 structure at Qaṣr Ibrîm, was built from the beginning entirely of mud brick. The average size of the bricks was 36 × 19 × 8 cm.[42] Although House 172 directly adjoined House 177 on the east, the two buildings did not share a common wall; the brick east wall of House 172 was built face-to-face with the stone west wall of House 177 (see fig. 9). That House 172 was built later than its neighbour is attested by the fact that the outer face of its east wall (i.e. the face abutting against House 177) was very rough and unfinished, in contrast to the other outer wall surfaces. All of the walls were uniformly 55 cm thick, i.e. the width of one header brick and one stretcher brick. Interior walls had been covered with a very hard, smooth pink plaster,[43] and this in turn had been whitewashed. Only the parts of House 172 immediately adjoining House 177 were reasonably well preserved. The east wall and adjoining parts of the north and south walls stood to a height of between 160 and 180 cm, while elsewhere the walls were generally not preserved to a height of more than 50 to 100 cm. House 172 was first excavated in 1969, and it was fully cleared and then dismantled in 1972.[44]

[39] For the original discovery see op. cit. For translations and commentary see Gerald M. Browne, *Old Nubian Texts from Qaṣr Ibrîm, III* (Egypt Exploration Society, Texts from Excavations) (London, in press). This find is described in Part 4, Chapter 1 as Cache no. 3.

[40] 74.1.30/6, nos. 1, 4, 5, 6, 7, 8, 9a, 9c, 16, 18, 23, and 30. See Browne, op. cit.

[41] 74.1.30/6, nos. 6 (AD 1188), 7 (AD 1191), 9a (AD 1199), and 8 (AD 1200). See Browne, op. cit.

[42] This is the typical size of X-Group and Early Christian bricks at Meinarti; see Adams, *Kush* 13 (1965), 155, n. 13.

[43] The colour derives in part from the fact that the plaster incorporates a large amount of pink sand from the west bank of the Nile. Similar plaster was employed in the Late Christian period at Meinarti; see Adams, *Kush* 12 (1964), 229.

[44] It is one of the buildings very briefly described by Plumley, *JEA* 56 (1970), 13.

House 172 was not an ordinary dwelling. More than half of its total area was occupied by a single large room (Room 1), which was far larger than any chamber in any other Late Christian house (pl. 4c). Adjoining Room 1 was an ingenious arrangement of smaller rooms which were used for storage and for access to a latrine (pl. 4d). The smaller rooms had all had brick vaulted roofs, but the very large Room 1 can only have supported a flat roof resting on timbers. A central masonry pillar within the room, and buttresses opposite it on the north and south walls, would have provided support for a central roof beam or beams, over which secondary beams and mud roofing material would have been laid. Although the house was provided with a stairway, this almost certainly gave access to a latrine platform and not to a second storey, for the house walls do not appear thick enough to support the latter.

Room 1 was entered at its north-east corner, from the same alleyway that also gave access to Houses 177 and 185 (see fig. 9). The doorway was nearly a metre wide, with a raised threshold consisting of a single cut stone slab into which deep votive grooves had been worn. From the threshold a second step of stone masonry led down to the floor within the room, which was originally at a level 30 cm below the threshold. Immediately opposite the door and adjoining the east wall was a baffle wall of brick, which screened the interior of the room from anyone looking in at the door. In the east and south walls, and also in the baffle wall, the horizontal brickwork was interrupted by a row of vertically laid bricks at a level 1 m above the floor. Room 1 had a very hard, wet-laid mud floor, which had been renewed many times in the course of occupation. In most cases this involved only the installation of 1 to 2 cm of new mud over the previous surface. The total number of refloorings could not be determined, but it may have been in excess of a dozen. The uppermost and latest floor in the room, however, was a relatively uneven surface, established on an accumulation of dry refuse. The total accumulation of material between the lowermost and the uppermost floors was about 55 cm

The floor in Room 1 exhibited a number of interesting features, some dating from the original construction and some from later modifications. In the original plan the floor was divided into eastern and western halves by a kind of low, rounded mud partition, 20 cm high, which ran across the room from north to south (see pl. 4c). In the course of later modifications the floor level was raised on the west side of the partition, but not on the east, until the whole western half of the room was a kind of dais 20 cm high. Still later the eastern half was also raised, resulting in a more or less level floor throughout the room. In place of the earlier mud ridge, a row of somewhat irregularly laid stones now separated the eastern and western halves of the room. These in their turn were buried under the final and uppermost floor.

In the original plan of Room 1 there was a small slab-lined firepit at the base of the east wall (fig. 9). The enclosing slabs projected 20 cm above the level of the original floor, but later, after the floor was built up, their tops were flush with the floor. In the final reflooring the firepit was buried altogether. Originally there was also a paving of small, irregularly laid stone slabs at the base of the central pillar, on its eastern side. This appears to be a place where a water jar rested. A small depression in the floor near the south-west corner, with a single slab in the bottom of it, may have been a rest for another pottery vessel.

In the course of a later reflooring, after the original dividing ridge had been covered over, a very low mastaba of mud was built in the northwest corner of Room 1. The main part of its surface was only 5 cm higher than was the surrounding floor, but it was considerably raised at the edges. In the eastern half of the room, at the same level, a slightly raised, round platform of mud had evidently served as the base for a stone quern (*rahaya*), though the apparatus itself was not found *in situ.* Both mastaba and quern platform were buried beneath the uppermost flooring in the house, but on this surface another quern platform was established in the middle of the room.

A stout, square wooden post stood upright in the eastern part of Room 1. It was not an original feature, but had been installed after the eastern floor level had been raised by 20 cm. Its original height and its purpose could not be determined, for after the house was abandoned the upper part of the post was hacked away. The small rooms along the south side of the house were as well built and finished as was Room 1, and they had the same hard pink plaster and whitewash. These rooms exhibited an ingenious arrangement of vaults and hidden crypts, repeating in miniature the kind of arrangements that are often found in Nubian 'castles' of the late mediaeval period.[45] At the south-west corner of Room 1, a small doorway with a raised brick threshold gave access to a narrow passage (Room 4). This proceeded southward, then turned eastward around a small interior store room (Room 3), and ended in a flight of brick-built steps. Only the two lowermost treads were preserved, but it was evident that the stairway had ascended eastward, first over a small vaulted crypt (Room 6) and then over the south end of Room 2, ending at a toilet chamber over Room 5 (see fig. 9). Access to the crypt under the stairs (Room 6) was by means of a very small aperture in the outside wall of the house, which would have allowed someone to reach in but not actually to crawl in.

[45] See Adams in Dinkler (ed.), *Kunst,* 142–52, and id., *Nubia,* 515–7.

Room 5, unlike the rest of House 172, was not built against the east wall of House 177 but against its south wall, so that it formed a projection from the otherwise square plan of the building (fig. 9). The reason for this is quite evident. Room 5 was a toilet chamber, and it was deliberately situated back-to-back with the toilet chamber (Room 7) in House 177. A small hole in the brickwork in House 172 connected with the cleanout hole that had previously been hacked through the stonework in House 177, as shown in the plan. There was a second cleanout hole in the east wall of Room 5, connecting with the outside of the house. Most of Room 5 was rather poorly preserved, but enough survived at the north end to show that the cess pit, comprising the lower portion of the room, had had a vaulted roof just over one metre above the level of the floor. The interior walls were without finish of any kind, as might be expected in a sewage pit. The toilet itself was undoubtedly in an overlying chamber, but no part of this was preserved. A large water jar (72.11.1/7) had stood in the angle of the passage (Room 4) leading to the toilet, for the convenience of those using the facility.

A rather wide but very low arched doorway in the southeast corner of Room 1 gave access to Room 2. Here again there was a raised threshold of bricks set on edge. At the south end of Room 2 a set of narrow, brick-built steps had ascended to the top of a low platform in the southeast corner of the room, with a vaulted niche underneath. As the room ceiling itself must have been quite low at this point, it is difficult to know what purpose the platform could have served. From Room 2, a narrow, arched doorway led into Room 3. The floors in the two rooms were contiguous, and there was no raised threshold separating them. Later however the floor in Room 3 was raised by 15 cm, and at this time a rough stone threshold was installed. Still later the doorway was blocked altogether with stones and mud mortar. Room 3 was devoid of features, but a large storage jar (72.11.1/2) rested on the original floor at its western end (pl. 4d).

House 172 yielded no significant documents. It is not difficult to guess, however, that Room 1 was built to serve as an audience chamber for the Eparch who lived in the adjoining house. The original floor partition and subsequent raising of the western half of the floor suggest that the western half of the room was reserved for the Eparch and his retainers, while the eastern half was occupied by his visitors and petitioners. The toilet facility would, of course, have been for the convenience of the Eparch and his guests, and Room 3 was perhaps a store room for food which could be served to visitors. The low platform in Room 2 might have been intended for a cooking apparatus, though no actual evidence of fires was seen in the room. Valuable documents could have been cached in the vaulted crypt (Room 6) beneath the stairs. While all this is necessarily speculative, the public function of the house is clearly proclaimed by the deep votive grooves worn into the threshold. Such grooves are found in and around the doorways of nearly all public buildings at Qaṣr Ibrîm, but not in private dwellings.

The upper fill was removed from House 172 without careful documentation or the collection of sherds, and for that reason it is not easy to reconstruct the later history of the building. Sherds found on and between the upper floor levels show that Room 1 continued to be used in the LC2 period, but it was almost certainly abandoned by the end of the period. The small southerly rooms may have been abandoned earlier, for before the end of the LC2 period they were dismantled down to a level about 60 cm above their original floors and were then overbuilt by the stone House 175 (see fig. 4). The doorway which had originally led from Room 1 into Room 4 may then have become an outside doorway; it was not blocked but was given a new, raised threshold of wood on top of its original brick threshold.

Dismantling of the southern rooms deprived House 172 of its toilet facility, but this was compensated by hacking a crude doorway through the east wall, giving access to the toilet chamber in House 177. The level of the doorsill suggests that this was concurrent with the last reflooring in House 177. It may have been at the same time that a small window was cut through the brickwork in the north wall of House 172. In view of the crudity of these modifications it is reasonable to conclude that House 172 by this time had ceased to have any public function.

The surviving evidence (as of 1972) does not give a clear indication of what happened to Houses 172 and 177 in the Terminal Christian period. They were almost certainly not in use, and may already have been partly filled with refuse by the end of the LC2 period. There is no evidence, however, that they were overbuilt, as were some neighbouring houses to the north. It was not until the Islamic period that their upper walls were systematically dismantled, and new houses built on top.

In sum, it may be surmised that House 177 was built early in the LC1 period, most probably immediately following the raid of Shams ed-Dawla. In the last years of the twelfth century it served as the residence of the Eparch Adam, who undertook a series of modifications in the house and also built House 172 alongside to serve as his audience chamber. Both structures apparently remained in use during part of the LC2 period, but they suffered considerable deterioration, and were probably no longer the eparchal residence. Before the end of the LC2 period both were abandoned and partly filled with refuse.

House 178. Another building that gave evidence of eparchal use was House 178, located just to the east of House 177 across a narrow alleyway (figs. 4 and 9). This structure had a very long and complex history, extending back to Meroitic times. Unfortunately the later phases of its history cannot be reconstructed very precisely, since the uppermost deposits and some of the walls were taken out in 1969 without very careful documentation.[46]

House 178 in Meroitic and X-Group times was a tavern, and was one of a row of contiguous structures extending along the east side of a narrow street. Its lower walls, to a height of 165 cm, were of well-dressed cut stone. Above that level the original walls were apparently of mud brick, whitewashed on the inside and fitted with ornamental stone window grilles.[47] The building had remained in use for a time in the Early Christian period but was then partially dismantled and filled in as were all of the houses in the plaza area between Churches 287 and 294 (see Ch. 1). The brick upper walls and the window grilles were pulled down, and their remnants were used to fill in the lower rooms as well as the street outside.[48]

At some time in the Late Christian period new walls of rough stone masonry were built on top of the older cut-stone walls in House 178 (pl. 5a).[49] The newly rebuilt house essentially reproduced the plan of the original, with some rearrangement of doorways and partitions (see fig. 11). In the rebuilt house there was no outside doorway at ground level, though there were interconnections between some of the interior chambers. One room had a small square aperture in the wall at ground level, suggesting the cleanout hole for a cess pit.[50] Along the west side of the house, three new rooms were added, resting not on older walls but on street deposit. These rooms had no doorways connecting with the rest of the house or with the outside (fig. 11). The whole complex of new and old rooms may well have been the cellars of a two-storey house, whose upper portion has vanished.

No Late Christian floor surfaces or deposits were left *in situ* after the 1969 excavations, and it was therefore not possible to determine how much of the earlier fill was dug back out at the time when House 178 was restored to use. It may be that the Late Christians merely took advantage of the older wall tops as footings and did not otherwise make use of the underlying building. For the same reason it is not possible to say how long House 178 was occupied in the Late Christian period. The excavator's report suggests that it was abandoned and filled over in the Terminal Christian period,[51] when large brick 'castle-houses' were built nearby.

In the absence of potsherd collections, Late Christian occupation in House 178 is attested chiefly by textual finds. Letters to the Eparch, in both Old Nubian (69/26; 69.2.11/2; 69.2.11/10; 69.2.16/4) and Arabic (69/25) were found in several of the upper rooms.[52] In addition, two fine brass basins (69/12, 69/51) of presumed Mamluk date were found buried beneath the floor in one of the corner rooms.[53] These finds not only attest to Late Christian occupation but suggest that House 178 was another eparchal residence, or at least a storehouse used by the Eparch.

House 849. There were no textual finds to identify this structure as an eparchal residence, but it was certainly larger and better furnished than were the typical Late Christian houses at Qaṣr Ibrîm. It was also one of the best-preserved houses, with walls standing in most places to a height of 150 cm or more. In part, this reflects the fact that the house, unlike most others at Qaṣr Ibrîm, did not have a very long history. It was built, occupied, destroyed by fire, and filled with refuse entirely within the LC2 period, which means in all probability within the span of a century. House 849 was excavated in the 1982 and 1984 seasons.[54]

The situation of House 849 was similar in many respects to that of House 763. It was built on sloping ground immediately next to the northern cliff edge, and its more northerly walls rested directly on *gebel* (fig. 12). The southern walls stood on a small accumulation of refuse and on the very denuded remnants of Roman or Meroitic brick structures. The northern outside wall was integral with the citadel fortifications, which extended in an unbroken line east and west of the house (see fig. 4). The west wall was abutted against a much older brick house, 848, which had already gone out of use when House 849 was built (pl. 5b). (See p. 41, above.) **The quality of construction in house 849 was better than that in any other Late Christian house.** The walls were relatively straight and were made from unusually large, roughly squared stone blocks, so that there was less use of chinking than in most other houses. All of the rooms were well and smoothly plastered, and the largest (Room 5) had a thick coat of

[46] For the original excavation report see Plumley, *JEA* 56 (1970), 13–5 and pl. XXII, 2.

[47] Op. cit., 16 and pl. XXIII, 4.

[48] For the earlier history of House 178 (formerly X-4) see Plumley and Adams, *JEA* 60 (1974), 217–9.

[49] See Plumley, *JEA* 56 (1970), pl. XXII, 2, and Plumley and Adams, *JEA* 60 (1974), pl. XLIII, 2.

[50] It was originally identified as a prison chamber; see Plumley, *JEA* 56 (1970), 14.

[51] Op. cit., 13.

[52] Op. cit., 14.

[53] Op. cit., 13–14 and pl. XXI.

[54] It is briefly mentioned in Adams, Alexander and Allen, *JEA* 69 (1983), 55.

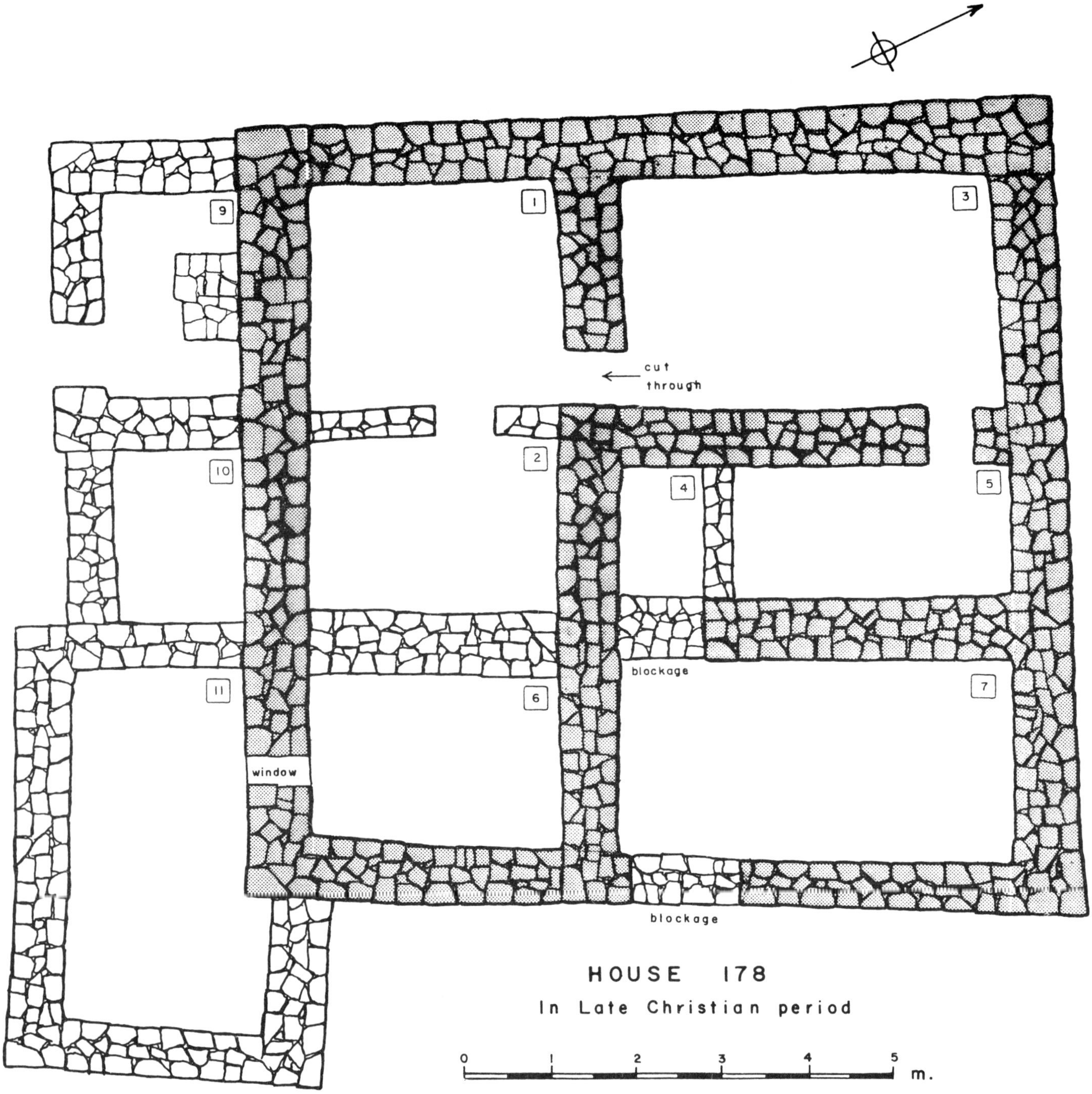

Figure 11. Plan of eparchal House 178. Shading indicates original Meroitic walls; unshaded areas are Late Christian additions. Figures in squares are room numbers.

whitewash. Individual walls were fairly uniform in thickness, but there was some variation from wall to wall, from a minimum thickness of 60 cm to a maximum of 90 cm

The house was entered through a very wide doorway near the south end of its east wall. This was originally 120 cm wide, with a stone masonry rebate on its south side and a threshold of small stone slabs. The threshold was at two levels, the upper (eastern) side being flush with the outside ground surface while the lower (western) half was 10 cm lower. This created a sill against which a door presumably closed, though no socket stone was found. In the course of a later renovation the width of the original doorway was reduced from 120 to 80 cm, by the insertion of brick masonry against its southern jamb (see fig. 12), and at the same

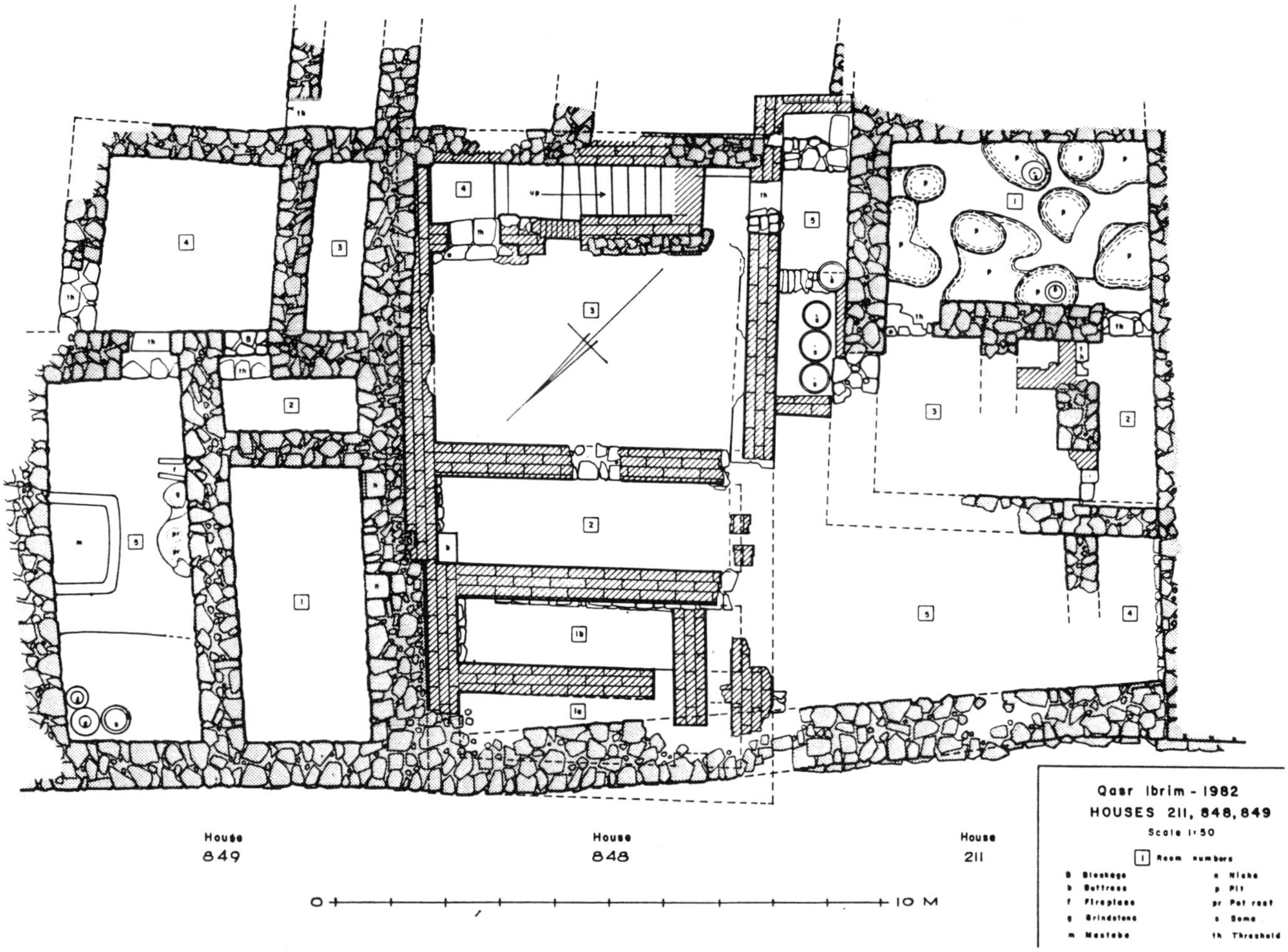

Figure 12. Plan of Houses 848, 849, and 211. Diagonal hatching indicates brick construction. Figures in squares are room numbers.

time the floor level within the room was raised by 10 cm. One of the doorways in the house had been fitted with a finely carved *uraeus* lintel of Meroitic type (82.3.4/88), undoubtedly salvaged from an older building. Its burned and broken pieces were widely scattered through the rubble fill in the house.

The first room to be entered from outside the house was a small entrance chamber (Room 4), without features. Surprisingly, neither of its two floor levels was very hard packed, and neither appeared to have been wet-laid. From Room 4, two doorways led into other parts of the house. A narrow doorway in the northwest corner gave access to a very small chamber (Room 2), hardly more than a closet. It is hard to know why the entry to this insignificant chamber required a rebate and a cut-stone threshold. One possibility is that this room originally housed a ladder giving access to the upper floor, since the house was not equipped with a stairway. An arrangement of this kind was found in a Late Christian two-storey house at Meinarti.[55] After a very short time, however, the doorway between Room 4 and Room 2 was solidly blocked with masonry, which was so well plastered over that no suggestion of a doorway remained visible. Thereafter Room 2 was merely a small cellar entered from above. It had been dug out and reused as a crypt in 'Bosnian' times, so that no Late Christian contents were found in it. To the north and to the south of this room were other cellars entered only from above (see fig. 12). Room 3 was a narrow but very stoutly built crypt, with no floor except the naked *gebel* surface. Like Room 2 it had been dug out and reused by the 'Bosnians,' and had no Late Christian contents.

Room 1, to the north of Room 2, was a large chamber with a number of interesting features. The original floor was a coating of mud laid directly in the *gebel* surface, which had a gentle but continual downward slope from south to north. Two round mud *somas* rested on the floor in the northeast corner of the room, and an upright pottery jar had been mortared into place

[55] Adams, *Kush* 13 (1965), 232–3 and fig. 4, B.

Plate 5. Houses of the Late Christian 1, Late Christian 2, and Terminal Christian periods. a, House 178 (formerly the tavern) from top of walls. b, Houses 848 (foreground) and 849 (background). c, Floor features in House 849, Room 5. d, Castle-house 169, resting on top of the Podium.

between them. Both *somas* contained a substantial quantity of acacia seeds, and one also contained cotton bolls.

The floor in Room 1 had been renewed twice, at levels 20 and 45 cm above the original surface (fig. 13). The new floors were smooth but not very hard packed; they had only a thin mud surface laid over soft refuse fill. These floors were laid at the north but not at the south end of the room, so that their effect was to level the originally sloping surface. After the final reflooring only the southernmost quarter of the room continued to have a flooring resting directly on *gebel* rock.

Resting on the uppermost floor surface, at the base of the east wall, were two *somas* of an unusual, square shape. They were found without contents. The two older *somas* in the north-east corner were now largely buried, only their rims continuing to project a short distance above the uppermost floor surface. A small, folded sheet of paper with Old Nubian writing was found under the floor beside the east wall; it was the only piece of text found in House 849. In the upper fill, all organic material had been destroyed by the burning of the house.

In the west wall of Room 1 were two niches, at a level about 100 cm above the floor (see fig. 12). Both were about 45 cm wide and 45 cm deep; their original height could not be determined because the tops were not preserved. At least one of the niches had been whitewashed. Since Room 1 was a cellar without lateral entrances, it might be supposed that one or both of the niches were meant for lamps, but in fact neither showed any traces of burning or oil spillage.

A second doorway from the entrance hall led into Room 5, the largest and most interesting room in House 849. Its entranceway was equipped in the beginning with stone jambs and a cut-stone threshold.

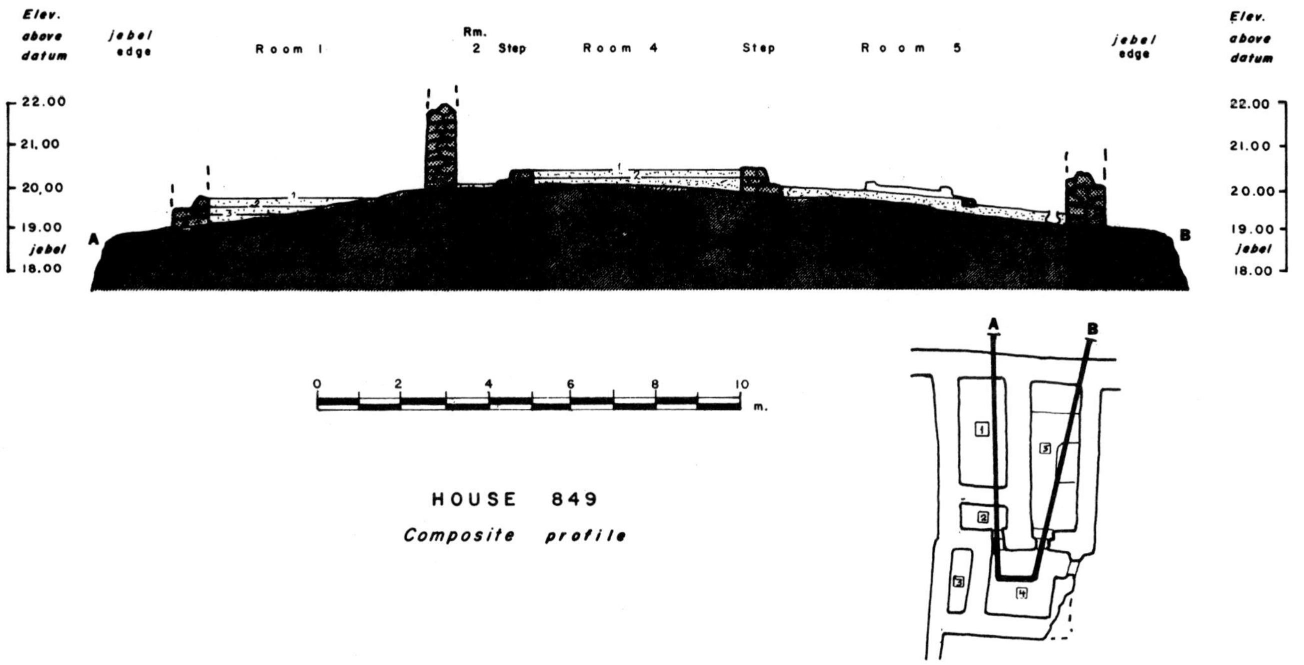

Figure 13. Composite profile of House 849, showing floor levels in each room.

From this there was a step down of 10 cm to an intermediate step, made of small stone slabs, and then a further step down of 10 cm to the floor of the room. At a later date the width of the doorway was reduced by 30 cm, by inserting brick masonry alongside its western jamb, and at the same time a new threshold of rough stone slabs was laid over the original. Presumably this was done at the same time when the outside doorway to Room 4 was reduced in size, and when a new and higher floor level was installed in Room 4. There was not, however, any concurrent raising of the floor level in Room 5.

Room 5 had only one floor throughout its history, and it was the only well-laid surface in House 849. It was a very smooth and hard-packed surface of mud with a considerable downward slope from south to north. At a point near the north end of the room a single line of bricks ran across the floor, beyond which there was a step down of 10 cm to a slightly lower floor level. In this northern area four large storage vessels had been buried. Two *somas* were buried so that their rims projected about 10 cm above the floor, while a third came just flush with the floor. The fourth vessel was a very large, decorated Meroitic storage jar with the top broken away (82.3.4/19). One *soma* contained a quantity of acacia seeds, while the other vessels had only soft earth fill.

The most interesting features were in the middle part of the room (pl. 5c). Adjoining the east wall was a mud mastaba 180 cm long and 125 cm wide, with rounded corners. Most of the upper surface was flat and was about 15 cm higher than the level of the room floor, but the outer edges were raised somewhat higher. Like the room walls, the sides and top of the mastaba had been whitewashed. Just opposite, along the base of the west wall, were several other built-in features. Two small upright slabs, set into the floor and projecting about 15 cm above it, may have served as a rest for some kind of container. This feature was apparently not a fireplace, for there was no trace of burning or ash around it, or anywhere else in the room. Just to the north of the slabs was a slightly raised area in the floor, where a large grinding mortar was embedded. Beside it were two round depressions. It may be hypothesized that the projecting slabs were a rest for a basket or tray of seeds to be ground in the mortar, while the round depressions were for the support of pottery vessels in which the ground flour could be placed.

The upper parts of House 849 had been destroyed by a fire, which had brought down the burned roof timbers and masses of mud-brick debris into the underlying rooms. Crushed beneath this material were more than 40 large and small pottery vessels, which had been resting on the floors at the time of the fire. The vessels were not entirely crushed, and it is evident that they had already been partly or even largely buried in soft earth before the roof came down. A few were actually preserved intact. In Room 1 there were at least 25 vessels (82/47; 82/153; 82/163; 82.2.27/15, 16, 18, 30; 82.3.1/35; 82.3.4/52), mostly large storage jars, which seem to have occupied most of the floor area except at the south end of the room. Room 5 had 20 or more additional vessels (82.3.1/41, 44, 46; 82.3.4/45, 55, 56), large and small, which seem to have been more or less randomly scattered over the floor and on the mastaba. These finds, accidentally preserved *in situ* by the fire, give some idea of what the contents of other Late Christian houses may have been like at the time of their occupation.

No traces of an upper storey survived *in situ,* but its presence can be inferred from three factors: first, the ground-floor walls were exceptionally thick in comparison with those in other Late Christian stone houses; second, there were three ground-floor rooms (Rooms 1, 2, and 3) that could be entered only from above; finally, the fill material within the stone house consisted very largely of broken and disarticulated brick. It is difficult to know where this material could have come from if not from an upper storey. It did not appear to be the remains of fallen vaults, for the bricks lacked the distinctive finger-marked grooves that are characteristic of Nubian vaulting bricks.[56] Moreover, the quantities of burned timber found in the debris make it evident that House 849 had had a wooden roof supported on squared palm logs. It was obviously the burning of this roof that resulted in the destruction of the house.

Unlike many of its neighbours, House 849 had not been used as a refuse dump after its abandonment, for its lower walls were almost entirely buried in fallen rubble from the upper walls. It was, however, used as a place of burial. A single adult individual, wrapped in a shroud, was interred within the rubble fill in Room 6 (Burial 1078). The burial position and the east-west orientation of the body show that this occurred in the Christian and not in the Islamic period. Still later, in 'Bosnian' times, the small Rooms 2 and 3 were dug out and used as storage crypts, and then were loosely refilled with stones. Finally a new 'Bosnian' house was built on top, using the wall tops of House 849 as footings.

The Terminal Christian 'castle-houses'

The last structures to be built at Qaṣr Ibrîm in the Christian period were three massive brick buildings (169, 170, and 171) in Zone B, close to the western battlements (fig. 5). They were excavated and dismantled in 1964, 1966, and 1969, without very precise documentation.[57] However, the structures were of a type which made its appearance all over Nubia in the fourteenth and fifteenth centuries, and a number of inferences can be made about them on the basis of other known buildings.[58] A Terminal Christian dating for the Qaṣr Ibrîm buildings is suggested by their stratigraphic position, their architectural type, and the finding of a cache of dated manuscripts under one of them.

Terminal Christian 'castle-houses' were always two-storey structures with a square or rectangular plan. They were either built entirely of brick, as at Qaṣr Ibrîm, or with stone lower walls and brick upper walls, as at several places in the *Batn el-Hajjar.* [59] Most and sometimes all of the ground-floor rooms were blind cellars, accessible only from above. Sometimes there were doorways connecting some of the ground floor rooms with each other, but not with the outside. At one corner of the house there was usually a small sewage chamber beneath an upstairs toilet. A distinctive feature of many Terminal Christian houses was the presence of a small room so ingeniously concealed within the thickness of the walls that it might escape detection by marauders.[60]

Ground-floor rooms were spanned by mud-brick vaults, and there were usually additional small vaulted crypts in the angles between the vault crown and the enclosing side walls.[61] These, like the cellars themselves, were entered from the floor above. At Kulubnarti, where a part of the second storey was preserved in several houses, there were small square hatchways, closed by slabs, giving access from above both to the small crypts and to the large cellars.[62] At Kulubnarti, access to the upper floors of the 'castle-houses' was by means of a doorway at the second-storey level, which could only be reached by means of a retractable ladder. Otherwise, the upper-storey arrangements were similar to those on the ground floors of one-storey Late Christian houses. About half of the total floor area was occupied by one or two large rooms, while the remaining area was given over to smaller rooms. There was nearly always an L-shaped passage leading from the large chambers to a toilet chamber at the rear of the house. The upper-storey rooms sometimes had flat, timbered roofs and sometimes vaulted roofs. In at least two cases there was a parapet projecting above the level of the second-storey roof.

The ingenious design and regular construction of the Terminal Christian 'castle-houses' suggests that they were the work of a small group of professional builders. It is an interesting fact, however, that no two of them were precisely identical in plan. Although

[56] See Somers Clarke, *Christian Antiquities in the Nile Valley* (Oxford, 1912), 24. See also Geoffrey S. Mileham, *Churches in Lower Nubia* (Eckley B. Coxe Junior Expedition to Nubia, 2) (Philadelphia, 1910), 8.

[57] For the preliminary reports see Plumley, *JEA* 52 (1966), 9–10; id., *JEA* 56 (1970), 13; and especially Frend, *JEA* 60 (1974), 33–6, 40–1.

[58] For discussion see Adams, *Nubia*, 514–8, and especially Adams in *Archéologie du Nil Moyen* 6 (1994), 11–46.

[59] For references see Adams in *Archéologie du Nil Moyen* 6 (1994), 37–39.

[60] Op. cit.

[61] See Adams, *Nubia*, 516–7 and fig. 80, sections A-A and B-B.

[62] Adams, *Kulubnarti* I, ch. II.

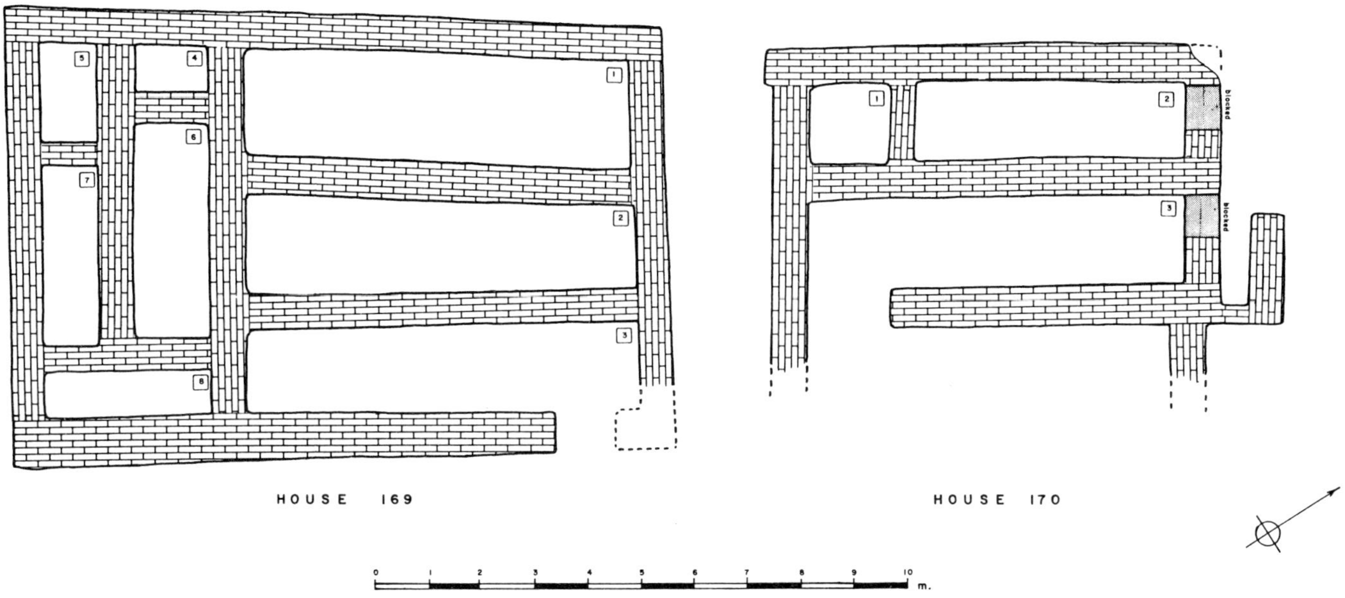

Figure 14. Plan of Terminal Christian brick houses 169 and 170. Figures in squares are room numbers.

widely scattered throughout Lower and Upper Nubia, there were seldom more than three or four 'castle-houses' in any one community. At Meinarti,[63] Kasanarti,[64] and Kulubnarti [65] they coexisted with other, older houses that continued in use, but the evidence for this is not so clear at Qaṣr Ibrîm. Apart from the three 'castle-houses,' only the two small Houses 206 and 207, in Zone D, gave evidence of occupation in the Terminal Christian period. However, other Terminal Christian houses might have been destroyed in the course of the general overbuilding of the Islamic period.

House 169. The three brick 'castle-houses' at Qaṣr Ibrîm extended eastward from the fortification walls in Zone B in a nearly straight line (fig. 5). The most westerly house, 169, seems to have had all of the classic features of the Terminal Christian 'castle-house' (see fig. 14). It had been built directly on top of the Qaṣr Ibrîm Podium, which served as a footing for its western and southern walls (pl. 5d). The published account of Professor Frend describes walls 50 to 55 cm thick,[66] but the plan shows a thickness of 70 to 80 cm,[67] and this seems more consistent with the size and height of the building. Only the ground-floor rooms were preserved. There were three very large and five smaller chambers, none of which communicated with any of the others or with the outside. (The doorway at the northeast corner, shown in Figure 14, was not an original feature but had been cut through at a later date.) A quantity of maize found in one room[68] suggested that it had been dug out and reused as a storage crypt in 'Bosnian' times. The walls in House 169 were preserved to a maximum height of 135 cm and thus gave no indication of the method of roofing or of the second-floor plan. That a second floor was present may be confidently inferred from the lack of any doorways at the ground floor level.

The published description speaks of a two-storey brick tower raised on top of the walls of House 169.[69] The north, west, and south walls involved a continued use, and probably a heightening, of the original walls of House 169, but the interior arrangements were quite different. The tower had only two large vaulted chambers on the ground floor, each measuring 3.5 m wide by 8 m long. There was no surviving trace of a connection between the two rooms, or between them and the outside. The upper storey apparently consisted of a single large chamber, about 8 m. square, which on account of its size must have been unroofed. There appears to have been a window in the west wall, commanding a view upriver from Qaṣr Ibrîm.

Nothing was found in the tower which could furnish an accurate date. In view of its situation on top of a partially dismantled and filled-up Terminal Christian house, it can hardly have been earlier than the latter half of the fifteenth century. It was almost certainly the last building erected at Qaṣr Ibrîm prior to the coming

[63] Adams, *Kush* 12 (1964), 231–3.
[64] Op. cit., 222.
[65] Adams, *Kulubnarti* I, ch. II.
[66] Frend, *JEA* 60 (1974), 36.
[67] See op. cit., 35, fig. 2.
[68] Op. cit., 34.
[69] Op. cit., 33–4.

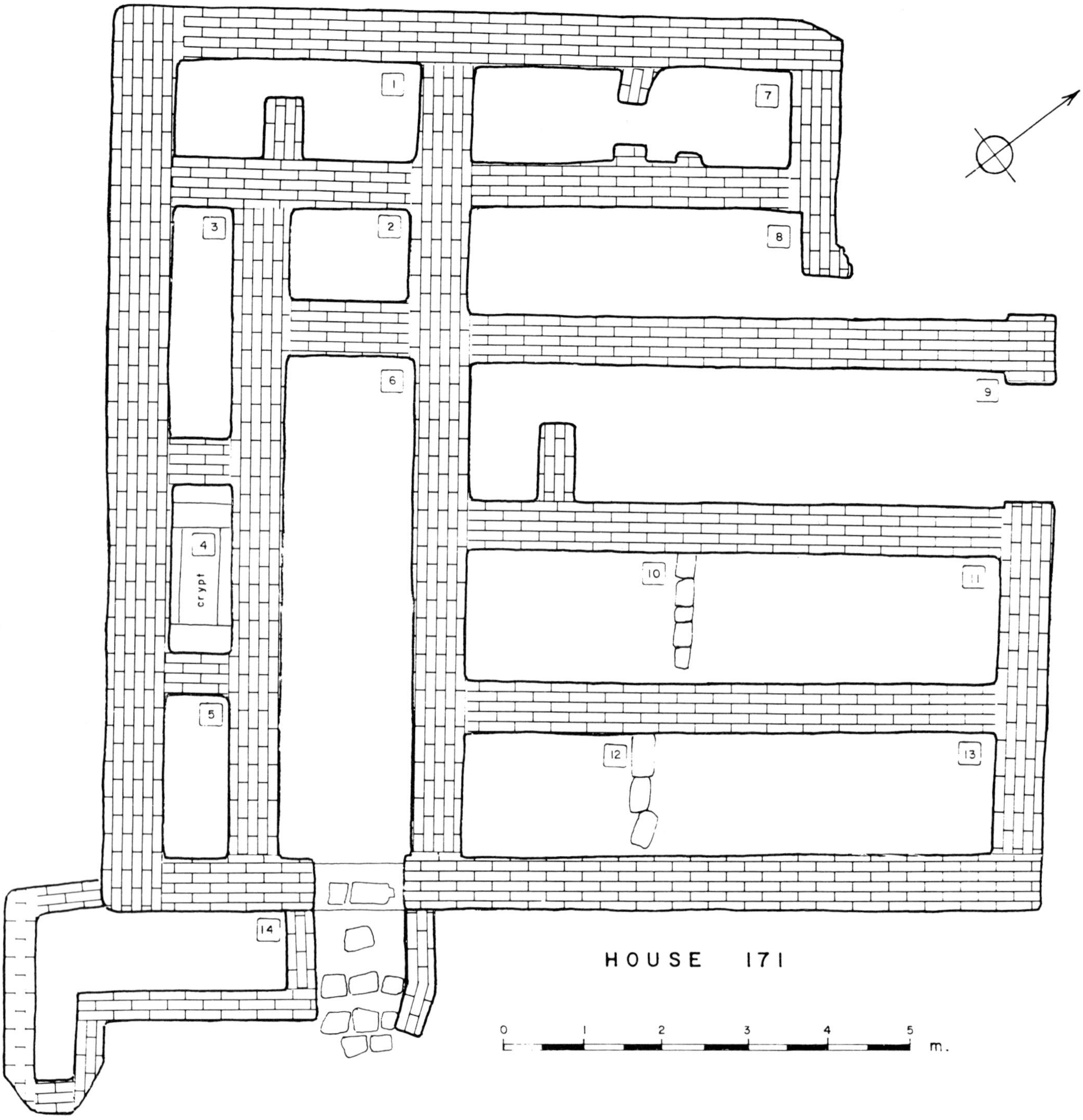

Figure 15. Plan of Terminal Christian brick house 171. Figures in squares are room numbers.

of the 'Bosnians,' and it may well have continued to be used by them after their arrival. Apparently no plan of the tower was made prior to its dismantling in the excavations of 1964.

House 170. This building stood just to the east of House 169, separated from it by a narrow passage (fig. 14). From the surviving records it is not possible to form a very clear picture of this house, for the excavator's plan is evidently incomplete.[70] There appear to have been three large ground-floor rooms running in an east-west direction. Two of the rooms were connected with each other by a wide doorway, while the third could be entered from the outside through a much narrower door. This had no jambs, rebate, or sills, and it was almost certainly a later intrusion rather

[70] Cf. op. cit., 35, fig. 2. For the description see op. cit., 40–1.

than an original feature. There was also one small square room at the northwest corner of the house, which may have been a cess pit beneath a toilet. Either just within or just outside this house, the 1964 excavations uncovered a cache of Old Nubian documents (64/23) that had been buried in a sealed jar (64/22).[71] Like the manuscripts in House 177 they were legal documents from the late mediaeval Kingdom of Dotawo. The dates ranged in time from AD.1281 to 1464; the latter must of course be the *terminus post quem* for the burial of the cache.[72]

House 171. This was the largest of the Terminal Christian 'castle-houses,' and stood slightly to the east and north of House 170. The surviving notes on this building are extremely sketchy,[73] but the excavator's plan appears to be complete (fig. 15). The published description states: 'Some of the original vaulted roofs were still in position. Although the purpose of this structure is not entirely clear, the absence of doorways and windows would suggest that it was probably a storehouse or magazine ... The discovery of a pot containing four leather scrolls written in Old Nubian [66A/45], concealed in the wall of this structure,[74] suggests that the building may be dated to the last period of organized Nubian Christianity.'[75]

The plan shows a large square building, measuring about 11 m. on a side, with an inset at the north-east corner. The ground floor was divided into somewhat unequal halves by a wall running across the house from north to south. To the east of this wall were five fairly large rooms having an east-west orientation; to the west were six smaller rooms on a north-south axis. One of the small western chambers had a brick-lined crypt beneath the floor. The plan shows the eastern room walls to be abutted against the wall separating them from the western rooms, suggesting that the latter were built first.

In the original plan there was apparently no interconnection between any of the ground-floor rooms. However, at least one of them seems to have had an outside entryway from the beginning. The plan shows a fairly wide door with a stone threshold slab, giving access to one of the western rooms, and roughly built stone steps leading up to the doorway. The plan also shows doorways leading into two other ground-floor rooms, but these were apparently not original features.

All of the 'castle-houses' at Qaṣr Ibrîm had undergone significant modification at some point in time after their construction. Doorways were somewhat crudely hacked into and between some of the ground-floor chambers, and they were then put to use as ordinary dwellings.[76] The same thing was found to have happened in the 'castle-houses' at Meinarti[77] and Kulubnarti.[78] The buildings, as originally designed, were certainly difficult of access, and it would appear that after a time considerations of convenience overcame those of security. The refuse within the houses suggested in each case that this happened within the Terminal Christian period; it was not the work of post-Christian squatters. Perhaps in these last mediaeval years the Nubians were so impoverished that they had nothing left that was worth hiding.[79]

[71] Reported in Plumley, *JEA* 50 (1964), 5 and pl. II, 2, and in Frend, *JEA* 60 (1974), 42–3. From the surviving documentation I have been unable to reconstruct the precise location of this find. Professor Frend places it in a building *underlying* House 170, but this seems impossible in view of the dates appearing on the documents. Moreover, I can find no plan of a house corresponding to Professor Frend's description. Professor Plumley at one point speaks of the scrolls as being buried under a stairway (*JEA* 60 (1974), 5), but elsewhere describes them as buried under the north wall of House 170 (in Kazimierz Michalowski, (ed.), *Nubia, récentes recherches* (Warsaw, 1975), 105). None of the plans prepared by Mr. Kenneth Frazer shows a stairway either in House 170 or in any underlying structure. My best guess is that the scrolls were buried in a small masonry-lined pit, roofed over with palm timbers, either just within or just outside one of the outer walls of House 170.

[72] For discussion of the content of the scrolls see Plumley in *Études nubiennes* (Institut français d'archéologie orientale, Bibliothèque d'étude, 77) (Cairo, 1978), 234–8. See also Plumley in Michalowski (ed.), *Nubia*, 104–6.

[73] Plumley, *JEA* 56 (1970), 13.

[74] The precise location within the building is not recorded. For discussion of the scrolls see Plumley in Michalowski (ed.), *Nubia*, 105.

[75] Plumley, *JEA* 52 (1966), 9–10.

[76] Op. cit., 10; Frend, *JEA* 60 (1974), 36, 41.

[77] Adams, *Kush* 12 (1964), 233.

[78] Adams, *Kulubnarti* I, ch. II.

[79] See Adams, *Nubia*, 544–6.

CHAPTER 3
STORAGE FACILITIES

During much of its history, Qaṣr Ibrîm was more important as a place for storage than as a place for living. The fortified mountain-top was not a convenient place to carry on most day-to-day activities, but it offered unusual protection both from human and from natural enemies. Most importantly food stores, buried in crypts or simply in holes in the ground, were safe from the moisture and the insect pests that are prevalent everywhere in the Nile flood-plain. Thus while only certain parts of the citadel were used as dwelling areas in the Late Christian period, nearly all parts (except the church interiors) were used for storage purposes. Five kinds of storage facilities were found in the Late Christian occupation levels:

Store rooms in ordinary houses. All of the larger and better-preserved Late Christian houses had at least one room designed primarily for storage. In two-storey houses, both brick and stone, a considerable part of the ground floor space was given over to storage cellars that could only be entered from above. Architectural details have already been described in Part 2, Chapter 2. Very little was found in any of these rooms, and it is not certain whether they were meant primarily for the storage of food, of family valuables, or both. Storage of food was presumably in *somas* or large pottery jars, which were found *in situ* in a number of houses. Two rooms in House 849, which was destroyed by fire, had had at least 45 pottery vessels resting on their floors at the time of destruction (pl. 6a). These, however, were empty of contents, as were most of the vessels and *somas* found in other houses.

Above-ground storehouses. While storerooms were common in ordinary houses, the building of above-ground structures purely for storage was not a usual practice of Late Christian times. In Zone A there was one roughly built stone structure (191), comprising two small rooms, that may have been intended for storage. Nearby, two rooms in an old X-Group house (189) had been replastered and restored to use as storerooms. Both of these structures may have been partly subterranean, but they appear to have had walls projecting above ground level as well. Neither had any significant contents when excavated.

Stone-lined and brick-lined crypts. In plaza areas adjoining their dwellings, the Late Christians made a regular practice of sinking deep storage pits into the filled-up remains of older houses. Sometimes they dug out and reused the whole of a small room, as in the Early Christian houses 210 (formerly EC1–6) and 235 (formerly EC1–24). Each of these had originally been a multi-room, above-ground dwelling, but by Late Christian times they had been deeply buried in refuse. The Late Christians in each case dug out a single room for use as a storage crypt, leaving the adjoining rooms unexcavated. In other cases, previously built storage crypts were refurbished. A particularly interesting and well-preserved example was represented by Unit 188 (formerly X-33 and LC1–11), shown in figure 16. Here, two deep crypts had been sunk in X-Group times into the filled-up remains of a still older Meroitic building (226). As originally built, the crypts had lining walls of mud brick, and both the walls and the floors were whitewashed. The Late Christians dug out all but the lowermost 35 cm of the X-Group refuse fill and put in new flagstone floors at this level (fig. 16). They also heightened the original walls by the addition of 50 to 60 cm of rough stone masonry, which was mud-plastered but not whitewashed. The crypts were then roofed over with timbers. In one of the two rooms the Late Christian roof was found fully intact; it consisted of four acacia logs overlaid with a continuous roofing of *jerid* (palm-leaf ribs) and small sticks, which were sewn in place with a wrapping of palm fibre cord (pl. 6c). The whole structure was then covered with a single large square of plaited matting made of halfa grass and this in turn was covered with mud. Access to the crypt was through a hole 35 cm square in the centre of the roof, which could be closed by a stone slab. The two crypts in Unit 188 held no valuables; they were entirely filled with soft, wind-blown material. Nearby, three small sub-floor crypts in the abandoned X-Group House 190 (formerly X-30) were also dug out and restored to use in Late Christian times.

In larger buried rooms, the Late Christians dug out a part but not all of the room fill in order to make storage crypts. Typically a deep hole would be dug alongside a buried wall or in a room corner, and the parts of the hole that did not adjoin an older wall would then be enclosed by brick masonry. The shape of such crypts thus tended by be half-round, if they adjoined a straight wall, or quarter-round, if they were in an older room corner. Examples of this kind were Units 192, sunk into a buried X-Group house, and 766, sunk into the buried Late Christian House 763 after it had been filled with refuse in LC2 times (see Part 2, Ch. 2).

a

b

c

d

Plate 6. Storage facilities. a, Pots *in situ* in House 849, Room 1. b, Late Christian masonry-lined storage crypts. c, Intact roof of logs and *jerid,* covering Late Christian storage Crypt 188. d, Storage pits in Cathedral Street.

Crypts were nearly always smoothly mud plastered, but were not whitewashed as in the X-Group and Early Christian periods.

The accurate dating of storage crypts is obviously a difficult matter. All of the Late Christian crypts had been filled either with a deliberate filling of stones and rubbish or with an accidental filling of wind-blown material, and only one (Unit 235) contained a pottery vessel of LC1 date. Dating in other cases was suggested either by stratigraphy (identification of the ground surface from which the crypts had been sunk) or by the finding of Late Christian sherds in the fill material. The number of these was seldom large, and did not permit a precise dating of crypts as between the LC1, LC2, and TC periods.

Storage under floors. For reasons of security, the Christian inhabitants at Qaṣr Ibrîm buried certain of their valued goods beneath their house floors. They did not, however, build regular sub-floor storage crypts, as did their predecessors in X-Group times.[1] Most commonly they simply dug small or large holes through the mud paving of their floors, inserted various objects in them, and refilled the holes with earth. Most of the Late Christian floors at Qaṣr Ibrîm had at least one such intruded pit and may have had more than one (cf. fig. 12, House 211). The preferred location for storage pits was at the base of one or another of the walls, especially in room corners. Very few of the sub-floor pits had any contents at the time of their excavation, but one pit in House 763 held a cache of dom nuts.

Very occasionally, valuables were actually sealed beneath the mud paving of the house floors. In House 785, Room 1, more than a dozen small bowls and cups of Early Christian date were sealed over when Floor 4 was laid in on top of the earlier Floor 5. Even larger

[1] See Plumley and Adams, *JEA* 60 (1974), 215.

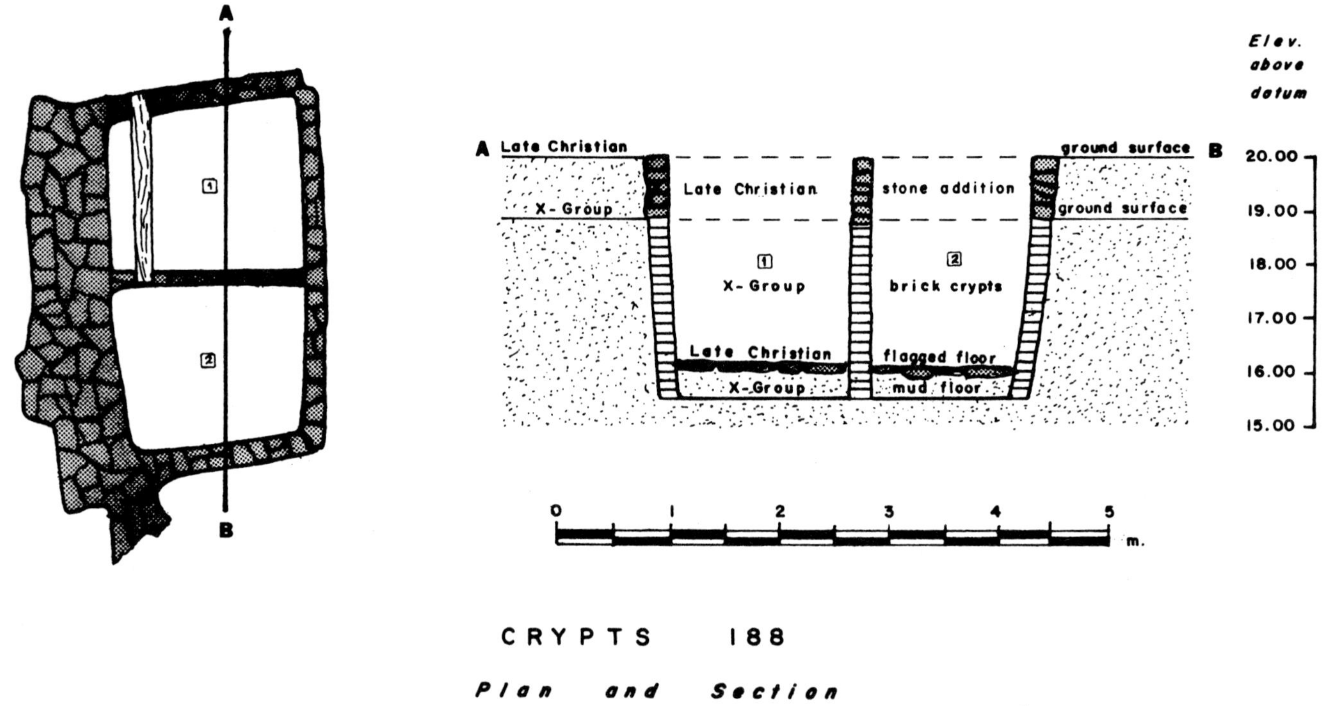

Figure 16. Plan and profile of X-Group/Late Christian crypts 188.

caches of pottery were sealed in this fashion in some of the Late Christian houses at Meinarti.[2] It may be conjectured that this represented a kind of dead storage, tantamount to our own consignment of disused goods to an attic or lumber-room. In short, these were obsolete or surplus goods that the owners could not quite bring themselves to dispose of.

Pits. The most common of all storage facilities were simple pits in the ground, usually about 1 m in diameter and 1 to 1.5 m deep. The digging of such pits apparently began in Meroitic times and continued without interruption until the final abandonment of Qaṣr Ibrîm in 1811. The number of pits specifically attributable to the Late Christian period cannot be accurately estimated, but it certainly was in the hundreds.[3] Late Christian pits were especially heavily concentrated in the plaza areas 356 and 764 and in the filled-up house remains west of the Cathedral (Zone C) (pl. 6d). In these places there was not a square metre of ground that had not been dug through by at least one storage pit.

Late Christian pits were usually lined in the bottom with several pieces of plaited basketry or matting. These were never wholly intact; they were broken pieces of worn-out carrying baskets or floor or roof mats. There were usually two or three, and sometimes as many as five or six, basketry fragments in each pit. (Technical details of the basketry will be more fully considered in Part 3, Chapter 3.) Apart from the basketry lining, there were no artifactual contents in any of the Late Christian pits. However, close examination of the basketry fragments revealed grains of wheat, millet, and barley, leaving no doubt that the pits were intended primarily for grain storage. In a few cases, dom nuts were also found in the pits.

Pits were presumably open only for brief periods when their contents were being inserted or removed and at other times were filled in. The fact that the basketry linings were left *in situ* when the pits were otherwise empty shows that they were meant to be reused, while the fact that they had all been filled in shows that they were not left standing open at times when nothing was buried in them. Indeed, walking in any of the Late Christian plaza areas would have been extremely hazardous if any number of the pits had been left open (cf. pl. 6d). Pits were normally filled with a mixture of midden refuse and stones; much of it evi-

[2] See Adams, *Kush* 12 (1964), 230 and pl. LI, b.

[3] Storage pits were not systematically numbered and recorded before the 1976 season. In the excavations between 1976 and 1984, a total of 20 pits were found that could be specifically attributed to the Late and Terminal Christian periods, but there were many additional pits of uncertain date that in all probability were also Late Christian.

dently the same rubbish material that was taken out when the pits were first dug. Unlike the brick-lined and stone-lined storage crypts, there is no evidence that pits were ever roofed over.

Accurate dating of pits is, for obvious reasons, even more problematical than is the accurate dating of crypts. The Late Christian pits were mostly dug into X-Group and Early Christian refuse deposits. Since they were largely refilled with the same material that was taken out when they were dug, their sherd content was little different from that of the surrounding matrix and consisted largely of X-Group and Early Christian wares. Only the occasional tell-tale sherd of Late Christian date gave evidence of the actual time of their digging. Textiles seem to provide a more reliable clue, for Late Christian pits were often found to contain significant numbers of textile fragments which can be identified as late.[4] Dating is also indicated in some cases by stratigraphy. In Plazas 356 and 764, the surfaces into which the pits had been dug could be fairly accurately dated to the LC1 period. In Zone C, the pits were dug into filled-up Classic Christian houses but were themselves overbuilt later by houses of the Islamic period, so that by process of elimination they must belong to the Late Christian period.

[4] Late Christian textiles will be more fully discussed in Part 3, Chapter 6.

CHAPTER 4
THE CHURCHES

QAṢR IBRÎM was a major religious centre throughout the Middle Ages, as it was also in pagan times. The little mud-brick Temple of Taharqa (287), equipped with an apse and a narthex at the beginning of the sixth century, may very well have been one of the first churches built in Nubia, and the even smaller Cupola Church (839) may well have been the last. In between those times at least two and possibly three other churches were built within the citadel area, and of these the Cathedral (293) was the most imposing architectural monument of mediaeval Nubia.

Textual records from the beginning of the Late Christian period list no fewer than seven churches at Ibrîm, variously dedicated to the Apostles, Gabriel, Kollouthos, the Holy Trinity, Mary, Michael, and Peter (see Part 4, Ch. 8, table 21). It is not certain that all these buildings were located on the mountain-top, where no more than five church buildings can be identified archaeologically. The Mary Church is unquestionably to be identified with the Cathedral,[1] but none of the other churches that are mentioned in texts can be specifically matched with any of the buildings preserved archaeologically.

The Qaṣr Ibrîm churches will be the subject of a special volume to be published later, and for that reason will not be described in detail here. However, it is necessary to say enough to establish their place in the architectural scheme and in the daily life of the community. To put them properly in their context a few words must be said first about Nubian church architecture in general.

The development of Nubian church architecture

Organizationally, the church in Nubia was integrally a part of the Coptic Orthodox Church of Egypt. Its bishops were appointed from Alexandria (later from Cairo) and were responsible directly to the Coptic Patriarch. Architecturally and liturgically, however, there were distinctive local traditions almost from the beginning. Five major stages in Nubian church development can be recognized, and only the first two of these have close parallels in Egypt.[2]

Some of the earliest Nubian churches were converted from pagan temples. These buildings exhibited no very consistent plan, since they had necessarily to adapt themselves to the architectural peculiarities of the temples in which they were built. Often their only added feature was a small apse of brick construction built into an older sanctuary chamber or inserted between two columns. In addition there was usually a brick-built pulpit adjoining a column or wall just in front of the apse. Converted churches of this type are designated as Type T.[3]

The earliest deliberately built churches in Nubia were similar to contemporary churches in Egypt. They were basilican in plan, fairly elongate, and nearly always oriented with the sanctuary to the east. Here the altar was located within a rather small apse. On either side of it were other small chambers (conventionally designated as the sacristy and the baptistry, though their function often cannot be determined) which were entered directly from the apse. A peculiarity of all Nubian churches was that the apse was embedded within a rectangular mass of masonry, rather than being enclosed by a curving wall. The earliest churches were entered at the west end, where there was usually, but not always, a narthex chamber. Most of the buildings originally had a flat, timbered roof resting on monolithic columns of granite. Some of the largest of the churches were cathedrals and were distinguished by the presence of two aisles on either side of the nave in place of the usual one. Early churches with an entry at the west end are designated as Type 1.[4]

Distinctive local features began to appear in the Nubian churches after the seventh century. The narthex was replaced by small rooms in the north-west and south-west corners of the building, and one of these usually carried a stairway leading to a tower or to the roof. Entry was now through symmetrically placed doors in the north and south walls, rather than at the

[1] On the testimony of Abu Salih in the thirteenth century. See B. T. A. Evetts and A. J. Butler, trans., *The Churches and Monasteries of Egypt and Some Neighbouring Countries* (Oxford, 1895), 266.

[2] The discussion here follows that of W. Y. Adams in *JARCE* 4 (1965), 87–139. This typology has been challenged by Przemyslaw Gartkiewicz and by Peter Grossmann, both of whom propose alternative schemes. See Gartkiewicz in Kazimierz Michalowski (ed.), *Nubia, récentes recherches* (Warsaw, 1975), 49–64, and Grossmann, *Elephantine II* (Abteilung Kairo, Archäologische Veröffentlichungen 25) (Mainz, 1980), 75–111. The typologies of Gartkiewicz and Grossmann are both based on art-historical principles rather than on empirical evidence, and for that reason I prefer to retain the older scheme.

[3] Adams, *JARCE* 4 (1965), 101–3.

[4] For discussion of the type and its subtypes see op. cit., 103–6.

TABLE 6
TYPOLOGY OF NUBIAN CHURCHES

Type*	Dates of construc.	Area (m²)	L-W† ratio	Details of plan and construction: East end	West end	Roof construction
T	550–600	475	1.6:1	Small apse inserted in sanctuary chamber or between columns	Highly variable	Original flat temple roof supported on columns
1a	550–750	160	1.6:1	Small apse enclosing altar; direct access from apse to sacristy and baptistry	Doorways at west end; usually narthex chamber	Flat, timbered roof supported on monolithic columns
1b	550–750	160	1.6:1	Small apse enclosing altar; usually direct access from apse to sacristy and baptistry	Doorways at west end; sometimes narthex chamber	Flat roof on columns or vaulted roof on piers
2a	650–800	220	1.7:1	Elongate apse enclosing altar; entry to sacristy and baptistry from apse, aisles, or both	Small corner rooms, one enclosing stairway to roof. Doorways in north and south walls	Vaulted roof on piers; nave notably wider than aisles
2b	650–800	150	1.5:1	Small apse enclosing altar; entry to sacristy and baptistry from aisles only	Small corner rooms, one enclosing stairway to roof. Doorways in north and south walls	Vaulted roof on piers; nave and aisles same width
3a	750–850	220	1.7:1	Converted from Type 2a churches by insertion of tribune in apse. Altar relocated in front of apse, screened by *higab*. Entry to sacristy and baptistry from aisles	Small corner rooms, one enclosing stairway to roof. Doorways in north and south walls	Vaulted roof on piers; nave notably wider than aisles
3b	750–1250	190	1.5:1	Passage east of apse, connecting sacristy and baptistry. Small apse without tribune. Altar just under or just outside apse, screened by *higab*. Entry to sacristy and baptistry from aisles	Small corner rooms, one enclosing stairway to roof. Doorways in north and south walls	Flat roof on columns (early only) or vaulted roof on piers. Sometimes central cupola
3c	750–1250	150	1.4:1	Passage east of apse, connecting sacristy and baptistry. Small apse filled by tribune seats. Altar in front of apse, screened by *higab*. Entry to sacristy and baptistry from aisles only	Small corner rooms, one enclosing stairway to roof. Doorways in north and south walls	Vaulted roof on piers; central dome common
4	1250–1500	80	1.2:1	Eastern passage rare. Sanctuary chamber occasionally apse, usually square. No tribune; altar located within sanctuary chamber. *Higab* rare. Sacristy and baptistry entered from sanctuary, from aisles, or both	Rooms at both western corners, one corner only, or none. Sometimes stairway to roof. Doorways in north and south walls	Vaulted, with central cupola projecting above adjoining roofs
?5	1400–1500	25	1.2:1	Sanctuary, sacristy and baptistry combined in a single transverse chamber. No eastern passage. Altar adjoins eastern wall	Western rooms present in two examples, absent in one. Doorways in north and south walls	Vaulted. Two examples had central cupolas

*See Adams in *JARCE* 4 (1965), 87–139.
†Ratio of length to width.

TABLE 7
QAṢR IBRÎM CHURCHES IN THE LATE CHRISTIAN PERIODS

Building no.	Former no.	Name	Periods of use	Type*	Area (m²)	Construction	Years excav.	Reports JEA
287	Church 3	Taharqa temple-church	XC1–TC	T	90	Mud brick with rough stone nathex	1972	60: 228–236
293	Church 1	Cathedral	EC1–TC	1a	450	Cut stone	1963 1964	50: 3–4
294	Church 2	Second church	LC1–LC2	3b	75	Rough stone	1966 1978	52: 10 65: 38
839	—	Cupola church	LC2–TC?	4	55	Rough stone	—	None†

*See typology of W. Y. Adams in Table 7.
†Decribed by Somers Clarke, *Christian Antiquities in the Nile Valley* (Oxford, 1912), 81, and Ugo Monneret de Villard, *La Nubia medioevale*, Vol. I (Cairo, 1935), 109–110.

west. Brick-vaulted roofs, resting on stout masonry piers, replaced the older flat roofs resting on columns. Churches having these characteristics are designated as Type 2.[5]

Beginning in the eighth century, there were major changes in the arrangements at the east end of the church building. The apse was now usually filled by a tribune (stepped choir seats), and this necessitated the removal of the altar to a point further west, within the nave. It also made impossible any direct passage from the apse to the sacristy or baptistry; these two side chambers were now always entered from the adjoining aisles. However, the sacristy and baptistry were connected to each other by means of a narrow passage which ran across the east end of the building behind the apse. Finally the area surrounding the altar was screened from the body of the church by the building of a *higab* (ikonostasis), usually of brick masonry. Normally this enclosed the west end of one or both of the aisles as well as of the nave. Churches having the above described features are designated as Type 3.[6]

A new and radically simplified form of church began to appear in Nubia in the thirteenth century. There was no eastern passage connecting the sacristy and the baptistry, and the shape of the sanctuary chamber was more often square than apsidal. There was no tribune, with the result that the altar could be returned to its original position near the eastern end of the building. In some of the earlier churches of this type there is still some evidence of a *higab*, but it seems to have disappeared later on. There were still western corner rooms in the earlier buildings, but these too disappeared later. One of the most distinctive features of the late Nubian churches was a tall cupola dome rising over the middle of the nave; for this reason they are often called cupola churches. These buildings are designated as Type 4.[7] They have no counterparts in Egypt but seem to have been inspired by contemporary architectural developments in Syria, Anatolia, and Greece.[8]

Throughout the Middle Ages there was continual reduction in the size of the Nubian churches. The earliest churches generally had a floor area of 200 m² or more, while the average floor area in the churches of Type 4 was under 100 m². There was also a reduction in the average ratio of length to width. The early churches were relatively elongate, while the plan of many of the cupola churches was almost square. Some of the last churches to be built were tiny structures having a floor area of less than 30 m², and having the sanctuary, sacristy, and baptistry combined into a single transverse chamber (Type ?5).[9] Table 6 gives more detailed information about the various types and sub-types of Nubian churches.

Four of the five main Nubian church types were represented at Qaṣr Ibrîm. However, three of the buildings shared a distinctive anomaly in that they exhibited the same north-east to south-west orientation that is found in all of the secular buildings on the site. Presumably this was because the oldest of the churches (287) had to retain the orientation of the pagan temple which it preempted, and the builders of the later nearby churches felt compelled to follow suit. Elsewhere in Nubia churches nearly always had a straight east-west

[5] For discussion of the type and its subtypes see op. cit., 106–10.
[6] For discussion of the type and its subtypes see op. cit., 110–16.
[7] For discussion of the type and its variants see op. cit., 116–9. These churches were designated by Somers Clarke as Type B, in contrast to all churches of basilican type (Types 1–3) which he collectively designated as Type A. See *Christian Antiquities in the Nile Valley* (Oxford, 1912), 32.
[8] Adams, *JARCE* 4 (1965), 118.
[9] Op. cit., 119–20.

orientation, and this was true of the Qaṣr Ibrîm Cupola Church (839) which was located outside the citadel walls.

After the eighth century the great majority of Nubian churches were decorated with coloured murals. Among the well-preserved paintings at Faras it was possible to recognize four successive decorative styles, spanning the period between the eighth and the fourteenth century.[10] Other well preserved murals were found in the churches at Tamit,[11] Abdallah Nirqi,[12] Abdel Qadir,[13] Sonqi,[14] and Kulubnarti.[15] However, only one of the Qaṣr Ibrîm churches retained any traces of painted decoration.

Church 287 (the Taharqa Temple-church)

The Temple of Taharqa at Qaṣr Ibrîm was a modest affair of mud-brick, very similar in plan to the Taharqa Temple at Semna.[16] About half of its total area was occupied by a forecourt having four sandstone columns. To the east of this was a somewhat smaller sanctuary chamber, flanked on one side by a very narrow magazine and on the other side by a stairway. Two other small magazines at the east end completed the building.[17] For some reason, all of the magazines had already been abandoned and filled with refuse before the end of the Meroitic period, with the result that only the forecourt and sanctuary remained in use.

The Taharqa Temple appears to have been converted into a church in the very early sixth century. A curving shell of stone masonry was inserted within the sanctuary chamber, converting its original rectangular shape into that of an apse (fig. 17). The space between the back of the new apse wall and the older sanctuary wall was filled with rubble containing sherds of late X-Group types (index clusters X2 and XC1[18])—one of several indications that the conversion of the building took place at a very early date. The apse from the time of its first building was occupied by stepped choir seats, a feature commonly referred to in Nubia as a tribune.[19]

The original Taharqa forecourt provided the main body for the new church, the original columns serving to separate the nave from the aisles. To enlarge the building, a narthex of rather rough stone masonry was added to the west end of the old temple, where previously a second Meroitic temple of stone (290) had stood. Much of the stone used to build the narthex wall consisted of fragments of the older temple. At some time after its original building, the narthex was divided into three roughly equal parts by brick arcading. Entrance to the church was through doors at the extreme west end of the north and south walls. The plan and interior features of Church 287 are shown in figure 17 and plate 7a.

Church 287 was equipped with a highly distinctive altar of stone. It was made from two large pieces of Aswân pink granite, both of which had been shaped in pagan times into the form of miniature temple pylons. Most likely they were barque stands from the dismantled Meroitic stone temple. One stone was inserted top down in the church floor, and the other rested on its side on top of it (fig. 18). A third miniature pylon of granite was laid into the floor to form a flagstone immediately in front of the altar.[20] There was a second, conventional altar of mud-brick masonry at the east end of the south aisle. Denuded remains of a small pulpit of stone masonry were found adjoining the north-east pillar of the forecourt, in the conventional position where pulpits were usually placed in Nubian churches. The sanctuary area, comprising the east end of the nave and of the south aisle, was screened from the rest of the church by a *higab* of mud-brick (see fig. 17). This was not an original feature, for prior to its building the two eastern columns in the nave had been notched to receive a wooden *higab*, or possibly just an altar rail.

Conventional Nubian churches always had a sacristy and a baptistry flanking the apse on either side, but within the original Taharqa Temple there were no rooms that could be converted for those purposes. To remedy this deficiency the early Christians built three additional rooms adjoining the south side of the temple-church. They were constructed of stone masonry similar to that of the narthex and were probably built at the same time, though their floor levels were substantially higher than those in the remainder of the church. Two of the rooms, 13 and 14, were

[10] See especially Kazimierz Michalowski, *Faras* (Warsaw, 1974), 28–41.

[11] Università degli Studi di Roma, Missione Archeologica in Egitto, *Tamit (1964)* (Rome, 1967).

[12] Paul van Moorsel *et al., The Central Church at Abdallah Nirqi* (Leiden, 1975).

[13] Griffith, *LAAA* 15 (1928), 63–82 and pls. XXV-XLVII.

[14] Donadoni in Erich Dinkler (ed.), *Kunst und Geschichte Nubiens in Christlicher Zeit* (Recklinghausen, 1970), 200–16.

[15] Adams, *Kulubnarti*, I, Ch. III.

[16] Dows Dunham and Jozef M. A. Janssen, *Semna Kumma* (Second Cataract Forts, 1) (Boston, 1960), 12–13 and Map VII.

[17] For the plan see Plumley and Adams, *JEA* 60 (1974), 230.

[18] For ceramic index clusters and their use in dating see William Y. Adams, *Ceramic Industries of Medieval Nubia* (Memoirs of the UNESCO Archaeological Survey of Sudanese Nubia, 1) (Lexington, 1986), 627–32.

[19] This term is somewhat unsatisfactory because in French and Italian usage it refers to overhead galleries rather than to choir seats in the apse. See Adams, *JARCE* 4 (1965), 95, n. 1.

[20] For illustrations of the altar see Plumley and Adams, *JEA* 60 (1974), 234, fig. 5, and pl. L, 1.

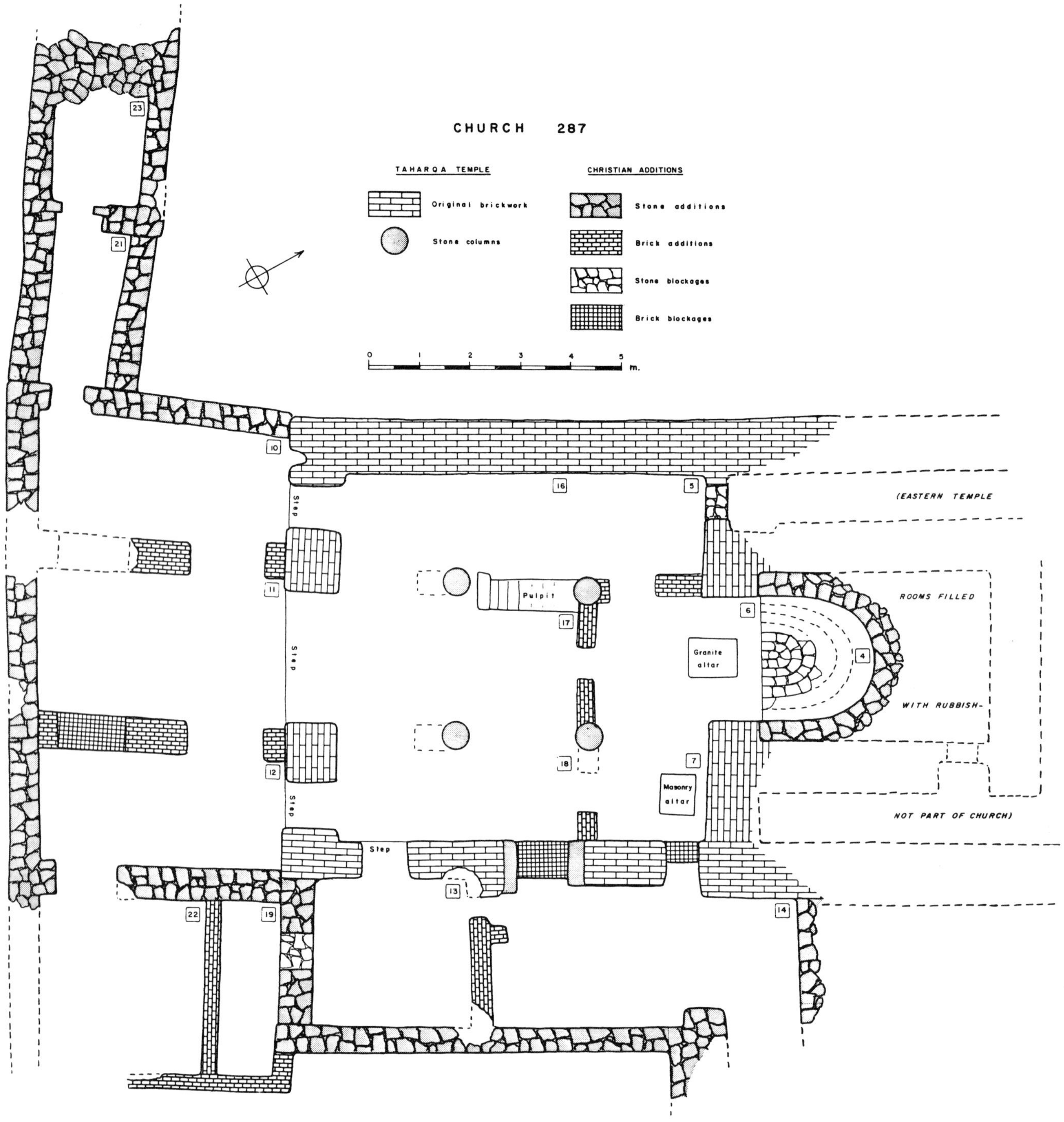

Figure 17. Plan of Taharqa Temple-Church 287. Figures in squares are room numbers.

entered from the body of the church through doorways cut through the mud-brick of the original temple wall. Room 14, whose doorway opened into the sanctuary area, was probably a sacristy; the function of Room 13 could not be determined. To the west of both these rooms was Room 22, originally an antechamber adjoining the southern church door. At some later date it was divided in half by a brick partition, and the more easterly half (Room 19) became a toilet or at least a urinal chamber. In Late Christian times, however, this was disused and filled with rubbish.

All parts of the church, including the narthex and the added southern chambers, had a well-laid floor of large, irregularly shaped sandstone slabs (pl. 7a). This was evidently not an original feature in the body of the church or in the narthex, for remnants of an older floor

a

b

c

d

Plate 7. The smaller churches. a, Interior of the Taharqa Temple-church 287, looking toward the sanctuary. b, The South Church 294, seen from the northwest corner. c, The small Temple 289, which may have been converted into a church. d, The Cupola Church 839, which stood below the fortification walls.

Figure 18. Altar in the Taharqa Temple-Church 287.

were found underneath it. At least in places the older floor seems to have been paved with water-worn cobbles, like the original floor in the church at Meinarti.[21]

There is no direct evidence as to how the temple-church was roofed. The nave and aisles (the original Taharqa Temple forecourt), if they were roofed at all, can only have had a flat, timbered roof, for the columns were too small and too far apart to support brick vaults or a dome. This would also have been true of the narthex in the beginning, though it could have been spanned by three parallel vaults after the insertion of its interior partitions. The apse was presumably covered by a semi-dome of brick vaulting, as was characteristic of nearly all Nubian apses.[22]

Church 287 was the only church at Qaṣr Ibrîm that bore any traces of painted decoration. The white-washed front of the tribune was adorned with wavy, vertical stripes in blue and yellow, perhaps intended to give a very impressionistic simulation of marble. Faint traces of similar decoration were also found in the body of the church and in the narthex, in places where they had been preserved because later walls were abutted against them. No traces of decoration survived on the north and south walls of the church, but the lower portion of a robed human figure could be made out on the west wall of the narthex. The robe was of a solid, red-violet color outlined in black. It is believed to represent an early style of Nubian church decoration, dating perhaps from the ninth century.[23] The general impression given is that Church 287 was decorated fairly early in its history and was never redecorated thereafter. One possible explanation for this is that the church in its later years was unroofed; a possibility that also exists in the case of the Qaṣr Ibrîm Cathedral to be discussed below. It must be noted, however, that some fragments of brightly coloured and elaborately decorated plaster were found in the refuse fill within the church.

In the Early Christian period Church 287 was directly adjoined by other structures on its north, west, and south sides. It is presumed that these were part of a monastic complex, since Nubian churches were never directly adjoined by secular buildings[24] The south doorway then seems to have given access to some of the monastery chambers rather than to the outside. In

[21] See Adams, *Kush* 13 (1965), 166 and pl. XXV, b.

[22] William Y. Adams, *Nubia, Corridor to Africa* (London, 1977), 483.

[23] Michalowski, *Faras*, 29.

[24] Adams, *JARCE* 4 (1965), 90.

the Classic Christian period, however, all of the adjoining rooms were deliberately dismantled and filled over to leave the church free-standing.

For the general public, access to Church 287 was apparently through a narrow doorway at the northwest corner of the narthex. This was approached through a series of small antechambers (Rooms 21, 23, and 30), each at a slightly higher level than the room to the south of it. They were not coeval with the first building of the narthex but were added slightly later, apparently at the same time when the adjoining monastery chambers were built. The purpose of the antechambers was perhaps to provide access to the church without going through any of the monastery rooms adjoining it. However, the antechambers remained standing long after the other parts of the monastery were dismantled. They had the same kind of flagstone floor as had the main body of the church.

While some of the features of Church 287, such as the flagstone floor, were clearly not original, it is not possible to say when they were added. As long as it was in use, the building was kept deliberately clear of refuse, so there were no stratified deposits to tell the story of growth and decay. The entire filling of the building, from the floor to the tops of the walls, consisted of soft material without any discernible difference in content from bottom to top. The story outside was very different, for refuse began to accumulate against the outer walls of the temple long before it became a church, and the process continued throughout the Christian period. By X-Group times the sanctuary chamber was already at least semi-subterranean, in that the adjoining magazines were already deeply filled with rubbish. In Christian times refuse gradually accumulated around the western end of the building as well, and by the time of its abandonment the church floor was a least a metre below the ground level outside. This undoubtedly accounts for the generally good preservation of the lower walls. The 'Bosnians' eventually dismantled the parts of the walls that still projected above ground level, but they, of course, left *in situ* those parts that were already buried.

Church 287 did not have the dense, apparently deliberate filling of midden that was found in many Late Christian houses (see Part 1, Ch. 1). Instead, much of the fill material appeared to be wind-blown. It consisted of fine, soft earth with a heavy admixture of straw, chaff, and rags, but without a large content of sherds and stones. The sherds present were largely of LC2 and TC wares. These circumstances suggest that the building may have stood open but disused for a considerable time in the Terminal Christian period. Within the fill were a number of more or less compacted surfaces, possibly representing times when the area was used for winnowing or other outdoor activities. Eventually, very early in the Islamic period, a small house of rude stone masonry was erected within the still standing walls, on top of the straw deposit, as other houses were built in the Cathedral (Church 293) and the small Meroitic temple at the east (289). Still later, however, the upper walls as well as the 'Bosnian' partitions were dismantled, and the whole area became an open courtyard (735). It was one of the few areas at Qaṣr Ibrîm that was not overbuilt by a dense cluster of 'Bosnian' houses, a fact which may indicate that the church walls remained standing until a fairly late date.

Church 287 was discovered and excavated in 1972,[25] and further subfloor testing was carried out in 1984. Because of its historic significance, there are no plans to dismantle this building in order to excavate the underlying deposits.

Church 293 (the Cathedral)

The Qaṣr Ibrîm Cathedral was by far the most imposing building that was left standing when the community was abandoned in 1811. It stood on the highest elevation on the site, and its walls towered over the surrounding 'Bosnian' houses as they must earlier have towered over the dwellings of the Christian period. After abandonment the building became a landmark for visitors, and there are many descriptions, drawings, and photographs of it from the nineteenth and early twentieth centuries.[26] In its heyday the Qaṣr Ibrîm Cathedral was rivalled in size only by those at Faras and Old Dongola,[27] but in the artistic quality of its construction and carved decoration it stood alone.

The exact date when the present cathedral was built is uncertain, but it must certainly have been fairly early in the Christian period. There are arguments in favour of both a seventh century and an eighth century dating.[28] It was built on top of a number of abandoned X-Group houses, which were largely dismantled at the time of its construction. The foundations of the east and south walls were cut through older buildings and deposits and rested directly on bedrock. At the west end of the building this was only a few centimetres

[25] For the original excavation report see Plumley and Adams, *JEA* 60 (1974), 228–36.

[26] For a partial listing see Ugo Monneret de Villard, *La Nubia medioevale*, I (Cairo, 1935), 117.

[27] The three buildings were very nearly identical in size, measuring approximately 20 × 25 m. For Faras see Kazimierz Michalowski and Georg Gerster, *Faras, die Kathedrale aus dem Wüstensand* (Zurich and Cologne, 1967), 97. For Old Dongola see Gartkiewicz, op. cit., 52.

[28] These arguments are based not on stratigraphy but on typology; that is, on architectural peculiarities of the building itself. They are too complex to be pursued here, but will be fully discussed in a subsequent volume dealing with Qaṣr Ibrîm in the Early Christian period.

below the floor level, but at the east end it was more than three metres lower, because of the natural slope of the *gebel.* It was this condition which made possible the construction of deep subterranean crypts beneath the sacristy and baptistry at the east end of the church.

The Cathedral walls were faced inside and out with regularly shaped and carefully dressed sandstone blocks, closely fitted so that no mortar was visible between them. However, the walls had an inner core of stone rubble and mud mortar, and this was the only bonding holding together the two dressed stone faces.[29] The foundations and lower courses were made from large blocks of yellow sandstone, quite obviously taken from the Meroitic temple (290) which had once stood adjoining the Taharqa Temple (287). These were sufficient to carry the walls up to a height about 2 m above the ground. Above that height they were continued upward with somewhat smaller blocks of pink sandstone, quarried at a nearby site on the mountain-top. The south wall and, presumably, also the north wall were pierced by a line of at least six rectangular windows, at a level about 3.5 m above the ground. String courses of wood, with carved decoration, were set into the inside and outside wall facings at the level of the windowsills, and again at the level of the lintels, which were also of wood. Above that level, the uppermost walls were built of quite small sandstone blocks resembling large bricks. The south wall of the Cathedral is still standing to a height of 5 m, which appears to be its full original height (pl. 8a).

The interior plan of the Cathedral comprised a very wide nave with two much narrower aisles on either side of it (fig. 19). The width of the nave (6 m) was greater than the combined width of the two aisles on either side. This was evidently not the original design of the builders, for the half-round apse which terminated the nave was underlain by foundations of an earlier, narrower apse. The later apse, like the rest of the church, was well and solidly constructed of stone masonry. It was fairly close to half-round in plan, in contrast to the rather elongate apses commonly found in Nubian churches.[30] From the time of its first construction it was filled by a tribune, also built of well-dressed stone blocks. This necessarily meant that the adjoining sacristy and baptistry had to be entered from the aisles, rather than from the apse as was usual in early Nubian churches.

The sacristy chamber, to the north of the apse, was devoid of features. The baptistry also was featureless except for a large baptismal tank sunk into the floor and recessed slightly into the north wall of the room. The sides of the tank were of stone masonry, while the floor was formed by a very large Meroitic funerary stela.[31] Both the sides and the bottom were heavily plastered. There was a wide passage behind the apse, such as is found in many Nubian churches of later date (Type 3), but in the Cathedral it was walled across the middle, with only a narrow doorway providing communication between the sacristy and the baptistry.

The nave of the Cathedral was separated from the adjoining inner aisles by two lines of monolithic granite columns. These had stood on granite bases set into the floor, and they were crowned by elaborately carved granite capitals (pl. 8d–e). All but one of the columns had fallen, but they were found lying whole or in pieces on the church floor, as were several of the capitals. The inner aisles were separated from the outer aisles not by columns but by well-laid stone arcading. The arches, of which two have survived at the southern side of the building, were almost perfectly half-round (pl. 8b). Their capstones, and also the stones halfway up on either side, were decorated with carved stone rosettes or crosses. Many other elements of carved stone decoration were found among the fallen building material in the Cathedral. It is apparent from the surviving masonry piers that there was arcading parallel to the west wall as well as to the north and south walls, thus setting off a kind of narthex area at the west.

There were three symmetrically placed doorways in the west wall of the Cathedral, opening onto a stone-flagged terrace. A fourth doorway gave access to a square tower which adjoined the building at the southwest corner. This was apparently an integral feature of the original building, not a later addition. Within the tower, a stairway ascended in a counter-clockwise direction around a central masonry pier. The lower steps were of cut stone, while the upper steps were formed of wooden timbers set into the side walls. Fragmentary evidence suggests that there was originally a tower at the northwest corner of the cathedral as well, but this had almost certainly fallen or been dismantled before the late mediaeval period.

The Cathedral also had an original doorway near the west end of the south wall, opening into the narthex. A similarly placed doorway in the north wall was almost certainly a later addition, made at the time when the floor level in the church was raised to cover over the fallen columns (see below).

At the east end of the Cathedral, the sacristy and baptistry were underlain by whitewashed, brick-vaulted crypts 3 m high. Access was by means of well-built stone stairways, which descended beside the north and south walls of the building (pl. 8c). The crypts were floored directly on *gebel,* and each had a series of rock tombs cut below the floor. There were four such tombs in the southern crypt, and two in the

[29] For discussion of the masonry see Somers Clarke, *Christian Antiquities*, 76–7.

[30] See Adams, *JARCE* 4 (1965).

[31] See Plumley, *JEA* 50 (1964), 4.

a

b

c

d

e

Plate 8. The Cathedral. a, Exterior view of the south wall. b, Interior view showing arches separating the nave from the south aisle. c, Stairway to the southeast crypt. d, Interior view, looking down the nave toward the sanctuary. e, Interior view before removal of fallen columns and other architectural debris.

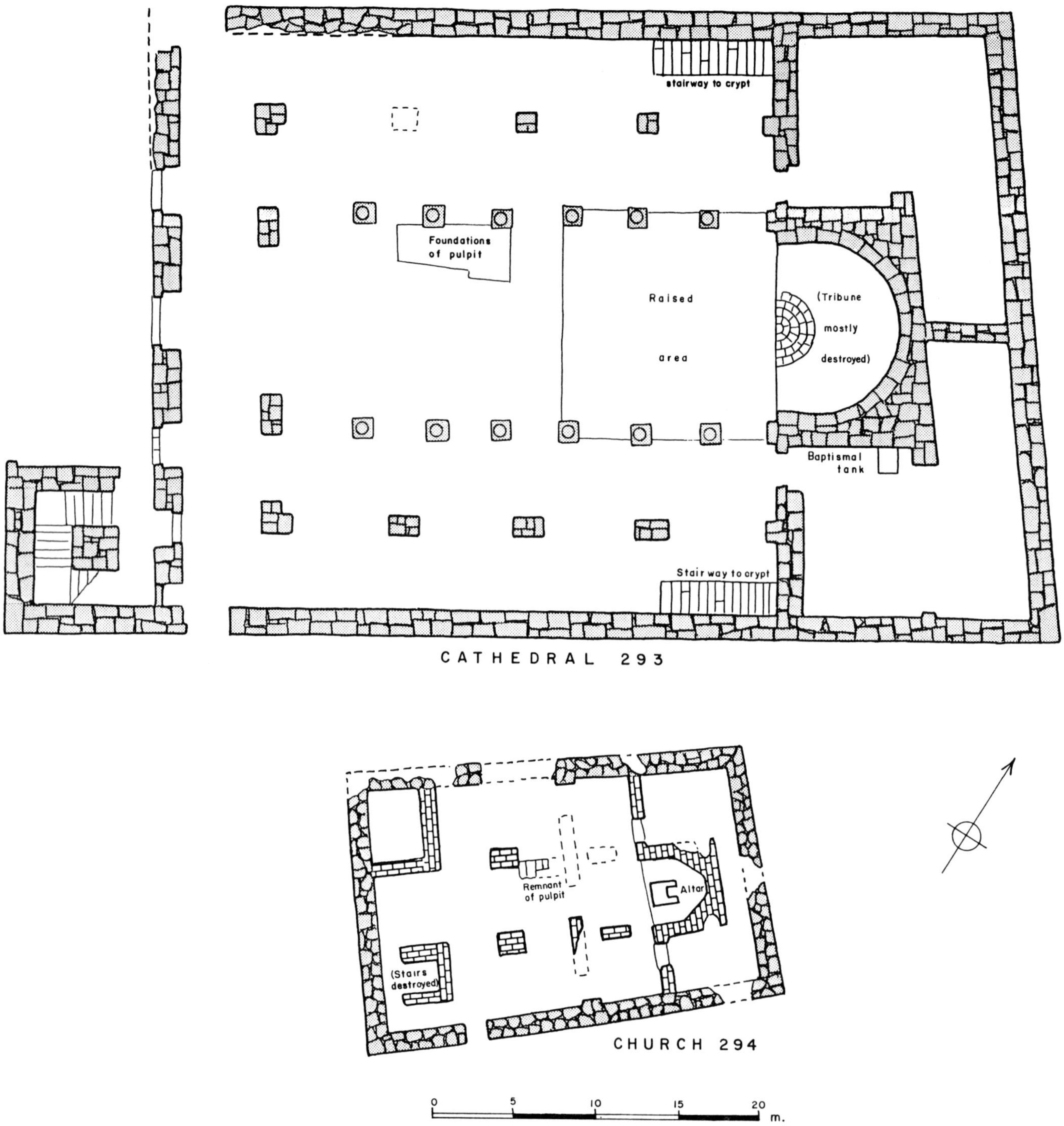

Figure 19. Plan of Cathedral 293 and South Church 294, in Late Christian 1 period. Stone construction indicated by shading; brick construction indicated by simulated brick.

northern. Three of the tombs were found to contain intact burials, but there were no accompanying objects to furnish a date for the interments.

The Cathedral did not have a masonry *higab* of the usual kind. A substantial area in front of the apse, enclosed by the first three columns on either side of the nave, was raised 15 cm higher than the rest of the church floor, and this area was surrounded either by a light wooden *higab* or by a simple rail mounted on wooden posts. Nothing survived except the sockets in which the wooden posts had rested. Within the raised and enclosed area there was no surviving trace either of an altar or of a triumphal arch. Just outside the enclosure were the foundations of a rather crude stone-built pulpit, adjoining two of the columns on the north side of the nave. The entire church was floored with neatly cut and fitted rectangular paving stones. These were somewhat variable in size, but two intersecting lines of absolutely uniform paving stones formed a kind of cross design in the middle of the floor.

Whether or not the Cathedral ever had painted decoration is problematical. Parts of the interior stonework exhibited the same fine finish as did the exterior, and there were various carved decorative elements of stone and wood that were certainly not meant to be plastered over. No traces of paint or plaster can be seen in the interior today, and none were noted either by Somers Clarke[32] or by Monneret de Villard[33] in the course of their visits. However a much earlier visitor, Father Henniker, reported seeing a painted representation of St. John in 1822.[34]

How the Cathedral was roofed is very much an enigma. Abu Salih, in his thirteenth century *Churches and Monasteries of Egypt and Some Neighbouring Countries*, reported of Qaṣr Ibrîm: '... there is a large and beautiful church, finely planned, and named after our Lady, the Pure Virgin Mary. Above it is a high dome, upon which rests a large cross.'[35] This information, like much of that in Abu Salih, was evidently obtained at distant second-hand[36] and cannot be relied on. There is nothing in the surviving arrangement of columns and piers that could possibly have supported a dome, even of wood.

The widely spaced monolithic columns and the rather thin stone piers also could not have supported brick vaulting. It is evident therefore that the Cathedral must have had a roof of wood. The six-metre span over the nave would almost certainly have required the use of trusses. Wooden roofs resting on columns were fairly common in the earliest Nubian churches, when coniferous timber from the Levant was still reasonably accessible. After the eighth century, however, nearly all Nubian churches were built with brick vaults resting on masonry piers. Even in many of the older churches, the columns were pulled down and replaced by piers and vaults when the original wooden roofs had to be replaced because of deterioration. This was presumably because, in the disturbed political conditions of Tulunid and later times, timber could no longer be obtained from the mountains of the Levant.[37] Qaṣr Ibrîm appears to have been one of the very few places in Nubia, if not the only one, where an original wooden roof was never replaced by a vaulted one.

There are two possible explanations for this anomaly. One is that, in the moisture- and vermin-free environment of the mountain-top, the original roof actually survived *in situ* for a period of eight centuries. The alternative possibility is that, during its later years, parts or all of the Cathedral were unroofed. The latter eventuality is suggested by the seeming absence of painted decoration on the walls, and by the fact that parts of the arcading along the south aisles seem to have fallen down and not afterward to have been rebuilt.[38] It is further noteworthy that, by the time Bishop Timotheos was interred in the fourteenth century, the north crypt had entirely filled with soft, apparently wind-blown earth (see below).[39] It is very unlikely that this would have occurred had the building still been enclosed.

The Qaṣr Ibrîm Cathedral belongs clearly to Nubian Church Type 1a, all of whose members are cathedrals.[40] The building is divergent, however, in having a passage behind the apse. Elsewhere in Nubia this feature did not make its appearance until the middle of the eighth century or later, and it was absent from the earliest cathedrals at Faras[41] and Old Dongola.[42] Another anomaly is the north-east to south-west orientation of the Qaṣr Ibrîm Cathedral, which is found nowhere else in Nubia except in the two immediately neighbouring churches at the same site.

The Cathedral underwent various modifications in the course of its long history. A considerable amount of the north wall fell away and was rather clumsily rebuilt, as were areas along the top of the east wall. A new doorway, with its threshold at a high level, was cut through the north wall at its western end. At some point in time there was a fire which destroyed some of the roof and a part of the arcading,[43] and it appears that some of the arches were not afterwards rebuilt. None of these developments can be securely dated, but the fire and partial destruction of the interior may well have been the work of Shams ed-Dawla, whose attack on Qaṣr Ibrîm in 1172/3 is recorded by Abu Salih.[44]

Over the centuries it is evident that the vaulted crypts beneath the sacristy and baptistry gradually became filled with earth. After the northern crypt was entirely filled, it became the burial place for a certain Bishop Timotheos, who died shortly after the year

[32] Somers Clarke, *Christian Antiquities*, 75–8.

[33] Monneret de Villard, *La Nubia*, I, 117–20.

[34] Fr. Henniker, *Notes During a Visit to Egypt, Nubia, the Oases, etc.* (London, 1824), 160.

[35] Evetts and Butler, op. cit., 266.

[36] Cf. op. cit., xiv–xv.

[37] See discussion in Adams, *JARCE* 4 (1965), 91.

[38] Cf. Somers Clarke, *Christian Antiquities*, 77.

[39] See J. Martin Plumley, *The Scrolls of Bishop Timotheos* (Egypt Exploration Society, Texts from Excavations, Memoir 1) (London, 1975).

[40] Adams, *JARCE* 4 (1965), 103–5.

[41] Cf. Michalowski and Gerster, *Faras,* 97.

[42] Gartkiewicz, op. cit., 52.

[43] See Anderson and Adams, *JEA* 65 (1979), 38.

[44] Evetts and Butler, op. cit., 267.

1372. His body was found buried in the fill of the stairway leading to the crypt, under its covering arch.[45]

Taking all the evidence together, I think everything points to the probability that the Cathedral was set on fire during the raid of Shams ed-Dawla, resulting in the destruction of its wooden roof. Some of the supporting columns and arches may have come down at the same time. Since the roof could not effectively be replaced, either with wood or with vaulting, and since the free-standing columns were now unstable, most of the remaining columns were also pulled down after the raid was over. The fallen columns, along with a mass of burned wood and manuscript material which lay on the floor, were then buried in earth.[46] Finally a new earth floor was established on top of this deposit,[47] as was done also at Faras after the original cathedral columns were pulled down.[48] From this time onward the building was open to the sky, with the result that the crypts gradually became filled with wind-blown deposit. If the foregoing interpretation is correct, then we have to picture the Cathedral throughout the Late and Terminal Christian periods as being unroofed, without standing columns, and having a plain mud floor.

Finally, after 1550, the 'Bosnian' garrison appropriated the Cathedral for its own use. The two most southerly aisles were converted into a mosque, by hacking a rather crude *mihrab* niche into the south wall of the building, and constructing a *minbar* (pulpit) immediately beside it.[49] It may be that this was the only section of the building that retained any part of its roof. Other parts of the Cathedral were put to use as ordinary dwellings by building various interior partitions of stone masonry within the walls. It may also have been the 'Bosnians' who blocked the original doorways leading from the aisles to the sacristy and baptistry.

The Cathedral was excavated in the 1963 and 1964 field seasons.[50] Additional, detailed architectural studies were carried out by Przemyslaw Gartkiewicz in 1972 and 1978.[51] For obvious reasons there are no plans to dismantle the Cathedral, which will presumably be the chief attraction should Qaṣr Ibrîm ever be opened to tourism.

Church 294 (the South Church)

This modest structure stood immediately beside the Cathedral on its southern side (fig. 19; pl. 7b). It was the most poorly preserved of the Qaṣr Ibrîm churches, having been largely dismantled and overbuilt with houses in the Islamic period. The walls nowhere stood to a height of more than 95 cm, and some of them at the north-west corner had been dismantled down to the foundations.

Stratigraphic evidence shows that Church 294 was built in the LC1 period. However, it may have been built on the site of an older destroyed church of red brick. The foundations and the floor were underlain at many places by a dense rubble of broken brick, painted and inscribed plaster, and hundreds of burned and torn fragments of religious manuscripts.[52] From these indications it is possible to suggest that the original church on the site was one of those destroyed by Shams ed-Dawla, as reported by Abu Salih,[53] and that Church 294 was built immediately afterward to take its place.

The exterior walls to a height of 70 cm were built of rough stone masonry, generally similar to that in the neighbouring Late Christian houses (see Ch. 4). Above that height they were of mud-brick. The foundations were of small stones laid upright, except that there were four mud bricks laid horizontally at each of the four corners of the building. The apse and the interior walls were entirely of brick. The average size of the bricks was 36 × 18 × 8 cm, as in the nearby House 172 (see Part 2, Ch. 2).

In most respects Church 294 exhibited the typical form of the Classic Nubian church (Type 3). However, there was no tribune in the apse, and for that reason the building is assigned to the rather uncommon Subtype 3b rather than to the more usual Subtype 3c.[54] Another peculiarity was that the apse had decidedly angular contours (see fig. 19) instead of the usual oval or half-round shape. This was apparently made necessary because deep niches were let into the masonry of the apse structure both from the sacristy and from the baptistry. Apart from these there were no preserved features in either of the corner rooms. Both were entered from the body of the church through rather narrow doorways with raised thresholds. The nave and aisles were separated from each other by four symmetrically placed brick piers, which could have supported a central dome. There were, as usual, small rooms at the north-west and south-west corners of the church, and the latter carried a stairway.

The lowermost courses of the altar were preserved *in situ*. It was built of plastered and whitewashed brick, and measured 40 cm square. There was a hollow within the altar which could be reached through a small

[45] Plumley, *The Scrolls*.

[46] Plumley, *JEA* 50, 4.

[47] Op. cit. See also J. Martin Plumley and Gerald M. Browne, *Old Nubian Texts from Qaṣr Ibrîm*, I (Egypt Exploration Society, Texts from Excavations, Memoir 9) (London, 1988), 2.

[48] See Michalowski, *Kush* 12 (1964), 202–3.

[49] Somers Clarke, *Christian Antiquities*, 77.

[50] For the preliminary report see Plumley, *JEA* 50 (1964), 3–4.

[51] Anderson and Adams, *JEA* 65 (1979), 37–8.

[52] See Plumley, *JEA* 52 (1966), 11–12; Plumley and Adams, *JEA* 60 (1974), 214 and pl. XLII, 2; Anderson and Adams, *JEA* 65 (1979), 40–1.

[53] Evetts and Butler, op. cit., 267.

[54] See Adams, *JARCE* 4 (1965), 112–4.

aperture at its east side. (A similar recess in an altar at Faras was found to contain a chalice.[55]) The altar, as originally built, stood just within the apse, but in the course of a later reflooring it was relocated at a point slightly further to the west so that half of it was beneath the apse and half outside it. There were traces of a mud-brick *higab* adjoining the south-east nave pier, screening the sanctuary area from both the nave and the south aisle. The corresponding feature on the north side of the nave had not been preserved. The lowest steps of a brick pulpit structure remained in situ at the north side of the nave (fig. 19).

Church 294 originally had a hard-packed mud floor. Both it and the walls were whitewashed, but there were no surviving traces of decoration anywhere except in the apse. Here was preserved a single horizontal red stripe which might conceivably have been the lower border of a painting. At a later date the body of the church had been refloored with roughly laid flagstones, but this paving apparently did not extend into the sanctuary area or the eastern corner rooms. Still later, however, the floor area within the apse was raised by 15 cm, and it was at this time that the altar was relocated slightly further to the west.

Most of the deposit within Church 294 was removed in 1966[56] without very careful documentation, and for that reason it is not possible to trace the later history of the building with any certainty. Mr Kenneth Frazer, who planned the church, evidently did not believe that it had remained in use until the end of the Christian period, for his 1966 site plan bears the notation 'Church abandoned at end of 1st L/C period.'[57] The reasons for this conclusion are not stated.

Church 294 was discovered and largely excavated in 1966. Additional subfloor testing was carried out in 1972, and the building was dismantled in the 1978 season.[58]

Church 289(?) (the small temple)

There may just possibly have been a fourth church within the citadel walls at Qaṣr Ibrîm. At the eastern extremity of the site there stood a very small stone temple, 289, whose date of construction is uncertain. Like the Taharqa mud-brick temple, it may have been converted into a church. There are two reasons for this supposition: first, the building was left standing throughout the Middle Ages, whereas the larger Meroitic temple 290 was entirely dismantled; second, the uppermost courses of masonry, surmounting the pylon gate, were evidently not part of the original construction (pl. 7c). They were formed of well-shaped but very small stone blocks identical to those in the upper Cathedral walls (see above),[59] and they were probably made at the same time. If the temple did become a church, this may also explain why the Late Christians refortified this part of the citadel, which otherwise shows no evidence of Late Christian activity.

The pylons and the north wall of Temple 289 remained in a good state of preservation as recently as 1976. However, the interior walls had been largely pulled down by the 'Bosnians,' who built houses of their own within the temple just as they did in the Cathedral. Thus, no specifically ecclesiastical features could be recognized within the building, and its use as a church remains conjectural. The lake waters finally reached the temple foundations after 1976, and it has since been largely destroyed by wave action.

Church 839 (the Cupola Church)

This minuscule structure stood by itself on a small natural terrace outside and below the eastern citadel walls. It was never investigated by the E.E.S. Expedition, and it disappeared under water between the 1966 and 1969 seasons. Fortunately it was visited earlier by Somers Clarke[60] and Monneret de Villard[61] both of whom published plans and brief descriptions. Monneret de Villard also published two photographs, of which one is reproduced here (pl. 7d).[62] These records are the sole basis for the plan and description given here.

Church 839 was still very well preserved in 1930, as can be seen in Monneret's photographs (see pl. 7d). Most of the walls stood to their full original height, and a part of the central cupola was still preserved. The walls were of rough stone construction to a height of 120 cm and above that were of mud-brick. The building had the characteristic skewed plan found in many Late Christian dwellings (see Part 2, Ch. 2).

The plan (fig. 20) shows a Late Christian church (Type 4) of a very late subtype.[63] There were no western corner rooms, no stairway, no pulpit, and no *higab*. The sanctuary at the east end of the building was square, but it was surmounted by a semi-dome resting on squinches, which can be seen in one of the

[55] Michalowski, *Kush* 13 (1964), 196 and pl. XXXIX, a.

[56] See Plumley, *JEA* 52 (1966), 10.

[57] Unpublished document among Qaṣr Ibrîm site records.

[58] Anderson and Adams, *JEA* 65 (1979), 38.

[59] For an illustration see C. L. Woolley, *Karanòg, the Town* (Eckley B. Coxe Junior Expedition to Nubia, Vol. 5) (Philadelphia, 1911), pl. 12.

[60] See Somers Clarke, *Christian Antiquities*, 78 and 80.

[61] See Monneret de Villard, *La Nubia*, I, 109–11.

[62] Op. cit., II, pl. LV.

[63] Cf. Adams, *JARCE* 4 (1965), 116–8.

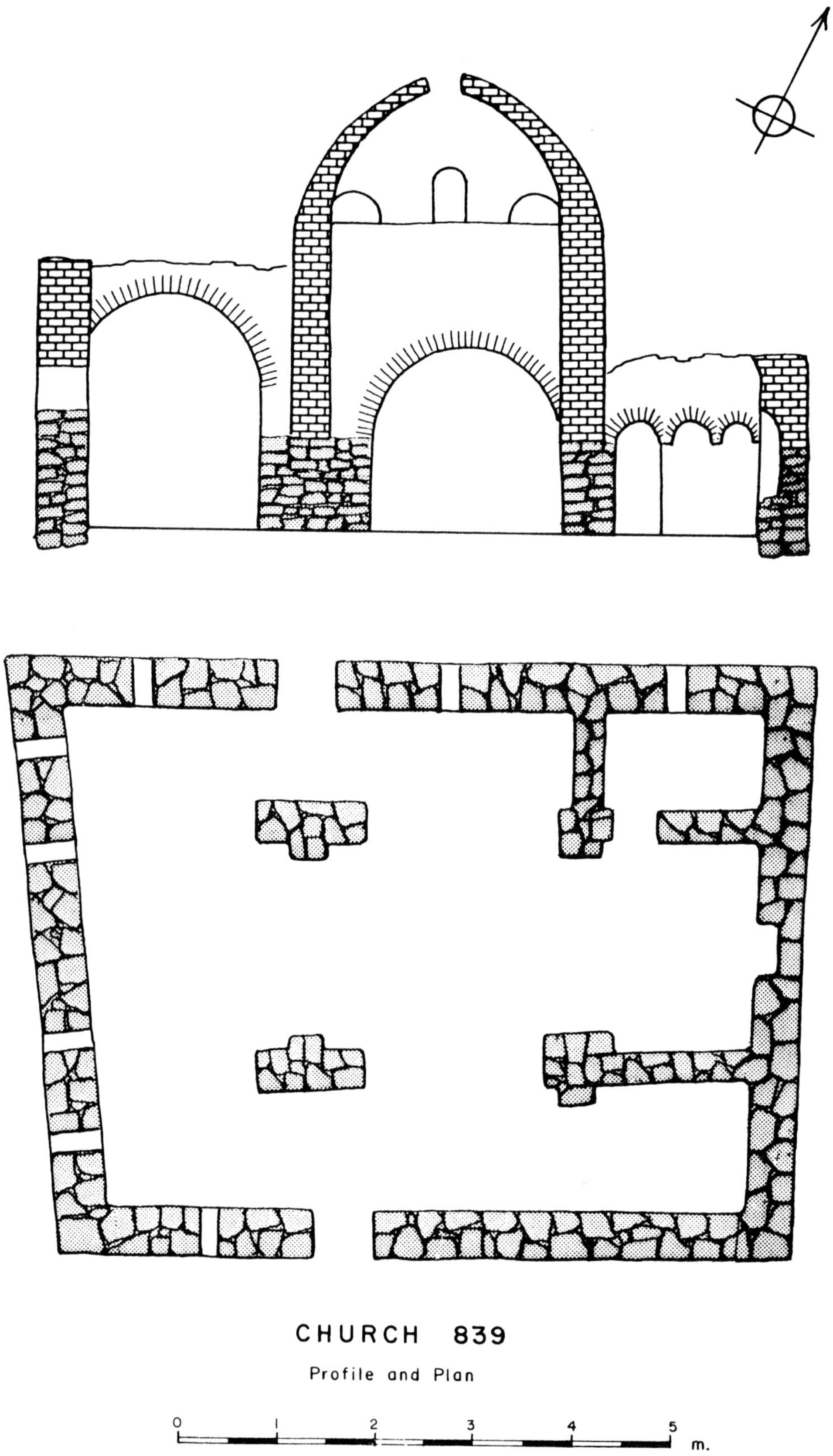

Figure 20. Elevation and plan of Cupola Church 839 (after Somers Clarke, *Christian Antiquities in the Nile Valley* (Oxford, 1910), pl. XIX). Stone construction indicated by shading; brick construction indicated by simulated brick.

published photographs[64] There was an arched niche at the back (east) end of the sanctuary, but the plan gives no indication of an altar. From the sanctuary chamber a doorway led directly into the sacristy on the north. However, the corresponding room on the south side was entered from the south aisle. The building had a number of narrow windows high in the walls; the plan shows four in the west wall and three in the north. Only one window was preserved on the south side, as other parts of the wall were broken down. The church was whitewashed on the inside, but apparently bore no traces of painted decoration.

The Cupola Church must be assigned on typological grounds to the Terminal Christian period. More direct dating is provided by two painted inscriptions on the interior walls, giving the name of Bishop Merki (the Nubian equivalent of Marcos).[65] His name also appears on two of the last known documents from the Kingdom of Dotawo (see Part 1, Ch. 2), dated respectively 1464 and 1484.[66] If it was actually Merki who commissioned the church, then it must have been one of the last ecclesiastical buildings ever erected in Nubia. It may be, therefore, that the entire history of Nubian church architecture is encompassed between the Taharqa Temple-church and the Cupola Church at Qaṣr Ibrîm.

Functional relationships among the churches

Although chronological evidence is somewhat tenuous, there are clear indications that at least three of the Qaṣr Ibrîm churches, 287, 293, and 294, were in use concurrently during the LC1 period, and probably also in the LC2 period. In Terminal Christian times the two smaller churches, 287 and 294, may have gone out of use, perhaps about the same time when the Cupola Church (839) was built. Obviously nothing can be said about the small Temple 289, if indeed it ever became a church.

It seems reasonable to assume that there was some division of function among the three or four churches within the citadel walls. All of the major Nubian cathedrals had smaller churches built alongside them. This would suggest that, like most cathedrals in Europe, they did not serve as parish churches but were reserved for special and specially exalted functions. It is further noteworthy that most of the cathedrals seem to have lacked *higabs* of the usual mud-brick type, screening the sanctuary area from the view of the congregation. It may, therefore, be that the cathedral interiors were accessible only to the clergy, who were privileged to witness the holy service in its entirety. Since, on the testimony of Abu Salih, the Cathedral at Qaṣr Ibrîm was dedicated to the Virgin,[67] the most important ritual celebrated there may have been the Feast of the Assumption.

The original parish church at Qaṣr Ibrîm was presumably the Taharqa Temple-church, since it almost certainly preceded all the others. At a later date, however, this may have become primarily a monastery church, and it was perhaps then that a new church was built alongside the Cathedral. As already noted, the original church beside the Cathedral was apparently of red brick, to be replaced at a later date by Church 294. It is interesting to note that both at Qaṣr Ibrîm and at Faras there were red-brick churches on the south side of the cathedrals;[68] they were apparently the only churches in Lower Nubia constructed in this fashion. A building date of 930 was recorded on a dedicatory stela in the Faras church.[69]

The monastery walls surrounding the Taharqa church were pulled down at the end of the Early Christian period, and thereafter all three of the churches on the citadel stood free of adjoining structures. What special function the temple-church then performed can only be conjectured. Inscriptions on a nearby mountain-top[70] show that Qaṣr Ibrîm in the Middle Ages was a major place of pilgrimage for the Nubian clergy, and it may be that the temple-church, as the oldest church in Nubia, had some special role in the pilgrimage ritual.

The situation of the Cupola Church, standing alone outside the citadel walls, was anomalous, but it was an anomaly found elsewhere in Nubia as well. At Faras East,[71] at Serra,[72] at Abdel Qadir,[73] at Qasr Ico,[74] at Gendal Irki,[75] and at Kulubnarti[76] there were also small churches of a late type which stood at a considerable remove from the communities which they were pre-

[64] Monneret de Villard, *La Nubia*, II, pl. LV, right.

[65] Op. cit., I, 110.

[66] See Plumley in Michalowski (ed.), *Nubia, récentes recherches*, 105.

[67] Evetts and Butler, op. cit.

[68] See Michalowski, *Kush* 12 (1964), 195–6, 203.

[69] Op. cit., 203.

[70] See Plumley and Adams, *JEA* 60 (1974), pl. LI.

[71] See Geoffrey S. Mileham, *Churches in Lower Nubia* (Eckley B. Coxe Junior Expedition to Nubia, vol. 2) (Philadelphia, 1910), 38–40 and pls. 27–28. See also Monneret de Villard, *La Nubia*, I, 166, figs. 171–172.

[72] Mileham, *Churches*, 42–7 and pls. 32–5; Monneret de Villard, *La Nubia* I, 200–4.

[73] Griffith, *LAAA* 15 (1928), 63–82 and pls. XXV–XLVII.

[74] Francisco Presedo Velo, *Antigüedades de la isla de Kasar-Ico* (Comité Español de la Unesco para Nubia, Memorias de la Misión Arqueológica, 1) (Madrid, 1963), 14–29 and pls. I–XIII.

[75] Somers Clarke, *Christian Antiquities*, 50–2; Monneret de Villard, *La Nubia*, I, 224–5.

[76] Somers Clarke, *Christian Antiquities*, 48–50; Monneret de Villard, *La Nubia*, I, 233–4; Adams, *Kulubnarti*, I, Ch. III.

sumably meant to serve. There is no obvious explanation for this situation, for there was no lack of space within most of the communities. All of the buildings in question apparently date from the late Dotawo era, after the breakup of Makouria and the loss of effective communication with the Coptic hierarchy in Egypt. All of them are notable, too, for the simplicity of their interior arrangements. Possibly there arose, in these last years of Nubian Christianity, a kind of simplified and purely Nubian rite, and the physical separation of the church was one of its liturgical features. An alternative possibility is that the late churches were situated at a distance simply because they were so frequently subject to Muslim depredation.[77]

The Cathedral cemetery

For obvious reasons, the main Qaṣr Ibrîm cemeteries were always outside the fortification walls. In the wadis east and west of the town there were enormous cemeteries containing both pagan and Christian graves.[78] Another group of graves extended over a considerable area of the desert terrace to the south of the citadel. Here again there appear to be Christian graves, although none have so far been excavated.

Early in the Christian period a cemetery was prepared within the town area itself, immediately adjacent to the cathedral. Earth fill was deposited so as to form a kind of raised terrace, which was supported along its west and south sides by a stout stone retaining wall. Access to the terrace was by means of a wide stairway at the southwest corner.[79] The cemetery terrace had, as it were, two components. In the eastern portion, close to the walls of Church 294, there were only a few centimetres of earth fill laid directly on *gebel*, and any graves that were made here had either to be cut into the rock or built above the ground. However, this area of high-standing *gebel* terminated abruptly in a straight escarpment, the result of quarrying in pre-Christian times. The consequence was to leave a vertical rock face about 4 m high.[80] The *gebel* surface west of the escarpment was, therefore, at a level well below that to the east. The whole of this difference was later made up with earth fill, which the Early Christians brought in to replace the quarried-away stone and to form a single, level terrace adjoining the Cathedral.

Only three burials were actually found in the area of soft, deep earth fill in the western portion of the terrace. Two of these were typically featureless Christian interments.[81] Far more important and interesting were a series of tombs cut into the *gebel* rock in the eastern part of the terrace, close to the wall of Church 294. Here six large chamber tombs (295–300) had been cut in a neat row. They were not dug downward from above but were cut horizontally into the rock from its previously sculptured western escarpment.[82] To the north of them, another rock-cut tomb (365) was actually located partly under the Cathedral tower. The chambers were, on the average, 3.5 m long and 2 m wide, with somewhat narrower doorways at the western end which were designed to be closed with stone slabs. Within, the chambers were quite variable in height. In one case the builders had broken through the upper ground surface, and as a result had been obliged to cover the tomb with brick vaulting. Outside four of the tombs there were masonry-lined *dromoi* extending down from ground level to the tomb door, indicating that the chambers were designed for multiple interments. Two bodies were in fact found in one of the tombs.

Still farther east, immediately beside the west wall of Church 294, were additional, above-ground tomb chambers of red brick (369, 370). One of these had been whitewashed on the inside, and bore painted inscriptions from the four gospels in Sahidic Coptic.[83] All of the above-ground tombs as well as the rock-cut chambers had been thoroughly ransacked in antiquity, almost certainly during the raid of Shams ed-Dawla.[84] As a result, only two intact bodies were found.

Two vaulted brick tombs (366 and 367) directly adjoined the western face of the Cathedral tower. One tomb had been very largely destroyed, while the other contained three intact bodies wrapped in embroidered linen. This tomb also had been whitewashed and decorated with inscriptions in Sahidic Coptic.[85] One more vaulted brick tomb was found on the north side of the Cathedral (965). It held the body of a very tall, very old man, tightly bundled in three shrouds and then bound criss-cross with linen tapes, somewhat after the fashion of Egyptian mummies.[86]

With one or two exceptions the tombs in the Cathedral cemetery were much more elaborate than was usual in Christian Nubia, and it can hardly be doubted that this was a burial place reserved for high ecclesiastical dignitaries.[87] No tombstones were found *in situ*, but one of the plundered rock tombs held no fewer than five redeposited stelae, along with a great

[77] For discussion see Adams, *JARCE* 4 (1965), 118.

[78] See A. J. Mills, *The Cemeteries of Qaṣr Ibrîm* (Egypt Exploration Society, Excavation Memoir 51) (London, 1982), especially pl. I (frontispiece).

[79] Plumley, *JEA* 52 (1966), 12 and pl. V, 3.

[80] See op. cit., pl. V, 2.

[81] See Adams, *Nubia*, 480.

[82] See Plumley, *JEA* 52 (1966), 11 and pl. V, 2.

[83] Op. cit., 10–11.

[84] Op. cit.

[85] Originally reported by Plumley, *JEA* 50 (1964), 4.

[86] For a closely parallel example, from mediaeval Egypt see H. E. Winlock and W. E. Crum, *The Monastery of Epiphanius at Thebes*, I (New York, 1926), pl. XI, c.

[87] Cf. Plumley, *JEA* 52 (1966), 10.

many loose pages from religious manuscripts.[88] The stelae were those of Bishops of Ibrîm and Qurta, dated in the tenth and eleventh centuries.[89] Probably they had originally adorned five of the tombs cut into the *gebel* face. A sixth stela, found in the loose fill nearby, was that of Bishop Marianos of Faras.[90] This might indicate that Qaṣr Ibrîm was the preferred place of burial for clerics from other parts of Nubia as well.

None of the tombs in the Cathedral cemetery can be attributed to a Late or Terminal Christian date. By this time, in fact, the terrace retaining walls and the access stairway were largely or entirely buried in refuse. It may be hypothesized that most of the tombs were plundered by Shams ed-Dawla's raiders, and thereafter no further use was made of the cemetery within the town walls. The Christians, it seems, subsequently gathered up the displaced tombstones, along with whatever manuscript pages had escaped destruction, and redeposited them in one of the reopened tombs. This certainly did not take place in post-Christian times, for the 'Bosnians' would have taken no such pains. Indeed, they repeatedly employed Christian tombstones as building blocks in their own houses.[91]

[88] Op. cit., pl. VI.

[89] Op. cit., 11 and pl. IV, 5.

[90] Op. cit., p. 11. Marianos is otherwise well known from wall paintings and inscriptions in the Faras Cathedral; see Stefan Jakobielski, *Faras III* (Warsaw, 1972), 143–7, and Michalowski and Gerster, *Faras*, pls. 81–3.

[91] Cf. Plumley, *JEA* 61 (1975), 13.

CHAPTER 5
THE FORTIFICATIONS

In the modern era the most conspicuous architectural feature of the Qaṣr Ibrîm citadel was its fortification wall. As recently as 1969 it stood to a height of between 4 and 6 m along the southern and western margins of the site (pl. 9a). After 1969 the fortifications were gradually destroyed by a combination of rising water and wave action, and today only the walls at the western end of the citadel are still *in situ*. In anticipation of this destruction, salvage excavations were carried out at various places along the southern and western fortifications between 1974 and 1980;[1] these yielded much detailed information about the original construction and subsequent history of the walls.

The fortifications were originally built in Ptolemaic times, and they were enlarged and heightened twice during the interval of Roman occupation that followed a little later.[2] After the first century AD, however, they seem to have been neglected for the better part of a thousand years, and by the twelfth century they were certainly in an advanced state of decay. Much of their material had probably been robbed to build houses during the peaceful years of the earlier Middle Ages (see Part 1, Ch. 2). This is attested by the fact that most of the recently visible walls were of Late Christian construction, though resting on Ptolemaic and Roman foundations.[3] The original walls were reasonably well preserved only at the angles in the fortifications and in the vicinity of the two main gateways. The Late Christian walls were further heightened, and in some places repaired, in Islamic times, and they remained fairly intact until their final destruction in the 1970's (pl. 9b).

Both logic and concrete evidence suggest that the fortifications were rebuilt immediately after the raid of Shams ed-Dawla in 1172–3. There would have been no incentive to repair them earlier, for Nubia had been at peace since the conclusion of the *Baqt* treaty in the seventh century. However, the depredations of Shams ed-Dawla were part of a general anti-Nubian campaign on the part of Egypt's new Ayyubid rulers,[4] and the Nubians may well have anticipated the beginning of a new and more belligerent era. More direct testimony as to the date is furnished by the material used as filling behind the newly constructed fortifications (fig. 21). It included a rubble of burned brick, carved wooden architectural elements, painted and inscribed wall plaster, and a great many fragmentary religious manuscripts. Identical material was found beneath the Late Christian Church 294 (see Part 2, Ch. 4); it is believed to represent the wreckage of a church which Shams ed-Dawla is known to have destroyed.[5]

Wall construction

Ptolemaic and Roman construction. The Ptolemaic and Roman fortifications were walls in the full sense of the term. They were stoutly built affairs, about 3 m thick at the base, with dressed stone faces and an inner core of rubble [6] (see pl. 9b, 9c). The foundations were not laid on the level top of the mountain but on the slopes somewhat lower down, presumably in order to enclose a larger area. In many places the walls seem to have followed the alignment of an older set of revetments, built perhaps in Napatan times.[7] An irregular projection at the south-west corner of the citadel (see fig. 3) was necessary so that the walls could detour around the massive brick South Bastion (336) which was already standing there, and which probably dates back to pharaonic times.[8]

Because of their situation on sloping ground, somewhat below the summit of the mountain, refuse tended to accumulate very rapidly along the inner faces of the walls. It was quite obviously this circumstance which led the Romans both to thicken and to heighten the original walls, and yet by the time of their departure in the second century their own rubbish had very nearly engulfed the inner side of the fortifications. In places along the southern rampart the combined depth of Ptolemaic and Roman refuse was in excess of 4 m.[9] From being true walls, therefore, the fortifications had become essentially revetments, creating a level terrace

[1] See Plumley, *JEA* 61 (1975), 20–4 and pl. XIII; Plumley, Adams, and Crowfoot, *JEA* 63 (1977), 37–9; Anderson, Adams *et al.*, *JEA* 65 (1979), 33–5 and pl. IV, 3; Adams, Alexander and Allen, *JEA* 69 (1983), 56–9 and pl. VII.

[2] For more detail see Adams, *JARCE* 20 (1983), 95–104, and id. in Francis Geus and Florence Thil (eds.), *Mélanges offerts à Jean Vercoutter* (Paris, 1985), 9–17.

[3] We were mistaken in an earlier assumption that the reconstruction of the girdle wall was primarily 'Bosnian' work; see Plumley, Adams and Crowfoot, *JEA* 63 (1977), 37–8.

[4] See H. A. R. Gibb, *The Life of Saladin* (Oxford, 1973), 7.

[5] See B. T. A. Evetts and A. J. Butler, trans, *The Churches and Monasteries of Egypt and Some Neighbouring Countries* (Oxford, 1895), 267.

[6] See n. 2.

[7] Adams, Alexander and Allen, *JEA* 69 (1983), 57.

[8] See Anderson and Adams, *JEA* 65 (1979), 33–5 and pl. IV, 3.

[9] See especially Adams in Geus and Thil (eds.), *Mélanges*.

a

b

c

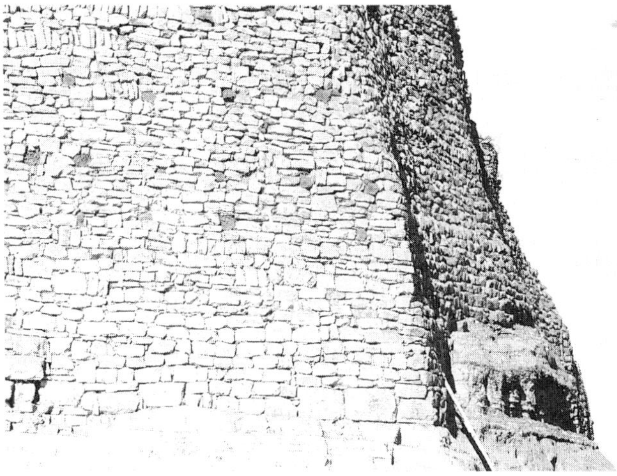

d

e

Plate 9. The fortifications. a, General view from the south; the blocked South Gate is at the extreme left. b, The South Bastion, showing 'Bosnian' and Late Christian rebuilding resting on older, pre-Christian remnants. The South Gate is at the left. c, The south end of the western fortifications. The South Gate is at the right. d, Detail of construction in the South Bastion. Ends of palm log tie-timbers can be seen in the upper part of the photo. e. The East Gate. The lower, decorative gateway was blocked with refuse fill in Late Christian times. The wide gateway directly above it was then the main entry to the site.

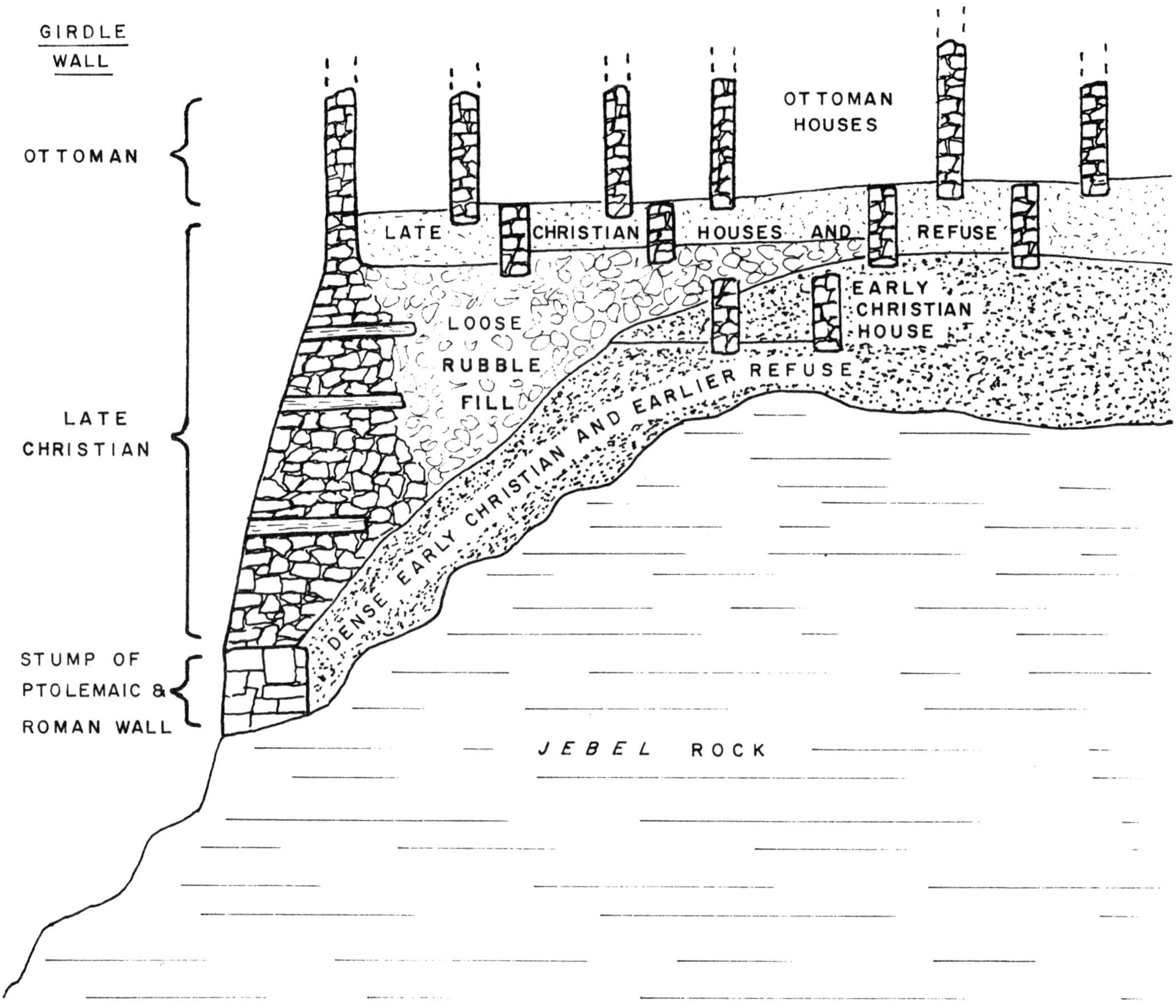

Figure 21. Schematic profile through the southwest fortification walls; not accurate to scale. This corrects the drawing in *JEA* 63, p. 38, where the reconstructed girdle wall is attributed primarily to the Ottoman ('Bosnian') period.

which enlarged the natural area of the mountaintop (fig. 21).

Late Christian construction. The Late Christian rebuilding was not so much an effort to heighten the walls as to restore them to their original state. Along the whole perimeter of the site they were rebuilt on the original foundations, though in some places these survived only to the height of a few courses. The Northwest Bastion tower, a small projection which had been added by the Romans, was also rebuilt, and later a house (206) was added beside it.[10]

The Late Christian walls, unlike their predecessors, were revetments rather than true walls from the beginning. They had a somewhat battered (sloping) outer face, from 1 to 2 m thick, composed of irregular and unshaped stone blocks. Here and there, fragments of decorated stone from older temples and churches were incorporated. The walls were laid up with mud mortar and a mass of stone and sherd chinking but were not plastered. In some places they were laid directly up against older deposits that had remained *in situ*, but more often it was necessary to fill in the space immediately behind them with rubble.[11] Potsherds found in this material, and in the chinking of the wall itself, help to establish the Late Christian dating of the walls.

[10] See Adams, Alexander and Allen, *JEA* 69 (1983), 56.

[11] The nature of the construction can be seen in Plumley, *JEA* 61 (1975), pl. XIII, 2.

The most distinctive feature of the Late Christian fortifications was their use of palm-log bonding timbers at regular intervals. These ran crosswise through the full thickness of the wall facing and projected back into the rubble fill behind the facing for a distance of 2 to 3 m (fig. 21). The outer ends of the timbers, where they came flush with the face of the wall, can readily be seen in plates 9b and 9d. The spacing of the timbers was not entirely uniform, and they were not used in places where there was *gebel* rock or older deposit immediately behind the wall facing. Along the southern bastion, where they were most conspicuous (pl. 9d), they were inserted at intervals of about one metre horizontally and slightly more than one metre vertically. It is these bonding timbers, among other things, that make it possible to distinguish the Late Christian construction both from the underlying Ptolemaic and Roman work and from the overlying 'Bosnian' additions. The 'Bosnian' construction was generally very similar to that of the Christians, but the stones employed were somewhat smaller, and there was no use of timbers. The 'Bosnian' additions, moreover, were true walls, which served to enclose houses built directly against the battlements.[12] Late Christian construction can be very readily identified in plates 9b and 9d. It is evident here that a large part of the southern and eastern walls was of Late Christian origin, while along the western ramparts there were large areas of 'Bosnian' repair.

On the north, the citadel was naturally protected by the adjoining cliff. At some time, however, the upper part of this had been deliberately quarried away so as to make it more nearly vertical. Before that time there had been rock-cut storage crypts alongside the cliff face, like the ones found in House 781 (see Part 2, Ch. 2). These were largely destroyed in the process of refashioning the cliff face, but the contours of their inner sides can still be made out. The reshaping of the cliff also truncated a flight of rock-cut stairs that earlier had descended at the northwest angle of the citadel, just to the east of House 763 (see Part 2, Ch. 2). There is no certain way of dating these modifications, but they could well have been a part of the general scheme of Late Christian refortification. The walls of several Late Christian houses (210, 211, 848, 849) were built directly alongside the newly reshaped cliff face.

The gates

The South Gate. The original, Ptolemaic and Roman gate was located at the south-west corner of the citadel. Here there was a tall doorway, 220 cm wide, spanned at the top by a heavy wooden timber.[13] In Roman times the width of the door was somewhat reduced by constructing a new masonry jamb at one side.[14] A very large and deep bolt socket in the eastern jamb showed that the gate could be closed by a heavy pivoting door. The walls at this point stood on rather steeply sloping ground, and the gate was reached from below by means of steps cut into the *gebel* rock.[15] These led down onto a small neck of level ground which connected the citadel with the desert terrace to the south, and from here additional rock-cut steps[16] led down toward the valley floor west of the site.

At some fairly early date, apparently in Meroitic times, the original South Gate was firmly blocked with masonry.[17] When the Late Christians rebuilt the fortifications, they took the precaution of adding a solid mass of additional masonry against the outer face of the blocked gateway, so that no trace of its presence was afterward visible (see pl. 9a).[18] It was probably also the Late Christians who hacked away the rock-cut steps leading to the South Gate.[19]

The East Gate. From Meroitic times onward, the main access to the citadel was through an ornamental gateway in the middle of the south-east wall, designated as the East Gate (pl 9e). This was spanned by a carved stone *uraeus* lintel, suggesting an origin in Meroitic times. The gate may have been built at the same time when the South Gate was blocked, but this can only be a matter of conjecture. The East Gate gave access to a large antechamber, 10 m long and 5 m wide, within which a flight of cut-stone steps ascended to a second doorway in the north wall of the chamber. It is not clear whether this opened into another room, or onto open ground within the fortifications.[20] The East Gate was approached from below by a zigzag pathway ascending from the valley floor to the east of the citadel.

By Late Christian times there must have been a deep refuse deposit within, and probably also outside, the East Gate, for the Christians did not restore it to use when they rebuilt the adjoining fortifications. Instead they built a somewhat wider gateway directly above the earlier one, as shown in plate 9e. It was the first

[12] Plumley, Adams and Crowfoot, *JEA* 63 (1977), 38, fig. C.

[13] See Plumley, *JEA* 53 (1967), 4, and id., *JEA* 56 (1970), 17–8 and pls. XXIV, XXV, 1.

[14] Plumley, *JEA* 56 (1970), 17.

[15] Op cit., 17 and pl. XXIV, 1.

[16] See Plumley, *JEA* 53 (1967), pl. II, 2.

[17] See Plumley, *JEA* 56 (1970), 17.

[18] See op. cit.; also Plumley, *JEA* 53 (1967), 4 and pl. II, 1.

[19] Plumley, *JEA* 56 (1970), 17.

[20] The East Gate was planned in 1969, but no excavations were carried out before 1974, when the structure was half under water. See Plumley, *JEA* 63 (1977), 21–4. The published plan for 1974 (op. cit., 23) shows structures from several periods, and the accompanying description is difficult to interpret.

entrance to the fortress which was large enough to admit horses and cattle without difficulty, and this may have been a consideration in its design. However, the gateway as it was preserved in the recent past may not have been entirely of Christian construction, for the masonry of its eastern jamb appeared to be 'Bosnian.' The preoccupation with defence which was elsewhere shown by the Late Christians makes it evident that the East Gate would have been provided with a stout closing door, or perhaps a pair of pivoting doors on either side, but actual details of the gates were not recorded prior to the time of their destruction by lake waters in the 1960's.[21]

The Podium Gate. From very early times there was another gateway in the middle of the west citadel wall, adjoining the Podium on its southern side. It could not be determined whether this was part of the original Ptolemaic plan, or was added later by the Romans or Meroites. The gateway, which was 150 cm wide, was closed by a pivoting wooden door which had left deep wear marks on the threshold stone from innumerable openings and closings. Immediately within, heavy stone-built steps ascended eastward beside the Podium, then turned southward for a short stretch, and then eastward again.[22]

The Podium Gate seems to have remained in use throughout the Middle Ages, for the steps were rebuilt in Early Christian times and again in Late Christian times. The Late Christian steps were adjoined on one side by a brick retaining wall, made necessary by the deep accumulation of refuse alongside the walls by this time. For the same reason the stairway was continued eastward considerably beyond the point where it had originally terminated, in order to surmount the later accumulation of refuse.

The Podium Gate was approached from outside by steps cut into the steeply sloping *gebel* directly below it. This was not an easy route of access, and it can have served only for fairly agile persons who were not burdened with heavy loads. The gate was blocked altogether in Islamic times, when the adjoining sections of the girdle wall were rebuilt for the last time.

[21] Kenneth Frazer's 1969 plan of the East Gate does not show the Late Christian upper gate.

[22] See Frend, *JEA* 60 (1974), 44–5.

CHAPTER 6
THE EVIDENCE OF ARCHITECTURE

QASR Ibrîm in the Classic Christian period would appear to have been a kind of acropolis, dominated by its three or four churches (287, 293, 294, and possibly 289). Surrounding the churches were large areas of open plaza, as well as a cemetery at the western end of the Cathedral. The number of residential structures was limited, and they may have been reserved entirely for the Eparch of Nobadia and for ecclesiastical officials. Commerce and everyday living activities were evidently confined to the lower town-site, along the riverbank. The hilltop fortifications were in an advanced state of disrepair, having received no attention since Meroitic or possibly X-Group times.

After the raid of Shams ed-Dawla in 1172–3, the character of the community changed rapidly. The first task undertaken by the inhabitants, after the raiders had departed, was evidently that of rebuilding the fortifications. This was probably accompanied by the demolition of a number of partially destroyed houses and at least one church, as well as the quarrying of a great deal of new stone. That this activity took place very shortly after the raid is indicated by the fact that large quantities of burned material and manuscript fragments from the Cathedral library were dumped into the fill material immediately behind the rebuilt girdle wall.

At least a few houses seem to have survived the general destruction. This was true specifically of the eparchal House 763, at the northern extremity of the site, which shows evidence of occupation both before and after the Shams ed-Dawla raid. Before long it was joined by increasing numbers of newly built houses, while other structures that had been disused and filled with refuse since X-Group or Early Christian times were dug out and restored to use. The formerly open plaza area between the Cathedral (293) and the Temple-Church (287) was gradually filled with houses, and additional structures were built along the northern perimeter of the fortifications. Yet the area west of the Cathedral, where a number of Classic Christian houses had stood, was never rebuilt; the burned-out remains of its earlier houses were levelled to make a new plaza. No trace of Late or Terminal Christian construction was found anywhere on the eastern portion of the site. It is possible that this area was kept clear to serve as a kind of open market space, since it was located just within the town gate (fig. 5). It is also possible, however, that the evidences of Late Christian occupation were obliterated when the area was densely overbuilt with houses in the Ottoman period.

In spite of the increasing number of secular dwellings, the Late Christian architectural remains at Qaṣr Ibrîm do not convey the impression of an ordinary town-site; particularly when they are compared with the contemporary town-sites of Meinarti,[1] Debeira,[2] Abkanarti,[3] and various others. A considerable number of the houses were eparchal dwellings at one time or another, and others must surely have been the residences of the Eparch's dependants and retainers (see Part 4, Ch. 8). There would still also have been a need to house at least a few ecclesiastical officials. In other words, the site in Late Christian times may have been chiefly an administrative centre, while everyday living and commercial activities were still carried out mainly in the lower town—presumably the 'Lower Ibrîm' mentioned in a number of texts. Yet wholesale restoration of the fortifications was probably meant to provide protection not only for eparchs and bishops but also for all the inhabitants of the community in the event of further military incursions. In short, Ibrîm in the Late Medieval period may perhaps be viewed as a kind of castle, permanently occupied only by its feudal lord and his retainers but available as a refuge to all those under his care. It would thus have justified the 'Qaṣr' which was later to be added to its name.

The storage function of the site evidently remained important and indeed may have increased in significance. Several of the Late Christian structures, both refurbished and newly built, were clearly meant for storage rather than as residences, and in addition pits were dug wherever open ground was available. The possibility exists that the inhabitants of the lower town retained the right to store their goods, perhaps in certain designated areas on the fortified hilltop, even though they could not maintain residences there.

The history of the hilltop community during its last mediaeval phase, the Terminal Christian period, is difficult to reconstruct. Only a very few of the Late

[1] See Adams, *Kush* 12 (1964), 222–39, and id., *Kush* 13 (1965), 148–76.

[2] See P. L. and Margaret Shinnie, *Debeira West* (Warminster, 1978).

[3] See Francisco Presedo Velo, *El poblado cristiano de la isla de Abkanarti* (Comité Español de la UNESCO para Nubia, Memorias de la Misión Arqueológica, 7) (Madrid, 1965).

Christian 1 and 2 dwellings show evidence of continued occupation during the last century of Nubian Christianity, and many were certainly abandoned, as perhaps were the Cathedral (293) and the South Church (294). However, three new buildings were erected during the Terminal Christian period, i.e. the massive vaulted structures of brick (169, 170, and 171) that occupied the Podium area, south and west of the Cathedral. To the extent that their plans can be reconstructed, they appear similar in design to two-storey brick buildings that were erected in many parts of Lower Nubia and the *Baṭn el-Hajjar* at about the same time, but at Qaṣr Ibrîm they mark a radical departure from earlier building traditions. Their surviving lower portions were certainly not residences and would seem to have been designed mainly to provide safe storage for goods. Any residential activity would necessarily have been confined to the upper storeys, as is specifically attested in the case of two-storey brick structures at Kulubnarti[4] and Dal.[5]

Since we have textual reference to the Eparchs of Nobadia at least as late as 1464, it seems reasonable to assume that the great brick structures of the fifteenth century were built at their behest and perhaps now became their main places of residence. At the same time the general abandonment of so many other dwellings might suggest that the eparchs were reserving the fortified hilltop more and more exclusively for their own use, and that it was beginning to assume the quasi-military function that became its dominant feature in the Ottoman period.

Paradoxically, while much of the archaeological and textual evidence from Qaṣr Ibrîm clearly bespeaks an élite centre, the character of the architecture does not. The irregular and sometimes almost flimsy quality of the stonework, even in some of the eparchal houses, has already been remarked (Part 2, Ch. 2). To our modern eyes it compares unfavourably with the brick architecture found in contemporary but less pretentious Nubian communities such as Meinarti[6] and Kulubnarti.[7] Even indoor toilet facilities were much less common at Ibrîm than at Meinarti.[8] It is noteworthy too that the eparchal residences—particularly 177 and 763—were not significantly larger or more pretentious than other dwellings of the same period. The cumulative evidence suggests that the dwelling, in and of itself, was not an important status symbol in late mediaeval Nubia. Status was perhaps proclaimed by residence on the mountaintop, rather than in the lower town, and not by the actual character of the dwelling itself.

Taking all of their characteristics into consideration, it seems that many of the Late Christian stone houses at Qaṣr Ibrîm were designed more for safe storage than for everyday living. This would account for the general absence of mastabas, fireplaces, and toilets, all of which are commonly found in late mediaeval houses elsewhere in Nubia. It can further be deduced that, in contrast to earlier times, there was no class of professional or of skilled stonemasons at Ibrîm in the Late Christian period. Not only were the houses somewhat irregularly built, but there was no use of cut stone for jambs, lintels, or sills, as was common in X-Group and Early Christian houses. The few cut-stone thresholds that were used were almost certainly robbed from earlier buildings. The rather clumsy repairs to the Cathedral (see Part 2, Ch. 4) are further evidence of the lack of skilled masons.

The Qaṣr Ibrîm churches seem to tell a story of the declining importance of Qaṣr Ibrîm as a religious centre in the late mediaeval period. Although the Cathedral may still have been used at times for special celebrations, such as the Feast of the Assumption, it was almost certainly in a state of considerable disrepair after the thirteenth century, with part of its north wall collapsed and at least part of its roof missing. The use of the adjoining South Church (294) in the Terminal Christian period is not clearly attested by the deposits found in it. The Temple-Church, or at least a part of it, seems to have remained in use until the end of the Christian period, and it may have been the principal church used by the few inhabitants who still resided on the mountaintop. For others, the little Cupola Church (839), half way down the mountain on its east side, may have been the designated place of worship for the ordinary folk of Ibrîm. It is of a distinctive, very late mediaeval type, and shares with many others of the same age the peculiarity of standing alone, at a considerable remove from the community.

It must be recalled again that the citadel remains at Qaṣr Ibrîm do not tell the full story of the late mediaeval community. There was also a settlement beside the riverbank, and it may have been here, rather than on the mountaintop, that the more ordinary folk lived, and that the typical activities of Nubian daily life were carried out.[9] Whether or not the remains of 'Lower Ibrîm'[10] would have resembled those within the citadel, or would have been more like other Nubian farming communities of the same period, will never be known.

[4] William Y. Adams, *Kulubnarti* I (Lexington, 1994), Ch. II.

[5] Author's unpublished field notes.

[6] See Adams, *Kush* 12 (1964), 222–39, and id., *Kush* 13 (1965), 148–76.

[7] See Adams, *Kulubnarti* I, Ch. II.

[8] Adams, *Kush* 13 (1965), 159.

[9] For evidence of pottery-making activity see Somers Clarke, *Christian Antiquities in the Nile Valley* (Oxford, 1912), 78–81.

[10] 'Lower Ibrîm' is specifically mentioned in one of the late mediaeval legal documents (74.1.30/6, no. 5) found on the site. See Gerald M. Browne, *Old Nubian Texts from Qaṣr Ibrîm* III (Egypt Exploration Society, Texts from Excavations) (London, in press).

PART 3
THE ARTIFACTUAL RECORD

CHAPTER 1
MATERIALS, INDUSTRIES, AND TECHNOLOGIES

The Late Christian 1 period was one of the most prosperous in Nubian history, to judge from the abundance and variety of its material remains. Peace with Egypt was quickly restored after the incursion of Shams ed-Dawla, and it was not seriously threatened again until the coming of Mamluk rule a hundred years later. In the meantime trade with Egypt continued to flourish, as it had in Fatimid times, under the supervision and encouragement of the Eparchs. The inhabitants of Qaṣr Ibrîm were especially favoured in the material sphere because the place was both a commercial entrepôt and a manufacturing centre. There is evidence of local industries in ceramics, weaving, basket-making, leatherwork, wood turning, and probably ironmongery. Imported manufactures included glass and glazed pottery, bronze work, silk and linen textiles, and various luxury items of wood, bone, and ivory.

In the Late Christian 2 period the picture began to change. Both Egypt and Nubia were impoverished by the political instability and military adventurism of the Mamluk era, and trade dropped off sharply. Conditions became still worse in the Terminal Christian period, after the breakup of the Kingdom of Makouria and its replacement by the shadowy Kingdom of Dotawo. By this time the predatory Beni Kanz had taken effective control of the most northerly parts of Nubia and also of the Aswân region, and their depredations were injurious alike to the Nile trade and the Red Sea trade.[1] By the fifteenth century hardly more than a trickle of goods was arriving from Egypt, and even local manufacturing declined sharply. In the last years of Nubian Christianity the country had reverted to something very close to a subsistence economy.[2]

In the chapters that follow, the material goods of late mediaeval Nubia will be considered primarily from a functional point of view, that is, in terms of what part they played in the life and activities of the community. In this introductory chapter, however, it seems desirable to take a more conventional archaeologist's approach and to talk about the different raw materials that were used and the ways in which they were worked. However, extended technological descriptions will not be given here, since they can be found in other, more purely technical works that will be cited at appropriate points in the text. Table 8 gives a comprehensive listing of materials and of the different kinds of objects made from them in the late mediaeval period.

Stonework

Mediaeval Nubia was several millennia removed from the Stone Age. Cutting tools and weapons were made of iron, and the art of flint knapping had long since been forgotten. The main continuing use of stone was as building material. Very little skill was exhibited in the construction of ordinary houses (cf. Part 2, Ch. 2), but ornamental elements such as columns, capitals, lintels, and jambs were another matter. Fragmentary decorative elements, adorned with crosses and various kinds of floral designs, have been found all over the site at Qaṣr Ibrîm, both in the churches and reused as building blocks in ordinary houses. Materials employed were either the pink granite of Aswân, or locally quarried sandstone. The rose-coloured sandstone which occurs naturally on the Qaṣr Ibrîm mountaintop was especially favoured for decorative elements. As previously noted, however, no decorative stonework can be attributed specifically to the Late Christian periods; it looks rather as if the art of skilled stonemasonry had died out by this time.

Apart from its use as building material, the main continuing use of stone was for grinding apparatus. The most common grinder was a rather large, shallow mortar which was used in conjunction with a small, spherical handstone. The preferred material for both mortars and handstones was black granite or some other hard, igneous rock, obtained from the Second Cataract area or from stream boulders in the desert wadis. A less common apparatus was the rotary quern (*rahaya*), made usually of sandstone. Local sandstone

[1] See William Y. Adams, *Nubia, Corridor to Africa* (London, 1977), 524–36.

[2] For discussion see op. cit., 521.

TABLE 8
CONSPECTUS OF LATE CHRISTIAN MATERIALS AND OBJECTS MADE THEREFROM
(* identifies materials and/or object categories that were often imported)

	STONE	
Fine-grained stone	**Sandstone**	
Grinders	Perforated weights	
Pounders	Stamps and seals	
Bowls*	Small discs and dice	
Hones	Architectural decorative elements	
Beads*		
	GOLD AND SILVER*	
	Rings	
	COPPER, BRONZE, AND BRASS	
Containers	**Tools and instruments**	**Ornamental**
Patera	Handle bindings	Pendant crosses
Bowls	Kohl sticks	Brooches
Spoons and ladles	Tweezers	Bracelets
	Thimbles	Rings
Coins		**Cult objects**
	IRON	
Cutting tools	**Other tools and instruments**	**Ornamental, etc.**
Knives	Bodkins	Pendant crosses
Saws	Needles*	Bracelets
Adzes	*Turiyas*	Rings
Sickles	Fishhooks	
Razors*	Handle bindings	**Miscellaneous**
	Buckles*	Nails
	Kohl sticks*	Arrowheads
	Tweezers	
	Problematical tools	
	CERAMICS	
Vessels	**Other utilitarian**	**Ornamental**
Pottery vessels and lids*	Tiles	Figurines
Lamps*	Spindle whorls	Pendant crosses
Censers	Stamps and seals	Pottery beads
Toilet fixtures	Sherd discs	Faience beads*
	UNFIRED MUD	
Somas	Loom weights	Figurines
Platters	Jar seals	
	GLASS*	
Bottles	Mirrors	Bracelets
Bowls	Coin weights	Beads
	WOOD	
Vessels and lids	**Miscellaneous implements**	**Toilet articles**
Troughs	Implement handles	Combs
Bowls	Awls	Mirror backings
Boxes*	Pulley wheels	
Buckets and barrels	Pegs and stakes	**Ornamental, etc.**
Lids and stoppers	Wedges	Hair pins
Spoons and ladles	Stamps and seals	Pendants
		Beads

TABLE 8 (*continued*)

	WOOD (cont.)	**Ornamental, etc. (cont.)**
Weaving implements	**Furnishings**	Figurines
Spindles and whorls	Furniture parts and knobs	Gaming pieces
Shuttles	Lock housings and bolts	Carved and painted tablets
Packing combs	Lock tumblers	Painted reeds
	Keys	Decorated gourds
Miscellaneous		Architectural elements
Saddles		
Arrows		
	TEXTILES	
Clothing*	Wall hangings	Potstands
Headgear*	Carpets*	Dolls
Bags		Balls
	BASKETRY AND COARSE FIBRE	
Basketry and matting	**Apparel, etc.**	**Unwoven fibre**
Baskets and lids	Sandals	Pot stands
Bags	Fans	Brooms and brushes
Sieves and strainers	Fly whisks	
Chair and bed webbing	Processional crosses	**Cordage**
Floor mats	Amulets	Rope and string
Straps	Wreaths	Sling (weapon)
	LEATHER AND SKIN	
Containers	**Apparel**	**Ornamental, etc.**
Waterskins	Garments and caps	Croziers
Bags	Boots and shoes	*Higabs*
Pouches and purses	Sandals	Necklaces
Sheaths for weapons		Book covers
Sieves	**Miscellaneous utilitarian**	Problematical decorated pieces
	Saddles and harness	
	Handles	**Material for writing***
	Straps	

BONE	**IVORY***	**HORN**	**SHELL**
Bracelets	Hair pins	Funnels	Spoons
Beads	Bracelets	Bracelets	Lamps
Rings	Gaming pieces	Rings	Beads
Turned handles			
Chest inlays			

PAPER*

was also used in small quantities for weights, stamps (for marking mud jar sealings), dice, and decorated gaming pieces. A few small fragments of carved stone vessels have been found in Late Christian deposits, but some of these are recognizably of pharaonic types, and they appear to have been accidentally redeposited from much earlier contexts. In pre-Christian times, semi-precious stones like carnelian and lapis lazuli were very much used for beads, pendants, and the like. However, it appears that in Christian times they gave way entirely to glass, and the lapidary art died out along with that of stonemasonry.

Nothing can be said with certainty about the tools and methods employed in stoneworking. The quarries on and near the Qaṣr Ibrîm mountain-top do not give evidence of very sophisticated quarrying techniques, and there are no impressions of wooden wedges such as were regularly used in Egypt. Iron tools and various abrasives would have been readily available for shaping the stone once it had been quarried.[3]

Soft metals

Two finger rings, one each of gold and of silver, were the only objects of precious metal found in the Late Christian deposits at Qaṣr Ibrîm. The general scarcity of precious metals suggests that these objects were imports from abroad. Lead has been found only in the form of small weights, attached to the edges of a fishing net.

Copper, bronze, and brass

The question of a local copper and bronze industry in Nubia is problematical. There are few good sources in copper anywhere in the area,[4] and tin would have been even harder to come by. Moreover, the number and variety of copper and bronze objects found at Qaṣr Ibrîm and other Nubian sites is not large. Probably the most common items are rather plain and simple finger rings. There are also small bowls of beaten bronze, and spoons, tweezers, and thin strips used as binding on implement handles. The general scarcity of these items, as well as the absence of readily available ores, suggests the probability that all of Nubia's copper and bronze was imported from Egypt during the mediaeval period. Brass made its first appearance at Qaṣr Ibrîm in the LC 1 period. It is represented mainly by two large and very fine ornamental bowls, which were almost certainly made abroad since they bear Arabic inscriptions (see Part 3, Chapter 3).

Iron

The famous iron works of Meroë have been much discussed, and lately also debated, in the archaeological literature.[5] It is a striking anomaly, however, that no direct evidence of iron working has been found at any other Nubian site, either of the Meroitic period or later.[6] Yet the abundance and variety of iron tools, taken together with the ready availability of ores, makes it a virtual certainty that there was local iron production in mediaeval Nubia.

At Qaṣr Ibrîm, iron ore would have been plentifully available from the ironstone layer which caps the nearby desert plateau. In the immediate vicinity of the site this has been systematically dug through with small holes (much too small for graves), which may be the result of mining activity. The smelting apparatus would presumably have been the tubular furnace of brick, with tuyères (forced-air intakes) at the base, which became general throughout the Nile Valley in Ptolemaic and Roman times.[7] Any iron smelting in the Qaṣr Ibrîm area would almost certainly have taken place on the Nile flood-plain rather than within the citadel, since large quantities of fuel as well as a certain amount of water would be required. All Nubian iron goods were forged rather than cast, for ancient and mediaeval furnaces would not produce temperatures high enough for casting.[8] There is no evidence of alloying to make steel.

Iron was the preferred metal for nearly all utilitarian purposes. The most common implements of iron found at Qaṣr Ibrîm were knives, sickles, needles, nails, arrowheads, and thin strips that would serve as binding on wooden furniture or on implement handles. Less common finds were *turiya* blades, fish hooks, buckles, and kohl sticks. The general absence of larger objects such as axes and chisels probably reflects only the fact that these items would be unlikely to be lost or abandoned.

Unfired mud

Apart from its use as building material, unfired mud from the Nile flood-plain was employed to make certain kinds of objects. The most common were *somas*; large, cylindrical storage vessels that might be up to 60 cm in diameter and up to 1 m in height. They were regularly used for the storage of grain, dates, and other perishables. *Somas* were made from Nile mud with a heavy admixture of dung. Other uses of mud were for loom weights and jar sealings, both of which employed a mixture of Nile mud and finer clays. Mud was also used to make small, rather crudely formed animal figurines, presumably for the amusement of children.

[3] For discussion of Egyptian stone-working techniques see A. Lucas and J. R. Harris, *Ancient Egyptian Materials and Industries,* 4th ed. (London, 1962), 50–74.

[4] For discussion see op. cit., 201–6.

[5] Trigger, *African Historical Studies,* 2 (1969), 23–50; Shinnie and Kense, *Meroitica* 6 (1982), 17–28; Tylecote, *Meroitica* 6 (1982), 29–42; Hermann Amborn, *Die Bedeutung der Kulturen des Niltals für die Eisenproduktion im Subsaharischen Afrika* (Frobenius-Institut, Studien zur Kulturkunde, 39) (Wiesbaden, 1976), 161–77.

[6] For discussion see especially Amborn, op. cit., 255–6.

[7] See Tylecote, op. cit., 35–41; Forbes in Charles Singer *et al., A History of Technology,* II (Oxford, 1956), 58–61.

[8] See Lucas and Harris, op. cit., 241.

Ceramics

Pottery was the most abundant and also the most elaborate of mediaeval Nubian manufactures. There were, in fact, two quite distinct industries, one producing hand-made and the other wheel-made wares. They are believed to represent, respectively, the output of female and of male potters.[9] Hand-made vessels were built up by moulding and were fired at rather low temperatures in open pits. Wheel-made vessels were thrown on a wooden kick-wheel, and, after appropriate drying in the sun, were fired in double-chamber updraught kilns. The technology of their manufacture is very well known, partly because several mediaeval kiln sites have been excavated[10] and partly because the industry survives in virtually unaltered form in Egypt today.[11] In Nubia, both the hand-made and the wheel-made wares were fashioned largely from Nile mud, although finer clays were generally employed in Egyptian pottery making. As a result the Nubian wares were technically inferior to those of Egypt, but they compensated for this deficiency by being much more consistently and more elaborately decorated.

It is presumed that hand-made pottery was locally produced by Nubian women all over the country, including at Qaṣr Ibrîm. There is also both direct and indirect evidence for the local production of wheel-made pottery. In 1912, Somers Clarke reported: '...south of the town...there are remains of a kiln and of masses of broken pottery, very much fine red ware with patterns in black...'[12] The reference is probably to the Late Christian decorated red and orange wares R17 and R11,[13] since very little decorated red pottery was made in earlier Nubian periods.[14] In addition, unfired vessels and kiln rejects have been found in the refuse deposits within the Qaṣr Ibrîm citadel itself.

To supplement their own ceramic products, the mediaeval Nubians regularly imported certain kinds of pottery vessels from Egypt. The most numerous and varied of these were the products of a factory at or near Aswân, whose output seems to have been destined largely for the Nubian trade. Aswân vessels were generally similar to those made in Nubia, but they were much more carelessly made and finished. They were nevertheless very popular at some periods (especially in LC 1 times), either because they were cheaper than the comparable local products or because they were made from better and harder clays.[15] There was also a considerable importation of brightly coloured glazed wares from Lower Egypt; these were apparently never produced either in Upper Egypt or in Nubia because of the absence of natron. Finally there were certain kinds of shipping containers, such as amphorae and pottery kegs, that were imported not for their own sakes but for the commodities they contained, such as wine, honey, oil, and salt.

Fired clay was used for a few other objects besides pottery vessels. These included sections of pipe, toilet fixtures, stamps (for marking mud jar sealings), discs made from ground-down potsherds, and occasional figurines.

Glass

One of the essential components in making glass is sodium carbonate, which occurs naturally in the form of natron. It is found throughout the limestone regions of Egypt but does not occur in sandstone-capped Nubia. For this reason it is assumed that there was no local glass industry, at least in the full sense of the term. The fairly common glass flasks found at Qaṣr Ibrîm are all of familiar Egyptian types and can be confidently identified as imports. The same is almost certainly true of the occasional mirrors.

Beads may possibly be another story. The finding of small lumps of brightly coloured glass, both at Qaṣr Ibrîm and at Meinarti, suggests that glass may have been imported in ingot form, for fashioning locally into beads. Glass beads were relatively common in the Late Christian levels at Qaṣr Ibrîm. A few are multi-coloured, but they display none of the decorative elaborateness seen in Meroitic and X-Group beads.[16] The various technologies of bead-making have been well described by Lucas[17] and need not be repeated here.

Wood

In mediaeval Nubia, as in most of the pre-industrial world, wood was the most versatile and most widely

[9] For extended discussion see William Y. Adams, *Ceramic Industries of Medieval Nubia,* Part I (Memoirs of the UNESCO Archaeological Survey of Sudanese Nubia, 1) (Lexington, 1986), Ch. 2 and Ch. 4.

[10] See op. cit., Ch. 3.

[11] See, among many other sources, Winifred Blackman, *The Fellahin of Upper Egypt* (London, 1927), 135–53, and Butzer, *Journal of Near Eastern Studies,* 33 (1974), 377–82.

[12] Somers Clarke, *Christian Antiquities in the Nile Valley* (Oxford, 1912), 79–81.

[13] See Adams, *Ceramic Industries*, Part II, 501–5.

[14] See op. cit., Part I, Ch. 11.

[15] For discussion of the Aswân wares see op. cit., Part II, Ch. 16.

[16] See especially C. Leonard Woolley and D. Randall-MacIver, *Karanòg, the Romano-Nubian Cemetery* (Eckley B. Coxe Junior Expedition to Nubia, vols. 3–4) (Philadelphia, 1910), 74–7 and pl. 40.

[17] Lucas and Harris, op. cit., 46–7.

used of all structural materials. Although wooden items are well preserved in the dry conditions at Qaṣr Ibrîm, it is usually only smaller items that are found. Evidently larger wooden elements, such as furniture and loom parts, were regularly recycled into smaller ones, or else burned for fuel, after they had served their original purposes. Therefore the items that have been recovered, numerous and varied though they are, cannot be taken as fully representative of the original inventory of woodwork.

The two ubiquitous trees in the Nile Valley are the wild-growing acacia (*Acacia spp.*), or *sunt,* and the cultivated date palm (*Phoenix dactylifera*). However, the very soft and fibrous wood of the date palm is practically useless for making any kind of implements or furniture, and it is evident that the great majority of Nubian wooden objects were made from the hard and fine-grained wood of the acacia. Other woods that might occasionally have been used were those of the sycamore (*Ficus sycamorus*), the tamarisk (*Tamarindus indica*), and the dom palm (*Hyphaene thebaica*).[18] Ebony from the southern Sudan was employed in a few luxury items such as combs, turned wooden boxes, and the fancier spindle whorls.

Wood was fashioned in three ways: by turning, by sawing, and by hewing with an axe, adze, or chisel. Hewn items were most numerous and varied; they included such things as implement handles, awls, spindles, shuttles, pegs and stakes, keys, stamps, and certain kinds of ornaments. After their initial shaping most items were given a smooth finish, probably by rubbing them with a piece of sandstone. Sawn items included large boards used in doors and furniture, smaller boards used to make boxes and buckets, wedges, and lock tumblers. Many of these items were also finished by sanding.

We do not know what kind of lathe was in use,[19] but the abundance and variety of turned goods at Qaṣr Ibrîm suggests the probability of local production. Included were wooden bowls, small boxes and lids, various kinds of furniture elements, spindle whorls, some of the fancier implement handles, bottle stoppers, pulley wheels, decorative hair pins, and gaming pieces which look very much like modern chess pawns. Composite items of wood included beds and chairs, saddles, and buckets. From the surviving evidence, it does not appear that the joiner's art was very highly developed.

Leather

The presence of a local leather industry at Qaṣr Ibrîm can be inferred from the finding of numerous offcuts left over from the making of shoes and bags. Whether hides were locally tanned, or were imported from elsewhere and turned into finished goods, could not be determined. The principal skins employed were certainly those of cattle, sheep, and goats, but there might also have been some use of pigskin and of camel skin. The tanner's art was evidently highly developed, for many of the surviving items of leather are very soft and fine.

The principal use of leather was probably for footgear. There was, in addition, a considerable variety of leather bags, pouches, and sheaths. Strap leather was used for handles, decorative and functional binding on baskets, saddle and harness straps, and probably for various other purposes. Ornamental uses of leather were for tooled book covers, *higabs* (small pouches into which amuletic texts were sewn), and small braided crosses. Some of the important legal documents found at Qaṣr Ibrîm were written on soft sheepskin, which evidently took the place of parchment. The few pieces of true parchment that have been found are mostly fragments of religious manuscripts in Greek or Coptic; they were almost certainly produced in Egypt.

Textiles

At Qaṣr Ibrîm, woven goods were enormously numerous and varied at all periods of history. They are however preserved almost entirely in the form of torn-up rags, making recognition of the original garment form impossible in most cases. We can, on the other hand, be certain in regard to the materials and the techniques employed.

Textile manufacturing was probably Qaṣr Ibrîm's most important industry. Cotton, wool, and goat hair were locally spun and woven, as attested by the finding of cotton bolls and hanks of unwoven woolen yarn. Additional textiles of linen and silk were imported from Egypt and from further abroad. The variety of textiles found in the Late Christian levels is truly astonishing, exceeding that from any earlier period. Undoubtedly this reflects the very high development of textile manufacture and trade throughout the mediaeval Near East.[20]

Spinning was done on relatively small, straight wooden spindles, equipped with an iron hook at the upper end and a turned wooden whorl just below it. This type of spindle is normally employed by rotating it between the palms, then allowing it to drop from the hands and turn freely.[21] Spindles and spindle whorls are among the commonest of all small finds at Qaṣr Ibrîm from the Meroitic period onward.

[18] See op. cit., 442–8.

[19] See op. cit., 450, and Aldred in Singer *et al.*, op. cit., 232–3.

[20] See Stone, *Aramco World Magazine,* 38, no. 3 (1987), 2–5

[21] See Crowfoot in Charles Singer *et al., A History of Technology,* I (Oxford, 1954), 424–5.

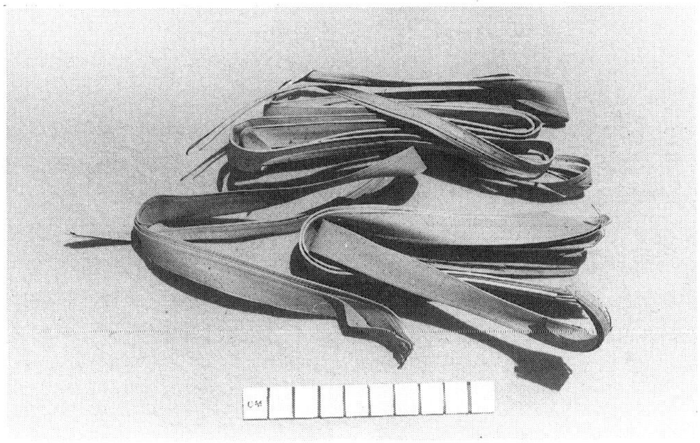

a

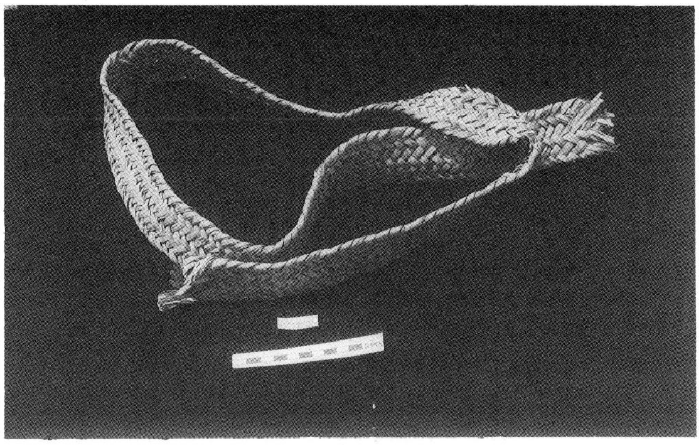

b

Plate 10. Basketry materials. a, Sections of split and folded palm leaf (82/499). b, A plaited basketry strip (82/119).

While the ancient Egyptians and the Meroitic Nubians both preferred undyed white fabrics for their clothing, with only a limited amount of decoration, the mediaeval Nubian textiles were often dyed in a variety of bright colours. The most common colours were blue and brown, but red, yellow, and green were also employed. Dyes that have been identified include madder (red and pink), weld and Persian berries (yellow), indigotin (blue), and tannin (brown).[22]

In mediaeval Nubian textiles, coloured designs were obtained by employing previously dyed yarns in the warp and weft. The most popular designs were simple stripes and checks. Some imported Islamic textiles had block printed designs, but this technique was not employed by the local weavers. Embroidery, which was a very common form of coloured decoration in the pre-Christian period, was very little used in mediaeval times. So-called Coptic textiles, with elaborate tapestry-woven panels and roundels executed on a plain linen background,[23] have almost never been found in Nubia.

Evidence in regard to the loom is necessarily inferential, for no actual loom parts have been found in Late Christian contexts at Qaṣr Ibrîm. However, the abundance of spindles and of spindle whorls leaves no doubt that much weaving was done locally. X-Group and Early Christian levels have produced a great many tear-drop shaped loom weights of mud, and from these it can be inferred that the upright, warp-weighted loom was in use.[24] However, only one loom weight has been found in a Late Christian context, and it seems probable that some other kind of loom was now preferred. Other weaving implements that have come to light in earlier levels include short wooden shuttles with tapered ends, and heavy combs for tamping the weft down or up. Long wooden rods with traces of yarn wrapping may have been heddles.

The mediaeval Nubian weavers employed either plain one-over-one or tapestry weaving techniques. A few specimens exhibiting twill weaving were probably imported. Woven cloth, both locally made and imported, was cut and sewn into tailored clothing, as attested by the finding of offcuts not only of local fabrics, but also of silk. Cloth was also used for various kinds of bags, bedding, and possibly for wall and door hangings. Three fragments of knotted carpet, almost certainly of Near Eastern origin, has been found. Rags of discarded garments were used to make pot-stands, dolls, and balls which may have been playthings for children.

Basketry and cordage

The date palm and the dom palm, while practically useless for structural wood, produced virtually everything that was needed for making basketry and cordage. The tough and pliant leaves, split into strips of suitable width, provided the basic material for plaited baskets and mats, and also the wrapping for coiled baskets (pl. 10a). Fibres from the long, woody fruit stem often provided the foundation bundle for coiled basketry. The loose, stringy outer fibres of the palm trunk were the basic material for making all kinds of rope. Apart from the various components of the date palm and dom palm, about the only other material that was employed for basketry or matting was the tall halfa grass that grows everywhere along the Nile flood-plain. Gathered into bundles, it was then plaited or twined into thick, soft mats that were often used for roof covering, and possibly for sleeping mats.

[22] Identified by George W. Taylor of the Conservation Laboratory, York Archaeological Trust for Excavations and Research, Ltd.

[23] Cf. Klaus Wessel, *Coptic Art* (New York, 1965), 181–233.

[24] See Crowfoot, op. cit., 427–8.

The mediaeval Nubians had a variety of baskets, mats, and trays, made both by the coiling and by the plaiting techniques. The presence of a local industry at Qaṣr Ibrîm is attested by the finding of wooden awls and of bundles of split palm leaves that were ready for weaving (see pl. 10a). Whether basket-making was commercially important or was merely a household craft is uncertain.

Basket-making is one of the very few mediaeval Nubian crafts that has survived almost intact down to modern times, and this has permitted a detailed ethnoarchaeological study of the techniques involved. In the present day some kinds of baskets are regularly made by men, others by women, and still others by both sexes. It has also been found that some kinds of baskets are made nearly everywhere, while others are important commercial items, widely traded from a few centres.[25]

The most common basket-making technique was that of plaiting, which is essentially simple over-and-under weaving[26] Sections of palm leaf were plaited into long rectangular strips, from 3 to 20 cm wide (pl. 10b), and these were then sewn together at the edges to make flat mats and various kinds of carrying and storage baskets. Sandals and certain kinds of bags were also made by plaiting. Decoration was occasionally achieved by weaving together previously dyed leaves of black, red, and natural colour to produce intricate geometric designs.

In the coiling technique, one end of a bundle of stiff, woody foundation fibres was tightly bound around with a wrapping of split palm leaf. The flexible bundle was then itself wound into a tight coil, held together because the spiral wrapping on each section of coil was stitched through the wrapping of the adjoining coils.[27] Decoration was sometimes achieved by varying the pattern of wrapping and stitching, and sometimes by using alternate sections of coloured and undyed wrapping. The most common decorative colour was black, but brown and red wrapping may also have been used. Strips of fine leather were sometimes also introduced into the wrapping, especially at the centres and at the edges of baskets, for decorative effect. The most common coiled items were flat jar covers, but small conical, cylindrical, and even square baskets were also made by coiling.

Twining is a basketry technique in which rigid elements such as withes or canes are bound together by weaving flexible elements around and through them.[28] A few twined trays and sandals have been found in the pre-Christian levels at Qaṣr Ibrîm, but twined items from the Late Christian period are restricted to a few simple mats.

Cordage had, as everywhere, a wide variety of uses. Fine string was spun mostly from cotton, but the preferred material for all heavier cordage was palm fibre. Scraps of rope of various sizes were found throughout the Late Christian deposits at Qaṣr Ibrîm. They were occasionally unplied, but much more commonly were two-plied.

Horn, bone, ivory, and shell

Horn, bone, ivory, and shell were used only to a very limited extent, and almost entirely for decoration. Large cross-sections of cow horn were cut and smoothed into bracelets, and smaller ones into finger rings. Finger rings were also cut from sections of animal bone. Both bone and ivory were lathe-turned into small decorative elements that look like gaming pieces of some sort. They were also cut into small strips or plaques, adorned with carved designs, that were probably attached as inlays to chests or other furniture. Cowrie shells, drilled through for suspension, were popular as beads. The scarcity of all these items suggests that they were not locally manufactured at Qaṣr Ibrîm.

Writing materials and technology

The basic writing material of pre-Christian and Early Christian Nubia was papyrus, but by Late Christian times this had given way entirely to paper. Among several thousand whole and fragmentary texts from Late and Terminal Christian contexts, fewer than 100 are on any material other than paper, and only five (all in Coptic) are on papyrus. The main exceptions to the use of paper are religious texts, which are often on parchment,[29] and legal documents which were sometimes executed on soft skins. The former are largely in Greek and Coptic, the latter entirely in Old Nubian.

The source of Nubia's paper has not been identified, but it was almost certainly not local. However, paper-making was apparently widespread throughout the Arab domains by the ninth century,[30] and it was probably from one or more of these sources that paper came to Nubia. That it was a scarce and precious commodity is attested by the regularity with which scraps of

[25] See Driskell in *American Research Center in Egypt Newsletter*, no. 134 (1986), 20–2.

[26] For the technology see J. M. Adovasio, *Basketry Technology* (Chicago, 1977), 99–123.

[27] For the technology see op. cit., 53–98.

[28] For the technology see op. cit., 14–52.

[29] For an interesting discussion of the relationship between parchment and early Christianity see Harold I. Innis, *Empire and Communications* (Toronto, 1972), 116–40.

[30] *Encyclopaedia Britannica*, 14th ed. (Chicago, 1958), 17, 229.

paper were reused, if there was any blank space left on them. This phenomenon accounts for the very large number of seemingly bilingual texts, in Arabic and Old Nubian. In the great majority of cases there is really no connection between the two texts; they simply represent a reuse of available paper. No actual writing instruments have been found in Late Christian deposits, but pointed pens made from reeds have been found in the overlying Ottoman levels. Ink was presumably made from soot, as it still is in Egyptian and Nubian villages today.[31]

[31] Cf. J. Spencer Trimingham, *Islam in the Sudan* (London, 1949), 117.

CHAPTER 2
AGRICULTURE, ANIMAL HUSBANDRY, AND FOODS

THE excavation of village sites usually provides little information about farming and livestock practices, since these activities were carried out at some remove from the communities themselves. This is particularly true in the case of Qaṣr Ibrîm, which was not really a farming community. The inhabitants were the provincial élite of Lower Nubia: the merchants, artisans, clerics, and administrators, though many were probably landholders as well. The excavations have, in any case, yielded only a very few artifacts that can be related to food production activities. On the other hand, the dry conditions at the site have resulted in the preservation of many traces of the actual foods that were consumed. Household artifact finds also give evidence of how foods were prepared and stored.

Agriculture and plant foods

Agricultural implements

Farming implements are represented only by a single small iron *turiya* (pl. 11a) and by small, curved iron blades which may have been either sickles or saws (pl. 11b).[1] In addition, irrigation by means of the *saqia* is attested by the finding of a good many fragmentary and one complete *qadus* (*saqia* pots) in the domestic refuse.[2] This does not mean of course that irrigation was actually carried out on the mountain-top, but rather that cracked and misshapen *qadus* were occasionally put to secondary use as storage vessels.

Plant food remains

Plant food remains are found primarily in the form of residual deposits that were left in the bottom of storage pits; occasional deposits of seeds are also found in the domestic refuse layers. In addition, barley and sorghum chaff forms a substantial part of the midden deposit everywhere on the site. On the basis of this evidence we can identify several different grains that were grown in late mediaeval Nubia. Then, as now, sorghum was the single most important food crop. The two races *Sorghum bicolor bicolor*, race *durra*, and *Sorghum bicolor bicolor*, race *bicolor*, are about equally well represented in the late mediaeval deposits, although there is some evidence that *durra* was gradually supplanting *bicolor* in importance. Only slightly less important was hulled barley (*Hordeum vulgare*). Wheats were apparently less important in the diet, although at least two species were cultivated: a free-threshing tetraploid wheat similar to durum wheat (*Triticum cf durum*) and a hexaploid similar to bread wheat (*Triticum cf aestivum*). Also of lesser importance were common millet (*Panicum miliaceum*) and bulrush millet (*Pennisetum typhoides*).

Pulses also contributed significantly to the mediaeval as to the modern Nubian diet. The most important was the termis bean (*Lupinus albus*), but peas (*Pisum sativum*), lentils (*Lens culinaris*), and cowpeas (*Vigna unguiculata*) have also been identified among the Qaṣr Ibrîm food remains. Sesame (*Sesamum indicum*) and the castor bean (*Ricinus communis*) were both probably major sources of oil. Other food crops that have been identified in the Qaṣr Ibrîm deposits include a cucurbit, probably cucumber (*Cucumis cf sativus*), water-melons (*Citrullus lanatus*), onions (*Allium cepa*), and garlic (*Allium sativum*).[3]

Imported commodities

The importation of various exotic foodstuffs and beverages is attested by the finding of distinctive, Egyptian-made pottery vessels in which these commodities were shipped. We know from this evidence that wine was imported in enormous quantities in pagan and Early Christian times, both from Upper and from Lower Egypt.[4] There is evidence also for the importation of honey, oils, and salt.[5] By contrast, the volume of exotic shipping vessels occurring in Late Christian

[1] For parallel examples that have been identified as saws see W. M. Flinders Petrie, *Tools and Weapons* (London, 1917), pl. L. For an example from Nubia that has been identified as a sickle see A. J. Mills, *The Cemeteries of Qaṣr Ibrîm* (Egypt Exploration Society, Excavation Memoir 51) (London, 1982), pl. LXXXVI, no. 5.

[2] See William Y. Adams, *Ceramic Industries of Medieval Nubia,* Part I (Memoirs of the UNESCO Archaeological Survey of Sudanese Nubia, I) (Lexington, 1986), 105. For fuller discussion of *qadus* (pl. *qawadis*) and their use see H. E. Winlock and W. E. Crum, *The Monastery of Epiphanius at Thebes,* Part I (New York, 1926), 64–5 and pls. XVII, C; XVIII.

[3] For an excellent discussion of foods consumed in a mediaeval Egyptian monastery see Winlock and Crum, op. cit., 144–9; for agricultural practices see op. cit., 160–3.

[4] See William Y. Adams, *Nubia, Corridor to Africa* (London, 1977), 362–4, 418, 452.

[5] Op. cit., 137.

deposits is relatively small. Importation of amphorae—the principal wine containers of earlier times—had apparently ceased altogether. The only containers that might have served for the importation of wine were curious keg-like vessels of Ware U12,[6] that were apparently made at the Middle Egyptian site of Ballas[7] (pl. 18d). They are found in fairly considerable numbers in the Late Christian 1 deposits, comprising 7% of the total sherd complex, but diminish to only 2% of the sherd complex in the Late Christian 2 and Terminal Christian periods. The possibility that these vessels originally contained wine is suggested by the presence of inked graffiti on the shoulders, which may have identified the vintage. On the other hand the interiors are not resinated, in contrast to the wine amphorae of all earlier periods.

Animal husbandry and animal foods

Artifactual remains

The only registered artifacts which may relate in any way to animal husbandry are three apparent pieces of saddles and one apparent piece of a bridle. The saddle fragments, if such they are, are rather stout, curved pieces of wood covered in leather, which in one case is tooled. This suggests a riding rather than a pack saddle, but the pieces are too small to permit any reconstruction of original shapes.

A stoutly woven band of goat hair, 9 cm wide and 24 cm long (pl. 11c), is probably a fragment of a saddle girth. At the unbroken end it terminates in a stout loop made of twisted leather thong; presumably there was another such loop at the other end. The woven band is brown in colour, but has two decorative stripes in white. A shorter fragment of another girth is somewhat more colourful.[8]

Plate 11d shows some pieces of highly ornamental leather strapwork that are probably parts of a bridle. At least some of the many other fragments of leather strap and of goat hair and palm-fibre rope found at Qaṣr Ibrîm are probably parts of bridles, harnesses, or animal leads, and some of the numerous wooden pegs and stakes were probably for tethering (for descriptions see Part 3, Chapter 4).

Dung

Sheep and goat dung is ubiquitous in the Late Christian, as in all earlier deposits at Qaṣr Ibrîm, and is found both in the streets and plazas and in the houses themselves. There can be little doubt that the animals were regularly kept within the citadel, and sometimes within the houses, as is common throughout the Near East today. Horse, donkey, and camel dung have also been found in street and plaza deposits, but we have not identified any structure of the Late Christian period that could have served as a stable or corral. Given their rather heavy water and feed requirements, it is unlikely that any of the larger domesticated animals were regularly kept on the mountain-top at Qaṣr Ibrîm. Their dung is probably the evidence of intermittent visits, when they brought up supplies from the valley below.

Animal bone

Animal bone was fairly abundant in the Late Christian deposits and included the bones of sheep, goats, pigs, cattle, horses, donkeys, and camels. Of these, sheep *(Ovis aries)* and goat *(Capra hircus)* bones are by far the most numerous. There can be little doubt that sheep, goats, pigs, and cattle were all eaten; the evidence in the case of the other species is less certain. However, the bones of all the different species were found disarticulated and widely scattered through the refuse, in the manner characteristic of kitchen refuse.

Fishing

Fishing activity in the Late Christian period is attested by two large, barbed iron fishhooks, very little different in design from those in use today (pl. 11e).[9] Also found was a fragment of cotton and flax netting, which may be part of a fish net (pl. 11f).[10]

Food preparation and storage

Methods of food preparation and storage are suggested both by artifactual and by architectural finds.

Milling apparatus

By far the most common artifacts relating to food preparation, in all levels at Qaṣr Ibrîm, are the heavy

[6] Adams, *Ceramic Industries*, Part I, 107.

[7] Op. cit., Part II, 574–5.

[8] For details on weaving techniques employed in the girths see Part 3, Chapter 6.

[9] For contemporary parallels see Donald S. Whitcomb and Janet H. Johnson, *Quseir al-Qadim 1978: Preliminary Report* (Cairo, 1979), pl. 69, v-x and aa-bb. For parallels from various other parts of the ancient world see Petrie, *Tools and Weapons*, pls. XLIII–XLIV.

[10] For a parallel see Winlock and Crum, op. cit., 71 and pl. XXII, b.

a

b

c

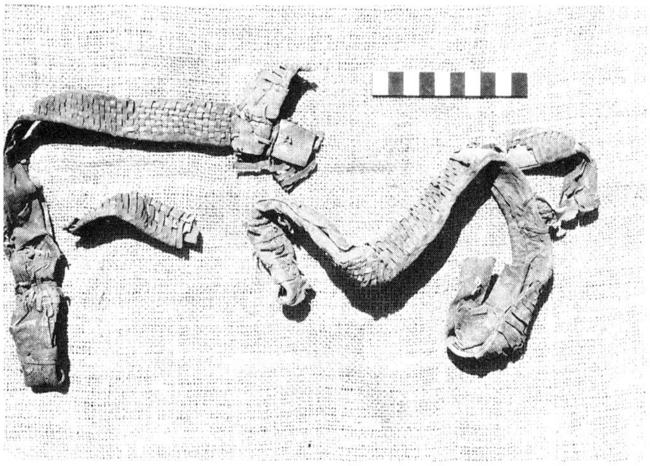

d

e

f

Plate 11. Objects associated with agriculture and food production. a, Iron *turiya* blade (76.2.29/8). b, Iron sickle blades (78.2.2/146, 82/316). c, Fragment of saddle girth (84.1.7/8). d, Fragments of decorated leather bridle (66A/376). e, Iron fishhook and section of heavy line (78/21). f, Fragment of fishnet (78.2.26/31).

stone mortars and associated pounding stones employed in the grinding of grain. The mortar is usually a large, flattish, water-worn cobble of granite or some other igneous material, that has had a shallow concavity pecked into its upper surface. Other than this the natural shape of the cobble is usually unmodified, and, therefore, sometimes quite irregular. The maximum exterior diameter of the stone is usually about 40 cm, while the diameter of the grinding concavity is about 25 cm, with a depth of 5–10 cm. The 'pestle' used in conjunction with the mortar was most commonly a perfectly spherical granite ball, about 7 cm in diameter. A great many of these were found in the fill of House 849, along with a mortar which was let into the floor. Some of the handstones have a more elongate form, and one is in the shape of a tapered cylinder.

An alternate method of grinding grain was by means of the rotary sandstone quern *(rahaya)*, having a fixed lower disc and a revolving upper disc, both about 40 cm in diameter (pl. 12a).[11] Parts of three of querns were found in House 849, and small fragments of others were unearthed elsewhere in the Late Christian deposits.

Sieves and strainers

Two fairly well preserved conical basketry strainers were found, measuring respectively 9 cm and 12 cm in diameter (pl. 12b). It is possible that these were used in the making of *merissa* beer. More problematical are two fragmentary items that may be parts of fine meshwork sieves. One is woven from fine strips of leather, forming a mesh of about 2 mm. The meshwork is attached to a curved, plaited leather rim. The surviving segment of rim suggests that the original sieve was round and had a diameter of about 36 cm. Another fragment of meshwork, woven from horsehair, measures about 18 × 20 cm, and has a mesh of about 1.2 mm. No part of the rim survives to indicate the original shape.

Funnels

Funnels were made from the cut-off ends of cow horn, and usually measured about 9 cm in length. Only two of these were found in the Late Christian deposits.

Spoons and ladles

Simple spoons were carved from acacia wood, as shown in plate 12c.[12] The typical length was about 15 cm overall. A much larger wooden specimen, of which only the bowl survives, was probably a ladle. Nile mussel shells were sometimes also used as spoons, the only modification being a slight rounding off of one end.

Cooking vessels

Cooking was apparently carried on almost entirely in pottery vessels; there is no evidence for the use of iron. Cooking pots were mostly more or less hemispherical in shape, with diameters ranging from 16 to 32 cm. The great majority of the vessels were hand-made, but there were also a few much finer pots of imported Aswân Ware (Ware U6).[13] These vessels will be more fully described in the next chapter. In addition to pots, flat earthenware griddles *(dokas)* were used for the baking of *durra* bread, as they are today throughout the Sudan.[14] Fragments of *dokas* were abundant among the ceramic refuse, but no complete specimens were found, and their precise shape is uncertain. The Late Christian deposits included also a single very small copper *patera* (pl. 12d), whose use in cooking is uncertain.

Fireplaces

Fireplaces were by no means a regular feature of the Late Christian houses; they were in fact found only in Houses 172 and 849. In each of these cases, however, the fireplace was very small, and was more probably intended for warmth than for cooking. The absence of ash deposits in the houses is also remarkable. It seems very probable, therefore, that the great majority of cooking in Late Christian times was done out of doors. It should be recalled, however, that in many cases we have recovered only the lower floors of what were originally two-storey houses (cf. Part 2, Ch. 2). The possibility thus exists that cooking was done on the now destroyed upper floors.

Storage

As we saw in Part 2, Chapter 3, Qaṣr Ibrîm was an important regional storage centre, because of the protection that it provided both from marauders and from moisture. Food surpluses were stored all over the site in a variety of circumstances and containers. The various kinds of Late Christian storage structures have already been described in Part 2, Chapter 3. Food for more immediate use was also stored within ordinary

[11] For contemporary parallels see Donald S. Whitcomb and Janet H. Johnson, *Quseir al-Qadim 1980: Preliminary Report* (Malibu, 1982). pl. 72, a–b.

[12] For parallel examples see Petrie, *Tools and Weapons*, pl. LXXIV, 85; id., *Objects of Daily Use* (London, 1927), pl. XXXIII.

[13] Adams, *Ceramic Industries*, Part II, 559–60.

[14] Op. cit., Part I, 104.

a

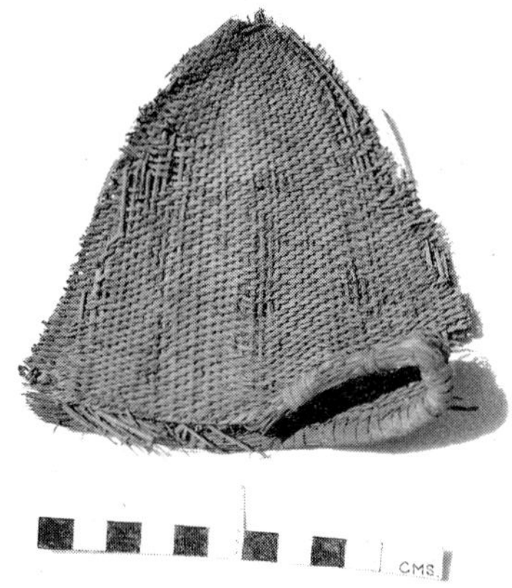

b

c

d

Plate 12. Food preparation and serving equipment. a, The upper, rotating element of a stone quern (*rahaya*) (82.3.4/120). b, A basketry strainer for beer (*merissa*) (78/107). c, A wooden spoon (72/82). d, A copper *patera* (64/19).

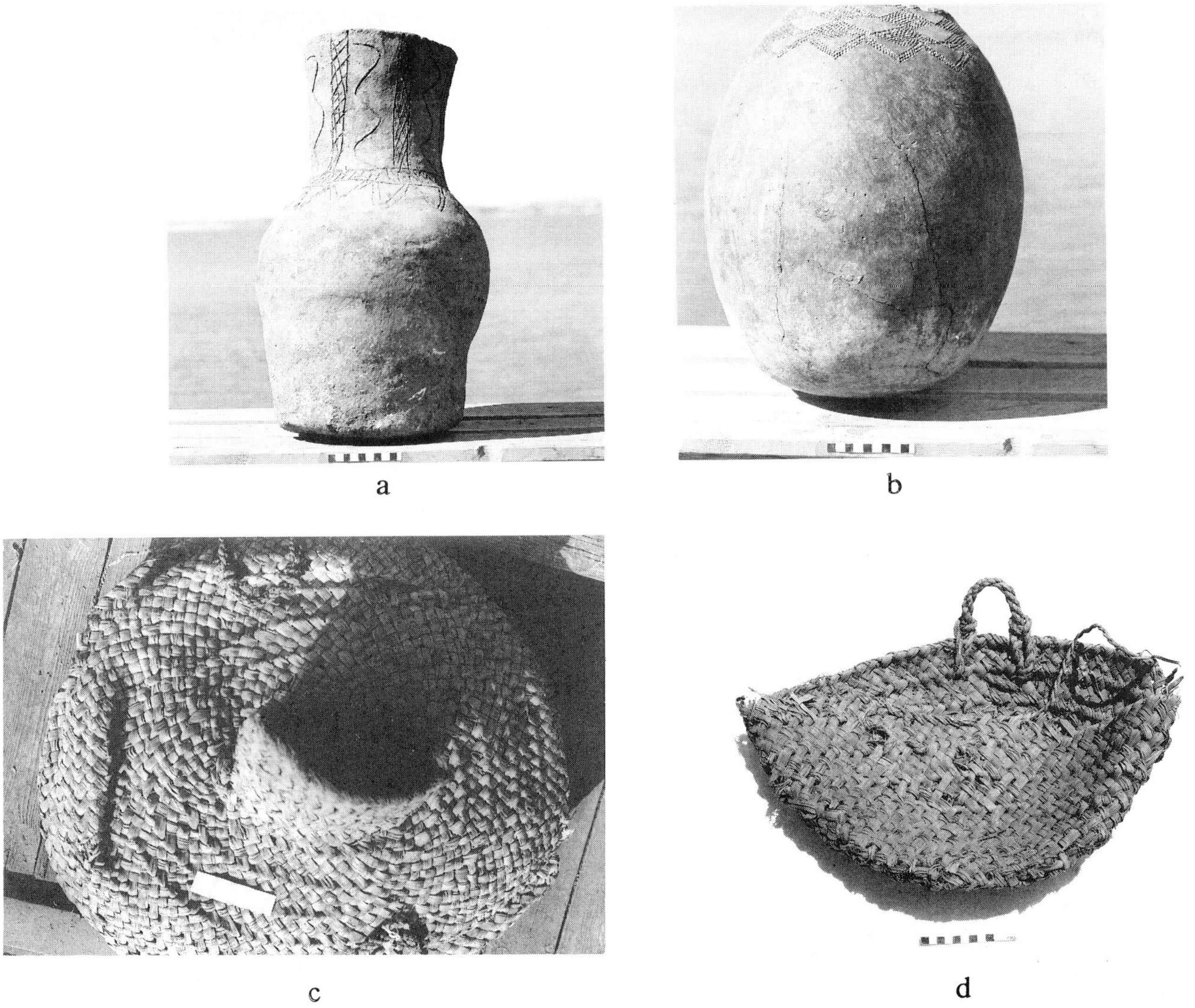

Plate 13. **Food storage facilities.** a, Large hand-made storage jar, Ware H4 (n/r). b, Large hand-made storage jar, Ware H6 (72.11.1/7). c, Plaited bottle-shaped storage basket (72.2.21/10). d, Plaited carrying basket (*guffa*) (78/777).

houses. Among the common food containers were large unfired mud silos *(somas)* that were apparently used both for grain and for dates (pl. 3b).[15] Also employed were very large pottery jars of various shapes (pl. 13a, 13b), and very large, bottle-shaped baskets (pl. 13c). Not uncommonly, jars and baskets containing grain were buried under house floors. These containers will be more fully described in the following chapter.

[15] For further discussion see Winlock and Crum, op. cit., 51–3 and pls. XIII, XIV.

CHAPTER 3
CONTAINERS

THE importance of Qaṣr Ibrîm as a storage centre has already been remarked (Part 2, Ch. 3). It is not surprising, therefore, to find that containers of one sort and another are the most abundant of all artifactual remains on the site. More than 100 different kinds of containers were in use, made variously of stone, metal, pottery, glass, unfired mud, wood, leather, textiles, and basketry. In this chapter the different kinds of containers will be described according to the materials employed in their manufacture.

Stone

Six fragments of stone vessels were found in the Late Christian levels at Qaṣr Ibrîm: two of alabaster, one each of granite and of steatite, and two of unidentified material. Three of the six specimens belong to what are recognizably much earlier types, dating in two cases from the pharaonic era and in one case from the X-Group. Their presence in the Late Christian deposits is presumably due to accidental redeposition, and this may well be true of the other fragments as well. There is no convincing evidence for the making and use of stone vessels at Qaṣr Ibrîm or anywhere else in late mediaeval Nubia.

Pottery

Town-site excavations usually do not yield large numbers of whole pottery vessels. The 205 whole or restorable vessels that were found in the Late and Terminal Christian levels at Qaṣr Ibrîm were mostly stray individual finds, found in many cases buried under house floors. In a few cases the vessels had served as repositories for documents (pl. 14a). In only one instance were large numbers of vessels unearthed in a single deposit. The LC 2 House 849 had burned with most of its contents *in situ,* and almost 50 whole and restorable vessels were found in two of the ground-floor rooms (pl. 14b). However, information about pottery containers is afforded not only by whole vessels, but also by the much more numerous potsherds found in the same deposits. While whole pots give information about the various wares and vessel forms that were in use, the sherd counts give information about their relative frequencies (cf. table 9). The total number of sherds that were recovered, classified, and counted from the late mediaeval deposits was in excess of 20,000. Here the various wares and their frequencies will be discussed first, and specific vessel forms afterward.

It may be useful to recall at this point the chronological designations that are used throughout the present work. LC1 refers to the Late Christian I period (c. 1173–1300 AD); LC2 refers to the Late Christian II period (c. 1300–1400); TC refers to the Terminal Christian period (c. 1400–1500).

The major pottery families

Nearly all of the pottery used by the late mediaeval Nubians falls into five main categories or families:[1] Nubian wheel-made wares (Family N), Nubian hand-made wares (Family D), Aswân factory wares (Family A), Middle and Lower Egyptian factory wares (Family L), and Lower Egyptian glazed wares (Family G). These wares and their histories and characteristics have been discussed at length in W. Y. Adams, *Ceramic Industries of Medieval Nubia.*[2] Consideration will be given here only to their occurrence at Qaṣr Ibrîm:

Nubian wheel-made wares (Family N) comprised about 65% of the total sherd complex in the LC1 and LC2 periods, dropping to only 37% in the TC period. These wares were used for all kinds of large and small vessel forms, both utilitarian and decorative. Smaller forms, especially bowls and vases, were usually decorated in the rather elaborate Late Christian Styles N.VIA or N.VIB (pl. 14c), or in the simpler and bolder Terminal Christian Style N.VII (pl. 14d).[3] A few vessels of earlier manufacture, decorated in the Classic Christian Styles N.IV and N.V, also remained in use.[4] Large utility vessels were nearly always undecorated.

[1] For discussion of the system of pottery classification involving families, ware groups, and wares see William Y. Adams, *Ceramic Industries of Medieval Nubia* (Memoirs of the UNESCO Archaeological Survey of Sudanese Nubia, 1) (Lexington, 1986), Part I, 64–5.

[2] Op. cit.

[3] For descriptions and illustrations see op. cit., Part I, 249–51, 335–52.

[4] For descriptions and illustrations see op. cit., Part I, 245–9, 309–34.

a

b

c

d

Plate 14. Pottery vessels. a, Decorated jar containing documents, Ware R11 (64/22). b, Pots *in situ* on floor of House 849, Room 1. c, Decorated jar, Ware R11, Style N.VIa (64/22). d, Decorated bowl, Ware W14, Style N.VII (66A/36).

TABLE 9
PERCENTAGE DISTRIBUTION OF POTTERY FAMILIES AND WARE GROUPS IN LATE AND TERMINAL CHRISTIAN LEVELS AT QAṢR IBRÎM

	Percentages by period		
	LC 1	LC 2	TC
Family D: Hand-made wares			
Earlier ware groups	1.5		
Ware Group D.III: Later Christian hand-made wares	6.0	6.0	40.0
Total hand-made wares	7.5	6.0	40.0
Family N: Nubian wheel-made wares			
Earlier ware groups	3.0	2.5	2.0
Ware Group N.V: Post-Classic wares	2.5	t	t
Ware Group N.VI: Late Christian wares	5.0	6.0	4.0
Ware Group N.VII: Terminal Christian wares	t	6.5	3.5
Ware Group NU: Undecorated utility wares	44.0	49.0	25.0
Unidentified as to ware group	8.5	1.0	2.5
Total Nubian wheel-made wares	63.0	65.0	37.0
Family A: Aswân wares			
Earlier ware groups	2.0	1.5	1.5
Ware Group A.III: Early Islamic wares	1.5	1.0	t
Ware Group A.IV: Later Islamic wares	16.0	16.0	6.0
Unidentified as to ware group	0.5		0.5
Total Aswân wares	19.0	18.0	8.0
Family L: Middle and Lower Egyptian factory wares			
Ware U12: Ballas keg ware	7.0	2.0	2.0
Ware U13: Fostat *qulla* ware	1.0	4.0	5.5
Total Middle and Lower Egyptian factory wares	8.0	6.0	7.5
Family G: Lower Egyptian glazed wares			
Earlier glazes	0.5		
Group G.II: Later gloss wares	1.5	1.0	2.0
Group G.IV: Mamluk wares		2.0	5.0
Other glazes	0.5		
Total glazed wares	2.5	3.0	7.0
Unidentified wares		2.0	0.5
Totals	100.0%	100.0%	100.0%

t = trace

Nubian hand-made wares (Family D) comprised only 7% of the total sherd complex in the LC1 and LC2 periods, rising to no less than 40% in the TC period. The latter figure is not due entirely to an increase in hand-made pottery production; it reflects also a substantial decline in the production of wheel-made vessels, which were to disappear altogether after AD 1500. Hand-made vessels were overwhelmingly utilitarian, mostly cooking pots and jars (pl. 15a), with a few small and simple cups and bowls. They were usually rather crudely formed, with notably thick vessel walls. All but the largest vessels had either a red or a black slip, and burnished surfaces. In the Terminal Christian period many red vessels were decorated with geometric designs in black and white (Style D.III) (pl. 15b).[5]

[5] For description and illustrations see op. cit., Part I, 239–40, 264–9.

a

b

c

d

Plate 15. Pottery vessels. a, Hand-made cooking pot, Ware H4 (66.2.9/3). b, Decorated hand-made storage jar, Ware H7, Style D.III (76.2.14/6). c, Aswân-made cooking pot, Ware U6 (82.2.27/34). d, Fragments of decorated Aswân-made vase, Ware W12, Style A.IV (82/156).

Aswân wares (Family A) contributed importantly to the Nubian ceramic complex throughout the mediaeval period. In the LC1 and LC2 periods they comprised about 18% of the total sherd count, dropping to 8% in the TC period. Aswân wares were prized chiefly for their hardness, which exceeded that of any Nubian-made pottery. The most abundant of the Aswân wares in all the late mediaeval periods was a plain brownish utility ware (Ware U6), used almost entirely for cooking pots (pl. 15c).[6] However, in the LC1 period there were also considerable numbers of smaller forms such as bowls and vases, similar in general to the contemporary Nubian vessels and like them usually decorated, though in a rather casual style (Style A.IV) (pl. 15d).[7] These vessels virtually disappeared after about AD 1250.

Middle and Lower Egyptian factory wares (Family L). This group actually includes only two quite distinct wares, imported from different places and at different times. Ware U12, apparently made at Ballas in Middle Egypt, is found only in the form of distinctive pottery 'kegs' (pl. 18d).[8] These unusual vessels may have served for wine importation. They were fairly numerous in the LC1 period (7% of the total pottery complex) but much less so (2%) thereafter. Ware U13, apparently made in the Fostat area, was used only for *qullas* (filter-neck water jars), very similar to those still made at Fostat today.[9] Sherds of this ware comprised only 1% of the pottery complex in the LC1 period but increased to 4% in the LC2 and TC periods.

Glazed wares (Family G) seem to have come entirely from Lower Egypt, or still further abroad. The great majority were probably made at Fostat, a famous pottery manufacturing centre near modern Cairo.[10] The late mediaeval glazed wares fall into two main groups. Those of Group G.II are very fine and brightly coloured and were evidently made in imitation of Chinese porcelain. They generally have a very light-coloured fabric and decoration in blue and/or black on white.[11] The glazes of Group G.IV are much heavier and coarser, with a dark brown fabric and decoration in earth tones such as brown, yellow ochre, and brownish green (pl. 16a, 16b).[12] Glazes of both groups are sufficiently numerous to suggest that they were made in Egypt rather than further abroad. There were, in addition, a few sherds of more exotic glazed wares, made perhaps in Syria or Anatolia, and a few fragments of genuine Ming porcelain. Glazes altogether comprised about 3% of the total pottery complex in the LC1 and LC2 periods, increasing to 7% in the TC period.

The main form classes

The 205 registered vessels from the Late and Terminal Christian levels exhibit 103 different vessel forms belonging to 18 form classes, according to the system of form classification published by Adams in *Ceramic Industries*.[13] A tabulation of the number and percentage of vessels in each form class and in each of the major pottery families is given in table 10:

Cups and goblets (Classes A and B) were relatively rare and were equally divided between rather crude hand-made specimens and finer, usually decorated specimens in the Nubian wheel-made wares.

Plain bowls (Class C) were relatively common and occur in 14 different forms. The general absence of decoration on these vessels suggests a utilitarian function, presumably for food serving. The largest number of plain bowls are in the Nubian wheel-made group, but there are also several hand-made specimens and three bowls of Aswân ware.

Footed bowls (Class D) are the most common of all the Late Christian vessel-form classes, numbering 38 catalogued specimens and 18 different forms. The largest number of footed bowls are in the Nubian wheel-made wares and the glazed wares, though there are also some footed bowls in the Aswân group. Footed bowls nearly always have interior decoration, which in many cases is quite elaborate (pl. 16c, 16d), suggesting that their use may have been as much ornamental as utilitarian.

Vases (Class F) were another very common vessel form class in the later mediaeval period. At Qaṣr Ibrîm in the Late and Terminal Christian deposits they numbered 31 vessels in 9 different forms. These vessels are found almost entirely in the Nubian wheel-made family and generally have elaborate decoration (pl. 17a, 17b). Their function, if any, is unknown; they may have been primarily decorative.

Small pots (Class G) is a kind of catch-all designation for small, closed vessel forms of unknown use. There were 6 of these, in 5 different forms, in the Late Christian deposits. All of the different pottery families are represented among them.

[6] See op. cit., Part II, 556, 559–60.

[7] For description and illustrations see op. cit., Part I, 254–5, 371–6.

[8] See op. cit., Part II, 573–5.

[9] See op. cit., Part II, 576–8.

[10] See op. cit., Part II, 585–97.

[11] See op. cit., Part II, 592–4.

[12] See op. cit., Part II, 595–7.

[13] Op. cit., Part I, 101–7.

a

b

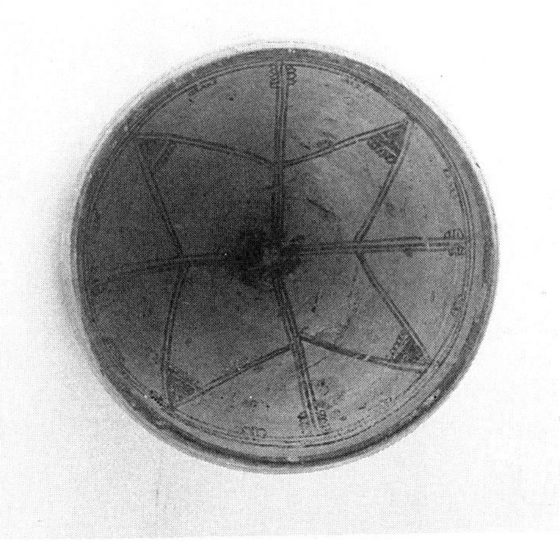

c

d

Plate 16. Decorated footed bowls. a, Glazed bowl, Ware G.IV, top view (64/30). b, Side view of **a**. c, Nubian-made bowl, Ware R11, Style N.VIa (64/28). d, Nubian-made bowl, Ware R11, Style N.VIa (82/148).

a

b

c

d

Plate 17. Nubian decorated vessels. a, Classic Christian vase, Ware R7, Style N.IVa (78/212). b, Late Christian vase, Ware R22, Style N.Va (66A/44). c, Terminal Christian pilgrim bottle, Ware R26, Style R26 (66A/34). d, Lid of unrecognized ware and style (80/649).

TABLE 10
DISTRIBUTION OF REGISTERED VESSELS BY FORM CLASS AND FAMILY

Form class	Family D	Family N	Family A	Family L	Family G	Totals	%*
A. Cups	4	3				7	3.4
B. Goblets			3			3	1.5
C. Bowls	6	10	3	1		20	9.7
D. Footed bowls	2	20	5		11	38	18.5
E. Plate				1		1	t
F. Vases		30			1	31	15.1
G. Small pots	3	2	1			6	2.9
I. Jugs		2	3			5	2.4
K. Pilgrim bottles		4	1			5	2.4
Q. Lids	2	5		1		8	3.9
T. Basin		1				1	t
U. Pots	26	2	5	1		34	16.6
V. *Qadus*	4	9	1			14	6.8
X. Footed jars			3			3	1.5
Y. Storage jars	9	13				22	10.7
Z. Amphorae		1	2			3	1.5
ZZ. Kegs				3		3	
Totals	56	101	28	8	12	205	
Percentages*	27.4	49.2	13.7	3.9	5.8		100.0

*Percentage of all registered pottery vessels
t = trace

Qullas, or filter-neck water bottles (Class H) are not represented by any whole specimens, but their presence is attested by distinctive and easily recognized sherds. The Egyptian-made utility Ware U13 was used almost entirely for *qullas,* and sherds of this ware were found in very considerable quantities, especially in the Terminal Christian level. Sherd finds indicate that there were also a few decorated *qullas* among the Nubian wheel-made wares.

Jugs and pilgrim bottles (Classes J and K) were uncommon in the Late and Terminal Christian periods; only 10 vessels were found in the two classes together. All but three of the specimens are in the Nubian wheel-made wares and have painted decoration in Style N.VIA or N.VII (pl. 17c). Two jugs and one pilgrim bottle are in the Aswân Ware U6 and are undecorated.

Lamps (Class P) will be discussed in part 3, Chapter 5, along with other household furnishings.

Lids (Class Q) of pottery were not numerous in the Late and Terminal Christian periods; the great majority of vessel covers were apparently of basketry. Of the 8 pottery lids that have been recovered, 2 are hand-made, 4 are in the Nubian wheel-made wares (pl. 17d), one is glazed, and one is unidentifiable as to ware.

Pots (Class U), used mainly for cooking, are among the most common of vessels and are represented by 16 different forms. Of the 34 cooking pots that have been registered, 26 are hand-made (pl. 18a), and another 5 are in the distinctive Aswân utility Ware U6 (pl. 18c). Since they were often used over a fire, pots very rarely had painted decoration, though several of the hand-made vessels bore simple incised or punched designs.

Jars (Class W) are vessels generally similar to pots but have a narrower mouth and frequently a neck. They were probably used mostly for holding and serving liquids. Fourteen jars were found in the Late and Terminal Christian levels in 9 different forms. The majority of jars are in the Nubian wheel-made wares and are undecorated, but there are also several hand-made specimens.

Storage jars (Class Y) are similar in form to the jars of Class W but are very much larger in size. They seem to have been used mainly for grain storage. These again are found almost entirely in the Nubian wheel-made (pl. 18b; see also pl. 14b, foreground) and the hand-made wares; the latter are usually decorated in Style D.III (pl. 15b).

a

b

c

d

Plate 18. Utility vessels. a, Hand-made cooking pots, Ware H4 (72.10.311 and 72.10.15/16). b, A large storage jar, Ware U10, with scratched graffito on the shoulder (66.3.7/2). c, An imported amphora of Aswân Ware U6 (78.2.18/6). d, Imported keg-like vessels from Ballas, possibly for wine.

Amphorae and kegs (Classes Z and ZZ) were extremely numerous in the pagan and Early Christian periods, but much less so from Classic Christian times onward. In the Late and Terminal Christian deposits at Qaṣr Ibrîm they are represented only by three amphorae (pl. 18c) and three kegs, all but one of which are Egyptian imports. It should be noted, however, that these very large and thin-walled vessel forms are not often preserved intact, and the best indication of their relative frequency is afforded by sherd counts. On this basis we can say that amphorae were indeed scarce, while kegs for a time were reasonably common. The Ballas utility Ware U12 was used almost entirely for kegs (pl. 18d), and sherds of this ware comprised no less than 7% of the total pottery complex in the LC 1 period, diminishing to 2% in the LC 2 and TC periods.

Unfired mud

The main use of unfired mud was for making large storage silos (*somas*). These were most commonly cylindrical in shape (pl. 3b); less commonly they were in the form of a tapered cylinder, and a few had rounded bottoms and sides like large jars.[14] They might be up to 60 cm in diameter, and up to one metre in height. *Somas* were only very occasionally buried in the ground; much more commonly they stood upright in the store rooms of houses. Vestigial food remains that have been found in them include grains, chickpeas (*hummus*), dates, and dom nuts.

In the X-Group and Early Christian periods, when wine importation was plentiful, mud was used extensively for the stoppering of amphorae and other jars containing liquids. In the Late Christian deposits no actual mud sealings have been found except for those on jars which contained documents (pl. 14a; see also Part 4, Chapter 1). Nevertheless, the Late Christian deposits have yielded a considerable number of stone, ceramic, and wooden stamp-seals that were evidently made to leave seal impressions on mud (see Part 3, Chapter 8), leaving no doubt that the use of mud for sealing was still a common practice.

Glass

Glass was not abundant in the Late Christian levels at Qaṣr Ibrîm, and evidently did not play a very important part in the community's material inventory. Surprisingly, the volume and variety of glass was less than that found in the Late Christian levels at Meinarti, a smaller and less important site.[15] All of the glass that has been recovered appears to be of Egyptian origin.

The LC1, LC2, and TC levels yielded 223 fragments of glass that were individually registered; 33 of these came from the single House 785. The fragments are nearly all very small, and in only 26 cases is it possible to hazard any kind of guess as to the original vessel form. Of the 26 identifiable pieces, by far the largest number (20) are fragments of small ointment or perfume flasks of well-known Egyptian types. Three main types seem to be present:

(a) vessels of a pale green colour, having a nearly square cross-section and straight sides. Two of these were found nearly intact (pl. 19b, 3);

(b) vessels of a dark blue colour, having a round cross-section and a somewhat tapered body form (pl. 19a, 4 and 5);

(c) vessels having an opaque black body with marvered decoration in white. The cross-section is nearly square, and the body tapers down to a pointed bottom (pl. 19a, 2).[16]

Apart from the small flasks, there appear to be five pieces of larger bottles, three bases of tumblers (pl. 19c, 2 and 4), and twelve pieces either of tumblers or of bowls. In none of these cases could the original vessel shape be precisely determined.

While we can say little about vessel forms, it is possible to be a bit more specific about the different glass fabrics that were employed. For the Christian period as a whole we have developed a descriptive typology involving 10 types and 34 varieties (that is, subtypes) of glass fabrics, but only 6 of the types and 22 of their varieties are represented in the later Christian deposits. Nearly 70% of all the Late Christian specimens belong to Type 5 (fine, monochrome glass), Type 6 (mould-blown glass with textured surface), and Type 7 (thick and coarse monochrome glass). A complete enumeration of the types and the numbers of their representatives is given in table 11. By far the most common colours are various shades of green, but shades of blue, yellow, pink, wine, brown, and black also occur, along with fully transparent glass. Decorative techniques include the use of trailed threads and marvering,[17] as

[14] For further discussion see H. E. Winlock and W. E. Crum, *The Monastery of Epiphanius at Thebes,* Part I (New York, 1926), 51–3 and pls. XIII, XIV.

[15] Author's unpublished excavation records.

[16] For other fragments of these see Donald S. Whitcomb and Janet H. Johnson, *Quseir al-Qadim 1980: Preliminary Report* (Malibu, 1982), pl. 58, cc, ee, mm–pp.

[17] Marvering is a technique in which a fine thread of molten glass, different in colour from the main vessel body, is trailed around the vessel body, then is rolled flat so that it forms a stripe of contrasting colour which does not alter the contours of the vessel surface. See Harden in Charles Singer *et al.* (eds.), *A History of Technology,* II (Oxford, 1956), 340.

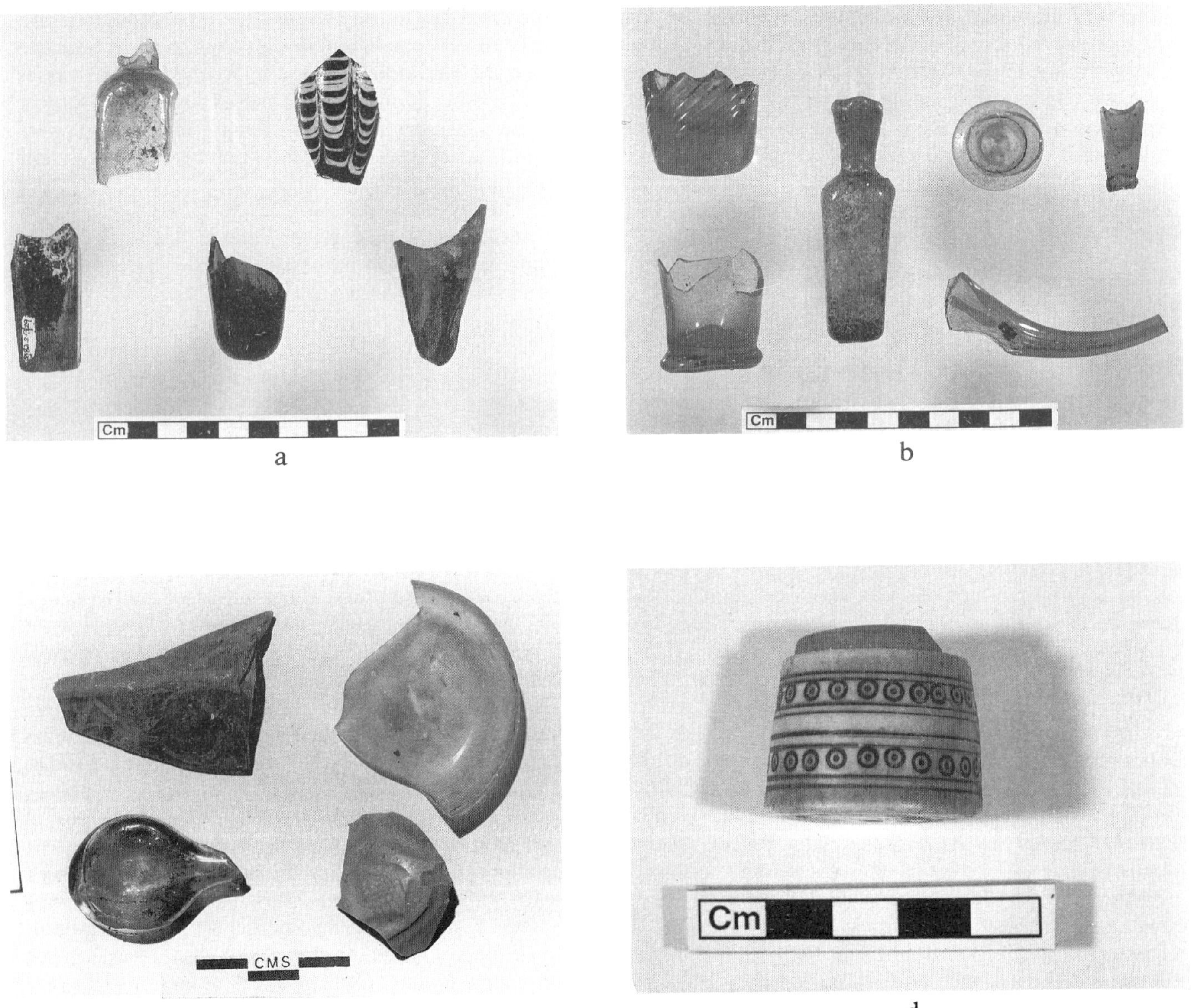

Plate 19. Glass vessel fragments; ivory box. a, Flask fragments (82/87). b, Flask and tumbler fragments (64/157, 82/87, 72.10.22/5, 72.11.2/4). c, Bowl fragments (right) (84.2.15/33). d, Miniature turned ivory box (69/24).

TABLE 11
GLASS TYPES FOUND IN LATE CHRISTIAN LEVELS AT QAṢR IBRÎM

Type and variety	Number of specimens
Type 1. Good quality clear glass with appliqué blue bands	
Var. 1. Blue band around rim	5
(Other varieties)	1
Total Type 1	6
Type 2. Opaque black or wine body with white trailed decoration	
Var. 1. Marvered white stripes combed vertically	6
Type 3. (Not found in Late Christian deposits)	
Type 4. (Not found in Late Christian deposits)	
Type 5. Fine, monochrome glass without moulded decoration	
Var. 1. Emerald green	8
Var. 2. Blue green	17
Var. 3 Transparent	7
Var. 4. (Not found in Late Christian deposits)	
Var. 5. Yellow-green	3
Var. 6. Pale green	13
(Other varieties)	5
Total Type 5	53
Type 6. Mould-blown surface patterning	
Var. 1. Oval or hexagonal indents	20
Var. 2. Vertical fluting	16
Var. 3. Diagonal or curving fluting	4
(Other varieties)	1
Total Type 6	41
Type 7. Monochrome, coarse textured glass with numerous bubbles	
Var. 1. Blue green	13
Var. 2. Pale green	26
Var. 3. Transparent	4
Var. 4. Amber	1
Var. 5. (Not found in Late Christian deposits)	
Var. 6. Dark green	14
(Other varieties)	2
Total Type 7	60
Type 8. Small, black opaque bottles	1
Types 9 and 10. (Not found in Late Christian deposits)	
Untyped specimens	56

well as various kinds of surface patterning produced by mould-blowing. No unmistakable examples of cut glass were found, and there is only one fragment with painted decoration, again in contrast to the findings from Meinarti.[18]

Metal

Vessels of copper, bronze and brass were evidently scarce and prized luxury items at Qaṣr Ibrîm, for only 11 whole and fragmentary specimens were found altogether in the Late and Terminal Christian levels. Their number did, however, include two of the most extraordinary vessels even found on the site. They are two large ornamental basins of brass, each measuring approximately 30 cm in diameter and 14 cm in depth (pl. 20). Each vessel has a flat, out-flared rim bearing a band of ornate, stamped decoration on its upper surface (pl. 20c, 20d). The decoration is divided into segments including *rinceau* (vine-wreath), *guilloche*, interlace, open flowers, prancing animals, and short segments of Cufic inscription. In addition to the rim designs, one basin also has a small roundel of floral decoration in the middle of the bottom, and the same vessel originally had three large bosses, sculptured like human faces, attached to the exterior (pl. 20a, 20b).

The two brass vessels were found, one inside the other, buried beneath the floor of House 178, a building which we have tentatively identified as an eparchal residence (see Part 2, Ch. 2).[19] Also found in the same building, although in the post-abandonment fill, was a smaller brass dish, essentially a shallow cylinder 10 cm in diameter and 2.5 cm in height. It also has a slightly everted flat rim but bears no decoration. From elsewhere on the site comes one additional, small fragment of a brass dish or pan, having a flat, everted rim decorated with rows of punched dots.

Other metal vessels were made of copper or bronze rather than of brass. Eight fragments have been found in the Late and Terminal Christian deposits, but the pieces are too small in all cases to permit a definite identification of the original form. One small bowl of bronze appears to have been embellished with vertical fluting on the vessel body, the result of hammering in a mould. No vessels or vessel fragments of iron were found.

[18] Author's unpublished excavation records.
[19] See Plumley in *JEA* 52 (1966), 13–14 and pl. XXI.

a

b

c

d

Plate 20. Brass vessels. a, Brass basin, side view (69/11). b, Same as **a**, bottom view. c, Brass basin, top view (69/12). d, Detail of rim decoration on **c**.

Wood

Containers of wood fall into three major categories, the first comprising carved or turned bowls and dishes, the second small, lathe-turned cylindrical boxes and lids, and the third buckets and/or barrels. Also described here, for want of a more suitable category, are roughly hewn wooden stoppers and a single small trough. Nearly all of the wooden containers found in the Late Christian levels are made of acacia wood.

Bowls and dishes

Fifteen fragments of wooden bowls and dishes were found in Late and Terminal Christian deposits. Most appear to have been lathe-turned and are well finished. Whether or not any kind of varnish was used is not clear. The most common shape is a simple hemisphere (pl. 21a, 1 and 3),[20] but at least two specimens had, in addition, a ring foot.[21] The largest bowl for which dimensions can be recovered had a diameter of 15 cm and a height of 7 cm. One small fragment of a cylindrical bowl retains traces of painted decoration in an elaborate floral frieze, and another fragment also has traces of paint. There is also a fragment of a shallow cylindrical dish having around the outside a carved zigzag frieze.

Unique among the wooden vessels found at Qaṣr Ibrîm is a very large wooden tripod dish, having a diameter of 38 cm and a height of 7 cm (pl. 21c, 21d). The body appears to be lathe-turned, with decorative incised grooves around the outside walls. Three stout, round feet were subsequently attached to the bottom by means of dowel pins. The vessel was evidently a prized possession, for it had at some time been broken and then was mended with two splints nailed across the lower surface (pl. 21c). Like so many other Late Christian luxury goods, it was found in one of the eparchal houses (House 177).

Turned boxes and lids

Small, cylindrical, lathe-turned boxes and lids of wood were relatively common in the Ottoman period (cf. pl. 21a, 2), but only one whole and two very fragmentary specimens were found in Late Christian levels. The complete specimen is a miniature toilet box, measuring just 4 cm in diameter and 2.5 cm in height. The sides as well as the lid have painted decoration in green and brown, and the lid is fitted on the underside with a tiny mirror (see pl. 34e). Late Christian levels also produced 19 other turned lids of wood, which might have been fitted either to boxes or to narrow-mouth pottery vessels. Some of the lids are merely flat discs, inset on the underside so as to fit snugly down into a vessel orifice; others have a central knob (pl. 21b, 21e).[22] The majority of lids measure between 3 and 7 cm in diameter; a couple have diameters slightly in excess of 10 cm.

Stoppers

In addition to fine turned wooden lids, the Late Christian levels also yielded a number of more roughly shaped wooden stoppers. These are more or less spherical or cylindrical knobs, having a cylindrical projection designed to fit down into the mouth of a bottle or small-mouth jar.

Buckets and/or barrels

A number of wooden pieces from the Late Christian levels are evidently fragments of small barrels or, more probably, buckets, formed of curved wooden staves fitted into a round base disc. In no case were any of the parts found in assembled form, but two bases and six fragmentary staves have been recovered. The two base pieces have diameters respectively of 12.5 and 15 cm. The six staves all measure between 2.5 and 4 cm in width, and the three longest have lengths of 18, 18, and 19 cm, though this does not appear in any case to be the full original length. The staves were not mortised into grooves in the base disc, as in modern barrels; they were fastened against the outer edge of the base by means of wooden dowel pins (fig. 22), which were found *in situ* in several of the staves and in one of the bases. Unstained areas on the outer surface of one of the staves show where the surrounding hoops had been fitted, but it could not be determined whether the hoops were of iron or were made of split withes.[23]

Trough

The Late Christian levels also yielded a small, roughly made wooden trough, 48 cm long and 17 cm wide, which had been made by hollowing out the interior of a palm log. It is unlikely that this was meant as an animal feeder, since it was found on the floor of one of the eparchal houses (House 763).

[20] For contemporary parallels see Donald S. Whitcomb and Janet H. Johnson, *Quseir al-Qadim 1978: Preliminary Report* (Cairo, 1979), pl. 71, e, o.

[21] For contemporary parallels see op. cit., pl. 71, p; Whitcomb and Johnson, *Quseir al-Qadim 1980*, pl. 68, h. k.

[22] For other examples of lids see Whitcomb and Johnson, *Quseir al-Qadim 1978*, pl. 71, g–h; Whitcomb and Johnson, *Quseir al-Qadim 1980*, pl. 69, j–m.

[23] For a similar wooden bucket from mediaeval Europe see Symonds in Singer *et al.*, op. cit., 255, fig. 230.

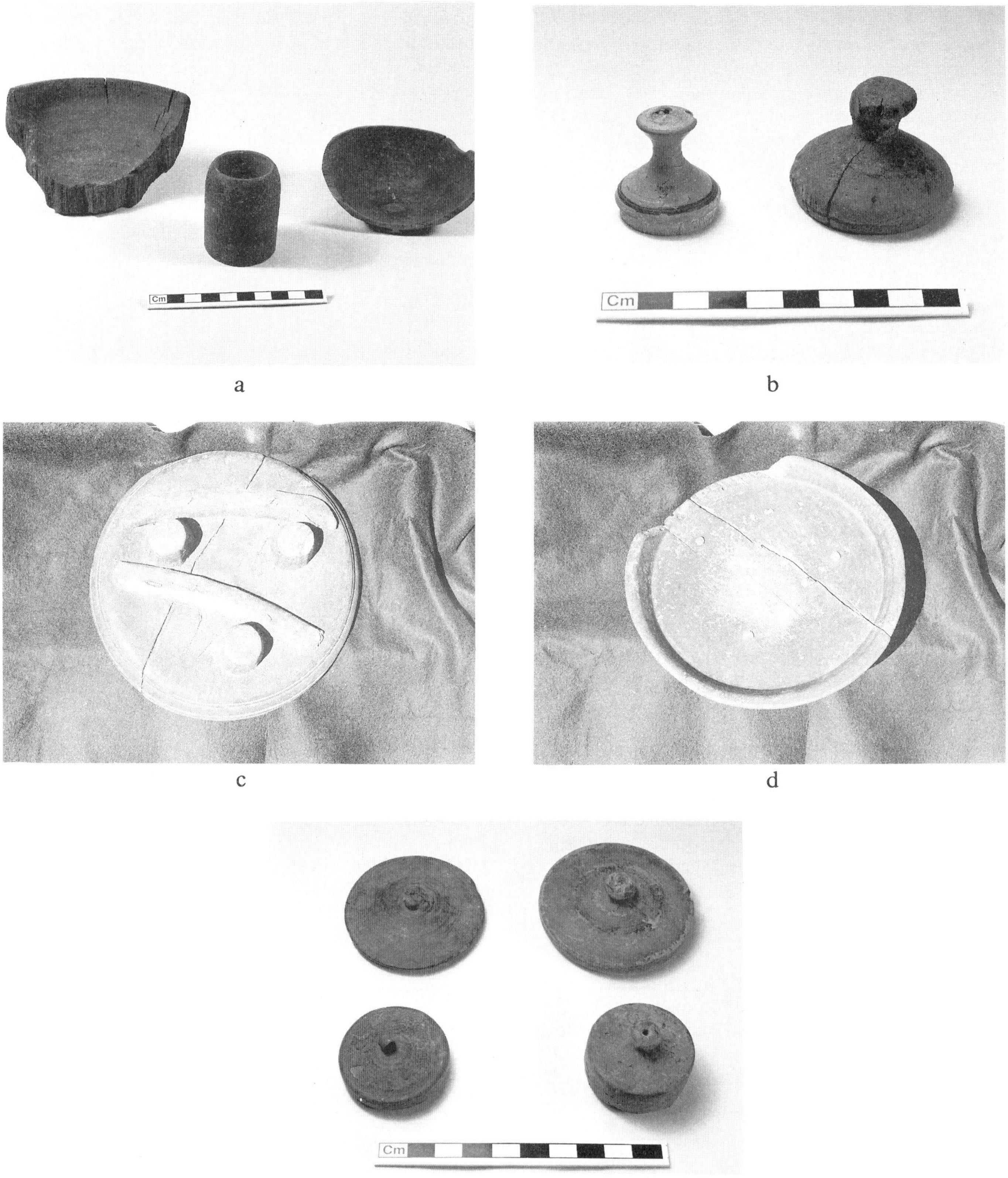

Plate 21. Wooden vessels and lids. a, Turned wooden bowls (64/208, 76.2.14/7, 82/185). b, Turned wooden lids (72/24). c, Tripod dish, bottom view (69/19). d, Same as **c**, top view. e, Turned wooden lids (78/487, 78/488, 82/183).

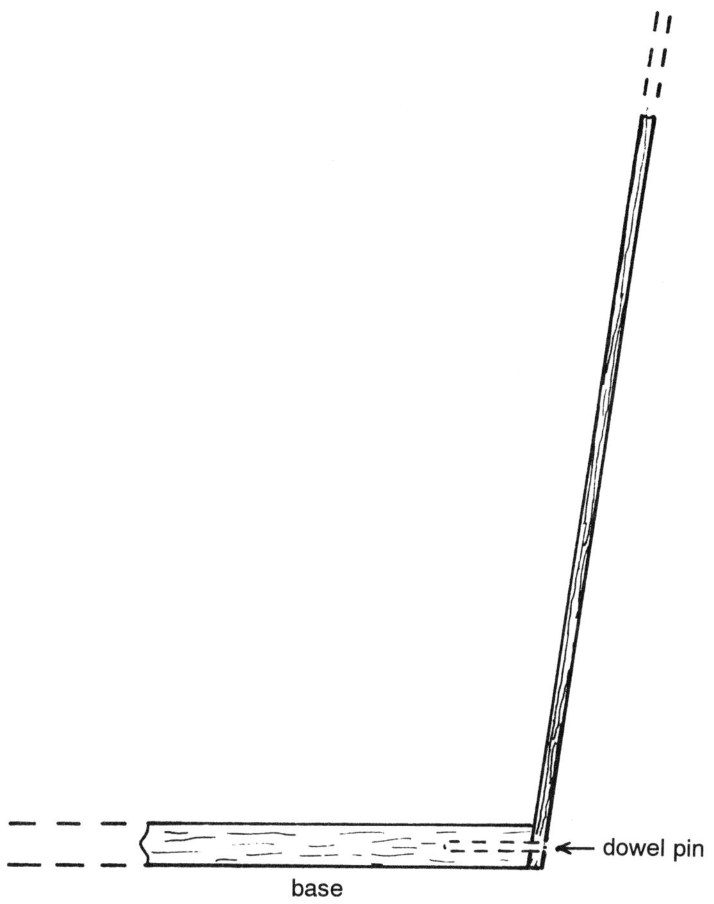

Figure 22. Schematic profile of wooden bucket, to show method of construction.

Ivory

Turned boxes were not made only of wood. Plate 19d shows a tiny, cylindrical ivory box, 2.5 cm in diameter and beautifully decorated. The inset rim shows that it was originally equipped with a lid. It must have housed some especially precious cosmetic.

Basketry

Baskets represent, after pottery, the most common and most varied class of containers found at Qaṣr Ibrîm. Included in this category are large, plaited carrying and storage baskets, plaited bags, small coiled baskets, and coiled basketry platters and lids. The various techniques of basket-making have been described in Chapter 9.

Plaited carrying and storage baskets

Plaited carrying baskets, closely similar in design to the *guffa* or *zanbil* of today, were common in all levels at Qaṣr Ibrîm (pl. 22a).[24] Eleven examples were registered from the Late and Terminal Christian deposits, but these undoubtedly represent only a small fraction of the actual finds, for a great deal of the lining found in the bottom of storage pits appeared also to consist of *guffa* fragments (see Part 2, Ch. 3). Diameters of the most complete baskets vary from about 30 to about 60 cm, and depths from about 15 to about 30 cm. Most carrying baskets were undecorated, but occasionally simple designs in black were worked into the plaiting just below the handles (pl. 22b). In addition to conventional *guffas,* there is a single example of a square plaited bag with carrying handles (pl. 22c). It measures 18 × 22 cm.[25]

[24] For a contemporary example see Whitcomb and Johnson, *Quseir al-Qadim 1978*, 200, fig. 22. For examples from Roman Egypt see W. M. Flinders Petrie, *Objects of Daily Use* (London, 1927), pl. XLI, nos 167 and 168.

[25] For a somewhat similar example from ancient Egypt see Petrie, op. cit., pl. XLI, no. 157.

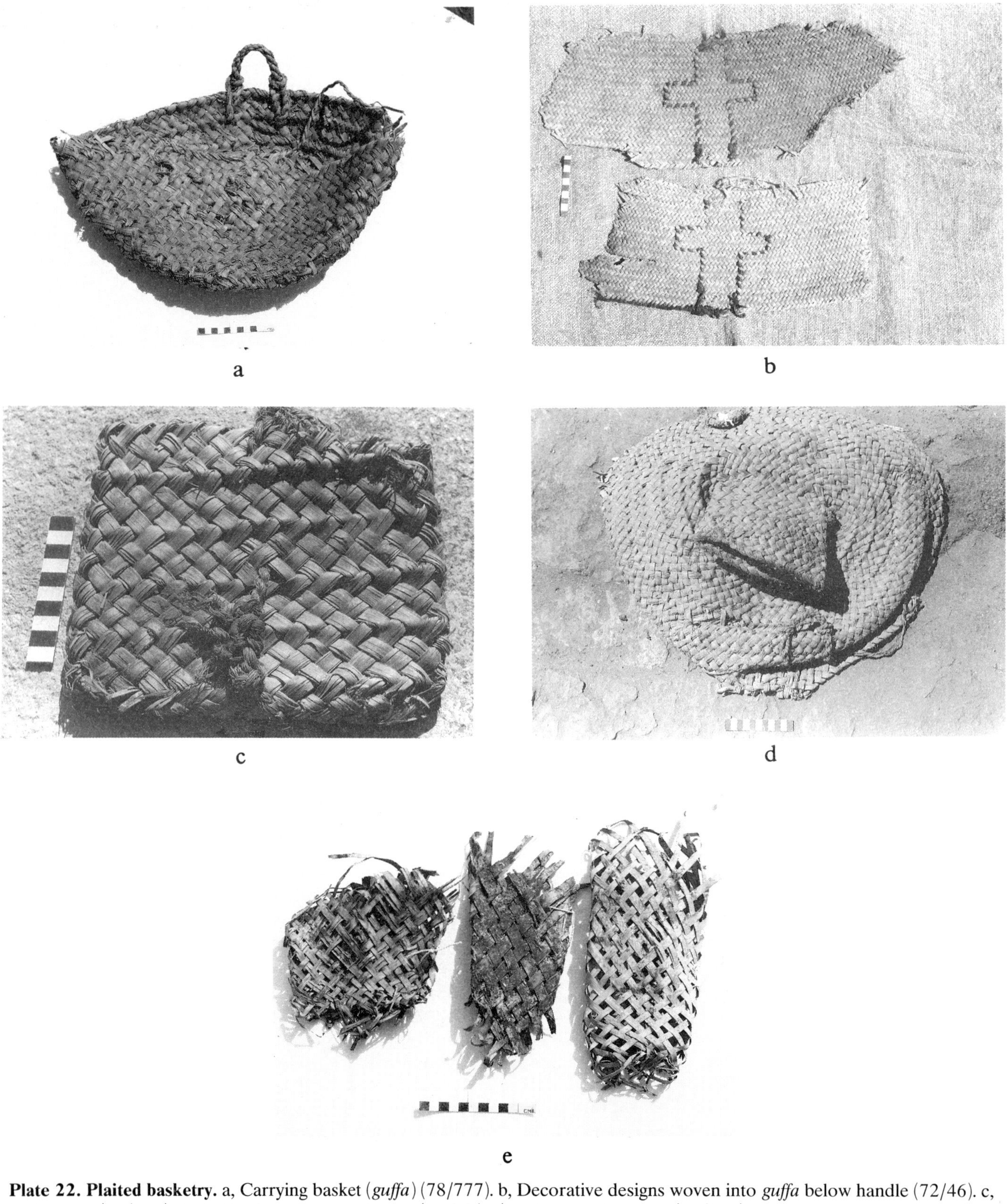

Plate 22. Plaited basketry. a, Carrying basket (*guffa*) (78/777). b, Decorative designs woven into *guffa* below handle (72/46). c, Plaited bag (76/107). d, Bottle-shaped storage basket (76.2.2/10). e, Small plaited bags (78/570).

Similar in design to the *guffas,* but larger in size, are bottle-shaped storage baskets, of which two were found nearly intact (pl. 13c, 22d). The lower part of the basket is little different from an ordinary *guffa,* while the upper part tapers upward to a narrow cylindrical neck. Attached at opposite sides of the body, just above the middle, are carrying handles of twisted rope. Diameters of the two intact specimens are respectively 58 and 47 cm. One of storage baskets had been buried beneath the floor of one of the eparchal houses (House 177) and was full of *durra* seeds when found.

Plaited bags

The Late Christian levels yielded 12 examples of open-work bags made by a loose, continuous plaiting technique (pl. 22e). Most are somewhat elongate in form, measuring between 30 and 35 cm in length and 12 to 15 cm in width, although none of the specimens appears to be wholly intact. We are not certain what purpose these bags might have served, but in modern Nubia similar bags are used in the preparation of *bouza* liquor from dates. In Egypt, however, they are called *sosul,* and are used to convey small gifts that are given on festival occasions.

Coiled baskets

Coiled baskets occur in a variety of sizes and forms. Many larger specimens are simple, slightly concave dishes (pl. 23a), of which the largest single example has a diameter of 47 cm.[26] Deeper coiled baskets are pan-shaped, with sloping sides and a flat bottom. Of six examples found in the Late Christian levels, five have a diameter of approximately 15 cm, and depths ranging from 5 to 8 cm. A variant form, shown in pl. 23b, has a small round bottom and outflared sides. This specimen has leather covering on the bottom and around the rim, and also has a decorative zigzag pattern of leather stitched into the sides.[27] Leather adornment, especially in the bottom and around the rim, is found in many coiled baskets.

Many of the Late Christian coiled baskets are miniatures, as shown in plate 23c–f. Plate 23c shows a bottle-shaped specimen with a height of 3.3 cm; pl. 23d shows a jar-shaped basket, 8 cm high, equipped with its own tiny lid; pl. 23e shows a kind of basketry box measuring 9 × 14 cm, with a height of 6 cm. Plate 23f shows a fragment of a small pan-shaped basket, 6.8 cm in diameter, with fine decorative stitching in black on the natural tan background. This specimen is believed to represent the standard Nubian measure for one handful of grain. Another miniature coiled basket (not illustrated) employed a spindle whorl as a lid.

Lids

Coiled lids and covers of one sort and another are among the most common of all basketry finds at Qaṣr Ibrîm. The Late and Terminal Christian levels yielded no fewer than 21 registered examples. The largest number are simple flat discs, which range in diameter up to 41 cm, though the majority have diameters between 5 and 15 cm (pl. 24a).[28] There are, in addition, lids of a more conical shape, very much like pottery lids, with a projecting flange made to fit down into the opening of a jar or basket (pl. 24b). Finally, some lids are in the shape of a shallow cylinder with a flange that was apparently meant to fit around the outside of a vessel mouth (pl. 24c).

Basketry lids not uncommonly have sewn leather centres, and may also have leather binding around the edges (pl. 24b and pl. 24d). The most ornate of Late Christian lids, shown in plate 24e, has a decorated leather overlay and also a fringe of cotton strings hanging from the outer edge. The diameter of the lid is 9.5 cm; the maximum length of the descending strings is 21 cm.

Stopper

Plate 24f shows a thick, more or less solid mass of coiled palm leaf which is presumed to be a stopper for a narrow-mouthed jar or bottle. The diameter is 6.4 cm.

Problematical basket

An unusual object of twined basketry is shown in plate 25a. It is more or less conical, with the rigid members drawn out and doubled over at the narrow end to form a kind of loop. This specimen bears some resemblance to the strainer shown in plate 12b, except that the doubled back-rods are suggestive of some kind of a handle. If so, the narrow end must have been the top rather than the bottom of the basket, and it may have been some kind of a large conical lid.

[26] For other examples of coiled basketry from Nubia see P. L. Shinnie and Margaret Shinnie, *Debeira West* (Warminster, 1978), pl. XXX, b–d. For some other examples of coiled basketry from the ancient world see Petrie, op.cit., pl. XLI, nos. 153–6.

[27] For examples of this kind of basketry decoration in the modern Sudan see C. G. and Brenda Z. Seligman, *Harvard African Studies* 2 (1918), 185ff., pls. I–III; and Sterns in the same volume, 194–6 and pls. I–III.

[28] For other contemporary examples see Whitcomb and Johnson, *Quseir al-Qadim 1978*, 203, fig. 23.

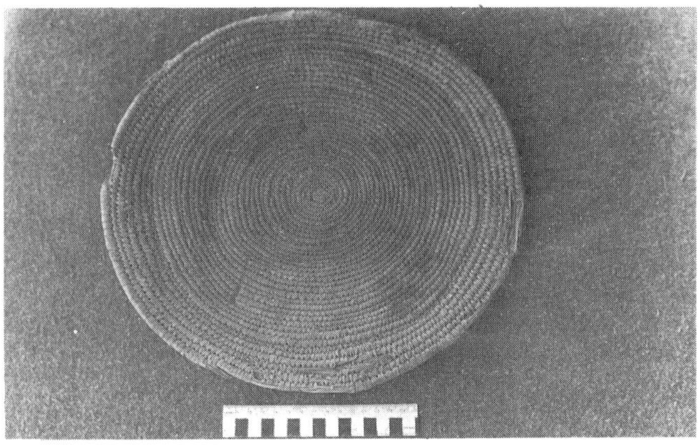

a

b

c

d

e

f

Plate 23. Coiled basketry. a, Wide, shallow coiled basket (80/584). b, Decorated conical basket, inverted (82/95). c, Miniature bottle-shaped basket (78/552). d, Miniature jar-shaped basket with lid (66A/54). e, Miniature box-shaped basket (78/562). f, Fragment of decorated basket (84.1.6/24).

Plate 24. Basketry lids and stopper. a, Flat, coiled lids (82/99). b, Flanged lid with leather-wrapped rim, top view (76.2.9/52). c, Flanged lid, underside (82/95). d, Flat lid with sewn leather centre and leather-wrapped rim (82/99). e, Lid with fancy leather fringes (84/418). f, Basketry stopper (84/422).

Textile

A good many cloth bags may have been in use at Qaṣr Ibrîm, but any large ones would in the end have been torn up for rags, as were nearly all other textiles (see Part 3, Ch. 1). There is, however, one scrap of cotton cloth, 33 cm long, that has spiral leather binding all along one edge, and that may be tentatively identified as part of the rim of a large bag. For the rest, the only cloth bags that have been recovered in recognizable form are small specimens. Six of these were found in the Late and Terminal Christian levels. All are more or less rectangular in shape and are made from a single piece of cotton cloth, folded at one side and sewn along the other side and across the bottom. The bags in all but one case are rather roughly sewn, and the open ends are unhemmed; probably they were made from scraps of previously used material. One is of solid blue cloth, one has blue and white stripes, one has a black and a red stripe, and the others are undyed. Sizes range from 2.9 × 5.7 cm in the smallest example to 10 × 28 cm in the largest.

Four of the seven small bags have either a drawstring (pl. 25b) or a tie string for closure. The largest bag is the only one which had a hemmed top, and the edge was turned and stitched to the outside rather than inside (pl. 25d). When it was found it contained two rectangles of blue and white checked fabric, 23 × 10 cm and 31 × 14 cm, each one neatly folded to fit inside. One bag was found to contain a fine brown powder, tentatively identified as henna, and another contained a pinkish granular material. It is possible that the use of the bags was at least partly amuletic.

Several fragments of woven goat hair have been found which probably were originally bags, but no specimen which is recognizably a bag has been recovered from the late mediaeval period. However, one complete and two fragments of knotted bags have been recovered from this period. The whole specimen is 24 cm long and 40 cm in circumference around the top (pl. 25c). It is made of undyed flax in a diagonal pattern of closely spaced knots. The top of the bag is finished off with 14 loops, which originally may have held a drawstring. The bottom of the bag ends in a tassel. One of the other specimens consists of the tassel only, although it is slightly more elaborate than the ending on the complete bag (pl. 26b). The third fragment is made of undyed cotton, instead of flax, and consists of the lower part of the bag with a decorative tassel. The execution of these bags shows that considerable skill was required to make them, and their very high quality indicates that they must have been greatly valued. It is possible that the flax bags were originally imported to Qaṣr Ibrîm, and that the cotton bag is a local copy.

Three bags have been recovered which are unlike any others from Qaṣr Ibrîm. The most complete example, measuring 33 × 24 cm, is made of one piece of cotton cloth, folded and then seamed on two sides with maroon wool yarn. Centred on each side of the bag is a five-pointed star, roughly outlined in running stitch, in the same maroon yarn (pl. 26d). The top is rough, but the piece seems to be complete, to judge by the centred decoration. The other two specimens, one of which is made from linen and one from cotton, are basically the same but less complete (pl. 26c).

Leather

Leather containers from the Late Christian levels include waterskins, miscellaneous soft bags, sewn pouches and purses, and sheaths for knives and daggers. Also described here, for want of a better place, are leather handles that were probably made for attachment to baskets or bags.

Waterskins

Waterskins, loaded on donkeys or camels, were probably the principal means of conveying water from the Nile to the Qaṣr Ibrîm mountain-top. If so, we may assume that their number was once fairly plentiful. A good many of the unsewn fragments of soft leather that have been found on the site are likely to be remnants of waterskins, but positive identification is impossible unless a large part of the bag is preserved. We assume, however, that any piece of soft leather showing extensive patching is probably part of a waterskin, since patching would not be a critical necessity for any other kind of leather container.

Six leather pieces from the Late and Terminal Christian levels have been tentatively identified as remnants of waterskins. One is nearly complete, and measures approximately 35 × 47 cm. As is common in waterskins, all of the sewing is on what is now the inside, i.e. the original skin was turned inside out before the belly slit and legs were sewn up, after which it was turned back right side out. Like most Qaṣr Ibrîm waterskins, this specimen has been heavily patched. Another, substantially smaller water bag has a handle of braided rope attached at two places (pl. 26a). Other possible waterskin fragments are too small to permit positive reconstruction of the original size or shape.

Bags

A great many pieces of soft leather show various kinds of stitching, but could not be identified as waterskins either because their shape is wrong or because they are not tightly sewn. In only one case is it possible to reconstruct the complete form of the bag. It is a large, flat pouch, measuring 60 × 55 cm, and is made from two

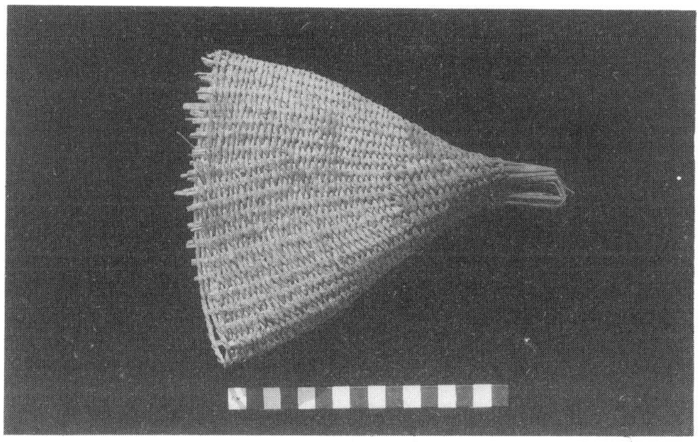

a

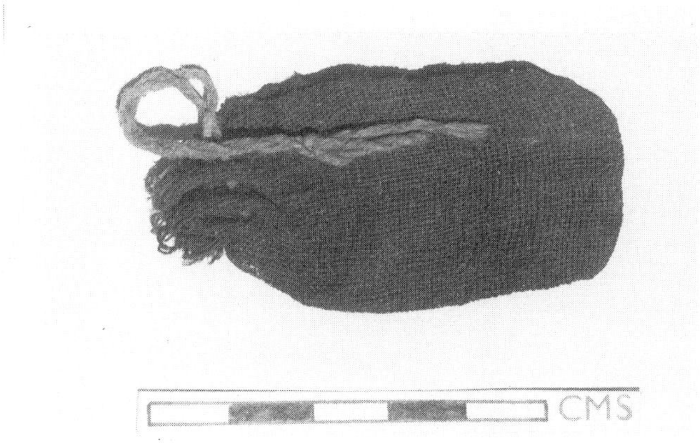

b

c

d

Plate 25. Basketry and textile containers. a, Problematical, conical basket (82/101). b, Small textile bag with drawstring (80/942). c, Knotted bag (82T/506). d, Bag with hemmed top (82T/426).

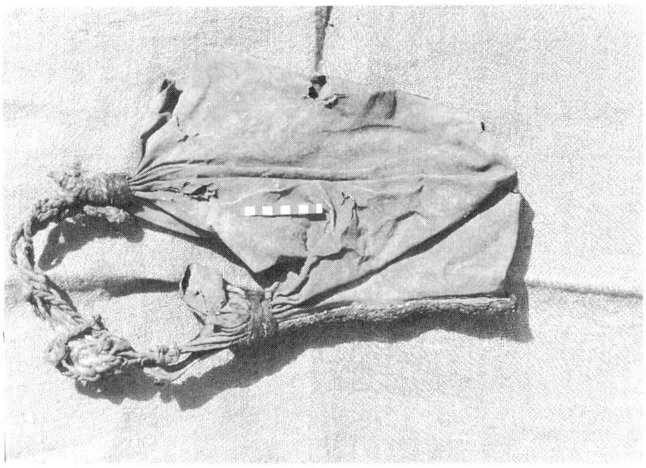

a

b

c

d

Plate 26. Waterskin; textile bag elements. a, Fragment of waterskin with handle (82/531). b, Cloth bag tassel (72.10.18/5). c, Cloth bags with sewn decoration (82T/703, 82T/363). d, Cloth bag with sewn decoration (82T/285).

thicknesses of leather. The open side appears to have been reinforced with an added strip of leather and may have had handles attached at opposite sides. There are, in addition, three pieces that are interpreted as fragments of bag rims. They have in each case one straight-cut edge which is reinforced with an extra strip either of leather or of cloth. Finally there are four round leather pieces, stitched around the edges, that are thought to be bag-bottom pieces, though other interpretations are also possible (e.g. coverings for basketry lids). Their diameters are respectively 11, 12.4, 18, and 24 cm.

Small pouches and purses

In this category are a number of small, flat containers of sewn leather. One (not illustrated) appears to have been oval in shape, although the open end is missing. The surviving portion is made of two identical pieces of fine leather, sewn together with very fine stitching all around the curved edge. The width at the widest point is 12 cm. Another very small pouch has an elongated oval shape, with flaps projecting from the upper end at both sides (pl. 27a). The purpose of the small, triangular flap is uncertain; the larger, spade-shaped flap was evidently meant to close over the mouth of the pouch. Slits at each side of the body suggest that the pouch was meant to be threaded onto a belt. The dimensions of the specimen when closed are 4.5 × 6 cm. An even smaller oval pouch is shown in plate 27b. It has an opening at the narrow end. One side is adorned with a cross-shaped pattern and a lozenge, done in very fine leather stitching.

Sheaths

The category of sheaths includes a couple of very long, narrow bags of soft leather, having preserved lengths respectively of 32 and 20 cm. One specimen has no side seam and was evidently made from the leg skin of an animal. Presumably these were sheaths for some sort of long, pole-like objects; they are too soft to have served either as scabbards or as quivers. More conventional sheaths for knives and/or daggers are shown in plate 27c–e. The specimen shown in plate 27c is actually a wooden sheath covered in tightly sewn leather. It measures 23 cm long and 4 cm wide and was evidently made for a long bodkin-like dagger. The much smaller specimen shown in plate 27d is rather crudely sewn from four separate pieces and is clearly made for a curved arm-knife of the kind formerly worn by nearly all Nubian men.[29] Plate 27e shows a still smaller sheath, probably made for a straight arm-knife such as is often carried by Beja tribesmen today.[30] It has both stitched and tooled decoration.

Handles

The Late Christian levels produced two sections of stout cord braided from fine leather thongs, involving at least 8 separate thongs in one case, and 12 in the other. The diameters of the cords are respectively 8 and 15 mm. The better preserved specimen measures 19 cm in length, and is wound around with narrow reinforcing strips of leather near both ends. It is bent into a half-circle, and almost certainly was some kind of a handle attached to a large basket or bag. This is the presumed use of the other specimen as well.

Gourd

The use of gourd containers is common throughout tropical Africa,[31] but only a few specimens have been found at Qaṣr Ibrîm. It seems that they were prized imports, presumably from the south, for in several cases broken gourds had been stitched back together. From the Late Christian levels we have two elongate gourd bottles, one of which has a carrying handle attached at the top (pl. 28a). The length of the illustrated specimen is 37 cm. Several other fragmentary gourds also bore remnants of handles. One gourd had been cut off along a straight line to form a kind of small bowl (pl. 28b). Several small fragments of gourd bear remnants of fine incised decoration (pl. 28c), a practice which is also common in Africa today.[32]

[29] Cf. J. L. Burckhardt, *Travels in Nubia* (London, 1819), 142: 'As soon as a boy grows up, his first endeavor is to purchase a short, crooked knife, which the men wear tied over the left elbow, under their shirt…' For illustrations see Thomas Legh, *Narrative of a Journey in Egypt and the Country Beyond the Cataracts* (London, 1817), following 200 and 204. For an illustration of curved arm-knife blades from mediaeval Nubia see Shinnie and Shinnie, *Debeira*, pl. XLI, a.

[30] Sheaths for curved and straight arm-knives were found at Quseir al-Qadim; see Whitcomb and Johnson, *Quseir al-Qadim 1980*, pl. 71, e–f.

[31] See Sterns, *Harvard African Studies* 1 (1917), 193 and n. 1

[32] Op. cit., 193–6; Friedrich Ratzel, *Völkerkunde* (Leipzig, 1885), 1, 378; Wilfrid D. Hambly, *Source Book for African Anthropology*, Part II (1937), 620 and 623.

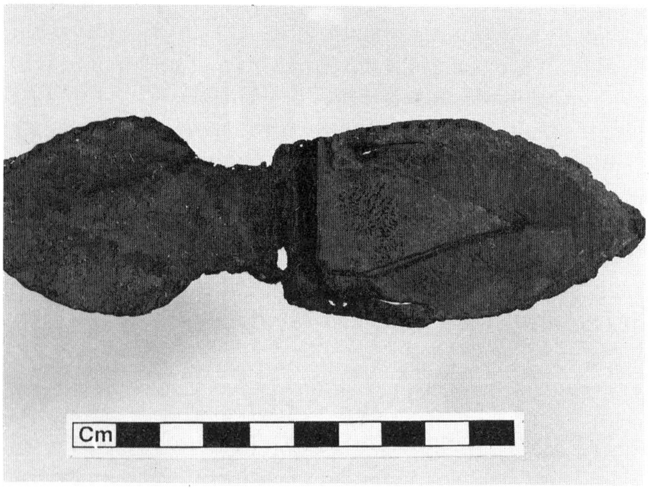

a

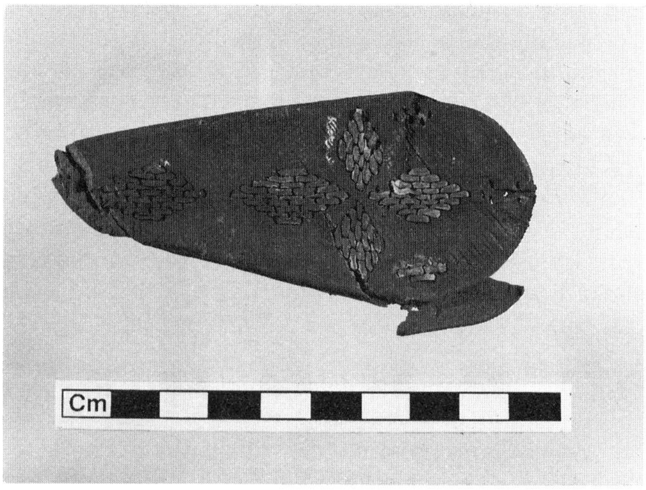

b

c

d

e

Plate 27. Leather pouches and sheaths. a, Small leather pouch, with lid folded open (82/555). b, Small leather pouch with sewn decoration (82/515). c, Knife sheath of wood covered with leather (78/53). d, Curved knife sheath (lower) (72/65). e, Knife sheath with stitched and tooled decoration (78/51).

a

b

c

Plate 28. Gourd containers. a, Small gourd bottle with suspension string (69/58). b, Gourd bowl, inverted (76.2.26/12). c, Gourd fragments with incised decoration (78/472).

CHAPTER 4
TOOLS, IMPLEMENTS, AND WEAPONS

THIS chapter will describe a wide variety of objects, made from many different materials, that were used to perform utilitarian tasks about the household, or in the streets and plazas. Many are implements that were used to produce or to manipulate other objects; none were apparently prized possessions in and of themselves. At the conclusion of the chapter weapons will also be considered, since they are not numerous enough to warrant a separate chapter.

Cutting tools, handles, and hones

Cutting tools in the late mediaeval period were made exclusively of iron. Registered specimens include knives, saws, and a single axe or adze head, as well as various wooden handles and fittings.

Knives

Six iron knives were found in the Late Christian deposits, of which three are shown in plate 29a. As can be seen, the blades are of various sizes and shapes, as in modern kitchen knives. Blade lengths for the illustrated specimens vary between 7 and 12 cm; overall lengths of three other specimens are 13, 20, and 21 cm.[1] All of the knives were evidently fitted with wooden handles, though in three instances they are not preserved. Handles are typically round in cross-section. The handles of two specimens are comprised of two sections, fastened through the shank of the blade with iron rivets. In another specimen the blade merely has a short tang which is inserted into the end of the handle, and this was evidently the case also with two of the blades which currently lack handles (pl. 29a, 2 and 4).

Saws or sickles

The serrated, curved iron blades shown in plate 11b may be either saws or a sickles; parallel examples of both have been illustrated by Petrie.[2] A similar but much more corroded blade (not illustrated) was found set into a rather roughly shaped wooden handle, having a length of 20 cm.

Axe or adze

A single iron axe or adze blade is illustrated in plate 29b. The length of the surviving piece is 7 cm, with a width of 5 cm. The straight-across fracture may follow the alignment of a socket hole; if so, this was an axe rather than an adze.

Implement handles and fittings

The Late Christian levels produced various pieces of round wooden rod that are undoubtedly handles for knives or awls. In several cases the socketing holes for a blade are clearly evident, and in one specimen a small fragment of the blade tang is preserved. The handles are in all cases carved rather than lathe-turned, but they vary considerably in the quality of their finish. Plate 29c shows a well-finished example having a section of spiral grooving cut into the wood.[3] The handles are mostly round in cross-section, with diameters ranging from 1.2 to 3.6 cm, although one specimen has a flattened oval cross-section. The wood in most cases is acacia. Lengths of the intact specimens range from 6.0 to 17.5 cm

Also found in the Late Christian deposits were a number of small iron and bronze rings, comprised of a thin strip of metal bent into a circle and riveted onto itself. There are eight iron and four copper or bronze examples. The diameters are typically between 2.0 and 3.2 cm and the widths of the bands between 0.5 and 1.0 cm. These are certainly not finger rings. We assume that they were meant as bindings for wooden handles, although none was actually found affixed to a handle.

Hones

The Late Christian levels produced three thin, rectangular pieces of slate or greywacke that are interpreted as hones for knives. The most complete example (plate 29d, lower) measures 4.1 × 13.9 cm, and has a perforation at one end. Another fragmentary specimen, measuring 2.5 × 6.5 cm as preserved, is also drilled at one end.

[1] For parallel examples from Roman Egypt see W. M. Flinders Petrie, *Tools and Weapons* (London, 1917), pl. XXVIII, nos. K 207–10.

[2] For saws see op. cit., pl. L, nos. F 30–1; for sickles see op. cit., pl. LV, nos. S 27–8.

[3] For a parallel to this particular handle, forming part of a drill, see op. cit., pl. LI, no. m 15.

a

b

c

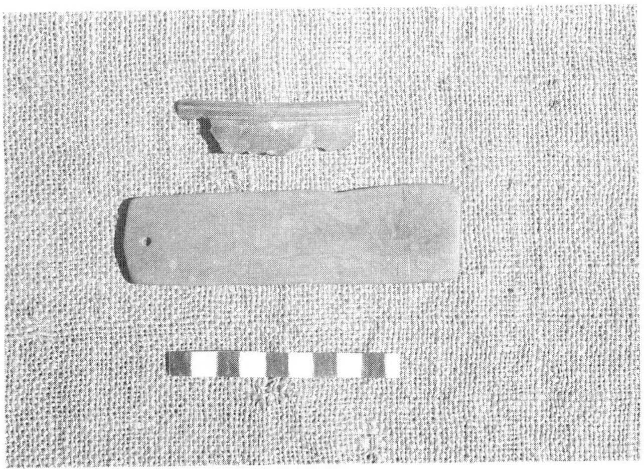

d

Plate 29. Cutting tools and accessories. a, Iron folding razor (at left) and knives (72/145, 72/13, 72/513, 82/324). b, Iron axe or adze blade (69/40). c, Turned wooden tool handle (78/424). d, Stone knife sharpener (lower) (72/52).

Sewing, spinning, and weaving equipment

The importance of the textile industry at Qaṣr Ibrîm is attested by many finds, not least by the number of implements connected with sewing, spinning, and weaving that have been found on the site. They include needles, awls, spindles and whorls, shuttles, a loom weight, a weft packing comb, and perforated wooden blocks that were probably used in card-weaving.

Needles

Needles of the Late Christian period are of two quite different kinds. Iron needles (pl. 30a) were presumably used in sewing cloth, and perhaps leather, since one specimen is 9 cm long. Another, smaller specimen has a length of 4.1 cm.[4] Somewhat larger and flatter wooden needles, made from palm ribs, must have been used in basket making. Two intact specimens measure respectively 13.5 and 14.0 cm in length.[5]

Thimble

The Late Christian levels produced a single bronze thimble, remarkably similar in appearance to modern thimbles (pl. 31d, left). The diameter is 1.6 cm, and the length 1.5 cm.[6]

Awls

Awls from the Late Christian period are made exclusively of wood. They differ from wooden needles in having a round rather than a flattened oval cross-section and in lacking an eye (pl. 30b). They are also slightly larger than needles. Of six intact specimens that were registered, five have lengths between 14.5 and 17.7 cm; the sixth is 21 cm long. Maximum diameters are typically a little less than one centimeter.[7] It can be difficult to distinguish between awls and the polished wooden hairpins that were so much favoured by earlier Nubians (see Part 3, Ch. 7), and that are still worn by Beja tribesmen today. As a rule of thumb we have classified as an awl any polished, pointed wooden rod that lacks carved decoration, and as a hairpin any piece with decoration.

Spindles and whorls

These are by far the most common of all household implements at Qaṣr Ibrîm, in the Late Christian levels and in most others. Registered Late Christian finds include 9 complete specimens (that is, including both the whorl and at least part of the shaft), 2 shafts without whorls, and 68 whorls without shafts. Of the latter 61 are of wood, 6 are made from ground potsherds, and one is of sandstone.

The typical Nubian spindle of the Late Christian period is a polished wooden shaft about 30 cm long, although individual specimens vary in length between 22 and 38 cm. Diameters are consistently between 0.6 and 0.7 cm. A small iron hook is thrust into the distal end, as shown in plate 30d. The whorl is attached immediately above the distal end (pl. 30c, 30d).[8] One Late Christian specimen has two whorls, one immediately above the other.

Qasr Ibrîm spindle whorls are anomalous in Nubia in that the great majority of them are made of lathe-turned wood.[9] Most commonly they have a more or less quarter-round profile (pl. 30c, 30e), but various other shapes also occur (pl. 30d). We have developed a typology involving a total of thirteen spindle whorl types that are regularly found at Qaṣr Ibrîm, of which two types are made from potsherds and the remainder from wood (fig. 23). The single most common Late Christian type is 8a, followed closely by Types 7b and 8b. All three of these types are often made of ebony and decorated with incised concentric grooves, as shown in plate 30e. Whorl diameters are fairly consistently between 4 and 5 cm, though a few specimens are slightly smaller and a few slightly larger.

At mediaeval Nubian sites other than Qaṣr Ibrîm, drilled potsherd discs are found by the hundreds, and undoubtedly these constituted the main form of spindle whorl. At Qaṣr Ibrîm, by contrast, only half a dozen potsherd whorls were found throughout the Late Christian levels (pl. 30f). Diameters are slightly larger than in the case of the wooden whorls, ranging between 5 and 8 cm. Sherds of the heavy, undecorated utility wares seem to have been preferred for making pottery whorls.

[4] For iron needles from mediaeval Egypt see Donald S. Whitcomb and Janet H. Johnson, *Quseir al-Qadim 1978: Preliminary Report* (Cairo, 1979), pl. 69, f–g. For parallels from Roman Egypt see Petrie, *Tools*, pl. LXII, nos. N 24–5.

[5] For wooden needles from mediaeval Egypt see Donald S. Whitcomb and Janet H. Johnson, *Quseir al-Qadim 1980: Preliminary Report* (Malibu, 1982), pl. 69, v–w. For other parallels from Egypt see Petrie, *Tools*, pl. LXVI, nos. N 118–20.

[6] For a parallel example, presumed to be from Roman Egypt, see Petrie, *Tools*, pl. XLIV, no. N 110.

[7] For other wooden awls from mediaeval Egypt see H. E. Winlock and W. E. Crum, *The Monastery of Epiphanius at Thebes,* Part I (New York, 1926), pl. XX, B.

[8] For parallel examples from Roman Egypt see Petrie, *Tools*, pl. LXVI, nos. N 143–147.

[9] For other turned wooden spindle whorls from mediaeval Egypt see Winlock and Crum, op. cit., pl. XV, b; J. E. Quibell, *Excavations at Saqqara (1908–9, 1909–10)* (Cairo, 1912), pl. LIV, 1 (top row).

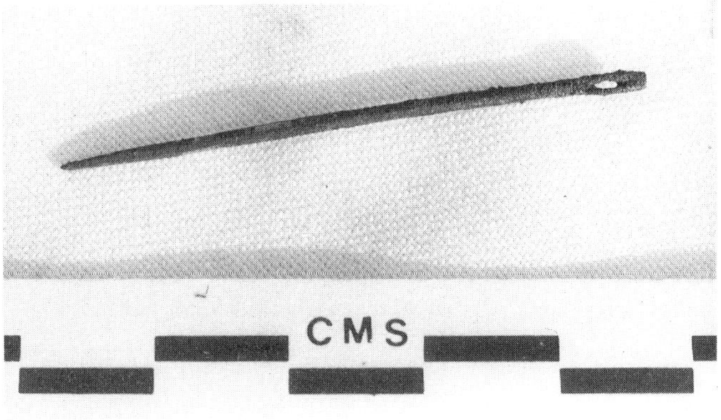

a

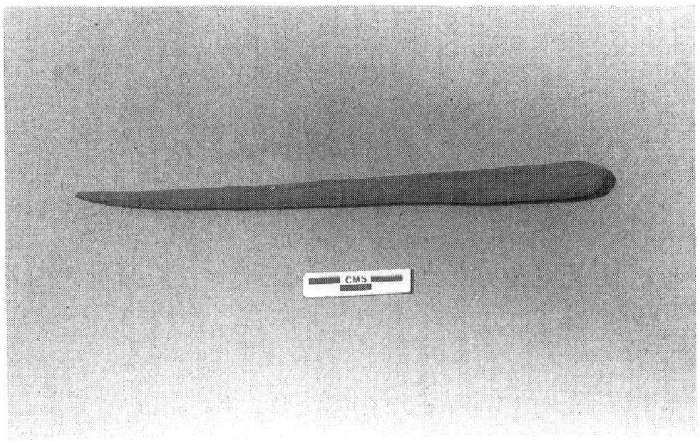

b

c

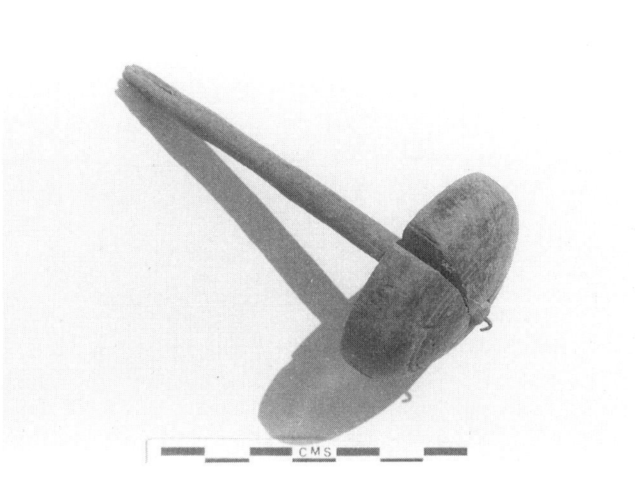

d

e

f

Plate 30. Textile equipment. a, Iron needle (82/328). b, Wooden awl (82/188). c, Wooden spindles (66/165, 82/81). d, Wooden spindle showing iron hook (82/81). e, Wooden spindle whorls (82/83). f, Potsherd spindle whorls (82/86).

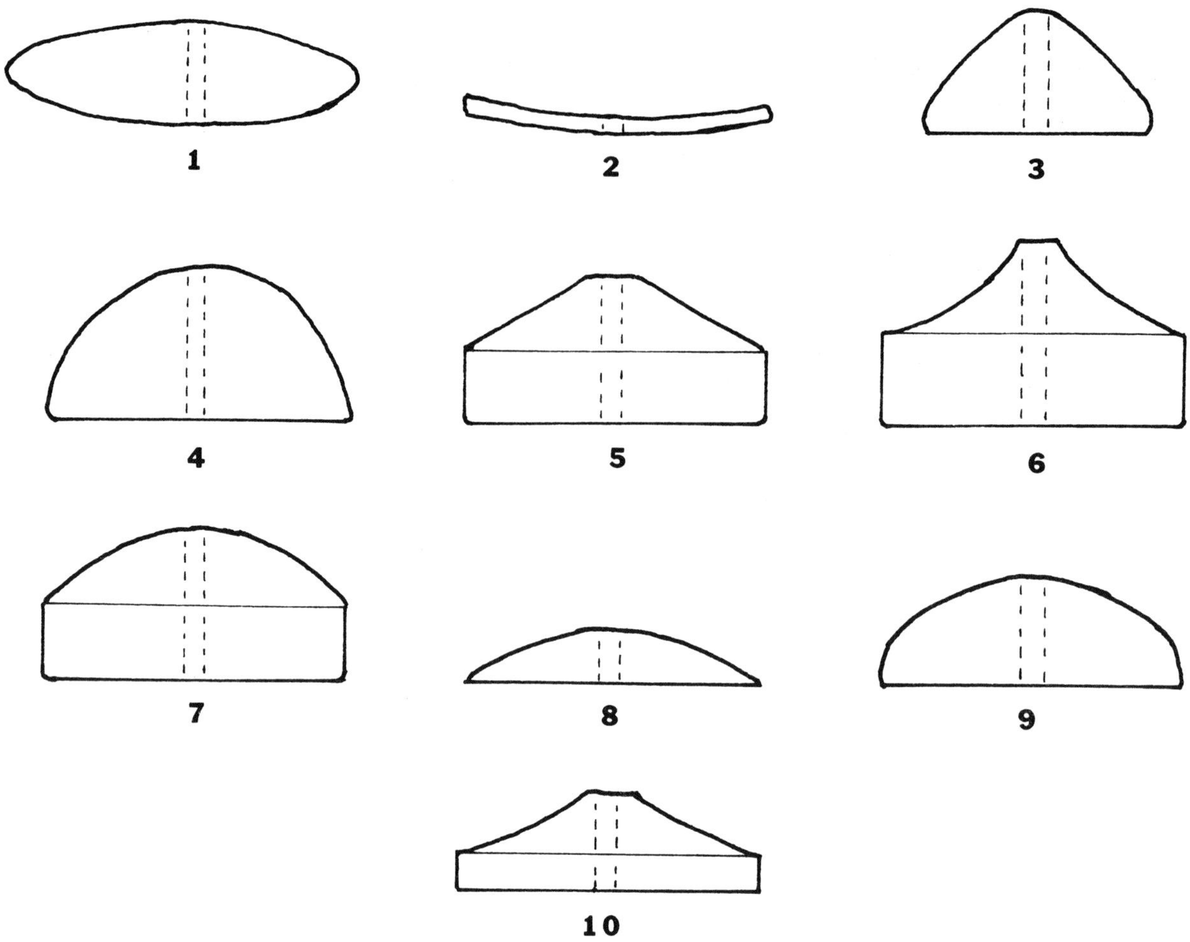

Figure 23. Major spindle-whorl types (R. C. Allen typology). **1**, stone; **2**, drilled potsherd; **3**, unbaked clay; all others turned wood.

Shuttles

Several fairly elaborate shuttles, having notched ends and carved decoration, have been found in the X-Group levels at Qaṣr Ibrîm.[10] Nothing comparable has been found in the later horizons. However, two pieces of polished wooden rod from the Late Christian levels have been interpreted as shuttles (pl. 31a). They are virtually identical in length (35.5 cm) and in diameter (1.5 and 1.6 cm). From the middle they taper very slightly in width toward the two ends, which are carefully rounded off.[11] The use of these implements as shuttles is suggested in part by the fact that both specimens are noticeably dirtier at both ends than in the middle, a fact indicating that they were regularly handled by the two ends.

Loom weight

While drop-shaped loom weights of mud were extremely common in the pre-Christian levels at Qaṣr Ibrîm, only a single example has been registered from a Late Christian context (pl. 31b). Given the absence of other, similar specimens, the possibility must be considered that this weight was recovered from an earlier occupation deposit and was put to a secondary use in the Late Christian house where it was found. It seems clear, at all events, that the warp-weighted loom was not the primary weaving apparatus in Late Christian times.

Packing comb

The weaver's comb is an implement used from time to time during the weaving process to pack the newly woven strands of weft tightly down upon the warp. Several wooden weaving combs have been found at Qaṣr Ibrîm, including one from the Late Christian levels (pl. 31c). It has a width of 15.4 cm and a length of 23.7 cm, including the handle.[12] The spacing between the teeth is approximately 0.5 cm As in most such implements, the grooves between the teeth are cut

[10] See Plumley and Adams, *JEA* 60 (1974), pl. XLVII, 1.

[11] For other shuttles from mediaeval Egypt see Quibell, op. cit., pl. LIV, 1.

[12] For parallel examples from mediaeval Egypt see Petrie, *Tools*, pl. LXVI, no. N 151; Quibell, op. cit., pl. LIV.

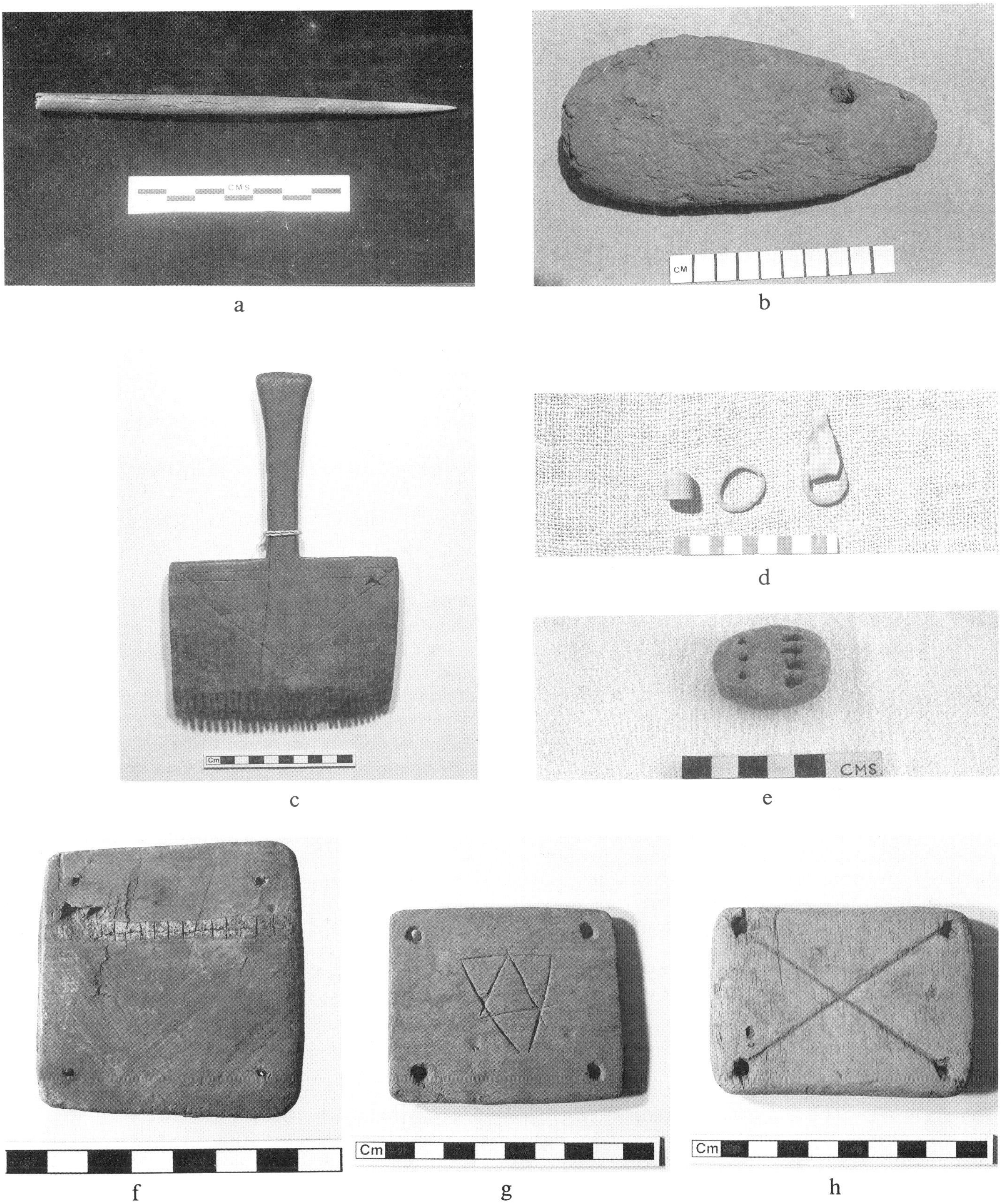

Plate 31. Textile equipment. a, Wooden shuttle (82/219). b, Mud loom weight (82/299). c, Wooden packing comb (78/502). d, Bronze thimble (left) (72/25). e, Ceramic string-making implement (78/413). f, g, h, Wooden card-weaving tablets (69/31, 72/470).

at an angle to the thickness of the wood, so that they are, in effect, deeper at one side than at the other. Both faces of the comb have simple incised decoration, as shown in plate 31c.

Weaving tablets or cards

Card-weaving, or tablet weaving, is a special technique used to produce fine woven straps and sashes; one such strap is described and illustrated in Part 3, Chapter 7.[13] The 'loom' consists simply of a number of wooden tablets ('cards'), perforated with a few symmetrically placed holes through which the warp is strung. The Late and Terminal Christian levels at Qaṣr Ibrîm have yielded two fragmentary and four complete specimens of wooden tablets that are interpreted as card-weaving apparatus (pl. 31f–h). Dimensions of the largest specimen are 10 × 8.5 cm, and of the smallest 7 × 5.5 cm. All the tablets are perforated with holes at each corner; two also have simple incised decoration (pl. 31g–h).

? String-making implement

A small oval pottery disc, perforated with one line of four holes and one line of three holes, may have served to hold and to separate the individual strands of yarn as they were twisted into 3-ply or 4-ply cord (pl. 31e). The disc has diameters of 3.4 and 3.6 cm and is made from hand-moulded, baked clay, not from a reused potsherd.

Lifting, pulling, and fastening apparatus

This category includes a variety of rather simple, utilitarian objects. While their precise function in many cases is problematical, we believe that in the broadest sense they were used to lift, pull, or fasten other objects, or animals. These items appear to be strictly utilitarian, in that they have no decoration and in most cases are no more carefully finished than was necessary to perform their intended jobs.

Pulley wheels

Two lathe-turned wooden spools, having a rather large centre-bore, are interpreted as pulley wheels (pl. 32a). The dimensions in the two cases are nearly identical: 7.6 cm in diameter and 2.9 cm in thickness.[14] There is no clear indication of where and how pulleys might have been used at Qaṣr Ibrîm, especially during the Late Christian period when no construction involving large building blocks was undertaken. It should be recalled, however, that the northern cliff face was very nearly vertical, so that some kinds of cargoes might have been hoisted directly from the river to the mountain-top by means of block and tackle.

Weights

Several objects of stone have been found which probably served in one sense or another as weights. The largest is a perforated block of sandstone with a rounded end, measuring 27 × 13 × 6 cm (pl. 32b). The general shape is similar to that of Nubian boat anchors, but the size is considerably smaller. Probably this specimen was used as a counterweight in conjunction with a block and tackle. Another possible weight is a small, thick disc of sandstone, 8.4 cm in diameter and about 4 cm thick, perforated with an irregular hole through the centre. Still more problematical, but probably functioning in some sense as a weight, is a pair of joined ironstone concretions tied around the narrow waist with a length of cord (pl. 32c). The overall length of the piece is 12.1 cm.

Pegs and stakes

Among the most common artifacts at Qaṣr Ibrîm are sharpened wooden sticks, which are designated as pegs if they have enlarged head-knobs (pl. 33a), and as stakes if they are simply sharpened sticks. On the basis of this distinction 22 objects from the Late Christian levels have been identified as pegs, 15 are identified as stakes, and 7 are pointed end fragments that could have belonged to either. The wood in all cases appears to be acacia.[15]

Pegs are typically knife-carved, as shown in plate 33a. They are never very well finished or polished and may have a rounded, a triangular, or a rectangular cross-section. The three largest pegs, measuring respectively 75, 45, and 43 cm in length, were probably used as animal tethering posts. All other pegs are substantially smaller, although varying considerably in length. It is possible that two functionally distinct groups are present: a group of medium-sized pegs, from 16 to 32 cm long, and a group of small pegs, from 8 to 12 cm long. These objects might have served a variety of purposes: as tent pegs, for staking out hides to dry, for staking out the horizontal loom, or as hanging pegs inserted into house walls.

Stakes also appear to fall into two size groups. There is a group of four large stakes, ranging in length from 28 to 38 cm, and a group of fifteen smaller stakes, from

[13] See also Winlock and Crum, op. cit., 71 and pl. XXII, C.

[14] For a mediaeval pulley wheel complete with block see Quibell, op. cit., pl. LIV, 2 (top left). For other Egyptian examples see Petrie, *Tools*, pl. LXXV, nos. W 143–4; Whitcomb and Johnson, *Quseir al-Qadim 1978*, pl. 70, u–v.

[15] For other examples from mediaeval Egypt see Winlock and Crum, op. cit., 70 and pl. XX, B.

a

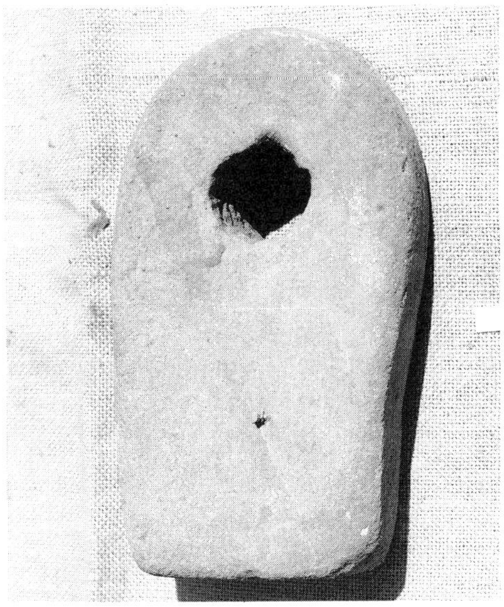

b

c

Plate 32. Lifting and pulling apparatus. a, Wooden pulley wheel (82/198). b, Perforated stone weight (78.2.12/57). c, Weight made from a natural concretion (82.2.2/44).

8 to 18 cm long. Many stakes are indistinguishable from pegs without heads, but others are more crudely made, involving only the removal of the bark from a natural wooden limb and the sharpening of one end. Both pegs and stakes often, but by no means always, show evidence of hammering at the blunt end.

Wedges

The Late Christian levels have yielded eight examples of roughly shaped wooden wedges, of which four are shown in plate 33b. The lengths are remarkably uniform, ranging between 7.0 and 10.1 cm, while the widths vary between 1.6 and 3.4 cm. Most of the wedges are somewhat tapered in width as well as in thickness toward the pointed end.[16] The wood in all cases is acacia. The heads of all the wedges are extremely battered, and in several cases the pointed ends also show extensive damage. Most probably these implements were used in the splitting of stone building blocks, and possibly also of building timbers.

Leather straps

The refuse deposits at Qaṣr Ibrîm have yielded a great many fragments of cut leather, of which some are pieces of strap. Presumably these were parts of harnesses, belts, or handles. Only seven fragments were actually registered from the Late Christian levels, but the number of unregistered scraps was probably far larger. One fragment of a large belt, 35 cm long and 1.6 cm wide, has two centrally placed perforations as in a modern belt, showing that it was originally fitted with a tongued buckle.

Cordage

Palm-fibre rope was undoubtedly the principal fastening material at Qaṣr Ibrîm, and scraps of rope are legion throughout the occupation deposits. The rope was most commonly two-plied but occasionally was three-plied. However, scraps of cordage were not individually registered unless they were attached to some recognizable artifact; hence it is not possible to give any estimate of the overall volume of material involved. For illustrations of sections of rope, attached to other artifacts, see plates 11e, 22a, 22d, 24e, 25b, 32c, 34d, 49c, and 49e.

Some fine cordage was also made from braided leather, as shown in plate 33c. In this piece one of the original ends is preserved. It comprises a single strip of leather, 2.5 cm wide, which just below the end is cut into three strands which are then braided together. Another, wrapped bundle of thongs is shown in plate 33d. For additional illustrations of leather cordage see plates 11d, 46a, 46b, 47a–c, 48e, 53a, and 57a.

After palm-fibre rope, the most common material for cordage is goat-hair. The initial element is always two-plied; multiples of these are twisted together to create cordage of various strengths. The principal size found is made of four elements, about 7 mm in diameter. Goat-hair cords may also contain eight, twelve or even more elements. Fine cotton cordage also occurs. Some specimens are made of plies twisted together; in other cases 4, 6 or 8 elements are worked together in a type of braiding technique. They measure between 5 and 7 mm in diameter.

A unique specimen of cordage is composed of numerous green and yellow wool yarns organized into three groups and plaited, very much as hair is plaited. The surviving piece is 30 cm long, 1.5 cm wide and 0.8 cm thick. Cordage is also sometimes made of twisted lengths of cotton fabric plied together or plaited.

Chain

From the Late Christian levels comes one short section of chain, made from fine copper or bronze wire 0.15 cm in diameter. The individual links are in the form of a figure '8,' and each is twisted 90° at the midpoint. The surviving piece is 5 cm long. This very fine chain could not have supported much weight; it might have been part of the suspension for a lamp or censer.[17]

Buckles and rings

A final category of fastening apparatus consists of metal buckles and rings that were presumably used in conjunction either with leather straps or with ropes. Five examples were recorded from the Late Christian levels, of which three are shown in plate 33e. All of the illustrated specimens are made of iron, but another specimen, similar in other respects to plate 33e, 2, is made of brass.[18] Two of the buckles have a narrow place in the middle of the cross-member (cf. pl. 33e, 1) where a tongue must have been attached, though in neither case is the tongue preserved.

Toilet articles

Toilet articles from the Late Christian levels include razors, combs, kohl sticks, tweezers, and mirrors. Some

[16] For the best parallel example from Egypt see Petrie, *Tools*, pl. LXIX, no. B 36.

[17] Cf. Paul Van Moorsel *et al.*, *The Central Church of Abdallah Nirqi* (Leiden, 1975), pl. 25.

[18] For the closest parallels from Egypt see W. M. Flinders Petrie, *Objects of Daily Use* (London, 1927), pl. XLIII, no. 36.

a

b

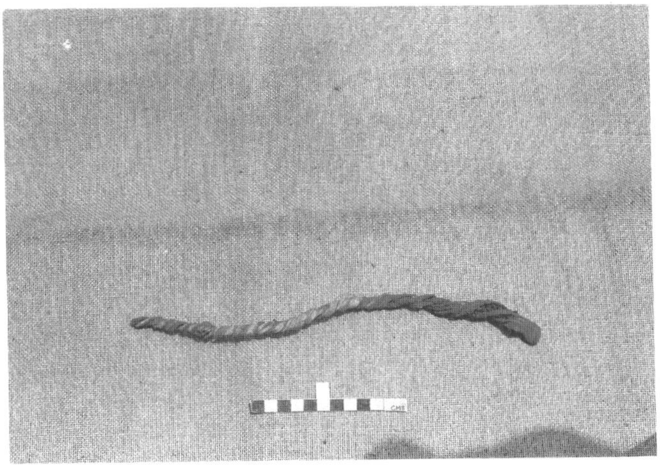

c

d

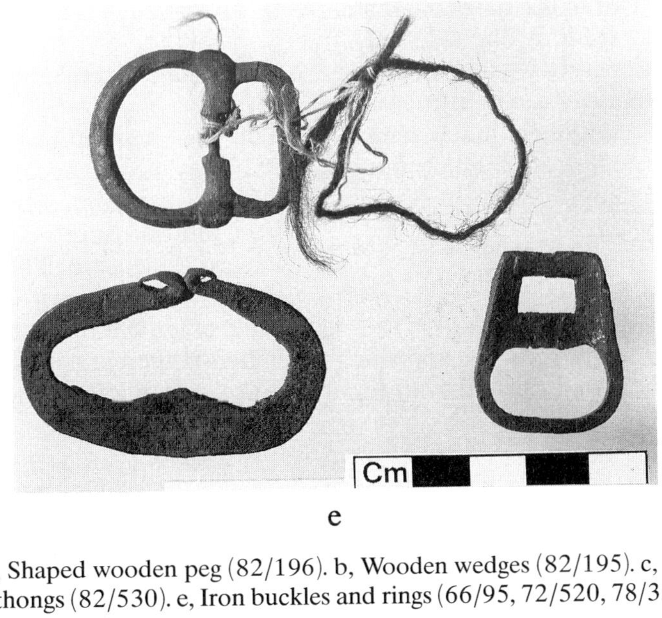

e

Plate 33. Fastening apparatus. a, Shaped wooden peg (82/196). b, Wooden wedges (82/195). c, Section of braided leather cord (78.2.12/6). d, Bundle of leather thongs (82/530). e, Iron buckles and rings (66/95, 72/520, 78/351).

of the small glass perfume flasks and the tiny lathe-turned wooden boxes described in Chapter 10 should undoubtedly also be included in the category of toilet equipment.

Razors

The Late Christian levels yielded two articles that have been identified as razors. One, shown in plate 34a, has a markedly curved blade set into a rather crudely fashioned wooden handle. The blade is designed to fold against the side of the handle, as shown in the photograph; obviously it could not be folded up within the thickness of the handle, as in modern pocket-knives. The length of the handle is 14.5 cm, and the blade (measured straight) is 10 cm long. Another possible razor is a thin iron blade, 12.5 cm long, having a slight angle in the middle. We assume at least that it was some kind of toilet implement, although its use as a razor is problematical.

Combs

Wooden combs are very common finds at Qaṣr Ibrîm. Twelve whole and fragmentary specimens were recovered from the Late and Terminal Christian levels (pl. 34b). The majority are closely similar to wooden combs that are still sold in Egypt today; they have very fine teeth along one side and somewhat coarser teeth along the other (pl. 34b, 1–3 and 5). Dimensions are typically about 6 × 8 cm, although slightly smaller and slightly larger specimens occur. The finest combs are made of ebony and often have decoration in the form of incised concentric circles on the smooth faces between the toothed areas.[19] Two of the Late Christian combs are aberrant in having teeth at one side only. However, the very small specimen shown in plate 34b, 4 appears to have been refashioned from a fragment of an original two-sided comb. Another, much larger comb appears to have been made from the beginning with teeth only at one side. Only a fragment of this specimen is preserved.[20]

Kohl sticks

The use of small, decorated metal rods for applying make-up (kohl) to the eyelids is well attested both for ancient and for mediaeval Egypt and Nubia.[21] Kohl sticks found in mediaeval Nubian sites are usually made of bronze.[22] However, five of the six specimens from the Late and Terminal Christian levels at Qaṣr Ibrîm are of iron. Plate 34c shows a typical though unusually well-preserved example, which is rounded at both ends and has an ornamented section, square in cross-section, in the middle. Two other iron kohl sticks are similar in design, and all three are between 14.5 and 16.7 cm in length.[23] There is also a smaller kohl stick, 9.5 cm long, which differs from the others in having one round and one pointed end. This may possibly be a surgical instrument, since similar instruments were used for eye surgery in Roman times. Another iron pin, 6.5 cm long and pointed at both ends, may be either a surgical instrument or a kohl stick.

Tweezers

The two small pairs of tweezers that were found in Late Christian contexts are shown in plate 34d. The lower specimen (pl. 34d, 2) is made of iron and is suspended from a small iron ring.[24] The much more decorative upper specimen, made of bronze, has a short length of cotton string attached.[25] Lengths of the tweezers are respectively 4.5 and 7.0 cm

Mirrors

The only two glass mirrors that were found in Late Christian levels were both fitted to the undersides of tiny, lathe-turned wooden box lids (pl. 34e). The mirror diameters are respectively 2.5 and 2.9 cm.[26]

Problematical implements

The two small implements shown in plates 35a and 35b may be connected in some way with sewing or weaving activities. They are cut from thin sheets of iron, and measure respectively 5.8 and 5.0 cm in the longest dimension. The small, pointed and apparently tanged object shown in plate 35c is cut from a thin sheet of copper or bronze. It was evidently meant to be hafted at the blunt end, but is certainly not a projectile point in view of its length (7.2 cm) and the thinness of

[19] For numerous parallels from Roman and mediaeval Egypt see op. cit., pls. XX–XXI, esp. nos. 19–33. See also Whitcomb and Johnson, *Quseir al-Qadim 1978*, pl. 70, f. j; id., *Quseir al-Qadim 1980*, 331 and pl. 69, a–e.

[20] Cf. Petrie, *Objects*, pl. XX, nos. 6–12.

[21] See op. cit., 26.

[22] Cf. P. L. Shinnie and Margaret Shinnie, *Debeira West* (Warminster, 1978), 74 and pl. XXXVIII, a. See also Petrie, *Objects*, pl. XXIII, nos. 47–9.

[23] For other iron kohl sticks from Nubia see Kent R. Weeks, *The Classic Christian Townsite at Arminna West* (Publications of the Pennsylvania–Yale Expedition to Egypt, 3) (New Haven, 1967), 68.

[24] For very closely parallel examples see Petrie, *Tools*, pl. LXIV, nos. Y 38–40, Y 50–2.

[25] For somewhat comparable examples see op. cit., pl. LXIV, nos. Y 42–3.

[26] For parallel examples from Roman Egypt see Petrie, *Objects*, pl. XXIX, nos. 44–5.

a

b

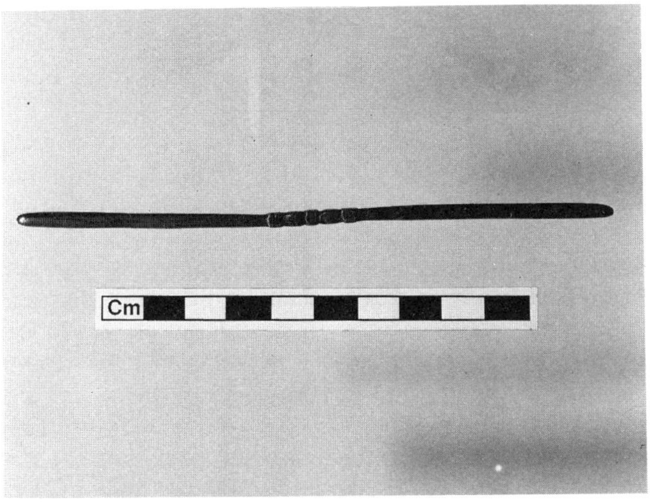

c

d

e

Plate 34. Toilet articles. a, Folding razor (72/145). b, Wooden combs (66/61, 66/65, 66/88, 69/43, 69/54). c, Iron kohl stick (69/45). d, Bronze (top) and iron tweezers (66/67, 66A/22). e. Miniature mirror set into underside of wooden lid (78/512).

the metal. Plate 35d shows a section of heavy iron rod, turned at a right angle, whose purpose is also unknown.

Weapons

Ancient Nubia was traditionally the Land of the Bows,[27] and the skill of Nubian archers was still celebrated when they repulsed an Arab attack on Dongola in AD 652.[28] The following centuries were, however, a time of prolonged peace, interrupted only briefly by the incursion of Shams ed-Dawla in 1172–3. It may have been during this interval that the Nubians lost the warlike propensity for which they were earlier famous. At any rate, warlike paraphernalia are notably scarce in the mediaeval levels at Qaṣr Ibrîm, notwithstanding the effort expended in rebuilding the girdle wall (see Part 2, Ch. 5).

Arrows

The bow and arrow were undoubtedly the chief projectile weapons of the mediaeval Nubians, as of their ancestors. However, only three arrowheads and six fragments of arrowshafts were found in the Late and Terminal Christian levels. The arrowheads are all of iron (pl. 36a), while the shafts are made of a hard, polished wood that has not been identified. One arrowhead is attached to a section of shaft 16.6 cm long. It is one of three shaft fragments which were found close together, and which may all be pieces of the same arrow. One of the shaft fragments is wrapped around at one point with fine gut.

Sling

One of the most interesting weapons found at Qaṣr Ibrîm is a stone-throwing sling made from two-ply palm-fibre rope (pl. 36b). The piece is intact except that the finger-loop at one end is missing. The length when fully extended is 141 cm.[29]

?Throwing stick

A flattened, curved wooden stick, 55 cm in length, may possibly have been some kind of throwing stick analogous to a boomerang (pl. 36c).

Arm knives

In the nineteenth century arm knives were part of the standard equipment of every Nubian male.[30] No actual examples have been found at Qaṣr Ibrîm,[31] but the two leather sheaths illustrated in plates 27d and 27e were unquestionably made to house arm knives similar to those of the more recent past.

?Naphtha bombs

These are very small, more or less pear-shaped ceramic bottles, having a short neck and a very thick body (pl. 39c).[32] One complete and four fragmentary examples were found in the Late Christian levels. All are made of hard, imported pottery wares somewhat like the Aswân utility Ware U6 (see Chapter 11), but more than one ware may be represented. Three of the vessels have a purplish, almost metallic lustre on the exterior surface, but it is not a true glaze. Two specimens have moulded decoration in the form of small bumps, possibly to provide a better hand grip.[33]

A peculiarity of these vessels is that they have a pointed but very thick and heavy bottom, so that they were clearly never meant to stand upright. More probably they were designed to be thrown as projectiles. While the use of the Qaṣr Ibrîm specimens cannot be determined with certainty, they bear a close resemblance to the 'naphtha pots' that were part of the regular equipment of Near Eastern armies in the late Middle Ages. Filled with burning naphtha ('Greek fire'), they were thrown over the walls of besieged cities in order to set fire to their buildings.[34] The one intact specimen from Qaṣr Ibrîm showed clear evidence of burning, although actual naphtha residues were not detected. Evidence of burning was not seen on the other specimens.

The Ibrîm specimens might possibly have been part of the defensive arsenal of the inhabitants, although they would have been of limited use as defensive weapons. More probably the vessels are 'souvenirs' either of the Shams ed-Dawla raid in 1171–2, or of one of the Mamluk raids of the fourteenth century.

[27] Cf. Walter B. Emery, *Egypt in Nubia* (London, 1954), 144.

[28] See William Y. Adams, *Nubia, Corridor to Africa* (London, 1977), 450–1.

[29] For an ancient Egyptian sling see Petrie, *Tools*, pl. LI, no. V 14.

[30] See Thomas Legh, *Narrative of a Journey in Egypt and the Country Beyond the Cataracts* (London, 1817). Following 200, 204; J. L. Burckhardt, *Travels in Nubia* (London, 1819), 142.

[31] For examples of mediaeval Nubian arm knife blades that have been found see Shinnie and Shinnie, op. cit., pl. XLI, 2.

[32] These vessels were previously identified by me as pottery lamps, and were designated as Types P34–6; see op. cit., 154. For fragmentary examples see Donald S. Whitcomb and Janet H. Johnson, *Quseir al-Qadim 1980: Preliminary Report* (Malibu, CA, 1982), pl. 49, i–j.

[33] For parallel examples see Zayn Bilkadi in *Aramco World Magazine*, 46, 1 (1995), 27.

[34] For further discussion see ibid.

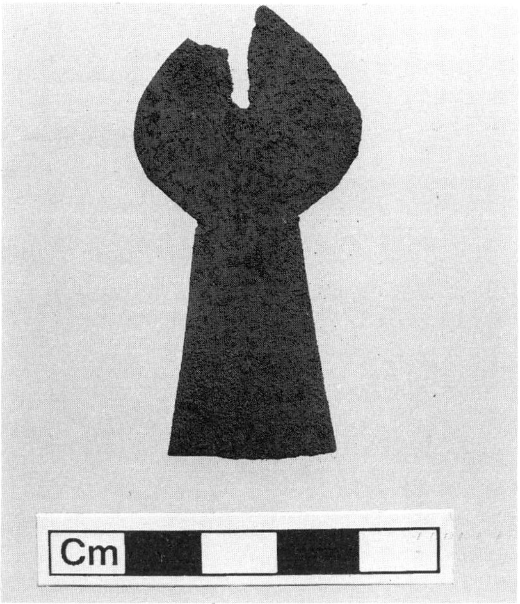

a

b

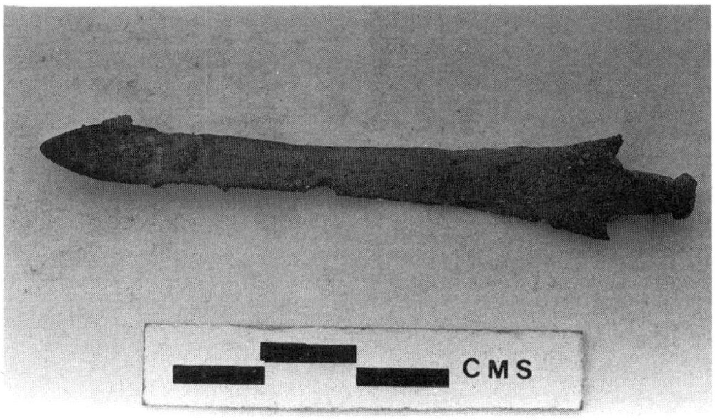

c

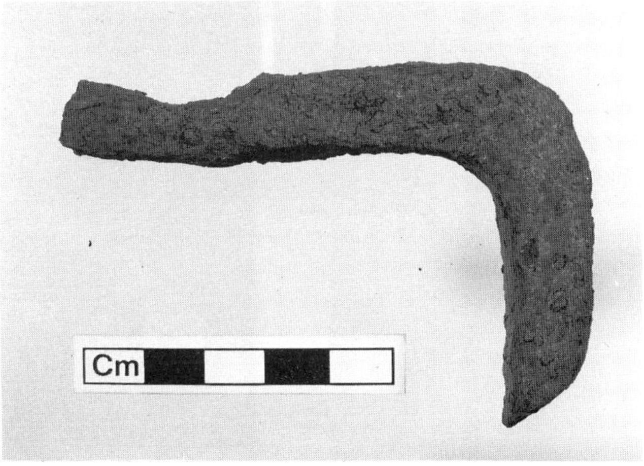

d

Plate 35. Problematical objects. a, Small problematical implement of sheet iron (82/356). b, Small problematical implement of sheet iron (82/357). c, Problematical object of bronze (82/383). d, Problematical bent iron bar (82/330).

a

b

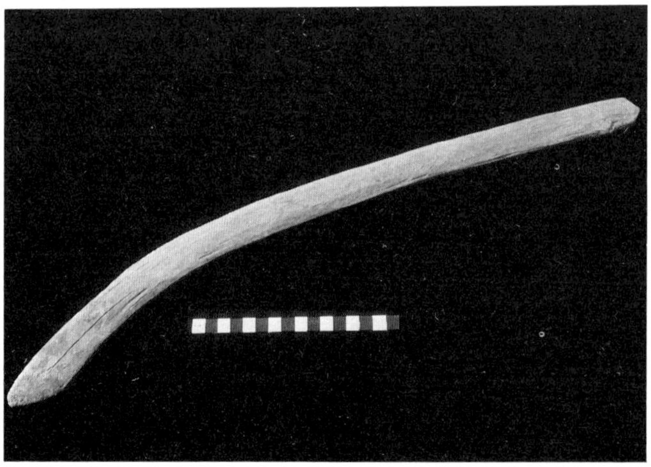

c

Plate 36. Weapons. a, Iron arrowhead (78/480). b, Sling made from palm-fibre rope (82/586). c, Curved throwing stick (82/56).

CHAPTER 5
HOUSEHOLD FURNISHINGS

APPARATUS for food storage and preparation were described in Part 3, Chapter 2, containers in Part 3, Chapter 3, and cutting tools in Part 3, Chapter 4. Other items that were part of the regular furnishing of late mediaeval houses at Qaṣr Ibrîm will be described and illustrated in the present chapter.

Furniture

Despite the tremendous abundance of artifactual material from Qaṣr Ibrîm, the absence of larger items of wood is conspicuous. This does not indicate that such items were never present, but rather that large pieces of wood that had served their original purposes were likely either to be refashioned into smaller objects, or else burned (see Part 1, Chapter 1). Thus, while it can be inferred that the mediaeval Nubians possessed various kinds of wooden furniture, our only direct evidence for them comes from a single bed or chair leg and various small pieces of carved or turned wood that may have been parts of chairs, beds, or chests.

Bed or chair leg

Figure 24 shows a stout piece of carved wood, 38 cm long, which is obviously the leg from a bed or chair. It is the only such item found in the Late Christian levels.

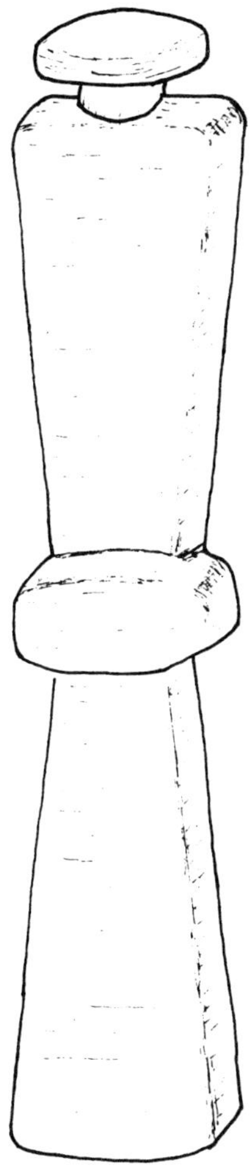

Figure 24. Wooden chair or bed leg, reg. no. 74/199. Length 38 cm.

Lathe-turned balusters

The mediaeval levels at Qaṣr Ibrîm have yielded a substantial number of ornate, lathe-turned wooden elements like the ones shown in plates 37a and 37b. The great majority are short segments, 10 to 12 cm long, having a tenon at both ends (pl. 37a, 1 and 2). A few have a rounded knob at one end and are evidently finials (pl. 37b, 2). The group of lathe-turned elements includes both relatively slender pieces that are fully round (pl. 37a)[1] and thicker pieces that are always found in quarter-round or 1/8-round segments (pl. 37b, 1 and 3).[2] Pieces of both kinds were common at the mediaeval Monastery of Epiphanius at Thebes; they are identified by the excavators as balusters respectively for chairs or benches and for flat wooden screens or door facings that were intended to be viewed from one side only.[3]

[1] For roughly comparable examples see W. M. Flinders Petrie, *Objects of Daily Use* (London, 1927), pl. XXIX, nos. 120, 121; J. E. Quibell, *Excavations at Saqqara (1908–9, 1909–10)* (Cairo,1912), pl. LIV.

[2] For closely comparable specimens see H. E. Winlock and W. E. Crum, *The Monastery of Epiphanius at Thebes* (New York, 1926), part 1, 56 and pl. XV, C. Other Nubian examples are illustrated in P. L. Shinnie and Margaret Shinnie, *Debeira West* (Warminster, 1978), pl. L.

[3] For extended discussion see Winlock and Crum, op. cit., 55–7.

a

b

c

d

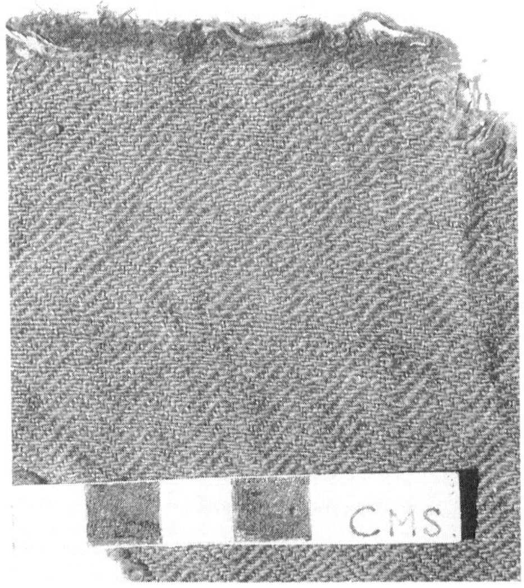

e

f

Plate 37. Furniture and bedding elements. a, Lathe-turned wooden balusters (66A/211, 66A/212, 66A/213). b, Sections of lathe-turned wooden baluster (66A/216, 66A/218, 66A/221). c, Turned wooden knobs (74.2.28/6, 80/765). d, Small carved rectangular elements of wood (69/72). e, Fragment of linen and cotton cushion cover (78T/60). f, Fragment of wool blanket (82T/333).

Turned knobs

Also found from time to time in the Late Christian levels are small, lathe-turned wooden knobs like those shown in plate 37c. These also are presumed to be furniture components, most probably finials.

Carved elements

Plate 37d illustrates three rather thin rectangular wooden panels, each measuring 6 × 8 cm. Each piece is identically decorated with incised parallel grooves, and each terminates at the top and bottom in a very thin flange that was evidently meant to be slotted into a wooden rail. These items are probably side panels from some kind of box or screen, or possibly a chair or bench. All three are almost certainly parts of the same original furniture piece.

Ivory inlay

The excavations produced one very small, thin fragment of ivory with carved decoration (not illustrated). It is believed to be part of the inlaid decoration from a chest.[4]

Toilet fixtures

One of the many anomalies at Qaṣr Ibrîm is the general absence of toilet fixtures, which were found in abundance at Meinarti and other late mediaeval Nubian sites.[5] Three of the Late Christian houses had toilet chambers (see Part 2, Ch. 2), but in none of them was a ceramic fixture found in place. The only examples of toilet fixtures are two fragments found in refuse deposits, one of which is illustrated in plate 40a.

Bedding

Recognizing the original components of bedding is difficult, since large textile pieces were used and reused and finally were torn up for rags. However, hundreds of rags have been found which were very roughly tacked together, involving from two or three up to seven or eight pieces in one large wad. The majority are wool rags, but cotton and linen rags were sometimes also treated in this way. It seems probable that these were used as padding of some sort, possibly as filling for mattresses or cushions. A number of fragments of what may have been cushion covers have also been recovered. They are of fustian, a fabric containing both flax and cotton (See Part 3, Ch. 6 for more detail). The weave is a diamond twill pattern in blue and white or in brown and white (pl. 37e). They have been tentatively identified as cushion covers because of their resemblance to finds from earlier and later periods, some of which still contained feather stuffing in the corners.

No textile find can be recognized with certainty as a mattress cover, and it is likely that the 'mattresses' were simply bundles of rags covered over with any large fabric. In fact, large fabric pieces could serve many functions, as Klunzinger noted in the nineteenth century when he and his companions were bedding down for the night: '...today [it] has already been used as a plaid, a head-covering, a fodder-cloth, a sack and a basket, and now becomes a carpet or a coverlet.'[6]

In addition to wool and cotton shawls that could be used as bedding, there were also flat-weave rugs and pile carpets. Flat-weave rugs are always of wool, well spun and tightly woven. They are generally colourful, using red, blue, yellow, tan, brown, and white in wide bands and tapestry-woven patterns. Three fragments of pile carpet have also been recovered from the Late and Terminal Christian periods. The patterns show only a small part of the whole but in general seem to be geometric. One example is made with a Ghiordes knot and may be a Caucasian type;[7] another uses the Spanish knot.[8]

There are a number of fabric specimens that may have been used as blankets, as well as serving other functions. They are of wool, in colours that include black, red, brown, dark brown, blue, green, orange, yellow, and the natural creamy colour of the undyed wool. Most blankets are decorated in plain bands, having one main colour which is used in alternation with bands of from one to four other colours (pl. 37f).

Fragments of quilting have been found which probably functioned as bedding. They nearly always comprise two layers of undyed or blue cotton cloth with cotton wadding between. The quilting stitches are in parallel rows, from 1 to 3 cm apart. At Gebel Adda quilts were used as outer wrappings on Late Christian burials. They are thought to be domestic items rather than specially produced for use in burial and were probably luxury house furnishings. The fabrics employed were striped cotton, checked linen and silk brocaded panels, all much more elaborate than any of

[4] For parallel but much better preserved examples see Petrie, *Objects*, pl. XLIX.

[5] See William Y. Adams, *Nubia, Corridor to Africa* (London, 1977), 491; Shinnie and Shinnie, op. cit., 106. For an illustration (incorrectly identified as an amphora stand) see Ugo Monneret de Villard, *La Nubia medioevale*, I (Cairo, 1935), 221, fig. 212.

[6] C. B. Klunzinger, *Upper Egypt: its People and its Products* (New York, 1878), 220.

[7] No. 78T/232.

[8] No. 78T/84.

the quilting found at Qaṣr Ibrîm, except that employed in caps (see Part 3, Ch. 7).[9]

Matting

The Late Christians made fairly extensive use of flat, plaited mats made from palm-leaf strips or, in a few cases, from palm-fibre cord. These are presumed to have been used originally as house furnishings, although they are preserved entirely in the form of large fragments that were reused as lining in storage pits (see Part 2, Ch. 3). Their original use is, therefore, necessarily conjectural.

Roof matting

The use of matting as a covering for lightweight roofs is common in modern Nubia[10] and seems to have been practised by the mediaeval Nubians as well. The roof of Late Christian Crypt 188 was covered with a large, thick mat made from bundles of halfa grass woven in a herring-bone pattern (see Part 2, Ch. 3).

Sleeping mats

Plate 38a illustrates one of two very large pieces of matting that were found in the lining of a Late Christian storage pit. Both pieces are about 2 m long but are incomplete. The warp in each case is made up of two-ply palm-fibre cord, through which loosely twisted strands of halfa grass are woven so as to form the main body of the mat. Closely similar, though slightly smaller, mats found at the Monastery of Epiphanius were identified as sleeping mats.[11]

One very unusual piece of matting, measuring about 40 × 64 cm, may be a fragment of a mattress. It consists of three separate layers of material sewn together with palm-fibre cord (pl. 38b). The central or foundation layer is comprised of twined basketry, involving a weft of flattened halfa grass stalks woven around and through a warp made up of rigid bundles of grass stalks. The result is a kind of mat that is flexible in one direction but not the other, i.e., it can be rolled up but cannot be folded. Masses of loose palm-fibre padding are sewn against both faces of the foundation mat by means of parallel rows of palm-cord stitching, passing through the padding from one side to the other. The piece is terminated at one end by a rigid wooden rod, around which the reed wefts are wrapped. A part of one straight side is also preserved; the other side and the other end are missing.

Floor mats

Late Christian storage pits have also yielded various fragments of flat, plaited matting made from palm-leaf strips, as shown in plate 38c. A second type is made from coarse woven hemp.[12] Both types are presumed to be fragments of floor mats.

Pot rests

Rings in which round-bottomed pottery vessels could be rested were made in various ways. The simplest example consists merely of a mass of palm-leaf strips loosely twisted into a circle (pl. 38d). Another specimen has a bundle of soft withes twisted into a circle and bound around with palm-leaf wrapping (pl. 38e). Other pot rests were made from cloth rags, twisted into a ring of soft cord and then wrapped around with other strips of rag. Pot rests from the Late Christian levels vary in diameter from 7 to 15 cm.

Lamps

Oil lamps were the basic lighting apparatus of the Nubians through most of their history. The oil used in them may possibly have been that of the castor bean, which is mentioned by several classical authors as the usual lighting oil of the Egyptians.[13] Olive oil, which was not produced locally in Nubia, would certainly have been too scarce and precious to be used in this fashion.

Nubian lamps were almost exclusively of pottery. In the course of time they underwent a distinct process of evolutionary development, as shown in figure 28. The common lamp of the Meroitic and X-Group periods was a small, closed vessel having a central hole for filling and a hole at one edge for the wick. Many imported specimens were mould-made and bore elaborate patterns of relief decoration on the upper surfaces. In the Early Christian period these gradually gave way to lamps shaped rather like a modern candle-holder, with a small central reservoir for oil surrounded by a broader, shallow dish in which the wick burned. These persisted in favour through Classic Christian times,

[9] Elisabeth Crowfoot, *Notes on the Nubian Textiles from Gebel Adda*. Unpublished manuscript on file in the office of the Director, Egyptian Department, Royal Ontario Museum, (Toronto, 1979), 5.

[10] See Horst Jaritz in Robert A. Fernea and Georg Gerster, *Nubians in Egypt* (Austin, 1973), 52.

[11] Winlock and Crum, op. cit., 72–4 and pls. XXIV–XXV.

[12] Fibre sample 84/17

[13] See A. Lucas and J. R. Harris, *Ancient Egyptian Materials and Industries,* 4th ed. (London, 1962), 332.

a

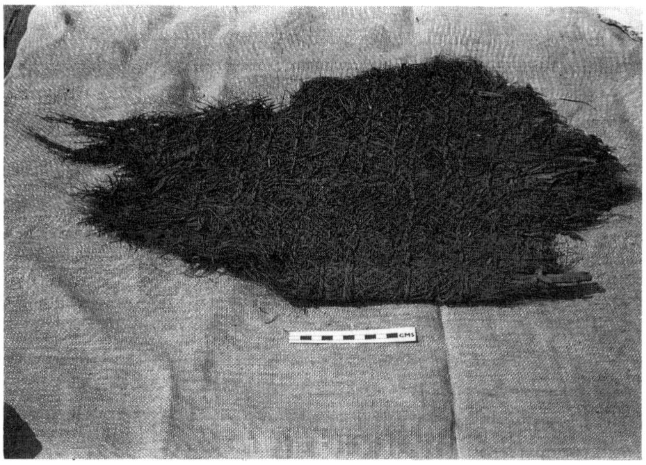

b

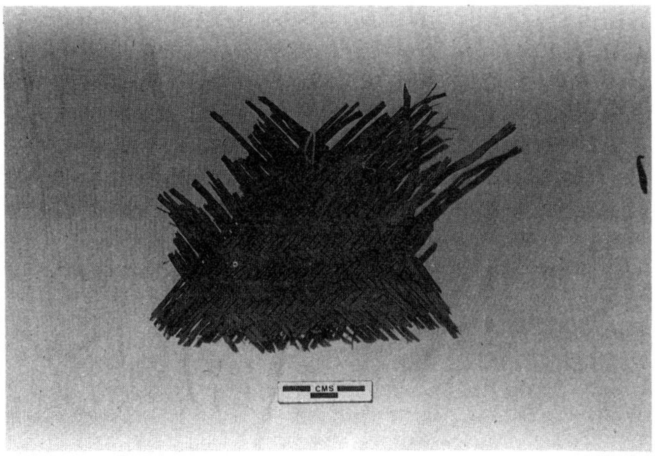

c

d

e

Plate 38. Palm fibre matting and pot rests. a, Large twined sleeping mat (78/681). b, ?Mattress fragment (82/92). c, Fragment of plaited floor mat (82/118). d, Pot rest of twisted palm leaf (78/293). e, Pot rest of wrapped palm leaf (82/109).

then gave way in turn either to simple open dishes or to miniature pottery bottles, though some more elaborate glazed lamps were also imported from Egypt. Finally, the lamps of the Terminal Christian and post-Christian periods were mostly small, simple and crude hand-made dishes.[14]

Two lamp forms were predominant in the Late Christian levels at Qaṣr Ibrîm: the simple dish or saucer and the small bottle. However, lamps of other forms were also in use:

Aswân saucer lamps. This type is the single most common lamp from the Late Christian levels; it is represented by eight registered examples and a much larger number of unregistered sherds. The vessel is a simple open dish, typically about 10 cm in diameter, having a flat bottom and out-flared sides (pl. 39a).[15] All of the registered specimens are of the Aswân utility Ware U6 (see Part 3, Ch. 3), and lack a slip or any kind of decoration. These vessels were not necessarily designed to serve exclusively as lamps, but all of them that were found at Qaṣr Ibrîm had been put to that use. Very small cups or goblets or Aswân ware[16] were also widely used as lamps at Meinarti.[17] Vessels of the same kind were also found at Qaṣr Ibrîm but only one showed evidence of use as a lamp (pl. 39b). The evidence in this case was unmistakable, since the cup had not one but several wicks hanging over the rim.

Bottle lamps. These are very small, more or less pear-shaped vessels having a short neck at the narrow end (pl. 39c).[18] One complete and four fragmentary examples were found in the Late Christian levels. A peculiarity of these vessels is that they have a pointed but very thick and heavy bottom. Originally, they were probably 'naphtha bombs' designed to be thrown over the battlements of besieged cities, and were discussed as such at the end of Chapter 4. However, there is some possiblity tht specimens found in Nubia, including at Qaṣr Ibrîm, were put to secondary use as bottle lamps.

All of the bottle lamps are made of hard, imported pottery wares. There is some resemblance to the Aswân utility Ware U6 (see Part 3, Chapter 4), but more than one ware may be represented. The vessels typically have a purplish, almost metallic lustre on the exterior surface, but it is not a true glaze. Two fragmentary specimens have moulded decoration in the form of small bumps, perhaps meant to simulate leaves.

Egyptian glazed lamps. From the Late Christian levels there are three fragmentary examples of Egyptian glazed lamps, of a type that is very common in the mediaeval deposits at Fostat.[19] The most common colour is light blue. One specimen appears originally to have been brown, though it is almost entirely covered by crusted oil.

Hand-made dish lamps. All of the common lamps of the Late Christian period discussed in the preceding paragraphs were foreign-made. The only lamp form that appears to have been locally made in Late and Terminal Christian times was a small, thick dish or bowl of hand-made ware, usually having either a red or a brown slip.[20] These vessels were extremely common at Meinarti and Kulubnarti,[21] but only one example has been registered from Qaṣr Ibrîm.

Broken vessel bases. Apart from the hand-made lamps just described, the Late Christians also made lamps from the broken-off bases of bowls, jars, and vases, after grinding off the broken edges to a relatively smooth contour. Lamps of this kind were common at Meinarti and Kulubnarti[22] but only four examples were registered from Qaṣr Ibrîm.

Older lamp forms. Four fragmentary lamps of X-Group and Early Christian types were found in the Late Christian deposits. It is possible that the Late Christian inhabitants found and reused older lamps, but more probably these represent accidentally re-deposited refuse.

Brushes

The Late Christian deposits yielded two rather crude brushes or hand-brooms, intended presumably for sweeping floors. One is made from a bundle of palm-leaf strips, bound around with palm-fibre cord at one end; the other is made from a bundle of small sticks (pl. 39d).[23]

[14] For further discussion of lamps and their development see William Y. Adams, *Ceramic Industries of Medieval Nubia* (Memoirs of the UNESCO Archaeological Survey of Sudanese Nubia, 1) (Lexington, 1986), Part I, 103–4, 150–4.

[15] Adams Types P28 and P29; see op. cit., 153.

[16] Adams Type P30; see op. cit., 153.

[17] Author's unpublished field records.

[18] Adams Types P34–36; see op. cit., 154. For fragmentary examples see Donald S. Whitcomb and Janet H. Johnson, *Quseir al-Qadim 1980: Preliminary Report* (Malibu, 1982), pl. 49, i–j.

[19] See Aly Bey Bahgat and Félix Massoul, *La céramique mussulmane de l'Égypte* (Cairo, 1930), pl. LVI, no. 1.

[20] Adams Types P22–27. See Adams, op. cit., 153.

[21] Author's unpublished field records.

[22] Op. cit.

[23] For parallel examples see Petrie, *Objects*, pl. XLII, no. 128; Winlock and Crum, op. cit., pl. XXIII, A (right).

a

b

c

d

e

Plate 39. Pottery lamps; miscellaneous objects. a, Saucer lamp of Aswân Ware W12 (82/121). b, Cup lamp of Aswân Ware W12, with multiple string wicks (66/132). c, Bottle lamp (or naphtha bomb) of Aswân Ware U6 (78/145). d, Straw hand-broom (82/470). e, Fragment of glazed tile (82/168).

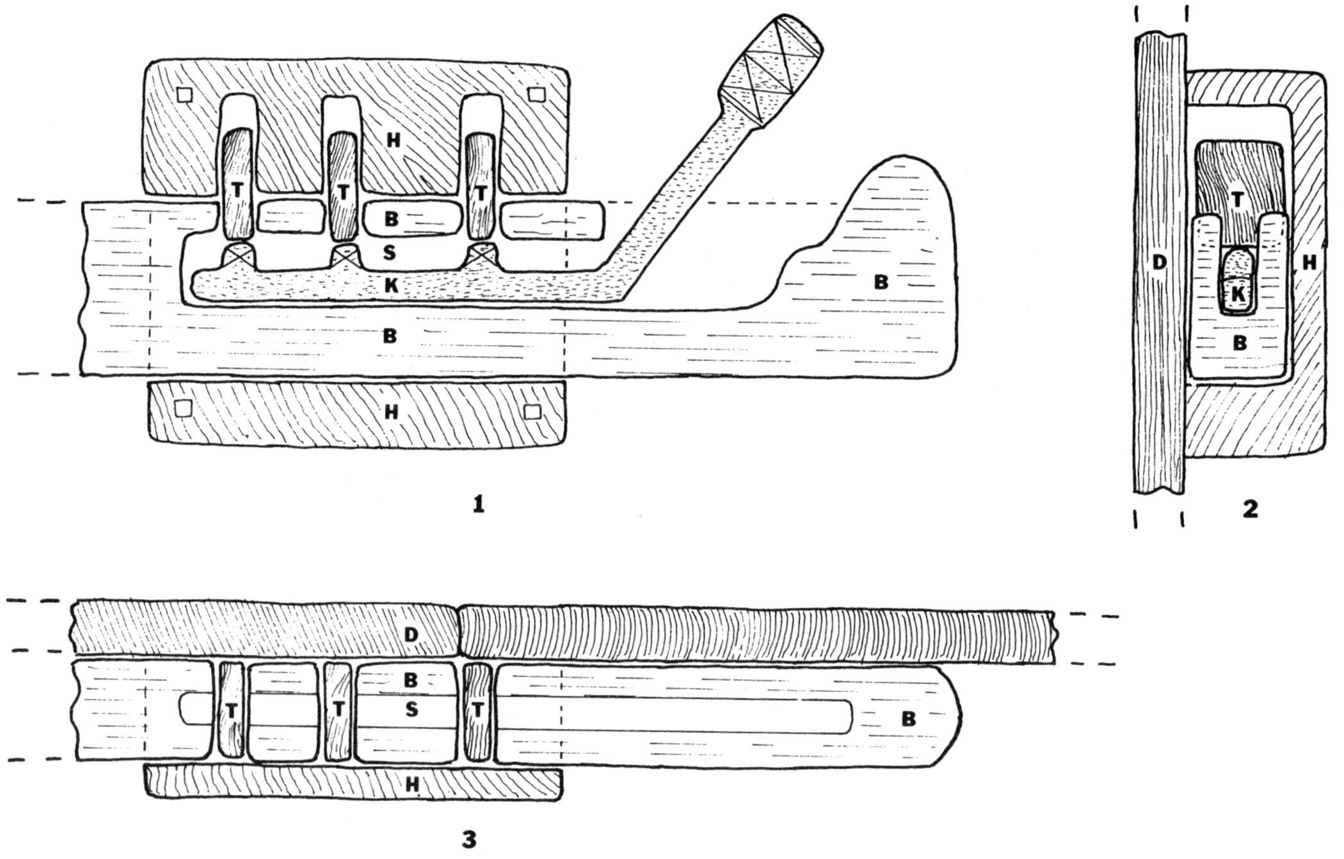

Figure 25. Cutaway diagrams to show operation of toothed key and lock mechanism. **1**, side view; **2**, end view; **3**, top view (key not inserted). **B**, bolt; **D**, door; **H**, housing; **K**, key; **S**, key slot; **T**, tumblers. Schematic diagrams not based on any actual specimen.

Miscellaneous household items

Other registered items that belong in the general category of household equipment include a sandstone block with a half-round depression, which evidently served as a door pivot; two square-shanked iron nails, with lengths of 5.5 and 9.2 cm; and a fragment of multicoloured glazed tile that is certainly of foreign origin (pl. 39e). The side of the tile illustrated in the photograph is decorated in blue, green, and red; the reverse is mostly plain white but exhibits a small remnant of a blue design. The size of the piece is 4.5 × 4.6 cm

Fragments of woven goat-hair tent panels are frequently encountered; one of the largest measures 102 cm × 48 cm (82T/332). It is dark brown with narrow white stripes near the two long edges, and occurring again closer to the centre of the panel.

Lock mechanisms

The principal door-locking mechanism employed by the mediaeval Nubians was identical to that which is still found in Nubian and Egyptian peasant homes today. It is made entirely of acacia wood, and consists of a stout bolt, a large housing through which the bolt is passed, and in which several small wooden tumblers are concealed, and a key for pushing back the tumblers (fig. 25). The tumblers move up and down within slots inside the housing and into matching slots in the top of the bolt. A stout wooden key has teeth spaced in such a way as to match the positioning of the tumblers. When the key is inserted into a hole in the housing, the teeth engage the lower ends of the tumblers and push them upward clear of the bolt, allowing it to be slid back and forth. Examples of housings, bolts, tumblers, and keys have all been found in the mediaeval levels at Qaṣr Ibrîm. Like virtually all finds on the site, these objects have been found disassembled and widely scattered through the refuse, not attached to the doors where they were originally fitted.

Housings

Mediaeval lock housings exhibit two slightly different designs. In one kind the bolt, when open, slides back into a recess within the housing itself (pl. 40b–c). In another kind, the bolt passes entirely through the

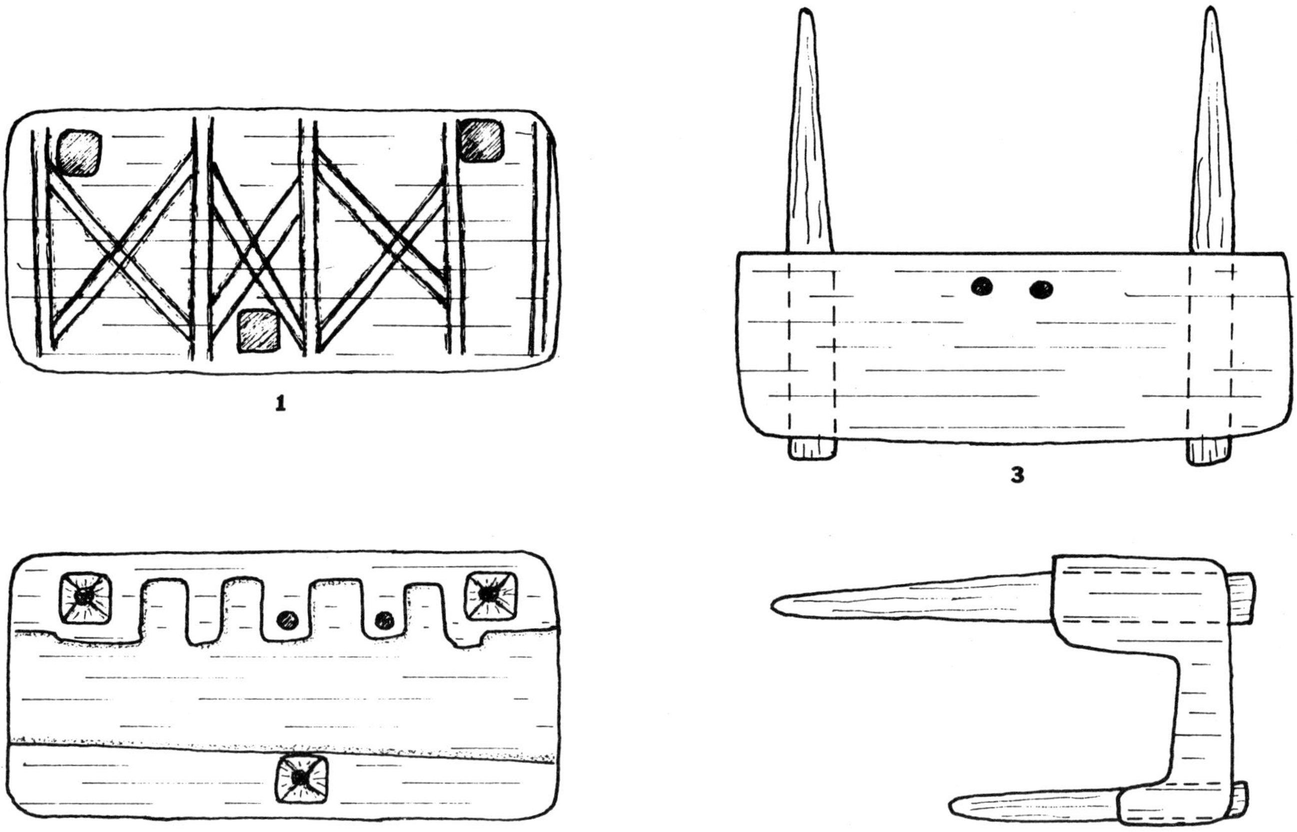

Figure 26. Wooden lock housing, reg. no. 78/54. **1**, exterior side view; **2**, interior side view; **3**, top view; **4**, end view. Length 28 cm.

housing (pl. 40d), which merely functions as a kind of staple to hold it against the face of the door.[24] This second type of housing is usual in Nubia today.[25] Plates 40b and 40c show respectively the exterior and the interior of a large housing of the first type. The two square holes which penetrate all the way through the wood are for stout, hand-wrought iron rivets that would have fastened the housing to the facing of a door. The three rectangular recesses visible in plate 40c would have housed the tumblers, and the long groove below them would have housed the bolt when drawn back. Note that there is a small carved monogram on the exterior face (pl. 40b, left). In mediaeval Nubia this was a common way of representing the name of St. Michael, whose blessing was probably invoked on the house and its contents.[26] The overall dimensions of the lock housing are 43.5 × 9.4 × 7.5 cm.

A large housing of the second type is illustrated in figure 26; its dimensions are 27.5 × 13 × 7.5 cm. Like modern Nubian housings, it has carved decoration on the outside face. A much smaller example of the same kind is shown in plate 40d.

Bolt

Plate 40e shows the only door bolt that has been found in a Late Christian context.[27] It was evidently part of a very simple lock mechanism, having only one or two tumblers. The length of the piece is 34 cm.

Keys

Wooden door keys are among the commonest finds at Qaṣr Ibrîm; 37 whole and fragmentary examples have been found in the Late and Terminal Christian levels

[24] For an illustration of an ancient housing and bolt that were found *in situ* see Elinor M. Husselman, *The Topography and Architecture, Karanis, Egypt* (University of Michigan, Kelsey Museum of Archaeology Studies, no. 5) (Ann Arbor, 1979), pl. 53, b. For another archaeological specimen from Egypt see W. M. Flinders Petrie, *Tools and Weapons* (London, 1917), pl. LXXV, no. W 133. For diagrams illustrating the lock mechanism see also Winlock and Crum, op. cit., 59; Shinnie and Shinnie, op. cit., 105.

[25] For more on modern Nubian door locks see Jaritz, op. cit., 51; Friedrich W. Hinkel, *Auszug aus Nubien* (Berlin, 1978), 40–1; and Marian Wenzel, *Nubian House Decoration* (London, 1972), *passim*. The latter book discusses the work of individual lockmakers, who are highly skilled specialists.

[26] For some of the innumerable variants see Adams, *Ceramic Industries*, 385.

[27] For parallel examples see Petrie, *Tools*, pl. LXXV, nos. W 124, W 133, and W 135; Husselman, op. cit., pl. 49, a.

a

b

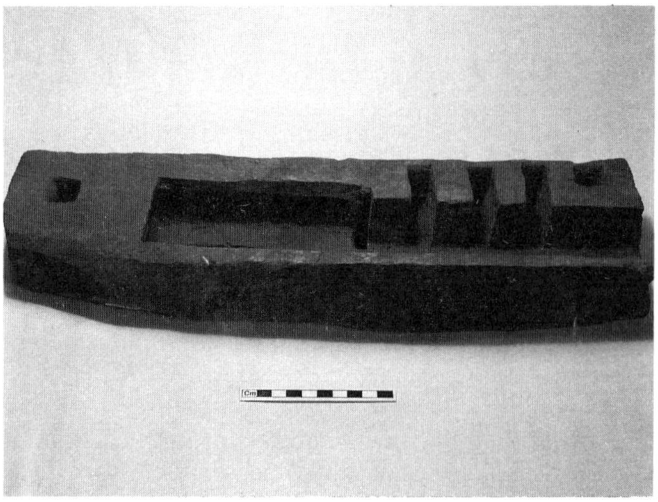

c

d

e

Plate 40. Ceramic toilet; wooden lock elements. a, Portion of ceramic toilet fixture (66.3.5/1). b, Wooden lock housing, exterior (82/55). c, Interior of **b**. d, Small wooden lock housing (66A/177). e, Wooden door bolt (78/64).

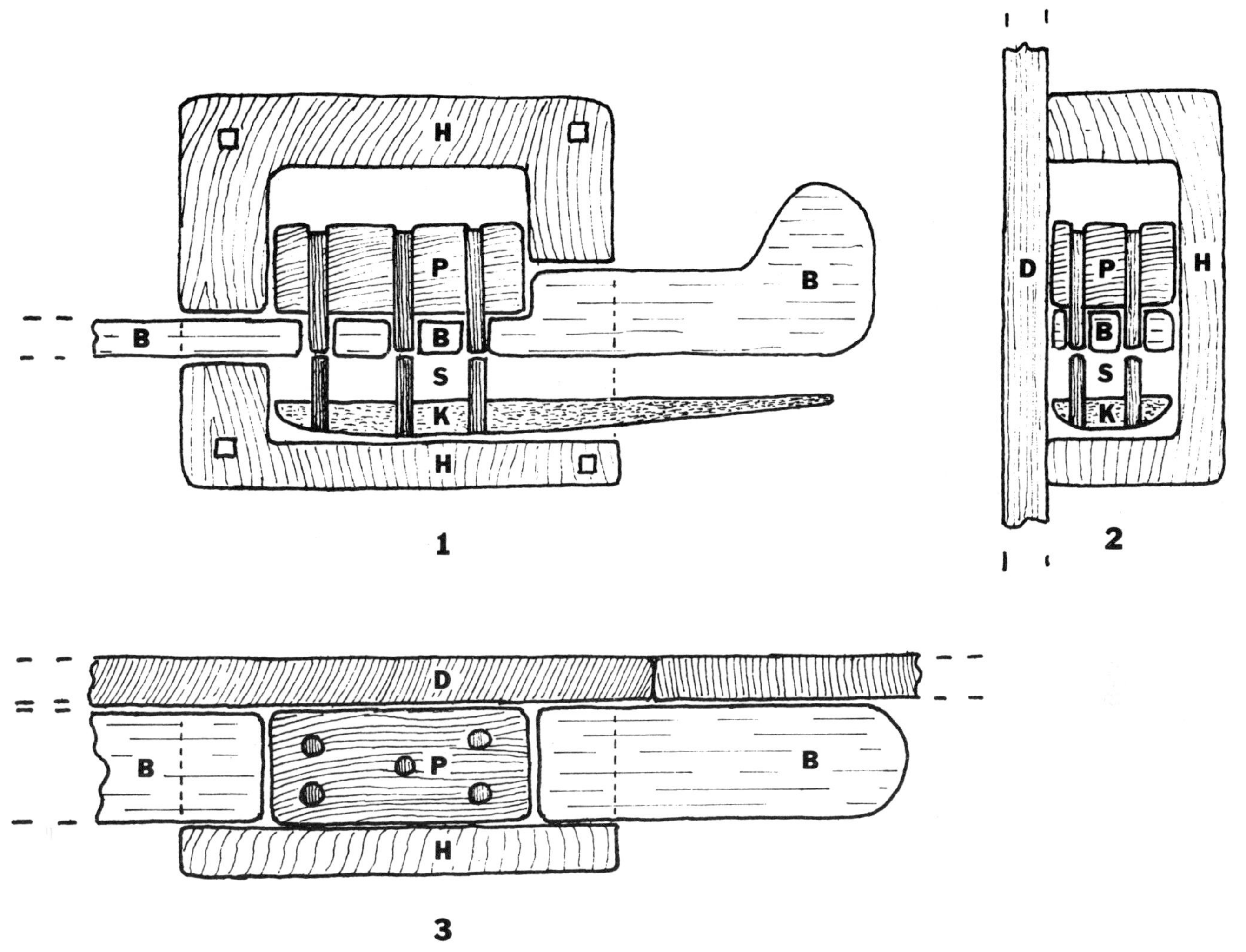

Figure 27. Cutaway diagrams to show operation of peg key and lock mechanism (Flinders Petrie interpretation). **1**, side view; **2**, end view; **3**, top view (key not inserted). **B**, bolt; **D**, door; **H**, housing; **K**, key; **P**, perforated block and tumbler pins; **S**, key slot. Schematic diagrams not based on any actual specimen.

alone. This is larger than the number of Late Christian houses and suggests the possibility that interior doors as well as street doors were often fitted with locks. The keys are of four basic types:

Simple toothed keys. By far the most common key type in the late mediaeval levels is the simple toothed key, illustrated in plate 41a.[28] The keys nearly always have either three or four teeth; they differ from each other mainly in the width and spacing of the teeth. An interesting feature of these keys is that they regularly have simple incised decoration. Many have knobs at the handle end, presumably where a suspension string could be tied. Lengths of the intact specimens range between 16 and 34 cm; the most common length is about 24 cm.

Tooth-and-peg keys. Some toothed keys have one or more of the teeth replaced by round wooden pegs inserted into the body of the key (pl. 41a, 1, 2, and 5). It seems evident in at least some of the cases that these were replacements for original teeth that had broken off.

Angled keys. These are similar to, but substantially larger than, straight-bodied keys. The four specimens that have been recovered from Late Christian levels all measure between 40 and 45 cm in length (pl. 41b).[29] Keys of this type are today most often used in conjunction with outside house doors, where an exceptionally heavy bolt and housing are employed.[30] The advantage of the angled design lies in the fact that the key can be thrust downward into a relatively short groove in the

[28] For parallel examples from Egypt see Petrie, *Tools*, pl. LXXV, no. W 133; Husselman, op. cit., pl. 54, a (upper).

[29] For other angled keys, but equipped with pegs rather than with teeth, see Petrie, *Tools*, pl. LXXV, nos. W 132 and W 140–2; Quibell, op. cit., pl. LIV; Husselman, op. cit., pl. 54, a (lower).

[30] Cf. Hinkel, loc. cit.; Jaritz, loc. cit.

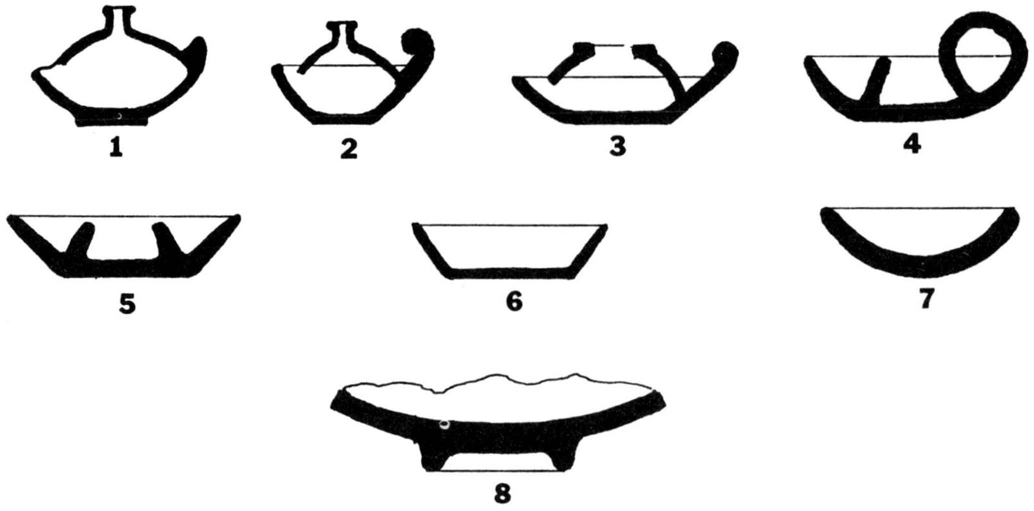

Figure 28. Evolution of Nubian lamp forms. **1**, X-Group; **2**, X-Group and Early Christian; **3**, Early Christian and Classic Christian I; **4**, Classic Christian I; **5**, Classic Christian II; **6**, Late Christian I (imported Aswan ware); **7**, Late Christian II and Terminal Christian (hand-made ware); **8**, Late Christian II and Terminal Christian (broken bowl base).

top of the bolt itself, which would not be possible with a straight-bodied key (cf. fig. 25).[31] Of the four Late Christian specimens that were found, two had been broken and mended, as shown in plate 41b.

Peg keys. These keys are different in design, and to some extent in principle, from the keys previously described. The body of the key is a relatively thin and flat piece of wood, between 20 and 30 cm in length, into which short, round pegs are inserted in various patterns.[32] Six examples were recovered from the Late Christian levels, of which four are shown in plate 41c. From top to bottom they had respectively five, four, five, and six pegs, though many of these are now missing. Unlike toothed keys, all of the peg keys have tapered handles, and all but one of them are drilled through the handle end for suspension. None bears any evidence of decoration.

Peg keys would have required a somewhat different lock mechanism from that previously described. According to Petrie's analysis these keys are pressed against the underside of the door bolt in such a way that the pegs penetrate into holes in the bolt itself, displacing very small round tumblers that had dropped down from a housing above (cf. fig. 27).[33] The bolt is then drawn back by pulling on the key itself. We have found no certain examples of bolts or housings to match these keys, but the very small perforated blocks, to be described below, may have been associated with them in some way.

Tumblers

Tumblers used in the common type of Nubian lock are nothing more than thin, roughly shaped rectangles of wood, as shown in plate 41d. Twenty-two examples were found in the Late and Terminal Christian levels. Their average size is about 3×4 cm, with a thickness of 1.5 cm. Most have a regular rectangular or square outline, but a few have one edge cut at an angle, as illustrated in plate 41d, 1, 2, and 6.

Perforated blocks

The Late and Terminal Christian levels yielded four small, perforated wooden blocks, illustrated in plate 41e. The lengths of all four specimens are between 3.6 and 4.8 cm, with widths and thicknesses slightly less. The blocks have respectively three, five, six, and ten holes placed close together. The use of these objects is uncertain, but the size and spacing of the holes is sufficiently close to the patterning of the pegs found on peg keys (pl. 41c) to suggest some connection between the two artifacts. Possibly these were tumbler housings, though they would, in turn, have had to be enclosed within a larger bolt housing.

[31] Cf. Hinkel, loc. cit.; Jaritz, loc. cit.

[32] For parallel examples from Egypt see Petrie, *Tools,* pl. LXXV, nos. W 136–8; Quibell, op. cit., pl. LIV; Donald S. Whitcomb and Janet H. Johnson, *Quseir al-Qadim 1978: Preliminary Report* (Cairo, 1979), pl. 72, a–b.

[33] Petrie, *Tools*, 59 and pl. LXXV, no. W 132; see also Winlock and Crum, op. cit., 59, fig. 19.

a

b

c

d

e

Plate 41. Wooden keys and lock elements. a, Simple toothed keys (69/41, 69/57, 78/364, 82/80). b, Angled key (78/359). c, Peg keys (69/141, 80/665, 82/80). d, Tumblers (82/197). e, Perforated blocks (72/440, 80/781, 82/21, 82/255).

CHAPTER 6
TEXTILE MATERIALS AND WEAVES
BY NETTIE K. ADAMS

THE conditions which make the site of Qaṣr Ibrîm so special for the archaeologist, namely, the extreme dryness which allows almost total organic preservation, have presented a challenge as well as an opportunity for the textile analyst. Probably few archaeological sites have yielded as many pieces of textile as has this one. In just one excavation season of eleven weeks (1980), 23,432 specimens of cloth were recovered, and the volume of textile finds from other seasons was nearly as large.

Rather than attempting to process a representative sample of the textile finds, it was decided to analyze and record every fragment. To aid in this massive endeavour, data forms were made up and a coding system was devised to express the basic structural attributes of cloth. These attributes include fibre, spinning direction of both warp and weft, weave type, thread count, colour, and types of borders and selvedges. Qualities such as the tightness of the spin and the spacing and diameter of the yarn are also noted. In addition, space is provided on the form for verbal descriptions and drawings of unusual weaves, colour relationships, and woven, embroidered, and printed patterns.[1]

The vast majority of our textile finds are small rags, which means that in most cases the original function of the fabric cannot be determined. This is directly attributable to the nature of the deposit on the site, i.e., refuse. Everything that has been preserved was either misplaced, forgotten, or discarded by its original owners. They recycled many of their larger garments into smaller things, like bags and children's clothing, but the ultimate fate of nearly every textile object was to be torn into rags. These were then used for all the things which paper towels, tissues, handkerchiefs, toilet paper, etc. are used for today. Occasionally we have found a complete textile object or garment, but in most of these cases they were too small to be made into anything else, or were simply lost.

Of course, some functions are intrinsic to the fabric itself, as in the case of carpet or net. In addition, by carefully noting such things as cut or shaped edges, the arrangement of seams and hems, and the placement of ties and buttons, we can infer the functions of many other specimens. We can also recognize that certain kinds of cloth were commonly used for certain kinds of garments, or for other purposes, even though the function of many individual specimens cannot be determined.

The fabrics discussed in this chapter came from 87 proveniences, all located within the walls of securely dated Late and Terminal Christian structures. Material from many other proveniences, whose stratigraphy is not absolutely secure, has been omitted. The 87 proveniences contained 3,123 recorded specimens, including more than 50 types of fabric. They ranged from the finest silks, to utility cotton, linen, and wool, to heavy mats and tent fragments made of woven goat hair. The fabric types have been grouped according to fibre content for discussion here.

Cotton fabrics

The cotton fabrics have been divided into twenty-one types, and these have been grouped into two basic groupings on the basis of spinning direction of the yarn—the first step in the production of woven cloth.

Fabrics made of S-spun yarn

Fabrics with S-spun yarn are those made from yarns in which the fibre is twisted in a clockwise direction. One of the most commonly found of the S-spun cotton fabrics is undyed and employs a balanced plain weave, i.e., a weave in which the warp and the weft are equally visible. This appears to be a continuation of the tradition of cotton-fabric production which began in Meroitic times. A variant of the type has small patterns embroidered in brightly coloured wool yarns—red, blue, green, and orange (pl. 42a). Most of the designs are geometric, although some have the appearance of Greek letters. We cannot be sure how this fabric was used, since only one piece has been found which proclaims its function. It is a small bag with the embroidered patterns occurring asymmetrically, and had obviously been remade from something else. Related to the foregoing type are two others, both of which were also common in Meroitic times. They differ only in regard to the weave. One employs a half-basket weave, having paired wefts, and the other is a full

[1] For detail on the recording methodology see Nettie K. Adams, 'Textiles from Qaṣr Ibrîm: A Window on Nubian Culture History,' 3–5. Paper delivered at the 1984 annual meeting of the Archaeological Institute of America, December 27–30, Toronto, Ontario.

basket weave, with both warps and wefts paired. The frequency of both types is minuscule, and they may simply have been rooted out of earlier levels by the mediaeval inhabitants for use as rags. Another fabric with S-spun yarns is weft-faced. The undyed cotton wefts are interrupted at regular intervals of 1 to 2 cm by two wool wefts of darker colour, giving the effect of a very narrow line in brown, black or rust. The yarn of this fabric is fairly thick, producing a solid cloth. It is not common, but occurs often enough to be a recognizable type (pl. 42b).

One S-spun fabric is very different in appearance from the others. The yarn is generally fine but irregular, and the plain weave, although close, is uneven, as if the wefts were poorly beaten. The fabric has an unskilled appearance in contrast to the other and better finished cotton fabrics. There are only minute amounts of this poorly made cloth in the Late Christian levels at Qaṣr Ibrîm, but it has been found more frequently in other late mediaeval sites in Nubia.[2] At Ibrîm itself it is more abundant in the late Ottoman period than it is earlier.

Fabrics made of Z-spun yarn

There are fourteen cotton fabric types in the Z-spun category, i.e., fabrics made from yarns in which the fibre is twisted counter-clockwise. Of these, thirteen have balanced weaves, while the remaining one has fine even yarns and is always warp-faced (pl. 42c). It has narrow blue and white stripes, with a wide blue stripe at the selvedge edge. Near the selvedge there is often a wider stripe of red, yellow or brown wool. The spinning and weaving is always very high in quality, giving the cloth a professional appearance. This one type accounts for 9.5% of all the fabrics recovered from LC2 deposits but is much less common both in the LC1 and in the TC periods.[3]

Another six types also have very standardized spinning and weaving styles, leading one to suspect that they were produced by professional weavers. They are all undyed, have Z-spun yarn, have a balanced plain weave, and differ from one another only in the diameter of the yarns and in their spacing (pl. 43a). Three of the types may be described as having respectively coarse, medium, and fine yarn closely spaced; the other three have similar grades of yarn, but it is more widely spaced and therefore has a more open fabric. All six of these types were used for long *galabiyah*-like garments. They are fairly rare in the LC1 period but increase in the course of time so that in the Terminal Christian period the type with closely spaced medium yarn accounts for 29% of the total cloth of that period.[4]

A final type of undyed cotton cloth with Z-spun yarns is made of very fine yarn widely spaced. We have found no clue as to the use of this fabric, but its delicate, diaphanous quality would hardly have been suitable for anything but luxury uses. It has been found only in the Terminal Christian period and accounts for less than 1% of the cloth from that period, but its frequency increases in the Ottoman period.

Three of the twenty-one types of cotton fabric with Z-spun yarns are of a solid blue colour. Again, they have a balanced plain weave, closely spaced, differing from one another in yarn diameter only. In fact, since they were dyed after weaving (piece-dyed), they may originally have been the same fabrics as the closely spaced undyed types discussed above. These too were used to make the long *galabiyah*-like garment. They are very rare or non-existent in LC1 contexts but are found with increasing frequency in LC2, and in the Terminal Christian period the medium and fine types of blue cloth amount respectively to 5.5% and 8% of the total fabric content.[5]

A very few examples of blue and white striped cotton have come from the LC and TC levels. They have Z-spun yarns and a balanced, slightly open plain weave. The stripes are arranged in clusters of 4–12, of various widths, and these are repeated at regular intervals. Blue and white checked designs are similarly arranged, a practice resulting in a repeating pattern of irregular checks (pl. 42d). A variant type has the addition of red or pink cotton yarns to one or both systems of warp and weft, producing a plaid pattern. There is also a regular check pattern which might be called a 'window-pane' check (pl. 25d). It is mostly white with two or three closely spaced blue warps and wefts crisscrossing at regular intervals, thus forming the boundaries of each 'pane'.[6]

[2] 6.4% of the 250 textile fragments from Kulubnarti, a late mediaeval site located in upper Nubia, are of this type. Statistical comparisons between Kulubnarti and the late Christian levels at Qaṣr Ibrîm are particularly valuable because every fragment of excavated textile has been recorded from both sites. The Kulubnarti collections are housed at the Museum of Anthropology, University of Kentucky (UKMA), Lexington, Kentucky.

[3] One specimen of this textile type was also found at Kulubnarti, no. UKMA 85.2.25, and several were found at Quseir al-Qadim, a site with late mediaeval occupation levels on the Red Sea. See Eastwood in Donald S. Whitcomb and Janet H. Johnson, *Quseir al-Qadim 1980* (Malibu, 1982), 288, 290 and nos. 214–7, 228.

[4] 22.4% of the textile fragments from Kulubnarti are of these 6 types. Six specimens of the same types are described by Ingrid Bergman in *Late Nubian Textiles* (Scandinavian Joint Expedition to Sudanese Nubia, 8) (Stockholm, 1975), 13, nos. 25/223, 25/226, 25/231, 178/1, 178/16, and 401/60; pl. 12: 3; pl. 13,14.

[5] Only 2.5% of the fabrics from Kulubnarti are blue-dyed cottons. One fragment is also cited in Bergman, op. cit., 13, no. 25/231 and pl. 13:2.

[6] There is one example from Kulubnarti: UKMA 85.2.35.1, 2. This type is illustrated by Brookner in Donald S. Whitcomb and Janet H. Johnson, *Quseir al-Qadim 1978* (Cairo, 1979), pl. 67a and fig. 13.

Plate 42. Cotton fabrics. a, Embroidered S-spun cotton (84T/452). b, Warp-faced cotton (84T/326, 84T/471). c, Left: early Z-spun cotton (84T/332); right: early Z-spun cotton with wool warp stripe (84T/432). d, Cotton checks (84T/428, 84T/521). e, Close-up of cotton checkerboard pattern (84T/328).

The striped and checked fabrics were originally worn as shawls or perhaps head-veils. A number of complete specimens have come from graves at Akhmîm.[7] Although they comprise only 4% of the Late and Terminal Christian fabrics at Qaṣr Ibrîm, their use increased markedly in the Ottoman period.[8] In addition to woven fabrics of cotton, there are also some examples of spun, grouped yarns. Some specimens are simply loosely twisted bunches of what were probably warp yarns. Others are tightly twisted and served as cordage. Three percent of the cotton fabrics comprise unique or nearly unique specimens which cannot be classified. Although statistically negligible, some are of sufficient interest to be discussed here. There are two fragments of a balanced plain weave red cloth. As with the blue fabric, this is probably identical to the closely spaced type of undyed material, which has been piece-dyed red after weaving. There is also one fragment of red and white checked fabric. A single piece of resist-dyed cloth has a repeating curvilinear motif on a dark blue ground. This type is more commonly found in Ottoman times and was surely imported to Qaṣr Ibrîm. Fabric of the same type has been found in late mediaeval levels at Quseir al-Qadim. An Indian origin has been suggested.[9]

Another cotton fabric with balanced plain weave is pale blue and dark blue with an all-over woven pattern which has the appearance of basket weaving (pl. 42e). Both the warp and weft have dark blue and pale-blue yarns arranged alternately. The appearance of basketry is effected by periodically interrupting the regular alternation of pale and dark blue by following every third dark-blue yarn with another of dark blue instead of pale blue. The arrangement in both systems is: 1 dark blue, 1 pale blue, 1 dark blue, 1 pale blue, 2 dark blue, 1 pale blue, and this sequence is repeated over the entire cloth. This material may have been imported.[10]

In conclusion, it seems evident that the majority of cotton fabrics were originally parts of garments, specifically including *galabiyah*-like gowns and head-veils. Some of these were very fine, while others were coarser and were probably for everyday utility wear. Other uses might have included household furnishing fabrics. In all probability the cotton fabrics with S-spun yarn were locally produced, while at least some of the Z-spun examples were certainly imported.

Linen fabrics

At Qaṣr Ibrîm linen fabrics are more plentiful in the late mediaeval period than at any time since the Roman. A popular linen type in LCl times was beautifully produced with regular, even spinning and weaving. It has a very close warp face, plain weave, and yarns are always S-spun (pl. 44a). It was used for tunics or *galabiyahs*, of which a number of fragments have been found with seams and hems. Also, one small bag was found made of this fabric. No colours have been found in this material.

A second type of linen fabric is usually undyed, but small amounts of coloured cloth are also found, exhibiting various shades of blue, bright orange, and pink. This material has a balanced plain weave, often fairly open. There are actually four subtypes, differing only in the spinning direction of the yarns, which may be S-spun, Z-spun, or a regular or irregular combination of the two.[11] In these cases the spinning direction of the yarn does not affect the appearance of the fabric. These fabrics comprise 20% of all the cloth found in LCl deposits but decrease to around 8% in the LC2 and TC periods. They were used for *galabiyah*-like garments and for small, close-fitting caps. Two specimens were made into narrow straps or cords with the long seam stitched with red wool yarns.

Linen fabrics with blue and white stripes and checks, including the 'window-pane' check, also occur. Their spinning directions are varied. The patterns, in general, are smaller and more regular than those found in cotton fabrics (pl. 44b). Material with tiny checks was used to make caps, and some hemmed fragments have also been found, indicating that the same material was also used for garments or other objects.[12] One piece of linen with a diamond twill weave is also present (pl. 43b). A linen strap with a chevron pattern was made using weaving tablets or cards instead of a loom (pl. 43c) (See plate 31f–h for photographs of weaving tablets or cards.)

Several fragments of very coarse, heavy warp-face material have been found; the pieces are so dirty and poorly preserved that not much can be learned about their use. The character of the yarn and the weave suggest that this fabric type would be most suitable for utility bags and floor mats (pl. 43d).

[7] Dr. Cherilyn N. Nelson, personal communication.

[8] For an illustration of this fabric as worn by an Egyptian woman in the 19th century see Edward Lane, *Manners and Customs of the Modern Egyptians* (London, 1895), 65.

[9] See Brookner, op. cit., 183 and pl. 66 n; Eastwood, op. cit., 288, 292; fig. 20, pl. 64 e, g. For a colour photo see Donald Whitcomb and Janet Johnson in *Field Museum of Natural History Bulletin*, 51, no. 6 (1980), 25.

[10] Eastwood describes what may be a similar fabric from Quseir al-Qadim. See Eastwood, op. cit., 289, no. RN 576.

[11] The same variation in the spinning direction of flax fabrics was found at Quseir al-Qadim. See Eastwood, op. cit., 286.

[12] A single example from Kulubnarti is UKMA 85.2.11. Linen stripes and checks are very numerous at Quseir al-Qadim. See Eastwood, op. cit., 289. For illustrations of similar fabrics see Brookner, op.cit., figs. 12 and 13; pl. 67.

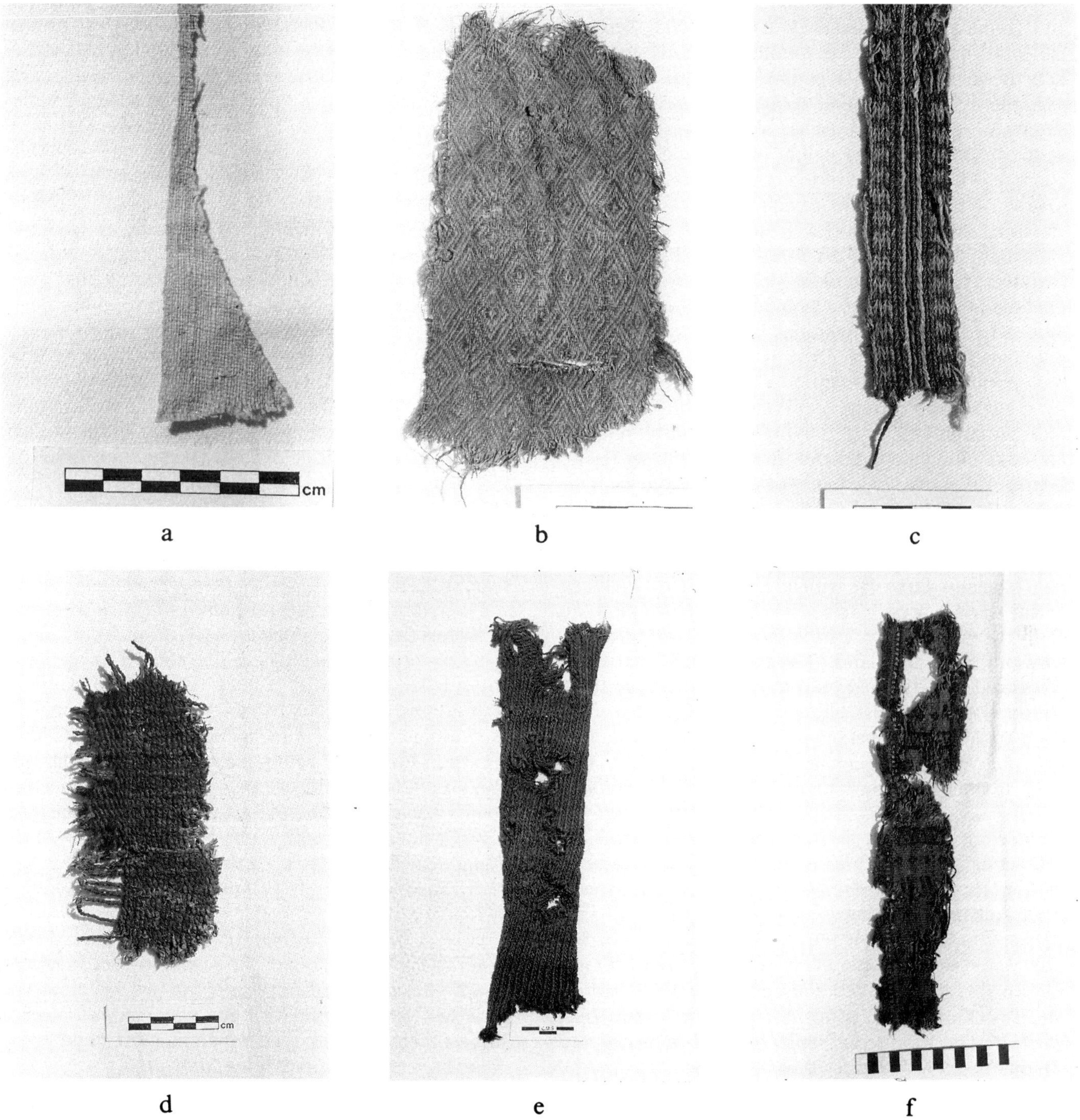

Plate 43. Textile weaves and types. a, Cotton offcut, Type C2 (82T/892). b, Linen diamond twill (82T/898). c, Tablet weave of rose silk with silver threads (82T/90). d, Flax fibre mat (82T/291). e, Knitted woollen tube (84T/297). f, Goat hair animal girth (84T/333).

Fustian is the final linen type to be discussed here; it has a flax warp and a cotton weft, generally in plain weave. The flax warp is almost always S-spun, although occasionally Z-spun flax warps are found; the weft is invariably Z-spun.[13] Fustian occurs most often undyed, but green, blue, and red or brown specimens have also been found. One piece has bands of alternating pale and dark blue, 4 cm wide, in the cotton weft. Fustian was used for trousers and also for a tunic-like garment. One example served as the neck facing of a child's dress. There are several specimens of fustian woven in a diamond twill pattern.[14] Two had clearly been used as cushion covers, as some of the feathers were still present. Other specimens of fustian twill give no clue as to their use. Fustian comprises between 1.7 and 2.7% of the textiles from the Late and Terminal Christian periods.

Linen, like cotton, seems to have been used largely though not exclusively for garments, many of which were of a very fine quality. There is very little evidence of a flax-weaving industry in Nubia, in the mediaeval period or at any time, and it therefore seems likely that the great majority of linen fabrics were imported.

Wool

Woollen fabrics account for almost one-third of the textiles found in the LCl period. In LC2 times their frequency had dropped to one-quarter, and by Terminal Christian times it was only 10%. The largest portion are S-spun and have a plain weave. The woollens fall into two basic categories: undyed and dyed.

Undyed woollens

Three groups of undyed woollens can be distinguished on the basis of colour. Some are dark brown—the dominant colour of the local Nubian sheep—while others are of a light, cream colour—the natural hue of 'white' sheep. In a third group each fragment exhibits a variety of natural colours, employing several shades of brown and 'white' in a random manner. These may have afforded a way for weavers to use up small amounts of yarn left over from other projects.

Dark brown wools are the most numerous at Qaṣr Ibrîm and are found from X-group times onward until the final abandonment of the settlement in 1811. The surviving fragments show no seams or hems, so the material must have been used much as it came off the loom. It probably had multiple uses: for simple garments that were worn wrapped or fastened around the body, for blankets, and for containers used to carry animal fodder, firewood, etc.[15]

The undyed brown woollens have yarn of varying diameters, and the finished material ranges from a coarse, heavy, solid fabric to a fine, open weave, with all gradations in between. The medium grade is by far the most common. It is sometimes found with bands embroidered in bright colours, including red, orange, blue, green, rust, and white (pl. 44c). The motifs are simple geometric figures: diamonds, chevrons, rectangles, bars, and X's. Sometimes small tassels of coloured yarn are placed at intervals along the embroidered band. In many cases the band is bordered on each side by 1 to 2 cm of blue wefts, replacing the brown; in one case the borders are red with countered twining in red and white.[16] The light coloured wool fabrics also vary from coarse to fine. Only one specimen has been found with embroidery. The variegated pieces range from medium to coarse and seem not to have been embroidered.

Dyed woollens with a balanced weave

All of the dyed woollen fabrics with a balanced weave (that is, with both warp and weft visible at the surface) can be divided into three groups: fabrics of a single colour, those with two or more colours arranged in bands, and plaids. All are characterized by fine yarns, loosely spaced. The banded and plaid textiles are much less common than those of a solid colour, and no features are present to suggest their function. Colours of the bands include cream and brown, cream and blue, tan and purple, and tan and red. For the plaids, red, green, and blue are used in varying amounts in both warp and weft to produce a large pattern (pl. 44d).

The group of solid-colour fabrics is much larger than the other two. Although many of these fabrics are without decorative or functional features, others have certain characteristics that suggest their use as head-veils. Their yarn is fine, tightly spun, and widely spaced, producing an open, delicate cloth. They are most commonly dark blue but occasionally are bright red, maroon, yellow, or one of several shades of green.

[13] Two specimens of fustian occurred at Kulubnarti; it was also found at Quseir al-Qadim. Eastwood, op. cit., 286. One specimen is mentioned by Bergman, op. cit., 13, no. 297/2 and pl. 12:4.

[14] See Eastwood, op. cit., 290.

[15] For an illustration of this type of fabric in use see C. B. Klunzinger, *Upper Egypt: its People and its Products* (New York, 1878), 53.

[16] Several examples of this type of embroidered wool were found at Kulubnarti: UKMA 85.2.14, 45, 49, 53, 57, 73, and 74. An example of countered twining bordered by red wefts can be seen in Christa C. Mayer Thurman and Bruce Williams, *Ancient Textiles from Nubia* (Chicago, 1979), 114, no. 119.

Plate 44. Linen and woollen fabrics. a, Warp-faced linen (82T/899, 82T/901). b, Tiny linen checks (82T/308). c, Embroidery on brown wool (82T/563). d, Woollen plaid (84T/470). e, Decorative bands on woollen head-veil (82T/913, 82T/453). f, Close-up of cotton decorative band on woollen head-veil (82T/296).

Small figures are sometimes embroidered in either white cotton or wool. On other specimens narrow decorative bands with floating wefts are woven in and extend across the full width of the piece (pl. 44e–f). The yarn for these bands often includes cotton, which may be white, red, or orange.[17] This fabric type accounts for almost 5% of the cloth from LC1 times, but its frequency drops in LC2 times, and by the TC period it comprises only 2/10 of 1% of all the fabric recovered.

Dyed woollens with a weft face

A second large group of dyed woollens differs from the fabric of the head-veils in several respects. Although a plain weave is once again employed, in all cases the weft is predominant. Often the wefts are so closely spaced that the warp yarns are completely covered, making a weft-faced cloth. Another difference is that wefts are of two or more colours used in alternation, so as to produce an overall pattern of coloured bands (pl. 45b). There is usually a basic weft colour which is the same as the colour of the warp, plus one or more additional colours alternating with the basic colour. Widths of the bands vary from no more than 2 mm to as much as 8–10 cm.

A vast range of colours is found: many shades of brown, tan, and cream; dark blue, medium blue, and pale blue; blue-green, bright green, grey-green, and yellow-green; yellow, gold or amber yellow, and mustard; red, maroon, purple, lavender, orange, and rust; and very occasionally black. Common combinations of colours include brown and blue, light brown and purple, pale and dark blue, and red and blue.[18] No evidence of shaping or sewing is visible on these fabrics, so it must be assumed that, if they were used as clothing, they were worn as mantles and wrapped or fastened around the body. They must surely have served also as blankets. Many fragments have been found loosely tacked together to make what may have been mattress pads and cushion stuffing. Another fabric has the same characteristics as the foregoing except that the warp is of undyed cotton, instead of wool. The banded wool weft is always very close, thus completely covering the cotton warp.

The banded woollens comprised 9.8% of the total material from the LC1 period, but had diminished to less than 1% by the Terminal Christian period.

Other woollens

Other woollen fabrics have been found in very small numbers, although they were much more common in the earlier Middle Ages. One type involves tapestry-woven elements. In this technique, wefts of different colours are used in discrete areas to form a pattern instead of moving across the entire width of the cloth to form a stripe or band. The tapestry technique goes back to Coptic, Meroitic, and Roman traditions, and the five specimens found in the late mediaeval deposits may, in fact, be survivals from earlier periods. The yarn is all S-spun and in many colours: dark brown, dark blue, rust, green, orange, yellow, red, purple, and cream.[19] The design figures include small ducks, flowers, crosses, squares, and a single large boat-shape or flattened crescent. This latter may possibly have come from a type of Coptic cloak, since a similarly shaped tapestry woven feature is found on a cloak from Illahun, in Egypt, where the design is located at the centre back, just above the bottom edge.[20]

Pieces of dark-brown wool with embroidery at the selvedge are probably also survivals from an earlier period. They have narrow patterns in red, blue, yellow, and cream wool yarn (pl. 45a). There are also two examples of woollen twill[21] and three fragments of knitted wool.[22] One of the latter was knitted in a tubular form (pl. 43e); another seems to have been part of a small bag. Nothing is known about the function of the other pieces. Finally, two fragments of felt have been found. Both are light brown and well made. The scraps give no hint of their use.

Wool was evidently the basic utilitarian material of mediaeval Nubia. It was used for the plain and simple garments of everyday wear, as well as for blankets, bedding, and containers of one sort and another. The great majority of mediaeval woollen material was certainly locally produced, although the fine head-veils and certain other luxury garments may have been imported.

Silk Fabrics

Fabrics containing silk are very rare in the mediaeval period, never comprising more than 1.7% of the total collection of textile material. The surviving fragments are mostly extremely small, and some have probably been reused. Three categories of silk fabrics will be dis-

[17] For descriptions of this fabric from Quseir al-Qadim see Eastwood, op. cit., 288 and 290, and pl. 62, 5.

[18] This type occurs at Quseir al-Qadim. (Eastwood, op. cit. 290.) See also Mayer Thurman and Williams, op. cit., 130, no. 153; 141, no. 176, and 145, no. 183.

[19] For short descriptions of tapestry weaves found at Quseir al-Qadim see Eastwood, op. cit., 288–9; for a photograph see Brookner, op. cit., fig. 11.

[20] A plan of this cloak which shows the tapestry woven element clearly is shown by Hero Granger-Taylor, *Textile History,* Vol. 13, no. 1 (1982), fig. 25.

[21] For woollen twills at Quseir al-Qadim see Eastwood, op. cit., 290, textiles RN 574 and RN 571, pl. 63, 3 and 4.

[22] Op. cit., 290, textile RN 577.

cussed here: a group made purely of silk, a second group which appears to the eye to be all silk but which contains cotton wefts, and a linen cloth which has the addition of silk in one or more discrete areas of the warp or weft.

Pure silk

Pure silk fabric occurs in several forms. Examples of the plain weave technique include a piece with a pale-blue balanced weave and an amber-coloured stripe along the selvedge, several pieces with narrow warp-face stripes in a variety of colours, and a resist-dyed specimen with cone shapes on a medium-blue ground.[23] More complex weaving techniques include twill weaves, satin, and a brilliant fragment which has a linear repeating pattern of yellow roosters with red eyes, beaks and wattles on a blue ground (pl. 45c). This latter specimen is a very good quality weft-face compound twill. Such a fabric was made on a drawloom and was imported. [24]

Silk and cotton

These fabrics appear at a distance to be of pure silk, but closer inspection reveals that the generally much more numerous silk warps are concealing cotton wefts (pl. 45d).[25] Satin is the most successful of these combinations of fibres. There are also warp-faced monochrome fabrics and stripes in black and white and blue and white. Fine twill weaves are also found.

Linen with silk

These fabrics are basically linen plain weaves with the addition of small amounts of silk decoration. Two of the specimens have silk warp stripes.[26] One of them, which was re-worked to make a garment for a child, has a stripe of red-silk warps 1 cm wide along the selvedges. The dress was enhanced by joining two selvedges with a decoratively stitched seam. The other has a patterned stripe of red, brown, and white silk in a float pattern over two wefts. Another piece of linen has silk used in a tapestry-woven weft band. This elaborately patterned decoration is in white, black, blue, red, light green, and mauve, with two lines of Arabic writing between three rows of repeating lozenge-shapes and arabesques (pl. 45e). It may originally have been the decoration on the sleeve of a tunic. The style is clearly of Fatimid origin (969–1171), and may have survived into late mediaeval times as a treasured family heirloom.[27]

Silk was undoubtedly reserved for the finest clothing, although the only specimen which is actually recognizable is a piece of a cap. All of the silk cloth was imported. Much of it certainly came from Egypt, but certain pieces may have been produced in the Levant, in Syria, or possibly even in China.

Goat hair

Textiles made of goat hair make up no more than 2% of the late mediaeval fabrics. The stiff hair was not suitable for clothing, but its strength and ready availability made it ideal for utility items such as ropes, straps, bags, mats or rugs, and tents. Collectively, these made an important contribution to the life of the community.

In contrast to the other fibres, most of which are simply spun, yarn produced of goat hair is S-spun and then plied, almost always in the Z direction. This adheres to the local tradition of spinning the the S direction and of plying in the opposite direction from the spin.[28] The basic Z-plied goat hair yarn was used to weave large bags and tent panels in a balanced plain weave. Black or very dark brown is always the main colour; white stripes or bands in the warp or weft are often added. Sometimes stripes of undyed cotton or flax are found also.

Several weft-faced specimens which were probably used as rugs have woven-in bands of yarn made from the hair of a small antelope, which has been tentatively identified as lechwe or duiker.[29] These animals are not found in Nubia today. If they were present in late mediaeval times, it would seem that a weaver was in an experimental mood, since antelope hair is short and bristly, and would have been very difficult to work with. It is also possible that these rugs were imported from the south, or perhaps from farther east.

A very close warp-faced fabric is also present. The wefts are concealed inside the warps and are often much coarser, giving the material a ribbed appearance

[23] For specimens of silk plain weave at Quseir al-Qadim see Eastwood, op. cit., 322, nos. 267b and 267c.

[24] The closest parallel to this specimen I have been able to find so far is a photograph, no. 8582.1860, in the photographic archives of the Victoria and Albert Museum in London. The attribution is given as Saracen.

[25] This fabric is called in Arabic *qotny*, and is thoroughly discussed by Homossani in *Ars Textrina*, 1 (1983), 265 ff.

[26] For similar fabrics found at Quseir al-Qadim see Eastwood, op. cit., 303, nos. 42, 48.

[27] For discussion of similar textiles in the Royal Ontario Museum see Golombek and Gervers in Veronika Gervers (ed.), *Studies in Textile History* (Toronto, 1977), 88, nos. 20–22 and photographs 115–7. See also Gervers in *Rotunda*, 11 (1978–79), 25–6; for excellent colour photographs see 28–9 therein.

[28] For an ethnographic description of goat-hair spinning see Crowfoot in *Sudan Notes and Records* 32 (1951), 73. For the production of plied yarns see Crowfoot in *Sudan Notes and Records* 4, no. 1 (1921), 25.

[29] Fibre identification by H. M. Appleyard.

Plate 45. Wool and silk fabrics. a, Selvedge patterns on brown wool (84T/195, 84T/314, 84T/357). b, Weft-faced wool with bands (82T/421). c, Close-up of rooster design on silk (82T/330). d, Fragment of silk and cotton (84T/4). e, Fatimid silk tapestry weave 78T/113). f, Goat-hair fabric (82T/331).

(pl. 45f). This material was used for bags, mats and rugs. A clever weaving technique was often employed, involving the use of paired wefts running in opposite directions. This served to strengthen the edges of the piece and, in the case of mats or rugs, would keep them from becoming frayed. A type of embroidery is sometimes found on this style of weave. It is done by wrapping certain of the exposed warp yarns with red, blue or cream-coloured wool thread. The patterns are mostly stepped arrangements. The same embroidery technique has also been found at Kulubnarti, in upper Nubia.[30]

Animal girths, which are flat straps about 10 cm wide, are also warp-faced. Some are simple black straps, but others have complementary warps in several colours which are manipulated to form geometric designs (pl. 43f) In addition to the natural black or dark brown, colours include white, yellow, orange, and pale blue. The weaving is done in such a way that the pattern appears in opposition on each side of the girth, i.e., a white area will be black on the reverse. Although the finished girths are more complex than the other types of goat-hair textiles, they were probably made in the simplest way, without even a loom. Among present-day bedouin peoples the warps are pegged out on the ground, and the weaver selects the yarns needed for the pattern with her fingers, lifting them with each pass of the weft.[31]

Goat hair was also used for thread, cordage, and rope. The basic Z-plied yarn was employed as a coarse thread for sewing heavy articles such as saddles, saddle girths, and bags, and was also used to tack wads of rags together for mattresses and cushions. Two groups of plies, S-twisted together, made a stout cord, and a continuation of the same process produced heavy rope suitable for tethering horses and tents, or tying loads and cargo.

Most of the goat-hair items from Qaṣr Ibrîm are similar or identical to things that are produced by bedouin peoples throughout the Middle East today.[32] In the Middle Ages, it seems probable that these items were obtained from the frequent Beja visitors to Qaṣr Ibrîm.[33]

Dyes

A sample of Late Christian textiles from Qaṣr Ibrîm was sent to the York Archaeological Institute for Excavation and Research, for analysis of the dyes employed.[34] Despite the variety of coloured materials and of colours, only four dyestuffs could be definitely identified; they seem to have been used alike for colouring cotton, linen, wool, and silk. The dyestuffs were madder, used for various shades of red and orange; indigo, for various shades of blue; and weld and Persian berries, both of which were used to produce shades of yellow. Green was produced by dyeing with weld and overdyeing with indigo, or vice versa, and purple was similarly produced by combining madder and indigo. These same dyes have been identified in textiles materials from earlier periods at Qaṣr Ibrîm and from other sites in Nubia.

[30] Embroidery of the same type occurs on one specimen from Kulubnarti: UKMA 85.2.92.

[31] Two examples of this type from Kulubnarti are UKMA 85.2.90 and 85.2.91. For a very close parallel, although from a much earlier time, see Lillian M. Wilson, *Ancient Textiles from Egypt in the University of Michigan Collection* (Ann Arbor, 1933), 47, no. 121 and pl. X. For a photograph which shows both sides of the foregoing specimen see Crowfoot in *Kush* 4 (1956), pl. 1, 1 and 2. For ethnographic descriptions of this type of girth weaving in the Sudan of the 1920's see op. cit., 34–8; also Crowfoot in *Sudan Notes and Records* 32 (1951), 71–6.

[32] See, e.g., Alois Musil, *The Manners and Customs of the Rwala Bedouins* (American Geographical Society, Oriental Explorations and Studies, no. 6) (New York, 1928).

[33] Grace Crowfoot concurred in this opinion when she wrote '...we may imagine that in that distant past also it was the dwellers in tents who wove the camel girths and not the craftsmen of the town...' Crowfoot in *Kush* 4 (1956), 35.

[34] Identification was made by Dr. George W. Taylor.

CHAPTER 7
DRESS AND ORNAMENTATION

How the mediaeval Nubians dressed is an interesting and in some respects a difficult question, since neither archaeology nor textual records provide very complete evidence. J. L. Burckhardt, one of the first European travellers of modern times, reported in 1819 that the people north of Derr wore a simple linen shirt,[1] while in more southerly areas they went largely naked.[2] The nakedness of the Nubians was remarked also by St. John in 1845[3] and even by Wallis Budge at the beginning of the twentieth century.[4] However, these conditions do not necessarily represent a continuation of mediaeval practices. They may only reflect the near paralysis of commerce, in textiles as well as in other goods, at the end of the Ottoman period.[5]

There are several reasons for believing that the mediaeval Nubians did not go habitually naked. First of all, such a practice would almost certainly have excited the comment, and disapproval, of the many mediaeval Arab historians who wrote about Nubia,[6] and in particular of Ibn Selim el-Aswâni, who visited the country in person.[7] Second, the *Baqt* treaty between Egypt and Nubia (at least in one of its recorded versions) called for the annual importation of a very large quantity of Egyptian textiles into Nubia.[8] Finally, there is the material evidence of the innumerable rags found at Qaṣr Ibrîm, most of which are certainly fragments of what were originally garments.

We are better informed in regard to headgear, and especially footgear, than we are in regard to bodily garments. Many caps were too small to have any secondary value as rags, and there was almost no secondary use to be made of worn-out shoes and sandals. These items were consequently discarded when they had served their original purposes. Larger garments on the other hand were so consistently torn up for rags when they were soiled or worn out that not a single specimen of an adult garment has survived intact, except for the very special habiliments in which the Bishop Timotheos was buried.[9] We are left to guess as to the form of mediaeval Nubian garments mainly from the tailored pieces of edging that have survived.

Garments

Fabric garments

To some extent we are able to reconstruct the appearance of garments by carefully noting such details as the cut shapes of the cloth and the presence of hems and seams. These features are found almost exclusively on cotton and linen fabrics—almost never on wool, except for the occasional mend. From this we conclude that the heavier woollen garments were simply rectangles of cloth which were worn draped over the body. Although this conclusion is based on negative evidence, our analysis of many thousands of textile fragments has shown that the seams and hems which occur so extensively on the cotton and linen goods are not present in any of the woolen specimens. With so much data in hand, it seems reasonable to suppose that if woollen fabrics had been cut and sewn into garments, we would have seen some evidence of it. It may be noted that our general impression of mediaeval Nubian clothing accords well with the written descriptions of clothing worn by the people of Upper Egypt in Ottoman times.[10]

Men's Clothing. The basic dress of Nubian men in mediaeval times was derived from the Roman tunic, and was a predecessor of the *galabiyah* worn today. A shirt-like garment of cotton or linen, it had wide flowing sleeves and reached almost to the ground. A round opening for the head was cut out, and this was always faced with another fabric, often of a contrasting colour. A slit opening extended some 20–25 cm down the front below the neck edge. Square gussets inserted on the bias in the underarm area allowed freedom of

[1] J. L. Burckhardt, *Travels in Nubia* (London, 1819), 141. For an illustration see Thomas Legh, *Narrative of a Journey in Egypt and the Country Beyond the Cataracts* (London, 1817), opposite 204.

[2] Burckhardt, op. cit.

[3] J. A. St. John, *Egypt and Nubia* (London, 1845), 425–6.

[4] E. A. Wallis Budge, *The Egyptian Sudan* (London, 1907), II, 425, 426, 429.

[5] See William Y. Adams, *Nubia, Corridor to Africa* (London, 1977), 609–14.

[6] See especially Giovanni Vantini, *Oriental Sources Concerning Nubia* (Heidelberg and Warsaw, 1975).

[7] For his account see Burckhardt, op. cit., 493–503.

[8] See op. cit., 512.

[9] See Crowfoot in Veronika Gervers (ed.), *Studies in Textile History* (Toronto, 1977), 43–51.

[10] C. B. Klunzinger, *Upper Egypt: its People and its Products* (New York, 1878), 17–20, 52; Edward W. Lane, *An Account of the Manners and Customs of the Modern Egyptians* (London, 1895), 46–67.

motion without ripping or tearing the underarm seam. This feature is not common in Late Christian times, but is seen in the Terminal Christian period. It may be that the technique came to Qaṣr Ibrîm with Islam. At Quseir al-Qadim, a Mamluk trading port on the Red Sea, a child's garment was found with underarm gussets; this would have been contemporary with the Nubian Late Christian I period.[11]

Most of the men's garments were made of undyed cotton or linen cloth, which must originally have been almost white; others were of dark blue cotton. The facings for the neck openings were of undyed linen, blue cotton, or blue-and-white striped linen in the case of undyed cotton garments, and of undyed cotton for the blue garments (pl. 46a). One fragment had a facing of 'printed' cotton, with a pattern produced by resist dyeing or block printing. Seams with no raw edges and neat hems indicate that the original sewing was of high quality; these garments were evidently made by skilled specialists. Belts, if worn, would probably have been no more than strips of cloth in a colour contrasting with that of the main garment—most often red. Scarves tied around the waist may also have served as belts.[12]

Probably the only undergarments worn by men were trousers. Those of the late mediaeval period were made of cotton, linen or fustian, a fabric having a flax warp and a cotton weft. They were very roomy, wide garments extending probably to just below the knee. They were gathered around the waist and tied with cords run through a casing made by folding the top edge over and sewing it down, leaving a neat opening for the two ends of the cord. Two types of waistband cords have been found. Some are simply doubled narrow strips of cotton cloth; others are made of sprang (pl. 46b). This is a looping technique which allows the cord to expand and contract with the body, so that it is very suited to use as a tie. Fullness was added to the trousers by means of a square gusset, with the direction of the weave placed at a 45° angle to the weave of the trousers. This bias cut allowed more freedom of movement than would a straight cut. The trouser leg openings included a short slit up the side, which was fastened closed with string ties attached to either side. A second type of fastening consisted of a small cloth button and a button hole or loop (pl. 46c).

In cooler weather men apparently wore a shawl or cloak over their main garment. Hundreds of fragments of woollen cloth have been recovered which could have served this purpose. Many have bands of two or three alternating colours. Bright hues of blue, red, green, yellow, pink, and more subtle variants of these occur. The natural colours of sheep's wool—dark brown and cream—were used both individually and mixed together to produce all the shades in between. Occasionally a single band of tapestry weave provided a more complex pattern. Other fabrics that could have been used as wraps include fine woollens with open weave and a plaid pattern in red, green and blue; and a brown and white checked cloth combining brown wool and white cotton.

Long outer garments which hung completely open in the front are described by both Klunzinger[13] and Lane[14] for nineteenth century Egypt. They could be worn by both sexes. If such garments were worn in mediaeval Nubia, their use was probably infrequent. Only one fragment which was surely open in the front has been found (76T/135). It consists of one side of the opening and hem, made of undyed cotton cloth and faced with the same material. There are many other fragments which could have been from similar garments but lack clearly indicative features. Most common are blue and white striped linen, and blue or undyed linen with silk stripes in red, green, white or dark brown.

The Clothing of Bishop Timotheos. The only intact garments that have survived from the Late Christian period are those in which Bishop Timotheos was buried in the north crypt of the Cathedral.[15] They appear to be his travelling clothes rather than his formal ecclesiastical robes, and they may, therefore, bear some relationship to the everyday clothing worn by other inhabitants at Qaṣr Ibrîm. However, it is believed that the Bishop died shortly after his arrival from Egypt,[16] so that his raiment probably did not include anything of Nubian manufacture. The following description has been furnished by Elisabeth Crowfoot, who has elsewhere published a very full description of the clothing of Timotheos:[17]

'His shroud, of undyed cotton, was doubled over his feet, tied round his neck, and fastened between by strings wound round 'buttons' of the cloth filled with earth. His uppermost garment was a voluminous bell-shaped hooded cloak of fine dark blue wool, largely disintegrated, though its exact cut was given by its well-preserved lining of red-brown cotton, with a facing of blue silk round hem and hood; a panel of silk tapestry in gold, white, black and blue decorating the back is of earlier date, re-used;[18] a scrap of the original blue wool,

[11] Donald S. Whitcomb and Janet H. Johnson, *Quseir al-Qadim 1980* (Malibu, 1982), pl. 63, 9.

[12] Lane, op. cit., 49.

[13] Klunzinger, op. cit., 19.

[14] Op. cit., 46, 49–50, 58; illus. 47, 50, 58.

[15] For the original find see Plumley, *JEA* 50 (1964), 3–4.

[16] See J. Martin Plumley, *The Scrolls of Bishop Timotheos* (Egypt Exploration Society, Texts from Excavations, Memoir I) (London, 1975).

[17] Crowfoot, op. cit.

[18] For a parallel example see I. Errera, *Collection d'anciennes étoffes égyptiennes* (Brussels, 1916), no. 437. The piece is tentatively dated 10th–12th centuries.

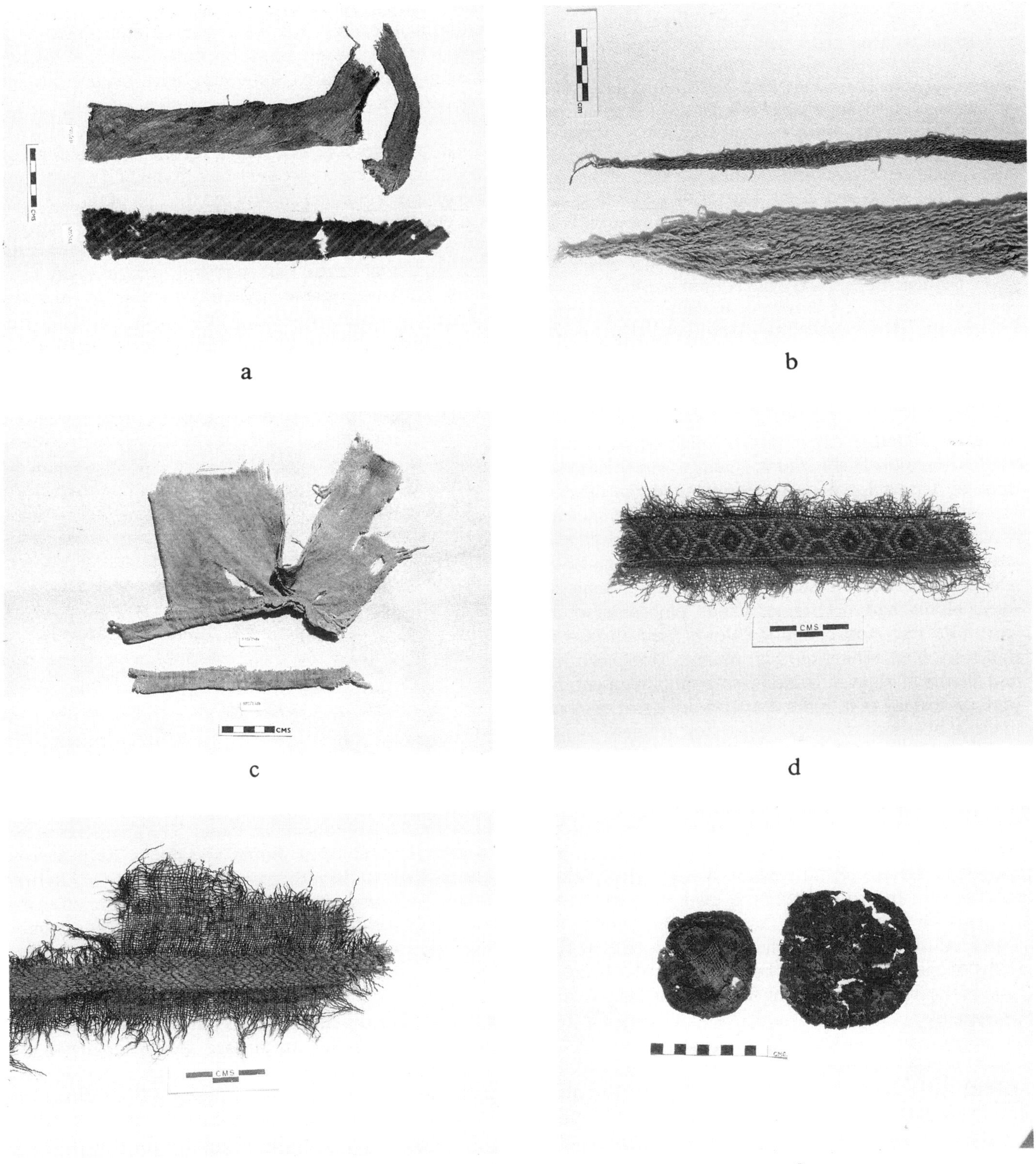

Plate 46. Fragments of textile garments. a, Neck facings of linen (82T/435, 82T/514). b, Waistband cords of cotton (82T/55, 82T/78). c. Trouser leg openings of fustian (82T/294a–b). d, Decorated band from head-veil, of wool (84T/135). e, Decorated band from head-veil, of wool (84T/134). f, Cotton caps (78T/241, 78T/261).

with a purple band and lines of silk embroidery with debased Kufic letters, probably came from above or below the panel.[19] A turquoise-blue fine cotton veil, wrapped turban-wise round his head under the hood, had slipped over his eyes. His tunic was well tailored, of the usual Late Christian-Islamic cut with continuous back and front centre panel, straight sleeves, slightly shaped side panels and under-arm gussets, close to that of the modern *galabiyah;* [20] it was of fine, undyed linen, lined throughout with cotton, the two layers made separately, held together by lines of running stitch at the seams and at the edge of the faced hem and sleeve-ends; the round neck was finished with a narrow bias-cut strip of blue and yellow or white striped cotton. His trousers, of medium-grade cotton, had a large triangular gusset between the legs, and a turned-over waistband, inside which were scraps of a drawstring in undyed wool sprang. Underneath he wore a narrow cotton body-belt, stitched together with white silk. A fine linen cloth, his *mappa*, with wide silk selvedges and bands of twill pattern in blue and white silk, was tucked into the front of his cloak.'

Womens' Clothing. It is possible that some women wore a long shirt like that of the men, as was sometimes done by Upper Egyptian women in Ottoman times.[21] However, the evidence for mediaeval Nubia is unclear. What is certain is that many women wore a dark brown seamless woollen cloth, wrapping it around the body and perhaps over the head in some fashion. Some of these cloths had decorative bands embroidered or woven in. The most common colours used in decoration were blue, white, red and orange. Motifs are X's and diamond shapes. In addition to this garment, or perhaps instead of it, some women wore a sort of cloak made of blue and white checked cotton or linen.[22]

Trousers would appear to have been worn by women as well as by men and were of the same general type.[23] Trousers of another style, with the legs gradually tapering towards the foot, are described by Klunzinger as sometimes being worn by Egyptian women in the nineteenth century. An apparently similar fragment from Qaṣr Ibrîm is made of dark-green fustian with an ankle-band faced in undyed cotton. A V-shaped slit is nicely finished and reinforced at the point of the V to keep the foot from tearing it open. One of the two ties for closing the slit at the ankle is still present.[24]

Other possible garments. A number of fragments of quilting have been found. They are most often two layers of undyed or blue cotton cloth with cotton wadding between. The stitching runs in parallel lines from 1–3 cm apart. The only specimen which has any additional features has what may be interpreted as a collar with a button and loop, below which is a fragmentary quilted area. This may have been a sort of padded jacket.

Children's clothing. Fragments recognizable as parts of children's garments are very rare in the LC1 period but become more numerous toward the end of the mediaeval era. This evidence may help to confirm the suggestion that the citadel was initially a religious and governmental centre with very few secular or lay residents but later became increasingly a place of ordinary residence as well.

Portions of several basic shirt-like garments have been found, suggesting that children's clothing was simply a smaller version of that worn by adults.[25] Most of the specimens are of undyed cotton cloth. The neck openings are often finished with a rolled hem instead of having a separate facing. However, two specimens do have neck facings. One is a dress of undyed linen faced with blue and white checked cotton; the other consists only of a blue and white striped linen facing, with narrow strips of silk remaining in the seam allowance. On the basis of such fragmentary evidence it is not safe to postulate that the entire garment was made from blue and black striped silk, though this remains a possibility.

Headgear

Many fragments of finely woven wool have been found, which might be parts of head-veils worn by women.[26] Most are of dark blue wool, but red, yellow, green and dark brown have also been found. The character of the weave is quite open. Some specimens have narrow decorative bands with geometric patterns (pl. 46d–e). These are sometimes embroidered, but more often are woven in with one or two colours. The most common type uses white cotton wefts, in addition to, or instead of, the blue wool wefts. The weaver picked up the warps in a selected sequence to create the patterned band. Other specimens have polychrome bands with the addition of red or orange wool along with the undyed cotton wefts.[27]

Headgear for men seems to have been limited to small caps. These are beautiful examples of skilled

[19] Cf. Gaselee, *Archaeologia* 23 (1924), 82, figs. 6–7.

[20] See Gervers in N. B. Harte and K. G. Pointing (eds.), *Cloth and Clothing in Medieval Europe* (London, 1983), 310, fig. 16.16.

[21] Lane, op. cit., 65–6.

[22] Op. cit., 63, illus. 65.

[23] Op. cit., 63.

[24] Klunzinger, op. cit., 52.

[25] For examples see Whitcomb and Johnson, *Quseir al-Qadim 1980*, 289 and 292–3, pl. 63, 9.

[26] Lane, op. cit., 59–60.

[27] For descriptions of head-veils found at Quseir al-Qadim see Whitcomb and Johnson, *Quseir al-Qadim 1980,* 288 and pl. 62, 5. For an illustration showing how they may have been worn see Klunzinger, op. cit., 53.

craftsmanship. The circular crown of the cap can be a single piece, often with patterns in coloured embroidery (pl. 46f). Another style of the cap crown is made of four, six, eight or even twelve sections of a circle. Attached to the outer edge of the crown is a band 6–8 cm wide. The caps are always lined and are often padded with cotton wadding, cloth, or even paper or light cardboard. Sometimes the caps are quilted in patterns. Occasionally soft cords of cotton or flax fibre are inserted between the two layers of fabric, which creates a three-dimensional pattern.

The one child's cap fragment comes from the end of the mediaeval period. What survives is the crown only, an unusual example with twelve sections instead of the more common four, six , or eight. Six of the sections are purple silk satin; these alternate with two sections each of green silk satin; of red, white and blue narrow stripes in silk and flax; and of yellow silk plain weave, although only one section of the latter was found. Originally, the cap was probably lined and had a band attached to the outer edge of the crown, but these two features are missing.

Leather garments

Although textile was clearly the preferred material for clothing, the mediaeval Nubians did not altogether disdain the wearing of leather. A number of leather pieces were found which appear to be parts of garments, although in most cases the remaining fragment is too small to permit an accurate reconstruction of the original garment form.

?Aprons The Late Christian levels at Qaṣr Ibrîm have yielded nine scraps of rather fine, soft leather showing traces of very fine stitching, often along curving seams. We assume that these are pieces of tailored leather garments; they are too thin and too finely sewn to be parts of waterskins. One piece includes a small gore. The complexity of the tailoring suggests that at least some of the pieces were made to fit the upper body. They may possibly be parts of work aprons, such as were worn by the monks at the Monastery of Epiphanius in Egypt.[28]

Tasselled skirts. In the early nineteenth century the tasselled leather skirt *(rahat)* was the main garment—often the only garment—worn by women in the more southerly parts of Nubia.[29] Fragments of these skirts are fairly common in the Ottoman levels at Qaṣr Ibrîm, but only four small fragments have been found in the Late Christian deposits. They consist of thin strips of leather descending from a knotted or interwoven waistband, as shown in plate 47a. The two largest fragments have tassels 12 cm in length, but this is probably not the full original length unless the skirts were worn by children.

Belts. The only definitely identified belt from the Late Christian levels is a plain leather strap, 65 cm long and 2.5 cm wide, which accompanied the burial of Bishop Timotheos in the Cathedral.[30] However, a good many of the fragments of leather strap described in Part 3, Chapter 4 are probably also parts of belts. A much more elaborate strap of finely woven leather, shown in plate 47b, should probably also be placed in the belt category. The preserved fragment is 34 cm long and 2.4 cm wide. It terminates at one end in a round thong comprised of palm-fibre cord, with fine leather braided around it. Presumably this was meant to be tied through a ring at the other end of the belt, as in the case of several leather belts found at the Monastery of Epiphanius.[31]

Problematical garment. Plate 47c shows an extraordinary object comprised of two identical pieces of fine, soft leather, elaborately decorated with leather stitching. The dimensions of each piece are 26 × 10 cm. As shown, the two sections are tied together with leather thongs at one end, but there are traces of thongs suggesting that they were originally tied at the other end also. The fancy ornamentation suggests that this was some kind of apparel, possibly a decorative neckpiece.

Buttons and toggles

Mediaeval Nubian garments, like modern Near Eastern garments, were probably fastened mainly by means of tie strings, belts, and perhaps soft balls of cloth that took the place of buttons. It seems unlikely that hard buttons were much used; otherwise more of them would have been found. There are, however, three objects from the Late Christian levels at Qaṣr Ibrîm that look like buttons. One is a potsherd disc, ground down from a fragment of hard Aswân ware and perforated with two holes (pl. 47d). The cotton string that was found attached to this suggests that it was being used for some kind of fastening, though not necessarily for clothing. The diameter is 2.2 cm. There are also two discs ground from white limestone and perforated with two holes; one of the two is shown in plate 47e. Diameters of the stone specimens are 1.9 and 3.5 cm.

[28] See H. E. Winlock and W. E. Crum, *The Monastery of Epiphanius at Thebes* (New York, 1926), I, 76 and pl. XXVI, A.

[29] See Legh, op. cit., 204–5; St. John, op. cit., 425–6. For illustrations see Wallis Budge, op. cit., I, 213, and II, 429.

[30] See Crowfoot, op. cit.

[31] See Winlock and Crum, op. cit., 77–8 and pl. XXVI, B.

a

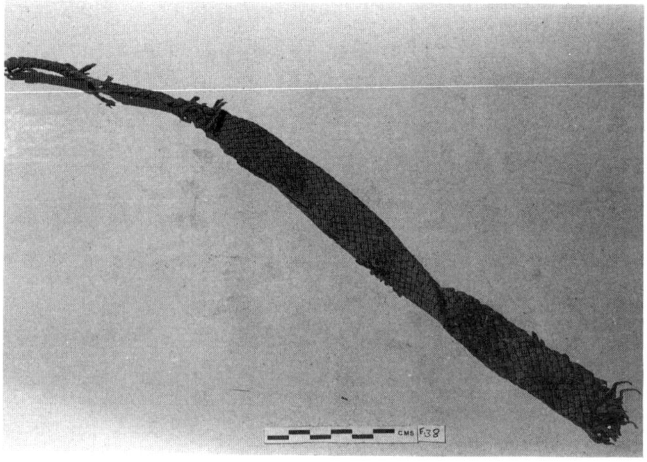

b

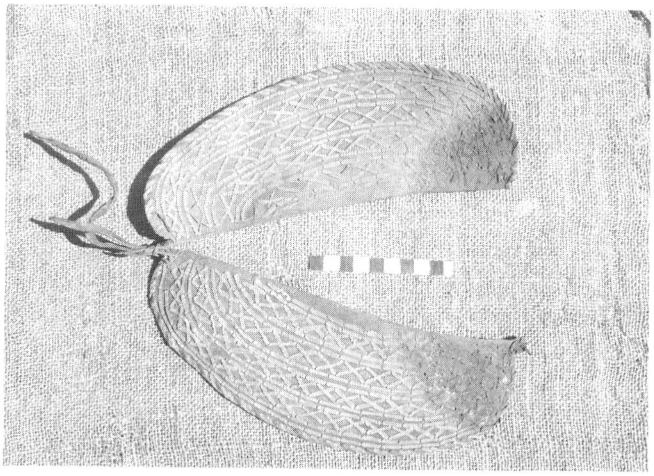

c

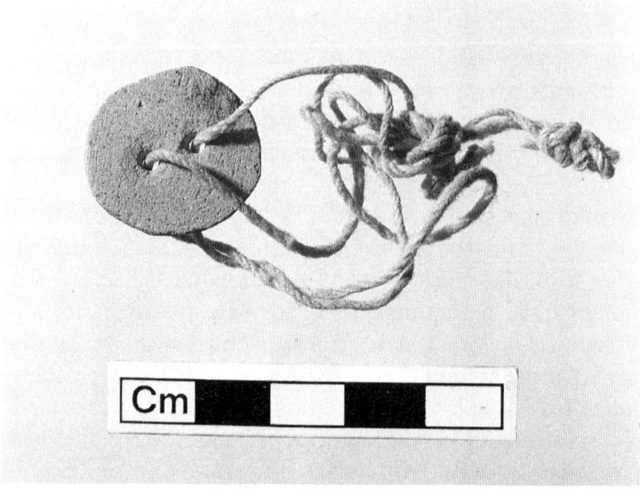

d

e

Plate 47. Leather garments; buttons. a, Fragment of *rahat* (78/614). b, Portion of woven leather belt (82/558). c, Decorated leather object of unknown use (72/47). d, Sherd button on string (78/413). e, Stone button (82/29).

Footgear

Because they had little value for any secondary purpose, discarded shoes and sandals are by far the most common items of wearing apparel found at Qaṣr Ibrîm. The Late and Terminal Christian levels alone have yielded, in whole or fragmentary form, 1 boot, 33 shoes, 28 leather sandals, and 29 palm-fibre sandals.

These different kinds of footgear probably served somewhat different purposes. The single boot that has been found seems to have been the property of an Eparch. Leather shoes, in general, were probably luxury possessions of the rich to be worn mainly on special occasions. Some of the best specimens may have been imported. Leather sandals, which commonly show evidence of very heavy wear, were probably the main footgear for hard outdoor use. Some of the palm-fibre sandals, on the other hand, show little evidence of wear and may have been the preferred footgear for indoor use.

Boot

Plate 48a–b shows a complete riding boot found in the Eparchal House 763. The upper portion is sewn from three pieces of soft, pebble-grained leather or pigskin. Along the top margin of the boot the pebble-graining has been stamped flat, leaving a smooth border 1.1 cm wide. The original stitching was done with two-ply flax thread, but the rear seam appears to have been somewhat crudely resewn at a later date. The sole is made of heavier leather than is the upper, and the heel has been reinforced internally with a second piece. The upward projection at the front of the knee shows that this was a riding boot, and a small projecting thong at the back of the heel may have been designed for the attachment of a spur. The boot had originally been dyed a red or maroon colour, although it is now much faded. The complete height of the piece is 47 cm. A second, fragmentary boot appears to have been very well made and stitched, but the surviving piece does not give a clear indication of the original form.

Shoes

The shoes worn at Qaṣr Ibrîm in the Late Christian period, like most other mediaeval shoes,[32] were made of relatively soft leathers and were of a design which today we should call slippers. They were not designed for hard use, though many had evidently been subjected to it, with clearly detrimental results. The soles are typically made from a single piece of fairly thick but pliable leather, or sometimes from two thicknesses of leather. The material is noticeably thinner and more pliable than that used in the making of leather sandals, to be described below. Uppers are made from thin and generally very soft leather. They are of several designs and may be made from one, two, or several pieces of leather. Uppers may be stitched to the sole in various ways;[33] in at least two cases a welt has been used. Stitching most commonly employs two-ply flax thread. Four of the five intact shoes vary in length between 23 and 27 cm; the fifth is 16 cm long and is evidently a child's shoe.

Plates 48c–f illustrate three shoes from the Late Christian levels, each exhibiting a somewhat different design. In the specimen shown in plates 48c–d the sole is comprised of two layers of leather separated by a layer of linen fabric. In another specimen, the inner lining has been turned back over the outer so as to form a rounded border along the top edge.[34] The shoe shown in plate 48f was evidently very finely made but has subsequently been much damaged. The upper appears to have been made from a single piece of leather, although the rear part of it is now missing. The front shows evidence of a very crude repair where the upper had become detached from the sole. The ornamental pointed 'tongue' is a feature found on a number of Late Christian shoes.[35]

The specimen shown in plate 48e is made from several small pieces of leather, stitched together with leather thongs. The sole is formed of two thicknesses of leather, held together by a central seam. The front part of the upper appears to have been rather crudely cut away at the top, while the rearward part still retains the original edge binding. The upper rises to a relatively high point, 9 cm above the sole, at the back of the heel. This is the only shoe that exhibits any suggestion of a fastening, although it is quite obviously not an original feature. Most of the thirty other shoes recovered from the Late Christian levels are much more fragmentary than the three specimens just discussed. Some were clearly similar in design to the illustrated specimens, but there were evidently shoes of other designs as well.

Study of the Late Christian shoes from Qaṣr Ibrîm suggests several conclusions. First, it is evident that these were scarce and prized items, for many specimens show evidence of extensive repair. Some of the finest shoes may, in fact, have come from one or another of the famous leather-working centres of the Islamic world. Second, the variety of designs suggests

[32] See Waterer in Charles Singer *et al.*, (eds.), *A History of Technology*, II (Oxford, 1956), 150–1, 177.

[33] See op. cit., 176.

[34] For a closely parallel example see Donald S. Whitcomb and Janet H. Johnson, *Quseir al-Qadim 1978: Preliminary Report* (Cairo, 1979), 192, fig. 14.

[35] Cf. Whitcomb and Johnson, *Quseir al-Qadim 1978*, pl. 71, h.

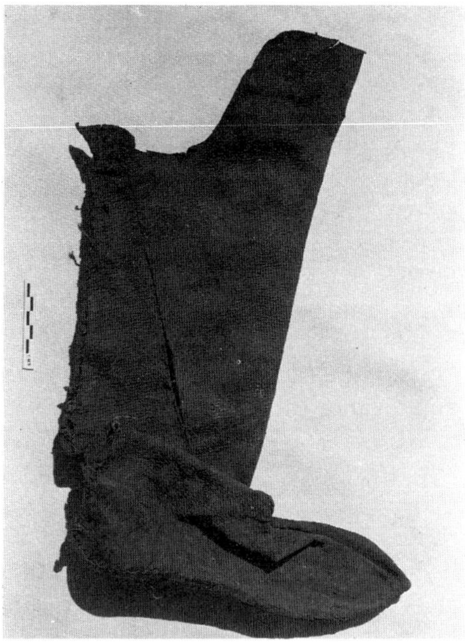

a

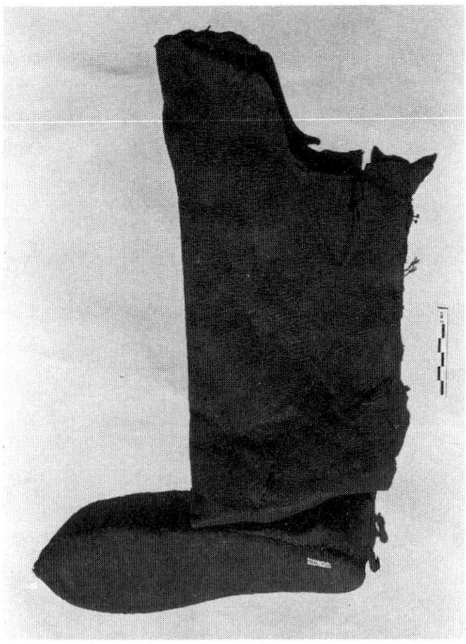

b

c

d

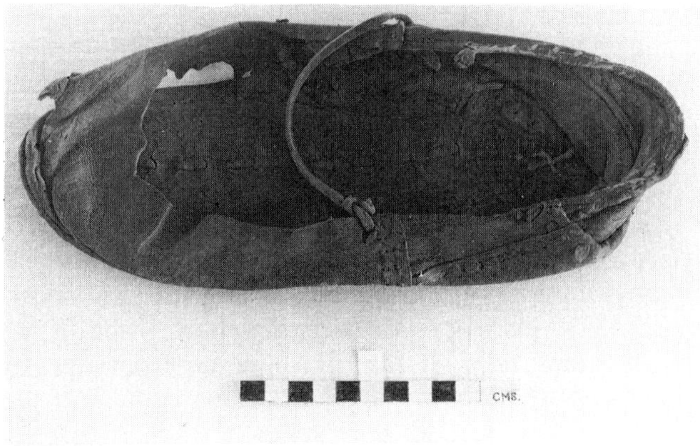

e

f

Plate 48. Leather boot and shoes. a, Leather boot, right side (82/598). b, Left side of **a**. c, Shoe (82/598). d, Shoe (78/466). e, Shoe (78/465). f, Shoe (78/466).

that the mediaeval Nubians may have expressed their individuality partly through their footgear, much as do modern wearers.[36] Finally, the condition of the heel portions shows that the wearers, like many Near Eastern peoples today, were in the habit of wearing their shoes like carpet slippers, with only the toe thrust into the shoe, while the rear portion of the upper was crushed down beneath the wearer's heel (cf. pl. 48d).

Leather sandals

Leather sandals appear to have been the preferred footgear for hard everyday wear. Those from the Late Christian levels are mostly very simple in design; they comprise a single piece of thick and relatively stiff cowhide with harness straps attached.[37] All but two of the eighteen intact specimens are between 19 and 28 cm in length and between 9 and 14 cm in width; the average dimensions are 22 × 10.5 cm Two smaller sandals, measuring 16 and 13 cm long, were evidently made for children.

In the most common form of leather sandal, shown in plate 49a, the sole is cut into two rounded 'lobes' with a somewhat narrower area in between. In some examples the toe is quite pointed, presumably for decorative effect. The harness is normally comprised of two leather straps fastened through holes in the sole. The straps are apparently designed to pass on either side of the middle toe or two toes (never the great toe), then to cross over the top of the instep and to fasten back into the sole on either side of the heel.

A slightly variant sandal design, also common in the Late Christian period, is shown in plate 49b. Here the sole is cut in such a way as to leave two rounded flaps which project upward on either side of the wearer's heel, and the harness is attached to these. The advantage of this design is that the harness is not fastened directly under that part of the sole which receives the heaviest wear, and thus it is less likely to wear our quickly. Curiously enough, sandals designed in this fashion always have a rounded rather than a pointed toe. The simplest of all sandal designs is that illustrated in plate 49c. It consists merely of a rounded rectangle of leather with attached harness, which in the illustrated specimen is made of palm cord rather than of leather. Several sandals of this kind were found in the Late Christian levels.

Fibre sandals

Fibre sandals are of two quite different kinds. The most common type is plaited from broad strips of palm leaf, as shown in plate 49d. The piece is originally made as a long, narrow strip of matting, slightly wider at one end than at the other; it is then doubled back on itself to form a doubled sole, as shown in the illustration. The extent of material that is doubled over varies from sandal to sandal; sometimes it is almost the full length of the sole and sometimes only the heel area. Quite possibly this was adjusted according to the foot size of the wearer. After doubling, a simple harness made of twisted palm leaf strips was attached. Many of the palm-leaf sandals have a pointed toe, while others are rounded like the specimen shown; still others are nearly straight.

There are only two examples of sandals woven from palm-fibre cord, as shown in plate 49e. These apparently represent the survival of an Early and Classic Christian sandal type. The weaving technique has not been analyzed in detail, but it appears that the twisted cords which make up the warp have also been doubled back and woven through to form the weft. In one specimen the heel area has been doubled over, as was the common practice with palm-leaf sandals.[38]

Fibre sandals are, on the average, slightly larger than leather sandals, varying from 18 to 30 cm in length, with an average length of 24 cm. In contrast to most of the other footgear found at Qaṣr Ibrîm, many of the fibre sandals show few signs of wear. In three instances, too, they were found in pairs, buried under house floors. It seems evident that this footgear was designed primarily for indoor use.

Ornamentation

Hair ornaments

The ancient Egyptians used both long-toothed combs and individual, decorated pins or skewers to help support their more elaborate coiffures.[39] Such hair ornaments are no longer found either in Egypt or in Nubia,[40] although they can still be observed among certain Beja tribesmen[41] as well as among more southerly African peoples.[42] They were evidently pop-

[36] Cf. also Waterer, op. cit., 177.

[37] For other leather sandals, of indeterminate type, see Whitcomb and Johnson, *Quseir al-Qadim 1980*, pl. 71, k–l. See also Winlock and Crum, op.cit., 75.

[38] For other rope sandals, rather different in design from those found at Qaṣr Ibrîm, see Whitcomb and Johnson, *Quseir al-Qadim 1978*, 200, fig. 21; Whitcomb and Johnson, *Quseir al-Qadim 1980*, pl. 71, o–p.

[39] Flinders Petrie, *Objects of Daily Use* (London, 1927), 24–6 and pls. XIX–XX.

[40] They are not described or illustrated by most of the 19th century travelers to Nubia; however see Friedrich Ratzel, *Völkerkunde* (Leipzig, 1885), I, 27.

[41] See especially F. L. James, *The Wild Tribes of the Soudan* (New York, 1883), 17. For illustrations see Wallis Budge, op. cit., I, following 174; K. M. Barbour, *The Republic of the Sudan* (London, 1961), pl. VIII.

[42] Cf. Ratzel, op. cit., 379, 447; Wilfrid D. Hambly, *Source Book for African Anthropology* (Field Museum of Natural History, Anthropological Series, Vol. 26) (Chicago, 1937), 616 and 625.

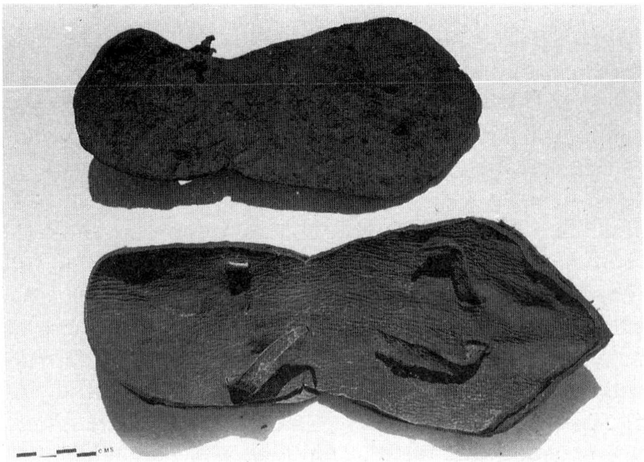

a

b

c

d

e

Plate 49. Sandals. a, Leather sandals (82/599). b, Leather sandal with leather thong (82/599). c, Leather sandal with rope thong (78/458). d, Plaited palm-leaf sandal (82/600). e, Woven palm-rope sandal (82/600).

ular in late mediaeval Nubia also, to judge by the number of long-toothed combs and decorative pins that have been found at Qaṣr Ibrîm and elsewhere. Most of the specimens from Qaṣr Ibrîm are of wood, which in some cases may be ebony. In Roman Egypt hair pins of bone, ivory, bronze, and even iron were also widely used, but they are rare in Nubia.[43] Most probably hair ornaments were worn only by Nubian males. It seems likely that women and girls braided their hair into innumerable fine plaits, as they still do today.

Decorative combs. Late Christian levels have yielded five whole or fragmentary long-toothed combs, of which four are illustrated in plate 50a. These objects may have served, in part, to hold masses of hair in place, but their main function was probably ornamental. The carved and decorated comb heads projected far above the hair to form a kind of crest, much like the ornamental combs (*peineta*) traditionally worn by Spanish ladies. All but one of the specimens from Qaṣr Ibrîm have some form of decoration, consisting in one case of incised criss-cross lines (pl. 50a, 1), in two cases of incised concentric circles (pl. 50a, 3), and in one case of perforations (pl. 50a, 2). The four large specimens all measure between 16 and 19 cm in length. The much smaller specimen (pl. 50a, 4) measures only 7.5 cm long and may have been worn by a youth.

Decorative pins. Plate 50b shows a selection of the ten wooden hair pins that have been found in Late Christian levels, and plate 50d (lower) shows the single intact ivory specimen. There are also two very fragmentary pins made either of bone or of ivory,[44] and a single shaft of a bronze pin. The length of the twelve intact pins varies between 12 and 25 cm, with an average length of 17.8 cm.

Body ornaments

Pendants and brooches. Plate 50e–f shows a heavy bronze brooch or pin that was evidently meant to be fastened to a garment. The punched design is actually one of the innumerable monograms on the name of St Michael,[45] surrounded by ornamental dots. Parts of the design retain traces of red pigment. On the back there are two small projecting bosses into which are set the two ends of a fastening shank that has since broken away.

Plate 50c shows an extraordinary wooden object that is quite obviously the legacy of a much earlier period. It is cut from a rather thick, flat piece of wood, 8.6 cm long and 1.1 cm thick. The design is the typical Meroitic *sa* or amulet that occurs so frequently both in pottery designs[46] and in textile decoration[47] from the Meroitic period. Although fairly carefully carved, the object shows no trace of painted decoration. It was originally perforated at one end, presumably for suspension, but the hole has subsequently been broken through at the top. Why the mediaeval Nubians recovered or retained this piece, and what they used it for, are problematical; it was found in the upper refuse fill of one of the LC 1 houses. Additional, ritual pendants, presumably worn by ecclesiastical officials, will be discussed in the next chapter.

Beads. Beads were undoubtedly the principal ornamentation worn by the mediaeval Nubians, as by most of their ancestors since prehistoric times. From the Late and Terminal Christian periods alone there are 116 registered finds of beads, and in a good many instances these, of course, represent a string or collection of beads rather than an individual find. The registered finds actually include 9 strings of glass beads, 60 individual finds of glass beads, 1 string combining glass and shell beads, 15 individual finds of pottery or frit beads, 2 stone beads, 2 wooden beads, 3 bone beads, and 11 cowrie shells.

It is evident, therefore, that glass was the overwhelmingly prevalent material used in Late Christian beads. The great majority are, however, simple spherical or tubular beads of opaque glass and of a single colour;[48] they lack altogether the decorative complexity found in Meroitic and X-Group beads.[49] By far the most prevalent colour is blue, suggesting that then as now this was the colour worn for protection against the evil eye. It is probable that many of the individually found blue beads were originally sewn as amulets to the clothing of children. Other relatively common bead colours are pale green and yellow; there are also a very few examples of white, orange, and black beads.

[43] Petrie, *Objects*, 24.

[44] For other mediaeval Nubian hair pins of bone or ivory see P. L. Shinnie and Margaret Shinnie, *Debeira West* (Warminster, 1978), pl. LI, and Kent Weeks, *The Classic Christian Townsite at Arminna West* (Publications of the Pennsylvania-Yale Expedition to Egypt, no. 3) (New Haven, 1967), 68.

[45] Cf. P. L. Shinnie and H. N. Chittick, *Ghazali—a Monastery in the Northern Sudan* (Sudan Antiquities Service Occasional Papers, no. 5) (Khartoum, 1961), 95. For illustrations see also William Y. Adams, *Ceramic Industries of Medieval Nubia* (Memoirs of the UNESCO Archaeological Survey of Sudanese Nubia, Vol. 1) (Lexington, 1986), Part I, 385.

[46] See Adams, op. cit., Part I, 275, fig. 127, Motif j.

[47] See N. K. Adams in *Wissenschaftliche Zeitschrift der Humboldt-Universität zu Berlin, Geisteswissenschaftliche Reihe,* 35 Jg., Heft 1, 21–6.

[48] Cf. Shinnie and Shinnie, op. cit., 82–4.

[49] See, for example, D. Randall-MacIver and C. L. Woolley, *Karanòg, the Romano-Nubian Cemetery* (Eckley B. Coxe Junior Expedition to Nubia, Vol. 4) (Philadelphia, 1910), pl. 40.

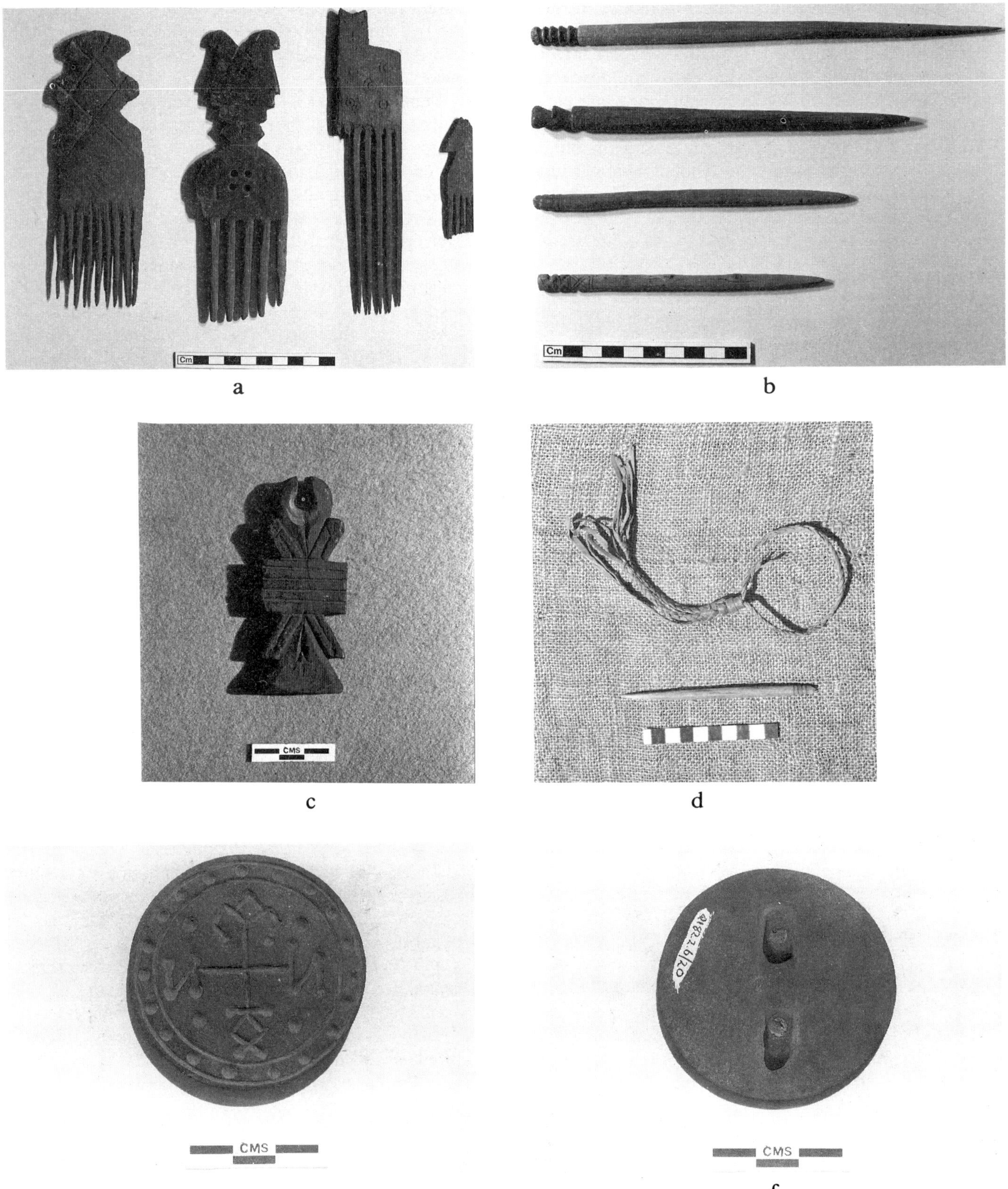

Plate 50. Hair ornaments; brooches. a, Decorative wooden combs, worn as hair ornaments (64/195, 66A/66, 66A/86). b, Decorative wooden pins, worn as hair ornaments (72/67, 72/168, 72/283, 78/496). c, Wooden pendant in shape of *sa* (82/205). d, Decorative ivory pin, worn as hair ornament (lower) (72/36). e, Copper brooch, top view (82/339). f, Underside of **e**.

Beads of translucent glass are much less prevalent than are opaque beads, numbering altogether fewer than two dozen examples. Once again the overwhelmingly predominant colour is blue. In the entire Late Christian collection there are only four varicoloured beads, of which one is pale green with a trailed white thread, one is purple with a marvered white thread, one is blue with projecting white spots, and one is green with white and blue spots.

Apart from glass, the only other common materials used for beads were faience or frit, and cowrie shells. All of the faience beads are pale to medium blue in colour. Cowrie shells are unmodified except for a small drilled hole.

The strings of beads that have been found are mostly fairly short, and could not have served as necklaces. Some of them might have been worn as bracelets, as in plate 51a, and others as earrings (pl. 51b). Plate 51c shows a single large, varicoloured glass bead threaded on a loop of copper wire, which is almost certainly an earring. A short string of beads was also found attached to a basketry lid, apparently purely for ornamentation.

Bracelets. Apart from the short bead strings that have just been mentioned, the mediaeval Nubians also wore various other kinds of wrist ornaments. Registered finds are not however very numerous, and all of them are fragmentary. Plate 51d illustrates one of three iron bracelets having rather simple hammered decoration. There is, in addition, a short segment of a bronze bracelet, having a flat inner surface and a rounded outer surface. Plate 51e shows one of three bracelets made from cut sections of cow horn. The illustrated specimen is very small and could only have been worn by a child; the other examples are nearly twice as large. From the Late Christian levels there is also a small segment of an ivory bracelet, square in cross-section and without decoration on the surviving fragment.

Also recovered from the Late Christian deposits were nine small fragments of varicoloured glass bangles of Islamic type. These objects are highly abundant in the Islamic levels at Qaṣr Ibrîm, but are so rare earlier that their occurrence before 1500 is considered problematical. None of the nine apparent Late Christian specimens was recovered from an absolutely secure context, and the possibility that they were accidentally displaced from overlying refuse deposits cannot be wholly discounted. It may be noted, nevertheless, that similar bracelets were found at Debeira West, where there is no evidence of post-Christian occupation.[50]

Rings. A final category of Late Christian body ornamentation consists of finger rings. Like the bracelets they are made from a variety of materials: bronze, iron,

[50] See Shinnie and Shinnie, op. cit., 89, 94.

Figure 29. Enlargement of design on signet ring, reg. no. 72/48.

silver, gold, faience, bone, and horn. However, 12 of the 19 registered specimens are made of copper or bronze. Of these, 10 are plain circlets, without bezels or ornamentation (pl. 52a), and the same is true of the single rings made of iron, bone, and horn. One slightly fancier bronze ring (pl. 52b) and one iron ring (pl. 52e, middle) are made from spirals of wire, hammered flat.

Two bronze rings have small projecting bezels. One has a simple design of punched dots on the upper surface. The other has a recessed top, presumably to receive a stone which is now missing. There is, in addition, a fragmentary stone ring, with a projecting bezel bearing the inscription ΧΠΘ (pl. 52d). This is almost certainly a kind of amulet rather than a signet ring. The letters ΧΠΘ are a cabalistic abbreviation for the name of St Michael,[51] and occur very frequently in mediaeval Nubian decorative art.

The two most elaborate rings from Late Christian contexts are made respectively of silver (pl. 52f) and gold (pl. 52c). The silver specimen appears to be a signet ring, with a fairly complex design (fig. 29) which incorporates familiar elements from mediaeval Nubian manuscript and pottery decoration. The gold ring has a setting for a bezel, which however is missing. There is, in addition, one very small fragment of what appears to be a faience signet ring.

Problematical object

An object which could not be illustrated is made from thin strips of leather woven through a framework of split palm canes, with sewn leather binding around the edges and across the middle. The preserved top edge is reinforced with a wooden rod. The dimensions as preserved are 18 × 21 cm. The use of the object is entirely conjectural; it is clearly too small to be a chair seat and too fieve. A fan has been suggested.

[51] See Shinnie and Chittick, op. cit., 95.

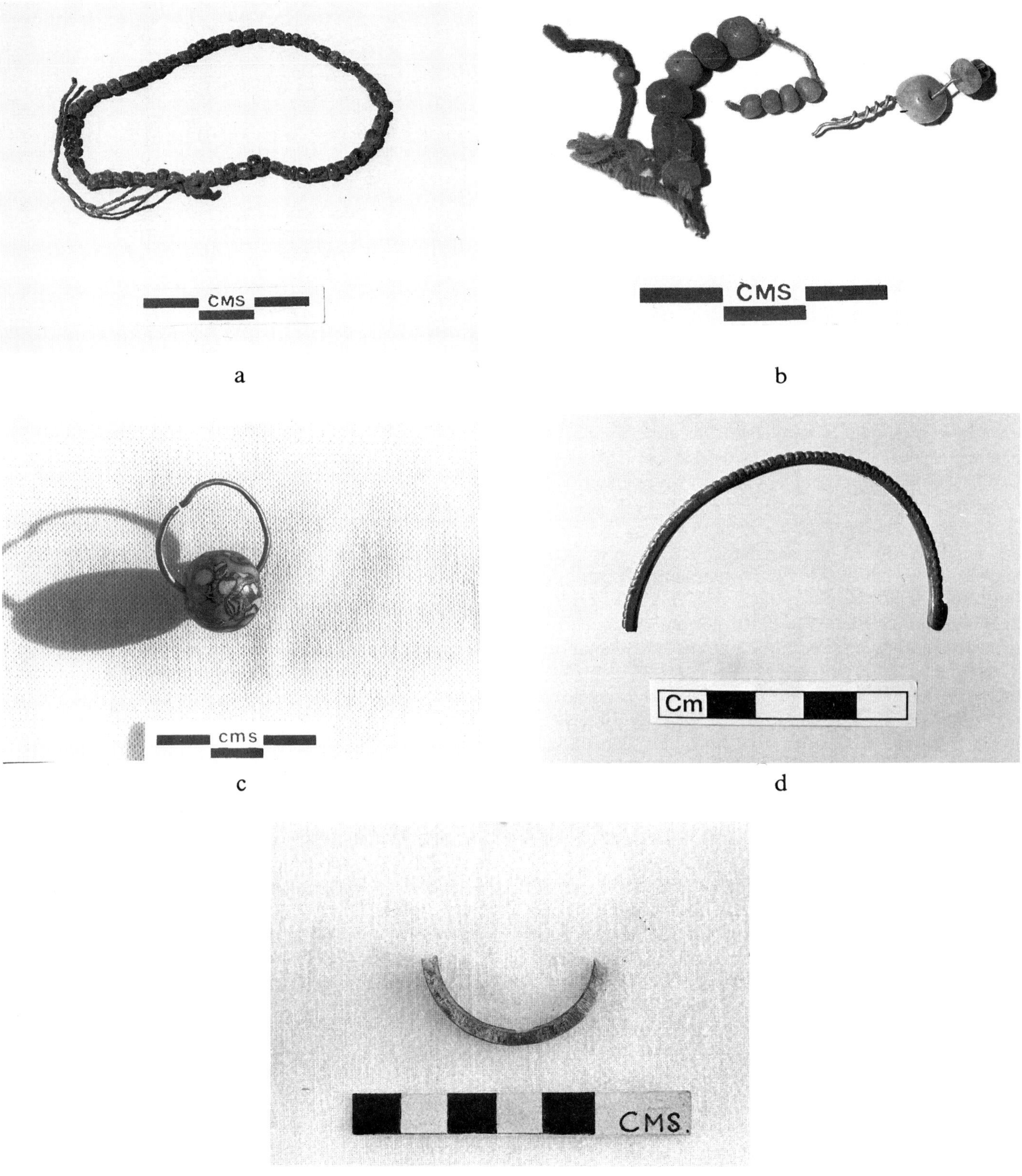

Plate 51. Beads and bracelets. a, String of glass beads (82/91). b, Short string of glass beads (82/91). c, Glass bead earring (84/647). d, Fragment of iron bracelet (82/352). e. Fragment of horn bracelet (78.2.6/22).

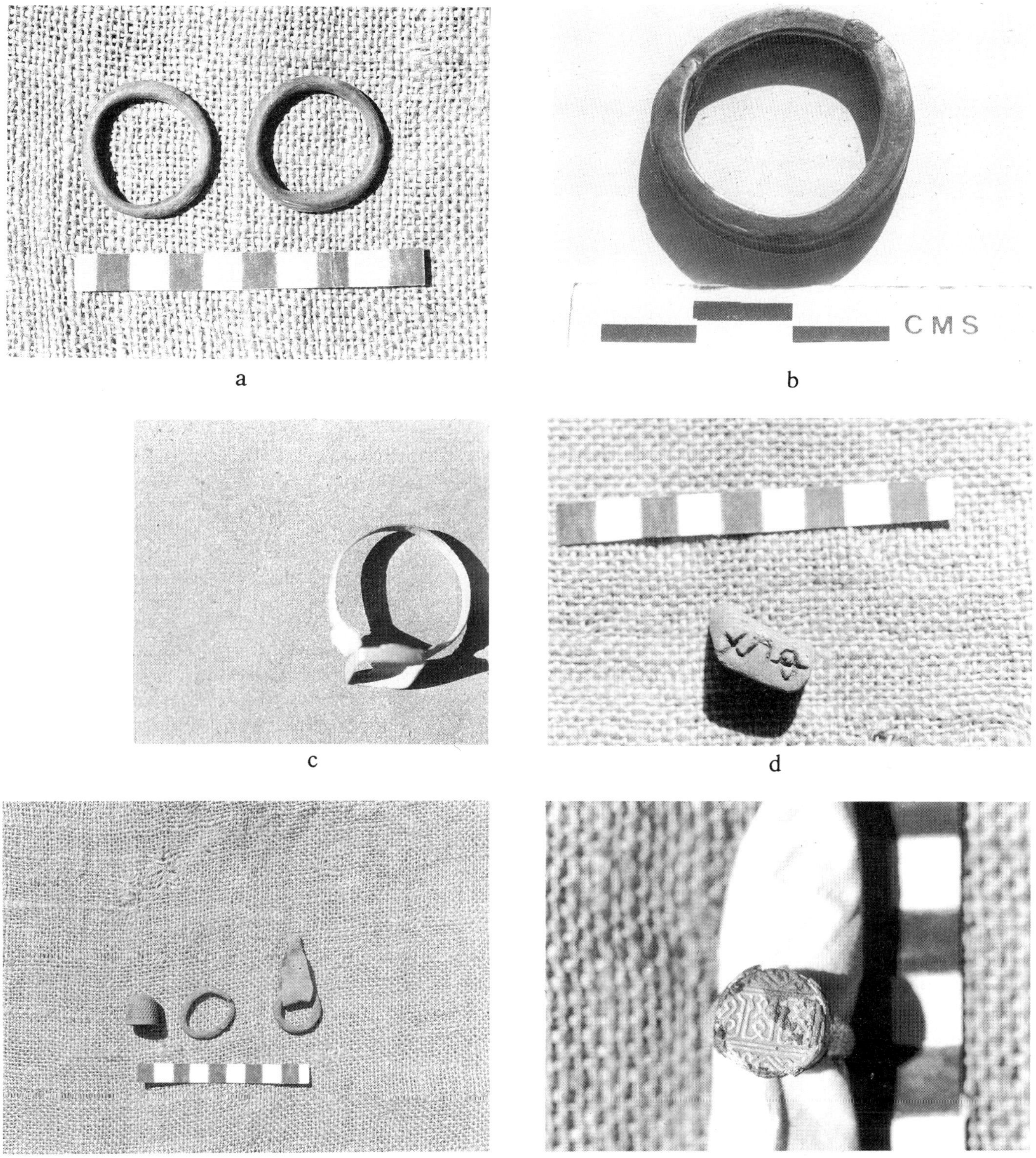

Plate 52. Rings. a, Bronze finger rings (72/253). b, Spiral-wound bronze finger ring (82/367). c, Gold ring with bezel missing (72/275). d, Stone amulet ring, top view (72/165). e, Iron ring (middle) (number lost). f, Silver signet ring (72/48).

CHAPTER 8
MISCELLANEOUS AND SPECIALIZED OBJECTS

THIS chapter will describe a variety of objects that do not fit readily into the categories described in previous chapters. In one way or another most of them are connected with the mental life of the mediaeval Nubians: religious, intellectual, artistic, or recreational.

Cult objects

The importance of Christianity to the mediaeval dwellers at Qaṣr Ibrîm is attested by many of their material remains; it finds expression in various kinds of cult objets no less than in texts, paintings, and religious architecture. The most common ritual objects are small crosses and amulets.

Crosses

The cross motif was used ritually and decoratively in a wide variety of forms:

The crosses of Bishop Timotheos. Plates 53a–b show a part of the paraphernalia that accompanied the burial of Bishop Timotheos, who died around 1372 and was buried in the north crypt of the Cathedral.[1] The bishop's staff had been suspended from a blue plaited cord, which at two points was twisted and sewn upon itself to form cross designs in string.[2]

Other processional and pectoral crosses. Plate 53f shows a copper or bronze cross which is probably a pectoral ornament, to judge by its suspension ring. It was found on the floor of the eparchal House 763.[3] The rather large and heavy cross shown in plate 53c has a central element of bronze, into which four iron legs are inserted. It has no loop or hole for suspension and must have been carried in the hand if, in fact, it is a processional cross. It was found in a refuse deposit of LC 1 age. Plate 53d shows part of a small, rather crude cross made from low-fired pottery, without any painted or relief decoration. There is no clear indication of how this cross might have been used; it is rather small for a processional cross.

Clothing ornaments. Plate 53e shows one of two thin sheets of stamped bronze exhibiting variations of the cross motif. The diameter of the larger piece is 5.5 cm; that of the illustrated piece is 3.5 cm. Probably these were originally sewn as decorations on garments.

Wooden finials. Use of the cross as a decorative furniture element is illustrated in plate 54a. This shows one of two nearly identical pieces of wood cut into a cross shape but without other decoration. Both pieces are complete except for a broken tenon at the lower end; the lengths are respectively 7.5 and 9.4 cm. They might possibly have adorned the top of a bishop's chair or chairs.

Palm crosses, amulets, and wreaths

A special category of ritual equipment comprises various objects made of palm leaf, which perhaps were carried in Palm Sunday and Easter Sunday processions. The most common of these are crosses, made by wrapping strips of split palm leaf as shown in plate 54b. The illustrated specimen is one of three found in Church 287, but other palm crosses were found in ordinary houses and in open plaza deposits.

Plates 54d (lower right) and 54e show small, carefully made objects made by interfolding strips of palm leaf back and forth over each other. The use of these meticulously made objects as amulets is conjectural, since they were found in refuse deposits, but it is difficult to conceive of any practical function they might have served.

One of the most unusual finds from Qaṣr Ibrîm is a collection of ornamental palm fronds that had been buried together beneath the floor of the Late Christian storehouse 235 (pl. 54c). Two of the fronds had been bent into a circle and loosely tied around with additional strips of leaf to make a kind of wreath. Another frond is twisted into a double loop. Three fronds have their individual leaves neatly plaited together, and there is one bundle comprising several fronds loosely tied together. The collection is completed by a palm centrum stick with a very small basket attached at one end. The whole collection probably represents equipment for a Palm Sunday or Eastern Sunday procession.

[1] For the original find see Plumley, *JEA* 50 (1964), 3–4.

[2] See Crowfoot in Veronika Gervers (ed.), *Studies in Textile History* (Toronto, 1977), 43.

[3] For other bronze crosses from Nubia see P. L. Shinnie and Margaret Shinnie, *Debeira West* (Warminster, 1978), pl. XXXIX, a–d.

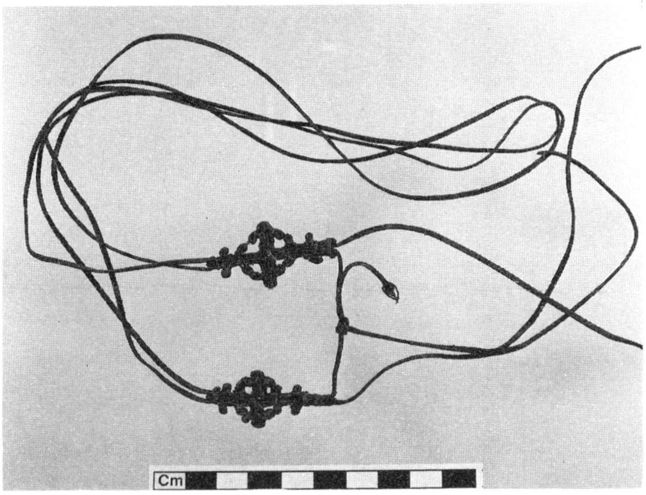

a

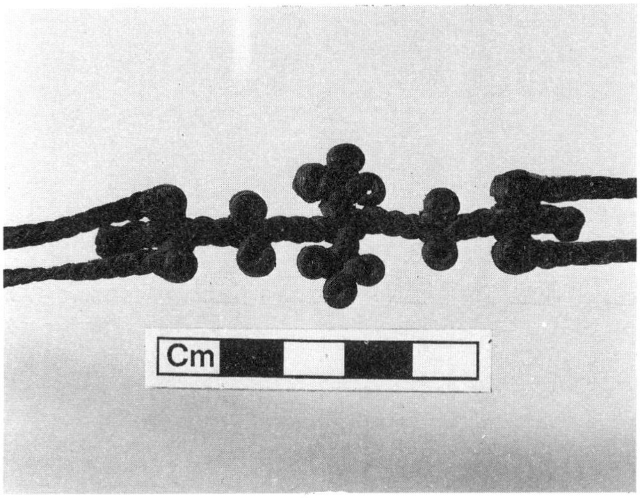

b

c

d

e

f

Plate 53. Crosses. a, Twisted cord crosses from costume of Bishop Timotheos (64/8). b, Detail of twisted cord cross from costume of Bishop Timotheos (64/8). c, Iron and bronze cross (66A/56). d, Ceramic cross (80/739). e, Small cross ornament of stamped bronze (66/94). f, Bronze pectoral cross (82/338).

a

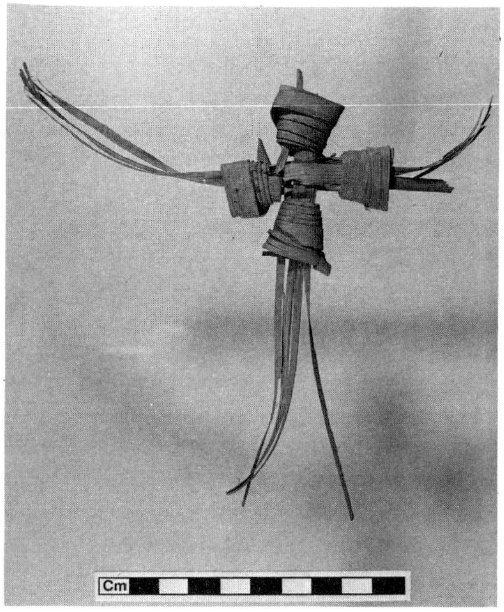

b

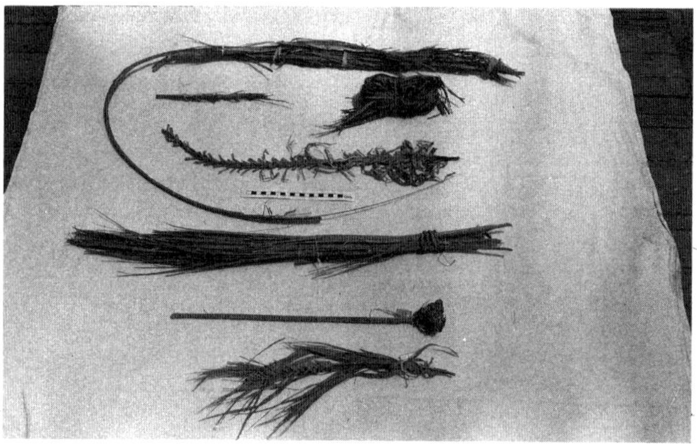

c

d

e

f

Plate 54. Wooden cross finial; palm crosses and amulets. a, Wooden cross finial (72/310). b, Palm fibre cross (72/317). c, Collection of processional palm fronds (78/34). d, Palm-leaf amulet (lower right) (76.2.4/12). e, Palm-leaf amulets (74/229, 76.2.4/12). f, Palm-leaf wreath (82/569).

Five additional palm leaf wreaths were found scattered at various points through the eparchal House 763. Three of the specimens are very large, having diameters between 55 and 60 cm; one of these is shown in plate 54f. Another wreath has a diameter of 40 cm, while a fifth is a miniature, only 4.8 cm in diameter. These objects, with their added tassels of palm leaf at regular intervals, appear clearly to be decorative, but their specific function is unknown. They are too large or, in one case, too small to have been worn on the head.

Icons

Plates 55a and 55b show respectively the front and the back of a tiny icon, 8.9 cm high,which is beautifully carved from some hard, dark wood. The more elaborately carved front side shows two holy figures; an adult man and an apparent child whose hand he is holding. The back is made to simulate a column with a decorated capital and plinth and with abbreviations for the names Jesus and Christ inscribed on the body of the column. This piece was found on the floor of the eparchal House 763. Plate 55c shows a fragment of a rather crudely carved icon, 14.5 cm tall, depicting one of the cavalier saints so popular in mediaeval Nubia.[4] It was found in the refuse fill of the eparchal House 178.

Statuettes

Statuettes and figurines evidently did not play an important role in the religious life of mediaeval Nubia, as they had in pre-Christian times. The four statuettes and statuette fragments that have been found in Late Christian contexts are all quite obviously legacies of much earlier periods. They were presumably cult objects at the time of their manufacture, but whether they retained any such function for their mediaeval owners is questionable. They may simply have been valued as curiosities or *objets d'art.*

Three fragmentary statuettes were found in the fill of the LC 1 House 185. One is the upper half of a typical pharaonic female figurine (pl. 55f), of which the surviving portion is 7 cm tall. There is also a very small nude female torso, apparently in classical style, carved in stone, and a more nearly complete male nude in bronze. These are respectively 6.5 and 6.0 cm tall.

A much more extraordinary find from the Late Christian period is a finely wrought standard of bronze, 41.6 cm high, which is topped by a classic head and torso of the youthful Dionysus (pl. 55d-e). Below the figure, the body of the standard is in the form of a square, fluted column, and from the base of it there projects the head of a leopard. Behind the Dionysus figure is a projection which attaches to a second, rounded column that extends upward above the level of the Dionysus head. In all probability this object originally formed one leg of a folding bronze tripod. It is closely similar to a number of finds from the X-Group royal tombs of Ballana and Qustul, which also exhibit Bacchic iconography.[5] A fifth or sixth century origin, therefore, seems likely. By Late Christian times the piece had evidently become detached from the remainder of the tripod, but was nevertheless retained as a prized possession of the Eparch Isra'il, in whose house (House 763) it was found. It had been buried under the floor, just below the threshold of one of the interior doorways.

Higabs

Higab is the Arabic word for a special kind of amulet: a religious text tightly folded and sewn up within a tiny leather pouch, which can then be attached by means of thongs to the wearer's person or clothing, or to some valued possession. The use of *higabs* is prevalent among both Christian and Moslem peoples in the Near East and Africa today.[6] In nineteenth century representations of Sudanese peoples they can often be seen tied just above the wearer's elbow.[7] *Higabs* were evidently popular also in the Middle Ages; they have been found abundantly both in the Late Christian and in the Ottoman levels at Qaṣr Ibrîm.

There are fourteen recorded examples of *higabs* from LC 1, LC 2, and TC levels. They are made in all cases from a single small rectangle of leather which is doubled over and then tightly stitched around all four edges. The typical size of the completed piece is about 4 cm square. On most of the specimens the folded-over edge of the leather projects a bit beyond the line of stitching, leaving a kind of sleeve through which a cord could be passed (cf. pl. 56a–d). In only three instances was any part of the actual cord found *in situ.* In one case it is a fine braided leather thong, which appears to be of a length to go around the wearer's arm (pl. 56d). One *higab* is unusual in being attached to a small bronze ring, 2 cm in diameter, instead of to a thong.

[4] See Griffith, *LAAA* 15 (1928), 80.

[5] See W. B. Emery and L. P. Kirwan, *The Royal Tombs of Ballana and Qustul* (Cairo, 1938), 350–3 and pl. 90. For more distant parallels from Herculaneum and Pompeii see H. Roux Ainé, *Herculaneum et Pompéi, recueil général des peintures, bronzes, mosaiques, etc.* (Paris, 1976), VII, part 2, 1–23.

[6] Cf. E. W. Lane, *Manners and Customs of the Modern Egyptians* (London, 1908), 575; E. A. Wallis Budge, *The Egyptian Sudan* (London, 1907), I, 217; Wilfrid D. Hambly, *Source Book for African Anthropology* (Field Museum of Natural History, Anthropological Series, Vol. 26) (Chicago, 1937), 373.

[7] See, for examples, G. A. Hoskins, *Travels in Ethiopia* (London, 1835), pls. I, III, XXX, XXXVIII, IXL.

a b

c

d

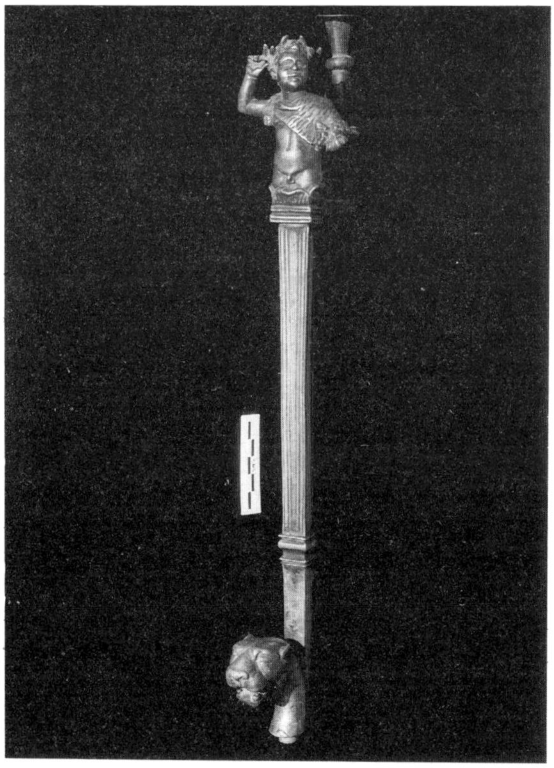

e

f

Plate 55. Icons and statuettes. a, Carved wooden icon, front view (82/206). b, Rear view of **a**. c, Crude wooden icon of cavalier saint (69/461). d, Detail of bronze Dionysus standard (82/49). e, Full view of **d**. e, Head and torso of Egyptian statuette (66/92).

a

b

c

d

Plate 56. Leather *higabs*. a, *Higab* (82/501). b, *Higab* (82/501). c, *Higab* (78/579). d, *Higab* with portion of tie-thong attached (82/501).

The more ornate *higabs* have fancy tooled decoration on one side, as shown in plates 56a and 56b. The second of these is unique in being folded back on itself a second time, prior to stitching. Plate 56c shows a much simpler and more crudely made higab without decoration. In this and several other examples the enclosed inscription had been removed in antiquity. In other instances the higab cases were not opened by us prior to surrendering them to the Egyptian authorities in division; we therefore have no information in regard to the actual inscriptions that were enclosed.

Other amulets

Apart from the *higabs* that have just been described, the Late Christian levels yielded a few other presumed amulets of a more purely animistic sort. Two of them are bundles of what appears to be human hair, sewn up in small leather tubes that are then tied off at each end. The lengths are respectively 7.7 and 8.5 cm. Somewhat more problematical, but presumably an amulet, is a small disc of shell, of an unidentified species, attached to a nicely braided leather thong (pl. 57a). Still more problematical is the curious object shown in plate 57b. It consists of a large, decorated potsherd of the Terminal Christian Ware R28 [8] and a tiny, flat piece of coiled basketry attached to it by a length of string. It is possible that this object is merely a toy.

Other presumed amulets consist simply of small objects or substances, perhaps supposed to have magical power, done up in cloth or yarn. One of the crudest is a chip of sandstone, possibly from a holy building, loosely wrapped in brown woolen yarn. Another is a small cotton bag containing a piece of corroded iron as well as a wad of flax yarn surrounding a lump of grey mineral; another is a small strip of linen cloth in which are tied up a cowrie shell, a bone bead, and a stone bead, all of white colour.

Figurines

Figurines from the Late Christian levels are few and fragmentary. Except for the 'heirloom' statuettes that were discussed previously, all of them appear to be of a purely secular nature. By far the most common are rather crudely modelled animal figurines, usually of unbaked clay but occasionally of low-fired pottery. In one instance the animal can be identified as a horse and in another as a camel; in other cases the species cannot be identified because the head is missing. Plates 57c and 57d show the bodies of very long-legged animals which might be giraffes or antelopes. One animal torso has a small detachable saddle.

Much less common than animal figurines are human figurines. The three registered examples include two small fragments of what appear to be female nudes, very crudely modelled, and a very stylized pottery figurine shown in plate 57e. The surviving portion is 7.2 cm tall and has areas painted in white and yellow.[9]

Sealing stamps

Among the various evidences of commercial activity at Qaṣr Ibrîm are the numerous sealing stamps found at the site. These of course were meant to leave distinctive impressions on clay seals, impressions that might indicate either the ownership of the sealed object or, in the case of jars and boxes, the nature of the content. Twenty-three sealing stamps, of many sizes and shapes, were recovered from the Late and Terminal Christian deposits. They are made variously of stone, pottery, and wood; these materials seem to have been used more or less interchangeably. Regardless of the material employed, the Late Christian sealing stamps fall rather clearly into four groups:

Large disc stamps. These are typically made in the form of a disc or drum, 4 to 7 cm in diameter and 2 to 3 cm thick. There are three examples of wood (pl. 58e and 58f), and one each of pottery (pl. 58b, 2) and of stone (pl. 58a, 3). Two of the wooden specimens have a design on either face and a groove around the outer edge of the disc.[10] As can be seen in the photographs, all but one of the disc stamps (pl. 58f) seem to be extremely worn or weathered.

Conical stamps. This group includes one stone and four pottery examples (pl. 58b, 3; pl. 58c–d). These specimens typically have a rather small round stamping face, with a long projecting handle behind it. Some of them are genuinely conical; others are more nearly bell-shaped, as shown in plate 58c. (Plate 58d shows the face of the same stamp.)[11]

[8] For the description see William Y. Adams, *Ceramic Industries of Medieval Nubia* (Memoirs of the UNESCO Archaeological Survey of Sudanese Nubia, 1) (Lexington, 1986), Part 2, 508 and 511–2.

[9] For mediaeval Nubian parallels see Shinnie and Shinnie, op. cit., pl. XLIV, b.

[10] For parallel examples see op. cit., fig. 104, no. 168; J. E. Quibell, *Excavations at Saqqara (1908–9, 1909–10)* (Cairo, 1912), pl. LV (top); W. M. Flinders Petrie, *Objects of Daily Use* (London, 1927), pls. LXI–LXII.

[11] For parallel examples see Shinnie and Shinnie, op. cit., fig. 104, nos. 423, 582, 712, and pl. XLIX, a; P. L. Shinnie and H. N. Chittick, *Ghazali—a Monastery in the Northern Sudan* (Sudan Antiquities Service Occasional Papers, no. 5) (Khartoum, 1961), 27.

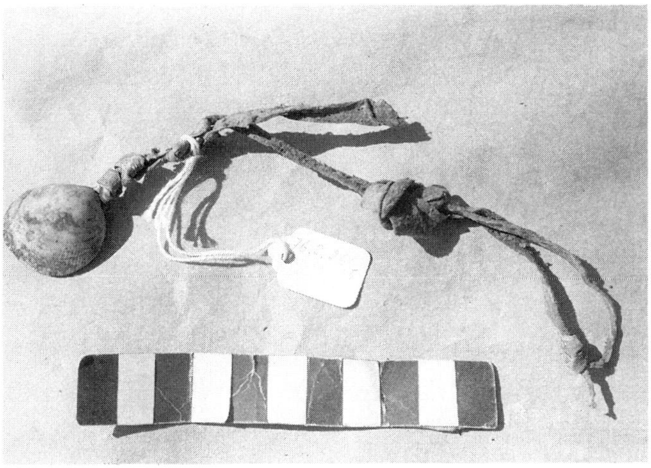

a

b

c

d

e

Plate 57. Amulets and figurines. a, ?Amulet comprised of a small shell attached to a braided leather thong (76.2.26/5). b, ?Amulet comprised of a small section of coiled basketry attached by a cord to a drilled potsherd, Ware R28 (76.2.9/7). c, Body and hind legs of mud animal figurine (n/r). d, Body and hind legs of a ceramic animal figurine (72/481). e, Head of a ceramic human figurine (78/397).

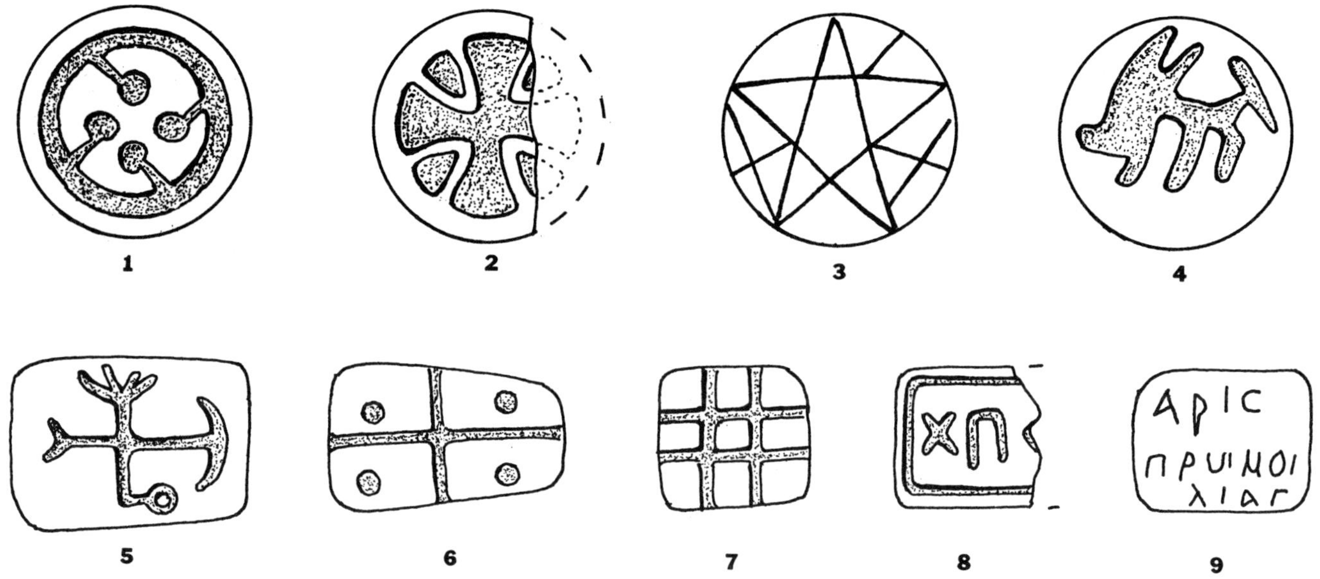

Figure 30. Designs on sealing stamps. **1**, stone; **2–3**, ceramic; **4**, wood; **5–8**, stone; **9**, ceramic.

Pyramidal stamps. These are the square or rectangular equivalents of the conical stamps. They have a small square or rectangular stamping face at one end, with an elongate handle behind it which is square or oblong in cross-section. There are four examples, all in sandstone. Plate 58a, 2 shows one of the pyramidal stamps in side view.[12]

Rectangular flat stamps. These are flat, rectangular pieces of stone (pl. 58a, 1 and 4), pottery (pl. 58b, 1), or wood (pl. 58g), having a stamping face on one or both sides. Six examples have been found in Late and Terminal Christian deposits. Lengths of the intact examples are 3.7, 4.8, and 6.5 cm.[13]

Other stamps. Not illustrated in a photograph is a fragment of a rather large pottery stamp, retaining part of an inscription of Greek, Coptic, or Old Nubian (fig. 30, 9). The piece was originally a flat slab of pottery, about 1 cm thick, having at least one cylindrical handle projecting at the back. Since no part of the outer edge is preserved, the original shape cannot be determined; it could have been round or square or rectangular.

There is also a very small copper or bronze disc, 1.4 cm in diameter, that has been interpreted as some kind of a seal. On one side it bears rather indistinct traces of a design, but it is too thin to be a coin.

Stamp designs. All of the Late Christian stamp designs that can be deciphered are illustrated in fig. 30. They can be roughly classified into five groups. The largest number are purely abstract geometric designs, with no obvious inscriptional content. There are three examples of apparently representational designs, one showing animal figures and two showing what appear to be highly stylized birds. These latter are the designs found on opposite sides of the very worn wooden stamp shown in plate 58e. In view of the condition of the piece, the interpretation of the designs is somewhat conjectural. A third group consists of designs that are partly geometric and partly inscriptional, i.e., Greek or Old Nubian letters have been attached to, or worked into, geometric patterns. A fourth group consists of simple combinations of letters, which are presumably abbreviations for names, and a fifth consists of actual short inscriptions. Because several of the registered stamps bear more than one design, the total of number of illustrated designs exceeds the number of individual stamps.[14]

Coins and coin weights

These objects are of interest in and of themselves, but they yield almost no information about the contexts in which they were found. Most of them came from refuse deposits, and many represent issues long antedating the late mediaeval period. Their occurrence in the Late Christian deposits may be due to accidental redeposition, or it may be that the Late Christian inhabitants found and retained them as souvenirs, as most of us would be inclined to do today.

[12] For parallel examples see Shinnie and Shinnie, op. cit., pl. XLIX, a.

[13] For parallel examples see Petrie, *Objects*, pls. LXI–LXII.

[14] For additional seal impressions, similar to many of those illustrated here, see H. E. Winlock and W. E. Crum, *The Monastery of Epiphanius at Thebes*, I (New York, 1926), 80.

Plate 58. Sealing stamps. a, Group of stone stamps (66/80, 74/18, 80/836, 64/156). b, Group of ceramic stamps (64/82, 72/37, 82/276). c, Ceramic stamp, side view (82/276). d, Bottom view of **c**. e, Weathered wooden disc stamp (82/276). f, Small wooden disc seal (78/106). g, Small rectangular wooden seal (78/406).

Coins

We have it on the authority of Ibn Selim el-Aswâni (c. 980) that Egyptian money circulated freely in tenth century Nubia,[15] and indeed *dirhem* are mentioned several times in Old Nubian texts from Qaṣr Ibrîm.[16] However, the use of coinage is not very well confirmed by archaeological finds, from Qaṣr Ibrîm or any other mediaeval Nubian site.[17] Only nine small bronze coins were found in the Late and Terminal Christian deposits, and of these at least three are of Roman date. Four others are of Mamluk date (thirteenth to fifteenth centuries AD), and two cannot be identified.

Plates 59a and 59c show the obverse and reverse of two Roman coins, respectively of Tacitus and of Antoninus Pius. Another Roman coin found in a Late Christian deposit can be dated roughly to the latter half of the fourth century but not to a specific emperor.

Only four coins are clearly coeval with the late mediaeval occupation at Qaṣr Ibrîm. Plate 59d shows the obverse and reverse of a coin of Sultan Bybars I, dated 658 AH (=AD 1260). Plate 59e shows the reverse of another Mamluk coin of fourteenth or fifteenth century date; the obverse in this case is illegible. A third specimen (not illustrated) bears the name of Shaban II (AD 1363–77), and a fourth can be attributed to the late fourteenth or early fifteenth century, but not to a specific reign.

Coin weights

Small, inscribed discs of glass, about the size of coins, are among the most distinctive products of Roman and mediaeval Egypt; according to Petrie they were never made in any other country.[18] They typically have one completely flat and undecorated side, while the opposite side bears a hot-stamped inscription surrounded by a raised border. In Egypt coin weights of the Omayyad, Abbasid, and Fatimid periods are very prevalent, but there seem to be no examples that can be securely dated to any later dynasty.[19]

Two complete coin weights and one fragmentary specimen were recovered from the Late Christian levels at Qaṣr Ibrîm. Plate 59f shows a weight, made of blue glass, bearing the name of the Fatimid Caliph al-Fa'iz (1154–60). Another, complete specimen (not illustrated) bears the name of the Fatimid ruler al-Hakim (996–1021). It is evident therefore that these coin weights, like many of the coins found at Qaṣr Ibrîm, originated at a time preceding the Late Christian period.

The very small coin weight shown in plate 59g is unique in having a central device, and around it the Old Nubian inscription ΕΠΑΡΧΟΥΒ ΝΟΥΒ, i.e., 'Eparch of Nobadia.' Also possibly decipherable are the letters ΓΟΔ, the Old Nubian word for 'lord.' (Unfortunately no part of the inscription can be made out in the published photograph.) The piece is of dark blue translucent glass, 2.0 cm in diameter. It and another fragment, found in a Classic Christian context, are the only known examples of mediaeval coin weights not inscribed in Arabic.

Writing equipment

Not illustrated here is a wooden pen case, 16 cm long and 3.5 cm wide. The recessed upper edge indicates that it was originally fitted with a closing lid.[20] The catalogue card states that there is an Arabic inscription on one side of the case, but no actual copy of it seems to have been made.[21] The Late Christian context of the find is nevertheless incontrovertible, for it came from a refuse deposit underlying one of the LC2 houses. It is the only example of writing equipment found in Late and Terminal Christian contexts at Qaṣr Ibrîm. There are also various pieces of blank paper, but they may be uninscribed portions of larger documents. There are in addition, rather surprisingly at so late a date, two sizable pieces of uninscribed papyrus.

Gaming equipment

This is necessarily a somewhat problematical category, since we do not really know what games were played by the mediaeval Nubians, or what equipment they used. In the case of dice our identification can be fairly secure, but other objects are assigned to the category of gaming equipment either because they resemble modern chess pieces, or because we cannot imagine what other purpose they could have served.

[15] See J. L. Burckhardt, *Travels in Nubia* (London, 1819), 495.

[16] They are rendered in Old Nubian as *tiram(i)* (personal communication from Prof. G. M. Browne).

[17] The mediaeval levels at Meinarti yielded only three coins, and all of them proved to be of Ptolemaic date (author's unpublished field notes). No coins have been reported from Debeira West, Arminna, or other mediaeval Nubian sites published thus far.

[18] W. M. Flinders Petrie, *Glass Stamps and Weights* (London, 1926), 1.

[19] Op. cit., 6. For other studies of Islamic coin weights see Stanley Lane-Poole, *Catalogue of Arabic Glass Weights* (London, 1891); Jungfleisch in *Bulletin de l'Institut d'Égypte*, 10 (1927–1928), 61–71; and Abdel-Rahman Fahmy, *Early Islamic Coin Weights* (Collections of the Museum of Islamic Art, 2) (Cairo, 1957).

[20] For a roughly parallel example see Petrie, *Objects*, pl. LVIII, no. 52.

[21] During the early excavation seasons the Qaṣr Ibrîm expedition usually did not include an Arabic philologist.

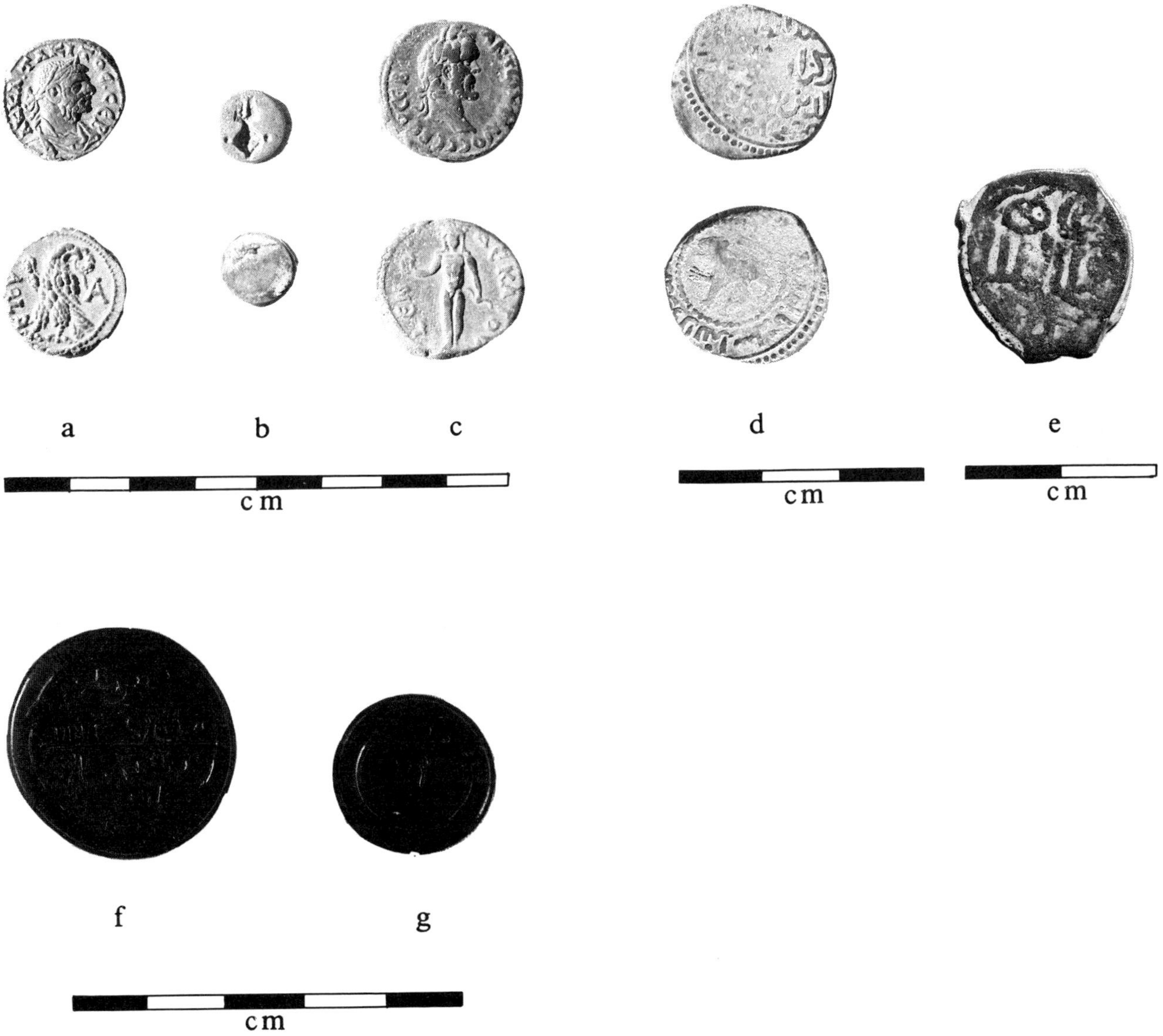

Plate 59. Coins and coin-weights. a, Roman bronze coin of Tacitus, obverse and reverse (66A/50). b, Very small, unidentified coin-like object of bronze (n/r). c, Roman bronze coin of Antoninus Pius, obverse and reverse (66A/50). d, Mamluk bronze coin of Bybars I, obverse and reverse (66/140). e, Mamluk bronze coin of unidentified ruler (72/20). f, Fatimid glass coin-weight of al-Hakim (78/412). g, Old Nubian glass coin-weight bearing the name of Eparch of Nobadia (78/119).

Lathe-turned counters

Late and Terminal Christian deposits yielded eight small, lathe-turned objects of wood, bone, and ivory that are presumed to be gaming counters of one sort or another. Three of the wooden specimens look remarkably like modern chess pawns, although they vary in height from 2.3 to 5.2 cm.[22] There are also two simple dome-shaped pieces, one of wood and one of ivory, that are somewhat reminiscent of the counters used in the ancient Egyptian game of *senet.* [23] A similarly shaped piece of white plaster might also be a gaming counter. The mediaeval Nubians could well have played chess, since the game was well known to the tenth century Arab author al-Mas'udi.[24] However, a good many other board games employing lathe-turned counters were also played in ancient and mediaeval times,[25] and the pieces found at Qaṣr Ibrîm could have belonged to any of them.

Rather different from any of the previously described pieces is the fragment of decorated bone ring shown in plate 60a. It is too large to be a finger ring and too small to be a bracelet, but its identification as a gaming piece is purely conjectural.

Sherd discs

It was a common practice of the mediaeval Nubians to grind down broken fragments of pottery into small, regular discs. The stamped central designs of Classic Christian saucers (Ware W5 [26]) were especially favoured for this purpose,[27] but Egyptian glazed wares were also popular (pl. 60b). The wares were obviously selected for their attractive appearance, but the use of the discs as gaming counters is, of course, conjectural.[28]

The Late and Terminal Christian levels yielded 14 examples of sherd discs; 7 made from Egyptian glazed wares, 2 from Nubian decorated wares, and 5 from other wares. Diameters range from 1.4 to 3.3 cm, with an average diameter of 2.2 cm. One disc has a geometric design, apparently a monogrammatic representation of the name Michael, incised into the upper surface (fig. 31); another has four small ground depressions symmetrically arranged.[29] These are not, in either case, part of the original decoration of the pottery vessel. In addition to discs, there is one example of a glazed sherd ground down to a rectangular shape, with rounded corners. The dimensions are 1.9 × 1.3 cm.

Figure 31. Design on sherd disc, reg. no. 78/106.

Dice

The Late Christian levels produced only one cubical die of sandstone, measuring 1.8 cm on a side (pl. 60d). The arrangement of the spots is the same as in modern dice, except that for 'two' the spots are arranged in a line across the centre of the face (· ·) rather than at diagonally opposite corners (. ˙).[30] A much more unusual find is an ivory or bone *talus,* the elongate die used in some Greek and Roman games (pl. 60e).[31] The piece is 6.4 cm long and is inscribed with patterns of small circles, rather irregularly placed, one on each of the four sides. There are three circles—two at one end and one at the other—on one face, while the face next to it has nine circles in a single cluster, the face next to that has nine circles in three separate clusters, and the last face has eighteen circles in two clusters of nine.

Problematical gaming equipment

Plate 60c shows a conical piece of bone, 7.5 cm long, decorated with small inscribed circles. The piece has been ground and polished down to its present shape, but it is not lathe-turned. This object was probably not a counter for a board game, since the bottom (i.e. the broad end) is not cut off straight. It may not be a gaming piece at all, though again it is difficult to think

[22] For parallel but apparently much older specimens see Petrie, *Objects*, pl. XLVIII, nos. 91–101.

[23] Op. cit., 51–4 and pl. XLVIII, nos. 151–8.

[24] See *Encyclopaedia Britannica,* 14th Ed. (Chicago, 1958), Vol. 5, 426.

[25] Petrie, *Objects*, 55–7 and pls. XLVII–XLVIII.

[26] See Adams, *Ceramic Industries*, 319.

[27] For numerous other examples see Shinnie and Shinnie, op. cit., 78, fig. 102, and pls. XLII, b; XLIII, b.

[28] But see Petrie, *Objects*, 54; Shinnie and Shinnie, op. cit., 78.

[29] Cf. also Shinnie and Shinnie, op. cit., pl. XLIV, a.

[30] For other dice see Petrie, *Objects*, 57 and pl. XLIX, nos. 234–84; Kent R. Weeks, *The Classic Christian Townsite at Arminna West* (Publications of the Pennsylvania-Yale Expedition to Egypt, no. 3) (New Haven, 1967), 68.

[31] See Petrie, *Objects*, 57 and pl. XLIX, nos. 230–2.

a

b

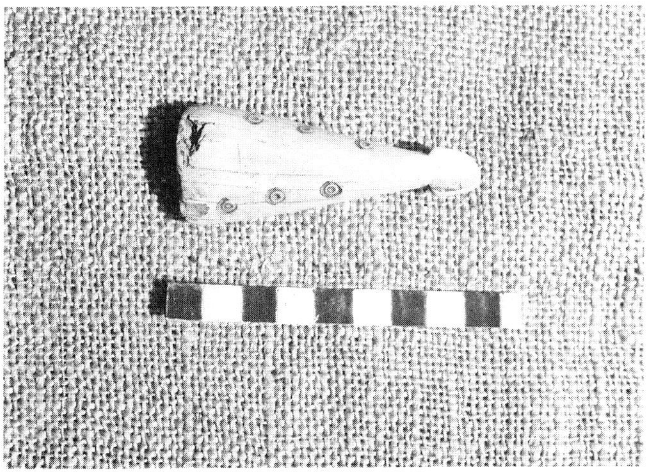

c

d

e

Plate 60. Gaming equipment. a, Fragment of turned bone ring (82/411). b, Ground sherd disc of glazed Ware G.II (82/74). c, Problematical gaming piece of bone, with inscribed markings (72/27). d, Sandstone die (78/406). e, Ivory *talus* (74/16).

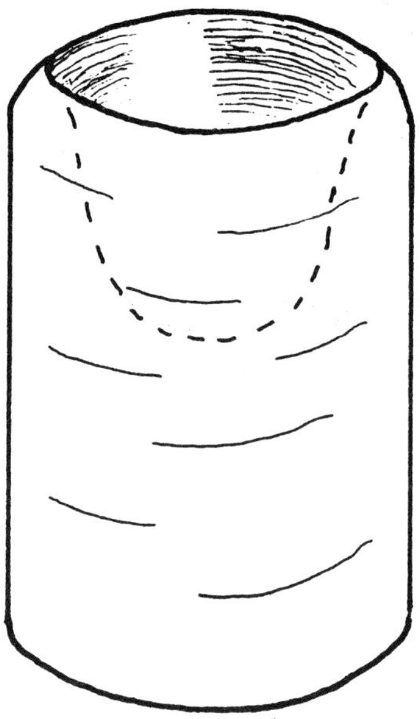

Figure 32. Wooden dice shaker (?), reg. no. 64/208. Height 6 cm.

of any other use. The small hollowed-out cylinder of wood shown in fig. 32 may have been intended as a dice shaker. It is 6 cm tall and 4.5 cm in diameter.

Playthings

Dolls and doll clothing

Nubian children at Qaṣr Ibrîm made rather crude dolls from crossed sticks, sometimes with the addition of a head modelled in mud. These figures were then clothed in garments sewn from discarded rags. No actual dolls were found in the Late Christian levels, but there are several examples of doll clothing, including the undecorated specimen shown in plate 61a. Another example was made of blue-, white-, and pink-checked cotton cloth. It is 6.5 cm long and measures 15 cm from sleeve end to sleeve end.

Balls

Mediaeval children played with balls made from bundles of rags sewn or tied together. Two examples were found in the Late Christian levels, of which one is shown in plate 61b. The diameters of the two balls are respectively 6 and 15 cm.[32]

Other playthings

Crude mud figurines of animals, presumably for the amusement of children, have already been described in an earlier section. There is in addition a small toy dish, 3.1 cm in diameter, modelled in mud (pl. 61c). The objects shown in plate 61d may be toy spindles, or possibly spinning tops. They seem in any case too small to have served any practical purpose, measuring only 3.0 and 3.6 cm in length. Finally, it appears that children made two miniature weavings (pl. 61e), crudely woven from brightly coloured yarns. They measure respectively 10 × 8 and 10 × 6 cm, excluding the fringed ends. Their small size and irregular edges suggest that one or two little girls had an early lesson in a useful skill.

[32] For parallel examples see op. cit., pl. LI, nos. 361–5.

a

b

c

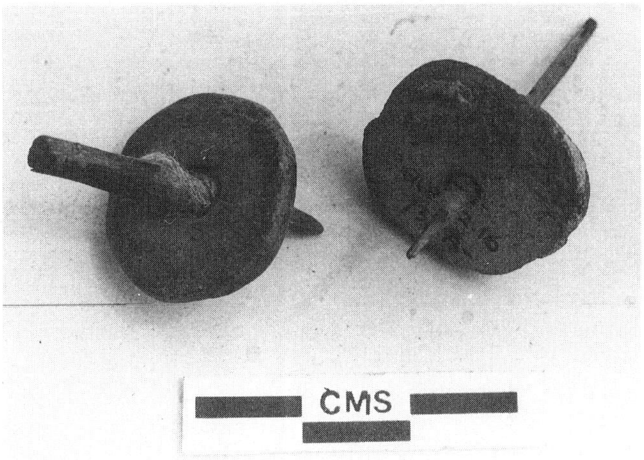

d

e

Plate 61. Playthings. a, Doll's dress of cotton (78T/10). b, Ball of wadded and wrapped rags (78.2.5/42). c, Miniature mud dish (82.2.28/58). d, Toy spindles, comprising drilled potsherds on wooden shafts (82/438). e, Miniature weavings (82T/580, 82T/698).

CHAPTER 9
UNIDENTIFIED OBJECTS AND FRAGMENTS

As always in archaeology, the excavations at Qaṣr Ibrîm have yielded a large number of whole and fragmentary objects whose use is problematical. Many fragments are simply too small for identification, while some seemingly complete objects may have been unfinished. There are, in addition, certain objects that appear to be finished, but whose function nevertheless remains enigmatic. This chapter will be concerned with two main groups of unidentified objects: whole objects of unknown function, and fragments that merit description because of the decoration they exhibit.

Problematical objects

Stone

Plate 62a shows a finely polished object made from some hard, dark igneous stone. It is in the form of a truncated cone, 4.7 cm in maximum diameter and has fairly deep depressions pecked into both of the two flat surfaces. A balance weight would be the obvious suggestion if there were only one pecked depression (to bring the stone precisely to the desired weight),[1] but the reason for two depressions is not obvious. Plate 62b shows a small schist pebble that has been rather crudely ground down to an oval shape and then incised with surrounding grooves in two directions, presumably so that it could be tied up in a string harness. Similar incised pebbles of schist were found at Kulubnarti.[2] Possibly they were weights for fishnets, since schist is an exceptionally heavy stone relative to its mass.

Metal

The Late Christian levels produced several scraps of sheet bronze and sheet iron, which were probably the raw materials of the metalsmith. There are, in addition, a few seemingly finished metal objects whose function cannot be identified. Two small, shovel-shaped iron plates are both reinforced with added metal along the curved edge, as shown in the specimen in plate 62c. Perforations at the corners along the straight edge suggest that the plates were once attached to something else, possibly to a wooden handle. The size of both pieces is 5.4 × 5.4 cm, but one is considerably thicker than the other. The three-armed bronze apparatus shown in plate 62d may be part of a suspension mechanism, from which chains would have descended to a lamp or censer.[3]

Pottery

The very small pottery object shown in plate 63a bears some resemblance to gaming counters that were described in the previous chapter, but it is perforated through from top to bottom by a very narrow hole, suggesting that it was once suspended on a string. The size and shape, however, do not suggest a bead; a plumb-bob is a more likely possibility.

Wood

The Late Christian levels yielded more than fifty unidentified objects of wood. The largest number are sticks, pointed or rounded at one end and sometimes perforated or notched at one or more points along the shaft. There are also sections of palm leaf centrum (*gerid*), notched or bound around with palm-leaf fibre. Possibly these are pieces of *sebit*, the frails that are so much used for carrying fruit and vegetables in Egypt today.

Leather

The number of unidentified objects of leather is also very large. Mostly they are fragments showing a certain amount of tailoring or stitching, but are not large enough to permit identification of the original object.

Matting

The flag-like object shown in plate 63b comprises a narrow strip of continuously plaited palm-leaf matting attached to a handle made from a palm leaf centrum (*gerid*). Only the lower edge of the plaited strip is original; the other edges have been torn or burned away, and the original size is, therefore, not determinable. As preserved, the length of the handle is 30 cm. A fly-whisk has been suggested.

[1] W. M. Flinders Petrie, *Ancient Weights and Measures* (London, 1926), illustrates some weights that are more or less in this shape (especially pls. III–IV).

[2] Author's unpublished field notes.

[3] Cf. Paul Van Moorsel *et al.*, *The Central Church of Abdallah Nirqi* (Leiden, 1975), pl. 25.

a

b

c

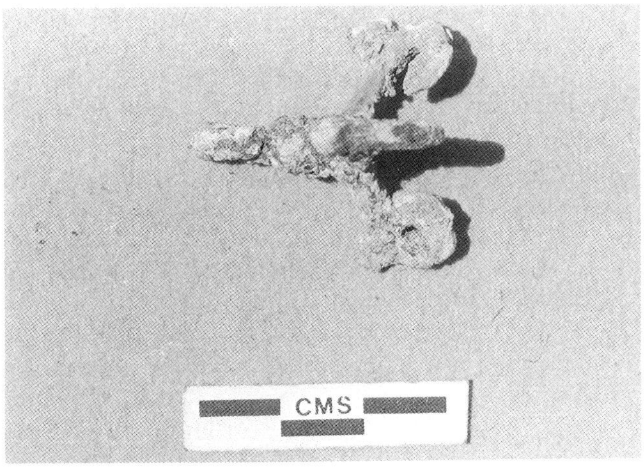

d

Plate 62. Unidentified objects. a, Polished stone disc, with conical depression; possibly a weight (78/631). b, Grooved schist pebble (80/905). c, Iron shovel-shaped object (84.2.2/343). d, Three-armed object of cast bronze (82/341).

Decorative elements

Stone architectural fragments

In building their stone houses the inhabitants at Qaṣr Ibrîm commonly availed themselves of material from older buildings, and in some cases this included fragments of blocks that had originally been carved and decorated. In Late Christian levels such blocks are found sometimes incorporated in the house walls, sometimes in the girdle wall, sometimes in the rubble where walls have fallen down, and sometimes as isolated finds in the refuse deposits. A good many fragmentary decorated blocks were employed when the girdle wall was rebuilt at the beginning of the Late Christian period. Some of them were probably wreckage from the churches and other buildings destroyed in the raid of Shams ed-Dawla a short time previously (see Part 1, Ch. 1). In no case is there any suggestion that decorated stone fragments were retained for their own sakes; their value was strictly as building material.

On the basis of their decorative iconography, fragments of carved stone can be attributed variously to pharaonic, Meroitic or X-Group, and Early Christian origins. It is likely enough that some of the older pieces had already been reused once or twice prior to their incorporation in Late Christian constructions. They must, nevertheless, be described among the Late Christian finds, since it was from these levels that they were recovered.

Among the finds attributable to a pre-Christian origin are at least four pieces of ornamental window grilles, such as had originally adorned the Meroitic Tavern (House 178),[4] and one piece of a *uraeus* lintel. Such objects are very common in all the mediaeval levels—not surprisingly since in earlier times there had been at least four Meroitic temples at Qaṣr Ibrîm. Also attributable to a Meroitic origin are three pieces of small lion statues, of which two evidently belong to the same statue.[5] It is shown in side and front views in plate 63c–d.

More probably attributable to an Early Christian date are two small pieces of finely sculptured alabaster or marble, which may be fragments of altar tops or fonts.[6] Finally there are several sandstone blocks of irregular shape, having one smooth surface that retains all or part of an incised geometric design. These are obviously remnants of what had originally been larger and more regular ashlar blocks. Several of them were found built into the blockage which the Late Christians added to the original South Gate (see Part 2, Ch. 5).

Decorated wood

From the Late Christian levels there are various small wooden fragments with carved or painted decoration. The most elaborate of them is a piece of coniferous wood with part of a carved frieze shown in plate 64a, 1. This may possibly be a detached fragment from one of the decorative wooden string courses that were built into the Qaṣr Ibrîm Cathedral;[7] alternatively, it may be part of a piece of furniture. Plate 64a, 2 shows part of a stick of soft wood, with a painted design in black on a white background. Plate 64b shows two fragments of halfa-grass reed, with very ornate painted decoration. The design is executed in dark red on the natural wood background. Possibly the two pieces are part of the same original object, since they were found close together.

Metal

Plate 64c shows a small piece of very thin sheet iron that has been cut or stamped to an elaborate decorative pattern. The two straight sides and the end with two perforations are original; the opposite end has been broken off. Because of its thinness, as well as the presence of perforations, there is a presumption that this piece was originally attached to something else; possibly it was a decorative element nailed to a wooden surface. However, the two straight edges appear to have been ground off to a considerable sharpness, as though the object had been put to secondary use as a razor.

Pottery

Plates 64e and 64f show respectively the upper and lower surfaces of what was originally a thick disc of low-fired pottery, about 12.5 cm in diameter. The surviving part of the upper surface is inscribed with the name MIXAHΛ as well as two of the monogram devices that are so common in Late Christian decoration.[8] The lower surface has a fairly intricate design of stamped crosses within an incised grid and with an incised central roundel. Very little of the design within the roundel is preserved, but it is possible to make out the legs of a prancing animal.[9] It looks as if a handle

[4] See Plumley, *JEA* 56 (1970), 16 and pl. XXIII, 4.

[5] For the original find see Plumley, *JEA* 52 (1966), 12 and pl. IV, 3.

[6] For Early Christian marble altar tops see Alfred J. Butler, *The Ancient Coptic Churches of Egypt* (Oxford, 1884), II, 7–11, and H. G. Evelyn White, *The Monasteries of the Wadi 'N Natrun,* Part III (New York, 1933), 18, 215–16 (Metropolitan Museum of Art Egyptian Expedition Publications, Vol. 8).

[7] See Somers Clarke, *Christian Antiquities in the Nile Valley* (Oxford, 1912), 15–6.

[8] See William Y. Adams, *Ceramic Industries of Medieval Nubia* (Memoirs of the UNESCO Archaeological Survey of Sudanese Nubia, 1) (Lexington, 1986), Part 1, 385.

[9] For parallels in pottery decoration see op. cit., 319.

a

b

c

d

Plate 63. Unidentified and decorative objects. a, Bell-shaped ceramic object (78.2.13/46). b, 'Flag' of matting attached to stick (78/756). c, Meroitic lion statue, side view (66/99). d, Front view of **c**.

a

b

c

d

e

f

Plate 64. Decorative fragments. a, Carved and painted wooden fragments (66A/211, 66A/212). b, Painted reeds (82/478). c, Small decorative element of stamped sheet iron (84/480). d, Decorative element of carved bone (80/930). e, Fragments of pottery ?bread stamp, upper view (66/98). f, Underside of **e**.

may originally have been attached at the middle of the upper surface; if so, this should probably be identified as some kind of a stamp. The British Museum accession card (no. 1971, 8-1, 1) identifies it as a bread stamp, for reasons that are not explained.

Bone

Plate 64d shows a small decorative object of carved bone, 5.2 cm long. The upper and lower roundels each contain a somewhat nondescript, beardless face, possibly surrounded by a nimbus. In the upper figure the arms of a cross can be seen projecting at the sides and top of the head. The piece originally had a further upward projection, for it is broken away at the top edge. The back is flat and undecorated, presumably because the piece was affixed as an ornament to some larger object. This is suggested also by the four small holes through the upper roundel, three of which retain traces of wooden (or horn?) dowels.

Leather

Plate 65a shows a fragment of fine, black leather which may be part of a book cover. It has two intersecting rows of small cut-out squares, through which decorative leather strips are interwoven. Plate 65b shows a kind of pennant of soft reddish-brown leather with rather fine incised decoration in three registers. The designs in the upper and lower registers incorporate both crosses and crescents; the eight-pointed star in the middle register occurs also in mediaeval Nubian pottery decoration.[10] There are small perforations at all three corners, suggesting that the piece was originally tacked or stitched to something else. The leather roundel shown in plate 65c originally served as backing for a design executed in different coloured silks, which were stitched to the leather with fine thread. Most of the design is now missing, but remnants of pink, yellow, and blue silk remain here and there, and the surviving pattern of stitch holes gives an idea of the original complexity of the decoration. The diameter of the piece is just under 13 cm.

Plate 65e shows a very unusual fragment of decorative leather consisting of three layers sewn together. The lowest layer is a simple backing, rounded at one end. On top of it is a second layer consisting of a single sheet of leather cut into a rather elaborate cut-out pattern. On top of this, individual leather strips have been sewn down in such a way that they exactly reproduce the underlying cut-out pattern, except that they are slightly narrower. The stitching is done with an additional narrow leather thong, of which only traces remain. It is easy to guess that the decorative pattern originally involved leathers of different colours, but no trace of colour variation is now discernible. The purpose of this object is entirely unknown.

Paper

The fragment of heavy paper shown in plate 65f may be part of a book cover. It is actually comprised of two sheets of paper bonded together, an inner, very glossy sheet and an outer sheet that is somewhat fibrous. The outer surface is red-purple in colour with embossed decoration comprising a very ornate floral design within a rectangular frame. The size of the piece is 5.2 × 6.5 cm.

Plate 65d shows a scrap of paper decorated with a very casual design in red and black. The arrangement vaguely suggests a floral design, with stems and one blossom in red and other blossoms and leaves in black. (Only the black can be made out clearly in the photograph.) Another scrap of paper (not photographed) has crudely drawn animal figures—apparently an elephant in yellow and a bird in brown. Yet another very small scrap retains part of a drawing of a human face.

[10] Op. cit., 334, lower left.

a

b

c

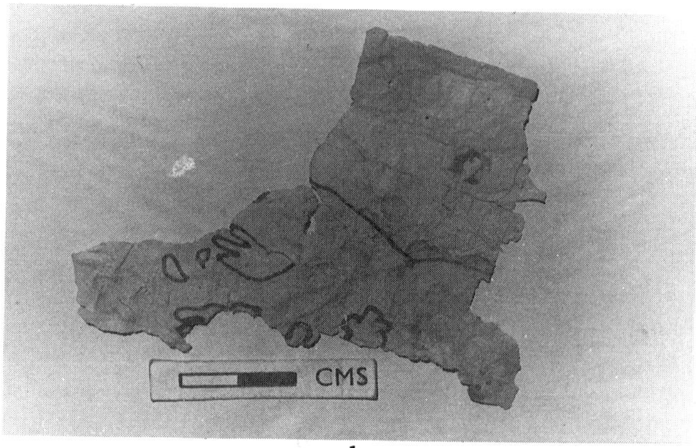

d

e

f

Plate 65. Decorative fragments. a, Portion of leather book cover, with sewn decoration (82/601). b, Small, triangular leather 'pennant' with incised decoration (78/41). c, Leather roundel with sewn decoration in silk thread (84/706). d, Fragment of paper with floral design in ink (80/146). e, Decorative leather object with cut-out design (82/558). f, Fragment of paper book cover, with embossed decoration (84.1.29/43).

CHAPTER 10
THE EVIDENCE OF THE ARTIFACTS

In terms of both numbers and variety the artifacts recovered from Ibrîm far exceed those from any other mediaeval Nubian site; perhaps even from all other Nubian sites combined. They include many artifact types that have never previously been found in Nubia, and, as such, they have added immeasurably to our knowledge of everyday material culture in the late Middle Ages. However, this circumstance cannot be taken simply as evidence of an especially prosperous community; it is much more a reflection of the extraordinary conditions of preservation at Qaṣr Ibrîm. In general, insofar as comparisons can be made, the kinds of tools, containers, and household furnishings that were used by the people at Ibrîm appear to have been little different from those used in other late mediaeval communities up and down the Nile.

The material inventory

The following is a brief resumé of what we have learned from the late mediaeval artifactual remains at Qaṣr Ibrîm:

Agriculture, animal husbandry, and foods

Artifactual remains relating to food production were not very numerous, as might be expected. Ibrîm was not an agricultural village in the same sense as were most other Nubian communities. Crops were raised on the Nile flood-plain rather than on the mountain-top, and farming tools as well as animals were mostly kept down below, near where they were needed. On the other hand, there is very abundant evidence of food storage and processing in the form of storage pits, grinding apparatus, and the chaff resulting from winnowing operations.

More informative than artifactual finds are the remains of foods themselves. There are bones from seven species of domesticated animals, as well as from fish. In addition, more than twenty kinds of plant foods have been identified—some for the first time in mediaeval archaeological contexts.

The evidence of pottery 'kegs' suggests that a fair amount of wine was still imported in the LC1 period, though its volume was considerably less than in the earlier Middle Ages. In the LC2 and TC periods the importation of wine virtually ceased. There are, however, basketry strainers indicative of the local production of beer. In general, the evidence points to a fairly abundant and varied diet at Qaṣr Ibrîm. Comparisons with other Nubian sites cannot be made in this regard, since food remains have not been recovered from any other site.

Containers

The most numerous containers at Qaṣr Ibrîm, as in all Nubian sites, were those of pottery. At least thirty-five different wares and more than a hundred vessel forms were in use. The wares and forms differ in no significant way from those found in other sites of the same age; indeed, there is a remarkably close correspondence between the ware-distribution figures from Ibrîm and those from other Nubian sites where detailed pottery tallies were recorded.[1]

During the LC1 and LC2 periods, the most numerous and varied wares were the Nubian wheel-made wares (Family N), some of which at least were locally produced. Next in importance were the cheap, mass-produced imports from Aswân (Family A), which also occurred in a variety of wares and forms. Collectively they constituted about one-fifth of all the pottery used in the LC1 and LC2 periods. Hand-made wares (Family D), probably all of local manufacture, were relatively unimportant in the LC1 and LC2 periods. In the TC period however they came to make up some 40% of the total ceramic inventory—not so much because their numbers increased as because the numbers of the fancier wares drastically declined.

Glazed wares (Family G) were imported mainly from Lower Egypt. They consisted almost entirely of small bowls, decorated in a wide variety of colours and colour schemes. These wares comprised only about 3% of the total ceramic inventory in the LC1 and LC2 periods but increased to 7% in the TC period. Among the glazed-ware sherds of the Terminal Christian period are a few specimens of non-Egyptian origin, possibly Syrian or Anatolian, and a few sherds of Chinese Ming porcelain. These latter wares have not

[1] See William Y. Adams, *Wissenschaftliche Zeitschrift der Humboldt-Universität zu Berlin, Geisteswissenschaftliche Reihe,* 35 Jg., Heft 1 (1986), 32–33; and id., *Ceramic Industries of Medieval Nubia* (Lexington, 1986), 617 (Memoirs of the UNESCO Archaeological Survey of Sudanese Nubia, Vol. 1).

been found at other Nubian sites, except Gebel Adda;[2] they seem to represent one of the very few examples of genuinely élite goods at Qaṣr Ibrîm.

Glass, like glazed pottery, came mainly from Lower Egypt. In contrast to the pottery, however, fragments of glass were less abundant than expected in the Late and Terminal Christian levels. Both the quantity and the variety of glass vessels were less that at the contemporary site of Meinarti.[3] The vessel forms that could be identified were mainly perfume flasks and other small bottles. The reasons for their relative scarcity are not easy to fathom, since both the vessels and their contents should have been among the luxury goods enjoyed by the high-status residents at Ibrîm.

Basketry ranked next to pottery as a material for containers. The number and variety of basketry containers is enormous, and they exhibit many different techniques of manufacture. Plaiting was used mainly for large carrying and storage baskets, similar to modern *guffas,* while coiling was the preferred technique for food covers and for small notion-baskets and their lids. At least some of the baskets of both kinds were certainly locally made. Unlike the pottery finds the basketry from Ibrîm has substantially enlarged our knowledge of mediaeval Nubian material culture, since basketry has generally not been preserved at other sites. Whether similar baskets would have been in use at sites other than Ibrîm is of course unknown but seems very probable, since the baskets from Ibrîm appear to be everyday rather than luxury goods.

Wood was not important as a material for containers. There were a few fragments of small wooden food bowls, but the majority of wooden containers were very small lathe-turned notion-boxes and their lids.

The most important use of leather was for waterskins. These must have played an important part in the daily life of the community, since large quantities of water had to be carried every day from the riverbank to the mountain-top. Leather was also used to a small extent for pouches, purses, and sheaths. Again there is no basis for comparison with other Nubian sites, where leather goods have not been preserved.

Containers of metal had almost no role at Qaṣr Ibrîm, apart from the two fancy brass basins which must have been a present to the Eparch from some Egyptian dignitary.[4] There are no remains of iron vessels and only a few small scraps of bronze and brass. For the Nubians, fancy painted pottery seems to have taken the place of the ornamental silver, bronze, and pewter vessels that were so much favoured by mediaeval Europeans.

Tools

Among the various tools and utensils found at Qaṣr Ibrîm by far the most abundant are those associated in one way or another with textile manufacture. They include needles and awls, spindles and whorls, shuttles, and loom parts. These objects leave little doubt that there was a textile manufacturing industry on the mountain-top, in contrast to most other manufacturing activities which were probably carried out in the lower town. The abundance of fancy lathe-turned wooden spindle whorls and the proportional scarcity of whorls made from ground potsherds stand in contrast to the situation at other Nubian sites of the same age.

Household utensils are not at all numerous, and consist mainly of iron knife blades and wooden handles. Toilet articles, however, are fairly abundant, as in many Nubian sites. They include kohl sticks, razors, combs, mirrors, and tweezers.

There is an abundance of lifting, pulling, and fastening apparatus, including pulley wheels, wooden stakes and pegs, wedges, and cordage. Much of this material was probably used in connection with tethering animals and with putting up tents.

Weapons of any kind are extremely scarce, but among them is the unique example of a nearly compete sling found in House 781.[5]

Household furnishings

Beyond any doubt, the most numerous household furnishings are wooden lock parts and keys. Similar items have not been preserved in other Nubian sites but have been recovered from many mediaeval Egyptian sites. They are little different from the lock mechanisms used today in Nubian and Egyptian villages.

Movable items of furniture have not been found at Qaṣr Ibrîm, except for a single bed or chair leg. This is not surprising, since large items of wood were regularly recycled into smaller items, or burned, after serving their original purpose. However, the abundance of lathe-turned wooden balusters suggests either that the local people were well supplied with rather fancy furniture, or else that these items were locally produced for export. Other examples of household furnishing include floor mats, sleeping mats, fragments of cushions and carpets, and lamps. Apparently there was no specially made bedding; blankets sewn together served for both mattresses and bedclothes.

[2] Personal communication from Nicholas B. Millet.
[3] Author's unpublished field notes.
[4] See Part 3, 117 and pl. 20.
[5] See Part 3, 114 and pl. 36, b.

Textiles

Archaeologically, the prosperity of mediaeval Nubia is nowhere better attested than in the textile remains. The people of Ibrîm made regular use of a wide variety of fabrics, some locally woven and others imported, apparently from various foreign sources. The materials, both local and imported, exhibit a wide range of qualities, of weaving and patterning techniques, and of colour combinations. Bright colours are a conspicuous feature of the late mediaeval textiles.

Wool was the primary material for simple, everyday garments and for various other uses, such as bedding and bags. Most woollens were locally produced, but some of the finest examples may have been imported. Cotton and linen were both used mainly for finer garments, including *galabiyehs,* trousers, head-veils, and caps. The coarser cotton fabrics and perhaps also some of the finer ones were made locally; linen and some of the fine cottons were imported. Imported silk was used for some of the finest garments, though in some cases they may have been tailored locally. Heavy, utilitarian items of goat hair, such as tents, bags, and saddle girths, were probably obtained in trade from the Beja or other nomads.

Dress

Even though nearly all textiles were torn up, in the end, for rags, we can draw many conclusions about the dress of the mediaeval Nubians from the Ibrîm finds. It is evident that the people, unlike Nubians of the more recent past, did not go largely naked; they were well supplied with garments of both locally made and imported cloth. Men generally wore a kind of tunic or short *galabiyeh,* and sometimes also a small, decorative cloth cap. Women's dress is less well attested, but it seems that at least sometimes they wrapped themselves in a length of untailored woolen cloth, something like the *hulaliya* worn by Egyptian women in the 19th century.[6] A head veil may have covered the head and shoulders. Both sexes might also wear baggy trousers of Turkish type as a kind of undergarment.

Footgear for both sexes consisted mainly of rather crude leather sandals for outdoor wear and more finely made basketry sandals for indoor wear. More elaborate leather shoes were probably imported from Egypt and were fancy-dress wear for the wealthy few.

The most common ornaments were glass beads, which were strung into necklaces, bracelets, and earrings. Also popular were decorative wooden hair combs and pins, similar to those worn by the Beja today.

Miscellaneous and specialized goods

There is a considerable variety of cult objects, including crosses made from various materials and used in various ways. These objects may have been more numerous at Ibrîm than at other Nubian sites because of the special status of the place as a pilgrimage centre. Also prevalent are amulets, and especially *higabs,* comprising a religious or magical text sewn up in a small leather pouch and worn on the body. Stamp seals are especially numerous, of many different shapes and made from a variety of materials. They seem to bear testimony to the importance of Ibrîm as a commercial centre, at least in the LC1 period. On the other hand, coins from the mediaeval levels are extremely scarce. Gaming equipment includes dice, and turned wooden counters like chess pieces. A number of rather crude dolls, cloth balls, and very crude mud figurines of animals were presumably amusements of children.

Economic systems

The artifacts from Qaṣr Ibrîm and other Nubian sites, and their spacial distributions, give evidence of four different economic systems in operation:

1. A local subsistence economy, in which each household produced most of its own food as well as certain very simple manufactures, like cordage and pegs, and probably at least some clothing;
2. A local barter economy, in which specialists within the community produced various goods, to be exchanged locally for food and other commodities. Products that may have circulated in this fashion include hand-made pottery, some of the more utilitarian wheel-made wares, certain kinds of basketry, many items of clothing, sandals, iron tools, and most leather goods;
3. A regional market economy, in which certain goods were produced at specialized manufacturing centres, and were then widely traded throughout Nubia, at least from Aswân to Dongola. Goods involved in this trade included textiles made and exported from Ibrîm, the Aswân pottery wares and perhaps some fancy leather goods and basketry from Aswân, the decorated Late and Terminal Christian pottery wares from a centre or centres within Nubia that have not been identified,[7] and perhaps leather goods and turned wooden boxes from other, as yet unidentified centres.
4. An international market economy, in which exotic goods were imported from Lower Egypt and the

[6] See E. W. Lane, *The Manners and Customs of the Modern Egyptians* (London, 1908), 51–3.

[7] See Adams, *Ceramic Industries*, 53–4.

Red Sea by way of the great entrepôt at Aswân. The goods that entered Nubia in this fashion included glazed pottery, beads and other items of glass, and perfumes, oils, and spices. The main exports from Nubia were undoubtedly slaves but may also have included dates, hides, and perhaps tropical exotica such as ebony wood and ostrich feathers.

The local barter economy and the international market economy are both well attested by textual finds, as will be seen in Part 4, Chapter 8. The Eparch of Nobadia was rather heavily involved in both, and travelling Egyptian merchants also played an important role in the international trade. On the other hand, there is not a hint as to the organization of the regional economy. Probably it was in the hands of entrepreneur-boatmen, as in the Nubia of recent times.[8]

Economy and society

The élite status of Qaṣr Ibrîm among Nubian communities, so clearly attested in the documentary sources, is not reflected in the material sphere, either in the houses or in their surviving contents. The same is true in regard to social stratification within the community. On the basis of archaeology alone we cannot discern that some households at Qaṣr Ibrîm were significantly better off than others, nor can we say that the Imbrîmers as a group were materially better off than the residents of Meinarti,[9] Kasanarti,[10] or Debeira.[11]

This circumstance might lead us to conclude that the mediaeval Nubians were not a materialistic people, or at least that they did not choose to express status differences by material ostentation. However, any such conclusion can be accepted only with reservations. For all the abundance of their material content, the deposits at Qaṣr Ibrîm were, in the last analysis, no more than rubbish heaps, like the deposits at all other Nubian townsites. Probably not more than a dozen of the artifacts (exclusive of documents) found in the Late Christian levels were things that had been deliberately preserved. A few others may have been accidentally lost, but the great majority had simply been thrown away because they were considered to have no value.

We cannot assume, in other words, that the refuse deposits at Qaṣr Ibrîm provide us with a full sample of the material goods that were actually in use. The most prized of all luxury goods, such as items of jewelry and of gold and silver, would surely have been carefully preserved, and handed on from generation to generation. They might, in the end, have been melted down, but they would not have been thrown away.

[8] Cf. Reisner, *Bulletin of the Museum of Fine Arts,* 27 (1929), 66.

[9] See Adams, *Kush* 12 (1964), 222–39; id., *Kush* 13 (1965), 148–76.

[10] See Adams, *Kush* 12 (1964), 218–22.

[11] P. L. Shinnie and Margaret Shinnie, *Debeira West* (Warminster, 1978).

PART 4
THE TEXTUAL RECORD

CHAPTER 1
THE FINDS AND THEIR PRESERVATION

THE Late and Terminal Christian levels at Qaṣr Ibrîm have yielded over 70 complete written documents, and perhaps 1000 textual fragments.[1] They are written in Greek, Coptic, Old Nubian, and Arabic and are inscribed variously on papyrus, paper, parchment, soft leather, potsherds, and stone. After registration on the site, these texts, or facsimiles of them, have been passed along for study to appropriate specialists in the various mediaeval languages; they will eventually form the basis for a special series of publications.[2] The intention in the present volume, therefore, is not to offer detailed translations or commentaries on the Late Christian texts but only to extract from them such cultural and historical information as may supplement the archaeological record, enlarging and correcting the view of mediaeval life at Qaṣr Ibrîm that has been developed in the preceding chapters. Translations of a few representative documents will be given, without philological commentary, in Part 4, Chapters 3 through 7, dealing respectively with administrative, legal, commercial, religious, and private texts. The overall historical and cultural implications of the late mediaeval texts will be briefly considered in Chapter 8.

The total number of texts and text fragments recovered at Qaṣr Ibrîm far exceeds that from all other Nubian sites combined. Two factors have contributed to this fortunate circumstance: first there are the unparalleled conditions of preservation, already described in Part 1, Chapter 1; second, Qaṣr Ibrîm was not a peasant village but a major administrative, commercial, and ecclesiastical centre, whose literate population would undoubtedly have been far greater than that found in most other Nubian communities.

The number of whole and fragmentary texts is so large that it is possible to subject these remains to a kind of quantitative analysis, much as is done with potsherds and textile fragments, in addition to the more usual analysis of their individual content. Thus, we can calculate the proportionate numbers of documents devoted to religion, to administrative and commercial affairs, to private correspondence, and the like, at different periods in history, even when we cannot recover the actual messages in many of the individual fragments. We can also trace the continual process through which Greek and Coptic were replaced by Old Nubian and Arabic. In this way nearly every textual find, no matter how fragmentary, may contribute something to our understanding of life and history at Qaṣr Ibrîm.

Such quantitative evidence must obviously be treated with a certain caution; at best it can furnish only a very approximate indication of the numbers and proportions of texts that were originally present. Almost certainly, many individual fragments are parts of the same original document. Unfortunately, the special constraints of working at Qaṣr Ibrîm rarely allow us time enough to try fitting together the hundreds of individual text fragments, unless they happen to be found in close proximity.[3] It is also probable that not all of the pieces are of Late Christian origin. The wholesale destruction of ecclesiastical documents during the Shams ed-Dawla raid of 1172–3 (see Part 1, Chapter 1) left behind an enormous volume of fragmented, scattered, and burned religious texts,[4] and some of these must inevitably have found their way into the rubbish deposits of the immediately succeeding period (pl. 66b). Finally there is a problem of inconsistent docu-

[1] This figure is necessarily an estimate. In the early excavation seasons it was a common practice to register a great many individual text fragments under a single number, without specifying the actual number of fragments involved. The total number of Late and Terminal Christian texts and text fragments that is specifically recorded on registration forms is 753; see table 13.

[2] These will appear in the series of *Egypt Exploration Society, Texts from Excavations.* Three volumes dealing with Qaṣr Ibrîm texts have already appeared: *The Scrolls of Bishop Timotheos,* edited by J. Martin Plumley (1st Memoir, 1975), *Arabic Documents from the Ottoman Period at Qaṣr Ibrîm,* edited by Martin Hinds and Hamdi Sakkout (8th Memoir, 1986), and *Old Nubian Texts from Qaṣr Ibrîm,* I, edited by J. Martin Plumley and Gerald M. Browne (9th Memoir, 1988). Two additional volumes on the Old Nubian texts, edited by Gerald M. Browne, are in press, and a volume on the mediaeval Arabic texts, edited by Elizabeth Sartain, is in preparation.

[3] The Qaṣr Ibrîm Expedition has no magazine where finds can be retained for later study; they must all be surrendered to the Egyptian Antiquities Organization immediately at the close of each excavation season.

[4] See Plumley, *JEA* 50 (1964), 3; Frend, *Jahrbuch für Antike und Christentum,* 29 (1986), 66.

mentation. In the early excavation seasons it was a common practice to register a number of individual text fragments under a single number, without specifying the actual number of pieces involved. I have, therefore, had to treat each of these registrations as though it involved only a single find. Since 1978 the number of pieces registered under each number has been meticulously recorded, and these figures are the basis of the statistical calculations in this and succeeding chapters. However, since the Terminal Christian deposits were virtually all taken out in seasons before 1978, the volume of documentary finds from that period is almost certainly under-reported.[5]

Conditions of discovery and preservation

Textual finds from the Late and Terminal Christian periods fall into two quite distinct categories: deliberately preserved archives and discarded writings. The latter are by far the more numerous, but they are frequently too fragmentary to yield much information individually. Although the original language can nearly always be recognized, it is possible to say something about the actual content in only about half the cases, and the number of specimens from which a coherent message can be recovered is much smaller still. Deliberately preserved archives on the other hand consist very largely of complete documents, whose informational value is sometimes enormous.

Archival caches

Five major caches of documents have been found in the Late and Terminal Christian levels. They are listed in summary form in table 12, and may be briefly described here:

1. Nine complete leather scrolls were found sealed in a decorated vase (Late Christian Ware R11 [6]) that was buried alongside the LC2 and TC House 169.[7] They are written in Old Nubian on a soft, tanned skin that is probably either goatskin or gazelle.[8] These documents have not yet been fully analysed, but they appear to be official and legal in character, very similar to the contents of archive no. 3 (described below).[9] The dates range from 1281 to 1464, the latter being the last recorded date for any Christian document from Qaṣr Ibrîm.[10]

2. Another decorated vase of Ware R11[11], buried under the LC2 House 171, contained four more leather scrolls written in Old Nubian. Unfortunately, the leather in these specimens had become very hard and brittle and could not be unrolled for study.[12] Up to the present time nothing definite can be said about the content. It may be noted however that all of the other leather scrolls found in archival caches at Qaṣr Ibrîm are official or legal documents.

3. The most important of all the Late Christian archival caches came from the eparchal House 177, dating from the LC1 period. Buried under the floor in a sealed jar of imported Egyptian ware (not definitely identifiable as to origin) were 10 soft leather scrolls, 1 paper scroll, 6 letters on parchment, and 17 letters on paper (pl. 66c–d).[13] The contents of this find are partially summarized in table 18; they include 1 royal proclamation, 1 royal letter of recommendation, 9 eparchal orders for the disbursement of grain and other commodities, 5 letters from church officials, 13 legal instruments relating to the sale or transfer of property, 2 records of the release of slaves or servants, and 3 property lists. All but one of the documents are in Old Nubian, and several of them bear dates, ranging in time from 1155 to 1199.[14] The single paper scroll is a letter in Coptic from the Nubian king to the Coptic Patriarch in Alexandria.[15]

4. The same House 177 also yielded a cache of letters that had been buried under a mastaba just inside the house entrance. There were indications that they had originally been sealed in a jar, but this had subsequently been crushed, leaving the documents somewhat scattered and not in the best of condition.[16] They are all on paper and include at least three letters in Old Nubian

[5] For further discussion of the problems involved in the study of textual finds from Qaṣr Ibrîm see Plumley in Kazimierz Michalowski (ed.), *Nubia, récentes recherches* (Warsaw, 1975), 101.

[6] For the dating of pottery wares see Appendix A.

[7] Registration number 64/23. For the original report of the find see Plumley, *JEA* 50 (1964), 5 and pl. II, 2.

[8] See Plumley in *Nubia, récentes recherches*, 105.

[9] For preliminary discussion see Plumley in *Nubia, récentes recherches*, 105–6; and in *Études nubiennes; colloque de Chantilly, 2-6 Juillet 1975* (Institut français d'archéologie orientale, Bibliothèque d'étude, 1978, 77), 234–8.

[10] Plumley in *Études nubiennes*, 235.

[11] For the dating of pottery wares see Appendix A.

[12] Excavation number 66.2.24/6; registration number 66a/45. For the original report of the find see Plumley, *JEA* 50 (1964), 9–10; see also Plumley in *Nubia, récentes recherches*, 105.

[13] Excavation number 74.1.30/6; Egyptian Museum registration numbers 90225–90232. For the original report of the find see Plumley, *JEA* 61 (1975), 7 and pl. I, 2, pl. II.

[14] For preliminary discussion see especially Plumley in *Études nubiennes*. For complete translations and commentary see Gerald M. Browne, *Old Nubian Texts from Qaṣr Ibrîm* III (Egypt Exploration Society, Texts from Excavations; in press).

[15] Plumley in *Études nubiennes*, 232.

[16] Excavation number 74.1.29/11; registration number 74/12. For the original report of the find see Plumley, *JEA* 50 (1964), 3–4 and pl. I, 2.

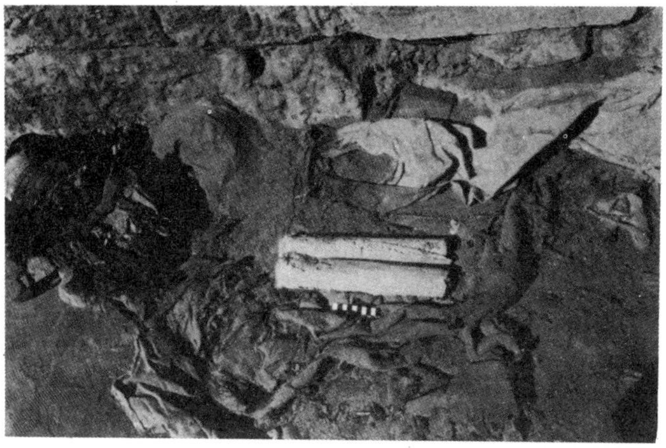

a

b

c

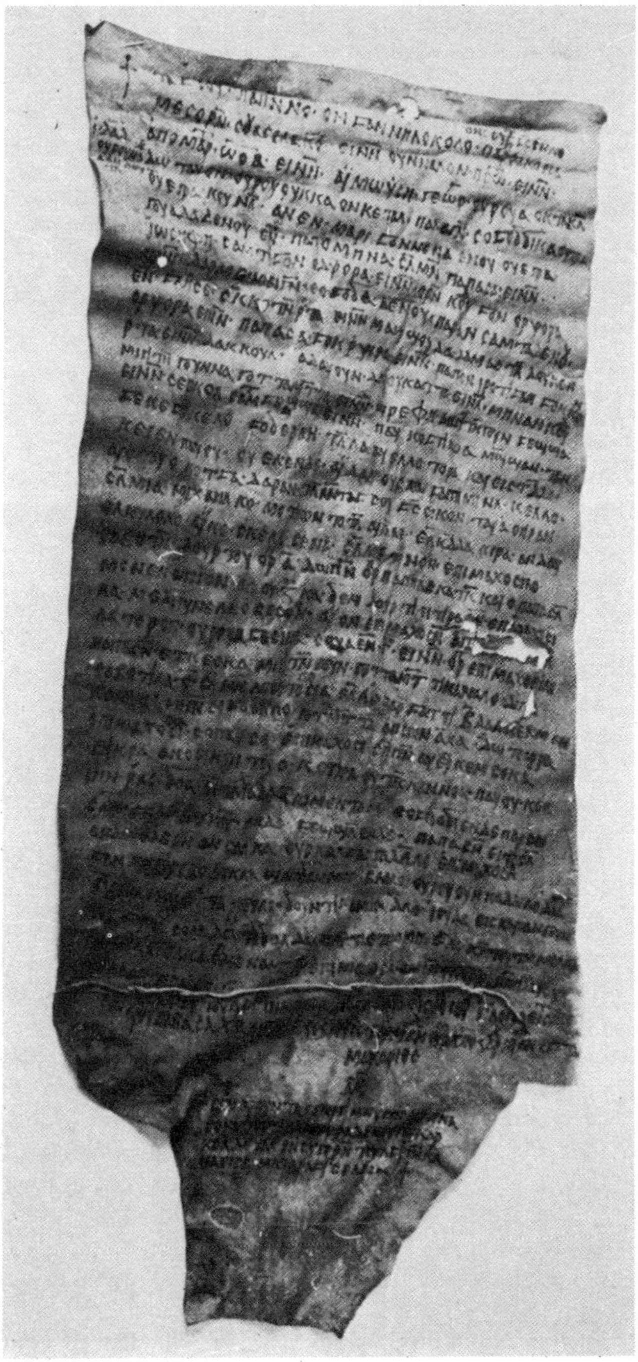

d

Plate 66. Textual finds. a, The scrolls of Bishop Timotheos, *in situ* (64/11). b, Religious manuscript fragments found under the South Church (Church 294). c, Pot containing Old Nubian cache of legal documents (74.1.30/6). d, Old Nubian legal document found in **c**.

TABLE 12
MAJOR LATE AND TERMINAL CHRISTIAN ARCHIVAL CACHES

No.*	Stratig. context	Provenance	Description	Excav. no.†	Reg. no.‡
1	LC2 or TC	Alongside House 169	9 Old Nubian scrolls in jar	(none)	64/23
2	LC2	Under House 171	4 Old Nubian scrolls in jar	66.2.24/6	66a/45
3	LC1	Under House 177	34 miscellaneous documents in jar	74.1.30/6	(several)
4	LC1	Under mastaba, House 177	11+ Arabic and Old Nubian letters	74.1.29/11	74/12
5	LC2	Cathedral	Coptic and Arabic consecration documents of Bishop Timotheos	(none)	64/11

*As listed in text of Part 4, Chapter 1, pp. 214–6.
†Day-number assigned in field
‡Official number in Antiquities Register

and eight in Arabic. Several of the latter are addressed to the Eparch of Nobadia or his deputies and deal with commercial and administrative matters.[17]

5. Sometime late in the fourteenth century, a certain Bishop Timotheos was interred in the rubbish-filled North Crypt of the Cathedral. Buried alongside him were his documents of consecration from the Coptic Patriarch: two very long paper scrolls of which one is in Coptic and one in Arabic (pl. 66a).[18] They had been executed in the Hanging Church of St. Mary in Cairo in the year 1371 or 1372.[19]

Most of the archival caches included documents of several kinds: administrative, legal, and commercial. For example, one cache (no. 3, above) included documents that were written variously by a King of Dotawo, three different Eparchs of Nobadia, one vice-eparch, one bishop, three priests, one archdeacon, and one elder (?), and they range in time over nearly half a century.[20] The largest number of deliberately preserved documents are evidently 'file copies' of letters that were sent by civil or ecclesiastical officials, but there are also some letters that were received by them.

The reason for the preservation of documents is not always obvious. Some caches (e.g. no. 3, above) contained documents dealing with relatively trivial matters, along with others of much more obvious importance. Further compounding the mystery is the fact that some of the archival storage jars were evidently opened and reclosed several times, to judge from the wide range of dates on the documents they contained; this would have given ample opportunity for the discard of obsolete documents.

Other complete and nearly complete documents

In addition to deliberate caches, a few complete or nearly complete documents were preserved by accident among the rubbish deposits in the Late Christian levels. They include seven individual pages from religious texts, written on parchment: six in Old Nubian and one in Coptic (pl. 66b). There is also one religious text and one legal deposition on paper in Old Nubian. Eight additional documents are letters to or from the Eparchs of Nobadia, of which six are in Old Nubian and two in Arabic. The largest number of these documents came from the refuse fill in the eparchal House 763, which also yielded enormous numbers of fragmentary texts[21] (see table 13). Some complete documents have also been recovered from storage pits in the Central and West Plazas. Whether these represent deliberate or accidental preservation is uncertain, given the fact that the fill in storage pits typically consists of rubbish. It may be noted that the same filling material that yielded a few complete documents also contained large numbers of fragments.

Fragmentary texts

Fragments of discarded text are found nearly everywhere in the deposits at Qaṣr Ibrîm, along with potsherds, basketry fragments, rags, and other discarded rubbish. Of the total of 44 houses and churches attributable to the Late and Terminal Christian periods, no fewer than 33 have yielded at least one fragment of text. However, a very high proportion of the texts have come, as might be expected, from the five eparchal

[17] Translations of several of the Arabic documents have been prepared by Elizabeth Sartain, and are presented in Part 4, Chapters 3 and 5.

[18] Registration number 64/11. For the original report of the find see Plumley, *JEA* 50 (1964), 3–4 and pl. I, 2.

[19] For full translations and commentary see Plumley, *Scrolls of Timotheos.*

[20] See n. 14.

[21] See Adams, Alexander and Allen, *JEA* 69 (1983), 54.

TABLE 13
SOURCES OF LATE AND TERMINAL CHRISTIAN TEXTUAL FINDS

Provenances	Number of texts/Languages								
Eparchal houses	Old Nubian	Nubian + Arabic	Nubian + Greek	Nubian + Coptic	Arabic	Arabic + Coptic	Coptic	Greek	Totals
172	1				8				9
177	16				13			1	30
178	4				1		2	3	10
763	169	57			118		5		349
849		2			2				4
Totals	190	59			142		7	4	402
%*	*63*	*68*			*53*		*18*	*31*	*56*
Adjoining houses									
169	9				1				10
171	5				4				9
211	20	2			16		5		43
785	6	3		2	14		3	3	31
848	10	1	2		9				22
Totals	50	6	2	2	44		8		115
%*	*17*	*7*	*40*	*40*	*17*		*21*	*23*	*16*
Church 287	6				10				16
%*	*1*				*4*				*3*
Plazas									
356	5				8				13
358	13	4		1	19		3	2	42
Totals	18	4		1	27		3	2	55
%*	6	5		20	10		8	15	8
All other provenances	38	18	3	2	42	1	20	4	128
%*	*13*	*20*	*60*	*40*	*16*	*100*	*53*	*31*	*17*
Grand totals	302	87	5	5	265	1	38	13	716

*Percentage of all texts in the language indicated, from Late and Terminal Christian levels only

houses and their immediate surroundings. Table 13 shows that 56% of all Late and Terminal Christian text fragments have come from the eparchal houses, and another 16% have come from five houses directly adjoining them. Indeed, the single eparchal House 763 yielded almost half of the total of Late Christian text fragments, as well as a number of whole documents.[22] The physical preservation of the textual fragments is generally excellent. Only a very few are so discoloured or so fragile that they cannot be read. On the other hand, all of them have been torn up, often into very small pieces, and this makes it impossible in the great majority of cases to recover more than a fraction of their meaning. Sources of the fragmentary texts, and the languages employed therein, are shown in table 13.

A note about dates

A word must be said in conclusion about the dating of the various documents that will be discussed and translated in succeeding chapters. All of the texts were

[22] Op. cit. The total of 1,279 documents reported for House 763 in the original publication does not correspond to that in table 13 because it includes a substantial number of Classic Christian documents, not covered in the present report.

recovered from what are, archaeologically, Late or Terminal Christian contexts. They were associated with houses whose occupation belongs mainly if not entirely to the period after 1172/73—the nominal starting point for this monograph. Yet many of the individual documents bear slightly earlier dates, extending back in some cases to the beginning of the twelfth century. This is true, for example, of all of the dated documents contained in cache no. 4 The Old Nubian texts in cache no. 3 bear dates both before and after 1172. Rather than arbitrarily dividing up these collections, discussing some documents while ignoring others, it has seemed to me preferable here to discuss all texts found in Late Christian archaeological contexts, regardless of their actual dates of writing. It must, therefore, be borne in mind that some of the events and personalities mentioned in the texts were not actually coeval with the architecture and artifacts described in earlier chapters of this monograph, though the general conditions of life reflected in the texts were probably very much the same before and after 1172.

CHAPTER 2
MATERIALS, LANGUAGES, AND SCRIPTS

THE use of paper was introduced to Nubia sometime in the Classic Christian period; by Late Christian times it had virtually supplanted all other writing materials. Among a thousand or so whole and fragmentary texts from Late and Terminal Christian deposits, fewer than 100 are on any material other than paper. The few examples of parchment that have been found are mostly religious texts, which in many cases appear to be relics of older documents, not originating in the Late Christian period.[1] This must surely be true also of the five small Coptic fragments on papyrus. Within the Late Christian period itself, the main exceptions from the general use of paper were legal instruments in Old Nubian, which were sometimes executed on soft skins. There are also a very few administrative letters on parchment. No examples of inscriptions on wood have been found, although several are known from the Classic Christian period,[2] and the only inscriptions on pottery are incised owner's graffiti [3] which are not ostraca in the full sense of the term. Stone no doubt continued to be used for funerary inscriptions, but no tombstones of secure Late Christian date have been found at Qaṣr Ibrîm.[4] Table 14 shows the numbers of texts in different languages written on different materials. (For further discussion of writing materials and technology see Part 3, Chapter 1).

Languages and their uses

Old Nubian was certainly the spoken language of mediaeval Nubia,[5] but no fewer than four languages were sometimes employed in written communications: Old Nubian, Arabic, Coptic, and Greek. The latter two, at least in the later middle ages, were used almost entirely for religious texts,[6] while Arabic was largely a mercantile and diplomatic language, used in commercial dealings with Muslims, both in Egypt and within Nubia itself. Not surprisingly, Old Nubian was used for a wider variety of communications, both public and private.[7]

Examples of all four of the aforementioned languages have been found in the Late and Terminal Christian levels at Qaṣr Ibrîm (table 14), though in very uneven proportions. The number of Greek and Coptic examples is so small as to suggest that these may be surviving remnants from earlier periods. On the other hand Arabic and Old Nubian are almost equally represented, suggesting either a very high degree of bilingualism or a very mixed population at Qaṣr Ibrîm in the late mediaeval period. Probably both of these things were true so some extent: the Eparch and his agents had necessarily to employ Arabic in commercial dealings with the Egyptians, but there may well have been Egyptian merchants or diplomats resident at the site as well.

In all four of the mediaeval languages, the great majority of texts conform to some kind of recognizable literary formula or convention. This makes it possible to classify the documents into a number of discrete categories, as listed in table 15. There are broad categories of administrative, legal, commercial, religious, and personal documents, and subdivisions in each of these. Subsequent discussion of the texts, in Chapters 3–7 will follow the aforesaid classificatory scheme. It should be evident, however, that the categorical boundaries are not hard-and-fast; some documents inevitably fall into more than one category. Obviously, too, such minute categorization is possible only in the case of complete or nearly complete documents. Fragments, if they are classifiable at all, can only be placed in a few very broad and general categories, as shown in table 16. In fact, more than three-fourths of the Late Christian text fragments are too small to permit any categorization of their content.

Table 16 shows the number of texts and text fragments in the four mediaeval languages, and the broad categories of usage to which they can be assigned.

[1] For an interesting discussion of the relationship between parchment and early Christianity see Harold I. Innis, *Empire and Communications* (Toronto, 1972), 116–40.

[2] See Anderson, Adams *et al.*, *JEA* 65 (1979), 41.

[3] For discussion see William Y. Adams, *Ceramic Industries of Medieval Nubia* (Memoirs of the UNESCO Archaeological Survey of Sudanese Nubia, 1) (Lexington, 1986), 256–7, 385–6.

[4] At Qaṣr Ibrîm, tombstones occur largely in the form of broken fragments reused as building blocks in the walls of the Ottoman period houses. Almost none of these can be accurately dated.

[5] See Shinnie in A. M. Abdelgadir (ed.), *Studies in Ancient Languages of the Sudan* (University of Khartoum, Sudan Research Unit, Sudan Studies Library, no. 3) (Khartoum, 1974), 42–3.

[6] In the earlier middle ages Coptic was also used to some extent as a commercial language in Nubia; see op. cit., 44–5.

[7] For further discussion of multilingualism in Nubia see William Y. Adams, *Nubia, Corridor to Africa* (London, 1977), 484–8; Shinnie, op. cit.; Shinnie in Robin Thelwall (ed.), *Aspects of Language in the Sudan* (New University of Ulster, Occasional Papers in Linguistics and Language Learning, no. 5) (Coleraine, 1978), 82–96.

TABLE 14
DISTRIBUTION OF TEXT FINDS ACCORDING TO LANGUAGE AND WRITING MATERIAL

Languages	Paper	Soft skin	Parchment	Papyrus	Potsherd	?
Old Nubian	271*	24	5		2	
Old Nubian + Arabic	85*		2			
Old Nubian + Greek	1		4			
Old Nubian + Coptic	2		3			
Arabic	265*					
Arabic + Coptic						1
Coptic	3	5	24	5		
Greek	3		10			
TOTALS	630*	29	48	5	2	1
%	*88*	*4*	*7*	*1*		

*Figures incomplete because of incomplete field recording

TABLE 15
CLASSIFICATION OF LATE MEDIAEVAL TEXTS FROM QAṢR IBRÎM

- Administrative texts (Chapter 3)
  - Royal proclamation
  - Eparchal correspondence
    - Disbursement orders
    - Other decrees
    - Letters to eparchs
  - Ecclesiastical administration
    - Royal letter of recommendation
    - Bishop's consecration documents
    - Episcopal and priestly correspondence
- Legal texts (Chapter 4)
  - Property management and transfer
    - Sales of land
    - Cession of land
    - Rental of land
    - Sale of unspecified property
    - Donation of property
    - Release from purchase
  - Commercial contracts
  - Release of slaves and servants
  - Depositions
  - Property lists
- Commercial texts (Chapter 5)
  - Eparchal correspondence
  - Private commercial correspondence
- Religious and magical texts (Chapter 6)
  - Biblical texts
  - Homilies, sermons, etc.
  - Islamic texts
  - Magical texts
- Personal correspondence (Chapter 7)

What stands out at once in this tabulation is the preponderance of administrative and commercial texts over all others, including religious texts. This presents a striking contrast to the situation in Classic Christian times, when the overwhelming majority of texts were religious in character.[8] The Late and Terminal Christian texts, like the architectural remains, testify to a diminished religious function, and possibly an increased administrative function, after the Shams ed-Dawla raid. Among the the decipherable Late Christian texts there are at least twenty, in Old Nubian and Arabic, addressed to or from the Eparchs, and dealing with administrative matters, as against only seven addressed to or from any ecclesiastical official. It may further be noted that among the numerous pilgrim's inscriptions on the nearby mountain-top there are none datable to the Late Christian period,[9] a fact suggesting that Qaṣr Ibrîm was no longer a major focus of religious pilgrimages. The following is a discussion of the individual languages and their uses.

Greek

At least in the earlier Middle Ages, the liturgical language of the Nubian church was Greek rather than Coptic or Nubian.[10] At Qaṣr Ibrîm, its use is attested by the finding of a great many fragments of Greek MSS

[8] Due to the fact that the very extensive remains of the Cathedral Library belong to the Classic Christian period.

[9] See Plumley and Adams, *JEA* 60 (1974), 235 and pl. LI; Plumley in Paul van Moorsel (ed.), *New Discoveries in Nubia* (Nederlands Instituut voor het Nabije Oosten, Egyptologische Uitgaven, 2) (Leiden, 1982), 108–9.

[10] See Adams, *Nubia*, 485; Plumley in *New Discoveries*, 107.

TABLE 16
DISTRIBUTION OF TEXT FINDS ACCORDING TO LANGUAGE AND CONTENT

Languages	Administrative & commercial	Archival & legal	Religious & literary	Private & misc.	Undetermined
Old Nubian	39	33	16	5	209
Old Nubian + Arabic	16		3	5	63
Old Nubian + Greek			2		3
Old Nubian + Coptic	1		1		3
Arabic	7	2	3	1	252
Arabic + Coptic					1
Coptic			6		32
Greek			5		8
TOTALS	63	35	35	11	572
%*	*9*	*5*	*5*	*2*	*79*

*Texts in this category as a percentage of all Late and Terminal Christian texts

among the destroyed remnants of the Cathedral library.[11] On the other hand only 18 examples of Greek have turned up among the hundreds of text fragments from the Late and Terminal Christian periods. Thirteen of these are purely in Greek; 1 is bilingual Greek and Old Nubian,[12] and 4 are primarily Old Nubian texts, with a few added lines of Greek. Of the 18 Greek or partly Greek texts from Late Christian deposits, all of those that can be recognized are religious in character, though only one appears to be Biblical.[13]

These characteristics raise a strong possibility that the few Greek texts from the Late Christian period are actually remnants of the destroyed Cathedral library, which accidentally found their way into the later deposits. It is difficult to date the Greek texts on palaeographic grounds, since there is little mediaeval Egyptian or Nubian material for comparison, but according to Dr J. David Thomas '...there is quite a lot of Coptic material which is palaeographically similar and some of which is datable to the ninth to twelfth centuries. I see no difficulty in [the] suggestion that the Greek material is all pre-1173; indeed it could well be as early as the ninth century or the tenth in some cases...'[14]

We are left, therefore, with no unequivocal evidence for the use of Greek, even as a liturgical language, after the time of the Shams ed-Dawla raid in 1172–73. The Nubian clergy must have learned their Greek locally, since Greek was not used in the Egyptian church, and it is possible that the destruction of the Cathedral library left little or nothing in the way of instructional materials for further training in Greek. However, Greek graffiti have been found in the churches at Abdel Qadir[15] and Kulubnarti,[16] both undoubtedly of Late Christian date.[17] Greek might also have remained in use as the principal language of tombstone inscriptions,[18] since in this case there would have been plenty of models to copy from. However, very few tombstones bearing late mediaeval dates have actually been found in Nubia, and none has been found at Qaṣr Ibrîm. There has been some debate as to whether the Greek of the mediaeval Nubian texts was similar to that used in other parts of the Near East at the same time, or was a kind of local pidgin.[19] Unfortunately the few Late Christian texts from Qaṣr Ibrîm are much too fragmentary to shed any light on this question.

[11] See Plumley in Kazimierz Michalowski (ed.), *Nubia, récentes recherches* (Warsaw, 1975), 103; Frend in *Études nubiennes; colloque de Chantilly, 2–6 Jouillet 1975* (Institut français d'archéologie orientale, Bibliothèque d'étude, 77 (Cairo), 1978),95. See also Frend, *Jahrbuch für Antike und Christentum,* Jg. 29 (1986), 66.

[12] Browne, *Sudan Texts Bulletin* 3 (1981), 9–19.

[13] Personal communications from Dr J. David Thomas and Professor K. H. Kuhn, both of the University of Durham.

[14] Personal communication from Dr J. David Thomas, University of Durham.

[15] See Griffith, *LAAA* 15 (1928), 67.

[16] Adams in Erich Dinkler (ed.), *Kunst und Geschichte Nubiens in Christlicher Zeit* (Recklinghausen, 1970), 149; id., *Kulubnardi* I (Lexington, 1994), ch. IX.

[17] Frend's assertion that Greek graffiti were recorded by Monneret de Villard in the Late Christian Cupola Church (839) is in error; Monneret states specifically that the graffiti were in Coptic. See Frend, *Byzantinoslavica,* vol. 33 (1972), 229; Ugo Monneret de Villard, *La Nubia medioevale* (Cairo, 1935), I, 110. However, at an earlier date Somers Clarke reported seeing both Coptic and Greek graffiti in the Cupola Church. See *Christian Antiquities in the Nile Valley* (Oxford, 1912), 81.

[18] See Adams, *Nubia,* 485–8; Oates, *JEA* 49 (1963), 161–71; Zilliacus, *Studia Orientalia,* 28, no. 15 (1964), 14.

[19] See Plumley in *Nubia, récentes recherches,* 106; Zilliacus, op. cit.; Oates, op. cit.

Coptic

The Coptic language had no official status in the Nubian church; there is a suggestion that it was understood only by those clerics or monks who were of Egyptian nationality, or had been trained in Egypt.[20] At Qaṣr Ibrîm, the situation of Coptic in the Late Christian period appears to have been generally similar to that of Greek. The number of surviving texts is slightly larger, totalling forty-four examples, but again they are nearly all religious, and the majority are on parchment. Texts that have been specifically identified include parts of the gospels of John and Luke and a homily concerning the Devil and St Michael.[21] The hands, where they can be identified, employ square or rounded uncials, suggesting an origin substantially earlier than the Late Christian period.[22] Once again there is a strong probability that these are surviving fragments of the Cathedral library, dating from the Classic Christian period or even earlier. The five Coptic texts on papyrus—the only examples of papyrus found in the Late Christian levels—must surely be of much earlier date.

There are, nevertheless, a few evidences for the continued use of Coptic as a living language. The most important of these is a letter written by the Nubian king to the Coptic Patriarch, recommending a certain person for a church appointment.[23] Another important document is the consecration scroll of Bishop Timotheos which was buried alongside him late in the fourteenth century.[24] There is also a fragment of a letter in Coptic addressed to the 'Orthodox Bishop of Ibrîm,' which contains one phrase in Old Nubian.[25] It must be noted, however, that these latter documents were not actually written at Qaṣr Ibrîm itself, while the king's letter to the patriarch was written at the very beginning of the Late Christian period. Thereafter, the only secure evidence for the continued local use of Coptic is offered by the Coptic graffito recorded by Monneret de Villard in the Ibrîm Cupola Church (839).[26]

Old Nubian

Old Nubian, the spoken language of mediaeval Nubia, was obviously the principal medium of written communication as well. Fifty-three percent of the surviving Late Christian texts from Qaṣr Ibrîm are in Old Nubian, or in combinations of Old Nubian and Arabic, Greek, or Coptic (see table 13). These texts are the remnants of all kinds of documents: religious, literary, administrative, commercial, legal, and personal. Almost two-thirds of them were found in one or another of the eparchal houses; the majority were evidently written either to or from the Eparchs of Nobadia. A number of the legal texts are on soft skin, but the vast majority of Old Nubian documents are on paper.

In spite of its obvious affinity to the present-day Mahasi (Nobiin) Nubian language,[27] Old Nubian remains the least understood of the mediaeval Nubian languages.[28] While considerable progress has been made in its decipherment in the recent past,[29] many aspects both of vocabulary and of grammar remain problematical. The translations and interpretations presented in this volume are, therefore, to be regarded as provisional and subject to future correction.

Many Old Nubian documents—even those written to and from the eparchs—are rather informal in tone and might almost be characterized as 'semi-official.' They were evidently written between individuals who knew each other well, personally as well as officially, and their protocols are relatively brief and perfunctory. 'I greet you,' 'I pay homage to your fathership,' 'I greet your sonship,' 'I greet your lordship, blessed by King and by God,' and 'In the name of God' are typical openings, after which the writer gets directly down to business. It is apparent in at least some of the cases (as in a letter from a bishop to an eparch) that the kinship terms employed in the salutations are figurative rather than literal. In addition to official matters there are frequently rather cryptic references to past events or to persons, and the writer often ends by sending greetings to various individuals who were evidently known to both sender and recipient.

[20] Adams, *Nubia*, 485; Jakobielski in Erich Dinkler (ed.), *Kunst und Geschichte Nubiens in Christlicher Zeit* (Recklinghausen, 1970), 31-2.

[21] See Lafontaine, *Le Muséon*, 92 (1979), 37-60.

[22] Personal communication from Professor K. H. Kuhn, University of Durham.

[23] See Plumley in *Études nubiennes*, 232.

[24] See J. Martin Plumley, *The Scrolls of Bishop Timotheos* (Egypt Exploration Society, Texts from Excavations, First Memoir) (London, 1975).7-26.

[25] Personal communication from Professor G. Michael Browne, University of Illinois.

[26] Monneret de Villard, op. cit., I, 110.

[27] For discussion of the modern language see Werner Roland, *Grammatik des Nobiin* (Hamburg 1987); for its historical affinities see Thelwall in Christopher Ehret and Merrick Posnansky (eds.), *The Archaeological and Linguistic Reconstruction of African History* (Berkeley, 1982), 39-52.

[28] See Gerald M. Browne, *Old Nubian Texts from Qaṣr Ibrîm*, II (Egypt Exploration Society, Texts from Excavations; in press), i.

[29] See Browne in *Bulletin of the American Society of Papyrologists*, 16 (1979), 249-56; 17 (1980), 37-43 and 129-41; 18 (1981), 55-67; 19 (1982), 9-37. See also various works by Fritz Hintze cited by Browne in op. cit. 6 (1979), 249.

The meaning of many passages in the Old Nubian letters is obscure. This is probably due in part to uncertainties of translation. However, there seems also to be an extremely terse, almost short-hand style of composition in many documents, taking for granted a lot of common knowledge on the part of writer and reader. Some allusions are evidently metaphoric, and their significance is no longer clear.

Arabic

The conduct of commercial relations with Egypt and with Muslims was one of the chief duties of the Nubian eparchs,[30] and the language employed for that purpose would almost necessarily have been Arabic. Since Qaṣr Ibrîm was the principal residence of the eparchs, the finding of a considerable number or Arabic letters is to be expected. The total volume of this correspondence is nevertheless surprising. The number of documents purely in Arabic from the Late and Terminal Christian periods (265) is only slightly less than the number purely in Old Nubian, and there are an additional eighty-seven documents combining the two languages (see table 13). All of the purely Arabic texts are on paper.

While Old Nubian was put to all kinds of uses, the overwhelming majority of the Arabic texts are concerned with commerce in one sense or another. Several were written to the eparchs by Egyptian commercial agents in and around Aswân; they exhibit a rather flowery, quasi-diplomatic style not found in the Old Nubian documents. However, there is at least one private letter and some very small fragments of Islamic religious texts. Some of the latter may be remnants of amuletic texts that were sewn up in *higabs* (see Part 3, Chapter 8). The presence of these texts raises the possibility that there were Egyptians or other purely Arabic-speaking Muslims resident at Qaṣr Ibrîm itself in the Late Christian period.

Bilingual texts

Textual finds from the Late and Terminal Christian periods include ninety-eight fragments bearing inscriptions in more than one language. All of them are incomplete, but enough is preserved to permit a partial reading in twenty-seven cases. By far the largest number are, as might be expected, in Old Nubian and Arabic; they seem for the most part to involve the same kinds of commercial and administrative correspondence that are predominant in the single-language texts.

The great majority of the 'bilingual' texts appear to represent nothing more than an opportune reuse of available paper, so that there is no actual connection between the texts in the two languages. There is no surviving example that unmistakably exhibits the same text in Old Nubian and Arabic, though in the case of some of the smaller scraps this possibility cannot be wholly ruled out. In three cases the Old Nubian text is religious in character, while the Arabic is not; in one case the reverse is true.

There are also five bilingual texts in Old Nubian and Greek, and five in Old Nubian and Coptic. As nearly as can be determined they are all religious in character, though most of the fragments are rather small. Five specimens are on parchment and the remainder on paper. At least some of them are genuine bilingual texts, repeating the same message in two languages. The best preserved specimen is a page from a parchment psalter in Old Nubian and Greek. According to the translator, 'For the most part the translation runs sentence by sentence, with two oblique strokes separating the Greek from the Old Nubian. The latter tends to be fairly literal, and it lacks the interpretive flair associated with Griffith's Lectionary.[31] On several occasions the translator appears to have misunderstood the Greek original...'[32] There is also a paper fragment containing Old Nubian and Greek, which is described as 'possibly part of a bilingual service book.'[33]

Changes in language usage over time

Table 17 shows the numbers of text finds in different languages, respectively from the Late Christian 1, Late Christian 2, and Terminal Christian periods. The most immediate impression conveyed by this table is one of declining literacy, since 56% of texts have come from the LC1 period, 29% from the LC2 period, and only 5% from the TC period. (Another 10% of texts are clearly of late mediaeval date but cannot be placed within a specific period). These figures must not be taken absolutely at face value, since the LC1 period was longer in duration than either of the two succeeding,[34] and it also seems that the overall population at Qaṣr Ibrîm was continually diminishing throughout the later mediaeval periods, if we can judge by the extent of the surviving architectural remains (see Part 2, Chapter 1). Notwithstanding these considerations, it is probable

[30] See Adams, *Nubia*, 464–6.

[31] See Gerald M. Browne, *Griffith's Old Nubian Lectionary* (Papyrologica Castroctaviana 8, 1982).

[32] Browne in *Sudan Texts Bulletin* 3 (1981), 10. For other bilingual psalter texts see Plumley, *Sudan Texts Group Circular* 2 (1979), and Anderson and Adams, *JEA* 65 (1979), 41 and pl. VI, 1.

[33] Personal communication from Professor G. Michael Browne, University of Illinois.

[34] For a discussion of the respective dates see Part 1, Chapter 1.

TABLE 17
DISTRIBUTION OF TEXT FINDS ACCORDING TO LANGUAGE AND PERIOD

Languages	Late Christian 1	Late Christian 2	Terminal Christian	Undetermined	Totals
Old Nubian	191	88	2	21	302
%*	*44*	*42*	*6*	*29*	
Old Nubian + Arabic	55	27		5	87
%*	*13*	*13*		*7*	
Old Nubian + Greek	4		1		5
%*	*1*		*3*		
Old Nubian + Coptic	5				5
%*	*1*				
Arabic	106	91	28	40	265
%*	*33*	*43*	*83*	*54*	
Arabic + Coptic	1				1
Coptic	27	5	1	5	38
%*	*6*	*2*	*3*	*7*	
Greek	11			2	13
%*	*2*			*3*	
TOTALS	400	211	34	73	716
%†	*56*	*29*	*5*	*10*	

*Texts in this language as a percentage of all texts from the period indicated (vertical column)
†Texts from this period as a percentage of all late mediaeval texts (horizontal row)

enough that literacy really was declining, since political conditions in the LC2 and TC periods were increasingly chaotic,[35] and trade was disrupted by the predations of Arab and Beja nomads.[36]

Textual finds in Greek and Coptic have come almost entirely from the LC1 period, further strengthening the suggestion that they are mainly remnants of the previously destroyed cathedral library. The proportions of Old Nubian and Arabic are roughly the same in the LC1 and LC2 periods, with Arabic showing only a slight gain at the expense of the indigenous language. In the Terminal Christian period, however, we find that 83% of all the surviving documents are in Arabic. As in all periods, they are overwhelmingly commercial in character. The general absence of religious texts from the Terminal Christian period may be taken as testimony to the parlous condition of Nubian Christianity during the century preceding its final disappearance.[37]

[35] See Adams, *Nubia*, 508–31.
[36] Op. cit., 531–2.
[37] Op. cit., 539–44; Adams in Kazimierz Michalowski (ed.), *Nubia, récentes recherches* (Warsaw, 1975), 11–17.

CHAPTER 3
ADMINISTRATIVE TEXTS

Administrative texts are here defined as those relating to the exercise of civil or ecclesiastical authority. The two categories are not always sharply distinct, for the Nubian eparchs had religious as well as secular duties,[1] and in the later years of Nubian Christianity there was an increasing convergence of the church and the state.[2] Qaṣr Ibrîm was in any case the chief centre of both civil and religious administration in late mediaeval Lower Nubia; it was the residence of both eparchs and bishops, as well as of many subordinate officials. The number of texts that can be classified as administrative is, therefore, substantial. Most of the complete documents have come from one or other of the archival caches found in the eparchal houses, as described in Part 4, Chapter 1; a few have also been preserved accidentally in rubbish deposits.

Administrative documents were written or issued by Kings of Dotawo, eparchs, vice-eparchs, *domestikoi*, bishops, priests, and archdeacons;[3] there are also letters addressed by private individuals to various of these functionaries. The administrative documents are mostly in Old Nubian, and the great majority are on paper, though there are examples also on leather and on parchment. They can be subdivided into several categories, which will be discussed individually.

Royal proclamation

Unique among all the documents found at Qaṣr Ibrîm is a proclamation issued by King Moses George of Dotawo, in the year 1155. It is inscribed in Old Nubian on soft leather, and is one of the large cache of official documents that had been sealed in a jar and buried in the eparchal House 177.[4] The text runs as follows:

Proclamation of Moses George, King of Dotawo [5]

It is written in the name of the Father, the Son and the Holy Spirit, it being the 29th of the month of Mesori, it being the first of the moon, it being year 871 (of the era) from the Martyrs. I, Moses George, called King, and nephew of King David, who also hold the Kingship of Dotawo as well as the office of Eparch of Palagi,

My mother Mari being Queen Mother and also Gouad,
Papo Mêna being Bishop of Ibrîm,
Iosêphi being *Tricliniaris* of the *Domesticus* Elect (?),
Orinkouda being *Tricliniaris* of No,
Darme being Eparch of Nobadia and *Domesticus* of Faras,
Nilêse being Potentiary (?) of Sikko(l)ti,
Massouda Damastil being *Tricliniaris* of Douksi,
Papasa being *Oeconomus* (?),
Papon, Iroti, being Potentiary (?) of Nan-Nokko,
Dakkoul being *Meizoterus* (?) of Adauou,
Mênankouda being Silentiary (?) of Nobadia,
Sirephê being *Ñess* of Nobadia,
Serkol being *Ñess* of the *Domesticus*,
under their care standing all the authorities:

Until he comes upon authorization (?) from God, who is the Saviour, no one is to speak in opposition and utter a denial against me, as all are under my care, and they come and proclaim the holy name of God. Whereas the *Tot* of Michaêlko(l) and (?) Motiko(l) in Ibrîm approached me through my chiefs and besought me in the matter of the Epimachus-church of Ibrîm West, asking me to free from servitude the Epimachus-church, which—when it gives to the Bishop wine which is more than (?) one unit of wine each Thaboti and the Bishop rejects it—sends each year 7 cubits (?) of wormwood; whereas I, when concern for the Epimachus-church entered my heart, when it was the 3rd month since I had become King, regarding the wine which, in the matter of the Epimachus-church, the Bishop was wont to receive through the office of the Silentiary (?) of Nobadia—I caused that, on the evening of the 9th of Thaboti, there be taken to the Epimachus-church from Dotawo (?) 1 (cubit [?] of) wormwood for the Silentiary (?) through the Eparch of Nobadia, if he (the Silentiary) did not deposit it together with the 2 *parñatt* of wheat from the Apostles-church of Ibrîm, in order that Epimachus might arise, come and place the four corners (?) of the nation for care under my feet: because of the power of his (?) authority there shall come against the Epimachus-church neither Eparch nor *Domesticus* of Faras nor Silentiary (?) nor *Ñess* nor anyone whom the Bishop sent. Truly if one speaks against and denies my statement, let Epimachus stab him with his spear, (2) let him die through the King's curse, (3) let him have a heart attack, (4) let him receive a share with Judas Iscariot the Wounder (?) of Mankind and the Betrayor, (5) let him not find anyone who knows

[1] See William Y. Adams, *Nubia, Corridor to Africa* (London, 1977), 464–6.

[2] Op. cit., 534.

[3] In most documents the titles are actually given in their Old Nubian forms rather than in these Greek or English equivalents; see Part 4, Chapter 8, table 20.

[4] Listed as archive no. 3 in Part 4, Chapter 1.

[5] Excavation number 74.1.30/6, no. 2. For the official translation and commentary see Gerald M. Browne, *Old Nubian Texts from Qaṣr Ibrîm*, III (Egypt Exploration Society, Texts from Excavations; in press).

him amongst the assembled people, and (6) let Epimachus on the day of judgment come great in battle against him.

And to this certified document, through the cross (?) of kingship ..., in 3 places I affixed the cross (?):

I, Papasa, *Chartelarius*, *Oeconomus* (?), Goukarko(l), Archimandrite of the Archangel Michael, and Archimandrite ... through (?) the Blessed King.

With God! I, Ounta, Great Scribe of George Moses the King and Goukarko(l), wrote and witnesses this certified document.

Eparchal correspondence

The largest number of administrative documents are letters written either from or to the Eparchs of Nobadia, or their deputies. They fall into several categories, as described below:

Disbursement orders

Among the various titles sometimes associated with mediaeval Nubian officials is that of 'keeper of the grain.'[6] In the case of the Eparchs of Nobadia, the importance of this function is attested by a considerable number of letters, which appear to be orders for the disbursement of grain, either from public stores or from the eparch's personal store.[7] There is also mention of dates in two documents and of wine (in very small quantities) in two. It is not certain that all of these letters were issued by the eparchs, though they all seem to have an official or semi-official character. At least seven of the disbursement orders bear the actual subscripts of eparchs, and another was issued in the name of a vice-eparch; there are several others whose authorship is uncertain. All of these documents are in the Old Nubian language. Rather surprisingly, five of them are on parchment and the remainder on paper. The disbursement orders have come mainly from an archive buried in the eparchal House 177 (74.1.30/6),[8] but some were recovered also from rubbish deposits. The following are three fairly typical specimens of the *genre*:

Letter from Eparch Gabrielkouda to Tapara [9]

I greet (you). What about (?) the 56 (artabs of) millet? Give 10 *artabs* to Loukasi, yourself take 5 *artabs*, give 1 *artab* to Atareti. Get and send (?) all the grain to Topara. Also, through this measure which you have on deposit, take out 40 *artabs* and be glad that you have them. If you come to the shoemaker Kroda, do not at all do anything bad, and don't let anything be taken. And truly, coming upon conditions (?) that have turned out as we hear, if you have come for a division (?), woman, come and winnow, and scatter (the chaff) and keep (the grain). One who comes through such conditions (?) is not covered (?).

(Address) Gabrielkouda, Eparch of Nobadia, to Tapara, *thel* ( ) of Katine.

Letter from the Eparch Adam to the Vice (?)-Eparch Soueti[10]

I pay homage to your lordship, blessed by God. As for that grain of yours in Ibrîm, which I offered in four *oupri*, I was not alone, but it was I; Mogôdikoña, son of Koudi-Pesa; and Iêsê, son of Magiti (who offered the grain). And the witnesses of the fact that we offered (the grain) are the best (?) men of Ibrîm:

Anaê
Ornourta
Isou, Priest
Darme, Priest
Ñapin-Ata, Deacon.

There being 5 *artabs* and 5 bushels of grain in one *oupri*, after Isou the Priest and with him Anna, being my (agent) from the Deacons, deposited one *artab*, you (?), giving him 1 *artab*, received 4 *artabs* and 5 bushels, and from the second *oupri* 2 *artabs* of barley and 8 bushels of wheat. I received what is his, and they received Ajjeji's present supply of water. Also, the rest of the wheat that you received does not require your cleaning. If you wish, draw (some water) for me, or have those who live outside draw it. And those four *artabs* and five bushels that you received are Ajjeji's.

(Address) Adam, Eparch of Nobadia, *Domesticus* of Pachoras, to Soueti, Vice (?) -Eparch of Terp (?).

Letter from the Eparch Adam to the Architriclinus Douddi(l)[11]

I pay homage (to you). There is 1 (bale of) hay that Kettoudi gave to my mother. Let it be ... Yes (?). There is 1 new (bale)

[6] Old Nubian *souni-* (see Part 4, Ch. 8, table 20). In legal documents from the archive 74.1.30/6, the title is associated twice with the King of Dotawo, once with the king's brother, and once with an official for whom no other title is given. There is no actual document in which the Eparch of Nobadia is named as Keeper of the Grain.

[7] For other food disbursement orders see also Griffith, *Proceedings of the British Academy,* 14 (1928), 129, and Zyhlarz in *Studies Presented to F. Ll. Griffith* (Oxford, 1932), 189–90.

[8] Listed as archive no. 3 in Part 4, Chapter 1.

[9] Excavation number 78.1.26/43 (also separately recorded as NI/14). It is written on paper, and was recovered from a storage pit in the West Plaza, datable to the LC1 period. For the official translation and commentary see Gerald M. Browne, *Old Nubian Texts from Qaṣr Ibrîm*, II (Egypt Exploration Society, Texts from Excavations; in press).

[10] Excavation number 74.1.30/6, no. 9c. It is written on paper, and was part of the archive cache buried in a jar in House 177, listed in Part 4, Chapter 1 as archive no. 3. For the official translation and commentary see Browne, *Old Nubian Texts*, III.

[11] Excavation number 74.1.30/6, no. 30. It is written on parchment, and was part of the archive cache buried in a jar in House 177, listed in Part 4, Chapter 1 as archive no. 3. For the official translation and commentary see Browne, *Old Nubian Texts*, III.

belonging to Argate, your mother. You gave them to my mother, as I know. Being reluctant to give (them) to her (agent) who was about to come, I took the dates and gulped them down. Come and give out 6 artabs of dates. And now, if they give (them) to her (agent), come forth; if they are reluctant to give, assign them to her young daughter.

(Address) Adam, Eparch and Eiksi(l), to Douddi(l), *Architriclinus.*

Other eparchal decrees

The document translated below gives further testimony to the economic activities of the eparchs. It is unusual among eparchal letters, both because of its length and because of the variety of topics covered. Although many of its allusions are obscure, the principal concern appears to be with the movement of various goods.

Letter from Eparch Masi to Elonna [12]

I greet your lordship, blessed by King and by God. From the property that they receive, without my knowledge they send nothing. God is good to you. And if Kouda comes and takes it, and if I am speechless (?), let him rejoice, as he goes on the wide river. As for the ship, he didn't call it to leave, did he? And the ship captain himself said that we received the property, and that the deputy of the *sonoj* delivered the five letters to me. And in none of the matters of the ship is the captain involved without my perceiving. And he will take them with them (or: him) onto my ship. Don't you cease harvesting (?) Send me seed for a hundred (days?). Yet I also sent this without a water-wheel. Look for a water-wheel and bring it. As for your standing (?) crop, I have nothing bad done to it. May God make your years numerous. You alone will see when you come whether I am good or am bad. And as I keep what I receive, may I not sit idle (?) over your affairs. You have put me in charge of your mares. And my daughter Miskine is coming. In truth, pay homage to Isaac. I greet Nodann, son of Tilleura, I greet Isaac. —And why did I answer, saying that you should bring seed for twenty days? Send it quickly!

(Address) Masi, Eparch of Nobadia, *Domesticus* of Pachoras and Eikshi, to Elonna.

Letters to the eparchs

Most of the letters written by the eparchs are, obviously, in Old Nubian, though Arabic was sometimes employed in dealing with Egyptian merchants.[13] Presumably most of the letters received by the eparchs were also in Old Nubian. It is a curious fact, however, that the largest number of letters to the eparchs that have survived, including many that were deliberately preserved, are in Arabic. Most are commercial/diplomatic letters written by Egyptian officials in the Aswân area; these will be discussed in Part 4, Chapter 5. However, the late mediaeval population of Lower Nubia also included permanently settled Muslims, and these, like the Christian Nubians, addressed the Eparch of Nobadia as their suzerain.

Although the great majority of eparchal correspondence in Arabic dates from the Classic Christian period, there are at least three surviving letters in Arabic from Late Christian contexts which involve official or business dealings between Muslim residents and Nubian officials. Two of the documents were not originally addressed directly to the eparch, but they must eventually have come to his attention, since they found their way into the eparchal archives buried in House 177.[14] One letter appears to be from a minor emir of the Beni Kanz; it requests that the eparch write a letter confirming him in the possession of his territory in Lower Nubia. The document is actually addressed to Ubaydallah, Secretary to the Eparch, who must have been a Muslim scribe employed specifically to handle correspondence in Arabic.[15] Another letter, again probably from a Kanzi, requests the return of two slaves (?) in accordance with existing agreements.[16] The salutation is missing, but the formal style of the document suggests that it was addressed to an eparch or other high official.[17] A third letter, addressed originally to a minor Nubian functionary, involves a problem about land rental and has attached to it a copy of the original rental contract.[18] All of these documents probably reached the eparch because he was officially charged with the conduct of relations with Muslims, both within and outside Nubia.[19]

Ecclesiastical administration

Royal letter of recommendation

One of the more extraordinary administrative documents from Qaṣr Ibrîm falls on the boundary between

[12] Excavation number 78.1.19/14 (also separately recorded as NI/15). It is written on paper, and was recovered from a storage pit in the Central Plaza, datable to the LC1 period. For the official translation and commentary see Browne, *Old Nubian Texts*, II.

[13] See Plumley in Kazimierz Michalowski (ed.), *Nubia, récentes recherches* (Warsaw, 1975), 106.

[14] Listed as archive no. 4 in Part 4, Chapter 1.

[15] Excavation number 74.1.29/11, no. 7. The letter is in fragmentary condition, and is still awaiting a full translation.

[16] i. e. presumably the terms of the *Baqt* treaty; see J. L. Burckhardt, *Travels in Nubia* (London, 1819), 511.

[17] Excavation number 74.1.29/11, no. 6. The letter is in fragmentary condition, and is still awaiting a full translation.

[18] Excavation number 74.1.29/11, no. 4. The letter is in fragmentary condition, and is still awaiting a full translation.

[19] Adams, *Nubia*, 464.

the civil and ecclesiastical domains. It is a letter from the King of Nubia to the Coptic Patriarch, commending a certain person for consecration to a bishopric in Nubia. The preserved copy of the king's letter is written on a paper scroll in Coptic with Greek subscriptions.[20] There are several blank spaces in the text (identified by [ ] in the translation below) which were evidently meant to be filled in later. Presumably they were completed in the official draft before it was sent, but not in the file copy that was retained at Ibrîm. The letter was one of the thirty-four official documents buried in a jar in House 177 (archive no. 3)[21] and is the only one not written in Old Nubian. The translation follows:[22]

Letter from King Moses George to Apa Mark, Patriarch of Alexandria

In the name of the All-Holy Trinity of One Substance, of the Father, the Son and the Holy Spirit, giving life to all [ie. in the universe], a single Mission, a single Lordship, a single [ ], a single counsel, a single power and command, a Trinity of three hypostaseis standing perfect, of three persons equal to one another in glory and suffering, the Trinity in Oneness and the Oneness in Trinity: This it is which we worship and to which we send day and night glory, praise and thankfulness in the highest, because this alone it is on which we place our hopes: Hail to the power of the Holy Trinity, Amen.

First of all: we pay homage to the angel of the holy altar of the contemplation, evangelic and apostolic, the martyr of Holy Mark; and secondly we similarly pay homage to and greet your holy hands many times and above all. Now we beseech your honoured and lofty fatherhood: do not be wise and protective to yourself alone, but become our guide, that you may instruct me in the upright way of your prayers for us always, for Jacob the Apostle says that the request of the just has power and works also in the way in which Elijah begged and so saved the people, and also as Benjamin [?] begged and so destruction ceased, and it was accounted to him as a mark of justice on our behalf. And now, Holy Father, continue to pray for the just kings in order that we may receive strength over everyone who hates us and may be saved, together with all the Christian people, through your holy prayers, Amen.

After all this, I want you to know, my honoured and blessed father,whether ..., I have agreed to send to your blessed and honoured Lordship and Father a man whose name is Iêsou, regarding whom I have found that he is worthy of this holy liturgy. And now take [him] up and ordain him Bishop of the Tabernacle [Greek: skênê] forever; fill him with the Holy Spirit and your words. I beseech the [literally: your] justice of your Virgin Mary and our Lord Jesus Christ our King and our true God, in [ ] that He look upon us in openness, mercy and compassion, the He take away every war, every disturbance, every earthquake, every affliction, every temptation and every confusion, through the raising of your holy hands to God, the Creator of the universe, He Whom you worship and beseech that He [verb omitted] upon me, concerning [my] palace, all my land, all the Christian people who dwell in it, and all my army, through the ambassadorship of the Mistress of us all, Mary Theotokos ... with prayers of ... the archangel Michael, the prayers of the archangel Gabriel, the prayers of the archangel Raphael, and the blessings of [literally: with] the Holy Mark, the contemplation, evangelic and apostolic, the [?] Martyr, and all the blessings, Amen.

The letter has no fewer than three subscripts, of which the first is in Coptic and the other two in Greek:[23]

(Coptic subscript)

A letter to the Archbishop. May his holy blessings come upon us, Amen. I, Eiñitta, do obeisance, and I greet a multitude of times holy footstools of thy feet and thy holy hands. Remember, O lord father, in thy holy prayers until God forgives me all my sins. We wrote on the 20th day of the month of Thoth, after the Martyrs 903. In the peace of God. Amen.

[689; i.e. Michael [24].]

(First Greek subscript)

Moses and Geor(ge), King and most pious, Christ-loving and Church-loving, and Loving-the-poor, and lover of men and lover of strangers, and good and mild and kind and generous and one who behaves uprightly and foster-father and most revered and of all the Barbaroi our King (of) Arouda and Makoura and Nobadia and Dalmat(ia) and Axum and Autocrator of the people of the Lord. God be guardian. Many be the years in the Lord. Greetings.

[20] For a facsimile of the Greek subscript see Plumley in *Études nubiennes* (Institut français d'archéologie orientale, Bibliothèque d'étude, Vol. 77) (Cairo, 1978), 238.

[21] Excavation no. 74.1.30/6A; listed as archive no. 3 in Part 4, Ch. 1.

[22] For this translation I am indebted to a personal communication from Professor Gerald M. Browne.

[23] Translation of the subscripts furnished by J. M. Plumley (personal communication). A second translation by Gerald M. Browne (personal communication) varies slightly, but without effect on the meaning.

[24] For a discussion of the rendering of names into numerical cryptograms see P. L. Shinnie and H. N. Chittick, *Ghazali—a Monastery in the Northern Sudan*, (Sudan Antiquities Service, Occasional Papers, no. 5) (Khartoum, 1961), 95.

(Second Greek subscript)

(To) Apa Markos by the mercy of God the great Archbishop of the city of Alexandria and the city of Babylon and Nobadia and Arouda and Makour(ia) and Dalmatia and Axum; Judge of the world. In the Lord, Greetings. Many be the years. From the creation of the world [ ]. From the birth of (?) [ ]. After the Martyrs [ ]. After the Saracens [ ]. In the Lord, Greetings. Written [or, I wrote] [ ].

The elaborate protocols and flowery style of this document stand in obvious contrast to the rather informal language of the Old Nubian documents discussed earlier. It may be surmised, however, that they are embellishments of the Coptic scribe who actually wrote the letter. No such personage is actually named, but it can reasonably be assumed that no Nubian king in the twelfth century had a sufficient command of Coptic to write such a letter.[25] Plumley surmises that the king's seeming claim to sovereignty over Alodia, Makouria, Nobadia, Dalmatia,[26] and 'all the barbarians' represents an error on the part of the scribe, who at some point in the writing confused the protocols of the sender (i.e. the king) with those of the recipient (the Coptic Patriarch.)[27] In Old Nubian documents the same Moses George is identified simply as King of Dotawo.

Bishop's consecration documents

Among the documents relating to church administration must be mentioned the consecration scrolls of Bishop Timotheos, which were buried alongside him in the north crypt of the Cathedral.[28] They consist of two long paper scrolls, each nearly 5 m in length, which bear essentially the same text in Coptic and in Arabic. They were issued by the Coptic Patriarch in Cairo in 1371 or 1372.

The consecration scrolls of Bishop Timotheos have been published in full by Professor J. M. Plumley,[29] and their text need not be repeated here. The translator's précis is however worth quoting:

Each Scroll contains a Letter Testimonial ... from the Patriarch Gabriel IV (A.D. 1370–8) to the people of Nubia informing them that he had consecrated for them a new bishop, Timotheos, in place of their deceased bishop, Athanasios, and instructing them to receive and enthrone Timotheos in his see.

At the end of each Scroll are the autograph witnesses of the bishops who were present at the rites and ceremonies performed on behalf of the newly consecrated bishop. Two of the witnessing bishops were present at his consecration and two at his subsequent enthronement. In the Coptic Scroll the autographs are written in Coptic, and in the Arabic Scroll in Arabic. An interesting addition to the Coptic witnesses is a passage in passable Greek by the hand of a fourth bishop. Unfortunately there are a number of lacunae in this passage, which have been caused by holes in the paper...

When the Scrolls were first rolled up, brief notes in Arabic were placed along the outer edge of each document. Before unrolling it was possible to read the words, 'By the hand of the Fatherly Patriarch Gabriel of the great city of Alexandria' [although the subscript shows that the documents were actually executed in the Hanging Church of St Mary in Fustat].

Finally, on the back of the Arabic Scroll ... are the remains of seven lines containing a rough but incomplete table of dates'[30]

Plumley further observes that 'The text of the Coptic Scroll is essentially the same as that contained in a fourteenth-century Coptic-Arabic manuscript in the Bibliothèque Nationale in Paris. This bilingual manuscript (Arab. 203) has been described as an encyclopedia of the ecclesiastical science of the Coptic Church.'[31]

Episcopal and priestly correspondence

One of the eparchal archives buried in House 177 (74.1.30/6) included five letters written in Old Nubian to or from church officials,[32] and another such document was found in the rubbish in House 763. Although two of the letters are written on parchment, the reason for their deliberate preservation is obscure, since they do not appear to deal with matters of great consequence. Three letters have to do with summons or invitations to visit; two are like many of the eparchal letters in that they are concerned mainly with disbursements of grain. One letter, from the Bishop of Pachoras (Faras) to the Bishop of Sai, seems to be an injunction to redistribute property. The following are translations of three specimens:

[25] For discussion of the restricted use of Coptic see Adams, *Nubia*, 485.

[26] Identified by Plumley with Ptolemais in Libya; see *Études nubiennes*, 236.

[27] Personal communication, 14 May 1988.

[28] For the report of the original discovery see Plumley, *JEA* 50 (1964), 3–4 and pl, I, 2.

[29] J. Martin Plumley, *The Scrolls of Bishop Timotheos* (Egypt Exploration Society, Texts from Excavations, Memoir I) (London, 1975)

[30] Op. cit., 4.

[31] Op. cit., 21.

[32] Listed as archive no. 3 in Part 4, Chapter 1.

Letter from Tapara, the Great Priest, to Eioñoka[33]

I greet (you). Take Papon-Penti, and if he gives you the lovely *asousi* in which I was dressed, come out and eagerly (?) call the King. I am remaining—it is good (to do so), but as for you, without remaining, come. And if you come here and come up to the river, I shall send Koudi downstream to you. If you are reluctant, remain, letting Penti come out, to whom I, going downstream, shall eagerly (?) hasten. Speak as befits a Father (?). Until I come to you, I continue not to judge ..., I greet all your people. If you do not send (him), let Askim (?) come out.

(Address) Tapara, the Great Priest, to Eioñoka.

Letter to Iêsousinkouda, Archdeacon, from Mineria (?)[34]

I greet (you). During the winter (?) month did you fail to find justice as to the face-value (?) originating through you? Truly you have failed to find this. For Annil-Soñoja there is 1, for Aman-Kose there is 1, for the daughter of Eve there is 1. These too send out. You, Iêsousinkouda alone, taking 2 from the threshing-floor by the great measure of Eiou my mother, take and bind them, and take and exchange them for seed. At the time of the grain (?)-sale, sell them at ...-value and exchange them for seed, in order that (?) you may deposit (the money taken in) amongst what you receive. And again, sell them in exchange for clothing at ...-value, and send (what you receive). Truly if he judges you again, write a letter to me. I am staying until he gives me the property. And you are an offering on my head, and the offering (?) is in hand (?). I pay homage to Papasa. And justice has found your children.

(*Address*) To Iêsousinkouda, Great Deacon and Priest, (from) Mineria (?)

Letter from Bishop Arôn of Pachoras to Bishop Isou of Sai[35]

I pay homage to the altar of the Virgin Mary Theotokos, and again I greet your brothership. God is good to you, and he has kept you upon your throne. Accordingly, this writing of the Christians and the one who recites it have pugnacity in your kingdom: for they come to you. And as for you, as you sacrifice (your) glory for the sake of God and the Holy Father, go around to all those who take away, and take away (from them) and give to those who have faith. And as for Pent ( ), who exults, affectionately kiss his eyes, because they are God's suppliants. Proclaim salvation in God, and receive praise from the Holy Father and his people: they are my suppliants.

(*Address*) Abba Arôn, Orthodox Bishop of Pachoras, to Abba Isou, Orthodox Bishop of Sai.

Lists of church property

One of the eparchal archives buried in House 177 (74.1.30/6)[36] included three documents that appear to be property lists. Two of them are mere listings of names, followed by numbers; in one case there are names of churches as well as of private individuals. A much more detailed document gives a listing of lands and other properties owned by the Jesus-Church of Touggili. While these documents clearly relate to church administration, they are more appropriately dealt with under the heading 'legal texts,' in the next chapter.

[33] Written on parchment; excavation number 74.1.30/6, no. 20. For the official translation and commentary see Browne, *Old Nubian Texts*, III.

[34] Written on paper; excavation number 74.1.30/6, no. 31. For the official translation and commentary see Browne, *Old Nubian Texts*, III.

[35] Written on paper; excavation number 74.1.30/6, no. 15. For the official translation and commentary see Browne, *Old Nubian Texts*, III.

[36] Listed as archive no. 3 in Part 4, Chapter 1.

CHAPTER 4
LEGAL TEXTS

AMONG all the whole and fragmentary documents from Qaṣr Ibrîm, there is none that can be recognized specifically as a proclamation of law. The texts that are here classified as legal are, rather, records and/or instruments. As usual, the largest number of them have to do with the ownership, management, or transfer of property. All but a few of the legal documents are in the Old Nubian language.

The style of the legal documents is rigidly formulaic, in this respect differing markedly from both administrative and commercial documents. Most begin with the formula 'In the name of the Father, the Son and the Holy Spirit,' and then go on to name a long list of public officials, starting always with the reigning King of Dotawo and his mother. After them are named various other officials of Dotawo, Nobadia, and other places which in many cases are no longer identifiable. The largest number of officials named in any one document is nineteen, and the average number is about ten. The reason for these citations is not clear, since the named officials were not actually witnesses to the documents, and in many cases can hardly have been aware of their existence. Perhaps the protocols were meant to demonstrate that the scribe was well-informed and reliable.

Following the body of the document there is always a separate list of witnesses, ranging in number from five to thirty on individual documents. The average number of witnesses named is about fifteen. Interestingly, several of the sales contracts include a detailed listing of payments in food or wine that were made to the scribe and/or the witnesses, as if to suggest that these were among the provisions of the contract. Some documents end by invoking a curse against anyone who shall deny their legitimacy.

Not surprisingly, legal texts are the most numerous of the documents preserved in eparchal archives. Of the thirty-four documents buried in a jar in House 177 (74.1.30/6),[1] eighteen are classifiable as legal texts. A summary inventory of these is given in table 18. It seems probable that the nine scrolls preserved near House 169 (64/23)[2] and the four scrolls buried under House 171 (66a/45)[3] were also mainly legal in character. It is noteworthy too that many of the legal texts are written on leather—an indication that they were meant to be preserved.

Property management and transfer

Documents relating to the management and transfer of property include several deeds of land sale, one cession of land for a five-year period, one contract for the rental of land, one record of the sale of unspecified property, one donation of property, and one document releasing the contracting parties from a sales contract.

Sales of land

Contracts for the sale of land were executed on behalf of both male and female vendors, and male and female buyers. The properties are described in the texts with varying degrees of specificity, but no actual measure is given in any case. There are mentions of land sown to various kinds of crops, as well as date groves, orchards, acacia land, thorn land, and possibly a clay deposit. One sale included a house, one included at least one *saqia,* and one seems to involve a small plot of land within a church; possibly a burial plot.[4] In some cases the sale involved shares in a plot rather than outright ownership. The sums received in exchange for the land in nearly all cases were pieces of gold and/or silver, which may or may not have been actual coinage (see Part 4, Chapter 8). Recognizable coinage denominations *(dirhem)* are mentioned in some of the property lists discussed at the end of this chapter but not in any of the sales contracts. The smallest price mentioned for any piece of land is one piece of gold; the largest is twenty pieces. In lieu of gold, one woman received a camel, an ox, and a slave. The following are three particularly interesting examples of land sale contracts:

Sale of land[5]

With God. In the name of the Father, the Son and the Holy Spirit, Amen: this certified document is written in the year 907 (of the era) from the Martyrs, it being the 5th of the month of Hathyr, it being the 24th of the moon, King Moses George being King of Dotawo,

[1] Listed in Part 4, Chapter 1 as archive no. 3.

[2] Listed in Part 4, Chapter 1 as archive no. 1.

[3] Listed in Part 4, Chapter 1 as archive no. 2.

[4] However, intramural burials are exceedingly rare in Nubian churches.

[5] Excavation number 74.1.30/6, no. 7. For the official translation and commentary see Gerald M. Browne, *Old Nubian Texts from Qaṣr Ibrîm*, Vol. III (Egypt Exploration Society, Texts from Excavations; in press).

TABLE 18
OLD NUBIAN LEGAL DOCUMENTS INCLUDED IN THE ARCHIVE 74.1.30/6

No.[1]	Material	Content	Sex[2]	Off.[3]	Wit.[4]
		Sales of land			
3	Leather	Private sale of agricultural land	M	10	11
5	Leather	Private sale of land; cession of land	M	14	14 + 30[5]
7	Leather	Private sale of land and house	F	19	24
1	Leather	Private (?) sale of land	?	13	27
9a	Leather	Private sale of a plot of land in a church	F	19	13 + 7[6]
8	Leather	Sale of church-owned land by eparch	M	19	22
16	Paper	Private sale of garden plot	M	3	9
23	Paper	Private sale of land by a woman to her children	F	—	14
14	Paper	Private sale of land to several buyers	M	—	8
		Cession of land			
11	Paper	Five-year cession of a plot of land	M	—	13
		Sale of unspecified property			
13	Paper	Sale by man of his children's (?) property	M	—	12
		Donation of property			
26	Paper	Donation of property to brother by a man entering the church	M	—	8
		Release from sale contract			
4	Leather	Release of a man from private sale contract	M?	9	12
		Release of slaves and servants			
18	Leather	Freeing of a male slave	M	7	21
6	Leather	Release of a servant to another man (?)	?	16	5
		Property lists			
22	Paper	Detailed list of properties belonging to a church	—	—	—
24	Paper	List of personal names, with sums of money or commodities owned by or due them	—	—	—
21	Parchment	List of church names and personal names, followed by numbers	—	—	—

[1] Individual number assigned to document. See Gerald M. Browne, *Old Nubian Tests from Qaṣr Ibrîm*, III (Egypt Exploration Society, Texts from Excavations; in press).
[2] Sex of vendor, donor, or party executing contract.
[3] Number of officials named in protocol
[4] Number of witnesses
[5] Thirty additional witnesses are named in an appendix to the original document
[6] Seven additional witnesses are named in an appendix to the original document

Mari being Queen Mother
Douddil being *Architriclinus*
Papannê, of Sai, son of Annako(l), being Great Scribe,
Papannê being *Oeconomus* (?)
Tapara being *Ñess* of Atwa,
Darme, son of the Great Priest, being *Domesticus* Elect (?),
Gabrielinkouda being *Meizoterus* (?) of Adauei,
Papo Thôma being Bishop of Ibrîm,
Adam, Eparch of Nobadia, (an office) which he also holds together with the office of *Domesticus* of Faras,
Marinkouda, *Tot* of Irtan-Ñal, being *Tricliniaris* of the Eparch,
Dipikkil being Scribe,
Sikamê being *Ñess* of the *Domesticus*,
Orin-Papasa being Silentiary (?),

David, son of Ennoua, being *Ñess*,
Zachari being *Ñess* of Odjo,
Dollisil being *Meizoterus* (?),
Persel being *Ñess* of the Town,
Eptaeiri being *Gous* of Mosmosi,
And under their care standing the Elders of the Church.

I, Kapopi, daughter of Touññesi, competent in my eyes, in my hands and in my feet, rejoicing and exulting, being barren in respect to daughter and son, not being subject to litigation (?), as regards all the land that I inherited from my mother, without denial I sell to Neuesi, daughter of Adama and Anenkoli, all the land that is mentioned in this document, and the house itself which is included. And the plots are these, firstly:

On the east are 3 plots in ..., on the west is 1 water-wheel in a plot for irrigation, on the south are 3 wadis in lupine;

On the south is the land of Mousen-Asti, and on the north is the land of the Jesus-Church, on the south is 1 water-wheel in a plot of lupine.

On the south is the land of the Apostles-Church, and on the north is the land of Asti, on the north is 1 waterwheel in a plot of lupine;

On the south is the land of Matte, and on the north the boundary is the land of the Timakkis, there are 2 water-wheels in a plot of golden millet (?), one third is mine;

On the south the boundary is the land of Severius, on the north the boundary is the land of Irtin-Asi of (?) Mosmosi, on the east everything belongs to the plot in ...

On the south is the land of Iezekiasi, and on the north is the land of Eiongi the Priest;

On the northeast is the acacia plantation one third is mine, in the thorn patch one third is mine, in the dried-up water-course one third is mine, in the plot of Douwwi a half is mine (I hold it together with Enomedjou);

On the south is the land of Anieion-Asti, and on the north is the land of Enon-Asti, in the cotton field (?) and in the cultivated depression of the orchard everything is mine;

On the south is the land of Anieion-Asti, and on the north is the land of the Peter-Church, there is 1 plot in the cotton field (?), one third is mine;

On the south is a stone for threshing (?), and on the north is the land of Ñejin-Asi, and there are 2 plots in ... of the orchard of tassi-trees, one third is mine;

On the south is the land of the Ñejin-Asi, and on the north is the land of the Peter-Church, and the name of the plot is 'That which is Datti's,' (consisting) of 1 plot;

On the south the boundary is the 'Mud (?) of the Animals,' and on the north is the land of the Jesus-Church.

The price that I received is, firstly: 1 male camel named 'Nubian,' 1 ornamental precious stone, 1 silver ring. I entered (into the agreement) without assistance. And moreover it is 1 slave (that I received). And the eye-witnesses to this are:

Sonoja-Thôma, son of Papsi,
Darme, Makihil (?)
Darme, Ouataphil,
Touskonkouda, son of Koudin-Pesa,
Tapara, Priest,
Darme, Priest,
Ornourta, Priest,
Napre, Priest,
Iêsousinkouda, Archdeacon,
Soñoja, Deacon,
Ajola, Deacon,
Anil,
Anaĉ,
Barin-Ogja, Deacon,
Chaêl-Soñoja,
Papi, Priest,
Tapara, Bishop of Ori,
Zachari,
Eiramil,
Eio,
Iskoei,
Isê, son of Abrami,
Eiodisi, Priest of the Jesus-Church of Kaki.

What they ate and drank is: 5 *pati* of *touskil*, 1 *komi* of wine, 1 *komi* of *anapiti*, 100 loaves, 1 jar of *gide* in ... of one kettle.

I, ordering Aera and Loukasi son of Zôsima to write this certified document, witnessed it.

I, Massouda, Deacon, who has the George-Church of the West, assembling and sitting with my elders, wrote and witnessed.

If one writes, deposits and proclaims the certified document, (his fee) is 1 roast of lion (?); if he does not eat, it is 1 *komi* of *anapiti*, 1 *pati* of *touskil*.

(Docket) The certified document concerning the property of Kapopi of Ibrîm.

Sale of church-land[6]

It is written in the name of the Father, the Son and the Holy Spirit, on the 4th of Tobi, on the 7th of the moon, it being year 915 (of the era) from the Martyrs, Basil being King of Dotawo, holding also the office of Keeper of the Granaries,

[names of the Queen Mother and seventeen other officials follow]

I, Ñonnen, daughter of Mêna, sell to Massouda Choiak-eiksil 1 plot—which consists of the 4th plot—at the 4 feet of the altar in the Stauros-Church of Mosmosi, a plot which I inherited from my father. And the price that I received from the hand of Darme, Timakkis, is 6 (pieces of) gold. And the witnesses of this are, firstly:

[names of Papo Mêna, Bishop and eleven other witnesses follow]

And I, Iôdisi, Great Priest and Timakkis, ordered to write, wrote and witnessed.

[6] Excavation number 74.1.30/6, no. 9a. For the official translation and commentary see Browne, *Old Nubian Texts*, III.

(Appendix)

As for the testimony of Ñonnen, the witnesses of the fact that Persi and her mother bought the plot of the Stauros-Church are:

[names of seven witnesses follow]

We sold it ... to Masal, and the witnesses of the one who purchased the plot of the Stauros-Church this (?) year are those mentioned in this document.

Sale of land[7]

As for Enomariamê, daughter of Pella, who inherited her share in the palm grove (?), which comprises one palm tree in their land: her people bought it, and those who bought it are:

Titta, being from her children, whom they ... -ed,
Kona-Awisil, being from her children, who ... -ed,
Tourki, being from her children,
Kapopi, daughter of Papsinen, being from her children,
Sonoja, son of Dollisil, being from her children,
Kitol, being from her children,
Dyssan, being from her children,
Doulousta, being from her children, whom they ... -ed.

The witnesses:

[names of Ajjeje, *Ñess* of Atwa, and thirteen other witnesses follow]

Each and everyone who is in the town of Addo are witnesses; all the people of the town are witnesses.

Cession of land

The document translated below seems to be the only one of its kind:

Cession of land[8]

I, Mouhoumeti, with his friend Teulote, say to his son: regarding his land that lies both on the west and on the east, giving it to Massouda, Choiak-eiksil, for 2 (pieces of) gold, I cede it to him for 5 years. And afterwards, giving him his wages (?), I shall release him from any other work (?) that arises thereafter (?) from this land. And the witnesses of this are:

[names of Mena, Bishop, and eleven other witnesses follow]

I, Ajola, Deacon, wrote and witnessed. The Timakkis ...

Rental of land

An Arabic document found in 1974 appears to be a contract for the rental of land.[9] While it has not yet been fully translated, Elizabeth Sartain provides the following information:

'... as far as I can tell, a Nubian official is sub-letting part of his Egyptian landgrant (*iqta'*) on a Nile island to a tenant farmer, for one year. The letter accompanying this contract appears to be a report by the Nubian's son (or agent? ...) on the unsatisfactory state of affairs on his land—it looks as if his tenant has been driven off and a less worthy farmer has taken his place, and the plough has been removed from the island.'[10]

Sale of unspecified property

Sale[11]

I, Isakê, representative of Maia, write in the name of the Father, the Son and the Holy Spirit: to Mariamê, I—the nation have taken [witnesses?]—sold that which is the possession of hers and mine, and to Oeila, her husband sold that which is from the children, and I did not put anything of mine in the children's sale. The witnesses of this are, firstly,

[names of Papo Marian, Bishop of Kourte, and ten other witnesses follow]

I, Tillinminne, wrote and witnessed. Whoever of Mariami's scribes will disparage me by saying that I am not the writer (?) of my document, may he become estranged from God, and may what is in the 7th seal (?) of the Apocalypse come forth against him.

Donation of property

Donation[12]

I, Pasine—since the Mary-Church of Ibrîm seeks me—gave (my) share, eight (pieces of) gold, to my brother and his wife. Truly if my father asks, I will give to him. Let whoever will deny this give 20 (pieces of) gold. The witnesses of this are:

[names of eight witnesses follow]

Release from sale contract

Release from sale[13]

It is written in the name of the Father, the Son and the Holy Spirit, King Moses, Koudil, being King of Dotawo,

[names of the Queen Mother and seven other officials follow]

I, Tiri, and my son Eno have written this: We release Eigali—the nation having approached [as witnesses?]—from the pur-

[7] Excavation number 74.1.30/6, no. 23. For the official translation and commentary see Browne, *Old Nubian Texts*, III.

[8] Excavation number 74.1.30/6, no. 11. For the official translation and commentary see Browne, *Old Nubian Texts*, III.

[9] Excavation number 74.1.29/11, no. 4.

[10] Personal communication from Elizabeth Sartain.

[11] Excavation number 74.1.30/6, no. 13. For the official translation and commentary see Browne, *Old Nubian Texts*, III.

[12] Excavation number 74.1.30/6, no. 26. For the official translation and commentary see Browne, *Old Nubian Texts*, III.

[13] Excavation number 74.1.30/6, no. 4. For the official translation and commentary see Browne, *Old Nubian Texts*, III.

chase made in God's name and amounting to 16 (pieces of) gold. And he himself, not liking it and getting rid of it at a 50% loss, gave it back to us, without denial. And the witnesses of this are, firstly,

[names of Soueti, *Meizoterus* (?) and eleven other witnesses follow]

I, Ajola, Deacon, wrote and witnessed on behalf of Adama. And whoever will deny this utters a denial against God. Let him be cursed and not blessed.

Release of slaves and servants

One of the eparchal archives in House 177[14] included two unusual documents written on leather. One is clearly an order for the manumission of a slave, who was henceforth to have the status of a 'Nubian.' The second document is more problematical; it seems to involve the release of a servant (or slave?) to the charge of another man.[15] The following is a translation of the first document:

Release of a slave[16]

In the name of the Father, the Son and the Holy Spirit, George Moses the King, Papelli, being King of Dotawo,

[names of the Queen Mother and five other officials follow]

And the word of God being secure in the whole [nation (?)].

I, Kapopi of Ibrîm, releasing this slave, Apa, keep him as a Nubian. He is amongst those who wish (to be free). And he does not have his son (with him). And if he frees his son, with God's help I will cause him to accompany him. And whoever will cause me to enslave him, may he become estranged from God, and may the seventh seal (?) come forth against him, and let him die through the King's curse. And the witnesses of this are:

[names of the son of the Bishop of Ibrîm, Sonoja, and nineteen other witnesses follow]

I, Darme, Great Priest, wrote and witnessed this document.

Deposition

The document translated below does not appear to have been part of a deliberately preserved archive. It was found in the rubbish deposits in House 763, the residence of the Eparch Isra'il. The original is written on paper, in Old Nubian

Deposition[17]

In the name of the Lord! This is the testimony of Iosephi, the Great Scribe of Kush (?), which Kosma gave, and which his daughter Marime spoke:

First, writing a letter to Megali, who is (?) soñoj, having given it to the horn-dealers (?), I wrote, in the presence (?) of Chael, saying that he should give us the price. And Megali sent a letter, saying that they hastened in a boat, with orders to receive the horn-dealers (?). And I sold it to Israel at the appropriate (?) time. And Israel—while I sat in another garb of mourning (?)—had it taken away. And after he deposited it in the village, sitting for 2 months, he eats dates, gulping them down. And I wrote a letter to him, saying: 'And after the horn-dealers (?)—as you acted wrongly (?)—deposited it through the deputy of the soñoj, where were you up to the time when it was received?' And after they themselves informed me, I went onto the boat in which they came to see. Israel, putting me in the boat, went to the Ñonnen, acting wrongly (?) himself, and after he himself went, reaching the 9th village in the 5th day, he caused much to be done. After he recrossed (?) the water, I wrote him a letter, and coming in shame (?), I did not receive the price.

Iosephi, the Great Scribe, is witness.

[names of six other witnesses follow]

Property lists

The larger of the two eparchal archives buried in House 177 (74.1.30/6)[18] included three documents on paper that appear to be property lists. They are not witnessed and do not have the same formulaic character as do the legal instruments that have previously been discussed; nevertheless they should probably be classed in the broadest sense as legal documents. Two of them are mere listings of names, followed by numbers; in one case there are names of churches as well as of private individuals. A much more detailed document gives a listing of lands and other properties owned by the Jesus-Church of Touggili. This text is of extraordinary interest both because it refers to several different kinds of productive properties, and because these seem to have been rather widely dispersed in different parts of Lower Nubia. Translations of the list of church properties and of one of the other lists are given here:

[14] Listed in Part 4, Chapter 1 as archive no. 3.

[15] Excavation number 74.1.30/6, no. 6. For the official translation and commentary see Browne, *Old Nubian Texts*, III.

[16] Excavation number 74.1.30/6, no. 18. For the official translation and commentary see Browne, *Old Nubian Texts*, III.

[17] Excavation number 82.1.25/19B. For the official translation and commentary see Gerald M. Browne, *Old Nubian Texts from Qaṣr Ibrîm*, II (Egypt Exploration Society, Texts from Excavations; in press).

[18] Listed in Part 4, Chapter 1 as archive no. 3.

List of church holdings[19]

These are the lands of the Jesus-Church of Touggili that are in Nobadia, firstly:

1 water-wheel in Tamit East, which belongs to the Michael-Church of Ibrîm: on the south the boundary is the land of Tamitikon-Asti, on the north the boundary is Lower Tamit;

1 water-wheel north of the meadow (?) in Tamit East: on the north the land of Tamitin-Asti, on the south the boundary is the land of Silimokki, encompassing the property of the Domesticus of Faras in the enclosure (?) on the island of Arminna, until it comes to the land of Iraein-Asti; there is 1 water-wheel;

1 water-wheel in Ibrîm: on the north the boundary is the Raphael-Church of Kopagi, on the south the boundary is Lower Penti;

1 water-wheel in Tonde: on the south the boundary is the land of the Kollouthos-Church, on the north the boundary is the Michael-Church of Toundi;

1 water-wheel in Sirin-Gisir, Ibrîm West: on the south the boundary is the land of the Apostles-Church, on the north the boundary is the land of the Gabriel-Church of Ibrîm;

6 streams (?) above the wide watercourse, Ibrîm North: on the north the boundary is the land of the Kollouthos-Church, on the south the boundary is the land of the George-Church of Ibrîm West;

1 clay-area (?) in Ibrîm: on the south the boundary is the land of Silimokki, on the north the boundary is the land of Pase;

2 fertilized areas (?) in Getti East: on the south the boundary is the high cornfield, on the north the boundary is the land of Epousin-Asti.

4 plots in the inlet (?) that belongs to the Andrew-Church of Touggili, in the depression of black iron (?);

[added entries below are in a different hand]

1 plot in front (?) of Sirin-Gisir: on the south the boundary is the land of Mousen-Asti, on the north the boundary is the land of Anion-Asti;

1 plot above the depression of Merkios: on the south the boundary is the land of Eisapen-Asti, on the north the boundary is a depression.

Itemized list[20]

Firstly: Tapara's: 1 (piece of) gold, 20 *dirhems*, wine
Darme's (who is from Gettin Gappitti): 6 (pieces of) gold
Titta's: 3 (pieces of) gold
Papasi's and Isou-Aggikouda's: 36 *dirhems*
Temsi's and Titta's: 31 and a half *dirhem*
Massouda's: 2 (pieces of) gold, 7 *dirhems*, a *morena* of wine
Ornourta's: 11 and a half
Sonoja's and Eirota's: 31 and a half

[next two entries written in another hand]

And Titta's (the daughter of Naei): 37 and a half
And Darme's: 1 (piece of) gold

[last three entries written in the same hand as first eight]

Nilêsa's: 35, wine
Einitta's: 23, in garlic (?)
And Nilêsa's: 12.

[19] Excavation number 74.1.30/6, no. 22. For the official translation and commentary see Browne, *Old Nubian Texts*, III.

[20] Excavation number 74.1.30/6, no. 24. For the official translation and commentary see Browne, *Old Nubian Texts*, III.

CHAPTER 5
COMMERCIAL TEXTS

MANY of the Old Nubian documents discussed in the last two chapters are concerned in the broadest sense with economic matters. It is a striking fact, however, that mediaeval documents relating specifically to commerce, i.e. to the commercial exchange of goods other than land, are almost exclusively in Arabic. It is difficult to escape the impression that the mediaeval Nubians were not a mercantile people, and that commerce was largely in the hands of itinerant and resident Arab traders.

Archived documents

The Fatimid period was a time of especially close relations, both diplomatic and commercial, between the Egyptian and Nubian governments,[1] a fact which is confirmed by the large volume of Arabic correspondence found in the Classic Christian levels at Qaṣr Ibrîm.[2] This cordial relationship evidently ceased during the Ayyubid regime, following the destructive raid of Shams ed-Dawla in 1172–73. At any rate there are no major archives of Arabic diplomatic or commercial documents from the Late or Terminal Christian levels. A small group of letters was found in the eparchal House 177,[3] but the two specimens which are dated belong to the late Fatimid (i.e. Classic Christian) rather than to the Ayyubid period. Since they were found in a Late Christian archaeological context, however, the possibility exists that some of the documents may be of post-Fatimid date. The contents of the letters have been thus summarized by Elizabeth Sartain, the translator:[4]

1. Letter: from Muslim merchant to son. Concerning consignment of spices, aromatics, and ?dyestuffs.
2. Letter: probably to eparch, from ? Compliments and best wishes in flowery style.
3. Letter: from ? to ? (Muslim merchants). Writer requests help to ensure the return of servants who ran away from him in Nubia, and other personal matters.
4. Contract: rent of land by Muslim from Nubian official, dated 1124–5.
Letter: from Muslim to same Nubian official, concerning some problem connected with the rented land.
5. Letter: from Muslim merchant to family, to tell them of his safe arrival in Soba, dated 1092–3.
6. Letter: probably to eparch, from ? a Kanzi, in official style, requesting return of two ... (slaves?) according to existing agreements.
Letter: difficult to piece together... Arabs, horses, Kanz al-Dawla are mentioned.
7. Letter: to Ubaydallah, Secretary of the Eparch, from ? a Kanzi, requesting letter confirming him in the possession of his territory.
8. Contract: frightful handwriting...I can only make out that it concerns the Nubian *mawla* (freedman, probably) of a *qadi*, dated 1121–2.

Fragmentary documents

Although the volume of official commercial correspondence from the Late Christian period is small, there is nevertheless a very large number of fragmentary Arabic texts (see table 16), most of which came from one or another of the eparchal houses (table 13). Their content can be determined only in a very few cases, but it seems likely, in view of what we know from the previous period, that many, if not most, relate to commercial dealings. Whether they involve official or private commercial dealings is, of course, conjectural.

[1] See Stanley Lane-Poole, *A History of Egypt in the Middle Ages* (London, 1901), 137–46.

[2] For discussion see Plumley in Kazimierz Michalowski (ed.), *Nubia, recentes recherches* (Warsaw, 1975), 106–7.

[3] Listed in Part 4, Chapter 1 as archive no. 4.

[4] Personal communication dated 7 January 1985.

CHAPTER 6
RELIGIOUS AND MAGICAL TEXTS

THE texts that are here classified as religious are all presumed to be canonical or formulaic, though in one or two cases they represent the only known exemplar of the text in question. Magical texts are included in this chapter also, since they are not numerous enough to warrant a separate chapter. However, texts relating to the organization of the church and its property have been classified as administrative rather than strictly religious, and are dealt with in Part 4, Chapter 3.

By far the most numerous and most interesting religious texts from Qaṣr Ibrîm have come from the Classic Christian levels; they were part of the apparently very extensive ecclesiastical library destroyed by the raid of Shams ed-Dawla in 1172–73. Many of the destroyed texts were found on the floor of the Cathedral,[1] others were deliberately or unintentionally dumped at various other locations on the site.[2] A collection of the Old Nubian religious texts has recently been published by Plumley and Browne,[3] and a few others have been published individually.[4]

By contrast, the Late and Terminal Christian levels have yielded fewer than two dozen texts that can be recognized as religious. All of them are fragmentary and were recovered from refuse deposits rather than from deliberately preserved caches. At least some of the texts may again be remnants of the Cathedral library, which accidentally found their way into the later deposits. The overwhelming majority have come from the LC1 levels, dating just after the Shams ed-Dawla raid, and the writing in several cases suggests a substantially earlier origin, perhaps in the in tenth or eleventh century. Indeed, there is no single religious text from the Late and Terminal Christian levels whose origin in this late period is certain.

Religious texts from the Late and Terminal Christian levels fall into four categories: Biblical fragments, non-Biblical Christian texts, Islamic canonical texts, and magical texts. Christian canonical texts are variously in Greek, Coptic, and Old Nubian; Islamic texts are in Arabic; magical texts are in both Old Nubian and Arabic. A descriptive list of the religious texts from Late Christian levels is given in table 19.

Biblical texts

Six Biblical fragments have been recovered. They are all on parchment and are evidently the remnants of much larger books. From the Old Testament there are fragments of Deuteronomy in Greek and of the Psalms in Old Nubian;[5] from the New Testament there are passages from Luke and John in Coptic, and from Mark and Jude in Old Nubian.[6] For further detail on these texts see table 19.

Non-Biblical Christian texts

A summary list of non-Biblical Christian texts is also given in table 19. Among those written in Old Nubian, there are three that are worthy of particular note, as follows:

Florilegium

Florilegia were a common *genre* of Byzantine literature, representing a kind of anthology of the most salient writings or sayings of particular individuals.[7] The specimen found at Qaṣr Ibrîm is preserved in three separate fragments, comprising in each case a pair of consecutive pages. Pages 32 and 33 lack the lowermost portions; pages 36 and 37 are complete and the final two pages lack the page numbers but are otherwise complete. The fragments thus cannot be joined to yield a continuous text, though they are obviously all parts of the same document. The translation of the surviving portions follows:[8]

(pages 32–33)

... as we (or: you) will be (?) finally in joy (?), because of the support of the great (?) ...

[1] For the original report of the find see Plumley, *JEA* 50 (1964), 3.

[2] See Plumley, *JEA* 52 (1966), 11 and pl. VI; Plumley and Adams, *JEA* 60 (1974), 214 and pls. XLII–XLIII; Plumley, Adams and Crowfoot, *JEA* 63 (1977), 44.

[3] J. Martin Plumley and Gerald M. Browne, *Old Nubian Texts from Qaṣr Ibrîm*, I (Egypt Exploration Society, Texts from Excavations, Ninth Memoir) (London, 1988).

[4] e.g. Plumley, *Sudan Texts Bulletin 2* (1980), 34–41.

[5] For translations and commentary on the latter see Gerald M. Browne, *Old Nubian Texts from Qaṣr Ibrîm*, II (Egypt Exploration Society, Texts from Excavations; in press).

[6] For translations and commentary on the latter see op. cit.

[7] See K. Krumbach, *Geschichte der byzantinischen Literatur*, 2nd ed. (Munich, 1897), 217–18.

[8] Excavation number 78.1.21/31 (= NI 5). For the official translation and commentary see Browne, *Old Nubian Texts*, II.

TABLE 19
RELIGIOUS TEXTS FROM THE LATE AND TERMINAL CHRISTIAN PERIODS

Excavation number	Sup. no.*	Description of content	Language	Material	Pub. ref.†
Biblical passages					
84.2.16/12A		Deuteronomy 32: 15–17 and 21–22	Greek	Parchment	
78.1.30/1 78.1.31/6	NI 35 NI 51	Psalms 26, 46, 83, 86, 90	Old Nubian	Parchment	1
84.1.24/15		Mark 11:1	Old Nubian	Parchment	2
82.2.23/90		Luke 13–25	Coptic	Parchment	
82.2.14/88 82.2.16/35		John 18:21	Coptic	Parchment	
78.1.21/32	NI 26	Jude 9–16	Old Nubian	Parchment	3
Non-Biblical texts					
78.1.19/13	GI 10	Eulogy on Michael	Greek	Parchment	
78.3.1/5	GI 21	Martyrology	Greek	Parchment	
78.1.23/11	GI 8	Hymn	Greek	Parchment	
76.2.28/16		Prayer book	Greek	Parchment	
76.2.25/21		Bilingual service book	Greek + Old Nubian	Paper	
82.2.28/2		Homily on Michael and the Devil	Coptic	Parchment	4
78.1.23/11	NI 21	Homily on Michael	Old Nubian	Parchment	5
78.3.13/12	NI 76	Encomium	Old Nubian	Parchment	6
78.1.21/31	NI 5	Florilegium	Old Nubian	Paper	7
78.1.21/30	NI 4	Theological text ?	Old Nubian + Arabic	Paper	
Unidentified					
69.2.9/1		???	Greek	Parchment	
69.2.10/8		???	Greek	Parchment	
72.10.24/13		???	Coptic	Paper	
Islamic texts					
82.1.28/14		???	Arabic	Paper	
82.2.25/34		???	Arabic	Paper	
Magical texts					
78.1.30/7	NI 16		Old Nubian	Paper	
78.2.12/65	NI 44		Old Nubian	Paper	
78.3.1/11	NI 58		Old Nubian	Paper	
78.3.4/31	NI 64		Old Nubian	Paper	
82.2.8/75		2 *Higab* texts	Arabic	Paper	

*Supplementary number
†Published translations and commentary as follows:
1. Gerald M. Browne, *Old Nubian Texts from Qaṣr Ibrîm, Vol. II* (Egypt Exploration Society, Texts from Excavations; in press).
2. Op. cit.
3. Op. cit.
4. Lafontaine in *Le Muséon*, vol. 92 (1979), 37–60.
5. Browne, op. cit.
6. Op. cit.
7. Op. cit.

And this is what he said, intending to release us from the servitude to sins through that to Jesus Christ: 'Perform servitude to the Lord, like (?) those who sit in fear and trembling,' David said ...

[about four lines missing at this point]

... being about to perform servitude to the Lord, as he said: 'It is good to hope in the Lord.' Let us not proceed, performing servitude to men, lest we enter onto the path of the desire of their evil. Let us not follow the eye's desire. The eye's (?) desire ...

[about four lines + two pages missing at this point]

(pages 36–37)

Because of envy sin has obtained power, and death has become king. Because of envy a good tree has produced bad seed. It is because of envy that they shed the blood of the innocent. He who has an envious and wrathful man as brother has as brother a poisonous serpent. However, he is good who, having (such a one), becomes king of the serpent and controls it; for whoever loves goodness is one who is in God's love and that of God's angels. But if he becomes anxious, he cannot see any illness. The sons of evil, ruling in evil through envy, place a blow upon the sons of God. He ...

[additional text missing at this point, including last page numbers]

... amongst those whom they will cause to assemble at last, because of ... seeing my affliction and my humility, he forgave me my every sin.

And this is what he said concerning holiness: Brothers, the Holy Book has said: 'Great is the holy man.'

And also, teaching, it says: 'Continue to become holy, because I am holy.' Let them testify until death, and let them keep our tribe from every form of destruction, as it is in the saying of Moses, the great prophet ...

The translator suggests that Chrysostom or pseudo-Chrysostom may be the original inspiration for the above quoted text.[9]

Encomium

This is a single fragment of parchment, bearing a text in Old Nubian on both sides. Neither the top nor the bottom of the page is preserved. According to the translator the text is an unidentified encomium, whose phraseology shows parallels to a number of known Greek texts:[10]

(*flesh side*)

... of one who has faith. Let us glorify his commemoration. For God himself who rules over all is also with us, together with the myriads of his holy angels, together with the archangels, together with ...

(*hair side*)

... together with the ... martyrs, the saints ..., the child-bearing women, together with the virgins, joyfully (?) ..., all the saints who are in the Old and New Testament: now, coming together in assembly, the powers from heaven ... the great ...

Homily on Michael

This text is preserved on a fragment of parchment which has on the opposite side a Greek hymn. The restoration of the text is largely hypothetical.[11]

... Truly, the one who has much gives joyfully according to his ability. But if I do not in fact have much, let me not go, being in poverty, but (?) receive the small offering of one who does not have much, who believes that Jesus Christ died on our behalf—as you see the good ... that our Lord caused (?) you to ... And now, desiring the heavenly instead of the earthly, through the request of the archangel Michael, who has kept our hearts for God and Lord ... our works joyfully ...

Homily on St Michael and the Devil

Unlike the three specimens previously discussed, this text is in Coptic. It comprises two almost complete, but non-contiguous, parchment folios, bearing portions of a homily on St Michael and the Devil.[12] A complete Coptic version of the same text is in the Pierpont Morgan Library in New York (M 592) and has recently been published by Lafontaine.[13] The first of our two folios contains most of the following text:[14]

I.2. The matter is marvellous and too difficult for man to understand. However, your love forces me and my mind has been at a loss how I might be able to approach to this great topic which no one understands except the angels who see these very things in which you force me (to be engaged).

3. Pray, therefore, with all your sons before the Lord, that He send to me power from on high and open for me the portal of the word and the understanding and revelation of this great mystery in order that it may become clear that the words of the heretics are empty and their thoughts and their teacher Mani are filled with confusion.

4. Since you said that they told you that they established Michael (in power?) after they threw out the Devil, I say that the Devil is unworthy and that he never had this kind of respect and, what is more, he was never ever called an archangel. Moreover, some heretics have said that when God created Adam he ordered the whole legion of angels to come and adore man whom God had created. You won't tell me, will you, that it is necessary in God's eyes for a spirit to adore the earth. They claim, therefore, that He summoned the Devil to adore man. Mestema, who is the Devil, did not agree to adore man. On this account he was cast out of Paradise and Michael was set up in his place.

[9] Op. cit., 61.

[10] Excavation number 78.3.13/12 (=NI 76). For the official translation and commentary see op. cit.

[11] Excavation number 78.1.23/11 (=NI 21). For the official translation and commentary see op. cit.

[12] Excavation number 82.2.28/2, A and B.

[13] For the original Coptic text and a translation into Latin see Lafontaine, *Le Muséon* 92 (1979), 37–60.

[14] The English version presented here has been prepared at my request by Professor Louis Swift of the University of Kentucky, based on the Latin translation of Lafontaine (op. cit.). Numeration of the paragraphs follows that of Lafontaine.

5. Oh these words, full of blasphemy and of blasphemies which heretics conjure up in their minds.

II.1. But you, oh man of God, flee from all these words which are empty. Give me a mind which is awake and ears which hear well this theme, while we consider your prayers which have been directed to us according to God's will. Your heart will be convinced about this question which you asked us, and afterwards it will become apparent to you that the whole system of the heretics' thought has no substance.

II.2. And your heart will be filled with this word that God was not at peace with the Devil when He created man. Because of the wickedness and perversity that was in the Devil's heart, he was opposed to God and to the order of angels before God created man, nor did the Devil know when God created Adam.

3. Come now to us, oh great priest of Moses, and teach us the things which are appropriate and inform us and direct my mind and our hearts to this theology which is deep and full of every mystery.

4. For it is written in Genesis that in the beginning God created heaven and earth. But the earth was not visible and the things pertaining to it had not yet been created. And the spirit of God moved over the waters. God, however, created all the heavenly angels to praise Him in song. The first creature, however, is the Devil.

5. The earth, however, was brought from the waters but was not yet visible. Before man was created on the earth, God did not yet divide the waters: one part (of the waters) was in the depths of the earth; the other part over the firmament. Darkness was spread over the depths of the earth.

Our second folio contains most of the following text:

IV.5. God took earth from earth; He created Adam and placed him in Paradise. He took Eve from the side of him whom he created.

6. When the Devil saw man, he trembled in fear and struck him. He did not know what he was doing, but he came close to see what man was and where he was. He saw that man is more beautiful than all the creatures and all the living things that God created.

7. The Devil marveled and said, 'Great is the injustice done to me. I have left heaven; I have come to this place to rule, and in order to rule and in order that my power might be exercised over myself and over my followers. Behold God has created in this place another king whose form I do not recognize. He is neither an angel, nor without a body, as we are. But, behold, I see that God comes, asking for him each day and loving him. I will sit down in this place until I know what is the nature of this form.'

V.1. The Devil did as he intended. He sat down with all those who are his companions from Paradise.

2. God came seeking Adam. God said to Adam, 'Behold I have given you every tree that is in Paradise in order that you may eat from all of them, and I have given also the Tree of Life, which is in the middle of Paradise. But from the Tree of the Knowledge of Good and Evil you shall not eat because on the day in which you eat from it, you will die.'

3. When, therefore, the Devil heard these things, as God spoke to Adam, he rejoiced and said, 'I know that God hates disobedience. I will approach Adam and speak to his heart, and I will see whether he will eat from the Tree of Knowledge of Good and Evil so as to die, and I will rule in this place without opposition.'

4. The deceiver approached Adam. He was not able to get near him because of the glory which surrounded him, but he approached the serpent and entered into him, and the serpent was made his instrument, and he approached Eve and spoke to her.

Although it was found archaeologically in a Late Christian context,[15] this document is clearly a survival from much earlier times. Lafontaine has estimated a sixth or seventh century date for the original composition.[16] The sermon is evidently directed against the Manichaean form of dualism, and is meant to instruct the hearers in regard to the correct place of the Devil in Christian theology.[17]

Islamic texts

Two fragmentary Arabic texts found in 1982 were identified by Professor Martin Hinds as religious in character, but no translation is available for either.[18]

Magical texts

Fragmentary magical texts both in Old Nubian and in Arabic have been recovered from the Late Christian levels. Probably these were originally contained in *higabs,* i.e. they were sewn up in small leather pouches and worn by individuals for protection (see Part 3, Chapter 8). The Old Nubian specimens exhibit two characteristics that are common also in Greek magical papyri of an earlier period: certain letters, and especially vowels, are repeated in a seemingly meaningless progression, and some of the repeated letters are drawn with small circles appended to their extremities.[19] One fragment may be tentatively rendered as follows:[20]

[15] House 211, Room 1, in the refuse fill above the uppermost occupation floor.

[16] Lafontaine, op. cit., 39–40, n. 1.

[17] Op. cit., 38–9.

[18] Excavation numbers 82.1.28/15 and 82.2.25/34.

[19] See Hans Dieter Betz, *The Greek Magical Papyri in Translation* (Chicago, 1986).

[20] Excavation number 78.3.4/31 (= NI 64). Translation furnished by courtesy of Gerald M. Browne (personal communication).

A man of bad birth...
OOOOO AAAAA
EEEE EE
EEEE EE
EEE...
EEEE
EEE
EEE

One magical text employs a combination of Old Nubian and Coptic.[21]

The excavation catalogue for 1982 lists also two *higab* texts in Arabic,[22] which have not yet been translated.

[21] Excavation number 78.3.4/31 (= NI 64).
[22] Excavation number 82.2.8/75

CHAPTER 7
PERSONAL CORRESPONDENCE

AMONG the Old Nubian and Arabic texts from Qaṣr Ibrîm there are a good many fragments, and a few whole documents, that appear to be personal letters. The following are two Old Nubian specimens:

Letter to the daughter of Eiteine[1]

I greet (you). First: Except for you (?), I have had no one. You have I held like mother and like sister, and I praise (you) through (our) relationship. You do not know what the son of Doue is like. May he not come and ruin you. For your sake, take (him) and put (him) away. And I am going. I greet my mother. She is with me indeed. I broadcast (this fact) and send joy. When the people from the west and from the east arrived, they came with a proclamation (?) from my father: 'There is no empty letter for one who does not praise who your father is.' In truth, I pay homage to my son Jak (?); I pay homage to all who are assembled.

(Address) O daughter of Eiteine!

Letter from Basileios to Israel[2]

In the name of God! I inform you that your letter came on Sunday. When you hear, O holy one, do not be dejected (?); for I shall go. Sit together (?) and don't lose (?) heart when I go. Sit together; for (otherwise) I shall not sleep. I pay homage to Geo(rgi), I greet the shoemaker. Douññen ( ) sends his greetings.

Address) Basileio(s), friend ... to Israel, domesticus of Pachoras

[1] Excavation number 84.2.20/40. For the official translation and commentary see Gerald M. Browne, *Old Nubian Texts from Qaṣr Ibrîm*, II (Egypt Exploration Society, Texts from Excavations; in press).

[2] Excavation number 82.1.25/19. For the official translation and commentary see op. cit.

CHAPTER 8
THE EVIDENCE OF THE TEXTS

The late mediaeval textual finds from Qaṣr Ibrîm will undoubtedly furnish material for scholarly interpretation and debate for generations to come. For the time being they may be said to enrich our picture of mediaeval Nubian life without significantly clarifying it, inasmuch as they raise perhaps as many questions as they answer. This chapter will attempt, in a very general and preliminary way, to identify both some of the questions and some of the answers that they raise.

Politics and administration

The largest number or documents recovered from Qaṣr Ibrîm are official in one sense or another; to that extent they should all shed some kind of light on political conditions. Nevertheless, the evidence that they provide is in many ways baffling. At the outset we are confronted with a bewildering profusion of officials and titles, without any indication as to what their functions were. There seem too to be several different, partially interlocking bureaucracies, whose relationship to one another is far from clear. Only a few of the most salient problems presented by the administrative texts can be considered here.

The Kingdom of Dotawo

Throughout all of the late mediaeval texts from Qaṣr Ibrîm there is only a single mention of the Kingdom of Makouria, the nominal suzerain to which all of Nobadia was subject.[1] On the other hand the Kingdom of Dotawo is mentioned over and over again, in texts dating back at least as early as the eleventh century, and continuing until near the end of the fifteenth. But when we turn to the mediaeval Arabic accounts of Nubia, precisely the opposite is true: Makouria (al-Muqurra) is named repeatedly, but there is no single reference to Dotawo.[2] In the circumstances, the possibility that Dotawo is merely the local name for Makouria cannot be ignored.[3]

The Ibrîm texts provide evidence both for and against an identification of Dotawo with Makouria. Between 1155 and 1191 we have documents naming Moses George, George Moses, Moses, and George as King of Dotawo[4]—all of whom may or may not be the same individual—at a time when a George and a Moses are known to have ruled at Dongola.[5] A century later, however, we have a Piarl, a George Simon, and a Siti named as Kings of Dotawo,[6] at a time when Shekenda, Barak, Shemamun, and Abi Abdallah Kanz al-Dawla are known to have ruled at Dongola.[7]

Further evidence against an identification of Dotawo with Makouria is provided by the royal proclamation of Moses George discussed in Part 4, Chapter 3.[8] Here we find the king intervening in a relatively minor and strictly local administrative dispute at Qaṣr Ibrîm, which can hardly have interested the ruler at Dongola. Moreover, the various officials who are named in the document, as well as the witnesses, are all the same individuals who are mentioned in many other Old Nubian documents, and who were clearly local residents at or near Ibrîm. There can be little doubt, therefore, that the royal proclamation was issued in the general area of Ibrîm.

We must note, however, that while the King of Dotawo is named in more than two dozen documents, he is the author of only two of them, and there are no examples of epistles addressed to him. On the other hand, we have a large number of documents written by or addressed to the Eparch of Nobadia. This suggests that the king, although evidently resident somewhere in the area, was not installed at Ibrîm itself. The best hypothesis is probably still the traditional one, that the King of Dotawo resided at Gebel Adda (Addo in the Ibrîm documents), and indeed the name 'Dotawo' may be derived from 'Addo.'[9]

The question of how the Kingdom of Dotawo related to the Kingdom of Makouria is perhaps answered by the information, provided by two mediaeval Egyptian authors, that the High King of Nubia had thirteen lesser kings under his jurisdiction.[10] It is evi-

[1] See William Y. Adams, *Nubia, Corridor to Africa* (London, 1977), 462–71.

[2] See Giovanni Vantini, *Oriental Sources Concerning Nubia* (Heidelberg and Warsaw, 1975), 804–14.

[3] This is the belief of Ahmed Al Bushra (personal communication), but it is specifically denied by Stuart Munro-Hay, *Kings and Kingdoms of Medieval Nubia* (MS), 32.

[4] Plumley in *Études nubiennes, colloque de Chantilly, 2–6 Juillet 1975* (Institut français d'archéologie orientale, Bibliothèque d'étude, Vol. 77) (Cairo, 1978), 234–5.

[5] Munro-Hay, op. cit., 21–2.

[6] Plumley, *Études nubiennes,* 235.

[7] Munro-Hay, op. cit., 32.

[8] Excavation number 74.1.30/6, no. 2.

[9] See Adams, *Nubia*, 534–5.

[10] See Plumley, *Études nubiennes,* 239.

dent, in any case, that the suzerainty of Makouria rested rather lightly on the people of Ibrîm, since it is never mentioned in the texts. For the people of Lower Nubia the local King of Dotawo must have been a far more important figure than the distant potentate at Dongola, if we can judge by the number of textual citations.

A more difficult question concerns the relationship between the King of Dotawo and the Eparch of Nobadia, since in this case there can be no doubt that the two exercised authority within the same territory. In the various legal texts in which both king and eparch are named, the name of the king always heads the list, while that of the eparch usually occurs rather far down, after the queen mother and various tricliniares, potentiaries (?), and other officials. Yet it can hardly be doubted that the eparch was the most important person resident at Ibrîm itself. Moreover, he was not directly subject to the King of Dotawo but was appointed by, and was the personal representative of, the King of Makouria, as is made evident by Arabic letters addressed to him. The best suggestion is probably that the king and the eparch held dominion over clearly distinct spheres of activity, the king being the main source of civil and legal authority while the eparch was responsible for trade and for relations with Muslims in general.[11]

The Eparchate of Nobadia

Old Nubian texts from Qaṣr Ibrîm suggest that the Eparch of Nobadia was not the only eparch resident in Lower Nubia, for an Eparch of Palagi is also mentioned. The latter office was held at one time by the King of Dotawo himself.[12] It seems clear, nevertheless, that the Eparch of Nobadia was far more important than any other, and was something more than a *primus inter pares.* [13] He is the only eparch about whose responsibilities and activities we have any specific information, for he is mentioned repeatedly both in the Ibrîm documents and in previously known Arabic sources.[14]

The Qaṣr Ibrîm texts have raised an intriguing problem with respect to the Eparch's title. In Arabic documents the term 'eparch' never appears. The title which occurs most often in its stead can be read, in unpointed texts, either as 'Lord of the Mountain' (*sahib al-jabal*) or as 'Lord of the Horses' (*sahib al-khayl*). Until recently the reading 'Lord of the Mountain' was almost universally preferred, and it appears even in some pointed Arabic texts where the reading is unmistakable.[15] However, among the Qaṣr Ibrîm letters there are some addressed to the Eparch in pointed Arabic, in which the reading 'Lord of the Horses' is equally unambiguous. Two even give the title as 'Lord of the King's Horses.' This has led some scholars[16] to the conclusion that 'Lord of the Mountain' involves a misreading on the part of both mediaeval Arab chroniclers and their modern translators. However, Browne has recently observed that titles equivalent to both 'Lord of the Mountain'[17] and 'Lord of the Horses'[18] occur among the Eparch's Old Nubian honorifics. It seems clear therefore that no misreading has occurred; the Eparch simply enjoyed both titles—along with a great many others. Indeed, the Ibrîm texts suggest that the mediaeval Nubians had a passion for collecting titles, like earlier Egyptians.

In more than half of the Ibrîm legal documents the Eparch of Nobadia is named also as Domesticus of Faras. However, the conjunction was not an automatic one, for there are two documents that name a Domesticus of Faras different from the eparch. Other titles borne by some of the eparchs were those of Eiksi of Douksin, and Silentiary (?).[19] There is nothing in any of the texts to suggest that the eparchal office was ever hereditary, as has sometimes been suggested.[20]

One rather enigmatic document names Gabrielinkouda as Eparch of Nobadia '... holding all authority over Nobadia, Adama the Eparch establishing him in the Church of the Holy Trinity in the Town of Ibrîm.'[21] There seems to be an implication here that Adama nominated his own successor. However, in several later documents Adama continues to appear as Eparch, while Gabrielinkouda is named as Silentiary(?),[22] which must mean that Gabrielinkouda was no more than a temporary replacement for the regular Eparch, perhaps while the latter was away on business. Since we know that the eparchal functions were not primarily

[11] See Adams, *Nubia*, 464–6.

[12] As specified in the royal proclamation (74.1.30/6, no. 2) translated in Part 4, Chapter 3.

[13] Cf. Ibn Selim al-Aswâni, quoted in Adams, *Nubia*, 466.

[14] Usually under the title 'Lord of the Mountain' or 'Lord of the Horses;' see Vantini, *Oriental Sources*, 478–9, 602, etc.

[15] Op. cit.

[16] Plumley, *JEA* 56 (1970), 14; Elizabeth Sartain, personal communication.

[17] Old Nubian *soñoj*, equivalent to modern Nobiin *sa-ñajj*. See Gerald M. Browne, *Old Nubian Texts from Qaṣr Ibrîm*, III (Egypt Exploration Society, Texts from Excavations; in press), Introduction.

[18] Old Nubian *mourtin nodil* (personal communication from Gerald M. Browne). See also Browne, *Altorientalische Forschungen* (in press).

[19] This is Gerald M. Browne's less-than-certain translation of Old Nubian *gottamet(t)* (personal communication).

[20] Adams, *Nubia*, 466.

[21] Document 74.1.30/6, no. 6, dated A.D. 1288. See Browne, *Old Nubian Texts*, III.

[22] Document 74.1.30/6, nos. 1 (undated), 8 (A.D. 1200), and 9 (A.D. 1199). See Browne, *Old Nubian Texts*, III.

religious, the establishment of Gabrielinkouda in the Church of the Holy Trinity (which cannot be identified archaeologically) must mean that the acting eparch used the church as his official headquarters.

The eparch's official functions can be inferred to some extent both from the direct content of his correspondence, and from the kinds of documents that he retained in his archives. Clearly the promotion and supervision of international trade, between Egypt and the Kingdom of Makouria, was his single most important responsibility. In this capacity he acted as the personal agent of the Makourian king, and possibly of the King of Alwa as well.[23] But other documents suggest that the eparch was generally responsible for the welfare and protection of all Muslims within the territory of Nobadia, whether engaged in trade or permanently settled as landholders.

The disbursement of grain was evidently another important eparchal activity. It is not clear, however, whether in these circumstances he was acting in a public or in a private capacity; that is, whether grain was being paid out from public stores, or from his own private stores, as an aspect of his commercial dealings. Finally, the keeping of legal archives was evidently an eparchal function, even though he himself does not appear in any of the documents as a source of legal authority or judgment.

What emerges most clearly from the Ibrîm texts is that the eparch was, first and foremost, responsible for dealings with Egyptian Muslims, and these evidently included the fulfillment of the provisions of the *Baqt* treaty. The supervision of trade with Makouria, the protection of Muslims resident or travelling in Lower Nubia, the provision of slaves, and the return of runaway slaves are all matters of concern in the letters to and from the eparch, and they are all matters covered in the treaty.[24] The eparch was resident in Lower Nubia because this was the area where, under the terms of the treaty, Muslims were free to travel and to settle, but he was responsible to the king at Dongola because the latter was the original signatory to the treaty.[25]

An unresolved mystery concerns the survival of the eparchal office into the fifteenth century—after the disintegration of the Kingdom of Makouria.[26] Eparchs seem to be mentioned in a number of Old Nubian legal documents, dating as late as 1464,[27] yet there was certainly no king at Dongola, or probably even at Soba, who could have appointed them.

The bureaucratic officials

The Ibrîm texts present us with a prodigious roster of official titles, many of which have not previously been reported. Some are recognizably Byzantine titles, though it cannot safely be inferred that their holders performed the same functions as did similarly titled individuals at Byzantium itself.[28] Others are purely Nubian titles, which can nevertheless be translated into known English equivalents. Particularly enigmatic among these is the term 'shoemaker,' which occurs several times in contexts suggesting that it was some kind of title. Yet the reading 'shoemaker' seems secure, at least with reference to the meaning of the same words in modern Nubian.[29] There remains finally a large residue of Nubian titles that for the time being cannot be translated, since the meaning of the titles themselves is not clear, and nothing is known about the functions of those who bore them.

It may be further observed that some titles, like *domesticus,* are always associated with places (*Domesticus* of Faras, *Domesticus* of Tafa, etc.), others like *tricliniaris* are associated with hierarchic superiors (*Tricliniaris* of the Eparch, *Tricliniaris* of the *Domesticus* -elect, etc.), some may be associated either with places or with hierarchic superiors, and some, like *architriclinus* and *oeconomus*, never appear with any ascription. A complete list of bureaucratic titles, and the contexts in which they occur, is given in table 20.

Among the various titles it is possible to recognize a civil and an ecclesiastical bureaucracy, though some titles could perhaps be either civil of ecclesiastical. With such a proliferation of titles, however, the question also arises whether more than one civil hierarchy may be represented. It is possible that some of the named officials were dependents of the Makourian king, some of the King of Dotawo, some of the Eparch of Nobadia, and some, perhaps, of the Bishop of Ibrîm. The suggestion conveyed is not so much that of an organized bureaucratic hierarchy as of a vast patronage network, or more probably an interlocking set of patronage networks, rather like the court officialdom of ancient Egypt.[30] Elizabeth Sartain writes that 'It would appear that the ruling families of the region, whether Christian/Muslim Arabs/Egyptians or Christian/Muslim Nubians are all very closely linked by diplomatic, commercial, personal and evidently also marriage relationships. There is nothing unusual about this; it is the normal Middle Eastern mediaeval

[23] Adams, *Nubia*, 466; Plumley in Kazimierz Michalowski (ed.), *Nubia, récentes recherches* (Warsaw, 1975), 106.

[24] See Adams, *Nubia*, 451–2.

[25] Op. cit.

[26] Op. cit., 531–9.

[27] cf. especially Registration number 64/23, and Plumley, *Études nubiennes,* 234–5.

[28] See Ugo Monneret de Villard, *Storia della Nubia cristiana* (Pontificium Institutum Orientalium Studiorum, Orientalia Christiana Analecta 118) (Rome, 1938), 189–91.

[29] Old Nubian *soulouwi,* modern Nobiin *sulu* (personal communication from Professor G. M. Browne (15 Feb. 1988).

[30] Cf. Pierre Montet, *Eternal Egypt* (New York, 1968), 94–6.

TABLE 20
OFFICIAL TITLES MENTIONED IN QAṢR IBRÎM DOCUMENTS

	Associations[1]		
Title	Persons	Places	None[2]
Translatable titles:			
King (*Ourou*)	—	Dotawo	+
Queen mother (*Ñonnen*)	—	—	+
Keeper of Granarics (*Souñi*)	—	—	+
Great Scribe (*Sountouwe dauoul*)	—	Kush (?)	+
Epistolary Scribe (*Epistolin sountouwe*)	—	—	+
Scribe (*sountouwe*)	Eparch	—	+
Byzantine titles:			
Eparch (*Soñoj*)	–	Nobadia, Lower Nobadia, Palagi	+
Vice-eparch (*Sonñojou mar*)	—	Terpi	+
Domesticus (*Samet*)	—	Faras, Tafa	–
Domesticus-elect (?) (*Sametiño*(*l*))	—	—	+
Architriclinus (*Odñol daoul*)	—	—	+
Tricliniaris (*Odñol*)	Eparch, *Domesticus*-elect, Bishop	Douksi, No	–
Oeconomus (*Nok*(*k*) *eidñil*)	—	—	+
Silentiary (?) (*Gottamet*(*t*))	Nobadia	—	+
Potentiary (*Irt*)	Non-nokko, Nopkol, Sikkolti	—	–
Meizoterus (*Dau*(*ou*)*katt*)	Adau, Ibrîm	—	+
Untranslatable Nubian titles:			
Asti	Bishop	Nal	–
Choiak-eiksi	—	—	+
Eiksi	—	Douksin	+
Gouad	—	—	+
Goukarko	—	—	+
Goush	—	Masmas, Tharmousi, 'Town' (= Ibrîm?)	–
Kash	—	—	+
Koña	—	—	+
Koud	—	Nassa (?)	–
Ñess	*Domesticus*, *Domesticus*-elect	Nobadia, Atwa, Eistipi, Koudketi, Kourk, Mame, Odjo, 'Town' (= Ibrîm?)	+
Ñeshshigaueikkol	—	Nal	+
Outaphil	—	—	+
Siren	—	'Town' (= Ibrîm?)	–
Timakkis	—	Faras	+
Thel	—	Katkine	–
Tot	—	Addindan, Addo, Arminna, Faras, Ibrîm, Irten-Nal, Kisdawo, Kodippe, Michaelko, Motiko, Nal, Nissin-Nal,Tamit, Toshka, Ymo	–

TABLE 20 (*continued*)

Title	Associations[1]		
	Persons	Places	None[2]
Ecclesiastical titles:			
Bishop (*Papas*)	—	Ibrîm, Kourte, Ori, Sai	+
Great Priest (*Sorto daoul*)	—	—	+
Priest (*Sorto*)	—	—	+
Archimandrite (*Greek form used*)	—	—	+
Archdeacon (*Greek form used*)	—	—	+
Deacon (*Greek form used*)	—	—	+
Liturgist (*Jalligatt*)	—	—	+
Chartelarius (*Greek form used*)	—	—	+
Elder (*Gort*)	*Domesticus*	—	+
Fire-Sacrificer (?) (*Eigla mosil*)	—	—	+

[1] Persons or places with which the title is sometimes associated

[2] + means that the title sometimes occurs without association with a person or place; — means that the title never occurs except in association with a person or place

pattern, where the different religious and ethnic groups were closely interlinked by a variety of relationships.'[31]

There are some Nubian titles, particularly *tot* and *ñess,* that appear to be quite localized; the *tot* in particular might be comparable to the *omda* of today. The authority of such individuals could have derived from local tradition rather than from royal or eparchal appointment. However, there is no clear indication that any office was hereditary, except that of King of Dotawo. It seems that the organization of the mediaeval state was primarily bureaucratic rather than feudal.[32]

The Beni Kanz

From the twelfth to the fifteenth century the Beni Kanz were, intermittently, the scourge of Upper Egypt, and at times their hostility was directed against Makouria as well.[33] Their base of operations was in the far north of Nubia, within what was traditionally the territory of Nobadia. Since the Beni Kanz were naturally warlike, and since they were Muslim while the Nubians of Dotawo and Makouria were Christian, they might have been expected to feel a special hostility toward their southern neighbours, as in later times the Kenzi Nubians (descendants of the Beni Kanz) did toward the Mahas-Fadidja Nubians who dwelt to the south of them.[34] However, there is no suggestion of hostility between them and the Christian Nubians in the Ibrîm texts. Relations between the Kanz ed-Dawla, the leader of the Beni Kanz, and the Eparch of Nobadia were entirely friendly, and those Beni Kanz emirs who lived within the territory of Nobadia evidently acknowledged the authority of the eparch just as did his Christian subjects. There is no mention of any relationship between the Beni Kanz and the King of Dotawo, which may indicate that the far northern reaches of Nubia did not lie within the traditional confines of Dotawo.

International relations

Relations between Fatimid Egypt and the Nubian kingdoms were particularly cordial, as we know from contemporary Egyptian sources,[35] and this is reflected in much of the correspondence found at Ibrîm.[36] At the outset of Ayyubid rule the amicable relationship was shattered when Shams ed-Dawla pillaged Ibrîm (see

[31] Personal communication from Elizabeth Sartain.

[32] For discussion see S. N. Eisenstadt, *The Political Systems of Empires* (New York, 1963).

[33] See Adams, *Nubia*, 524–5, 531–2.

[34] Cf. J. L. Burckhardt, *Travels in Nubia* (London, 1819), 138.

[35] See Stanley Lane-Poole, *A History of Egypt in the Middle Ages* (London, 1901), 132–92.

[36] See Plumley in *Nubia, récentes recherches*, 106.

Part 1, Chapter 2), yet peace was shortly afterward restored, and was not again seriously threatened for more than a century. However, there is no correspondence between Nubian and Egyptian officials that can be dated with certainty to the Ayyubid period, and it seems clear that relations with Egypt were never again quite as close as they had been earlier.

Nowhere in the Late Christian documents from Qaṣr Ibrîm is there any direct reference to the political or diplomatic relations between the Nubian and Egyptian monarchies. It is particularly surprising that there is no single mention of the raid of Shams ed-Dawla, in spite of the enormous damage that it wrought at Ibrîm. It can only be supposed that the conduct of international relations was strictly the affair of the king at Dongola and did not concern either the King of Dotawo or the Eparch of Nobadia.

The economic sphere

If a high percentage of the mediaeval Nubian documents are in some sense political or administrative, it is also true that most of them shed some light, in one way or another, on economic conditions. There is information specifically in regard to land tenure, agricultural production and crops, local barter, and commercial relations with Egypt.

Land tenure and exchange

The Ibrîm texts give a picture of the Nubian land economy that hardly differs from that of modern times.[37] Land was held in innumerable, individually owned small plots, and the holdings of any individual (or of a church) might be widely dispersed in different areas. Despite the legal fiction that all land belonged to the king,[38] it seems that in fact plots were freely salable, though it is possible that the consent of the eparch or some other official may have been required. This at least is suggested by the retention of land sale contracts in the eparchal archives. The price of land was evidently rather low, since in two cases a plot was exchanged for one piece of gold and one piece of silver,[39] and one woman exchanged a whole series of parcels for a camel, a ring, a jewel, and a slave.[40] *Saqias* are mentioned in many of the land-sale documents, and clearly were as essential to the Nubian agricultural economy in mediaeval as in modern times.[41]

The local economy

Although Egyptian currency circulated legally in Nobadia,[42] it is evident that the country did not have a fully monetized economy. This is suggested both by the extreme scarcity of Islamic coin finds (in contrast to the enormous numbers of Roman coins found in earlier levels) and by the relative scarcity of documents referring to monetary transactions. Money seems to have changed hands chiefly in sales of land; transactions of such moment that they were routinely attested by ten or more witnesses, and the contracts of sale were retained in official archives for decades afterward. Probably money was much more a form of storable wealth than an everyday medium of exchange.

It can be inferred from the Ibrîm documents that the local economy operated largely on the basis of barter, as it did when Burckhardt visited the region 500 years later.[43] The commodity most often mentioned in Old Nubian documents is grain, which clearly in some cases was given in exchange for services or in payment of debt. There are references specifically to wheat, barley, and millet, as well as several letters referring to 'grain' without specifying the kind. In addition, several fragmentary letters mention 'bushels,' which presumably would have meant either grain or dry legumes such as lentils. Wine also appears as a commodity of exchange in two documents. In a number of instances the witnesses to legal documents were provided with bread, wine, and other foodstuffs; whether this should be regarded as a fee, or merely represents the feeding and entertainment of the witnesses while the document was being executed, is uncertain.

Units of currency which are mentioned in the land sale documents and property lists include 'pieces of gold,' 'pieces of silver,' and *dirhems* (*tirami* in Old Nubian). It is evident that these are not interchangeable terms, for one property record lists separately the holdings of the individuals in 'pieces of gold' and in *dirhems.* [44] 'Pieces of gold' and 'pieces of silver' seem moreover to have been of rather considerable value, since in two instances a parcel of land was exchanged for one of each.[45] Given the fact that no actual denomination or issue is named in the case of 'pieces of gold'

[37] See especially Hassan Dafalla, *Sudan Notes and Records,* vol. 50 (1969), 63–74, and id., *The Nubian Exodus* (London, 1975), 68–83.

[38] See Adams, *Nubia,* 463; also Laszlo Török in *Études nubiennes, colloque de Chantilly, 2–6 Juillet 1975* (Institut français d'archéologie orientale, Bibliothèque d'étude, 77) (Cairo, 1978), 296–7.

[39] Document 74.1.30/6, nos. 8 and 16.

[40] Document 74.1.30/6, no. 7.

[41] See especially Hassan Dafalla, *The Nubian Exodus* (London, 1975), 71–3, and Adams, *Nubia,* 51–3.

[42] Cf. the mediaeval account of Ibn Selim el-Aswâni, quoted in Burckhardt, *Travels,* 493–5.

[43] Op. cit., 137; see also Shinnie in *Études nubiennes, colloque de Chantilly, 2–6 Juillet 1975* (Institut français d'archéologie orientale, Bibliothèque d'étude, 77) (Cairo, 1978), 255–6.

[44] Document 74.1.30/6, no. 24.

[45] Document 74.1.30/6, nos. 8 and 16.

and 'pieces of silver,' whereas *dirhem* are mentioned by name, the possibility exists that the pieces of gold and silver were not coins at all, but were unminted ingots of metal. However, gold dinars are specifically mentioned in Arabic documents from the Fatimid period found at Ibrîm.[46]

Foreign commerce

Texts having to do with trade in manufactured goods, rather than with land sales or with the barter of grain, are almost exclusively in the Arabic language. This circumstance tends to suggest that the mediaeval Nubians, like their nineteenth century descendants,[47] were not much inclined toward commerce, leaving it for the most part in the hands of resident and itinerant Egyptian traders.[48] It is nevertheless evident that the supervision of this commerce was one of the principal duties of the Nobadian eparchs.

The commodity most often mentioned in Arabic documents is cloth, which evidently included both bolt goods and finished garments. Dye-stuffs, perfumes, and spices are also mentioned; all of these were clearly imports from Egypt to Nubia. Several Arabic letters mention slaves, though, as previously noted, the number of references is not as great as might be expected in view of the supposed importance of the slave-trade in the Nubian export economy.[49]

What is perhaps most gratifying about the Qaṣr Ibrîm commercial documents is the extent to which they confirm the testimony of mediaeval Arab travellers and writers. The *Baqt* treaty of 652, as recorded by Maqrizi,[50] had enjoined upon the Nubians the duty of providing safe conduct to Muslim merchants, and also of returning runaway slaves to them. Both of these considerations figure importantly in the Arabic letters to the eparch. Some mediaeval writers state also that the Nubians were to receive wine, barley, lentils, clothes, and horses from the Egyptians as their portion of the *Baqt* agreement;[51] all of these commodities are mentioned in the Ibrîm correspondence. Finally, Ibn Selim el-Aswâni had reported at end of the tenth century that Moslem merchants travelled freely in Nobadia, and even settled there, and that money was in circulation, whereas no merchant or cargo could pass onward into the territory of Makouria without the written permission of the king.[52] All of this is confirmed in the Ibrîm documents, though it is evident that the king's permission was granted, *de facto,* by the eparch.

The structure of society

Ethnic groups

Undoubtedly, the great majority of people in the Ibrîm region were Nubians, of the dialect group which may still have been called Nobadian in late mediaeval times, but which later would be called Nobiin (or Mahas-Fadidja).[53] These people were probably the sole inhabitants of most villages. Yet the Ibrîm texts make it clear that in Lower Nubia there were also resident and itinerant Egyptian traders,[54] and there may as well have been priests or bishops of Egyptian origin among the Nubian clergy.[55] Moreover, some members of the Islamic Beni Kanz had already settled in the far north, adding further to the ethnic diversity in Lower Nubia. The fact that the Beni Kanz emirs wrote to the Eparch of Nobadia in Arabic rather than in Nubian suggests that the Kenzi dialect was already too distinct from the Nobadian to be mutually intelligible.[56] Finally, such slaves as were present would probably have been drawn from the non-Nubian populations to the south or west of Nobadia and Makouria; this is implied by a deed of manumission in which a freed slave is henceforth to have the status of a Nubian.[57] We have, therefore, to picture an open, partly multi-ethnic society, with members of diverse ethnic groups probably resident at Ibrîm itself.

It is rather curious to find, among the Ibrîm documents, no reference to the Beja or to any of their individual subgroups, considering the large part that these peoples played in earlier Nubian history, and particularly at Ibrîm itself.[58] It may be that the Beja settlers in late mediaeval Nubia were assimilated into the Beni Kanz.[59]

The family and kinship

In modern times, all of the Nubian groups have exhibited a modified version of the patriarchal extended family,[60] which is found in one form or another among Arab peasants nearly everywhere.[61]

[46] Personal communication from Elizabeth Sartain.

[47] See Burckhardt, *Travels*, 132–48.

[48] Cf. op. cit., 493–5; Adams, *Nubia*, 60.

[49] See Adams, *Nubia*, 451–3, 471; Török in *Études nubiennes*, 298.

[50] See Burckhardt, *Travels*, 511–12.

[51] See op. cit., 512.

[52] Op. cit., 493–5.

[53] See Adams, *JEA* 52 (1966), 153–5; id., *Nubia,* 48.

[54] See also Burckhardt, *Travels*, 493.

[55] Adams, *Nubia*, 480, 485.

[56] For discussion see Adams, *JEA* 52 (1966), 153–5.

[57] Document 74.1.30/6, no. 18.

[58] See Adams, *Nubia*, 56–60.

[59] Op. cit., 524.

[60] Op. cit., 563–9.

[61] Op. cit.

However, there is no hint of any such corporate unit in the mediaeval texts. Land and other property holdings are always listed in the name of individuals, not of families, and it is evident that husbands, wives, and even children could own and even sell land and other property independently of one another. Notable too is the general absence of patronymics in the documents; they seem to be used only when necessary to establish the identity of particular individuals. This suggests that the ideology of familism was not particularly prevalent among the mediaeval Nubians, again in contrast to the situation in more recent times.[62]

Slaves

Slaves do not figure prominently in the mediaeval texts from Ibrîm, and they are mentioned much more often in Arabic than in Old Nubian documents. There is one deed referring to the receipt of a slave as part of the payment for several plots of land,[63] but it appears that the same individual was subsequently freed by his mistress.[64] It might be inferred that slaves were much too valuable for the trade with Egypt, and/or much too necessary to fulfill the conditions of the *Baqt* treaty, to permit the Nubians the luxury of retaining any number of slaves for themselves. Probably such few slaves as were present at Ibrîm were mainly personal servants.

Law

Legal instruments and formulae

The mediaeval Ibrîm documents convey the impression of a rather legalistic society, placing heavy emphasis on the maintenance of appropriate forms and formulae and on the keeping of records over long periods of time. In the case of land sale contracts, the execution of a deed in the proper legal form seems to have been a more important consideration than giving a very precise description of the property involved. The importance that was attached to land sale contracts is attested by the fact that they were commonly written on skin rather than on paper and were retained in the eparchal archives for periods exceeding fifty years.

The formula for nearly all land sale contracts begins by invoking the name of God, the Father, the Son, and the Holy Spirit. This is followed in many though not in all cases by the date of the document, which is given both in Coptic and in lunar months. The year is somewhat less often specified than is the month and day; when it is given it always relates to the Era of the Martyrs rather than to the Birth of our Lord.

The opening invocation is invariably followed by the naming of a long list of currently serving officials, beginning always with the King of Dotawo and the Queen Mother, followed by anywhere from two to seventeen other functionaries who are listed both by name and by title. These people are not identified as witnesses to the document, and in some cases can hardly have been aware of its existence. In the broadest sense, their naming appears to be part of the invocation; that is, it confers legitimacy on the document in the same way as does the opening invocation in the name of God.

Following the list of officials there is a relatively brief description of the land that was sold and the price paid for it. The metes and bounds of the property are rarely specified in any detail, which could suggest that disputes over land boundaries were not usually a problem. The typical document then concludes with the names of anywhere from five to thirty witnesses, always listed by name but frequently also by title. There is mention in several documents of the bread, wine, and other foodstuffs that were given to the witnesses in payment for their services. Sometimes also an elaborate curse is laid upon anyone who shall deny the legality of the instrument.

Apart from land deeds, there are a few other documents that exhibit a similar legal formula. One relates to a sale of unspecified property, and two to the release of slaves.

Inheritance law

The numerous contracts for the sale of land give the impression that laws in regard to inheritance were not very rigid. Yet there are indications that parents were not entirely free to dispose of their children's patrimony. In one of the sales contracts cited in Part 4, Chapter 4, a woman states that she is free to dispose of the property inherited from her mother because she is 'barren in respect to daughter and son.'[65] The frequency with which this same woman claims a one-third share in various properties suggests too that she had received her portion as part of some kind of standard inheritance apportionment, perhaps comparable to that which is found in Islamic law.

Religion and the church

By all indications Qaṣr Ibrîm in the Classic Christian period was a great centre of religious learning and

[62] See especially Adams in Mahjoub el-Bedawy and David Sconyers (eds.), *Sudan Studies Association Selected Conference Papers 1982–1984* (Washington, 1985), 40–51.

[63] Document 74.1.30/6, no. 7.

[64] Document 74.1.30/6, no. 18.

[65] Document 74.1.30/6, no. 7.

TABLE 21
CHURCHES MENTIONED IN QAṢR IBRÎM DOCUMENTS

Ibrîm	*Kaki*	*Touggili*
Apostles	Jesus	Andrew
Gabriel		Jesus
Holy Trinity	*Kopagi*	
Mary	Raphael	*Location not specified*
Michaal		Jacob
Peter	*Masmas*	John (?)
	Stauros	Jesus of the Mountain
Ibrîm West		Mena
Epimachus	*Toundi*	
Gabriel	Michael	
George		
Kollouthos		

activity; perhaps the most important one in Lower Nubia, since Faras seems to have been in decline after the eleventh century.[66] The Shams ed-Dawla raid of 1172–73 must have dealt a severe blow to the religious life of the community, involving as it did the wholesale destruction of documents and damage to many of the church buildings. Yet it is possible to conclude from the Old Nubian legal texts that the church was still thriving, at least in an organizational and an economic sense, at the beginning of the 13th century. The documents mention no fewer than twenty churches in the general vicinity of Ibrîm: six at Ibrîm itself, four at Ibrîm West (presumably across the river), and eight in other nearby localities (see table 21).

It is evident too that the churches owned very substantial amounts of land. We are exceptionally fortunate in possessing an itemized list of the holdings of the Jesus Church of Touggili, which was preserved among the eparchal archives in House 177.[67] The church properties included no fewer than five *saqias,* which evidently included also the land irrigated by them, since they are described in terms of territorial boundaries. The document is somewhat unclear in regard to other properties of the Jesus Church, but they seem to include six streams (?), one clay-area (?), two fertilizer areas (?), and at least four other plots. These various holdings were scattered at least from Tamit to Ibrîm (a distance of almost 50 km) and were located on both sides of the Nile. That the Jesus Church was not exceptional in its land holdings is suggested by the fact that lands belonging to six other churches are mentioned in the same document. Another property list seems to refer to sums of money owned by, or owed to, certain churches.[68]

Whether the church remained an important spiritual force in late mediaeval times is more problematical. Documents written to or by the priests are concerned largely with secular and administrative affairs, and there is a notable absence of the purely religious texts that were so prevalent in the earlier middle ages. There seems to be little doubt, at any rate, that the destruction of the cathedral library ended Qaṣr Imbrîm's role as a centre of religious learning. The absence of pilgrim's graffiti from the later Christian period is also suggestive in this regard.[69] In general, the textual evidence from Ibrîm tends to confirm the impression, conveyed also by architectural evidence, that the later mediaeval period was an increasingly secularizing age.[70]

The clerical officials

Among the clerical officials named in various Ibrîm documents are bishops, great priests, priests, archdeacons, deacons, elders, a liturgist, a *chartelarius*, and someone who seems to have had the pagan-sounding title of 'fire-sacrificer'[71] (table 20). For the most part these individuals appear only as witnesses to, or writers of, documents, and nothing else is said about them. Only the bishops and a few priests are associated with specific places; there are references to bishops of Ibrîm, Kourte, Sai, and Ori. It is noteworthy that there is no mention of a Bishop of Faras, suggesting that this once-famous see had already gone out of existence by Late Christian times.[72]

Among the witnesses to one document there appears the name of Papasa, 'Archimandrite of the Archangel Michael,'[73] which presumably means that he headed a monastery dedicated to the archangel. The location of the monastery is not given. Apart from this one reference, there is no mention of monks or monasteries in any of the Late Christian documents from Qaṣr Ibrîm, suggesting, as does much other evidence, that Nubian monasticism was very much in decline in the later mediaeval period.[74]

[66] See Adams, *Nubia*, 467–8.
[67] Document 74.1.30/6, no. 22.
[68] Document 74.1.30/6, no. 21.
[69] Cf. Plumley and Adams, *JEA* 60 (1974), 235; Plumley in Paul van Moorsel (ed.), *New Discoveries in Nubia* (Nederlands Instituut voor het Nabije Oosten, Egyptologische Uitgaven, 2) (Leiden, 1982), 108–9.
[70] See Adams, *Nubia*, 539–46.
[71] Document 74.1.30/6, no. 6.
[72] See especially Stefan Jakobielski, *Faras III* (Warsaw, 1972), 160–8.
[73] Document 74.1.30/6, no. 2
[74] Cf. Adams, *Nubia*, 480.

PART 5

SYNTHESIS

THE LIFE AND DEATH OF A LATE MEDIAEVAL COMMUNITY

For any archaeologist who is also and primarily an anthropologist, the ultimate goal of excavation is to try and bring the dead past back to life, so that ordinary men and women of today can picture themselves living in those bygone times and circumstances. With that goal in mind, I have tried in this final chapter to frame a kind of historical narrative of Qaṣr Ibrîm during the three or more centuries of the Late and Terminal Christian periods, based on the combination of architectural, artifactual, and textual finds and on what is known from mediaeval Arabic records. The picture as I present it involves a great deal of my own interpretation, and should not be regarded as a statement of established fact.[1]

When the troops of Shams ed-Dawla withdrew from Nubia in 1173, the citadel of Ibrîm was left a smoking ruin. The Cathedral roof had burned and collapsed, along with many of its supporting columns and arches, and the little red brick church alongside was even more severely damaged. Perhaps most disastrous of all, the community's treasured library of religious manuscripts was burned and scattered among the ravaged buildings. Most of the secular houses had suffered also; indeed there was hardly a building on the mountain-top that was left in habitable condition.

Under the Eparch's direction, the people of Ibrîm set about restoring their shattered community. Materials were not at hand for the reroofing of the Cathedral (193), so its fallen columns and arches were not re-erected. Instead they were buried, along with a mass of burned manuscript material, under a newly established dirt floor. From then onward the Cathedral was open to the sky and was perhaps used only for the celebration of special festivals. The red-brick church which had stood alongside the Cathedral was found to be wrecked beyond repair, and its remains were carted away and dumped behind the newly reconstructed girdle wall. Presently a new and simpler church (194) arose in its place, and this became, for a time, the community's main parish church. The old Taharqa Temple-church (287) also was restored to use, although like the Cathedral it was probably open to the sky in the later Christian periods.

[1] For a somewhat comparable reconstruction see C. L. Woolley, *Karanòg, the Town* (Eckley B. Coxe Junior Expedition to Nubia, Vol. 5) (Philadelphia, 1911), 6–9.

Of all the buildings on the mountain-top, the eparchal House 763 had suffered the least destruction from Shams ed-Dawla's raiders. It was soon reoccupied, and probably served as the residence of the Eparch who oversaw the work of reconstruction on the site. But other Classic Christian houses that had stood to the west of the Cathedral were never rebuilt. Their charred and ravaged remains were buried under refuse to form an open terrace, upon which there was no further building until the coming of 'Bosnian' troops in the sixteenth century.

Within a short time of the reoccupation, a new eparchal residence (177) was constructed in the formerly open plaza area between the Cathedral and the Temple-church. It was adjoined from the beginning by another stone building (185) which probably housed some of the Eparch's retainers, while a little to the east an older building (178), long buried under refuse, was dug out and put to use as a storehouse. The Eparch's residence was little different from other Nubian dwellings of the same period, comprising an irregular cluster of rather small and airless rooms—which is perhaps why he decided to add a separate, brick-built audience chamber (172) at the south side of his house. This was probably the work of Adam, who served as Eparch during the last twenty years of the twelfth century. He and his successors continued to live in House 177, and to receive visitors in House 172, at least until the end of the thirteenth century.

While the rebuilding of churches and houses required a major effort, an even larger task was that of restoring the ancient and long-neglected girdle wall. For many centuries the Christian inhabitants of Ibrîm had been in the habit of plundering the old fortifications for building stone, secure in the belief that the *Baqt* treaty would guarantee them against any threat from abroad. By the year 1172 only a few courses of the old Ptolemaic and Roman fortifications remained *in situ,* except where there were corners or gates in the older wall. But the raid of Shams ed-Dawla showed the Ibrîmers that their security was no longer assured, and the restoration of the fortifications became a top priority.

The work of reconstruction, directed by the Eparch, continued over a period of several years. Building stone was taken from many of the destroyed houses and churches on the mountain-top, and a great deal of additional material was quarried nearby. As the wall grew upward, the space behind it was simultaneously filled with rubble, so that the wall became a revetment or retaining wall for a nearly level terrace on the mountain-top. As an added safety precaution, the Late Christians concealed the old and long disused South Gateway behind a mass of stone masonry, and they chiselled away the rock-cut steps that had led up to it from below. Along the northern side of the citadel, the cliff face was also deliberately quarried away at several points to make it more nearly vertical. Finally, a gateway was constructed in the eastern portion of the girdle wall, in the same place where the gateway of late Meroitic and X-Group times had been located. This was the main access to the citadel throughout the Late Christian period, although there was also a small postern gate in the western wall, beside the Podium.

During the thirteenth century, the mountain-top was occupied mainly by the Eparch, his retainers, and ecclesiastical personnel connected with the Cathedral. There was a complex bureaucracy of civil and ecclesiastical officials, as well as their families and their personal slaves. A fair amount of both local and international trading activity was conducted by the Eparch, assisted by his Arabic-speaking scribe. In addition, certain manufacturing activities were carried out on the mountain-top—possibly under the Eparch's direction. These included the spinning and weaving of cloth, both of cotton and of wool, and apparently some basket-making, leather work, and perhaps wood turning.

The ordinary folk lived below, along the riverbank, where there were additional churches and where the manufactures of pottery, ironwares, and brick were carried out. Probably also there were storehouses for the various trade goods that arrived by boat from Aswân and from further south in Nubia. It seems, however, that many people had the right to use the fortress for the storage of their grain supplies, for underground storerooms and storage pits were dug all over the mountain-top, wherever there were no actual buildings.

The dwellers on the mountain-top were the elite of Lower Nubia, yet the material circumstances of their lives were hardly different from those of the villagers down below. Their houses, like all late mediaeval Nubian houses, were rather cramped and airless, although at least two of them had a second storey. They had pots, jars, baskets, and many kinds of tools in profusion, but these were the ordinary wares enjoyed by nearly all mediaeval Nubians. It may be, however, that the Ibrîmers were somewhat better dressed than their neighbours; a fair number of them possessed luxury garments of silk or of fine flax, as well as imported leather shoes.

The people of the citadel enjoyed a fairly varied diet of grains, vegetables, and several kinds of meat. Sheep and goats wandered freely through the narrow streets and in and out of the houses, and rubbish was allowed to accumulate as freely as in any peasant village. Larger animals were not kept within the fortress, but horses, donkeys, and camels brought water and supplies up from the riverbank via a winding trail which led up to the East Gate. The eastern end of the mountain-top was kept clear of houses, probably so that cargoes could be discharged and pack animals tethered there. It may have served as a kind of open market area.

Lower Nubia in the thirteenth century still acknowledged the suzerainty of the Kingdom of Makouria, as it had for more than 500 years. The King's local deputy, the Eparch of Nobadia, resided at Ibrîm, and presided over commercial and diplomatic relations with Egypt and with travelling Egyptian merchants. However, local authority was exerted also by the King of Dotawo, a vassal of the King of Makouria, who resided at Gebel Adda, a day's journey to the south of Ibrîm. Ecclesiastical authority was in the hands of the Bishop of Ibrîm and Faras, who like the Eparch resided chiefly at Ibrîm.

Relations between the Nubians and the Ayyubid rulers of Egypt were peaceable if not always very cordial; the very close relationship of Fatimid times was never restored. When the Mamluks came to power in Egypt in 1250, however, they began to intervene actively in Nubian affairs, launching several military expeditions upriver from Aswân in the late thirteenth and early fourteenth centuries. Although Ibrîm was not the specific target of these incursions, the local folk became more and more concerned for their security. As a result, the formerly open area between the Cathedral and the Taharqa Temple-Church gradually filled up with rather ramshackle houses, where the dwellers along the riverbank could take refuge in disturbed times or perhaps could reside permanently. The mountain-top ceased to be the exclusive preserve of the civil and ecclesiastical elite, and became a refuge for ordinary folk as well. In effect, the citadel was transformed from an acropolis to a castle.

In the later fourteenth century the Kingdom of Makouria virtually disintegrated, and parts of its territory fell under the rule of Arab nomads. In the north, the formerly vassal Kingdom of Dotawo now became sovereign in its own right, and Qaṣr Ibrîm as always was one of its two principal centres. The King of Dotawo continued to reside at Gebel Adda, while the principal bishop and the Eparch remained at Ibrîm. Meanwhile the predatory Beni Kanz, a warrior tribe of mixed Beja and Nubian ancestry, became *de facto* rulers both of Upper Egypt and of the most northerly portions of Nubia. Although they never actually threatened Dotawo, their depredations brought the once-flourishing Nile trade virtually to a standstill.

In these impoverished and disturbed circumstances

much of the population of Lower Nubia drifted away, to find refuge in the less vulnerable *Baṭn el-Hajjar* region to the south of the Second Cataract. The Eparch and his retainers held doggedly on, but they now had the mountain-top mostly to themselves. By the end of the fourteenth century all of the old stone houses at Ibrîm had been abandoned and in some cases dismantled, to be replaced by three very large, fortified brick castle-houses (169, 170, 171). Here the Eparch, the Vice-Eparch, the *Domesticus*, the Bishop of Ibrîm, and the other local officials 'holed up,' as it were, until the end of the fifteenth century, presiding over an increasingly impoverished and depopulated land. They nevertheless built themselves a new but very small church (839), perhaps because both the Cathedral and the South Church alongside it had now fallen into disuse. This structure was not erected within the fortress walls, but on a lower terrace outside them—a practice that was very common in late mediaeval Nubia.

In terms of sheer size, the fifteenth century brick castle-houses of the Eparch and his retinue were grander than anything that had preceded them. Yet in all other respects their circumstances were straitened, and they enjoyed fewer luxury goods than had their predecessors at any time in the mediaeval period. Yet somehow they held on at least until the year 1484, maintaining a semblance of order and control in an ever-shrinking island of Christian tradition, while Muslim warlords ravaged the territories both to the north and to the south of them. By the end of the fifteenth century, however, the last traces of civil authority and of Nubia's mediaeval civilization had come to an end, and the great brick houses on the Qaṣr Ibrîm mountain-top stood empty and abandoned. It was an empty fortress which the 'Bosnians' seized when they established Ottoman rule at Ibrîm in the sixteenth century.

APPENDIX A
CALCULATED DATES FOR LATE AND TERMINAL CHRISTIAN POTTERY WARES FOUND AT QAṢR IBRÎM

Ware No.	*Ware name*	*Earliest Appear.*[1]	*Main Production*	*Latest Appear.*[2]
	Family D: Nubian Hand-Made Wares			
Group D. III: Later Christian Domestic Wares				
H4	Later Christian Plain Utility Ware	950	1000–1600 +	?
H5	Later Christian Red Domestic Ware	950	1000–1600 +	?
H6	Late Christian Incised Red Domestic Ware	1150	1350–1600	?
H7	Late Christian Painted Red Domestic Ware	1150	1350–1600	?
H8	Later Christian Black Domestic Ware	?	1000–1300	1500
H14	Late Christian Painted White Domestic Ware	1150	1350–1600	?
	Family N: Nubian Wheel-Made Wares			
Group N. V: Post-Classic Christian Wares				
R21	Post-Classic Christian Polished Orange Ware	900	1000–1200	1300
R22	Post-Classic Christian Matte Red Ware	900	1000–1200	1350
W7	Classic Christian Heavy White Ware	850	850–1250	?
W20	Post-Classic Christian Polished Yellow Ware	900?	1000–1200	1300
W23	Post-Classic Christian Matte White Ware	?	1000–1200?	1300?
Group N. VI: Late Christian Wares				
R11	Late Christian Polished Orange Ware	1100	1150–1500	1600
R17	Late Christian Matte Red Ware	1100	1150–1500	1600
R19	Late Christian Heavy Decorated Ware	1100	1150–1500	1600
W15	Late Christian Matte White Ware	1100	1150–1500	1600
W16	Late Christian Polished Yellow Ware	1100	1150–1500	1600
Group N. VII: Terminal Christian Wares				
R20	Terminal Christian Heavy Red Ware	?	?	?
R26	Terminal Christian Polished Orange Ware	1250	1300–1500	1600
R27	Terminal Christian Dull Orange Ware	?	1300–1500?	?
R28	Terminal Christian Decorated Orange Ware	?	1300–1500?	?
W14	Terminal Christian Decorated White Ware	1250	1300–1500	1600
W18	Terminal Christian Thin White Ware	?	?	?
Group NU: Nubian Coarse Utility Wares				
U5	Christian Red Utility Ware	100	550–1600 +	?
U10	Later Christian Pink Utility Ware	850	1000–1500	1600
U14	Later Christian Slipped Utility Ware	850	1000–1400	1500
	Family A: Aswân Wares			
Group A. IV: Mediaeval Aswân Wares				
R13	Aswân Islamic Plain Red Ware	750	850–1250	1500
R24	Aswân Mediaeval Decorated Red Ware	?	950–1300?	?
W12	Aswân Mediaeval White Ware	750	950–1300	1400
U6	Aswân Mediaeval Grey Utility Ware	700	950–1500	1600
G.V	Aswân Mediaeval Glazed Utility Ware	1300	1350–1450	1500
	Family E: Lower Egyptian Mud Wares			
U21	Mamluk Heavy Utility Ware	1350	1400–1500	?
	Family L: Egyptian Drab Utility Wares			
Sub-family LB: Ballas Wares				
U12	Ballas Drab Utility Ware	400	1100–1500	1600
Sub-family LF: Fostat Wares				
U13	Fostat Ordinary Utility Ware	350	1300–1500	1600
U19	Fostat Decorated Utility Ware	?	1000–1150	?

APPENDIX A—continued
CALCULATED DATES FOR LATE AND TERMINAL CHRISTIAN
POTTERY WARES FOUND AT QAṢR IBRÎM

Ware No.	*Ware name*	*Earliest Appear.*[1]	*Main Production*	*Latest Appear.*[2]
	Family G: Glazed Wares[3]			
Group G. I: Earlier Gloss Wares		900	950–1100	1250
Group G. II: Later Gloss Wares		950	1100–1500	1550
Group G. III: Dull Wares		1000	1100–1500	1550
Group G. IV: Mamluk Wares		1200	1300–1500	1550

[1] Dates of earliest deposits in which some sherds of the ware have been identified

[2] Latest dates at which some vessels of the ware are believed to have remained in use. Stray sherds may be found in deposits of still later date.

[3] Dates given for whole groups only; not for individual wares

APPENDIX B
SYNOPTIC TABLE OF LATE MEDIAEVAL EXCAVATION PROVENANCES AND DATES AS DETERMINED BY CERAMICS[1]

No.	*Structure*	*Whole Bldg.*[2]	*Room 1*	*Room 2*	*Room 3*	*Room 4*	*Room 5*	*Room 6*	*Room 7*	*Room 8*
168	House 168	(No sherd collections)								
169	House 169	(No sherd collections)								
170	House 170									
	Upper fill		LC2	TC	TC					
	Lower fill			TC						
171	House 171									
	Upper fill	TC	TC							
	Floor	TC								
172	House 172		LC2	LC2			TC	LC1		
	Fill									
	Floor 1		LC2							
	Floor 2		LC2							
	Floor 3		LC1							
	Floor 4		LC1							
	Sub-floor	LC1								
173	House 173	(No sherd collections)								
174	House 174	LC2								
175	House 175	(No sherd collections)								
176	House 176	(No sherd collections)								
177	House 177									
	Fill		LC1						LC2	
	Floor 1			LC1	LC1				LC1	
	Floor 2			LC1	LC1				LC1	
	Sub-floor		LC1	LC1						
178	House 178	(No sherd collections)								
179	Structure 179	LC2								
180	Structure 180	(No sherd collections)								
181	Storage crypt 181	TC								
182	House 182	(No sherd collections)								
183	House 183									
	Upper fill		LC1	LC1						
	Level 2			LC1						
	Below Floor 1		LC1							
	Lowest fill			LC1						
184	House 184	(No sherd collections)								
185	House 185	(No sherd collections)								
186	House 186									
	Upper fill	LC2								
	Floor deposit	LC1								
187	Structure 187									
	Floor 1		LC2							
	Floor 2		LC1							
188	Storage crypts 188									
	Dist. upper fill		LC2							
	Lower fill		LC1	LC1						
189	House 189									
	Upper fill				TC					
	Fill to Floor 1		LC1	LC1						
190	Storage rooms 190									
	Below Floor 1		TC							
	Magazine fill				LC1					

APPENDIX B—continued

SYNOPTIC TABLE OF LATE MEDIAEVAL EXCAVATION PROVENANCES AND DATES AS DETERMINED BY CERAMICS[1]

No.	*Structure*	*Whole Bldg.*[2]	*Room 1*	*Room 2*	*Room 3*	*Room 4*	*Room 5*	*Room 6*	*Room 7*	*Room 8*
191	Structure 191	(No sherd collections)								
192	Storage cr. 192	(No sherd collections)								
194	House 194	LC1								
195	House 195	LC1								
197	House 197									
	Upper fill		LC1	LC2			LC1	LC1		LC2
198	House 198	(No sherd collections)								
202	House 202	LC1								
206	House 206									
	Phase 2a	TC								
	Phase 2	TC								
	Phase 1	TC								
207	House 207									
	Upper levels	TC								
	Lowest levels	LC2								
210	House 210									
	Fill									LC2
	Floor 1									LC2
	Floor 2									LC2
211	House 211[3]									
	Fill		LC1	LC1	LC1					
	Floor 1		LC1		LC1					
	Floor 2		LC1							
	Floor 3		LC1							
	Floor 4		LC1							
233	House 233	(No sherd collections)								
235	House 235									
	Fill		LC							
	Floor 1		LC1							
	Floor 2		LC1							
287	Temple-Church									
	Upper fill	TC								
	Lower fill	LC2								
	Floor 1	LC2								
293	Cathedral	(No sherd collections)								
294	South Church									
	Floor 2	LC2								
	Floor 3	LC2								
311	Northwest Bastion									
	Upper levels	LC2								
	Lower levels	LC1								
314	East Gate test	TC								
334	South Rampart St.									
	Uppermost fill	LC1								
356	Central Plaza									
	Uppermost level	TC								
	Middle levels	LC2								
	Lowest levels	LC1								

APPENDIX B—continued

SYNOPTIC TABLE OF LATE MEDIAEVAL EXCAVATION PROVENANCES AND DATES AS DETERMINED BY CERAMICS[1]

No.	*Structure*	*Whole Bldg.*[2]	*Room 1*	*Room 2*	*Room 3*	*Room 4*	*Room 5*	*Room 6*	*Room 7*	*Room 8*
358	West Plaza									
	N.E. Section	LC2								
	Levels 1–2									
	Levels 3–6	LC1								
	N.W. Section									
	Levels 1–2	TC								
	Levels 3–6	LC1								
	Central Section									
	Level 1	TC								
441	Pit 78/37 (441)	TC								
451	Pit 78/57 (451)	TC								
466	Pits 78/62 + 3	TC								
468	Pit 78/64 (468)	LC2								
505	Pits 78/102 + 105	LC1								
517	Pit 78/114	LC2								
763	House 763[3]									
	Fill		LC2	LC2	LC2		LC2		LC2	LC2
	Floor 1		LC1	LC1	LC2	LC2	LC1	LC2	LC1	LC2
	Floor 2		LC1	LC1	LC1	LC2	LC1	LC1	LC1	LC1
	Floor 3					LC1				
764	Plaza 764									
	Level 2	LC2								
766	Storage crypt 766									
	Fill		LC2	LC2						
777	Structure 777	LC1								
781	House 781									
	Fill		LC2	LC2	LC2					
	Floor 1		LC1	LC2	LC2					
	Floor 2		LC1	LC1						
785	House 785[4]									
	Pit fill			LC2						
839	Cupola Church	(No sherd collections)								
848	House 848[3]									
	Upper fill			LC	LC2		LC2			
	Lower fill			LC	LC1		LC2			
	Floor 1			LC1		LC1/2	LC2			
	Floor 2						LC1			
	Floor 3						LC1			
849	House 849									
	Fill		LC2	LC2			LC2			
	Floor 1		LC2	LC2			LC2			
	Floor 2		LC2							
	Floor 3		LC2							

[1] LC1 = c.1100–1300; LC2 = c.1300–1400; TC = c.1400–1500

[2] Where dating is given for a whole building, it applies mainly to post-abandonment fill material.

[3] These buildings also contained earlier deposits from the Classic Christian or even earlier periods, which are not included in the present chart.

[4] Additional sherd data from the 1984 excavations in House 785 are not available at time of writing.

APPENDIX C
COMPREHENSIVE TABLE OF LATE AND TERMINAL CHRISTIAN OBJECT FINDS[1]

Day no.	*Reg. no.*	*Material*	*Object*[2]	*Provenance*[3]	*Date*[4]	*Plate*
			RAW MATERIALS (Part 3, Ch. 1)			
Single palm leaf strips						
82.1.14/156	82/117	Palm leaf	Single strip	H763-R1-Fl 2	LC1	
82.1.13/26	82/570	„	Bundle of strips	H211-R1-Fl 1-P	LC1	
80.2.24/3	82/499	„	„	H211-R3-F	LC1	10a
82.2.28/77	82/499	„	„	H211-R2-F	LC1	
82.1.14/158	82/117	„	„	H848-R1-Fl 3-P	LC2	
82.2.17/61	82/580	„	„	H781-P	LC1	
Plaited palm leaf strips						
82.1.14/76	82/110	„	Plaited strip	H763-R7-Fl 2	LC1	
82.2.14/94	80/1026	„	„	H206-R7-L1	TC	
82.1.14/80	82/113	„	„	P840	LC	
82.1.14/140	82/111	„	„	H849-R1-Fl 2		
82.1.14/155	82/119	„	„	H211-P	LC2	10b
			AGRICULTURE, ANIMAL HUSBANDRY, AND FOOD PROCUREMENT (Part 3, Ch. 2)			
Farming implement						
76.2.29/8	—	Iron	Turiya blade	Pl 358-P	LC1	11a
Riding gear						
74.2.2/11	74/228	Leather	Saddle? (f)	H177-SFl	LC1	
78.2.6/49	78/615	Leather + wood	„ (f)	Pl 358 NW-L5	LC1	
82.1.25/9	82/72	„	„ (f)	H763-R7-F	LC2	
82.1.31/66	82/545	„	Stirrup and strap?	„	LC2	
66.3.14/3	66/376	Leather	Bridle? (f)	H184-SFl	LC1	11d
84.1.7/8	—	Goat hr. + leath.	Saddle girth? (f)	H211-R1-F	LC1	11c
84T/333	86/268	Goat hair	Saddle girth	H785-R4-L4	LC1	43f
Fishing gear						
78.1.17/5	78/21	Iron + palm fibre	Fishhook + line	Pl 358 NE-P	LC	11e
72.10.22/11	72/40	Iron	Fishhook	H186-F	LC2	
78.2.26/31	78/751	Cotton + flax	Fishing net	H196-P	LC2?	11f
Milling apparatus						
82.3.4/120	—	Stone	Quern upper stone	H849-R5-F	LC2	12a
82.3.4/122	—	„	Quern upper stone	H849-R5-F	LC2	
82.3.4/121	—	„	„ (f)	„	LC2	
78.2.6/46	—	„	Conical pounder	Pl 358 NW-L6	LC1	
82.2.27/61	—	„	Oval pounder	H848-R3-SFl 1	LC1	
82.3.3/7	82/284	„	Perforated pounder	H849-R5-SFl 1	LC2	
84.1.24/24	—	„	Spherical pounder	H785-R4-L3	LC1	
84.2.4/42	—	„	„	H785-R11-L1	LC1	
78.1.26/52	—	„	„	H235-F	LC1	
82.2.23/71	82/284	„	Hammerstone	H848-R3-F	LC1	
Strainers						
78.3.12/45	78/107	Basketry	Conical strainer	W283-0-L1b	LC1	12b
78.3.12/45	78/108	„	„ (f)	W283-0-L1c	LC1	
78.3.1/44	78/776	Leather	Sieve (f)	Pl 358-P	LC2	
82.2.8/56	82/490	Horsehair + flax	„ (f)	H763-R8-Fl 2	LC1	
Funnels						
72.10.22/7	72/411	Horn	Funnel	H186-F	LC2	
78.1.26/49	—	„	„ (f)	H235-F	LC1	

APPENDIX C—continued

COMPREHENSIVE TABLE OF LATE AND TERMINAL CHRISTIAN OBJECT FINDS[1]

Day no.	*Reg. no.*	*Material*	*Object*[2]	*Provenance*[3]	*Date*[4]	*Plate*
Spoons and servers						
—	64/19	Bronze	Patera	H169-F	LC1	12d
66.3.8/4	66/81	,,	Small spoon	H185-R5-F	LC1	
74.2.2/13	74/200	Wood	Spoon	H177-SFl	LC1	
72.11.4/2	72/82	,,	,,	H172-SFl	LC1	12c
72.10.22/8	72/412	,,	,, (f)	PL 735-F	LC2	
78.2.12/50	—	Mussel shell	2 Spoons	H202-R7-F	LC1	
78.2.8/78	78/645	,,	Spoon	H235-Fl 1	LC1	
78.1.26/54	—	,,	,, (f)	H235-F	LC1	
			CONTAINERS (Part 3, Ch. 3)			
Stone vessels						
80.3.6/22	—	Alabaster	Vessel (f)	H207-R1-L8	LC2	
72.11.2/16	—	Stone	Bowl (f)	H172-SFl	LC1?	
78.2.22/6	78/679	Steatite	Incised bowl (f)	Pl 358-P	LC2	
66.3.6/11	66/68	Stone	Small pot	H184-F	LC1	
—	66/29	,,	Unguent bottle	H171-R3-F	LC2	
82.2.2/22	82/294	Sandstone	Stopper	Pl 764-L2	LC2	
Pottery vessels[5]						
Cups (Class A)						
66.12.2/4	66a/284	Pottery[5]	Cup (H4)	H171-R6-Fl	LC2	
66.2.20/2	—	,,	,, (H4 or H8)	H171-0	LC	
66.2.9/4	—	,,	,, (H7)	H171-0	LC	
72.10.25/15	—	,,	Cup (H8)	Pl 356-F	TC	
—	72/568	,,	,, (R11)	H172-F	LC2	
—	66/132	,,	,, (R11)	?	LC	
66.2.24/2	66/147	,,	,, (W14) (f)	H171-R4	LC2	
Goblets (Class B)						
82.2.4/75	82/128	,,	Goblet (W12) (f)	H763-R8-Fl 2	LC1	
82.3.1/29	—	,,	,, (W12) (f)	H211-R1-F	LC1	
82.3.4/70	82/127	,,	,, (W12)	H211-R1-SFl 4-P	LC1	
Plain bowls (Class C)						
72.10.25/11	—	,,	Bowl (H5)	Pl 356-F	TC	
80.2.17/6	—	,,	,, (H5)	H206-R2-L33	TC	
69.2.15/7	—	,,	,, (H5)	Ch 294-0	LC	
82.2.21/16	—	,,	,, (H5) (f)	H210-R8-F	LC2	
66.2.19/7	—	,,	,, (H8) (f)	Pl 758-F	LC	
66.3.3/7	—	,,	,, (H8)	H184-F	LC1	
78.3.16/64	—	,,	,, (R13) (f)	H235-F	LC1	
—	64/31	,,	,, (R17?)	Ch 293-R1	LC	
—	66/510	,,	,, (R21) (f)	Tomb T2	LC1	
80.3.4/27	—	,,	,, (R25)	H207-R3-L28	LC1?	
66.3.8/2	66/79	,,	,, (W12)	H184 or 185-F	LC1	
82.2.9/42	—	,,	,, (W12) (f)	H763-R7-Fl 3	LC1	
—	64/167	,,	,, (W12) (f)	H169-0	LC	
—	66a/275	,,	,, (W14) (f)	?	LC	
66.2.16/4	66/35	,,	,, (W14)	H171-0	LC	
66.2.16/4	66/36	,,	,, (W14)	,,	LC	14d
82.3.1/48	82/149	,,	,, (U6)	H849-R5-Fl1	LC2	
82.2.4/76	82/167	,,	,, (G.l) (f)	H763-R8-Fl 2	LC1	
74.2.5/2	—	,,	,, (?)	H186-F	LC1	
—	64/212	,,	,, (?)	H169-0	LC	

APPENDIX C—continued
COMPREHENSIVE TABLE OF LATE AND TERMINAL CHRISTIAN OBJECT FINDS[1]

Day no.	*Reg. no.*	*Material*	*Object*[2]	*Provenance*[3]	*Date*[4]	*Plate*
Footed bowls (Class D)						
82.2.24/75	—	Pottery[5]	Footed bowl (H5) (f)	H210-R8-SFl 1	LC1	
80.2.28/6	80/503	„	„ (H7)	H206-R1-L14	TC	
69.2.11/9	69/48	„	„ (R5)	H178-R6-F	LC1	
78.1.26/3	—	„	„ (R5) (f)	Pl 358 NW-L5	LC1	
76.2.7/15	—	„	„ (R11)	H190-R2-C	LC1	
—	64/28	„	„ (R11)	H169-0	LC	16c
72.10.31/10	72/63	„	„ (R11)	H172-R6-F	LC1	
—	64/163	„	„ (R11)	Ch 293-C	LC	
78.2.20/3	—	„	„ (R11) (f)	Pl 358-P	LC2	
82.3.1/47	82/147	„	„ (R11) (f)	H849-R5-Fl	LC2	
82.3.1/46	—	„	„ (R11) (f)	„	LC2	
82.1.28/36	—	„	„ (R11) (f)	H763-R7-F	LC2	
82.3.1/33	82/148	„	„ (R17)	H849-R1-Fl 1	LC2	16d
82.3.4/55	—	„	„ (R17) (f)	H849-R5-F	LC2	
82.1.27/3	—	„	„ (R17) (f)	„	LC2	
66.3.17/1	66/126	„	„ (R21)	Tomb T3	LC1	
—	66/154	„	„ (R21) (f)	Tomb T2	LC1	
—	64/161	„	„ (W10)	H169-0	LC	
82.1.30/30	—	„	„ (W10) (f)	H763-R1-Fl 2	LC1	
69.2.8/1	69/20	„	„ (W12)	St 328-F	LC	
—	64/162	„	„ (W12)	H169-0	LC	
76.2.25/19	—	„	„ (W12)	H187-SFl-P	TC?	
82.3.1/35	—	„	„ (W12) (f)	H849-R1-Fl 1	LC2	
82.3.1/34	—	„	„ (W12) (f)	H211-R1-F	LC1	
82.2.2/26	—	„	„ (W20) (f)	H763-R8-Fl 2	LC1	
80.2.26/51	80/550	„	„ (W21) (f)	H206-R6-SFl	LC1	
—	72/498	„	„ (W21) (f)	Pl 256	LC1	
82.1.31/37	82/167	„	„ (G.I) (f)	H763-R7-F	LC2	
66.2.24/9	66/161	„	„ (G.II) (f)	Pl 758-F	LC	
—	66a/162	„	„ (G.II) (f)	?	LC	
—	64/137	„	„ (G.III)	Ch 293-C	LC	
—	66/144	„	„ (G.IIIA)	Tomb T2	LC1	
—	64/30	„	„ (G.IV)	H169?-F	LC	16a-b
—	64/29	„	„ (G.IV)	„	LC	
—	66a/156	„	„ (G.IV) (f)	?	LC	
—	66a/158	„	„ (G.IV) (f)	?	LC	
—	66a/157	„	„ (G.IV) (f)	?	LC	
74.1.30/4	—	„	„ (?)	H177-R2-SFl	LC1	
Plate (Class E)						
78.2.12/55	78/146	„	Plate (?) (f)	H202-R7-F	LC1	
Vases (Class F)						
66.3.19/6	66/136	„	Vase (R1?)	Tomb T2	LC1	
—	64/22	„	„ (R11)	H169-P	LC1	14a, c
82.2.28/25	82/54	„	„ (R11)	H849-R1-Fl 1	LC2	
82.2.27/35	82/53	„	„ (R11)	„	LC2	
—	64/21	„	„ (R11)	Ch 293-C	LC	
—	64/38	„	„ (R11)	H169-0	LC	
82.2.28/24	82/126	„	„ (R11)	H849-R1-Fl 1	LC2	
82.3.1/45	82/52	„	„ (R11)	H849-R5-Fl 1	LC2	
82.3.1/49	82/51	„	„ (R11)	„	LC2	
82.2.27/51	82/155	„	„ (R11)	H849-R5-Fl 1	LC2	

APPENDIX C—continued

COMPREHENSIVE TABLE OF LATE AND TERMINAL CHRISTIAN OBJECT FINDS[1]

Day no.	*Reg. no.*	*Material*	*Object*[2]	*Provenance*[3]	*Date*[4]	*Plate*
66.2.24/6	66/44	Pottery[5]	Vase (R11)	H171-R4	LC2	17b
—	72/499	„	(R11) (f)	?	LC	
82.3.1/44	—	„	„ (R11) (f)	H849-R5-Fl 1	LC2	
82.3.1/36	82/152	„	„ (R11) (f)	„	LC2	
82.1.27/2	—	„	„ (R11) (f)	H763-F	LC2	
82.3.4/45	—	„	„ (R11) (f)	H849-R5-F	LC2	
66.3.6/3	66/71	„	„ (R11) (f)	H184-F	LC1	
69.2.15/6	69/73	„	„ (R11 or R17)	Ch 294-0	LC	
78.2.8/96	78/141	„	„ (R11 or R17)	H197-R1-F	LC1	
78.1.25/13	—	„	„ (R21) (f)	H235-F	LC1	
78.3.11/6	78/212	„	„ (W6)	H197-R1-F	LC1	
82.3.1/37	—	„	„ (W10?) (f)	H848-R5-Fl 3	LC1	
76.1.25/2	76/12	„	„ (W14)	St 337-F	TC	17a
69.2.4/2	69/10	„	(W14)	H178-R9	LC2	
66.3.7/3	66/73	„	„ (W15)	H184-F	LC1	
82.1.27/1	—	„	„ (W16)	H763-R7-F	LC2	
78.2.11/8	78/143	„	„ (W23)	H235-Fl	LC1	
80.2.17/4	80/499	„	„ (U14?)	H206-R2-L33	TC	
66.2.14/2	66/31	„	„ (G.II)	H171-R4-F	LC2	
72.11.2/13	72/71	„	„ (?)	H172-R2-SFl	LC1	
Small pots and bottles (Class G)						
82.3.1/42	82/151	„	Small pot (U6)	H849-R5-Fl 1	LC2	
72.11.4/3	72/74	„	„ (?)	H172-R2-SFl	LC1	
69.2.5/2	—	„	Small jar (H4)	H171-R5	LC2	
66.2.14/3	66/30	„	Miniature jar (H5)	St 328-F	LC	
66.2.22/13	—	„	Small bottle (H4?)	Pl 758-F	LC	
66.3.1/9	—	„	Spouted pot (U12) (f)	St 738-F	LC	
Jugs (Class I)						
82.2.27/31	82/159	„	Jug (R19) (f)	H849-R1-Fl 1	LC2	
—	64/50	„	„ (R29)	Ch 293-C	TC	
82.3.1/50	82/150	„	„ (W12)	H849-R5-Fl 1	LC2	
82.3.4/52	—	„	„ (U6)	H849-R1-Fl 1	LC2	
82.3.1/43	82/154	„	„ (U6)	H849-R5-Fl 1	LC2	
Pilgrim bottles (Class K)						
66.3.6/3	66/385	„	Pilgrim bottle (R19)	Tomb T2	LC1	
82.3.4/56	—	„	„ (R19)	H849-R5-F	LC2	
66.2.15/2	66/34	„	„ (R26)	Ch 294-F	LC	17c
66.3.17/8	66/70	„	„ (W7?)	H184-F	LC1	
69.2.6/8	69/18	„	„ (U6)	H177-R1-F	LC1	
Beakers (Class L)						
84.2.15/7	—	„	Beaker (H1 or H4)	H785-R6-L4	LC1	
82.3.1/40	82/63	„	„ (?)	H849-R5-Fl 1	LC2	
Oil bottles (Class N)						
78.2.8/97	78/142	„	Oil bottle (?)	H235-F	LC1	
69.2.13/1	—	„	„ (R5)	H178-R4-F	LC1	

APPENDIX C—continued
COMPREHENSIVE TABLE OF LATE AND TERMINAL CHRISTIAN OBJECT FINDS[1]

Day no.	*Reg. no.*	*Material*	*Object*[2]	*Provenance*[3]	*Date*[4]	*Plate*
Lids (Class Q)						
78.2.8/28	—	Pottery[5]	Lid (H4)	Pl 358 NW-L6	LC1	
72.11.21/13	—	”	” (H7)	Ch 287-R12	TC	
80.3.10/14	80/649	”	” (R21)	H207-R2-L3	LC1	17d
82.3.3/116	—	”	” (R22) (f)	H848-R3-Fl 2	LC1	
69.2.8/4	69/33	”	” (R26?)	H177-R1-F	LC1	
82.3.4/24	—	”	” (U5)	H211-R1-Fl 2	LC1	
80.2.14/99	80/506	”	” (G.II)	H207-L13	TC?	
82.3.3/116	—	”	” (?)	H848-R3-Fl 2	LC1	
Basin (Class T)						
72.11.2/15	72/73	”	Basin (U5)	H172-R2-SFl	LC1	
Pots (Class U)						
82.3.4/23	—	”	Pot (H1)	H211-R1-Fl 2	LC1	
66.3.8/7	—	”	” (H1 or H4)	H185-R5-F	LC1	
72.11.5/23	—	”	” (H3)	Pl 356	TC	
69.2.13/3	—	”	” (H4)	St 328-F	LC	
82.1.25/72	—	”	” (H4)	H763-R8-F	LC2	
72.10.31/1	—	”	” (H4)	H172-0	LC	18a
66.3.3/2	—	”	” (H4)	H184-F	LC1	
66.3.3/2	—	”	” (H4)	H184-F	LC1	
66.2.20/1	—	”	” (H4) (f)	H171-0	LC	
76.2.15/12	—	”	” (H4?)	H171-SFl	LC1	
69.2.10/12	—	”	” (H4?)	H178-R6-F	LC1	
69.2.13/11	—	”	” (H4?)	St 358-F	LC	
66.2.9/3	—	”	” (H5)	H171-0	LC	
66.2.9/3	—	”	” (H5)	H171-0	LC	15a
66.2.9/3	—	”	” (H5)	H171-0	LC	
66.2.19/6	—	”	” (H5) (f)	Pl 758-F	LC	
66.2.21/13	—	”	” (H7) (f)	H171-0	LC	
74.1.31/6	—	”	” (H8)	H177-R2-SFl	LC1	
66.3.3/1	66/59	”	” (H8)	H184-F	LC1	
66.2.13/3	—	”	” (H8)	H171-R5-F	LC2	
69.2.6/4	—	”	” (H8)	H177-R9	LC1?	
69.1.28/2	—	”	” (H8)	H172-R1	LC2	
72.10.30/2	—	”	” (H8)	Pl 356	TC	
—	63/12	”	” (H8)	Ch 293-C	LC	
69.2.13/4	—	”	” (H8) (f)	St 328-F	LC	
66.2.23/6	—	”	” (H8) (f)	Pl 758-F	LC	
72.10.26/6	—	”	” (U6)	Pl 356-F	LC1	
82.3.3/32	—	”	” (U6)	H848-R3-SFl 4	LC1	
82.2.27/34	—	”	” (U6)	H849-R4-Fl 2	TC	15c
78.2.8/129	—	”	” (U6)	H235-R2-F	LC1	
72.10.26/5	—	”	” (U6) (f)	H176	LC1	
69.2.19/6	—	”	” (?)	H178-R6-LB	LC	
69.2.16/3	—	”	” (?)	H178-R3-F	LC1	
82.3.3/34	—	”	Pot or jar (U10) (f)	H848-R3-SFl 4	LC1	
Qadus (Class V)						
69.2.13/7	—	”	Qadus (U5)	St 328-F	LC	

APPENDIX C—continued

COMPREHENSIVE TABLE OF LATE AND TERMINAL CHRISTIAN OBJECT FINDS[1]

Day no.	*Reg. no.*	*Material*	*Object*[2]	*Provenance*[3]	*Date*[4]	*Plate*
Jars (Class W)						
69.2.16/9	—	Pottery[5]	Jar (H1?)	St 328-F	LC	
69.2.5/8	—	„	„ (H4)	H171	LC2?	
74.1.31/8	—	„	„ (H4)	H177-R1-SFl	LC1	
72.11.1/2	—	„	„ (H4) (f)	H172-R3	TC	
76.2.14/8	76/19	„	„ (W12)	H171-SFl	LC1	
74.1.31/9	—	„	„ (U5)	H177-R1-SFl	LC1	
82.2.25/75	—	„	„ (U5)	H210-R8-Fl 1	LC1	
74.1.31/7	—	„	„ (U5)	H177-R1-SFl	LC1	
82.3.4/21	—	„	„ (U5)	H849-R5-Fl 1	LC2	
74.2.4/14	—	„	„ (U5) (f)	H174-F	LC2	
82.2.8/55	—	„	„ (U10) (f)	H763-R7-Fl 2	LC1	
66.3.7/7	—	„	„ (U14)	H185-R3-F	LC1	
82.2.24/74	—	„	„ (U19) (f)	H848-R3-F	LC1	
82.3.2/92	82/135	„	„ (U19) (f)	H848-R5-Fl 2	LC1	
Footed jars (Class X)						
82.3.1/39	82/156	„	Footed jar (W12)	H849-R5-Fl 1	LC2	15d
72.11.2/14	72/72	„	„ (W12)	H172-R2-SFl	LC1	
82.3.1/38	82/163	„	„ (G.V)	H849-R1-Fl 1	LC2	
Storage jars (Class Y)						
66.3.1/2	—	„	Storage jar (H4)	H171-R4	LC2	
72.11.1/7	—	„	„ (H4)	H172	TC	13b
66.2.13/2	—	„	„ (H4) (f)	H171-R5-F	LC2	
76.2.15/12	—	„	„ (H4?)	H171-SFl	LC1	
69.2.4/3	—	„	, (H4 or 5)	H178-R9-F	LC2	
69.2.5/3	—	„	„ (H5)	H171-R5	LC2	
72.11.15/6	—	„	„ (H5)	Ch 287-R5	TC	
80.2.17/7	80/488	„	„ (H6)	H206-SFl	TC	
76.2.14/6	—	„	„ (H7)	H171-R3-Fl 1	TC	15b
82.3.4/19	—	„	„ (R32) (f)	H849-R5-Fl 1	LC2	
74.1.31/9	—	„	„ (U5)	H177-R1-SFl	LC1	
66.3.15/1	—	„	„ (U5?) (f)	H184 or H185	LC	
82.2.27/16	—	„	„ (U10)	H849-R1-Fl 1	LC2	
82.2.27/17	82/47	„	„ (U10)	„	LC2	
82.2.27/18	—	„	„ (U10)	„	LC2	
82.2.27/30	—	„	„ (U10)	„	LC2	
69.2.6/3	—	„	„ (U10)	H177-R9	LC1?	
66.3.7/4	66/74	„	„ (U10)	H185-R1-F	LC1	
66.3.7/2	—	„	„ (U10)	H184-R3-F	LC1	18b
69.2.6/2	—	„	„ (U10)	H177-R9	LC1?	
84.2.23/66	—	„	„ (U10)	H785-R6-L4	LC1	
66.3.7	—	„	„ (U10) (f)	H171	LC	
Amphorae (Class Z)						
78.2.18/6	—	„	Amphora (U6)	H195-R1-FL 1	LC1	18c
66.3.8/7	66/388	„	„ (U6)	H185-R5-F	LC1	
69.2.4/4	—	„	„ (U10) (F)	H178-R9-F	LC2	
Kegs (Class ZZ)						
82.2.27/15	—	„	Keg (U12)	H849-R1-Fl 1	LC2	
82.1.25/1	—	„	„ (U12)	H763-R8-F	LC2	
82.3.1/28	82/153	„	„ (?)	H849-R1-F	LC2	

APPENDIX C—continued

COMPREHENSIVE TABLE OF LATE AND TERMINAL CHRISTIAN OBJECT FINDS[1]

Day no.	*Reg. no.*	*Material*	*Object*[2]	*Provenance*[3]	*Date*[4]	*Plate*
Sherds of undetermined vessel forms						
82.3.3/115	—	Pottery[5]	Sherds (H3?)	H211-R1-Fl-P	LC1	
66.2.21/14	66/147	,,	Decor. sherd (R21)	H171-0	LC	
66.3.13/11	66/147	,,	,, (W5)	H184-F	LC	
76.2.18/13	—	,,	,, (W16)	H183-R2-F	LC1	
66.3.13/11	66/147	,,	Amphora neck (U2)	H184-F	LC	
82.2.4/77	—	,,	Sherds (W12)	H763-R8-Fl 1	LC1	
82.2.25/8	82/46	,,	Incised sherd (U5)	H210-R8-SFl 1	LC2	
82.3.2/83	82/270	,,	Incised sherd (U10)	H211-R1-Fl 3-P	LC1	
66.2.17/5	66/147	,,	Glazed sherd (?)	H169-0	LC	
69.2.10/6	69/29	,,	,, (?)	H178-R6-F	LC	
72.10.28/4	—	,,	Glazed sherds (?)	H175-SFl	LC	
72.11.2/11	—	,,	,, (?)	Pl 356	TC	
80.2.16/59	80/730	,,	Glazed sherd (?)	H206-R1-L16	LC2	
82.1.23/36	82/175	,,	,, (?)	H763-F	LC2	
82.2.6/18	82/172	,,	,, (?)	H763-R4-Fl 3	LC1	
82.2.8/9	82/167	,,	,, (G.Ic)	H763-R4-Fl 3	LC1	
82.2.17/65	82/171	,,	,, (?)	H781-R2-C2	LC2	
82.3.4/64	—	,,	Roman sherd	H848-R5-Fl 4	LC1	
82.3.4/82	82/273	,,	,,	H848-R5-SFl 2	LC1	
72.10.25/7	72/582	,,	Meroitic sherd	H174-F	LC2	
82.1.31/39	82/171	,,	Sherd (?)	H763-R7-F	LC2	
82.2.24/76	—	,,	,, (?)	H210-R8-SFl 1	LC2	
76.2.17/6	—	,,	Jar neck (?)	Pl 356-F	TC	
Mud vessels						
84.2.4/12	—	Mud	Small vessel	H785-R6-L4	LC1	
82.2.17/60	82/300	,,	Platter (f)	H781-R2-C2	LC2	
Mud stoppers and sealings						
80.2.17/5	—	,,	Jar stopper	H206-R2-L33	TC	
82.1.26/67	—	,,	4 Jar sealings	H763-R8-F	LC2	
82.1.30/38	82/181	,,	Jar sealing	H763-R1-Fl2	LC1	
82.1.31/50	—	,,	,,	H763-R1-F	LC2	
84.2.15/36	—	,,	,,	H785-R6-L4	LC1	
82.2.24/12	82/18	,,	,,	H484-R3-F	LC1	
82.2.25/83	82/181	,,	2 Jar sealings	H849-R1-F	LC2	
Glass vessels[6]						
Bottles						
82.1.30/6	82/87	Glass[6]	Bottle (?) (f)	H763-R1-Fl 2	LC1	19a
82.2.25/35	82/87	,,	,, (?) (f)	H849-R1-L1	LC2	19b
82.3.2/59	82/87	,,	,, (?) (f)	H849-R1-Fl 3	LC2	
82.3.2/59	82/87	,,	,, (?) (f)	,,	LC2	
82.3.4/3	82/87	,,	,, (5.2) (f)	H848-R3-SFl 2	LC1	
Kohl flasks						
—	64/157	,,	Kohl flask (5.2)	H169-0	LC	19b
69.2.15/5	69/62	,,	,, (?)	H178-R3-F	LC	
80.2.13/19	80/624	,,	,, (?) (f)	H206-R2-L33	TC	
80.2.14/52	80/624	,,	,, (2.1?) (f)	,,	TC	
82.2.28/37	82/87	,,	,, (7.6) (f)	H211-R2-P	LC1	
82.3.2/15	82/87	,,	,, (2.1) (f)	H848-R5-Fl 2	LC1	19a
82.3.2/56	82/87	,,	,, (10) (f)	H849-R5-F	LC2	
82.3.2/57	82/87	,,	,, (6.3) (f)	,,	LC2	19b
82.3.3/92	82/87	,,	,, (7.2) (f)	H211-R1-Fl 3	LC1	19a

APPENDIX C—continued
COMPREHENSIVE TABLE OF LATE AND TERMINAL CHRISTIAN OBJECT FINDS[1]

Day no.	*Reg. no.*	*Material*	*Object*[2]	*Provenance*[3]	*Date*[4]	*Plate*
Other small flasks						
—	64/309	Glass[6]	Small flask (?) (f)	H169-SFl	LC	19b
72.10.22/5	—	„	„ (?) (f)	H186-F	LC2	
72.10.24/10	—	„	„ (2.1) (f)	Pl 734	LC	
72.11.5/21	—	„	„ (2.1) (f)	Pl 356-L4	LC1	
74.1.30/1	—	„	„ (?) (f)	H177-R1-SFl	LC1	
82.2.25/35	82/87	„	„ (?) (f)	H849-R1-L1	LC2	
82.3.2/56	82/87	„	„ (5.3) (f)	H849-R5-F	LC2	
82.3.2/59	82/87	„	„ (?) (f)	H849-R1-Fl 3	LC2	
82.3.3/92	82/87	„	„ (6.2a) (f)	H211-R1-Fl 3	LC1	
82.3.3/92	81/87	„	„ (5.6) (f)	„	LC1	
84.2.9/12	—	„	„ (?) (f)	H785-R8x-L4	LC1	
84.2.15/33	—	„	Bowl (5.3) (f)	H785-R6-L4	LC1	19c
Glass sherds of undetermined vessel forms						
72.11.2/4	—	„	Sherd (?)	H172-SFl	LC1	19b
74.2.4/2	—	„	„ (?)	H186-F	LC2	
78.1.19/25	78/665	„	„ (?)	Pl 358 NE-P	LC1	
78.1.26/2	78/664	„	„ (5.6)	Pl 358 NW-L5	LC1	
78.1.30/55	78/665	„	„ (?)	H194-F	LC1	
78.2.5/28	78/664	„	„ (?)	Pl 358 NW-L6	LC1	
78.2.6/27	78/664	„	2 Sherds (5.1)	„	LC1	
78.2.6/27	78/665	„	„ (7.6)	„	LC1	
78.2.6/40	78/664	„	„ (5.3)	Pl 358 NW-L6-P	LC1	
78.2.8/87	78/665	„	„ (?)	H197-R1-F	LC1	
78.2.15/5	78/664	„	Sherd (6.1)	H196-0	LC2	
78.2.25/40	78/665	„	Sherd (?)	Pl 358-P	LC2	
78.3.1/19	78/664	„	4 Sherds (?)	H235-SFl 2	LC1	
78.3.4/8	78/665	„	Sherd (?)	H196-0	LC2	
78.3.8/4A	78/665	„	„ (?)	Pl 358-P	LC	
78.3.8/4B	78/664	„	„ (?)	„	LC	
80.3.9/28	80/625	„	„ (?)	H207-R3-L3	LC1	
82.1.26/34	82/87	„	„ (5.2?)	H763-R2-Fl 1	LC1	
82.1.23/35	82/87	„	3 Sherds (?)	H763-F	LC2	
82.1.24/44	82/90	„	2 Sherds (5.2)	„	LC2	
82.1.25/17	82/90	„	7 Sherds (6.2)	H781-F	LC2	
82.1.25/46	82/87	„	Sherd (1.1)	H763-F	LC2	
82.1.25/46	82/90	„	„ (5.2)	„	LC2	
82.1.26/69	82/90	„	„ (?)	H781-F	LC2	
82.1.25/85	82/90	„	„ (5.6)	H763-R7-F	LC2	
82.1.25/85	82/87	„	„ (?)	„	LC2	
82.1.30/17	82/90	„	14 Sherds (?)	H763-R4-Fl 2	LC1	19a
82.1.31/4	82/87	„	Sherd (6.1)	H763-R7-F	LC2	
82.1.31/38	82/87	„	„ (6.1)	„	LC2	
82.2.1/44	82/87	„	„ (?)	H763-R8-Fl 2	LC1	
82.2.2/16	82/87	„	„ (?)	„	LC1	
82.2.2/21	82/87	„	„ (6.3)	Pl 764-L2	LC2	
82.2.2/21	82/87	„	„ (2.1)	„	LC2	
82.2.2/21	82/90	„	„ (5.3)	„	LC2	
82.2.2/54	82/90	„	„ (?)	H763-R8-Fl 2	LC1	
82.2.3/6	82/87	„	2 Sherds (5.3)	„	LC1	
82.2.3/6	82/90	„	„ (5.6)	„	LC1	
82.2.3/29	82/87	„	Sherd (7.2)	„	LC1	19a
82.2.4/43	82/90	„	2 Sherds (?)	„	LC1	
82.2.6/17	82/87	„	Sherd (?)	H763-R4-Fl 3	LC1	
82.2.8/84	82/90	„	„ (5.6)	H763-R8-Fl 3	LC1	

APPENDIX C—continued

COMPREHENSIVE TABLE OF LATE AND TERMINAL CHRISTIAN OBJECT FINDS[1]

Day no.	*Reg. no.*	*Material*	*Object*[2]	*Provenance*[3]	*Date*[4]	*Plate*
82.2.8/85	82/90	Glass[6]	Sherd (7.3)	H763-R7-Fl 3	LC1	
82.2.14/86	82/87	,,	,, (6.2)	H763-F	LC2	
82.2.17/62	82/90	,,	,, (7.1)	H781-R2	LC2	
82.2.20/19	82/87	,,	2 Sherds (6.1a)	H210-R8-F	LC2	19a
82.2.20/19	82/87	,,	Sherd (5.2)	,,	LC2	
82.2.20/19	82/87	,,	,, (5.3)	,,	LC2	
82.2.20/19	82/87	,,	,, (6.1c)	,,	LC2	
82.2.20/19	82/87	,,	,, (6.2a)	,,	LC2	
82.2.20/19	82/7	,,	,, (7.3)	,,	LC2	
82.2.20/34	82/90	,,	,, (7.2)	H849-R4-F	LC2	
82.2.22/68	82/87	,,	,, (6.1e)	H849-R4-L1	LC2	
82.2.23/19	82/90	,,	2 Sherds (5.1)	H849-R4-SFl 1	LC2	
82.2.23/19	82/90	,,	Sherd (5.2)	,,		
82.2.23/19	82/90	,,	,, (7.2)	,,	LC2	
82.2.23/19	82/90	,,	3 Sherds (7.6)	,,	LC2	
82.2.23/24	82/90	,,	Sherd (5.5)	H210-R8-SFl 1	LC2	
82.2.23/26	82/90	,,	2 Sherds (7.1)	H848-R3-F	LC2	
82.2.23/44	82/90	,,	Sherd (6.1c)	H848-R2-F	LC1	
82.2.24/34	82/87	,,	,, (5.2)	H848-R3-F	LC2	
82.2.25/11	82/90	,,	,, (5.5)	H849-R1-F	LC2	
82.2.25/11	82/90	,,	5 Sherds (7.2)	,,	LC2	
82.2.25/11	82/90	,,	Sherd (7.4)	H849-R1-F	LC2	
82.2.25/15	82/87	,,	,, (5.6)	H848-R2-SFl-P	LC1	
82.2.25/15	82/90	,,	,, (6.2)	,,	LC1	
82.2.25/15	82/90	,,	,, (7.2)	H848-R2-SFl-P	LC1	
82.2.25/18	82/87	,,	,, (?)	,,	LC1	
82.2.25/66	82/87	,,	,, (5.7)	H849-R1-F	LC2	
82.2.25/66	82/90	,,	4 Sherds (7.2)	,,	LC2	
82.2.28/3	82/87	,,	2 Sherds (1.4)	H211-R1-F	LC1	
82.2.28/45	82/87	,,	4 Sherds (5.1)	H849-R1-Fl 1	LC2	
82.2.28/45	82/87	,,	Sherd (7.3)	,,	LC2	
82.2.28/56	82/87	,,	,, (?)	,,	LC2	
82.3.1/6	82/90	,,	,, (5.3)	H849-R1-Fl 2	LC2	
82.3.1/6	82/90	,,	,, (5.9)	,,	LC2	
82.3.1/89	82/90	,,	,, (?)	H211-R1-1	LC1	
82.3.2/9	82/90	,,	,, (7.1)	H848-R5-F	LC1	
82.3.2/16	82/90	,,	,, (5.1)	H848-R5-Fl 2	LC1	
82.3.2/16	82/90	,,	,, (5.6)	,,	LC1	
82.3.2/16	82/90	,,	,, (6.2)	,,	LC1	
82.3.2/16	82/90	,,	,, (7.1)	,,	LC1	
82.3.2/16	82/90	,,	,, (7.2)	,,	LC1	
82.3.2/35	82/90	,,	3 Sherds (6.2a)	H211-R1-Fl 3	LC1	
82.3.2/55	82/90	,,	Sherd (5.5)	H849-R5-F	LC2	
82.3.2/55	82/90	,,	,, (5.6)	,,	LC2	
82.3.2/55	82/90	,,	,, (6.2)	,,	LC2	
82.3.2/55	82/90	,,	,, (7.1)	,,	LC2	
82.3.2/55	82/90	,,	,, (7.2)	,,	LC2	
82.3.2/56	82/87	,,	2 Sherds (2.1)	,,	LC2	
82.3.2/57	82/87	,,	Sherd (5.3)	,,	LC2	
82.3.2/57	82/87	,,	,, (6.4)	,,	LC2	
82.3.2/57	82/87	,,	,, (7.2)	,,	LC2	
82.3.2/59	82/87	,,	,, (?)	H849-R1-Fl 3	LC2	
82.3.2/70	82/90	,,	,, (?)	H849-R5-F	LC2	
82.3.3/11	82/90	,,	,, (7.1)	H211-R1-Fl 4	LC1	

APPENDIX C—continued
COMPREHENSIVE TABLE OF LATE AND TERMINAL CHRISTIAN OBJECT FINDS[1]

Day no.	*Reg. no.*	*Material*	*Object*[2]	*Provenance*[3]	*Date*[4]	*Plate*
82.3.3/11	82/90	Glass[6]	Sherd (7.2)	H211-R1-Fl 4	LC1	
82.3.3/24	82/90	,,	4 Sherds (7.1)	H849-R4-Fl 1	LC2	
82.3.3/26	82/87	,,	Sherd (6.2)	H849-R5-SFl 1	LC2	
82.3.3/86	82/90	,,	,, (7.6)	,,	LC2	
82.3.3/91	82/90	,,	4 Sherds (6.3)	H211-R1-Fl 3	LC1	
82.3.3/94	82/87	,,	2 Sherds (6)	H849-R5-SFl 1	LC2	
82.3.4/39	82/90	,,	Sherd (7.2)	H211-R1-Fl 4	LC1	
82.3.4/44	82/87	,,	4 Sherds (6.2)	H211-R1-Fl 4-P	LC1	
84.1.24/20	—	,,	Sherd (6.2)	H785-R4-L2	LC1	
84.1.20/20	—	,,	,, (7.1)	,,	LC1	
84.1.22/13	—	,,	,, (5.6)	H785-R4-L1	LC1	
84.1.22/13	—	,,	,, (6.2)	,,	LC1	
84.1.22/13	—	,,	,, (?)	,,	LC1	
84.1.25/1	—	,,	4 Sherds (7.7)	H785-R6-L3	LC1	
84.1.26/23	—	,,	Sherd (1.1)	,,	LC1	
84.1.26/23	—	,,	,, (6.3)	,,	LC1	
84.1.28/16	—	,,	,, (5.1)	,,	LC1	
84.1.28/16	—	,,	2 Sherds (5.2)	,,	LC1	
84.1.28/16	—	,,	Sherd (6.1)	H785-R6-L3	LC1	
84.1.28/16	—	,,	,, (6.3)	,,	LC1	
84.1.28/16	—	,,	,, (7.1)	,,	LC1	
84.1.28/16	—	,,	3 Sherds (7.2)	H785-R6-L3	LC1	
84.1.28/16	—	,,	Sherd (?)	,,	LC1	
84.1.30/30	—	,,	,, (1.1)	H785-R4-L3	LC1	
84.1.30/30	—	,,	,, (6.1)	,,	LC1	
84.1.30/30	—	,,	,, (?)	,,	LC1	
84.2.4/4	—	,,	,, (5.6)	H785-R4-L4	LC1	
84.2.4/4	—	,,	3 Sherds (6.1)	,,	LC1	
82.2.4/4	—	,,	2 Sherds (7.2)	,,	LC1	
84.2.4/4	—	,,	Sherd (?)	,,	LC1	
84.2.4/11	—	,,	,, (?)	H785-R6-L4	LC1	
84.2.9/12	—	,,	,, (?)	H785-R8x-L4	LC1	
Copper, bronze, and brass vessels						
62.2.4/6	69/11	Brass	Basin	H178-R9	LC	20a-b
69.2.4/7	69/12	,,	,,	,,	LC	20c-d
69.2.12/4	69/51	,,	Pan	H178-R9-F	LC	
82.2.2/13	82/401	,,	Vessel (f)	H763-R8-Fl 2	LC1	
72.10.28/2	72/42	Copper	Bowl	H175-SFl	LC1	
82.2.3/38	82/401	Copper or bronze	,, (f)	,,	LC1	
82.3.3/122	82/403	,,	,, (f)	H211-R1-Fl 3	LC1	
76.2.9/10	—	Bronze	Small bowl	H178-F	LC	
72.10.29/6	72/53	,,	Vessel (f)	H172-R1-F	LC2	
72.10.30/7	72/521	,,	,, (f)	H174-0	LC	
78.1.16/13	—	Copper or bronze	,, (f)	W283-0-F	LC1	
Wooden vessels						
Food bowls, etc						
69.2.6/5	69/19	Wood	Footed platter	H177-R9	LC	21c-d
—	66/192	,,	Bowl (f)	H184-F	LC	
—	72/421	,,	,, (f)	Pl 356-L4	LC1	
76.2.11/11	—	,,	,, (f)	H171-R2-F	TC	
76.2.14/7	—	,,	,, (f)	H171	LC	21a
80.1.30/21	—	,,	,, (f)	H206-R1-L15	TC	
—	80/533	,,	,, (f)	H206-R6-L41	LC1	

APPENDIX C—continued
COMPREHENSIVE TABLE OF LATE AND TERMINAL CHRISTIAN OBJECT FINDS[1]

Day no.	*Reg. no.*	*Material*	*Object*[2]	*Provenance*[3]	*Date*[4]	*Plate*
82.2.4/30	82/185	Wood	Bowl (f)	H781-0	LC	
82.2.21/66	82/185	,,	,, (f)	H210-R8-F	LC2	
78.2.25/43	—	,,	Vessel (f)	Pl 358-F	LC2	
80.3.9/27	80/717	,,	,, (f)	H207-R2-L3	LC1	
82.1.30/56	82/229	,,	,, (f)	H763-R6-Fl 2	LC1	
82.2.3/50	—	,,	,, (f)	H763-R8-Fl 2	LC1	
82.2.21/60	82/185	,,	,, (f)	H849-R4-F	LC2	21a
82.3.2/90	82/185	,,	,, (f)	H848-R5-Fl 2	LC1	
Boxes						
69.2.6/6	69/15	,,	Miniature box	H177-R3-F	LC1	
82.2.28/68	82/185	,,	Box (f)	H211-R2-P	LC2	
Lids						
72.10.19/6	72/24	,,	Lid	H735-SF1	TC?	21b
76.2.16/7	—	,,	,,	H183-SFl 1	LC1	
76.2.16/17	—	,,	,,	,,	LC1	
78.1.26/51	78/488	,,	,, (f)	H235-F	LC1	
78.2.6/26	—	,,	,, (f)	Pl 358 NW-L6	LC1	
78.2.12/32	78/487	,,	,,	H197-R1-F	LC1	21d
78.2.12/32	78/488	,,	,,	,,	LC1	21d
78.2.12/45	78/511	,,	,,	H202-R4-F	LC1	
78.2.12/53	78/488	,,	,,	H202-R7-F	LC1	21d
78.2.21/25	78/488	,,	,,	H194-R16-F	TC	
82.2.23/70	82/183	,,	,,	H848-R3-F	LC1	
82.2.27/23	82/42	,,	,,	H849-R4-0	LC2	
82.2.28/62	82/232	,,	,,	H849-R1-Fl 1	LC2	
82.3.2/88	82/183	,,	,,	H849-R5-Fl 1	LC2	21d
82.3.2/89	82/183	,,	,,	,,	LC2	
82.3.3/95	82/183	,,	,, (f)	H849-R5-SFl 1	LC2	
82.3.4/4	82/183	,,	,, (f)	H763-R8-Fl 2	LC1	
82.3.3/118	82/183	,,	,,	H848-R5-Fl 4	LC1	
84.1.16/35	—	,,	,,	H785-R6-L4	TC	
Stoppers						
78.1.30/58	78/489	,,	Stopper	H194-f	LC1	
78.2.1/8	78/490	,,	,,	,,	LC1	
82.2.28/66	82/225	,,	,,	H211-R2-P	LC2	
82.2.28/67	82/225	,,	,,	,,	LC2	
82.3.2/98	82/227	,,	2 Stoppers	H849-R5-Fl 1	LC2	
82.3.3/96	82/227	,,	Stopper	H849-R5-SFl 1	LC2	
Bucket or barrel parts						
78.2.12/34	78/514	,,	Bucket or barrel (f)	H197-R1-F	LC1	
82.1.25/107	—	,,	,, (f)	H763-R7-F	LC2	
82.1.26/55	82/182	,,	,, (f)	H763-F	LC2	
82.1.31/61	82/182	,,	,, (f)	H763-R7-F	LC2	
82.2.23/68	82/182	,,	,, (f)	H848-R3-F	LC1	
82.2.25/78	82/182	,,	,, (f)	H849-R1-F	LC2	
82.3.1/86	82/256	,,	,, (f)	H211-R1-F	LC1	
82.3.2/75	82/182	,,	,, (f)	H848-R5-Fl 2	LC1	
Trough						
82.1.26/68	—	,,	Trough	H763-R5-Fl 1	LC2	
Ivory container						
69.2.10/13	69/24	Ivory	Miniature box (f)	H178-R7-F	LC1	19d

APPENDIX C—continued

COMPREHENSIVE TABLE OF LATE AND TERMINAL CHRISTIAN OBJECT FINDS[1]

Day no.	*Reg. no.*	*Material*	*Object*[2]	*Provenance*[3]	*Date*[4]	*Plate*
Basketry containers						
Storage baskets						
—	74/15	Basketry	Storage basket	H177-R1-SFl	LC1	
76.2.21/10	—	„	„ (f)	Pl 358 NE-Fl 2	LC	22d
Guffas						
72.10.11/15	—	„	Guffa	H734-SFl	LC	
76.2.15/4	—	„	„	H172-SFl-P	LC1	
76.2.15/9	—	„	„	H171-F	TC	
76.2.23/4	—	„	„	Pl 358 NE-Fl 2-P	LC	
78.1.17/33	78/777	„	„	Pl 358 NE-P	LC	13d, 22a
78.2.28/52	78/566	„	„ (f)	Pl 358 NE-L6	LC1	
82.1.14/98	82/94	„	„ (f)	H763-R8-Fl 2	LC1	
82.1.14/161	82/118	„	„ (f)	H211-R1-Fl 3	LC1	
—	72/46	„	2 Decor. frags.	?	LC1?	22b
76.2.11/5	76/107	„	Handled bag	H171-F	TC	22c
Plaited pouches						
78.3.1/35	78/570	„	3 Pouches (f)	H235-SFl 2	LC1	22e
80.3.14/39	80/566	„	2 Pouches (f)	H207-R1-L27	LC1	
82.1.14/81	82/96	„	Pouch	H210-R8-F	LC2	
82.1.14/82	82/96	„	„	H763-R7-F	LC2	
82.1.14/87	82/96	„	„	H848-R5-Fl 2	LC1	
82.1.14/88	82/108	„	„	H763-R8-F	LC2	
82.1.14/136	82/96	„	„	H211-R1-SFl 3	LC1	
82.1.14/137	82/96	„	„	H211-R1-Fl 1-P	LC1	
82.1.14/138	82/96	„	„	H211-R1-SFl 3	LC1	
82.1.14/152	82/94	„	„	H211-R1-Fl 1	LC1	
82.1.14/153	82/96	„	„	H211-R1-SFl 3	LC1	
82.1.14/154	82/96	„	„	H211-R1-Fl 3-P	LC1	
Coiled baskets						
66.2.30/6	66/54	Basketry	Cld. basket + lid	H171-R4	LC2	23d
72.11.15/24	—	Basketry + leather	Coiled basket	Ch 287-R6-F	TC	
—	74/229	Basketry	„	H177-SFl	LC1	
76.2.1/1	—	„	„	H192-F	LC1	
76.2.25/17	76/113	Basketry + leather	„	H187-SFl	LC1	
78.1.17/21	78/552	Basketry	„	Ch 287-0-P	LC	
78.1.26/41	78/551	„	„	H235-F	LC1	
78.2.1/18	78/552	„	„	H195-F	LC1	23c
78.2.8/83	78/562	„	„	H235-Fl	LC1	23e
78.2.8/83	78/604	„	„	„	LC1	
78.2.12/56	78/708	„	„	H197-R1-F	LC1	
78.2.16/6	78/552	„	„	P470-F	TC	
78.2.18/11	—	„	„ (f)	P468-F	LC2	
80.3.14/46	80/567	„	„	H207-R1-L16	LC2	
80.3.14/72	80/584	„	„	H207-R1-L8	LC2	23a
82.1.14/12	82/95	„	„	P776-F	LC2	23b
82.1.14/25	82/95	„	„	H763-R1-F	LC2	
82.1.14/18	82/95	„	„	H763-R2-Fl 2	LC1	
82.1.14/19	82/107	„	„	H211-R1-Fl 4	LC1	
82.1.14/23	82/95	„	„ (f)	H763-R8-Fl 2	LC1	
82.1.14/118	82/95	„	„	H849-R5-Fl 1	LC2	
82.1.14/159	82/95	„	„	H848-R5-Fl 1	LC1	

APPENDIX C—continued
COMPREHENSIVE TABLE OF LATE AND TERMINAL CHRISTIAN OBJECT FINDS[1]

Day no.	*Reg. no.*	*Material*	*Object*[2]	*Provenance*[3]	*Date*[4]	*Plate*
82.1.14/176	82/95	Basketry	Coiled basket	H848-R3-Fl 4-P	LC1	
—	82/95	,,	,,	H763-R1-Fl 2	LC1	
84.1.6/24	—	,,	,, (f)	H785-R6-L4	LC1	23f
84.1.6/34	—	,,	,, (f)	H785-R11-L1	LC1	
84.1.16/35	—	,,	,,	H785-R6-L4	LC1	
Baskets of unrecorded type						
72.10.28/8	—	,,	Basket (type ?)	H175-SFl	LC	
72.11.19/16	—	,,	2 Baskets (type ?)	Ch 287-R11-Fl	LC2	
—	82/101	,,	Basket (type ?)	H763-F	LC2	25a
Lids						
—	66/301	Basketry	3 Coiled lids	H169-0	LC	
—	66a/166	,,	Coiled lid	H171-F	LC2	
76.2.9/52	—	,,	,,	H190-C	LC1	24b
76.2.15/10	—	,,	,,	H171-SFl	LC	
78.2.8/91	78/769	,,	,,	H197-R1-F	LC1	
78.2.12/44	78/552	,,	,, (f)	H202-R4-F	LC1	
78.2.12/49	78/551	Basketry + leather	,,	H202-R7-F	LC1	
82.1.14/26	82/106	Basketry	,,	H763-R8-Fl 2	LC1	24a
82.1.14/41	82/99	,,	,, (f)	H763-F	LC2	
82.1.14/46	82/99	,,	,,	H848-F	LC2	
82.1.14/51	82/99	,,	,,	,,	LC2	
82.1.14/53	82/95	,,	,,	H849-R4-F	LC2	
82.1.14/60	82/99	,,	,,	P840-F	LC	24a
82.1.14/63	82/95	,,	,,	H781-R1-F	LC2	24a
82.1.14/115	82/99	,,	,,	H211-F	LC2	24a
82.1.14/125	82/104	,,	,,	H848-R5-Fl 1	LC1	
82.1.14/130	—	,,	,,	H848-R5-F	LC2	24c
82.1.15/166	82/95	,,	,,	H849-R1-Fl 1	LC2	24d
84.1.6/51	84/418	Basketry + leather	,,	H785-R6-L4	LC1	
Stoppers						
82.1.14/3	82/107	Basketry	Stopper	H763-F	LC2	
84.1.6/50	84/422	,,	,,	H785-R8xx-L5	LC1	24e
Textile bags						
78.2.6/35	78/415	,,	Small bag	Pl 358 NW-L5	LC1	
78.3.4/28	78/317	,,	,,	Pl 358-P	LC2	
78.3.20/66	—	Textile	,,	P505-F	LC	
78.3.28/64	—	,,	,,	Pl 358-P	LC2	
78.3.28/67	—	,,	,,	Pl 358 NW-L6	LC1	
80.2.28/81	80/942	,,	,,	H206-R6-L41	LC1	25b
82T/291	—	Flax + goat hair	Bag (f)	H763-R7-Fl 1		
82T/309	—	Flax cloth	,,	H763-R8-Fl 2	LC1	
82T/329	—	Cotton yarn	Knotted bag frag.	H763-F	LC2	
82T/331	—	Goat hair + wool	Embroidered bag	H763-F	LC2	45f
82T/425	—	Cotton cloth	Bag	H763-F	LC2	
82T/426	—	,,	Bag + folded cloth	H763-F	LC2	25d
82T/506	—	Flax yarn	Knotted bag	H763-R7	LC	25c
82T/906	—	,,	Tassel from bag	H211-R1-SFl 3	LC1	
Leather containers						
Waterskins						
72.10.18/5	—	Leather	Waterskin (f)	H732-SFl	LC	
78.2.20/57	—	,,	,, (f)	Pl 358-P	LC2	
78.3.1/46	—	,,	,, (f)	,,	LC2	
82.2.8/46	82/531	,,	,,	H763-R7-Fl 3	LC1	26a
82.3.4/196	82/529	,,	,, (f)	H211-R1-F	LC1	
78.2.6/48	—	,,	Waterskin? (f)	Pl 358-NW-L5	LC1	

APPENDIX C—continued

COMPREHENSIVE TABLE OF LATE AND TERMINAL CHRISTIAN OBJECT FINDS[1]

Day no.	*Reg. no.*	*Material*	*Object*[2]	*Provenance*[3]	*Date*[4]	*Plate*
Bags						
78.1.26/50	—	Leather	Bag (f)	H235-F	LC1	
78.2.5/43	—	Leather + wool	2 Bags (f)	Pl 358 NW-L7	LC1	
78.2.15/30	78/626	Leather + cotton	Bag (f)	H196-0	TC	
80.2.13/78	—	Leather	„ (f)	H206-R2-L7	TC	
82.1.25/108	82/526	„	„ (f)	H763-R7-F	LC2	
82.1.25/118	82/522	„	„ (f)	„	LC2	
82.1.25/118	—	„	„ (f)	„	LC2	
82.1.26/70	82/558	„	„ (f)	H781-F	LC2	
82.1.28/53	—	„	„ (f)	H781-R2-C	LC1	
82.1.31/56	82/532	Leather + flax	„ (f)	H763-R7-F	LC2	
82.2.16/68	82/532	„	„ (f)	H211-R8-SFl 4	LC1	
82.3.1/98	82/526	Leather	„ (f)	H211-R1-F	LC1	
82.3.1/99	82/530	„	„ (f)	H848-R5-F	LC2	
82.3.3/156	82/526	„	„ (f)	H848-R5-Fl 2	LC2	
78.1.18/10	78/627	Leather + cotton	Bag handle (f)	Pl 358 NE-P	LC	
82.2.28/79	82/528	Leather	„ (f)	H211-R2-F	LC1	
Pouches and purses						
78.1.22/25	—	„	Pouch (f)	Pl 358 NE-P	LC	
78.2.5/32	78/311	„	„ (f)	Pl 358 NE-L6	LC1	
82.3.2/119	82/526	„	„ (f)	H848-R5-Fl 2	LC2	
82.2.23/77	82/555	„	Purse	P843-F	LC	27a
Sheaths						
72.10.33/9	72/31	„	Sheath	H168-F	LC2	
72.11.1/10	72.65	„	„	H176-SFl	LC	27d
78.2.8/68	78/51	„	„	P515-F	LC1	27e
78.2.8/94	78/53	Leather + wood	„	H197-R1-F	LC1	27c
82.2.6/46	82/558	Leather	„ (f)	H763-F	LC2	
82.3.1/96	82/526	„	„ (f)	H211-R1-F	LC1	
82.3.1/97	82/515	„	„ (f)	„	LC1	27b
Gourd vessels						
69.2.13/2	69/58	Gourd	Vessel	H178-RF4-F	LC1	28a
78.2.8/79	—	„	„	H235-Fl	LC1	
82.2.21/62	82/444	„	„ (f)	H849-R4-F	LC2	
78.2.1/3	78/472	„	Decor. vessel (f)	H185-F	LC1	28c
78.2.6/28	—	„	„ (f)	Pl 358 NW-L6	LC1	
82.2.2/43	82/443	„	„ (f)	H763-R8-Fl 2	LC1	
82.2.3/19	82/444	„	„ (f)	P795-F	LC1	
82.3.2/65	82/443	„	„ (f)	H211-R1-Fl 3	LC1	
82.3.2/72	82/443	„	„ (f)	H848-R5-Fl 2	LC1	
76.2.26/12	—	„	Cup	C188-R1-F	LC1	28b
74.2.2/3	74/200	„	Decorated lid	H177-SFl	LC1	

TOOLS, IMPLEMENTS AND WEAPONS (Part 3, Ch. 4)

Cutting tools, handles, and hones

Knives						
69.2.5/7	69/14	Iron + wood	Knife with handle	H177-R2-F	LC1	
72.10.22/6	72/29	„	„	H186-F	LC2	
72.10.25/17	72/30	„	„	Pl 356	LC1	
72.10.12/5	72/13	Iron	Knife blade	P734-F	LC?	29a
72.10.17/14	72/513	„	„	P732-F	LC?	29a
82.3.2/79	82/324	„	„	H849-R1-Fl 3	LC2	29a

APPENDIX C—continued

COMPREHENSIVE TABLE OF LATE AND TERMINAL CHRISTIAN OBJECT FINDS[1]

Day no.	*Reg. no.*	*Material*	*Object*[2]	*Provenance*[3]	*Date*[4]	*Plate*
Saws or sickles						
78.2.12/3	78/62	Iron + wood	Saw/sickle + handle	H197-R6-F	LC1	
82.3.3/119	82/316	Iron	Saw or sickle	H848-R5-Fl 4	LC1	11b
Axe or adze						
69.2.10/1	69/40	,,	Axe or adze blade	H178-R6-F	LC1	
Tool handles						
78.2.6/42	78/432	Wood	Implement handle	Pl 358 NW-L6-P	LC1	
72.10.21/7	—	,,	,,	Pl 735-F	LC?	
78.2.12/52	78/424	,,	,,	H202-R7-F	LC1	29c
78.3.4/11	78/432	,,	,,	H196-0-P	LC2	
82.1.30/67	—	,,	,,	H763-R1-Fl 2	LC1	
82.3.1/92	82/251	,,	,,	H848-R5-F	LC1	
Metal ferrules for tool handles						
69.2.10/11	69/36	Iron	Ferrule	H178-R6-F	LC1	
69.2.11/6	69/39	,,	,,	,,	LC1	
69.2.11/13	69/38	,,	,,	H178-R2-F	LC1	
72.10.25/10	72/516	,,	,,	H168-F	LC2	
72.11.13/20	—	,,	,,	Ch 287-F	TC	
78.1.26/53	—	,,	,,	H235-F	LC1	
78.2.12/48	—	,,	,,	H202-R4-F	LC1	
82.3.4/129	82/370	,,	,,	H211-F1-Fl 4	LC1	
72.10.18/8	72/514	Copper or bronze	,,	P732-F	LC	
72.10.25/4	72/518	,,	,,	H175-F	LC2	
72.11.1/3	72/522	,,	,,	H174-SFl	LC2	
78.2.12/72	—	,,	,,	H202-R4-F	LC1	
72.11.1/13	72/523	,,	Small cap	H172-SFl	LC1	
Hones						
72.10.29/5	72/52	Slate	Hone	H172-R3-Fl	TC	29d
72.11.7/31	—	,,	,, (f)	Pl 356-L4	LC1	
80.2.28/25	80/816	,,	,, (f)	H207-R3-L6	LC1	
Sewing, spinning, and weaving equipment						
Needles						
72.10.23/1	72/33	Iron	Needle	H168	LC2	
82.1.24/8	82/328	,,	,,	H763-F	LC2	30a
—	63/65	Wood	,,	H169-R8	LC2	
72.10.25/16	—	,,	,,	Pl 356	LC1	
76.2.22/8	—	,,	,,	Pl 358 NE-L2	LC2	
78.2.8/84	78/496	,,	,, (f)	H235-Fl	LC1	
Thimble						
72.10.25/9	72/25	Bronze	Thimble	H734-SFl	LC2?	31d
Awls						
78.3.1/33	78/495	Wood	Awl	H235-SFl 2	LC1	
82.1.28/49	82/188	,,	,,	H781-R2-C	LC1	
82.1.29/49	—	,,	,,	,,	LC1	
82.2.2/47	82/188	,,	,,	H763-R8-Fl 2	LC1	
82.2.28/64	82/188	,,	,,	H211-R2-F	LC2	30b
82.3.1/81	82/254	,,	,,	H849-R5-F	LC2	
82.3.3/100	—	,,	,, (f)	H211-R1-Fl 3	LC1	
82.3.3/112	—	,,	,, (f)	H211-R3-F	LC1	

APPENDIX C—continued
COMPREHENSIVE TABLE OF LATE AND TERMINAL CHRISTIAN OBJECT FINDS[1]

Day no.	*Reg. no.*	*Material*	*Object*[2]	*Provenance*[3]	*Date*[4]	*Plate*
Spindles and whorls[7]						
—	66/75	Wood	Spindle + whorl[7]	H168	LC	
66.3.7/6	66/165	..	..	H184-F	LC1	30c
66.3.12/10	66/89	..	..	H184-SFl	LC1	
74.2.5/3	74/195	..	..	H186-Fl	LC1	
76.2.8/3	76/21	..	..	H190-R4-C	LC1	
82.2.3/35	82/81	..	.. (7b)	H763-R8-Fl 2	LC1	
82.2.3/35	82/81	..	.. (7b)	..	LC1	30c-d
82.2.3/35	82/81	..	.. (f)	..	LC1	
82.2.27/60	82/81	..	.. (8a) (f)	H848-R3-SFl	LC1	
82.1.31/53	82/188	..	Spindle stick?	H763-R7-F	LC2	
82.2.3/48	—	..	..	H763-R8-Fl 2	LC1	
80.2.14/48	80/618	Sandstone	Spindle whorl (f)[7]	H206-R1-L15	TC	
76.2.17/7	—	Ceramic	..	H183-R1-F	LC1	
78.3.8/1	78/517	..	.. (2)	Pl 358-P	LC2	
82.1.23/64	82/265	..	..	H763-F	LC2	
82.2.23/43	82/86	..	.. (1)	H848-R2-F	LC1	30f
82.2.28/53	82/86	..	.. (1)	H849-R5-F	LC2	30f
72.10.23/7	72/413	Wood	..	H168-F	LC2	
72.11.2/8	72/420	..	..	H177-R2-SFl	LC1	
74.2.2/8	74/195	..	..	H177-SFl	LC1	
74.2.4/9	74/195	..	..	H186-R1-F	LC2	
74.2.5/5	74/195	..	..	H186-P	LC2	
76.2.14/14	—	..	..	H171-F	TC	
76.2.16/14	—	..	..	H182-SFl	LC1	
76.2.25/18	—	..	..	H187-SFl-P	TC	
78.1.22/22	78/518	..	.. (8a)	Pl 358 NE-P	LC	
78.1.25/12	78/518	..	.. (7b)	..	LC	
78.1.25/14	78/517	..	.. (8b)	H235-F	LC1	
78.1.30/57	78/518	..	.. (8a)	H194-F	LC1	
78.2.5/29	78/518	..	.. (8a)	Pl 358 NW-L6	LC1	
78.2.6/20	78/517	..	.. (8a)	Pl 358 NW-L6	LC1	
78.2.6/41	78/518	..	.. (6a)	Pl 358 NW-L6-P	LC1	
78.2.6/41	78/518	..	.. (6b)	..	LC1	
78.2.11/7	78/517	..	.. (7b)	H235-Fl	LC1	
78.2.12/43	78/518	..	.. (7b)	H202-0-R4-F	LC1	
78.2.18/7	78/517	..	.. (8a)	H195-R1-Fl 1	LC1	
82.1.25/12	82/83	..	.. (8b)	H763-F	LC2	
82.1.25/13	82/83	..	.. (7b)	H763-R7-F	LC2	
82.1.25/13	82/83	..	.. (7b)	..	LC2	
82.1.25/13	82/83	..	.. (7b)	..	LC2	
82.1.15/13	82/83	..	.. (9)	..	LC2	
82.1.28/45	82/83	..	.. (9)	P774-F	LC	
82.1.28/47	82/83	..	.. (8a)	H781-R2-C	LC2	
82.1.28/47	82/83	..	.. (9)	..	LC2	
82.1.30/36	82/83	..	.. (7b)	H763-R1-Fl 2	LC1	
82.1.30/36	82/83	..	.. (7b)	..	LC1	
82.1.31/48	82/83	..	.. (7b)	H763-R7-F	LC2	
82.2.21/58	82/83	..	.. (8b)	H849-R4-F	LC2	
82.2.23/59	82/83	..	.. (8b)	H848-R3-F	LC1	
82.2.24/59	82/83	..	.. (8a)	H848-R3-F	LC1	
82.2.27/25	82/83	..	.. (8a)	P846-F	LC	

APPENDIX C—continued
COMPREHENSIVE TABLE OF LATE AND TERMINAL CHRISTIAN OBJECT FINDS[1]

Day no.	*Reg. no.*	*Material*	*Object*[2]	*Provenance*[3]	*Date*[4]	*Plate*
82.3.1/57	82/83	Wood	Spindle whorl (6b)	H849-R1-Fl 2	LC2	
82.3.1/57	82/83	„	„ (8c)	„	LC2	
82.3.1/66	82/83	„	„ (8a)	H848-R5-F	LC2	
82.3.1/70	82/83	„	„ (9)	„	LC2	
82.3.1/95	82/83	„	„ (?)	H211-R1-F	LC1	
82.3.2/6	82/83	„	„ (8a)	H848-R5-Fl 2	LC1	
82.3.2/6	82/83	„	„ (8a)	„	LC1	
82.3.2/6	82/83	„	„ (8a)	„	LC1	
82.3.2/6	82/83	„	„ (9)	„	LC1	
82.3.2/21	82/83	„	„ (8a)	H211-R1-Fl 2	LC1	
82.3.2/58	82/83	„	„ (8a)	H849-R5-Fl 1	LC2	
82.3.3/1	82/83	„	„ (7a)	H211-R1-SFl 3	LC1	30e
82.3.3/1	82/83	„	„ (8b)	„	LC1	30e
82.3.3/1	82/83	„	„ (8b)	„	LC1	30e
82.3.3/1	82/83	„	„ (8b)	„	LC1	30e
82.3.3/1	82/83	„	„ (8b)	„	LC1	30e
82.3.3/6	82/83	„	„ (6a)	H849-R5-SFl 1	LC2	30e
82.3.3/6	82/83	„	„ (9)	„	LC2	
82.3.4/57	82/83	„	„ (7a)	H211-R1-Fl 4	LC1	
82.3.4/57	82/83	„	„ (7b)	„	LC1	
82.3.4/57	82/83	„	„ (8a)	„	LC1	
84.1.28/24	—	„	„	H785-R6-L3	LC1	
84.1.29/2	—	„	„	P978-F	LC	
84.1.30/41	—	„	„ (f)	H785-R4-L3	LC1	
84.2.2/20	—	„	„	H785-R6-L4	LC1	
84.2.2/32	84/547	„	„	„	LC1	
84.2.4/45	—	„	„	H785-R4-L4	LC1	
84.2.15/30	—	„	„	H785-R6-L4	LC1	
Shuttles (?)						
82.1.28/60	82/219	„	Shuttle?	H781-R2-C	LC1	31a
82.3.1/87	82/248	„	„	H211-F1-F	LC1	
Loom weight						
82.3.3/136	82/299	Mud	Loom weight	H211-R3-F	LC1	31b
Packing comb						
78.2.15/11	78/502	Wood	Packing comb	H197-R2-F	LC2	31c
Weaving stick (?)						
—	69/131	„	Weaving stick?	H177-R1-F	LC1	
Card-weaving tablets						
69.2.8/5	69/31	„	Card-weav. tablet	H177-R1-F	LC1	31f
69.2.13/14	69/53	„	„	H178-R3-F	LC1	
72.10.28/2	72/22	„	„ (f)	H732-SFl	LC	
72.10.24/14	72/470	„	„	H177-Fl	LC1	31g
76.2.29/10	—	„	„	Pl 358-C	LC1	31h
82.3.3/102	82/234	„	„ (f)	H211-R1-Fl 3	LC1	
String-making implement (?)						
78.2.25/30	78/413	Ceramic	String-mkg. imp.?	Pl 358-NW-L6	LC1	
Flax hackle?						
82T/445	—	Flax cloth + thorns	Flax hackle?	H763-F	LC2	
Lifting, pulling, and fastening apparatus						
Pulley wheels						
82.2.4/24	82/198	Wood	Pulley wheel	H763-R8-Fl 2	LC1	32a

APPENDIX C—continued
COMPREHENSIVE TABLE OF LATE AND TERMINAL CHRISTIAN OBJECT FINDS[1]

Day no.	*Reg. no.*	*Material*	*Object*[2]	*Provenance*[3]	*Date*[4]	*Plate*
Weights						
78.2.12/57	—	Sandstone	Perforated weight	H202-R4-F	LC1	32b
82.2.25/85	82/295	,,	,, (f)	H849-R1-F	LC2	
82.2.2/44	—	Ironstone	Grooved weight	H763-R8-Fl 2	LC1	32c
82.1.25/105	82/308	Ceramic	Perforated weight	H763-R7-F	LC2	
Rivets						
82T/896	—	Lead, iron + flax	Rivets in flax strap	H211-R1-Fl 1	LC1	
Pegs						
69.1.29/4	—	Wood	Peg	H177-R7-F	LC1	
74.2.2/1	74/200	,,	,,	H177-SFl	LC1	
78.2.8/85	78/555	,,	,,	H197-R1-F	LC1	
80.2.14/95	—	,,	,	H206-R1-L15	TC	
78.3.1/34	—	,,	,,	H235-Fl 2	LC1	
82.1.25/104	82/196	,,	,,	H763-R7-F	LC2	
82.1.28/48	82/196	,,	,,	H781-R2-C	LC2	33a
82.1.30/54	—	,,	,,	H763-R6-Fl 2	LC1	
82.1.30/60	82/196	,,	,,	H763-R4-Fl 2	LC1	
82.1.30/70	82/196	,,	,,	H763-R2-Fl 2	LC1	
82.2.6/45	82/196	,,	,,	H763-R4-Fl 2	LC1	
82.2.8/51	82/196	,,	,,	H763-R7-Fl 3	LC1	
82.2.21/63	82/196	,,	,,	H849-R4-F	LC2	
82.2.21/69	—	,,	,,	H210-R8-F	LC2	
82.2.23/76	82/196	,,	,,	P845-F	LC	
82.2.25/69	82/196	,,	,,	H849-R1-F	LC2	
82.2.25/87	82/196	,,	,,	,,	LC2	
82.3.3/135	82/240	,,	,,	H211-R3-F	LC1	
84.2.4/43	—	,,	,,	H785-R4-L4	LC1	
84.2.5/36	—	,,	,,	,,	LC1	
84.2.5/36	—	,,	,, (f)	,,	LC1	
84.2.5/36	—	,,	,, (f)	,,	LC1	
Stakes						
74.2.2/5	74/200	,,	Stake	H177-SFl	LC1	
78.1.19/32	—	,,	,,	Pl 358 NE-L6-P	LC	
82.1.26/56	82/195	,,	,,	H763-F	LC2	
82.1.25/51	—	,,	,,	H781-R2-C	LC2	
82.1.28/56	—	,,	,, (f)	,,	LC2	
82.1.30/40	—	,,	,,	H763-R1-Fl 2	LC1	
82.1.30/63	82/195	,,	,,	H763-R4-Fl 2	LC1	
82.1.30/66	—	,,	,,	H763-R1-Fl 2	LC1	
82.1.31/52	82/188	,,	,,	H763-R7-F	LC2	
82.1.31/52	82/188	,,	,,	,,	LC2	
82.2.2/51	82/195	,,	,,	H763-R8-Fl 2	LC1	
82.2.3/51	82/195	,,	,,	,,	LC1	
82.2.3/51	—	,,	,,	,,	LC1	
82.2.25/76	—	,,	,, (f)	H849-R1-F	LC2	
82.2.25/77	82/195	,,	,, (f)	,,	LC2	
82.2.28/69	—	,,	,, (f)	H849-R1-Fl 1	LC2	
82.3.2/93	—	,,	,, (f)	H849-R1-Fl 3	LC2	
82.3.2/96	—	,,	,,	H849-R5-Fl 1	LC2	
82.3.2/96	—	,,	,,	,,	LC2	
82.3.2/96	—	,,	,,	,,	LC2	
82.3.2/99	—	,,	,, (f)	H849-R5-Fl 1	LC2	
84.2.5/34	—	,,	,, (f)	H785-R4-L4	LC1	

APPENDIX C—continued

COMPREHENSIVE TABLE OF LATE AND TERMINAL CHRISTIAN OBJECT FINDS[1]

Day no.	*Reg. no.*	*Material*	*Object*[2]	*Provenance*[3]	*Date*[4]	*Plate*
Wedges						
78.3.12/47	78/434	Wood	Wedge	W283-0-L1b	LC1	
82.2.10/63	82/195	„	3 Wedges	H763-R7-Fl 4	LC1	33b
82.2.10/63	—	„	Wedge	„	LC1	
82.2.21/70	82/195	„	„	H210-R8-F	LC2	33b
82.3.3/101	82/195	„	„	H211-R1-Fl 3	LC1	33b
82.3.4/101	82/195	„	„	H211-R1-Fl 4	LC1	33b
Leather straps						
82.1.24/61	82/519	Leather	Strap (f)	H763-F	LC2	
82.1.30/41	82/519	„	„ (f)	H763-R1-Fl 2	LC1	
82.2.28/72	82/548	„	„ (f)	H848-R1-Fl 1	LC1	
82.3.1/102	82/557	„	„ (f)	H848-R5-F	LC1	
82.1.28/52	82/558	„	Loop	H781-R2-C	LC2	
Leather thongs and cords						
78.2.12/6	—	„	Twisted cord	H202-R7-F	LC1	33c
80.3.13/63	80/983	„	„	H206-R2-L29	TC	
82.1.24/62	82/530	„	Bundle of thongs	H763-F	LC2	33d
82.2.1/59	82/540	„	Cord (f)	H763-R7-F	LC2	
82.2.2/49	82/520	„	„ (f)	H763-R8-Fl 2	LC1	
82.2.4/57	82/540	„	„ (f)	P797-F	LC1	
82.2.8/50	82/540	„	„ (f)	H763-R7-Fl 3	LC1	
82.2.8/50	82/540	„	„ (f)	„	LC1	
Cordage						
82.2.4/57	82/540	Goat hair	„ (f)	P795-F	LC1	
Chain						
82.2.25/14	82/340	Copper or bronze	Section of fine chain	H211-R3-F	LC2	
Buckles and rings						
66.3.13/7	66/95	Iron	Small buckle	H184-F	LC	33e
78.3.13/52	78/351	„	„	Pl 358-P	LC	33e
69.2.5/6	—	Bronze or brass	„	H171-0	LC	
72.10.25/3	72/517	Iron + leather	Fastening ring	H175-F	LC1	
72.10.26/2	72/520	Iron	„	Pl 356-F	TC	33e
Toilet articles						
Razors						
72.11.8/13	72/145	Iron + wood	Razor	Pl 356-L4	LC1	34a
82.2.23/96	82/336	Iron	Razor blade	H848-R3-F	LC2	
Combs						
66.3.5/2	66/61	Wood	Comb (f)	H184-F	LC1	34b
66.3.6/2	66/65	„	„	„	LC1	34b
66.3.12/8	66/87	„	„ (f)	„	LC1	
66.3.12/9	66/88	„	„ (f)	„	LC1	34b
69.2.10/5	69/23	„	„ (f)	H178-R6-F	LC1	
69.2.11/5	69/43	„	„	„	LC1	34b
69.2.13/5	69/54	„	„	H178-R4-F	LC1	34b
72.10.25/14	72/415	„	„ (f)	H172-F	LC	
72.11.21/8	72/430	„	„ (f)	Ch 287-R12-F	TC	
82.2.21/68	82/191	„	„ (f)	H210-R8-F	LC2	
82.2.28/61	82/189	„	„ (f)	H849-R1-Fl 1	LC2	
82.3.3/117	82/189	„	„ (f)	H848-R5-Fl 4	LC1	

APPENDIX C—continued

COMPREHENSIVE TABLE OF LATE AND TERMINAL CHRISTIAN OBJECT FINDS[1]

Day no.	*Reg. no.*	*Material*	*Object*[2]	*Provenance*[3]	*Date*[4]	*Plate*
Kohl sticks						
66.3.12/7	66/97	Iron	Kohl stick	H184-F	LC1	34c
69.2.11/3	69/45	,,	,,	H178-R6-F	LC1	
76.2.29/9	—	,,	,,	Pl 358-C	LC1	
78.1.24/36	—	,,	,,	P512-F	LC	
80.3.1/39	80/871	,,	,,	W323-F	LC	
72.10.28/9	72/44	Bronze	,,	H174-0	LC	
Tweezers						
—	66a/22	Iron	Tweezers	H171-F	LC	34d
66.3.6/1	66/67	Bronze	,,	H184-F	LC1	34d
Mirrors						
69.2.9/2	69/34	Wood + glass	Box lid with mirror	H178-R6-F	LC1	
78.1.26/44	78/512	,,	,,	Pl 358 NW-L5-P	LC1	34e
Problematical implements						
66.3.13/9	66/96	Iron	Prob. implement (f)	H184-F	LC1	
80.2.26/58	80/812	,,	,,	H206-R6-L41	LC1	
82.2.4/45	82/398	,,	,, (f)	H763-R8-Fl 2	LC1	
82.3.1/83	82/330	,,	,, (f)	H849-R5-F	LC2	35d
82.3.2/66	82/356	,,	,,	H211-R1-Fl 3	LC1	35a
82.3.2/103	82/357	,,	,,	H211-R3-F	LC1	35b
82.2.20/20	82/402	Copper or bronze	,, (f)	H210-R8-F	LC2	
82.2.20/23	82/383	,,	,,	H849-R4-F	LC2	35c
Weapons						
Arrows						
—	64/106	Iron	Arrowhead	H169-C	TC	
78.3.12/23	78/480	,,	,,	W283-0-L1b	LC1	36a
78.3.12/48	78/426	Wood	3 Arrows (f)	,,	LC1	
82.2.25/90	82/344	Wood + iron	,, (f)	H849-R1-F	LC2	
Sling						
82.2.16/70	82/586	Palm fibre rope	Sling	H781-R3-C	LC1	36b
Throwing stick						
82.1.30/35	82/56	Wood	Throwing stick	H763-R6-Fl 2	LC2	36c
			HOUSEHOLD FURNISHINGS (Part 3, Ch. 5)			
Furniture						
Chair or bed leg						
74.1.29/14	74/199	Wood	Chair or bed leg	H177-R1-SFl	LC1	
Balusters						
—	66a/221	,,	Baluster (f)	H184-F	LC1	37b
—	66a/222	,,	,, (f)	,,	LC1	37b
66.3.10/2	66/218	,,	,,	H184-0	LC	
66.3.10/6	66/216	,,	,,	,,	LC	37b
66.3.12/5	66/214	,,	,, (f)	,,	LC	
69.2.10/9	69/37	,,	,,	H178-R6-F	LC1	
72.10.28/3	72/416	,,	,, (f)	H172-R1-Fl 3	LC2	
72.11.26/15	72/435	,,	,,	Pl 356-L5-P	LC1	
76.2.15/11	—	,,	,,	H171-SFl	LC	
76.2.18/14	—	,,	,,	Pl 356-F	TC?	
78.1.16/5	78/592	,,	,, (f)	W283-0-F	LC1	
78.2.21/28	78/593	,,	,,	H197-R3-P	LC	
78.3.12/40	78/591	,,	,,	W283-0-L1b	LC1	
80.3.9/26	80/765	,,	,, (f)	H207-R2-L3	LC1	
80.3.10/26	80/766	,,	,, (f)	H207-R1-L27	LC2	

APPENDIX C—continued
COMPREHENSIVE TABLE OF LATE AND TERMINAL CHRISTIAN OBJECT FINDS[1]

Day no.	*Reg. no.*	*Material*	*Object*[2]	*Provenance*[3]	*Date*[4]	*Plate*
Knobs						
—	66a/223	Wood	Knob	H184-F	LC1	
69.2.11/8	69/44	,,	,,	H178-R6-F	LC1	
72.10.16/5	72/409	,,	,,	H732-SFL	TC?	
74.2.5/4	74/200	,,	,,	H186-FL	LC1	
76.2.19/10	—	,,	,,	C188-F	LC1	
80.3.10/35	80/765	,,	,,	H207-R2-L3	LC1	37c
82.2.25/68	82/224	,,	,,	H849-R1-F	LC2	
82.2.27/66	82/218	,,	,,	H848-R3-SFl 1	LC1	
82.3.2/78	82/237	,,	,,	H848-R5-FL 2	LC1	
Carved elements						
66.3.13/1	66/213	,,	Furn. element (f)	H184-F	LC1	37a
66.3.13/2	66/211	,,	,, (f)	,,	LC1	37a
66.3.13/2	66/212	,,	,, (f)	,,	LC1	37a
69.2.15/8	69/72	,,	3 Furn. elements	H178-R3-F	LC1	37d
Ivory inlay						
—	66a/226	Ivory	Carved inlay (f)	H184-F	LC1	
Problematical furniture pieces						
—	66a/224	Wood	Furniture piece? (f)	H184-F	LC1	
78.2.12/54	—	,,	,,	H202-R7-F	LC1	
80.2.26/50	80/778	,,	,, (f)	H206-R6-L41	LC1	
80.2.28/70	—	,,	,, (f)	H849-R1-Fl 1	LC2	
82.3.1/79	82/249	,,	,,	H849-R5-F	LC2	
82.2.3/37	82/378	Iron	Furniture fitting?	H763-R8-Fl 2	LC1	
Toilet fixtures						
66.3.5/1	—	Ceramic	Toilet fixture (f)	H184-R1-F	LC1	40a
82.2.10/50	—	,,	,, (f)	H763-R7-Fl 3-P	LC1	
Bedding						
76T/516	—	Wood cloth	Blanket	H170-F	TC	
78.2.1/40	78/681	Grass + cotton	Sleeping mat (f)	P514 lining	LC	38a
82.1.14/175	82/92	,,	,, (f)	H849-R4-P	LC2	38b
Floor mats						
72.10.29/3	72/46	Palm fibre	Floor mat (f)	H734-SFl	LC	
76T/513	—	Flax fabric	,, (f)	H171-R1-F	TC	
78T/251	78/280	,,	,, (f)	H197-R5-F	LC1	
82.1.14/36	82/118	Palm fibre	,, (f)	H763-R7-F	LC2	38c
82.1.14/103	,,	,,	,, (f)	H763-R7-Fl 3	LC1	
Rugs						
76T/514	—	Wool fabric	Rug (f)	H170-F	TC	
76T/515	—	,,	,, (f)	H170-F	TC	
76T/651	—	,,	,, (f)	Cr 188-R1-F	LC1	
84T/356	86/300	Goat + antelope hair	,, (f)	H785-R8xx-L4	LC1	
Pot rests						
78.1.21/29	78/293	Palm fibre	Pot rest	Pl 358 NE-P	LC	38d
82.1.14/112	82/109	,,	,,	H849-R1-Fl 3	LC2	38e
Lamps[8]						
Cup lamp						
66.3.19/20	66/132	Pottery[8]	Cup lamp (U6)	Tomb T3	LC1	39b

APPENDIX C—continued
COMPREHENSIVE TABLE OF LATE AND TERMINAL CHRISTIAN OBJECT FINDS[1]

Day no.	*Reg. no.*	*Material*	*Object*[2]	*Provenance*[3]	*Date*[4]	*Plate*
Saucer lamps						
—	72/75	Pottery[8]	Saucer lamp (W12)	?	LC	
76.2.29/5	76/97	,,	,, (W12)	Pl 358-C-F	LC	
82.2.21/1	82/121	,,	,, (W12)	H210-R8-F	LC2	39a
—	63/28	,,	,, (U6)	Ch 293-C-L2	LC	
—	63/29	,,	,, (U6)	,,	LC	
—	63/30	,,	,, (U6)	,,	LC	
69.2.16/1	69/65	,,	,, (U6)	H178-R3-F	LC1	
74.2.4/15	74/28	,,	,, (U6)	H101-SFl	LC	
Bowl lamps						
—	64/212	,,	Bowl lamp (?)	H169-0	LC	
72.10.19/5	—	,,	,, (H4)	H173-F	LC2	
76.2.11/12	—	,,	,, (?)	H171-R2-F	TC	
78.2.12/4	—	,,	,, (?)	H202-R7-F	LC1	
82.2.23/56	82/131	,,	,, (R11)	H849-R1-F	LC2	
82.3.1/41	—	,,	,, (R11)	H849-R1-Fl 1	LC2	
'Candle-holder' Lamps						
69.2.13/12	69/55	,,	'Candle-holder' lamp	H178-R5-F	LC	
78.2.5/33	—	,,	,,	Pl 358 NW-L6	LC1	
Bottle lamps						
—	66a/281	,,	Bottle lamp (U6) (f)	?	LC?	
—	66a/282	,,	,, (U6) (f)	?	LC?	
72.10.18/10	72/41	,,	,, (U6)	H172-F	LC2	
78.2.12/28	78/145	,,	,, (U6)	H196-R4-F	LC2	39c
82.3.4/69	82/63	,,	,, (H5)	H211-R1-SFl 4	LC1	
Egyptian glazed lamps						
66.2.20/4	66/280	,,	Glazed lamp (G.II) (f)	H171-R10-F	TC	
69.2.12/6	69/56	,,	,, (G.II)	H178-R7-F	LC1	
72.11.2/12	—	,,	,, (G.II?)	Pl 356-L4	LC	
'Recycled' X-Group and Early Christian lamps						
—	64/154	,,	Bowl lamp (R5?)	H169?	LC	
—	66a/58	,,	Frog lamp (W2)	Pl 758-F	LC	
69.2.12/5	69/49	,,	Min. bottle lamp (H1)	H178-R7-F	LC1	
72.10.11/14	72/45	,,	,, (R1?)	H734-SFl	LC?	
Unidentified lamp fragment						
80.2.19/52	80/681	,,	Lamp (?) (f)	H206-R2-L17	TC	
Censers						
72.10.10/4	—	,,	Censer (?) (f)	H734-SFl	LC?	
72.20.24/10	—	,,	,, (?) (f)	,,	LC?	
72.11.22/9	—	,,	,, (?) (f)	Ch 287-R10-F	TC	
82.2.21/7	82/164	,,	,, (H7)	H210-R8-F	LC2	
Brushes						
82.1.25/115	82/470	Grass stalks	Brush	H763-R7-F	LC2	39d
82.2.23/75	82/469	,,	,,	P845-F	LC	
Miscellaneous household items						
82.3.4/115	—	Wood	4 Door planks	H211-R1-Fl 4-P	LC1	
82.2.25/79	—	Sandstone	Door pivot stone	H849-R1-F	LC2	
66.3.10/4	66/123	Iron	Nail	H184-SFl	LC1	
78.3.12/20	—	,,	,,	W283-0-L1b	LC1	
82.3.2/80	82/168	Ceramic	Glazed tile (f)	H849-R1-Fl 3	LC2	39e
82T/332	—	Goat hair	Tent (f)	H763-F	LC2	

APPENDIX C—continued

COMPREHENSIVE TABLE OF LATE AND TERMINAL CHRISTIAN OBJECT FINDS[1]

Day no.	*Reg. no.*	*Material*	*Object*[2]	*Provenance*[3]	*Date*[4]	*Plate*
Locks and lock mechanisms						
Housings						
66.3.12/2	66/177	Wood	Lock housing	H184-F	LC1	40d
76.2.16/12	—	„	„	H183-SFl 1	LC1	
78.2.8/95	78/54	„	„	H197-R1-F	LC1	
80.1.29/54	80/763	„	„	H206-R1-L15	TC	
82.1.28/2	82/55	„	„	H781-R2-C	LC1	40b-c
Bolt						
78.2.12/67	78/64	„	Bolt	H196-R4-F	LC2	40e
Keys						
Simple toothed keys						
66.3.12/4	66/178	„	Key	H184-F	LC1	
69.2.11/7	69/41	„	„	H178-R2-F	LC1	41a
69.2.11/12	69/42	„	„	H178-R1-F	LC1	
69.2.13/6	69/57	„	„	H178-R4-F	LC1	41a
69.2.13/15	69/138	„	„ (f)	H178-R3-F	LC1	
72.10.18/9	—	„	„	H732-SFl	TC?	
72.10.12/15	—	„	„	H168-F	LC	
72.11.5/3	—	„	„ (f)	Pl 356 N-L4	LC1	
76.2.15/7	—	„	„	H171-SFl	LC	
78.2.8/80	78/371	„	„	H235-Fl	LC1	
78.3.12/43	78/364	„	„	W283-0-L1b	LC1	41a
—	78/377	„	„	H197-R1-F	LC1	
82.1.28/41	82/199	„	„ (f)	H781-R2-C	LC1	
82.1.30/59	82/80	„	„	H763-R4-Fl 2	LC1	
82.1.30/59	82/80	„	„ (f)	H763-R4-Fl 2	LC1	
82.1.30/59	82/80	„	„ (f)	„	LC1	
82.2.24/58	82/80	„	„	H848-R3-F	LC1	
82.2.24/58	82/80	„	„ (f)	„	LC1	
82.3.2/77	82/223	„	„	H848-R5-Fl 2	LC1	
84.1.28/23	—	„	„ (f)	H785-R6-L3	LC1	
Tooth-and-peg keys						
—	64/297	„	„	H169-F	LC2	
74.2.2/7	74/198	„	„	H177-SFl	LC1	
78.2.16/7	78/360	„	„	H197-R2-F	LC2	
82.2.28/60	82/80	„	„	H849-R1-Fl 1	LC2	
82.1.30/37	82/80	„	„	H763-R1-Fl 2	LC1	
82.3.1/67	82/80	„	„	H848-R3-F	LC1	41a
Angled keys						
66.2.9/6	66/9	„	„	H171-0	LC	
69.1.30/1	69/8	„	„	H177-R7-F	LC	
76.2.11/10	—	„	„	H171-R2-F	TC	
78.2.2/24	78/359	„	„	P515-F	LC	41b
Peg keys						
69.2.6/1	69/141	„	„	H177-R5-F	LC1	41c
72.11.13/18	—	„	„	Ch 287-F	TC	
80.3.10/28	80/665	„	„	H207-R2-L3	LC1	41c
82.2.21/59	82/80	„	„	H849-R4-F	LC2	41c
82.2.25/73	82/80	„	„	H849-R1-F	LC2	
82.3.2/97	82/227	„	„	H849-R5-Fl 1	LC2	

APPENDIX C—continued
COMPREHENSIVE TABLE OF LATE AND TERMINAL CHRISTIAN OBJECT FINDS[1]

Day no.	*Reg. no.*	*Material*	*Object*[2]	*Provenance*[3]	*Date*[4]	*Plate*
Locks and lock mechanisms						
Tumblers						
78.3.12/39	78/381	Wood	Lock tumbler	W283-0-L1b	LC	
82.1.24/63	82/197	,,	,,	H763-F	LC2	
82.1.25/113	82/197	,,	,,	H763-R7-F	LC2	
82.1.26/54	—	,,	,,	H763-F	LC2	
82.1.30/62	82/197	,,	,,	H763-R4-Fl 2	LC1	
82.1.31/62	—	,,	,,	,,	LC1	
82.2.3/49	82/258	,,	,,	H763-R8-Fl 2	LC1	
82.2.3/49	82/197	,,	6 Lock tumblers	,,	LC1	41d
82.2.25/67	82/197	,,	Lock tumbler	H849-R1-F	LC2	
82.3.2/95	82/197	,,	,,	H849-R1-Fl	LC2	
82.3.2/105	82/258	,,	,,	H848-R5-Fl 2	LC1	
82.3.3/139	82/485	,,	,,	H211-R1-Fl 3-P	LC1	
82.3.4/28	82/197	,,	,,	H849-R1-Fl	LC1	
82.3.4/100	82/197	,,	,,	H211-R1-Fl 4	LC1	
84.1.29/37	—	,,	2 Lock tumblers	H785-R4-L4	LC1	
84.2.5/35	—	,,	Lock tumbler	,,	LC1	
Perforated blocks						
72.10.18/6	72/440	,,	Perforated block	H732-SFl	TC?	41e
80.2.18/56	80/781	,,	,,	H206-R1-L32	TC	41e
82.2.21/72	82/21	,,	,,	H210-R8-F	LC2	41e
82.3.1/80	82/255	,,	,,	H849-R5-F	LC2	41e
Padlock						
69.2.10/10	69/35	Iron	Padlock (f)	H178-R6-F	LC1	

TEXTILES (Part 3, Ch. 6)[9]

66.3.3/4	—	Textile	Decorated frags.	St 738-F	LC
66.3.3/8	—	,,	,,	H184-F	LC1
82.3.7/3	82/572	Silk	Decorated strip	H763-F	LC2
82.3.7/9	82/572	Wool	Decorated square	H211-R3-SFl- 1	LC1
82.3.7/19	82/572	,,	,,	H848-R5-Fl 4	LC1
78.3.38/5	—	Flax	Painted cloth	Pl 358 NE-P	LC
82.3.4/72	82/23	,,	Inscribed cloth	H848-R5-Fl 2	LC1
82.2.6/61	82/497	Cotton	Bundle of cloth	H763-R8-Fl 2	LC1
84.1.7/22	—	Flax + cotton	,,	H211-R1-F	LC1
78.3.18/77	—	Wool	Spool of yarn	P517-F	LC2

APPENDIX C—continued
COMPREHENSIVE TABLE OF LATE AND TERMINAL CHRISTIAN OBJECT FINDS[1]

The following fragments were catalogued by a system of textile numbers rather than day numbers

Textile no.	*Reg. no.*	*Material*	*Object*[2]	*Provenance*[3]	*Date*[4]	*Plate*
76T/413	—	Flax	Checked cloth	H171-F	TC	
76T/414	—	,,	,,	,,	TC	
76T/418	—	Cotton + wool	Striped cloth	,,	TC	
76T/419	76/133	Cotton	Plaid cloth	,,	LC1	
76T/421	—	Cotton + wool	Striped cloth	,,	LC1	
76T/601	—	Wool	Weft-faced cloth	Ch 287-R22A-SFl	LC1	
76T/646	—	Cotton + wool	,,	H183-R2-L2	LC1	
76T/647	—	Cotton	Striped cloth	,,	LC1	
76T/652	—	Cotton + wool	Weft-faced cloth	C188-R1-F	LC1	
76T/650	—	Wool	,,	,,	LC1	
76T/707	—	,,	Plainweave	C188-R2-F	LC1	
76T/720	—	Cotton + wool	,,	H171-L3-F	LC2	
78T/8	—	Silk	Plainweave frag.	W305-F	LC2	
78T/176	—	Wool	Weaving wedge	H235-F	LC1	
(78T/210)	—	Silk + cotton	Plainweave	H197-R1-F	LC1	
78T/215	—	Cotton	Checked cloth	,,	LC1	
78T/177	—	Cotton + wool	Weft-faced cloth	H235-F	LC1	
80T/166	—	Flax	Striped cloth	H206-L21	LC1	
80T/167	—	Cloth fragment	,,	,,	LC1	
80T/246	—	Wool	,,	H206-L46	LC1	
82T/210	—	Flax + silk	Plainweave frag.	H781-R2-C	LC1	
82T/211	—	Cotton	,,	,,	LC1	
82T/212	—	,,	,,	,,	LC1	
82T/213	—	Cotton + wool	Striped cloth	H781-R2-C	LC1	
82T/214	—	Cotton	,,	,,	LC1	
82T/215	—	Wool	Polychrome cloth	,,	LC1	
82T/216	—	Cotton + wool	,,	,,	LC1	
82T/217	—	,,	,,	,,	LC1	
82T/218	—	,,	,,	,,	LC1	
82T/283	—	Flax	Checked cloth	H763-R4-Fl 2	LC2	
82T/292	—	Cotton + wool	Plainweave frag.	H763-R7-Fl 1	LC2	
82T/305	—	Silk	Striped cloth	H763-F	TC	
82T/307	—	Flax	Checked cloth	H763-R8-Fl 2	LC1	
82T/308	—	,,	,,	,,	LC1	44b
82T/323	—	Cotton	Warp-faced cloth	H763-F	LC2	
82T324	—	Flax	Orange cloth	,,	LC2	
82T325	—	,,	Plainweave frag.	,,	LC2	
82T/328	—	Cotton	Check pattern	,,	LC2	
82T/333	—	Wool	Weft-faced cloth	,,	LC2	37f
82T419	—	Cotton	Checked cloth	,,	LC2	
82T/420	—	Wool	Polychrome cloth	,,	LC2	
82T/421	—	Cotton + wool	,,	,,	LC2	45b
82T422	—	Cotton	Checked cloth	,,	LC2	
82T/427	—	,,	Plaid cloth	,,	LC2	
82T/428	—	,,	Checked cloth	,,	LC2	
82T/429	—	,,	Plaid cloth	,,	LC2	
82T/430	—	,,	Checked cloth	,,	LC2	
(82T/430)	—	,,	,,	H848-R3-Cr	LC1	
82T/431	—	,,	,,	H731-F	LC2	
82T/432a	—	Cotton + wool	Striped cloth	H763-F	LC2	
82T/432b	—	,,	,,	,,	LC2	
82T/436	—	Cotton	Very fine cloth	,,	LC2	
82T/437	—	Silk + cotton	,,		LC2	

APPENDIX C—continued
COMPREHENSIVE TABLE OF LATE AND TERMINAL CHRISTIAN OBJECT FINDS[1]

The following fragments were catalogued by a system of textile numbers rather than day numbers

Textile no.	*Reg. no.*	*Material*	*Object*[2]	*Provenance*[3]	*Date*[4]	*Plate*
82T/438	—	Cotton	Checked cloth	H763-F	LC2	
82T/439	—	Wool	Plainweave frag.	H763-F	LC2	
82T/442	—	Flax + cotton	Plainweave frag.	„	LC2	
82T/443	—	Silk	Striped cloth	„	LC2	
82T/448	—	Cotton	Plainweave frag.	„	LC2	
82T/697	—	Flax + cotton	Striped fustian	H848-R3-Fl 1	LC1	
82T/707	—	Cotton	Plainweave frag.	H848-R5-Fl 1	LC2	
82T/708	—	Flax	Striped cloth	„	LC2	
82T/712	—	Flax + cotton	Fustian	„	LC2	
82T/713	—	Cotton + wool	Striped cloth	„	LC2	
82T/714	—	Flax	Shroud fragment	„	LC2	
82T/894	—	Wool	Weft-faced cloth	H211-R1-Fl 1	LC1	
82T/895	—	„	Fringe + twining	„	LC1	
82T/900	—	Flax	Warp-faced cloth	H211-R1-Fl 3	LC1	
82T/901	—	„	„	„	LC1	44a
82T/907	—	„	„	H211-R1-Fl 3-P	LC1	
82T/908	—	„	Hemmed cloth	„	LC1	
82T/909	—	„	„	„	LC1	
82T/910	—	„	„	„	LC1	
84T/4	86/134	Silk	Striped cloth	P906	LC	45d
84T/325	86/411	Cotton	Checked cloth	H785-R6-L3	LC1	
84T/326	86/452	Cotton + wool	Weft-faced cloth	H785-R4-L2	LC1	42b
84T/332	86/393	„	Striped cloth	H785-R4-L4	LC1	42c
84T/466	86/414	Cotton	Checked cloth	Pl 939-NE	LC1	
84T/467	86/249	Flax	Plainweave frag.	„	LC1	
84T/470	86/349	Wool	Plaid cloth	„	LC1	44d
76T/417	76/134	„	Embroidered cloth	H171-F	TC	
76T/600	—	„	„	Ch 287-R22a-SFl	LC1	
76T/604	76/133	„	„	„	LC1	
76T/605	76/134	„	„	„	LC1	
76T/649	—	„	„	C188-R1-F	LC1	
78T/476	—	„	„	H197-R7-F	LC1	
80T/245	—	Flax	„	H206-R E-L36	TC	
82T/209	—	Cotton + wool	„	H781-R1-Fl 2	LC2	
82T/285	—	Cotton	„	H763-R4-Fl 2	LC2	
82T/433	—	Cotton + wool	„	H763-F	LC2	
82T/434	—	Cotton	„	„	LC2	
82T/703	—	Flax	„	H848-R3-Fl 1-P	LC1	
82T/893	—	Wool	„	H211-R1-Fl 1	LC1	
84T/140	86/356	„	„	H785-R6-L4	LC1	
84T/357	86/343	Wool + flax + cotton	„	H785-R8xx-L4	LC1	45a
76T/420	—	Cotton + wool	Tapestry weave	H171-F	LC1	
78T/113	78/279	Flax + silk	„	H195-F	LC1	45e
78T/477	—	Wool	„	H197-R7-F	LC1	
78T/490	—	„	„	H197-R5-F	LC1	
82T/304	—	„	„	H763-Rubble F	TC	
82T/441	—	„	„	H763-F	LC2	
84T/468	86/451	„	„	Pl 939-NE	LC1	
76T/415	—	Flax + silk	Float weave	H171-F	TC	
76T/706	—	Silk	Satin weave	C188-R2-F	LC1	
76T/719	—	Wool	Twill weave	H171-L3-F	LC2	
(78T/60)	—	Flax + cotton	„	H197-R1-F	LC1	37e
78T/133	—	Cotton	„	Ch 293-Narth-SF	TC	

APPENDIX C—continued
COMPREHENSIVE TABLE OF LATE AND TERMINAL CHRISTIAN OBJECT FINDS[1]

The following fragments were catalogued by a system of textile numbers rather than day numbers

Textile no.	*Reg. no.*	*Material*	*Object*[2]	*Provenance*[3]	*Date*[4]	*Plate*
78T/134	—	Silk + cotton	Satin weave	Ch 293-Narth-SF	TC	
(78T/250)	—	Flax	Float weave	H197-R7-F	LC1	
78T/475	—	Wool	Two-faced weave	H197-R7-F	LC1	
80T/102	—	„	Twill weave	H206-R C-L19	TC	
82T/312	—	Cotton	Pile weave	H763-R8-Fl 2	LC1	
82T/327	—	Flax	Float weave	H763-F	LC2	
82T/330	—	Silk	Compound weave	„	LC2	45c
82T/709	—	Flax + cotton	Twill weave	H848-R5-Fl 1	LC2	
82T/874	—	„	„	H849-R1-Fl 2	LC2	
82T/898	—	Flax	„	H211-R1-Fl 3	LC1	43b
82T/306	—	Cotton	Printed cloth	H763-R8-Fl 2	LC1	
82T/444	—	Silk	„	H763-F	LC2	
76T/602	—	Wool	Knitted fragment	Ch 287-R22a-SFl	LC1	
78T/478	—	„	„	H197-R7-F	LC1	
84T/297	86/247	„	„	P1044	LC1	
Miscellaneous Textile Items						
82T/101	—	Flax + wool	Narrow strap	Cr 766-F	LC2	
(82T/101)	—	„	„	H763-F	TC	
82T/290	—	Wool + cotton	Experimental wv.	H763-R7-Fl 1	LC2	
82T/310	—	Flax	Loom end	H763-R8-Fl 2	LC1	
82T/440	—	Wool	Cloth with twining	H763-F	LC2	
82T/698	—	Cotton + wool	Child's weaving	H848-R2-Fl 1	LC1	61e
82T/892	—	Cotton	Cloth offcut	H211-R1-Fl 1	LC1	43a
82T/899	—	Flax	Stitched rectangle	H211-R1-Fl 3	LC1	44a
84T/90	86/223	„	Tablet-woven braid	P932-L1	LC	

DRESS AND ORNAMENTATION (Part 3, Ch. 7)

Textile no.	*Reg. no.*	*Material*	*Object*	*Provenance*	*Date*	*Plate*
Fabric garments						
—	64/7	Flax + wool	Bishop's vestments	Ch 293-B376	LC2	
—	64/133	„	Garment fragments	„	LC2	
—	64/9	„	Handkerchief	„	LC2	
76T/650	—	Wool	Weft-faced cloth	Ch 293-B376	LC1	
78.3.28/3	—	Cotton	Infant's dress	Pl 358 NE-P	LC	
78.3.28/63	—	„	Loincloth (f)	H195-R1-F	LC1	
78.3.28/29	—	Flax	Garment neck (f)	Pl 358-P	LC2	
78.3.28/50	—	Cotton	„ (f)	„	LC2	
76T/416	—	Cotton + flax	„ (f)	H171-F	TC	
82T/284	—	Flax	Garment hem (f)	H763-R4-Fl 2	LC2	
82T/423	—	Flax + silk	Garment neck (f)	H763-F	LC2	
82T/435	—	Flax + silk + cot.	Neck and facing (f)	„	LC2	46a
82T/704	—	Cotton	Garment (f)	H848-R3-P	LC1	
82T/902	—	Flax	„ (f)	H211-R1-Fl 3	LC1	
84T/324	86/158	Silk + cotton	Garment facing (f)	H785-R6-L3	LC1	
Caps						
76T/599	—	Flax + silk + cot.	Padded cap (f)	Ch 287-R22a-SFl	LC2	
76T/717	—	Cotton	Cap (f)	H171-L3-F	LC2	
78T/88	—	Wool + flax + cot.	„ (f)	H202-R1-F	LC1	
78T/262	—	Flax	Cap center	H194-R16-F	TC	
78.3.28/8	—	Silk + flax + fur	Cap	P505-F	LC1	
78.3.28/14	—	Cotton	„	P517-F	LC	
78.3.28/23		Flax	„ (f)	H194--R16-F	TC	
82.2.28/45	82/557	Leather	„ (f)	H211-R2-F	LC1	

APPENDIX C—continued

COMPREHENSIVE TABLE OF LATE AND TERMINAL CHRISTIAN OBJECT FINDS[1]

The following fragments were catalogued by a system of textile numbers rather than day numbers

Textile no.	*Reg. no.*	*Material*	*Object*[2]	*Provenance*[3]	*Date*[4]	*Plate*
Trousers						
82T/294	—	Flax + cotton	Leg opening	H763-R7-Fl 1	LC2	46c
82T/295	—	„	„	„	LC2	
82T/311	—	„	„	H763-R8-Fl 2	LC1	
Belts						
76T/718	—	Cotton + wool	Embroidered (f)	H171-L3-F	LC2	
78T/473	—	Wool	Polychrome (f)	H197-R7-F	LC1	
80T/423	—	„	Sprang belt (f)	H206-A3-L13b	LC1	
80T/500	—	Silk + cotton	Belt tab (f)	H207-A3-L33	LC1	
Headveils						
76T/510	—	Wool	With dec. band	H171-SFl	LC1	
78T/474	78/280	Wool + cotton	With embroidery	H197-R7-F	LC1	
82T/296	—	„	With dec. bands	H763-R7-Fl 1	LC2	44f
82T/297	—	„	With dec. band	„	LC2	43e
82T/446	—	Wool	Brilliant red	H763-F	LC2	
82T/447	—	„	Dark blue	„	LC2	
82T/449	—	„	Ivory colour	„	LC2	
82T/450	—	„	Emerald green	„	LC2	
82T/451	—	„	Blue-green	„	LC2	
82T/452	—	„	Red	„	LC2	
82T/453	—	Wool + cotton	With dec. band	„	LC2	44e
82T/454	—	Wool	Dark blue	H763-F	LC2	
82T/455	—	Wool fibre + yarn	Blue	„	LC2	
84T/134	86/385	Wool + cotton	With dec. band	H785-R6-L3-SFl	LC1	46e
84T/135	84/595	„	„	H785-R6-L3-Fl	LC1	46d
Leather garments						
Aprons, etc.						
78.1.25/11	—	Leather	Apron? (f)	Pl 358 NE-P	LC	
78.1.25/29	—	„	„ (f)	„	LC	
78.2.15/4	—	„	„ (f)	H197-R5-F	LC1	
78.3.1/48	—	„	„ (f)	Pl 358-P	LC2	
80.2.28/84	80/985	„	„ (f)	H206-R6-L41	LC1	
Rahats						
78.2.15/31	78/614	„	Rahat (f)	H196-0-L3	TC	47a
78.2.20/45	78/614	„	„ (f)	H194-R16-F	TC	
78.2.26/27	78/614	„	„ (f)	H196-0-P	LC	
78.3.1/36	78/773	„	„ (f)	H235-SFl 2	LC1	
Belts						
—	64/10	„	Belt	Ch 293-B376	LC2	
82.2.3/36	82/558	„	„ (f)	H763-R8-Fl 2	LC1	47b
Decorative neckpiece?						
72.10.29/4	72/47	„	Neckpiece?	H174-SFl	LC	47c

APPENDIX C—continued
COMPREHENSIVE TABLE OF LATE AND TERMINAL CHRISTIAN OBJECT FINDS[1]

Day no.	*Reg. no.*	*Material*	*Object*[2]	*Provenance*[3]	*Date*[4]	*Plate*
Problematical fragments						
66.2.17/2	—	Leather	Garment frags.?	H169-0-F	LC	
78.1.19/33	—	,,	,,	P505-F	LC1	
78.1.19/35	—	,,	,,	,,	LC1	
78.2.12/30	—	,,	Garment fragment?	H197-R1-F	LC1	
78.2.26/33	—	,,	Garment frags.?	H196-0-P	LC	
78.3.9/16	—	,,	,,	Pl 358-P	LC2	
82.1.25/119	82/530	,,	,,	H763-R7-F	LC2	
Buttons						
78.3.1/32	78/413	Pottery	Button	H235-SFl 2	LC1	47d
80.3.8/45	80/905	Stone	,,	H206-R1-L5	TC	
82.2.28/65	—	,,	,,	H211-R2-F	LC2	47e
Footgear						
Boots						
78.3.12/44	78/462	Leather	Boot (f)	W283-0-L1b	LC1	
82.1.25/30	82/598	,,	,,	H763-R8-F	LC2	48a-b
Shoes						
76.2.17/11	—	,,	Shoe (f)	Pl 356-F	TC	
76.2.28/17	—	,,	,, (f)	H187-F	LC2	
78.1.19/34	78/466	,,	,, (f)	P505-F	LC1	48d
78.1.23/10	78/466	,,	,,	Pl 358-NE-P	LC	
78.1.25/30	78/466	,,	,, (f)	,,	LC	
78.1.25/30	78/460	,,	,, (f)	,,	LC	
78.1.25/30	78/460	,,	,, (f)	,,	LC	
78.1.28/12	78/466	,,	,, (f)	,,	LC	
78.1.28/12	78/466	,,	,, (f)	,,	LC	
78.2.5/31	78/466	,,	,,	Pl 358 NW-L6	LC1	48f
78.2.8/93	78/465	,,	,,	H197-R1-F	LC1	48e
78.2.12/29	78/466	,,	,, (f)	,,	LC1	
78.2.20/59	78/466	,,	,, (f)	Pl 358-P	LC2	
78.2.26/32	78/466	,,	,, (f)	H196-0-P	LC	
78.2.26/32	78/466	,,	,, (f)	,,	LC	
78.3.1/47	—	,,	,, (f)	,,	LC	
78.3.2/65	78/466	,,	,, (f)	,,	LC	
80.2.28/91	—	,,	,, (f)	H206-R2-L7	TC	
82.1.24/6	82/606	,,	,, (f)	P776-F	LC2	
82.1.24/73	82/606	,,	,, (f)	H763-F	LC2	
82.1.25/89	82/606	,,	,, (f)	H781-F	LC2	
82.1.25/89	82/606	,,	,, (f)	,,	LC2	
82.1.25/16	82/606	,,	,, (f)	H763-F	LC2	
82.2.4/29	82/606	,,	,, (f)	P797-F	LC1	
82.2.6/7	82/606	,,	,, (f)	,,	LC1	
82.2.10/4	82/606	,,	,, (f)	H785-R2-P	LC2	
82.2.14/80	82/606	,,	,, (f)	H763-F	LC2	
82.2.16/56	82/606	,,	,, (f)	P837-F	LC1	
82.2.23/41	82/606	,,	,, (f)	P845-F	LC	
82.3.1/105	82/606	,,	,, (f)	H848-R3-F	LC1	
82.3.1/106	82/598	,,	,,	,,	LC1	48c
82.3.1/107	82/606	,,	,, (f)	H848 R5 F	LC1	
82.3.1/108	82/606	,,	,, (f)	H211-R1-F	LC1	

APPENDIX C—continued
COMPREHENSIVE TABLE OF LATE AND TERMINAL CHRISTIAN OBJECT FINDS[1]

Day no.	*Reg. no.*	*Material*	*Object*[2]	*Provenance*[3]	*Date*[4]	*Plate*
Leather sandals						
—	64/126	Leather	Sandal	H169-Fl	LC1	
72.10.18/1	—	,,	,,	H732-SFl	TC?	
72.10.19/7	—	,,	,,	,,	TC?	
76.2.21/9	—	,,	,,	Pl 358 NW-L2	TC	
78.1.22/21	78/457	,,	,,	Pl 358 NE-P	LC	
78.1.26/46	78/460	,,	,,	H235-F	LC1	
78.2.6/47	78/457	,,	,, (f)	Pl 358 NW-L5	LC1	
78.2.8/92	78/458	,,	,,	H197-R1-F	LC1	
78.2.12/29	78/458	,,	,, (f)	,,	LC1	
78.2.18/26	78/460	,,	,, (f)	P468-F	TC	
78.2.20/59	78/460	,,	,, (f)	Pl 358-P	LC2	
78.2.21/4	78/458	,,	Pair of sandals	H198-0-F	LC	
78.2.26/28	78/458	,,	Sandal (f)	H196-0-P	LC2	49c
78.3.1/47	—	,,	,,	Pl 358-P	LC	
78.3.2/65	78/460	,,	,, (f)	,,	LC	
78.3.25/5	78/460	,,	,, (f)	H260-0	LC	
82.1.31/55	82/599	,,	,,	H763-R7-F	LC2	
82.1.31/59	82/606	,,	,, (f)	,,	LC2	
82.2.2/58	82/599	,,	,,	H763-R8-Fl 2	LC1	
82.2.2/58	82/606	,,	,, (f)	,,	LC1	
82.2.21/49	82/599	,,	,,	P840-F	LC	
82.2.21/49	82/606	,,	,,	,,	LC	
82.2.23/51	82/599	,,	,,	H849-R1-F	LC2	49a
82.2.23/51	82/599	,,	,,	,,	LC2	49a
82.3.1/104	82/599	,,	,,	H211-R1-F	LC1	49b
Fibre sandals						
72.10.22/10	—	Palm fibre	Pair of sandals	H182-SFl	LC1	
72.10.24/1	—	,,	,,	LC1 level	LC1	
72.10.25/13	—	,,	Sandal	H172-Fl	LC2	
74.1.31/4	74/228	,,	,,	H177-R6-SFl	LC1	
76.2.15/6	—	,,	,,	H171-SFl	LC	
76.2.22/6	—	,,	,,	Pl 358 NE-L2-P	LC	
76.2.23/3	—	,,	,,	,,	LC	
78.1.17/28	78/453	,,	,,	,,	LC	
78.1.17/28	78/459	,,	,, (f)	,,	LC	
78.3.13/80	78/459	,,	,, (f)	Pl 358-P	LC	
80.3.14/48	80/1015	,,	,,	H206-R2-L7	TC	
82.1.24/13	82/600	,,	,,	H763-R5-F	LC2	49e
82.1.25/11	82/600	,,	,,	H763-R7-F	LC2	
82.1.27/43	82/606	,,	,,	H763-F	LC2	
82.1.30/13	82/600	,,	,,	H763-R3-Fl 1	LC2	
82.1.30/20	82/600	,,	,,	H763-R4-Fl 2	LC1	
82.1.30/21	82/600	,,	,,	H763-R7-F	LC2	
82.2.3/40	82/600	,,	,,	H763-R8-Fl 2	LC1	
82.2.3/40	82/600	,,	,,	,,	LC1	
82.2.3/41	82/600	,,	,,	,,	LC1	
82.2.17/71	82/600	,,	,,	H781-R2-C	LC2	
82.2.28/88	82/600	,,	,,	P845-F	LC	
82.2.28/89	82/600	,,	,,	H211-R1-Fl 1	LC1	49d
82.3.4/176	82/600	,,	,,	H848-R5-Fl 4	LC1	
82.3.4/178	82/606	,,	,,	H211-R1-Fl 1-P	LC1	

APPENDIX C—continued
COMPREHENSIVE TABLE OF LATE AND TERMINAL CHRISTIAN OBJECT FINDS[1]

Day no.	*Reg. no.*	*Material*	*Object*[2]	*Provenance*[3]	*Date*[4]	*Plate*
Ornamentation						
Decorative hair combs						
—	64/195	Wood	Dec. hair comb	H169-R3	LC1	50a
66.3.6/10	66/66	,,	,,	H184-F	LC1	50a
66.3.12/1	66/86	,,	,,	,,	LC1	50a
69.2.10/3	69/22	,,	,,	H178-R6-F	LC1	50a
82.3.1/68	82/190	,,	,,	H848-R3-F	LC1	
Decorative hair pins						
72.10.22/12	72/36	Ivory or bone	Dec. hair pin	H186-F	LC2	50d
66.3.12/3	66/220	,,	,, (f)	H184-F	LC1	
78.2.8/67	—	,,	,, (f)	P515-F	LC	
72.10.28/6	72/34	Bronze	,, (f)	H175-SFl	LC	
72.11.2/2	72/67	Wood	,,	H172-SFl 1	LC1	50b
72.11.9/33	72/168	,,	,,	Pl 356-L4	LC1	50b
72.11.18/4	72/283	,,	,,	Ch 287-F	TC	50b
76.2.17/2	—	,,	,,	H183-R1-F	LC1	
76.2.22/2	—	,,	,,	Pl 358 NE-L3	LC1	
78.2.8/89	78/496	,,	,,	H197-R1-F	LC1	50b
78.2.12/51	78/495	,,	,,	H202-R7-F	LC1	
82.1.30/53	82/188	,,	,,	H763-R6-Fl 1	LC2	
82.2.20/21	82/188	,,	,, (f)	H849-R4-F	LC2	
82.3.1/88	82/254	,,	,,	H211-R1-F	LC1	
Pendants and brooches						
82.2.6/20	82/339	Copper or bronze	Brooch	H763-R4-Fl 3	LC1	50e-f
82.3.3/113	82/205	Wood	Pendant	H211-R3-F	LC1	50c
82T/326	—	Cotton, wool, reed	Necklace	H763-F	LC1	
Beads						
—	64/304	Glass	String of beads	H168-F	LC2	
78.1.21/11	78/608	,,	,,	Pl 358 NE-P	LC	
78.2.21/22	78/617	,,	,,	Pl 358-P	LC2	
82.2.10/35	82/91	,,	,,	H781-R2-L2	LC1	51a
82.2.25/36	82/89	,,	,,	H849-R1-L1	LC2	
82.3.2/73	82/91	,,	,,	H848-R5-Fl 2	LC1	
82.3.3/50	82/91	,,	3 Str. of beads	H848-R3-Fl 3	LC1	51b
84.1.31/13	—	Glass + shell	String of beads	H785-R9-L2	LC1	
—	66a/23	Wood, stone, fai.	Collection of beads	H171-W-F	LC2	
78.2.20/60	78/617	Shell, stone, bone	,,	Pl 358-P	LC2	
80.3.24/25	80/626	Stone	Bead	H207-R2-L3	LC1	
82.2.28/48	82/91	Bone	,,	H849-R1-Fl 1	LC2	
84.2.15/20	—	,,	,,	H785-R8xx-L5	LC1	
72.10.24/6	—	Cowrie shell	,,	H732-SFl	TC?	
82.3.1/8	82/89	,,	,,	H849-R1-Fl 2	LC2	
82.3.2/37	82/89	,,	,,	H849-R5-F	LC2	
82.3.3/37	82/89	,,	2 Beads	H848-R3-Fl 3	LC1	
82.1.28/18	82/89	,,	Bcad	II781-R2-C	LC1	
82.1.30/18	—	,,	,,	H763-R4-Fl 2	LC1	
84.1.28/25	—	,,	,,	H785-R6-L3	LC1	
84.1.29/38	—	,,	,,	H785-R4-L4	LC1	
84.1.30/43	—	Shell	2 Beads	H785-R4-L3	LC1	
82.1.25/18	82/89	Wood	Bead	H781-F	LC2	
78.2.13/21	78/618	Ceramic	,,	H202-R7-F	LC1	
80.3.10/87	80/904	,,	,,	H207-R1-L27	LC2	
82.3.4/26	82/308	,,	,,	H211-R1-F	LC1	
82.3.4/92	82/308	,,	,,	H210-R1-Fl 4	LC1	

APPENDIX C—continued
COMPREHENSIVE TABLE OF LATE AND TERMINAL CHRISTIAN OBJECT FINDS[1]

Day no.	*Reg. no.*	*Material*	*Object*[2]	*Provenance*[3]	*Date*[4]	*Plate*
84.1.28/25	–	Ceramic	Bead	H785-R6-L3	LC1	
80.2.24/51	80/626	Faience	,,	W305-0-F	LC	
82.1.25/18	82/89	,,	,,	H781-F	LC2	
82.2.3/7	82/89	,,	,,	H763-R8-Fl 2	LC1	
82.2.23/22	82/91	,,	,,	H210-R8-SFl 1	LC2	
82.2.28/5	82/89	,,	,,	H211-R1-F	LC1	
82.3.2/68	82/89	,,	3 Beads	H849-R5-F	LC2	
84.1.7/11	—	,,	Bead	H211-R1-F	LC1	
84.1.24/19	—	,,	,,	H785-R4-L2	LC1	
66.3.12/11	—	Glass	,,	H184-SFl	LC1	
78.1.16/11	78/608	,,	,,	W283-0-F	LC1	
78.1.19/26	78/608	,,	,,	P505-F	LC1	
78.1.24/20	78/608	,,	,,	P512-F	LC	
78.1.30/53	78/608	,,	,,	H194-F	LC1	
78.2.1/15	78/608	,,	,,	H195-F	LC1	
78.2.1/33	78/613	,,	,,	Ch 293-SFl	TC?	
78.2.6/29	78/607	,,	,,	Pl 358 NW-L6	LC1	
78.2.6/43	78/608	,,	,,	Pl 358 NW-L6-P	LC1	
78.2.8/15	78/613	,,	,,	P515-F	LC	
78.2.8/47	78/608	,,	,,	H197-R1-F	LC1	
78.2.12/46	78/618	,,	,,	H202-R4-F	LC1	
78.2.15/10	78/613	,,	,,	H196-0-F	TC?	
78.3.1/21	78/618	,,	,,	H235-Fl 2	LC1	
78.3.4/7	78/617	,,	,,	H196-0-P	LC2	
78.3.8/8	78/617	,,	,, (f)	Pl 358-P	LC2	
78.3.12/56	78/618	,,	3 Beads	W283-0-L1b	LC1	
80.1.24/29	80/626	,,	Bead (f)	H206-R1-L12	TC	
80.2.13/20	80/626	,,	,, (f)	H206-R2-L33	TC	
80.2.14/36	80/626	,,	,,	W304-F	LC1	
80.2.27/71	80/626	,,	,,	H206-R1-L14	TC	
80.3.4/20	80/628	,,	,, (f)	H207-R1-L8-P	LC2	
80.3.4/25	80/626	,,	,,	H207-R2-L3	LC1	
82.1.23/37	82/89	,,	,,	P776-F	LC2	
82.1.25/32	82/89	,,	,,	H763-R8-F	LC2	
82.1.25/41	82/89	,,	,,	,,	LC2	
82.1.25/48	82/89	,,	2 Beads	H763-F	LC2	
82.1.27/36	82/89	,,	Bead	H763-R8-Fl 1	LC1	
82.1.28/18	82/89	,,	,,	H781-R2-C	LC1	
82.1.30/18	82/91	,,	2 Beads	H763-R4-Fl 2	LC1	
82.2.2/7	82/89	,,	Bead	H763-R8-Fl 2	LC1	
82.2.8/86	82/91	,,	2 Beads	H763-R7-Fl 3	LC1	
82.2.9/36	82/89	,,	,,	H763-R7-Fl 3	LC1	
82.2.9/37	82/91	,,	Bead	H763-R7-Fl 3	LC1	
82.2.10/36	82/89	,,	,,	H781-R2-L2	LC1	
82.2.11/41	82/89	,,	,,	H781-R1-W	LC1	
82.2.21/11	82/89	,,	3 Beads	H849-R4-L2	LC2	
82.2.23/21	82/89	,,	2 Beads	H849-R4-SFl 1	LC1	
82.2.23/22	82/91	,,	Bead	H210-R8-SFl 1	LC2	
82.2.23/22	82/89	,,	,,	,,	LC2	
82.2.23/27	82/89	,,	,,	H848-R3-F	LC2	
82.2.24/33	82/89	,,	3 Beads	H848-R3-F	LC1	
82.2.27/38	82/89	,,	2 Beads (f)	P846-F	LC	
82.2.28/46	82/89	,,	4 Beads	H849-R1-Fl 1	LC2	
82.2.28/57	82/89	,,	2 Beads	H849-R1-W	LC2	

APPENDIX C—continued
COMPREHENSIVE TABLE OF LATE AND TERMINAL CHRISTIAN OBJECT FINDS[1]

Day no.	*Reg. no.*	*Material*	*Object*[2]	*Provenance*[3]	*Date*[4]	*Plate*
82.3.1/9	82/89	Glass	2 Beads	H849-R1-Fl 2	LC2	
82.3.1/10	82/89	,,	Bead	H211-R1-Fl 1	LC1	
82.3.2/64	82/89	,,	,,	H211-R1-Fl 3	LC1	
82.3.2/67	82/89	,,	5 Beads	H849-R5-F	LC2	
82.3.3/50	82/91	,,	3 Beads	H848-R3-Fl 3	LC1	
82.3.3/73	82/89	,,	Bead	H211-R1-Fl 3-P	LC1	
82.3.3/75	82/89	,,	,,	H21-R2-P	LC1	
82.3.3/105	82/89	,,	,,	H211-R1-Fl 4	LC1	
82.3.4/43	82/89	,,	,, (f)	,,	LC1	
82.3.4/63	82/89	,,	,,	H848-R5-Fl 4	LC1	
84.1.26/22	—	,,	,,	H785-R6-L3	LC1	
84.1.29/12	—	,,	,,	,,	LC1	
84.1.29/38	—	,,	,,	H785-R4-L4	LC1	
84.2.9/11	—	,,	,,	H785-R8x-L4	LC1	
84.2.20/26	—	,,	,,	H785-R12-F	LC1	
Earring?						
84.1.22/14	84/677	Copper + Glass	Earring?	H785-R8-L1	LC1	51c
Bracelets						
78.3.12/22	78/473	Iron	Bracelet (f)	W283-0-L1b	LC1	
82.3.3/123	82/352	,,	,, (f)	H211-R1-Fl 4	LC1	51d
84.1.30/42	—	,,	,, (f)	H785-R4-L3	LC1	
80.2.21/30	80/846	Copper or bronze	,, (f)	W304-0	LC?	
82.1.31/8	82/29	Limestone	Bracelet? (f)	H763-R7-F	LC2	
78.2.21/26	78/470	Ivory	Bracelet (f)	H194-R16-F	TC	
82.2.1/43	82/77	Bone	,, (f)	H763-R8-Fl 2	LC1	
78.2.6/22	—	Horn	,, (f)	Pl 358 NW-L6	LC1	51e
80.3.9/24	—	,,	,, (f)	H207-R2-L3	LC1	
84.1.26/2	—	,,	,, (f)	H785-R6-L3	LC1	
72.11.4/5	—	Glass	,, (f)	Pl 356-L4	LC	
78.1.30/54	78/657	,,	,, (f)	H194-F	LC1	
78.2.6/21	78/654	,,	,, (f)	Pl 358 NW-L6	LC1	
78.3.8/2	78/654	,,	,, (f)	Pl 358-P	LC2	
82.1.25/5	82/88	,,	,, (f)	H781-F	LC2	
82.1.30/2	82/88	,,	,, (f)	H763-0-F	LC	
82.1.31/5	82/88	,,	,, (f)	H763-R7-F	LC2	
82.2.22/38	82/88	,,	,, (f)	P845-F	LC	
82.3.2/69	82/88	,,	,, (f)	H849-R5-F	LC2	
Rings						
72.11.16/11	72/275	Gold	Signet ring	Ch 287-R12-F	TC	52c
72.10.29/8	72/48	Silver	,,	H172-R1-F	LC2	52f
72.11.9/19	72/165	Sandstone	,, (f)	Pl 356-L4	LC1	52d
82.2.3/3	82/367	Iron	Ring	H763-R8-Fl 2	LC1	52b
66.2.3/8	—	Copper or bronze	Ring	H171-F	LC2	
66.2.17/3	—	,,	,,	H169-0-F	LC2	
69.2.2/3	—	,,	,,	H177-R3-F	LC1	
69.2.8/6	69/47	,,	,,	H177-R1-F	LC1	
72.10.31/11	72/58	,,	,,	H174-SFl	LC2	52a
72.11.14/12	72/253	,,	,,	Ch 287-F	TC	
72.11.14/12	72/263	,,	,,	,,	TC	
72.11.26/26	—	,,	,,	Ch 287-R3	LC	
80.1.27/9	80/254	,,	,,	H206-R1-L15	TC	
82.2.26/33	82/36	,,	,,	H781-R3-C	LC1	

APPENDIX C—continued
COMPREHENSIVE TABLE OF LATE AND TERMINAL CHRISTIAN OBJECT FINDS[1]

Day no.	*Reg. no.*	*Material*	*Object*[2]	*Provenance*[3]	*Date*[4]	*Plate*
82.3.1/11	82/364	Copper or bronze	Ring	H211-R1-Fl 1	LC1	
82.3.2/71	82/364	"	" (f)	H849-R5-F	LC2	
69.2.5/5	69/152	Bone	"	H177-R2-F	LC1	
82.1.30/22	82/68	Horn	"	H763-R4-Fl 2	LC2	
76.2.5/16	—	Faience	" (f)	H190-C	LC1	
82.3.4/62	82/43	Agate	Ring bezel?	H848-R5-Fl 4	LC1	
Problematical object						
76.2.22/4	76/111	Leather + palm fib	Fan?	Pl 358-NE-L3	LC1	
MISCELLANEOUS AND SPECIALIZED OBJECTS (Part 3, Ch. 8)						
Cult objects						
Ornamental crosses						
—	64/8	Iron	Bishop's staff	Ch 293-B376	LC2	53a-b
66.3.3/5	66/56	Iron + bronze	Cross	H184-F	LC1	53c
66.3.10/3	66/94	Copper or bronze	"	H184-SFl	LC1	53e
72.10.31/4	72/59	"	"	Pl 356-F	TC	
82.2.2/14	82/338	"	"	H763-R8-Fl 2	LC1	53f
80.2.24/52	80/739	Ceramic	" (f)	W305-0-F	LC	53d
72.11.21/7	72/310	Wood	Cross finial	Ch 287-R12-F	TC	54a
72.11.15/12	72/266	"	"	Ch 287-R6-F	TC	
—	64/8	Braided twine	Dec. crosses	Ch 293-B356	LC2	
Palm-leaf crosses						
72.11.22/23	72/317	Braided palm leaf	Cross	Ch 287-R12-F	TC	54b
72.11.23/19	72/317	"	" (f)	Ch 287-R21-F	LC2	
72.11.25/1	—	"	" (f)	Ch 287-R21-F	LC2	
82.2.18/57	82/602	"	"	P1764-F	LC1	
82.3.1/109	82/602	"	"	H848-R3-F	LC1	
Palm-leaf amulets						
74.1.29/10	74/229	"	Amulet (f)	H177-R1-SFl	LC1	54e
76.2.4/12	—	"	"	Pl 358-L2	LC	54d
84.1.15/28	—	"	" (f)	H785-R4-L4	LC1	
Palm-leaf wreaths						
78.1.26/56	78/34	"	Group of fronds and wreaths	H235-F	LC1	54c
82.1.13/23	82/560	"	Wreath	H763-R8-Fl 2	LC1	
82.1.13/24	82/567	"	"	"	LC1	
82.1.13/33	82/569	"	"	"	LC1	54f
82.1.14/68	82/107	"	"	H763-R7-Fl 3	LC1	
82.1.26/61	82/582	"	"	H763-R8-F	LC2	
Icons						
69.2.11/11	69/46	Wood	Icon	H178-R7-F	LC1	55a-b
82.1.30/39	82/206	"	"	H763-R1-Fl 2	LC1	55c
Statuettes						
66.3.8/5	66/82	Bronze	Statuette (f)	H185-R5-F	LC1	
82.1.27/75	82/49	Brass	Tripod leg with statuette	H763-R8-Fl 2	LC1	55d-e
66.3.13/8	66/93	Stone	Statuette (f)	H185-F	LC1	
66.3.13/14	66/92	Faience	" (f)	"	LC1	55f

APPENDIX C—continued

COMPREHENSIVE TABLE OF LATE AND TERMINAL CHRISTIAN OBJECT FINDS[1]

Day no.	*Reg. no.*	*Material*	*Object*[2]	*Provenance*[3]	*Date*[4]	*Plate*
Higabs						
72.10.22/3	72/515	Leather	Higab	Pl 735	LC?	
72.10.23/11	72/532	„	„	H168-F	LC2	
72.10.24/5	72/39	„	„	H732-SFl	TC?	
72.10.25/5	72/519	„	„	?	LC?	
72.11.9/16	72/164	„	„	Pl 356 N-L4	LC1	
74.1.30/5	—	„	„	H177-R1-SFl	LC1	
—	—	„	„	Pl 358 NW-L3	LC1	
78.1.19/36	78/574	„	„	P505 F	LC	
78.2.15/6	78/581	„	„	H196-0-F	TC?	
78.2.18/14	78/579	„	„	P466-F	TC	56c
82.1.25/8	82/501	„	„	H763-R7-F	LC2	
82.2.3/2	82/501	„	„	H763-R8-Fl 2	LC1	56a
82.2.27/39	82/501	„	„	P846-F	LC	56b
82.3.4/40	82/501	„	„	H211-R1-Fl 4	LC1	56d
Miscellaneous amulets and cult objects						
66.3.3/9	66/370	Leather + hair	Small pouch containing hair	H184-F	LC1	
—	66/370	„	„	„	LC1	
82.2.6/60	82/491	Textile + iron + ?	Small sewn bag with misc. contents	H763-R7-F	LC2	
82.2.6/60	82/491	Yarn + mineral	Mineral wrapped in yarn	„	LC2	
82.2.28/4	82/491	Textile + stone	Stone wrapped in cloth	H211-R1-F	LC1	
76.2.9/7	—	Sherd + basketry	Amulet	Pl 358 NW-L1	TC	57b
76.2.26/5	—	Shell + leather	„	C188-R1-F	LC1	57a
78.2.8/90	78/52	Leather	Head of staff?	H197-R1-F	LC1	
Figurines						
69.1.29/3	69/7	Ceramic	Animal figurine (f)	H177-R5-Fl 1	LC1	
76.2.12/1	—	„	„ (f)	H171-R1-F	TC	
78.2.8/54	—	„	„ (f)	H235-F	LC1	
82.2.2/40	81/180	„	„ (f)	H763-R8-Fl 2	LC1	
82.2.28/63	82/180	„	„ (f)	H211-R2-F	LC2	
66.3.7/10	66/78	Mud	„ (f)	H184-F	LC1	
74.2.2/10	74/210	„	„ (f)	H177-SFl	LC1	
72.10.19/1	72/476	„	„ (f)	H732-SFl	TC?	
72.10.23/4	72/489	„	„ (f)	H168-F	LC2	
72.10.24/4	72/481	„	„ (f)	H734-SFl	LC?	57d
82.1.25/111	82/428	„	„ (f)	H763-R7-F	LC2	
76.3.1/14	—	Ceramic	Human figurine (f)	Pl 358 NE-L4	LC1	
78.1.24/18	78/397	„	„ (f)	P512-F	LC	57e
74.3.11/18	74/210	Mud	„ (f)	East Gate test	TC?	
—	64/125	„	Model shield?	H169-F	LC1	
Stamps and seals						
Large disc stamps						
—	64/156	Sandstone	Disc stamp	H169-F	LC1	58a
72.10.31/13	—	Ceramic	„	H174-SFl	LC2	
78.3.12/42	78/106	Wood	„	W283-0-L1b	LC1	58f
82.2.6/51	82/276	„	„	H763-R4-Fl 2	LC1	58e

APPENDIX C—continued
COMPREHENSIVE TABLE OF LATE AND TERMINAL CHRISTIAN OBJECT FINDS[1]

Day no.	*Reg. no.*	*Material*	*Object*[2]	*Provenance*[3]	*Date*[4]	*Plate*
Conical stamps						
74.2.2/16	74/230	Sandstone	Conical stamp	H177-SF1	LC1	
69.2.15/9	69/63	Ceramic	„	H178-R3-F	LC1	
72.10.26/4	72/37	„	„ (f)	H172-F	LC2	58b
82.2.2/55	82/276	„	„	H763-R8-Fl 2	LC1	58b
82.2.2/33	82/276	„	„	„	LC1	58c-d
Pyramidal stamps						
66.3.8/3	66/80	Sandstone	Pyramidal stamp	H184-F	LC1	58a
69.2.10/14	69/21	„	„	H178-R6-F	LC1	
76.2.4/9	—	„	„ (f)	Pl 358-L2	LC	
76.2.9/6	—	„	„	Pl 358 NE-L1	TC	
Rectangular flat stamps						
72.10.18/3	72/34	Limestone	Flat stamp	H732-SFl	TC?	
74.2.2/4	74/18	Sandstone	„	H177-SFl	LC1	58a
74.2.2/6	74/30	„	„	„	LC1	
80.2.24/27	80/836	„	„ (f)	W305-0-F	LC1	58a
—	64/82	Ceramic	„ (f)	H168-Fl	LC2	58b
78.1.29/7	78/406	Wood	„	H194-F	LC1	58g
Miscellaneous stamps						
66.3.13/3	66/328	Copper or bronze	Stamp	H184-F	LC1	
—	64/158	Sandstone	„	H169-F	LC1	
76.2.25/9	76/70	„	„	H187-Fl 2	LC1	
82.2.6/33	82/45	Ceramic	„ (f)	H763-R4-Fl 3	LC1	
Coins						
66.2.26/5	66/50	Copper or bronze	Roman coin	H171-R6-F	LC2	59a-c
72.11.9/29	72/386	„	„	Pl 356-L4	LC1	
72.11.9/29	72/386	„	Roman coin?	„	LC1	
72.11.27/4	72/359	„	„	Ch 287-R6-F	TC	
66.2.21/2	66/140	„	Islamic coin	H171-0-F	LC2	59d
72.10.22/4	72/20	„	„	H186-F	LC2	59e
78.2.1/41	78/43	„	„	Ch 293-SFl	TC	
82.1.29/2	82/605	„	„	Pl 764-F	LC2	
76.2.4/6	—	„	Unidentified coin	Pl 358 NE-L1	TC	
Coin weights						
82.3.3/39	82/40	Glass	Fatimid coin weight	H848-R3-Fl 3	LC1	
78.2.6/30	78/412	„	„ (f)	Pl 358 NW-L6	LC1	59f
78.3.15/15	78/119	„	Nubian coin wt. (f)	Pl 358-L9	?	59g
Writing materials						
72.11.9/22	72/166	Wood	Pen case	Pl 356-L4	LC1	
80.2.28/83	—	Papyrus	Blank papyrus (f)	H206-R6-L41	TC	
82.2.2/83	82/35	Paper	Blank paper (f)	H763-R8-Fl 3	LC1	
Gaming equipment						
Lathe-turned counters						
74.1.30/13	—	Ivory or bone	Turned counter (f)	H177-R6-SFl	LC1	
82.1.26/58	82/409	„	„	H763-R8-F	LC2	
82.2.20/5	82/411	„	„ (f)	H210-R8-F	LC2	60a
74.2.4/1	74/25	Wood	„	H186-F	LC2	
76.2.14/9	—	„	„	H171-SFl	LC1	
76.2.15/3	—	„	„	H171-W-F	TC	
82.1.25/106	82/20	„	„	H763-R7-F	LC2	
82.3./82	82/253	„	Counter	H849-R5-F	LC2	
82.2.25/71	82/74	Plaster	„	H849-R1-F	LC2	

APPENDIX C—continued

COMPREHENSIVE TABLE OF LATE AND TERMINAL CHRISTIAN OBJECT FINDS[1]

Day no.	*Reg. no.*	*Material*	*Object*[2]	*Provenance*[3]	*Date*[4]	*Plate*
Ground disc counters						
78.1.30/59	—	Potsherd[10]	Disc counter (?)	H174-F	LC1	
78.2.6/23	—	,,	,, (G.II)	Pl 358 NW-L6	LC1	
78.2.6/23	—	,,	,, (G.II)	,,	LC1	
78.2.13/60	—	,,	,, (W10)	H202-R7-F	LC1	
78.3.9/1	—	,,	,, (?)	W283-0-L1b	LC1	
82.1.26/7	82/74	,,	,, (G.I)	H763-R3-F	LC2	
82.1.28/17	82/74	,,	,, (G.II)	H781-R2-C	LC1	60b
82.1.28/38	82/74	,,	,, (G.III)	H763-R7-F	LC2	
82.2.2/12	82/74	,,	,, (G.II)	H763-R8-Fl 2	LC1	
82.2.3/4	82/74	,,	,, (G.I)	H763-R8-Fl 2	LC1	
82.2.13/26	82/74	,,	,, (?)	P831-F	LC	
82.2.17/64	82/74	,,	,, (?)	H781-R2-0-F	LC	
82.2.23/25	82/74	,,	,, (W5)	H210-R8-SFl 1	LC2	
84.1.26/27	—	,,	,, (U13)	H785-R6-L4	LC1	
82.3.3/38	82/74	,,	Rect. counter (G.I)	H848-R3-Fl 3	LC1	
Dice						
78.1.26/42	78/406	Sandstone	Die	H235-F	LC1	60d
74.1.31/5	74/16	Ivory or bone	Talus	H178-SFl	LC1	60e
Miscellaneous gaming equipment						
72.10.10/1	72/27	Bone	Gaming counter?	H734-SFl	LC?	60c
—	64/208	Wood	Dice shaker?	H168-Fl	LC2	
Playthings						
Doll clothing						
76T/705	—	Cotton cloth	Doll dress	Cr 188-F	LC1	
78.3.28/4	78T/10	Cotton textile	,,	Pl 358 NE-P	LC	61a
Balls						
78.2.5/42	—	Wool + flax text.	Ball	Pl 358 NW-L7	LC1	61b
78.3.28/71	—	Wool textile	,,	Pl 358 NE-P	LC	
Toys						
82.2.16/32	82/438	Wood + pottery	2 Tops?	H781-R3-C	LC1	61d
82.2.28/58	—	Mud	Toy dish?	H489-R1-F	LC2	61c

UNIDENTIFIED OBJECTS (Part 3, Ch. 9)

Stone						
78.2.8/82	78/631	Granite	Truncated cone	H235-Fl	LC1	62a
82.2.25/84	—	Sandstone	Shaped piece	H849-R1-F	LC2	
82.2.25/86	—	,,	,,	,,	LC2	
82.2.21/80	—	,,	Decorated fragment	H210-R8-F	LC2	
80.1.26/30	80/905	Steatite	Incised pebble	H206-R1-L12	TC	62b
78.3.5/5	—	Stone	Decorated pebble	Pl 358-P	LC	
66.3.5/6	—	Sandstone	Small trough	H184-R1-F	LC1	
82.2.20/6	82/294	Ironstone	Small concretion	H210-R8-F	LC2	
84.1.28/22	—	,,	,,	H785-R6-L3	LC1	
Metal						
Iron						
66.3.6/7	66/72	Sheet iron	Shaped piece	H184-F	LC1	
78.2.12/33	—	Iron rod	Small curved piece	H197-R1-F	LC1	
84.2.2/34	—	Thick sheet iron	2 shovel-shaped pieces	H785-R6-L4	LC1	62c

APPENDIX C—continued

COMPREHENSIVE TABLE OF LATE AND TERMINAL CHRISTIAN OBJECT FINDS[1]

Day no.	*Reg. no.*	*Material*	*Object*[2]	*Provenance*[3]	*Date*[4]	*Plate*
Copper or bronze						
82.2.25/88	82/341	Cast copper or bronze	3-armed attachment	H849-R1-F	LC2	62d
78.2.21/55	—	Sheet copper/bronze	Strip with perf.	H198-0-F	LC1	
78.3.12/53	—	„	„	W283-0-L1b	LC1	
78.3.1/54	—	„	Fragment	H235-Fl 2	LC1	
82.2.25/37	82/402	„	„	H849-R1-L1	LC2	
72.10.23/5	—	Copper/bronze rod	Serrated fragment	H168-F	LC2	
82.1.25/50	82/391	Copper/bro. wire	Curved piece	H763-F	LC2	
82.2.2/15	82/351	„	Loop	H763-R8-Fl 2	LC1	
Lead						
78.2.8/88	—	Sheet lead	Rectangular frag.	H197-R1-F	LC1	
80.2.18/35	80/868	„	Small disc	W305-0-F	LC1	
82.1.25/16	82/347	Lead	Small sphere	H781-F	LC2	
78.2.12/47	—	Lead?	Fragments of slag?	H202-R4-F	LC1	
Ceramic						
72.10.28/7	—	Ceramic	Smoking pipe? (f)	H175-SFl	LC2	
78.2.13/46	—	„	Bell-shaped obj.	H202-R7-F	LC1	63a
82.2.10/34	—	„	Brick	H781-R2-L2	LC1	
82.2.17/63	82/305	„	Spherical ball	H781-R2-0-F	LC	
82.2.23/20	82/308	„	2 Spherical balls	H849-R4-SFl 1	LC1	
82.3.2/84	82/138	„	Sherd on string	H848-R3-F	LC2	
Wood						
Blocks						
78.3.12/50	78/449	Wood	Block	W283-0-L1b	LC1	
78.3.12/58	78/425	„	„	„	LC1	
82.1.25/114	—	„	„ (f)	H763-R7-F	LC2	
82.2.8/47	—	„	„	H763-R8-Fl 3	LC1	
82.2.8/47	82/197	„	„	„	LC1	
82.2.15/55	—	„	„	P838-F	LC1	
82.2.21/64	—	„	„	H849-R4-F	LC1	
82.2.21/64	—	„	„	„	LC1	
Cylinders						
82.1.30/43	—	„	Cylinder	H763-R1-Fl 2	LC1	
82.1.30/61	—	„	„	H763-R4-Fl 2	LC1	
82.2.20/22	—	„	„ (f)	H849-R4-F	LC2	
Boards						
82.1.30/43	—	„	Board (f)	H763-R1-Fl 2	LC1	
82.2.3/55	—	„	„ (f)	H763-R8-Fl 2	LC1	
Perforated pieces						
78.1.16/3	—	„	Perf. board (f)	W283-0-F	LC1	
82.1.25/2	—	„	„ (f)	H763-R4-F	LC2	
82.2.3/55	82/208	„	„	H763-R8-Fl 2	LC1	
78.1.26/48	78/431	„	Flat perf. piece	H235-F	LC1	
82.2.15/57	82/239	„	Perf. stake (f)	P838-F	LC1	
74.1.29/13	74/200	„	Perforated stick (f)	H177-R1-SFl	LC1	
84.2.4/44	—	„	Perforated disc	H785-R4-L4	LC1	

APPENDIX C—continued
COMPREHENSIVE TABLE OF LATE AND TERMINAL CHRISTIAN OBJECT FINDS[1]

Day no.	*Reg. no.*	*Material*	*Object*[2]	*Provenance*[3]	*Date*[4]	*Plate*
Worked sticks						
80.2.25/57	—	Wood	Notched stick (f)	W305-F	LC1?	
82.1.25/110	82/238	,,	,, (f)	H763-R7-F	LC2	
72.10.9/3	72/404	,,	Polished stick	H734-SFl	LC?	
80.2.26/63	—	,,	,,	H206-R6-L41	TC	
82.1.25/120	—	,,	,,	H763-R7-F	LC2	
82.1.26/31	—	,,	Peeled stick	H763-R5-Fl 1	LC2	
82.1.28/63	82/24	,,	,,	H781-R2-C	LC1	
82.2.2/48	—	,,	,,	H763-R8-Fl 2	LC1	
82.2.21/65	—	,,	,, (f)	H849-R4-F	LC2	
82.3.1/93	82/250	,,	,,	H848-R5-F	LC1	
Sharpened sticks						
80.2.26/60	—	,,	Sharpened stick	H206-R6-L41	TC	
82.1.30/43	—	,,	,,	H763-R1-Fl 2	LC1	
82.1.31/58	—	,,	,,	H763-R7-F	LC2	
82.1.31/58	82/250	,,	,,	,,	LC2	
82.2.2/67	—	,,	4 Sharp, sticks (f)	H763-R8-Fl 2	LC1	
82.2.8/47	—	,,	Sharpened stick (f)	H763-R8-Fl 3	LC1	
82.2.9/12	—	,,	,,	H763-R7-Fl 3	LC1	
82.2.3/53	82/220	,,	,, (f)	H763-R8-F12	LC1	
Miscellaneous carved items						
76.2.19/6	—	,,	Rough carved knob	Pl 358 NE-L3	LC1	
76.2.24/1	76/74	,,	Carved phallus	Pl 358 NW-L2	TC?	
78.2.21/42	78/380	,,	Tapered rod	Pl 358-P	LC	
82.2.23/78	—	,,	Grooved rod	P845-F	LC	
82.1.25/109	82/210	,,	Shallow trough (f)	H763-R7-F	LC2	
82.1.26/60	—	,,	L-shaped piece (f)	H763-R8-F	LC2	
82.2.25/19	—	,,	C-shaped piece (f)	H848-R2-Fl 1-P	LC1	
Other wooden items						
76.2.21/7	—	,,	Cylinder with projecting sticks	Pl 358 NE-L3	LC1	
82.2.28/71	82/250	,,	Flat, curved piece	H849-R1-Fl 1	LC2	
82.1.25/117	82/468	Wood + palm fibre	4 sticks wrapped with palm cord	H763-R7-F	LC2	
84.1.24/6	—	,,	2 sticks tied with palm cord	H785-R4-L3	LC1	
82.1.25/121	82/216	Wood + leather	Stick in leather sheath	H763-R7-F	LC2	
Reed						
82.1.30/42	82/474	Reed	Notched reed (f)	H763-R1-Fl 2	LC1	
82.2.21/75	82/475	,,	,, (f)	P840-F	LC	
80.2.26/59	—	,,	Pointed reed	H206-R6-L41	TC	
Gourd						
82.1.24/7	82/43	Gourd	Perforated disc	P776-F	LC2	
Leather						
Decorated scraps						
78.2.25/41	—	Leather	Decorated scrap	Pl 358-P	LC2	
82.3.4/27	82/422	,,	2 decorated scraps	H211-R1-Fl 1	LC1	

APPENDIX C—continued

COMPREHENSIVE TABLE OF LATE AND TERMINAL CHRISTIAN OBJECT FINDS[1]

Day no.	*Reg. no.*	*Material*	*Object*[2]	*Provenance*[3]	*Date*[4]	*Plate*
Stitched fragments						
78.1.21/45	—	Leather	Stitched fragment	Pl 358 NE-P	LC	
78.1.28/11	—	,,	2 stitched frags.	,,	LC	
78.2.8/51	—	,,	3 Stitched frags.	Pl 358-NW-L6	LC1	
72.2.25/41	—	,,	Stitched fragment	Pl 358-P	LC2	
78.3.1/49	—	,,	3 Stitched frags.	,,	LC2	
78.3.12/51	—	,,	6 Stitched frags.	W283-0-L1b	LC1	
78.3.13/79	—	,,	2 Stitched frags.	Pl 358-P	LC	
80.1.31/80	—	,,	,,	H206-R7-L1	TC	
82.1.26/57	82/558	,,	Stitched fragment	H763-R8-F	LC2	
82.1.28/64	82/558	,,	,,	H781-R2-C	LC1	
82.1.31/57	82/529	,,	,,	H763-R7-F	LC2	
82.1.31/57	82/558	,,	,,	,,	LC2	
82.2.3/52	82/558	,,	,,	H763-R8-Fl 2	LC1	
82.2.3/52	82/519	,,	,,	,,	LC1	
82.2.4/56	82/558	,,	,,	P795-F	LC1	
82.2.6/42	82/526	,,	,,	P797-F	LC1	
82.2.6/44	82/530	,,	,,	,,	LC1	
82.2.8/48	82/558	,,	,,	H763-R7-Fl 3	LC1	
82.2.16/67	82/558	,,	,,	P837-F	LC1	
82.2.1/73	82/558	,,	,,	H210-R8-F	LC2	
82.2.23/72	82/549	,,	,,	H848-R3-F	LC1	
82.3.2/120	82/558	,,	,,	H848-R5-Fl 2	LC2	
82.3.3/148	82/558	,,	,,	H211-R1-Fl 3	LC1	
Offcuts						
78.1.21/45	—	,,	Offcut	Pl 358 NE-P	LC	
78.2.20/58	—	,,	6 Offcuts	Pl 358-P	LC2	
78.3.1/45	—	,,	21 Offcuts	,,	LC2	
Unworked scraps						
78.1.26/45	—	,,	10 Scraps	H235-F	LC1	
78.3.12/51	—	,,	2 Scraps	W283-0-L1b	LC1	
78.1.26/57	—	Sheepskin	Scrap	H235-F	LC1	
Miscellaneous						
82.2.2/50	82/435	Hide	Thick strip (f)	H763-R8-Fl 2	LC1	
78.2.26/34	—	Wool + leather	Textile fragment; leather patch	H196-0-P	LC2	
Palm fibre						
78.2.8/127	78/756	Woven palm leaf	Fly whisk?	H235-Fl	LC1	63b
80.2.25/59	80/1009	Palm fibre	Net edging? (f)	W305-F	LC1?	
78.2.12/5	—	,,	Section of rope (f)	H197-R1-F	LC1	
78.3.12/41	—	,,	,, (f)	W283-0-L1b	LC1	
82.2.3/54	82/540	,,	,, (f)	H763-R8-Fl 2	LC1	
80.3.13/64	—	,,	Twisted loop	W311-0-L7	LC1	
82.2.28/78	82/460	,,	Bung?	H211-R2-F	LC1	
Bone						
82.1.26/59	—	Bone	Rib bone	H763-R8-F	LC2	
Horn						
78.2.6/36	—	Horn	Gazelle horn	Pl 358 NW-L5	LC1	
Hair						
78.2.5/24	—	Hair	Bundle of hair	Pl 358 NW-L7	LC1	
78.2.6/38	—	,,	,,	Pl 358 NW-L5	LC1	
80.2.28/82	80/944	,,	Ball of hair	H206-R6-L41	TC	

APPENDIX C—continued

COMPREHENSIVE TABLE OF LATE AND TERMINAL CHRISTIAN OBJECT FINDS[1]

Day no.	*Reg. no.*	*Material*	*Object*[2]	*Provenance*[3]	*Date*[4]	*Plate*
Textile						
82T/424	—	Flax	Y-shaped pad	H763-F	LC2	
Decorative elements						
Stone architectural fragments						
66.3.12/6	—	Sandstone	Window grille? (f)	H184-SFl	LC1	
66.3.13/5	—	„	Window grille (f)	H184-F	LC1	
66.3.13/6	—	„	„ (f)	„	LC1	
69.2.6/7	—	„	„ (f)	H185-R7-F	LC1	
72.10.12/16	—	„	„ (f)	H168-F	LC2	
69.2.13/13	—	„	Carved capital	H178-R3-F	LC1	
82.3.4/88	—	„	Meroitic lintel	H849-R5-F	LC2	
72.10.10/5	—	„	Mero. carved frag.	H734-SFl	LC?	
80.3.10/51	80/662	„	Carved boss (f)	H207-L18	LC1	
66.3.13/10	—	Marble	Altar top? (f)	H184-F	LC1	
72.10.24/7	72/584	Alabaster	„ (f)	H732-SFl	TC?	
Statuary						
66.3.13/12	66/99	Sandstone	Lion statue (f)	H184-F	LC1	63c-d
66.3.13/13	66/99	„	„ (f)	„	LC1	
80.1.30/61	—	„	„ (f)	W304-F	LC1	
Decorated blocks						
66.3.5/8	—	„	Decorated block (f)	H184-F	LC1	
69.3.1/6	—	„	„	W313-0-F	LC	
69.3.2/1	—	„	„ (f)	„	LC	
69.3.2/2	—	„	„ (f)	„	LC	
76.2.9/1	—	„	„ (f)	H190-C	LC1	
76.2.14/5	—	„	„ (f)	H171-0-P	LC	
82.2.2/66	—	„	„ (f)	H763-R8-Fl 2	LC1	
82.2.25/82	82/69	„	„	H848-R2-F	LC1	
66.2.20/6	—	„	Votive block with carved footprint	H171-0-F	LC2	
Miscellaneous stone						
78.2.6/37	78/482	Alabaster	Carved fragment	Pl 358 NW-L6	LC1	
80.2.26/53	80/544	Sandstone	Miniature staircase	W305-F	LC1	
Decorative metal						
84.2.20/23	84/480	Sheet iron	Piece with fancy cut pattern	H785-R12-L1	LC1	64c
Decorative wood						
Carved items						
—	69/77	Wood	Block with cat's head impression	H178-R6-F	LC1	
78.2.19/6	78/70	„	Carved and painted animal head (f)	W304-F	LC1	
78.1.31/36	78/549	„	Carved post with foliate design (f)	H195-F	LC1	
82.2.2/46	82/240	„	Stake with incised herringbone des.	H763-R8-Fl 2	LC1	
—	66a/225	„	Carved fragment	H184-F	LC1	
76.2.19/9	—	„	Carved scrap	C188-F	LC2	
Turned fragment						
72.11.2/5	72/418	„	Turned fragment	H172-SFl	LC1	
Painted items						
66.3.10/5	66/93	„	Painted board (f)	H184-SFl	LC1	
78.1.16/4	—	„	„ (f)	W283-0-F	LC1	
82.3.5/85	82/219	„	„ (f)	H197-F	LC1	

APPENDIX C—continued
COMPREHENSIVE TABLE OF LATE AND TERMINAL CHRISTIAN OBJECT FINDS[1]

Day no.	*Reg. no.*	*Material*	*Object*[2]	*Provenance*[3]	*Date*[4]	*Plate*
Decorative reed						
72.10.25/12	72/414	Reed	Reed with beads inset (f)	H174-F	LC1	
84.1.24/25	—	,,	Reed with incised spiral design (f)	H785-R4-L3	LC1	
82.2.25/91	82/478	,,	Painted reed (f)	H849-R1-F	LC2	64b
Decorative pottery						
66.3.13/4	66/98	Ceramic	Stamped disc (f)	H184-F	LC1	64e-f
66.3.14/1	66/98	,,	,, (f)	H185-0-F	LC1	
78.2.11/16	—	,,	Part of painted model? (f)	H202-R6-F	LC1	
Decorative faience						
72.10.23/2	72/38	Faience	Scarab (f)	H168-F	LC2	
78.2.1/42	78/307	,,	,,	Ch 293-0-F	TC?	
78.1.14/19	—	,,	Small stud	P512-F	LC	
Decorative glass						
82.2.1/60	82/78	Glass	Uraeus bead	H763-R7-Fl 2	LC1	
Decorative bone						
80.2.26/49	80/930	Bone	Inlay element	H206-R6-L41	LC1	64d
Decorative leather						
78.2.1/19	78/41	Leather	Dec. 'pennant'	H194-F	LC1	65b
84.1.30/54	84/706	,,	Dec. roundel	H785-R6-L3	LC1	65c
82.2.2/23	82/558	,,	Dec. stitched item	Pl 764-L2	LC2	65e
82.1.31/51	82/515	,,	Dec. sheath? (f)	H763-R7-F	LC2	
Decorative paper						
66.3.3/6	66/278	Paper	Scrap with animal designs	St 738-F	LC	65d
80.1.22/34	80/146	,,	Scrap with floral designs	H206-W-F	LC	
82.2.8/80	82/24	,,	Scrap with human face design	H763-R7-Fl 3	LC1	
82.3.2/52	82/13	,,	Scrap with zigzag design	H848-R5-Fl 2	LC1	
80.1.31/92	80/282	,,	Scrap with stamped design	H206-R1-L1	TC	
84.21.29/43	—	,,	Book cover? (f)	H785-R6-L3	LC1	65f

INSCRIBED OBJECTS (Part 4, Ch. 1)[11]

Day no.	*Reg. no.*	*Material*	*Object*	*Provenance*	*Date*	*Plate*
Inscriptions on stone						
66.3.1/1	—	Sandstone	Block with hiero. inscription	H171-F	TC	
69.2.4/5	—	,,	,,	H178-R9-F	LC2	
72.10.22/2	—	,,	,,	Pl 735-F	LC	
72.11.29/18	—	,,	,,	Ch 287-R10-Fl	LC2	
76.2.26/14	—	,,	,,	C188-F	LC	
78.3.22/45	—	,,	,,	W304-F	LC1	
80.3.13/99	—	,,	,,	,,	LC1	
78.2.25/18	78/180	,,	Block with Meroitic inscription	Pl 358-P	LC	
78.2.1/9	—	,,	Greek tombst.? (f)	P514-F	LC	
78.2.21/5	—	,,	Coptic tombst. (f)	W282-0-F	LC1	
82.2.25/72	82/12	,,	,, (f)	H849-R1-F	LC2	

APPENDIX C—continued

COMPREHENSIVE TABLE OF LATE AND TERMINAL CHRISTIAN OBJECT FINDS[1]

Day no.	*Reg. no.*	*Material*	*Object*[2]	*Provenance*[3]	*Date*[4]	*Plate*
Ostraca						
78.2.7/8	78/251	Potsherd	Meroitic ostracon	Pl 358 NW-L6	LC1	
80.2.17/8	80/523	,,	Demotic ost. (f)	H206-R2-L33	TC	
80.2.18/16	80/523	,,	,, (f)	,,	TC	
76.3.1/20	—	,,	Greek ostracon (f)	St 334-F	LC1	
76.2.17/5	—	,,	Greek or Coptic ostracon (f)	Pl 356-L4	TC	
78.3.9/3	78/250	,,	,,	W283-0-L1b	LC1	
72.11.2/18	72/68	,,	Old Nubian ostracon	Pl 356-L4	LC1	
—	64/91	,,	Sherd with incised graffito	H169-F	LC2	
72.10.29/12	—	,,	,,	H185-F	LC1	
78.1.26/47	78/213	,,	,,	H235-F	LC1	
80.3.10/8	80/524	,,	,,	H207-R2-L3	LC1	
82.1.27/4	82/46	,,	,,	H763-R1-F	LC2	
Sealing						
82.2.4/44	82/39	Mud	Sealing with Arabic? text (f)	H763-R5-Fl 2	LC1	

[1] Not including text finds and certain unidentifiable objects

[2] (f) = fragment

[3] Abbreviations as follows: B = Burial; C = Crypt; Ch = Church; F = Fill; Fl = Floor; H = House; L = Leyel; NE = North-east section; NW = North-west section; 0 = Outside (exterior) deposit; P = Pit fill; Pl = Plaza; R = Room; SFl = Sub-floor; St = Street; W = Section of girdle wall

[4] LC = Late or Terminal Christian; no more precise dating possible. LC1 = Late Christian I (c. 1100–1300 AD; LC2 = Late Christian II (c. 130–1400 AD); TC = Terminal Christian (c. 1400–1500 AD). Dates are mostly calculated on the basis of ceramic deposits; see Appendix 2. Where ceramic evidence is lacking, dates are estimated on the basis of stratigraphic position or association with datable objects such as inscriptions, or on typology of the object itself. Objects found in deposits between room floors are given the same dating as the underlying floor.

[5] Pottery ware number is given in brackets following the name of the object. See Appendix A.

[6] Glass type is given in brackets following the name of the object.

[7] Spindle whorl type is given in brackets following the name of the object.

[8] Pottery ware of lamps is given in brackets following the name of the object.

[9] Items entered in object register only. The great majority of textile fragments are entered only in separate textile register.

[10] Pottery ware of sherd discs is given in brackets following the name of the object.

[11] Not including inscriptions on papyrus, paper, or skin.

BIBLIOGRAPHY

Adams, Nettie K. Textiles from Qasr Ibrim: A Window on Nubian Culture History. Paper delivered at the 1984 annual meeting of the Archaeological Institute of America, Toronto, December 27–30 (1984).

Adams, Nettie K. Textiles at Qasr Ibrim: an Introductory Quantitative Essay. *Wissenschaftliche Zeitschrift der Humboldt-Universität zu Berlin, Geisteswissenschaftliche Reihe* 35, Heft 1 (1986), 21–6.

Adams, William Y. Post-Pharaonic Nubia in the Light of Archaeology, III. *JEA* 52 (1966).

Adams, William Y. Sudan Antiquities Service Excavations in Nubia: Fourth Season, 1962–63. *Kush* 12 (1964).

Adams, William Y. Architectural Evolution of the Nubian Church, 500–1400 A.D. *JARCE* 4 (1965).

Adams, William Y. Sudan Antiquities Service Excavations at Meinarti, 1963–64. *Kush* 13 (1965).

Adams, William Y. Post-Pharaonic Nubia in the Light of Archaeology, III. *JEA* 52 (1966).

Adams, William Y. Invasion, Diffusion, Evolution? *Antiquity* 42 (1968).

Adams, William Y. Settlement Pattern in Microcosm: the Changing Aspect of a Nubian Village During Twelve Centuries; in K. C. Chang, ed., *Settlement Archaeology*, 174–207 (Palo Alto, 1968).

Adams, William Y. The University of Kentucky Excavations at Kulubnarti, 1969; in Erich Dinkler, ed., *Kunst und Geschichte Nubiens in Christlicher Zeit.*, 141–54 (Recklinghausen, 1970).

Adams, William Y. The Twilight of Nubian Christianity; in Kazimierz Michalowski, ed., *Nubia, récentes recherches*, 11–17 (Warsaw, 1975).

Adams, William Y. Correspondence. *The Geographical Journal* 142 (1976), 381–4.

Adams, William Y. *Meroitic North and South. Meroitica* 2 (Berlin, 1976).

Adams, William Y. *Nubia, Corridor to Africa* (London, 1977).

Adams, William Y. The Dead Community: Perspectives from the Past; in Art Gallaher, Jr. and Harland Padfield, eds., *The Dying Community*, 23–54 (Albuquerque, 1980).

Adams, William Y. The Coming of Nubian Speakers to the Nile Valley; in Christopher Ehret and Merrick Posnansky, eds., *The Archaeological and Linguistic Reconstruction of African History*, 11–38 (Berkeley, 1983).

Adams, William Y. Primis and the 'Aethiopian' Frontier. *JARCE* 20 (1983).

Adams, William Y. Adaptive Retrogress; the Retribalization of the Nubians in the Late Middle Ages; in Mahjoub el-Bedawy and David Sconyers, eds., *Sudan Studies Association Selected Conference Papers* 1982–4, 40–51 (Washington, 1985).

Adams, William Y. Ptolemaic and Roman Occupation at Qasr Ibrim; in Francis Geus and Florence Thil, eds., *Mélanges offerts à Jean Vercoutter*, 9–17 (Lille, 1985).

Adams, William Y. *Ceramic Industries of Medieval Nubia. Memoirs of the UNESCO Archaeological Survey of Sudanese Nubia*, 1 (Lexington, 1986).

Adams, William Y. From Pottery to History: the Dating of Archaeological Deposits by Ceramic Statistics. *Wissenschaftliche Zeitschrift der Humboldt-Universität zu Berlin, Geisteswissenschaftliche Reihe*, 35, Heft 1 (1986), 27–45.

Adams, William Y. Castle-Houses of Late Medieval Nubia. *Archéologie du Nil Moyen* 6 (1994).

Adams, William Y., J. A. Alexander and R. D. Allen. Qasr Ibrim 1980 and 1982. *JEA* 69 (1983).

Adams, William Y., and H.-A- Nordström. The Archaeological Survey on the West Bank of the Nile: Third Season, 1961–62. *Kush* 11 (1963).

Adovasio. J. M. *Basketry Technology* (Chicago, 1977).

Ainé, H. Roux. *Herculaneum et Pompéi, recueil général des peintures, bronzes, mosaiques, etc.* (Paris, 1976) (7 vols.).

Aldred, Cyril. Furniture: to the End of the Roman Empire; in Charles Singer *et al.*, eds., *A History of Technology*, vol. 2, 221–39 (Oxford, 1956).

Alexander, J. A., and B. Driskell. Qasr Ibrim 1984. *JEA* 71 (1985).

Amborn, Hermann. *Die Bedeutung der Kulturen des Niltals für die Eisenproduktion im Subsaharischen Afrika. Frobenius-Institut, Studien zur Kulturkunde*, 39 (Wiesbaden, 1976).

Anderson, R. D., W. Y. Adams *et al.* Qasr Ibrim 1978. *JEA* 65 (1979).

Bahgat, Aly Bey, and Félix Massoul. *La céramique mussulmane de l'Égypte* (Cairo, 1930).

Barbour, K. M. *The Republic of the Sudan* (London, 1961).

Bentley, O. and J. W. Crowfoot. Nuba Pots in the Gordon College. *SNR* 7, no. 2 (1924).

Bergman, Ingrid. *Late Nubian Textiles. Scandinavian Joint Expedition to Sudanese Nubia Publications, 8* (Stockholm, 1975).

Betz, Hans Dieter. *The Greek Magical Papyri in Translation* (Chicago, 1986).

Blackman, Winifred S. *The Fellahin of Upper Egypt* (London, 1927).

Brookner, J. Textiles; in Donald S. Whitcomb and Janet E. Johnson, *Quseir al-Qadim: Preliminary Report 1978*, 183–95 (Cairo, 1979).

Browne, Gerald M. Notes on Old Nubian. *BASP* 16 (1979), 249–56.

Browne, Gerald M. Notes on Old Nubian. *BASP* 17 (1980), 37–43, 129–41.

Browne, Gerald M. New Texts in Old Nubian from Qasr Ibrim, II. *Sudan Texts Bulletin* 3 (1981), 9–19.

Browne, Gerald M. New Texts in Old Nubian from Qasr Ibrim II. *BASP* 18 (1981), 55–67.

Browne, Gerald M. Griffith's Old Nubian Lectionary.

Papyrologica Castroctaviana 8 (1982).

Browne, Gerald M. The Old Nubian Verbal System. *BASP* 19 (1982), 9–37.

Brown, G. M. *Old Nubian Texts from Qasr Ibrim, II. Egypt Exploration Society, Texts from Excavations*, in press.

Brown, G. M. *Old Nubian Texts from Qasr Ibrim, III. Egypt Exploration Society, Texts from Excavations*, in press.

Browne, W. G. *Travels in Africa, Egypt, and Syria from the Year 1792 to 1798* (London, 1799).

Budge, E. A. Wallis. *The Egyptian Sudan* (London, 1907) (2 vols.).

Burckhardt, J. L. *Travels in Nubia* (London, 1819).

Butler, Alfred J. *The Ancient Coptic Churches of Cairo* (London, 1884) (2 vols.).

Butzer, Karl. Modern Egyptian Pottery Clays and Predynastic Buff Ware. *Journal of Near Eastern Studies* 33 (1974), 377–82.

Caminos, Ricardo A. *The Shrines and Rock-Inscriptions of Ibrim. Egypt Exploration Society, Archaeological Survey of Egypt, Memoir* 32 (London, 1968).

Clarke, Somers. *Christian Antiquities in the Nile Valley* (Oxford, 1910).

Crowfoot, Grace. Weaving and Spinning in the Sudan. *SNR* 4, no. 1 (1921), 20–38.

Crowfoot, Grace. The Sudanese Camel Girth in Double Weave. *SNR* 32 (1951), 71–6.

Crowfoot, Grace. Textiles, Basketry, and Mats; in Charles Singer *et al.*, eds., *A History of Technology*, vol 1, 413–47 (Oxford, 1956).

Crowfoot, Grace. The Sudanese Camel Girth. *Kush* 4 (1956), 34–8.

Crowfoot, Elisabeth. The Clothing of a 14th Century Nubian Bishop; in Veronika Gervers, ed., *Studies in Textile History*, 43–51 (Toronto, 1977).

Dafalla, Hassan. Land Economy of Old Halfa. *SNR* 50 (1969), 63–74.

Dafalla, Hassan. *The Nubian Exodus* (London, 1975).

Dinkler, Erich. Die deutschen Ausgrabungen auf den Inseln Sunnarti, Tangur und in Kulb; in Erich Dinkler, ed., *Kunst und Geschichte Nubiens in Christlicher Zeit*, 259–79 (Recklinghausen, 1970).

Driskell, Boyce N. Egyptian Basketry Technology in Cultural and Historical Perspective. *American Research Center in Egypt Newsletter*, no. 134 (1986), 17–23.

Driskell, Boyce N., Nettie K. Adams, and Peter French. A Newly Discovered Temple at Qasr Ibrim. Preliminary Report. *Archéologie du Nil Moyen* 3 (1988), 11–54.

Donadoni, Sergio. Les fouilles à l'Église de Sonqi Tino; in Erich Dinkler, ed., *Kunst und Geschichte Nubiens in Christlicher Zeit*, 209–18 (Recklinghausen, 1970).

Dunham, Dows, and Jozef M. A. Janssen. *Semna Kumma. Second Cataract Forts* 1 (Boston 1960).

Eastwood, Gillian. Textiles; in Donald S. Whitcomb and Janet E. Johnson, *Quseir al-Qadim 1980: Preliminary Report*, 285–326 (Malibu, 1982).

Eisenstadt, S. N. *The Political Systems of Empires* (New York, 1963).

Emery, W. B. *Egypt in Nubia* (London, 1965).

Emery, W. B., and L. P. Kirwan. *The Excavations and Survey between Wadi es-Sebua and Adindan 1929–1931* (Cairo, 1935) (2 vols.).

Emery, W. B., and L. P. Kirwan. *The Royal Tombs of Ballana and Qustul* (Cairo, 1938) (2 vols.).

Encyclopaedia Britannica. 14th ed. (Chicago, 1958).

Errera, I. *Collection d'anciennes étoffes égyptiennes* (Brussels, 1916).

Evetts, B. T. A., and A. J. Butler. *The Churches and Monasteries of Egypt and Some Neighbouring Countries, Attributed to Abu Salih, the Armenian* (Oxford, 1895).

Fahmy, Abdel-Rahman. Early Islamic Coin Weights. *Collections of the Museum of Islamic Art*, 2 (Cairo, 1957).

Forand, Paul. Early Muslim Relations with Nubia. *Der Islam* 48 (1971), 111–21.

Forbes, R. J. Food and Drink; in Charles Singer *et al.*, eds., *A History of Technology*, vol. 2, 103–46 (Oxford, 1956).

Forbes, R. J. Metallurgy; in Charles Singer *et al.*, eds., *A History of Technology*, vol. 2, 41–80 (Oxford, 1956).

Forbes, R. J. Power; in Charles Singer *et al.*, eds., *A History of Technology*, vol. 2, 103–46 (Oxford, 1956).

Frend, William H. C. Coptic, Greek, and Old Nubian at Q'asr Ibrim. *Byzantinoslavica* 33 (1972), 224–9.

Frend, William H. C. The Podium Site at Qasr Ibrim. *JEA* 60 (1974).

Frend, William H. C. The Greek Liturgical Papyri from the Cathedral at Q'asr Ibrim; in *Études Nubiennes*, 95–6. Institut français d'archéologie orientale, Bibliothque d'étude 77 (Cairo, 1978).

Frend, William H. C. A Eucharistic Sequence from Q'asr Ibrim. *Jahrbuch für Antike und Christentum* 29 (1986), 90–8.

Gardberg, C. J. *Late Nubian Sites. Scandinavian Joint Expedition to Sudanese Nubia Publications*, 7 (Stockholm, 1970).

Gartkiewicz, Przemyslaw. The Central Plan in Nubian Church Architecture; in Kazimierz Michalowski, ed., *Nubia, récentes recherches*, 49–64 (Warsaw, 1975).

Gaselee, S. Lettered Egyptian Textiles in the Victoria and Albert Museum. *Archaeologia* 23 (1924), 73–84.

Gervers, Veronika. Rags to Riches: Medieval Islamic Textiles. *Rotunda* 11 (1978–9), 22–31.

Gervers, Veronika. Medieval Garments in the Mediterranean World; in N. B. Harte and K. G. Pointing, eds., *Cloth and Clothing in Medieval Europe*, 279–315 (London, 1983).

Gibb, H. A. R. *The Life of Saladin* (Oxford, 1973).

Golombek, Lisa, and Veronika Gervers. Tiraz Fabrics in the Royal Ontario Museum; in Veronika Gervers, ed., *Studies in Textile History*, 82–125 (Toronto, 1977).

Granger-Taylor, Hero. Weaving Clothes to Shape in the Ancient World: the Tunic and Toga of the Arrigaton. *Textile History* 13 (1982), 3–25.

Griffith, F. Ll. *Karanòg, the Meroitic Inscriptions of Shablul and Karanòg. Eckley B. Coxe Junior Expedition to Nubia*, 6 (Philadelphia, 1911).

Griffith, F. Ll. *The Nubian Texts of the Christian Period. Abhandlungen der Königlichen Preussischen Akademie der Wissenschaften*, 1913, Phil.-Hist. Klasse, 8.

Griffith, F. Ll. Oxford Excavations in Nubia, XL–XLVIII. *LAAA* 13 (1926).

Griffith, F. Ll. Christian Documents from Nubia. *Proceedings of the British Academy* 14 (1928), 117–46.

Griffith, F. L. Oxford Excavations in Nubia. LVI–LXI. *LAAA* 15 (1928).

Griffith, F. Ll. Meroitic Studies VI. *JEA* 15 (1929).

Grossmann, Peter. *Elephantine II. Deutsches Archäologisches Instituts-Abteilung Kairo, Archäologische Veröffentlichen* 25 (Mainz, 1980).

Hambly, Wilfrid D. *Source Book for African Anthropology. Field Museum of Natural History, Anthropological Series*, 26 (Chicago, 1937) (2 vols.).

Harden, D. B. Glass and Glazes; in Charles Singer *et al.*, eds., *A History of Technology*, vol. 2, 311–346 (London, 1956).

Hasan, Yusuf Fadl. *The Arabs and the Sudan* (Edinburgh, 1967).

Henniker, Fr. *Notes During a Visit to Egypt, Nubia, the Oases, etc.* (London, 1824).

Hinds, Martin, and Hamdi Sakkout. A Letter from the Governor of Egypt to the King of Nubia and Muqurra Concerning Egyptian-Nubian Relations in 141/758; in Wadad el-Qadi, ed., *Studia Arabica et Islamica*, 209–16 (Beirut, 1981).

Hinds, Martin, and Hamdi Sakkout. *Arabic Documents from the Ottoman Period from Qasr Ibrim. Egypt Exporation Society, Texts from Excavations*, 8 (1986).

Hinkel, Friedrich. *Auszug aus Nubien* (Berlin, 1978).

Homossani, M. M. The Original Fabrics of Kaftan. *Ars Textrina* 1 (1983), 263–87.

Hoskins, G. A. *Travels in Ethiopia* (London, 1835).

Husselman, Elinor M. *The Topography and Architecture, Karanis, Egypt. University of Michigan, Kelsey Museum of Archaeology Studies*, 5 (Ann Arbor, 1979).

Innis, Harold I. *Empire and Communications* (Toronto, 1972).

Jakobielski, Stefan. Some Remarks on Faras Inscriptions; in Erich Dinkler, ed., *Kunst und Geschichte Nubiens in Christlicher Zeit*, 29–40 (Recklinghausen, 1970).

Jakobielski, Stefan. *Faras III* (Warsaw, 1972).

James, F. L. *The Wild Tribes of the Soudan* (New York, 1883).

Jaritz, Horst. Notes on Nubian Architecture and Architectural Drawings; in Robert A. Fernea and Georg Gerster, *Nubians in Egypt*, 49–60 (Austin, 1973).

John of Biclarum. *Chronicle*, ed. Th. Mommsen (Berlin, 1894).

John of Ephesus. *Ecclesiastical History*, trans. Payne-Smith (London, 1860).

Jungfleisch, Marcel. Les ralts discoïdes en verre. *Bulletin de l'Institut d'Égypte* 10 (1927–8), 61–71.

Kirwan, L. P. Studies in the Later History of Nubia. *LAAA* 24 (1937), 69–105.

Kirwan, L. P. Nubia and Nubian Origins. *The Geographical Journal* 140 (1974), 43–51.

Klunzinger, C. B. *Upper Egypt: its People and its Products* (New York, 1878).

Kronenberg, A. and W. Preliminary Report on Anthropological Field-Work 1961–62 in Sudanese Nubia. *Kush* 11 (1963).

Kronenberg, A. and W. Preliminary Report on the Anthropological Field-Work in Sudanese Nubia, 1962–63. *Kush* 12 (1964).

Krumbach, K. *Geschichte der byzantinischen Literatur*, 2nd ed. (Munich, 1897).

Lafontaine, Guy. Une homélie copte sur le Diable et sur Michel, attribuée à Grégoire le Théologien. *Le Muséon* 92 (1979), 37–60.

Lane, Edward W. *An Account of the Manners and Customs of the Modern Egyptians* (London, 1895).

Lane-Poole, Stanley. *Catalogue of Arabic Glass Weights* (London, 1891).

Lane-Poole, Stanley. *A History of Egypt in the Middle Ages* (London 1901).

Legh, Thomas. *Narrative of a Journey in Egypt and the Country Beyond the Cataracts* (London, 1817).

Lloyd, Seton. *Mounds of the Near East* (Edinburgh, 1963).

Lucas, A., and J. R. Harris. *Ancient Egyptian Materials and Industries*, 4th ed. (London, 1962).

Michalowski, Kazimierz. *Faras, fouilles polonaises 1961* (Warsaw, 1962).

Michalowski, Kazimierz. Polish Excavations at Faras—Fourth Season, 1963–64. *Kush* 13 (1964).

Michalowski, Kazimierz. *Faras* (Warsaw, 1974).

Michalowski, Kazimierz, and Georg Gerster. *Faras, die Kathedrale aus dem Wüstensand* (Zurich and Cologne, 1967).

Mileham, Geoffrey S. *Churches in Lower Nubia. Eckley B. Coxe Junior Expedition to Nubia*, 2 (Philadelphia, 1910).

Millet, Nicholas B. Some Notes on the Linguistic Background of Modern Nubian; in Robert A. Fernea, ed., *Contemporary Egyptian Nubia*, 1, 59–71 (New Haven, 1966).

Mills, A. J. *The Cemeteries of Qasr Ibrim. Egypt Exploration Society, Excavation Memoir* 51 (London, 1982).

Monneret de Villard, Ugo. *La Nubia Medioevale* (Cairo, 1935) (2 vols.)

Monneret de Villard, Ugo. *Storia della Nubia cristiana. Pontificium Institutum Orientalium Studiorum, Christiana Analecta* 118 (1938).

Montet, Pierre. *Eternal Egypt* (New York, 1968).

Munro-Hay, Stuart. *Kings and Kingdoms of Ancient Nubia.* MS.

Musil, Alois. *The Manners and Customs of the Rwala Bedouins. American Geographical Society, Oriental Explorations and Studies*, 6 (New York, 1928).

Norden, Frederick. *Travels in Egypt and Nubia*, trans. Tempelmann (London, 1757).

Oates, John F. A Christian Inscription in Greek from Armenna in Nubia. *JEA* 49 (1963), 161–71.

Petrie, W. M. Flinders. *Tools and Weapons* (London, 1917).

Petrie, W. M. Flinders. *Ancient Weights and Measures* (London, 1926).

Petrie, W. M. Flinders. *Glass Stamps and Weights* (London, 1926).

Petrie, W. M. Flinders. *Objects of Daily Use* (London, 1927).

Pliny. *Natural History*, trans. H. Rackham (Cambridge, MA, 1961) (10vols).

Plumley, J. Martin. Qasr Ibrim 1963–1964. *JEA* 50 (1964).

Plumley, J. Martin. Qasr Ibrim 1966. *JEA* 52 (1966), 9–12.

Plumley, J. Martin. Qasr Ibrim December 1966. *JEA* 53 (1967), 3–5.

Plumley, J. Martin. Qasr Ibrim 1969. *JEA* 56 (1970), 12–18.

Plumley, J. Martin. Qasr Ibrim 1974. *JEA* 61 (1975).

Plumley, J. Martin. The Christian Period at Qasr Ibrim, Some Notes on the MSS Finds; in Kazimierz Michalowski, ed., *Nubia, récentes recherches* (Warsaw, 1975).

Plumley, J. Martin. *The Scrolls of Bishop Timotheos. Egypt Exploration Society, Texts from Excavations*, 1 (London, 1975).

Plumley, J. Martin. New Light on the Kingdom of Dotawo; in *Études Nubiennes*, 231–41. *Institut français d'archéologie orientale, Bibliothèque d'étude* 77 (Cairo, 1978).

Plumley, J. Martin. Texts from Qasr Ibrim. *Sudan Texts Group Circular* 2 (1979).

Plumley, J. Martin. A Medieval Nubian Literary Text. *Sudan Texts Bulletin* 2 (1980), 34–41.

Plumley, J. Martin. The Christian Period in Nubia as Represented on the Site at Qasr Ibrim; in Paul van Moorsel, ed., *New Discoveries in Nubia*, 99–110. *Nederlands Instituut voor het Nabije Oosten, Egyptologische Uitgaven*, 2 (Leiden, 1982).

Plumley, J. Martin. New Evidence on Christian Nubia in the Light of Recent Excavations. *Nubia Christiana* 1 (1982).

Plumley, J. Martin, and William Y. Adams. Qasr Ibrim 1972. *JEA* 60 (1974).

Plumley, J. Martin, William Y. Adams, and Elisabeth Crowfoot. Qasr Ibrim, 1976. *JEA* 62 (1977).

Plumley, J. Martin, and Gerald M. Browne. *Old Nubian Texts from Qasr Ibrim, 1. Egypt Exploration Society, Texts from Excavations*, 9 (London, 1988).

Presedo Velo, Francisco. *Antigüedades de la isla de Kasarico. Comité español de la Unesco para Nubia, Memorias de la misión arqueólogica*, 1 (Madrid, 1963).

Presedo Velo, Francisco. *El poblado cristiano de la isla de Abkanarti. Comité español de la Unesco para Nubia, Memorias de la misión arqueológica*, 7 (Madrid, 1965).

Quibell, J. E. *Excavations at Saqqara (1908–9, 1909–10)* (Cairo, 1912).

Ratzel, Friedrich. *Völkerkunde* (Leipzig, 1885) (2 vols.).

Reisner, George A. Ancient Egyptian Forts at Semna and Uronarti. *Bulletin of the Museum of Fine Arts* 27 (1929), 65–75.

Robertson, John M. and Al-Abbas Mohammed. Meroitic Modelled Pottery; in P. L. Shinnie, ed., *Canadian Archaeology Abroad*, 85–96 (Calgary, 1976).

Roland, Werner. *Grammatik des Nobiin* (Hamburg, 1987).

St. John, J. A. *Egypt and Nubia* (London, 1845).

Säve-Söderbergh, Torgny. *Ägypten und Nubien* (Lund, 1941).

Säve-Söderbergh, Torgny. *Temples and Tombs of Ancient Nubia* (London, 1987).

Seligman, C. G., and Brenda Z. Seligman. The Kabâbîsh, a Sudan Arab Tribe. *Harvard African Studies* 2, 105–186 (Cambridge, MA, 1918).

Shinnie, P. L. Multilingualism in Medieval Nubia; in Abdelgadir M. Abdallah, ed., *Studies in Ancient Languages of the Sudan*, 41–7. *Sudan Research Unit, Sudan Studies Library*, 3 (Khartoum, 1974).

Shinnie, P. L. The Ancient Languages of the Northern Sudan; in Robin Thelwall, ed., *Aspects of Language in the Sudan*, 82–96. *New University of Ulster, Occasional Papers in Linguistics and Language Learning* (Coleraine, 1978).

Shinnie, P. L. Trade in Medieval Nubia; in *Études Nubiennes*, 253–64. *Institut français d'archéologie orientale, Bibliothèque d'étude* 77 (Cairo, 1978).

Shinnie, P. L., and H. N. Chittick. *Ghazali—a Monastery in the Northern Sudan. Sudan Antiquities Service, Occasional Papers*, 5 (Khartoum, 1961).

Shinnie, P. L., and François Kense. Meroitic Iron Working. *Meroitica* 6 (1982), 17–28.

Shinnie, P. L., and Margaret Shinnie. *Debeira West* (Warminster, 1978).

Sterns, F. H. Darfûr Gourds. *Harvard African Studies* 1, 193–6 (Cambridge, MA, 1917).

Stone, Caroline. Fabrics from the Middle East. *Aramco World Magazine* 38, no. 3 (1987), 2–5.

Strabo. *Geography*; trans. H. C. Hamilton and W. Falconer (London, 1954) (3 vols.).

Symonds, R. W. Furniture: Post-Roman; in Charles Singer *et al.*, eds., *A History of Technology*, vol. 2, 240–58 (London, 1956).

Thelwall, Robin. Linguistic Aspects of Greater Nubian History; in Christopher Ehret and Merrick Posnansky, eds., *The Archaelogical and Linguistic Reconstruction of African History*, 39–52 (Berkeley, 1982).

Thurman, Christa C. Mayer, and Bruce Williams. *Ancient Textiles from Nubia* (Chicago, 1979).

Török, Laszlo. Money, Economy, and Administration in Christian Nubia; in *Études Nubiennes*, 287–312. *Institut français d'archéologie orientale, Bibliothèque d'étude* 77 (Cairo, 1978).

Trigger, Bruce G. The Myth of Meroe and the African Iron Age. *African Historical Studies*, 2 (1969), 23–50.

Trigger, Bruce G. The Cultural Ecology of Christian Nubia; in Erich Dinkler, ed., *Kunst und Geschichte Nubiens in Christlicher Zeit* 347–86 (Recklinghausen, 1970).

Trimingham, J. Spencer. *Islam in the Sudan* (London, 1949).

Troupeau, G. La 'Description de la Nubie' d'Al-Uswani. *Arabica* 1 (1954), 279–88.

Tylecote, R. F. Metal Working at Meroe, Sudan. *Meroitica* 6 (1982), 29–42.

Università degli Studi di Roma, Missione Archeologica in Egitto. *Tamit* (1964) (Rome, 1967).

Van Moorsel, Paul, *et al. The Central Church of Abdallah Nirqi* (Leiden, 1975).

Vantini, Giovanni. *Oriental Sources Concerning Nubia* (Heidelberg and Warsaw, 1975).

Vantini, Giovanni. *Christianity in the Sudan* (Bologna, 1981).

Vantini, Giovanni. *Il cristianesimo nella Nubia antica* (Verona, 1985).

Waterer, John W. Leather; in Charles Singer *et al.*, eds., *A History of Technology*, vol. 2, 147–86 (London, 1956).

Weeks, Kent R. *The Classic Christian Townsite at Arminna West. Publications of the Pennsylvania-Yale Expedition to Egypt*, 3 (New Haven, 1967).

Wenzel, Marian. *Nubian House Decoration* (London, 1972).

Wessel, Klaus. *Coptic Art* (New York, 1965).

Whitcomb, Donald S., and Janet E. Johnson. *Quseir al-Qadim: Preliminary Report 1978* (Cairo, 1979).

Whitcomb, Donald S., and Janet E. Johnson. *Quseir al-Qadim 1980: Preliminary Report* (Malibu, 1982).

White, H. F. Evelyn. *The Monasteries of the Wadi 'N Natrun*, Part 3. *Metropolitan Museum of Art Egyptian Expedition Publications*, 8 (New York, 1933).

Wilson, Lillian M. *Ancient Textiles from Egypt in the University of Michigan Collection* (Ann Arbor, 1933).

Winlock, H. E., and W. E. Crum. *The Monastery of Epiphanius at Thebes*, Part 1. *Metropolitan Museum of Art Egyptian Expedition Publications* (New York, 1926).

Woolley, C. L. *Karanòg, the Town. Eckley B. Coxe Junior Expedition to Nubia*, 5 (Philadelphia, 1911).

Woolley, C. L., and D. Randall-MacIver. *Karanòg, the Romano-Nubian Cemetery. Eckley B. Coxe Junior Expedition to Nubia*, 3 (Philadelphia, 1910).

Zilliacus, H., R. Holthoer and A. Salonen. *Five Grave-Stelae from Sudanese Nubia. Studia Orientalia* 28, no. 15 (1964).

Zyhlarz, Ernst. Neue Sprachdenkmäler des Altnubischen; in *Studies Presented to F. Ll. Griffith*, 187–95 (Oxford, 1932).